Leading the Charge

Leading the Charge

Orrin Hatch
and 20 Years
of America

Lee Roderick

GOLD LEAF PRESS

Leading the Charge
© 1994 by Lee Roderick
All rights reserved.

No portion of this book may be reproduced in any form
without written permission from the publisher,
Gold Leaf Press, 2533 North Carson St. Suite 1544, Carson City, NV 89706.

Library of Congress Cataloging-in-publication Data

Roderick, Lee
Leading the charge : Orrin Hatch and twenty years of America/ by Lee Roderick
p. cm.
Includes bibliographical references and index.
ISBN 1-882723-09-0 :
1. Hatch, Orrin, 1934- . 2. Legislators—United States—Biography.
3. United States. Congress. Senate—Biography.
I. Title.
E840.8.H29R63   1994
328.73'092—dc20
[B]   94—2048
                                                 CIP

All Photos Used by Permission
Printed in the United States of America
Cover designed by Brian Bean

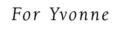

For Yvonne

Contents

Author's Note

Early in 1993, after preliminary research for this book, I wrote Senator Orrin Hatch to ask if he would grant an interview and perhaps give me access to some personal papers.

Several weeks went by with no response. Then, late one Friday afternoon, I received a telephone call from the director of Hatch's Utah office. "The Senator's in town this weekend. Can you meet with him tomorrow at 11 A.M.?" I could.

Arriving at the Federal Building in downtown Salt Lake City the next morning, I was surprised to find Hatch in a yellow pullover and slacks. In fifteen years of covering him as a journalist in Washington and Utah, I had never seen Hatch out of a coat and tie.

Hatch agreed to cooperate on the book already in progress. In fact, he said, how would I like to have access to *all* of his private writings? Wondering where the catch was, I cautiously asked how many pages he was talking about. The answer was stunning: well over ten thousand.

For most of his adult life, Hatch has kept extensive, highly detailed notes on important events in which he has been involved. Hatch offered me access to all those files—his personal papers, notes, correspondence, and other confidential materials.

I had not known Hatch beyond Capitol Hill and my journalist's skepticism surfaced. "Senator, of course I would love to have access to those resources," I told Hatch. "But I plan to write an *un*authorized biography, and you would have absolutely no control over what direction the book takes or what conclusions I draw."

"I agree," he said. "All I ask is that you look at my life with an open mind and be fair."

"That's all?" I asked.

"That's all."

Then he added one other thing: "I'll also talk to you as your book progresses if you have questions. But my time is extremely limited, so you'll have to interview me on my car phone as I drive to work."

"What time do you leave in the morning?" I asked.

"At about 6:30."

"Senator, that's 4:30 in Utah."

"How badly do you want to write your book?"

Obviously I wanted to write it pretty badly. Time has proved the wisdom of that decision. Hatch was as good as his word, giving me unprecedented access to his personal and often private world and asking nothing in return except that I describe it honestly. Why, as an ambitious politician, would Hatch take such risk? Obviously he was confident that, despite the warts, the open record as a whole would reflect well on him.

It has been a fascinating adventure. Readers of *Leading the Charge* will share a rare fly-on-the-wall look inside the U.S. Senate, to see how great issues have been and are decided, and how members of "the world's most exclusive club" sink or rise to the occasion.

Most readers, including my colleagues in the media, with few exceptions, won't recognize the Orrin Hatch of this book. I wouldn't have recognized him myself if I hadn't personally read those ten thousand pages, pored over thousands of other primary and secondary documents, and interviewed dozens of friends and foes who have known Hatch in many different settings. As a reporter I covered Hatch for years—and never knew him.

Orrin Hatch's sheer impact on the United States, for good or ill depending on your point of view, has made him one of the nation's premier political players of the last quarter of this century. He has been pivotal in many of the crucial public battles fought during that time. Yet, while Hatch is mentioned frequently in the media, rarely is he given more than cursory or grudging attention. From 1988 through 1992, Hatch's name appeared often in the *Washington Post* and *New York Times*. Yet the *Post* index—a measure of significant emphasis on a subject—lists Hatch a total of eight times during the five years, compared with Senator Edward Kennedy who is listed seventy-two times. For the same period, the *Times* index lists Hatch once—in 1988—and Kennedy thirty-nine times.

To many journalists and other outsiders, Hatch has a stiff personality that does not invite sympathetic inquiry. He is also a complicated man whose interests range from poetry to pugilistics and who defies categorization. Those traits are hurdles to understanding Hatch, and few observers have been willing to jump them.

There is another factor: We journalists say we write for our readers, but too often we write first to impress our colleagues in the media. Usually that means individuals of "liberal" political persuasion will be treated more fully and fairly in news coverage than will "conservatives" like Hatch.

While I was researching this book, a colleague at KSL television who was formerly assigned to Washington said, "I found Hatch one of the most open and decent people I dealt with all the time I was back there." Then he added quickly: "That's off the record. Don't tell the other reporters I said that." Such bias by no means is unique; I have seen it—and admittedly been part of it—in other newsrooms in Washington and Utah.

When Hatch first appeared on the political radarscope in 1976, he was labeled an "ultraconservative" despite his protests. It was a scarlet letter he wore for a decade or more, in the face of increasing contrary evidence. Hatch is, in fact, a mainstream conservative with a maverick bent. Opponents have also called him harsh, antiwomen, anticivil rights, and antilabor. Such labels obscure, more than define, Orrin Hatch.

This book was written neither to help nor to hurt Hatch but to reveal him, both as a private individual and a public figure, in the context of his time. The reader may judge whether that goal has been met.

Lee Roderick
April 5, 1994

Acknowledgements

THE AUTHOR THANKS HIS TWO TALENTED EDITORS for their invaluable assistance: Darla Isackson at Gold Leaf Press, who prodded him to think with *both* sides of his brain, and Lavina Fielding Anderson, who sharpened the book's focus. Thanks also to Linda Thomson for critically reading the manuscript and offering suggestions that invariably improved it.

Appreciation for research assistance goes to my son Eric Roderick, to Marsha Thomas at the University of Utah Law Library, and to Stephen W. Stathis at the Library of Congress.

The support of a number of other individuals made the difference between this book as a concept and as a reality. Curtis Taylor opened the door at Gold Leaf Press. Timely encouragement also came from friends and colleagues J. R. Allred, Sheri Dew, Cecelia Foxley, George Griner, Mark Hartshorn, Paul Norton, and Kirk Wessel.

Senator Hatch's staff was cheerfully helpful in locating various documents. Thanks in particular go to Ron Madsen and Melanie Bowen in Utah, and Paul Smith, Jeanne Lopatto, and Ruth Montoya in Washington.

Many current and former associates of Orrin Hatch—friends and critics alike—were generous with their time in offering insights into Hatch's career and personality. I am especially grateful for the assistance of Senator Edward Kennedy and former Senators Frank Moss, Jake Garn, and Paul Laxalt. Justice Clarence Thomas made an exception to his policy of not granting media interviews, for which I am sincerely grateful.

This book would have been written with or without the cooperation of Orrin Hatch. But the candor of Hatch and his wife, Elaine, in sharing both joyful and painful memories during more than a dozen interviews and in granting unrestricted access to thousands of pages of his private writings, made the experience especially rewarding.

To each of these individuals, I express sincere appreciation.

Prologue

IT WAS NEARLY MIDNIGHT, OCTOBER 20, 1988, but every corridor gleamed
with lights as Orrin Hatch hurried through the Capitol, heading for
the Senate chamber.

The close of a session obviously was at hand. After nine months of
sleepy deliberation, the 100th Congress was ending in a typical flurry of
long hours and short tempers, with billions thrown to the wind in a
rush to get home and campaign. The election was less than three weeks
away.

That's us, thought Hatch, glancing at two huge paintings in the
rotunda depicting the surrender of British generals John Burgoyne and
Charles Cornwallis. Republicans, he believed, were yielding too easily to
the Democratic majority.

Now that's more like it. He had reached the Senate side of the Capitol
and a painting of U.S. admiral Oliver Perry being rowed from his
sinking ship to another vessel on Lake Erie. Perry regrouped and
defeated the British fleet.

Hatch was looking for Ted Kennedy, but the Massachusetts senator
was hard to find—not in the cloakroom, nor on the floor. Then he heard
uproarious laughter outside the Senate chamber, beneath the press
gallery. It was a truism: To find Kennedy, follow the laughter.

Kennedy had been out celebrating. His imprint was on a lot of the
bills Congress had passed that session: stiffened measures to fight illegal
drugs, insurance for Medicare participants with catastrophic illness, an
overhaul of the welfare system, sixty days required notice before plants
could close, and strengthened enforcement for civil rights.

"Orrin!" yelled Kennedy as he saw Hatch coming.

"Theodoe!" Hatch yelled back. It was his pet name for Kennedy, even though "Ted" derived from Edward and not Theodore.

Senator Christopher Dodd of Connecticut was the other half of the laughter. The two carefree bachelors had been out to a favorite watering hole and were back, feeling no pain. Both were liberal Democrats, divorced Catholics, fast friends, and not known for inhibition. During one celebrated night of revelry, they had ripped each other's autographed photos from the wall of La Colline restaurant and smashed them. Kennedy's amorous escapades kept supermarket tabloids in hot copy.

Hatch joined his colleagues, and Kennedy wrapped a beefy arm around the Utahn's slender neck.

"Orrin, you've got to help me with the AIDS bill," said Kennedy. "That AIDS bill is really important. You've got to help me get the AIDS bill through."

Hatch nodded. Kennedy, arm still draped over Hatch, continued to repeat everything three times. "Come sailing with me up in Hyannis Port, Orrin. I've got a wonderful boat, you know. You'll love it. You've got to come up and sail with me."

The genial but blurred monologue continued for fifteen minutes, then Hatch cut in. "Ted, I've got a favor to ask."

"Done!" said Kennedy, with a sweep of his free arm.

"Well, you better hear me out first," cautioned Hatch. "Remember Frank Madsen, my former administrative assistant?"

"Sure, sure. Great guy."

"Frank is up in Boston—"

"My hometown!"

"—presiding over about 200 young missionaries for our church. And he'd like you and me to go up and speak to the missionaries at a conference."

"Done!" Another sweep of the arm.

"There's another thing," said Hatch.

"Just name it."

"He wants to know if you'll arrange to get Faneuil Hall for the conference."

"Done!"

Hatch, smiling but bone-tired, bade Kennedy and Dodd amiable goodnights, and drove to his home in Virginia. Next morning he woke earlier than usual, left immediately for Washington, and arrived at the office ahead of his staff. He turned on his word processor and began to keyboard: "Dear Ted . . ." Hatch outlined their agreement of the night before, climbed two flights of stairs, and slipped it under Kennedy's door.

That afternoon, Kennedy found Hatch in a committee room and approached urgently, waving Hatch's letter.

"Orrin, I have just one question," he said gravely.

"Yes, Ted?"

"What *else* did I agree to last night?"

They were the Senate's odd couple: Kennedy born to wealth and a political dynasty, Hatch to scarcity and obscurity. Kennedy living a reckless lifestyle, Hatch a model of rectitude. Kennedy the icon of American liberals, Hatch the Senate's conservative wizard. Only months after arriving in Washington, Hatch had privately assessed his Senate colleagues. He was complimentary to almost all of them. But Kennedy, wrote Hatch, was "one of the three or four I find basically nothing good to say about."

The story of how the two key legislators became warm personal friends is part of Washington legend, to be described from Hatch's perspective later in this book. Even as friends, they continued to fight fiercely over most issues. But on the occasions they reached agreement, locked arms, and marched together, Presidents and other members of Congress tended to step aside.

In a Congress full of plastic people, they were among the living. Neither their personal concern for colleagues nor their social consciences had shriveled behind a shield of cynicism or personal ambition. Beyond Capitol Hill, Hatch and Kennedy came to share each other's darkest hours and brightest triumphs. Kennedy taught Hatch to laugh. Hatch coached Kennedy back from the edge of self-destruction.

Both of them were an integral part of what has been called "the world's most exclusive club." This story of Hatch's life is also the story of the club itself—an insider's view of the powerful, quirky, wrangling, ego-centered, and emotionally intense institution whose decisions affect the daily lives of every citizen: the United States Senate.

In addition, this book is a history of the most important issues to face the United States during the past two decades, and how our leaders have dealt with them—issues such as proposed constitutional amendments, including the Equal Rights Amendment, massive federal deficits, ending the Cold War, the Supreme Court's landmark abortion ruling, the tumultuous replacing of two-thirds of the high court's justices, expanding civil rights laws, forced unionization, public lands, and other regional issues pitting the West against the rest of the U.S.

Finally, this book is a political narrative of the Senate and the Presidency covering the past twenty years—showing how we choose those who govern us and the gaps between their promises and performance. It details the successes and failures of Congress as well as those of four Presidents: Jimmy Carter, Ronald Reagan, George Bush, and Bill Clinton.

In 1977 Hatch and ninety-nine other men (the Senate was then an all-male bastion) brought their personal dreams, ideals, prejudices, and nightmares to the corridors of power. They had separate mandates from citizens in fifty states, and were thrown into a steaming political caldron, responsible for creating solutions to national problems without forsaking those citizens. Only a handful of senators at a time would distinguish themselves in balancing parochial interests with the national interest and in setting aside personal and political differences with colleagues to pursue the common good.

Behind the deceptively neat packages of legislation that made their way to the President's desk lay a jungle history of human need, power brokering, systematic logic, raw appeal to emotion, the making and calling in of favors, and the sculpting of compromise that are the biosphere of the political process.

This book shows that law-making often is not a pretty sight when viewed up close. The German statesman Otto Von Bismarck noted that two things were not fit for human eyes—the making of sausage and the making of laws.

In 1976, almost without a trace of political experience, Hatch was elected from Utah—a small state about as far removed from the political mainstream as it is possible to get. He has been reelected twice and is now a senior senator with political power in national affairs far out of proportion to his state's position.

Hatch is a man known for never breaking his word and yet a consummate deal-maker. He walks the corridors of power to the drumbeat of both conscience and compromise, routinely at risk of being misunderstood—and perhaps punished—on a given issue by either the Washington establishment or his constituents in Utah.

Annoyingly independent, Hatch takes predictable positions on fiscal and foreign policy matters but carefully weighs real human needs on social issues. He was despised by feminists for opposing abortion and for insisting there was a better way to obtain equality for women than a constitutional amendment. At the same time, he was denounced by conservative women for joining Democrats to help enact a sweeping child-care law. He also stunned conservatives in the early '90s by tramping the U.S., including traditionalist Utah, wearing a symbolic red ribbon to drum up support for research and treatment to fight AIDS.

It is easy to take issue with Hatch's approach. But its results are irrefutable. History would be different if Hatch had not served in the Senate. Here are some likely ways:

William Rehnquist probably would not be Chief Justice of the Supreme Court, and Clarence Thomas and Ruth Bader Ginsburg would not share that bench. Millions of American workers would have been forced into unions. The electoral college would have been abolished and the President elected by direct popular vote. The nation would not have much tougher criminal laws, a major child-care program, or easy access to cheaper generic drugs. In the name of civil rights, thousands if not millions more citizens would have suffered civil wrongs, also called "reverse discrimination." The Cold War would have been prolonged because the Soviet Union would not have been forced to abandon its war in Afghanistan when it did.

The roster of Hatch's friends was as eclectic as his political philosophy: Muhammad Ali and Oliver North, black inner city Bishop Smallwood Williams and Ronald Reagan, the late Senators Hubert Humphrey of Minnesota and James Allen of Alabama, establishment Democrats Tommy Corcoran and Jack Valenti, Republicans Jeanne Kirkpatrick, Henry Kissinger, Paula Hawkins, and Anna Chennault, novelists Patricia Cornwell, Scott Turow, and Robin Cook. And Clarence and Virginia Thomas.

The list of those who disliked Hatch at one time or another or had suffered his relentless prosecutory style was equally eclectic: Anita Hill, Mormon feminist Sonia Johnson, Interior Secretary Bruce Babbitt, ultra-conservatives Phyllis Schlafly and Paul Weyrich, Senate Majority Leader Bob Byrd, Senators Paul Tsongas, Howard Metzenbaum, Frank Church, and often Ted Kennedy.

One national publication called Hatch "an independent-minded and enigmatic politician whom Washington, with its penchant for pigeon-holing, is ill-equipped to understand."

The enigmas ran deep. For example, despite Hatch's aggressiveness and capability for rapier-like attacks, his Achilles' heel was a too-trusting nature that failed to discern the private agendas of "friends" whose misdeeds would cause him untold grief and sorrow. A tireless senator, he was also a tender father, whose private remorse over time lost with his children kept him constantly juggling to serve both them and the nation.

Early on Hatch was backed by the "New Right," which soon resented his independence and penchant for compromise rather than confrontation. Hatch, in turn, resisted tactics he considered unfair by both the left and the right, and baffled everyone with what he chose to support or oppose.

Yet the enigmas become more understandable in light of his back-ground, composed of equal parts poverty, service, driving ambition, and an insatiable appetite for work. The fabric of his makeup and memories begins with his childhood in a small patch of woods in Pittsburgh, continues westward over the Rockies for an education, weaves in two years of full-time service to his church, and then incorporates law school, and a return to Utah.

From there, against all odds, he would be sent to Washington as a remarkably innocent citizen-senator. He would become loved and hated, maligned by many and adored by others, the focus of vicious smear campaigns and the leading target of powerful special interest groups bent on unseating him. How could one man create so many enemies? What was the source of his strength? Could he be tough enough to lead many of the most important Senate battles of the past two decades and retain his humanity? What made him who he was? As Hatch neared the end of his third Senate term, the apparent paradoxes of his life and career were as intriguing as ever.

During his public career, Hatch would be as zealous as a missionary, as tenacious as a trial lawyer, and as aggressive as a prize fighter. He had, in fact, been all three.

Leading the Charge

Orrin Hatch
and 20 Years
of America

1

The Early Years

ORRIN'S GREAT-GRANDFATHER, Jeremiah Hatch, was one of the first white settlers in Utah's Ashley Valley, a verdant nook in the northeastern corner of the state near both the Colorado and Wyoming borders.

In the spring of 1878, Jeremiah built a cabin on a bench above the Green River, high enough to give him early warning of the area's twin menaces: outlaws (soon to include the notorious Harry Longabaugh, aka Butch Cassidy) and marauding Indians.

The Mormon colonizing president, Brigham Young, had sent him to Ashley Valley as a missionary and Indian agent, hoping Jeremiah could "civilize" the warlike Utes and convert them to Christianity. Unlike most frontiersmen, Young counseled kindness toward Native Americans, insisting it was more humane as well as cheaper to feed than to fight them. Jeremiah was widely known as a friend to the Indians, who called him "Uncle Jerry."

In 1879 a zealous U.S. Indian agent in Colorado named Nathan Meeker tried to force the Utes to shoot their beloved ponies and become instant farmers. The attempt cost Meeker and nine of his employees their lives in a bloody affair known as the "Meeker Massacre." Meeker's wife and daughter were captured and led away to the mountains by rampaging Utes, as Indian anger spilled across the Utah border.

Warned secretly by friendly chiefs, Jeremiah quickly helped erect a fort-village of eighteen log cabins in what is now the city of Vernal, and the Mormon settlers moved inside to prepare for what would be a long, grim winter.

Days after completing the fort, Jeremiah and his thirteen-year-old son Joe were in the badlands south of the valley hunting for horses. Suddenly Joe's pony bolted and tore off through the sagebrush out of control. Jeremiah spurred his horse and caught the other mount.

Jolting to a stop, Jeremiah saw the source of the pony's fright: a band of Indians, knives unsheathed, bearing down on them at full gallop. As the Indians closed in, Jeremiah's horse reared in terror, throwing Jeremiah's head, including his long trademark beard, backward in profile. Instantly recognizing Uncle Jerry, the Indians reined in their ponies.

As he met the Indians' eyes, Jeremiah quietly told Joe to go to a nearby knoll. Then he spoke in Ute: "You want blood. Take his blood. Go ahead, shoot my son!"

The Indians didn't move. Again he told them to shoot, and still they didn't move.

"You kill, drink blood!" he challenged a third time. Then he motioned toward the Colorado border and the White River agency where Nathan Meeker had been dragged behind a horse and then staked to the ground only days earlier. "Why kill my friends?"

Finally an Indian named Colorow answered. "My friend tell good. Indians go."

But Jeremiah talked the Utes into accompanying him and Joe back to the fort. There, the Indians were fed and a council was held around a large bonfire, with the men of the fort and the Indians smoking a peace pipe. Young Joe's reaction was not recorded.

"Thus," says one historian of those early days, "was a calamity averted that might have written in blood the early history of Ashley Valley." If the Indians had completed their murderous mission that day, feminists a century later wouldn't have had to worry about Orrin Hatch. Thirteen-year-old Josephus Hatch would live to father thirteen children, including, in 1904, Orrin's father Jesse.

Jeremiah, whose own grandfather of the same name fought in the Revolutionary War, had arrived in Utah by covered wagon in 1850 after joining The Church of Jesus Christ of Latter-day Saints (Mormon or LDS) in New England a decade earlier. The twenty-seven-year-old blacksmith was a natural, eloquent leader, with a calm demeanor and steady gaze. He and his wife, Louisa Pool Alexander Hatch, moved north to Cache Valley in 1862 with their growing family. When Louisa died in 1869, she left eleven children, including Joe who was nearly three. Jeremiah remarried the following year and, as the peculiar Mormon practice of polygamy spread, added a third wife six years later. He took both women with him to Ashley Valley, eventually had a family of thirty children, and lived out his days as one of Vernal's leading citizens.

Joe also stayed in Vernal but his civic record was not so shining. Reared by an older brother after his mother's death, Joe raised horses, sheared sheep, and worked in the coal mines to feed the thirteen children born to him and his wife, Martha Luella Thomas Hatch. By reports he was very much in love with her and gentle with his children.

But Joe had a fatal fondness for Demon Rum, despite the Mormon prohibition against alcohol. According to a family history, "Joe was hit over the head with a butt of a gun and it formed a blood clot on his brain, which later caused him to have seizures." The fight, confided a family member, occurred during a drunken brawl. Joe was eventually committed to the state mental hospital in Provo where, the family history adds cryptically, "he was killed" in 1915. Among the children he left behind was eleven-year-old Jesse, Orrin's father.

Martha Luella took in washing, ironing, and sewing. Then in 1919 she accepted a job at the Rainbow Mines, seventy-five miles southeast of Vernal, where a hundred men were mining Gilsonite. She managed the boarding house, setting an example of industriousness that would become a Hatch hallmark. Her day started at 5 A.M. when she fired up the kitchen stove. Often assisted by the children, she prepared three large meals for the miners, hanging up her dishcloth at 9 P.M.

Fifteen-year-old Jesse had his first full-time job, joining the other Gilsonite miners. At age seventeen, he moved to the tiny mining town of Hiawatha, about a hundred miles from Vernal toward the center of Utah, where he roofed new housing for the miners and boarded with the John Bernard Kamm family.

Kamm was a welder from Illinois whose family included a very pretty sixteen-year-old daughter, Helen. At the first sign of attraction between Helen and Jesse, her alarmed father whisked Helen back to Illinois to live on a farm with her mother's sister, "Aunt Nan," a straitlaced Methodist. Helen and Jesse had no chance to exchange addresses.

Kamm's quick action seemed to succeed. Helen had no way to reach her rough-hewn young man, and Jesse, meeting with Kamm's firm denials, returned to Vernal, then headed into Wyoming's oil fields as a wildcatter. But he was haunted by the memory of Helen, a spirited brunette with a beautiful figure, warm oval face, and sparkling dark eyes.

Within weeks, Jesse had borrowed train fare and headed for Illinois. A taxi driver, for a set fee, agreed to take him on a search for the farm, and they began crisscrossing Rural Route 7. Jesse's only clue was that "Aunt Nan" owned a farm. He didn't know that, after fifty years on the farm, she had given it up shortly after Helen's arrival and moved with the girl to nearby Jacksonville.

After searching every farm in the vicinity, Jesse on a hunch began looking in Jacksonville. But after winding through Jacksonville for some time, the taxi driver told Jesse to give up the search. Jesse talked the driver into trying one more house. As they approached the yard, he saw a young woman strolling up a path with a basket of freshly picked blackberries on her arm. It was Helen. Before the sun set, Jesse had borrowed a suit and they were married at the local courthouse.

"Our marriage was a surprise to both of us," Helen would recall seventy years later. "He didn't ask me and I didn't ask him. We just did it. I guess I married Jesse because he was the kindest man I ever knew."

They lived for several months in the Wyoming oil fields. Then, succumbing to petitions from her mother Oma, who had divorced Helen's father a dozen years earlier, they went by train to join Oma in Pittsburgh. They arrived November 1, 1923.

Pittsburgh was too busy flexing its muscles to take note of the poorly dressed, penniless young couple. Pennsylvania mined most of the nation's coal and produced most of its steel. Pittsburgh District was the heart of it all. The city's population had exploded in recent years and the building trade, in which Jesse planned to spend his future, was booming.

He landed a union card and a job as a wood lather. Jesse would become known across Pittsburgh as a master craftsman who could do all of the fancy lath and plaster work required in fine custom-built homes and commercial buildings.

The Hatches made a down payment on a small frame house in a working-class section of Homestead Park. Less than a year later, Jesse Morlan (Jess) was born. Four more children were born over the next eight years, but two of them died within the first few months of birth. The two survivors were daughters Marilyn, known as "Nubs," and Nancy.

Then ripples from the stock market crash reached their doorstep. By January 1931 one of every five Pittsburgh workers was out of work, and the housing industry halted in its tracks. Jesse and Helen's home was half-paid-for, but they had to abandon it. They lingered long enough for Helen to give birth on March 22, 1934, to their sixth child and second surviving son. They named him Orrin Grant over the protests of hand-some, ten-year-old Jess, who argued hard for "Samson" or "Moses."

Jess looked like his mother. Orrin favored his blond father, although he inherited his mother's dark, piercing eyes. His profusion of white-blond ringlets grew unchecked for two years before a first haircut, and his older sisters delighted in tormenting Orrin by patting his "wool."

Later he tried, to no avail, to plaster his locks into submission with soap or petroleum jelly.

By all accounts, Orrin was unusually quiet, thoughtful, and serious. He appears as a child or adolescent in twenty-three photographs in his mother's family album. In only two or three does Orrin betray a hint of a smile. He had a strong religious bent even as a tot. Helen recalls Orrin staring at a calendar depicting the crucifixion of Christ and singing all the lines of "The Old Rugged Cross," memorized from hearing it on the radio. His siblings describe him as a perpetual worrier who thought deeply about adult kinds of problems.

After losing their home to the Great Depression, Helen and Jesse scraped together a little money, bought a heavily wooded acre of land in Baldwin Borough, purchased secondhand materials, including lumber from a building partially destroyed by fire, and built their home, board by board with their own hands. Until they painted it white, one side of the two-story frame house advertised "Meadow Gold Ice Cream." At first the children all slept in a large second floor dormitory-like room. Orrin shared his bed with the two youngest children until he was eleven.

There was no gas, electricity, or other utilities for the first year. Helen cooked outside over cinderblocks, and the family answered nature's call at an outhouse seventy-five yards from their back door.

They planted apple and cherry trees and a large garden that supplied most of their food. Unable to afford a plow, family members hand-hoed the ground, raising corn, beans, tomatoes, squash, and beets. Helen applied the discipline, including occasional spankings, to see that all seven children shared the weeding and other chores. "Dad had such a gentle heart he couldn't bring himself to touch us," recalls Nancy. Orrin was generally a good worker but disliked weeding and looked for excuses to get out of it.

As adults her children would remember Helen far more for constant encouragement and open expressions of love than for her infrequent swats. Helen had the disposition of a saint, according to her children, invariably looking for the good in those around her and insisting that the children do likewise.

Orrin felt close to both parents but seemed to have a particularly close bond with his mother. She was fun, spirited, optimistic, and, in Orrin's mind, righteous without being self-righteous. When he was five, Orrin and a few friends hiked to Brentwood, two miles away, to buy candy at a dime store. "Orrin had sixty cents," recalled his mother. "When they returned, the other children all had big bags of candy. But Orrin had spent his sixty cents to buy *me* a 'diamond' solitaire engagement ring. He handed it to me and said, 'Now you will look like the other mothers.'" Helen kept the ring for more than a half-century as a prized keepsake.

Jess was sunny and gregarious. Orrin tagged after him with an affection bordering on worship, but relations with Nancy and Nubs were stormy. On a cold January morning when he was five, Orrin appeared at his parents' bedside, bundled in winter clothing. A stick slung over his shoulder hobo-style had a red bandanna filled with personal items knotted on the end. "Mom, I'm leavin' home," he announced, "Dem girls [Nancy and Nubs] are mean to me." With that he was off, before Helen could rouse herself to realize he might be serious.

Orrin was gone throughout the morning. Snow started to fall. Afternoon came and the storm intensified as his family scoured the area for him. Still no Orrin. Neighbors joined the frantic search. Finally, as night fell, the front door creaked open and Orrin shuffled in. He had hiked a ways, then doubled back to the chicken coop behind the house, where he had spent most of the day in a barrel of feed. When the chickens went noiselessly to sleep, his fear of the dark overcame his stubbornness. Helen covered Orrin with delousing powder, and Nancy and Nubs were noticeably kinder in coming weeks.

One summer day after his sisters teased him, he disappeared again. An extensive search located Orrin, asleep under the black cherry tree where slumber had overtaken him after he'd gorged himself on the sweet fruit. Sometimes they would find him asleep under his bed.

Admittedly, Nancy and Nubs relished teasing him, but they also grew up believing he was special. "I remember . . . going up to Orrin when he was about three and patting him on the head and telling him, 'You're going to be President someday,'" says Nancy. "I never told anyone else, but I never forgot it."

The family's financial condition was humble. Jesse searched for assorted odd jobs to keep them afloat. Breakfast invariably was oatmeal, and dinner frequently consisted of a thin soup of vegetables from their garden. But the Hatches' circumstances were no worse than those of their neighbors, who also were suffering the effects of the Great Depression.

Their social and financial status made an indelible impression on Orrin, who would refer to it often as an adult. His sisters, on the other hand, looked back on life in the family's wooded acre as almost idyllic. "I don't remember us as poor," says younger sister Frances Hatch Merrill. Nancy adds, "We always had plenty to eat." Jesse hung a long rope swing on a big walnut tree, and the children spent countless hours on it. A stream ran through the nearby woods and neighborhood kids loved to play "Tarzan" in the summers, swinging over the water on vines.

Even during the iciest winter days, the children walked to McGibney Elementary School, a half-mile from home. Orrin was self-conscious about his clothes, which were not as nice as those of most classmates, but he was an exceptional student. He had an amazing memory and excelled, especially in history and English. School was easy for Orrin, except math which he disliked intensely. A "B" in arithmetic during the last six weeks was all that marred an all-"A" report card for sixth grade from his teacher, Mildred Weyand.

The family's social life revolved largely around their church and the small band of fellow members and proselyting missionaries in the Pittsburgh area. They were members of The Church of Jesus Christ of Latter-day Saints, referred to as Mormons or LDS—short for Latter-day Saints.

Jesse had belonged since boyhood and Helen had been baptized several years after moving to Pittsburgh. Both were stalwarts in the congregation, though Jesse had found it painful to give up chewing tobacco, a habit proscribed by the Mormon health code known as the Word of Wisdom, which also outlawed coffee, tea, and alcohol. The congregation met in a former Jewish school that had been converted into a chapel. The Hatch family made the fifteen-mile round-trip twice each Sunday, attending Sunday School in the morning and worship services in the evening. From the age of three, Orrin and his siblings took their turns addressing the other children in short, simple talks delivered over a tiny pulpit in a Sunday School separate from the adult classes.

Helen had played the violin as a girl and instilled a love of music in her offspring. Somehow she saved enough money to buy an old upright piano, and nearly all the children learned to play it. Orrin sang from the time he could talk and—under protest—also took violin lessons. All of the Hatch children, including Orrin, also played the organ for congregational singing. Each child was baptized at age eight, the traditional age of "accountability" for Mormons.

Mormon missionaries, usually ages nineteen through twenty-one, came and went in Pittsburgh during two-year terms of service. They regularly visited the hospitable Hatches, often staying for a meal and taking Orrin's and Jess's bed while the boys slept on the floor. Later, Orrin suspected that their attention may have been spurred by his bevy of attractive sisters; but as a youngster, he idolized the youthful ministers. So did teenage Jess, who spoke with anticipation of serving his own mission like the other "elders." His other ambition was to be a pilot. He and his friends built a large collection of model airplanes, proudly displayed in the Hatch basement.

When America entered World War II, Pittsburgh, a patriotic, blue-collar city, responded with fervor. Thousands of its young men volunteered for service, including eighteen-year-old Jess Hatch, who joined the Army Air Force, planning to become a missionary later. Jess was assigned to the

Fifteenth Air Force in Europe as a nose gunner in a B-24 Liberator, the workhorse of the Allied bombing effort. He was decorated as one of the few GIs to shoot down a German jet from that exposed position and sent his family a photograph of his ten-man crew. Orrin kept the photo on a dresser in the bedroom he had shared with Jess.

The family prayed daily for Jess's safety and for an early end to the war. Then one evening, Helen and Jesse returned from a movie to find that a freak tornado had exploded over their house, knocking down fruit trees and blowing debris through the bedroom windows. Surveying the damage the next morning, Helen was startled to find a hole punctured through the glass covering Jess's Air Force photo, precisely over his face. She took it as a bad omen.

In February 1945, ten-year-old Orrin was playing in the woods across the road when he sensed that something was wrong. Racing to the house, he saw a uniformed serviceman standing with his stunned parents. Helen was sobbing. Jess's plane was missing in action in Austria. He was presumed dead, but the sad news would not be confirmed for years. Jess had been shot down twice before, both times returning to his base in Foggia, Italy, with the help of the underground, but this time it was for keeps. Jess was the only one of the eighteen servicemen from their neighborhood who would not eventually return home.

Orrin was inconsolable. Literally overnight a white streak appeared in his hair above the right side of his forehead. It was permanent. For days he stayed home from school. He couldn't force food down and his skinny body became even scrawnier. When Helen gave birth to her ninth child in 1946, they named the baby Jessica in her brother's honor. Four years later, Jess's remains were located in Vienna and returned to Pittsburgh for burial, renewing the family's grief. As the only surviving son, Orrin redoubled his efforts to contribute to the family, shoveling coal and helping his father build a new chicken coop. Orrin fed the chickens and sold eggs.

As a teenager, Orrin's most serious interest was competitive sports. He loved them all, but football was not a serious option for the slightly built youth. His legs were so skinny that he sometimes wore long pants even when playing games calling for shorts.

Grit he didn't lack. At twelve, Orrin decided basketball would be his standout sport. For months, he practiced dribbling and shooting baskets through a crude hoop mounted on a tree at the next-door neighbors' home. Shortly after enrolling at Baldwin High, a suburban school that included grades seven through twelve, Orrin tried out for the seventh-grade team.

"That's the first time I ever knew there was a difference between a volleyball and a basketball," he ruefully remembers. Orrin had been practicing all those months with the smaller one. Bewildered by the huge ball now standing between him and athletic glory, he was cut from the team.

Humiliated but doggedly determined, Orrin borrowed a scruffy leather basketball from a neighbor and began shooting again. A year later he made the team, getting limited playing time. Then, as a ninth grader, Orrin was named captain of the junior high team. He was still slender and wiry, stretching 118 pounds of skin and muscle over a frame that reached his full height of six-feet-two that year. A scrappy competitor, Orrin fouled out or was thrown out of no fewer than fifteen basketball games that season.

A family friend who encouraged Orrin to develop his athletic talent was Vernon Law, the great Pittsburgh Pirates right-hander, and a fellow Mormon. Law, nicknamed the "Deacon" by Pirates fans, would later win the Cy Young award as baseball's best pitcher. Law sometimes lived with the Hatches during the season, and said they were his greatest fans. The teenage Hatch idolized Law and never missed his games or the speeches he gave to church groups in the area. Helen Hatch said, "I think being around Vernon made Orrin believe he could be somebody and made him want to."

Friday nights often found Orrin and his father huddled around the radio, listening to the fights from Madison Square Garden. Inspired by great champions such as Rocky Graziano, Tony Zale, Sugar Ray Robinson, Gene Fullmer, Joe Louis, and Rocky Marciano, Orrin determined to improve his own body. He began a rigorous regimen of calisthenics and running, and took up amateur boxing. Jess had left a large khaki duffle bag at home and it became Orrin's punching bag. He filled the bag with sand and rags, hung it on a mulberry tree outside Helen's kitchen, donned twenty-nine-cent brown cotton garden gloves, and began walloping the bag. In time he came to pack a jarring punch for a youngster his size.

Orrin coveted his father's muscular build and found his own wiry frame a source of much frustration and embarrassment. But even in the rough part of town where they lived, he was known as a tough kid who, in a fistfight, never would admit he was beaten.

But he was not a rowdy. One of his favorite memories was attending performances of the Pittsburgh Symphony Orchestra, sitting high up in peanut heaven at the Syria Mosque. Helen and Jess would scrape together $18.75 for student season tickets, something teenage Orrin showed he appreciated by going to every concert so that not a penny of their sacrifice would be wasted.

Guest conductors he saw included Vladimir Bakilenokoff, Fritz Reiner, and Arturo Toscanini. World-class performers included Yehudi Menuhin, Isaac Stern, Vladimir Horowitz, and Artur Rubenstein. Orrin watched, enraptured, as Roberta Peters ("the most beautiful woman I had ever seen") made her debut in Pittsburgh. Before or after concerts, Orrin visited nearby museums and galleries, developing a love of art.

When Orrin turned sixteen in 1950, he became an apprentice in the Wood, Wire & Metal Lathers International Union. Like his father, Orrin was a loyal union member. Jesse later served for many years as president of Local 33L. Under his father's watchful eye, Orrin learned to make elliptical and gothic arches, plaster molding, suspended ceilings, fancy corners, high suspension floor lathing, and partitions. He also did rock lathing. Orrin worked at the trade each summer, eventually becoming a journeyman lather, and, like Jesse, a foreman on some jobs around Pittsburgh.

Orrin also was becoming politically aware. The Hatches, like most blue-collar families, were Democrats. "We thought President Roosevelt was the biggest hero that ever lived," recalled his mother. That view was widely shared by American laborers, especially in Pennsylvania where attempts to pass progressive measures desperately needed by workers before and during the Great Depression had been smothered by a Republican political machine that ruled the Commonwealth.

The nation's second richest state didn't elect a Democrat as governor or U.S. senator in this century until 1934. By then, despite its immense wealth, Pennsylvania ranked thirty-third among all states in amount of workmen's compensation, thirty-fourth in the length of time it took to receive compensation, fortieth in widows' compensation, and forty-fourth in medical assistance for injured workers.

As a teenager Orrin studied the injustices suffered by laborers in his state and elsewhere, reinforcing his growing loyalty to the Democrats. "I read books about the lives and times of Clarence Darrow, Samuel Gompers, and other great labor lawyers and leaders," he recalled. "I was appalled at how the men were bullied and pushed around by some of the great industrialists."

One day in the tenth grade, a teacher called on Orrin to read something on the blackboard. He couldn't. That was when his parents and teachers learned one secret of Orrin's fabulous memory: He had learned to retain in his head everything said in class because he was too nearsighted to see what teachers wrote on the board. Orrin started to wear glasses. New glasses helped Orrin's basketball performance, though with his aggressive style he often broke them while playing. "Being able to actually see the rim of the basket, instead of just an orange blur, seemed like the most wonderful thing in the world," he recalls.

He was the only junior to start on the Baldwin High varsity, but the team lost twenty-one straight games. A consolation for Orrin was his father's faithful attendance at nearly every home game. (Helen disliked sports.) "I always looked up to see if he was in the stands," Hatch recalls. "When he was there, I really tried harder than ever to play my best. Often it was a real sacrifice for him to attend, because he was so tired after doing physical work all day. But he was almost always there."

Jesse was a man of few words. If Orrin had starred, the most he'd say as they left the gymnasium together was, "Good game, son." If Orrin had played poorly, it was "Keep working on it. You did all right."

Orrin was developing into a fine player. There were hints of a possible college scholarship in his future. The summer after his junior year, Orrin and several other promising players joined a pickup league and began to hone their skills in earnest. Joining them was a new kid in town, Paul Wilcox—later an all-American at Davis and Elkins College; still later a professional player for Cleveland. The result was a dramatic turnabout in the basketball fortunes of Baldwin, a perennial patsy.

With Wilcox averaging about twenty-four points a game and Hatch feeding him the ball and usually scoring about fourteen more himself, Baldwin won the Triadic Conference championship for the first time. In the process, they twice beat defending Pittsburgh City champion Carrick High, with Orrin guarding Carrick's six-foot-eight center, "Meatball" Clark, holding him to four points in each game.

English teacher Eleanor Smith was the instructor who had the greatest influence on Orrin during that time. "She gave me a love for English literature which has been with me all my life," said Orrin, who corresponded with Smith for decades. "She was able to get across the idea and concept that English study creates lifelong benefits."

Orrin gained a reputation for rising to meet tough challenges. Another student was supposed to play a solo on a string bass in a school music festival but fell ill the day of the performance. The music director, a Mr. McElroy, talked Orrin into substituting for him—even though Orrin, a violinist, had never played the bass. McElroy coached Orrin for about an hour, and that evening Orrin played the solo flawlessly — receiving a standing ovation from the audience, who had been alerted to the situation.

During Orrin's senior year, he got his first taste of elective politics by being voted class vice president and winning a citizenship award. Baldwin High's mock presidential election heightened student awareness of the United States' presidential campaign. "In the first vote, [student] Senator Earl Lyons of New Jersey was in the lead with 53 votes," reported the school paper, "but because he did not have the majority vote of 66, the delegates had to vote again. Senator Hatch won the election. Congratulations." In a senior class poll published in the school newspaper, *The Purbalite*, Orrin was voted the "most likable" boy and, reflecting nostalgically on the school year, the same issue queried: "Can you imagine . . . Orin [sic] Hatch without a basketball?"

Next to his senior photo in the school yearbook was a thumbnail sketch:

> Basketball whiz . . . hardworking union man . . . plans to go to dental school . . . quite a musician . . . great sense of humor.
>
> Balthi, Orchestra, Key Club, Boys Leaders, Senior Class Officer, Hi-Y, Varsity Letterman, Football, Basketball, Intramurals.

Orrin didn't really plan to go to dental school. In fact, he didn't know what to do after graduation. He was seriously dating one of the few Mormon girls in the area. Perhaps he would attend a local college on a basketball scholarship, or marry immediately and work full-time as a lather. His parents panicked at that prospect. Denied much formal education themselves, they longed for their promising son to carry the Hatch colors to college.

Helen and Jesse thought LDS church-owned Brigham Young University in far-away Utah offered both a nurturing atmosphere and alternative distractions. They urged him to apply there. They promised to go along with the marriage if he was still in love after a year of college.

To sweeten the prospect, a $25 "citizenship" scholarship—one-third of a year's tuition—suddenly arrived from Utah. Orrin always suspected that his parents had engineered the scholarship and perhaps even paid for it. Nonetheless, seeing how much it meant to them, in the fall of 1952 he packed up and caught a ride west with a friend.

2

The Missionary

THE FORCE OF THE BLOW KNOCKED Hatch's head awkwardly backwards, his mouthpiece flying out of the ring. Jerry Muir, the BYU boxing instructor, was all over the dazed freshman, pummeling him with two uppercuts to the abdomen that hoisted him off the floor, a left jab to his face, and a crushing right hook to his head. Orrin doubled over and spat blood onto the canvas.

Welcome to BYU, Mr. Hatch.

Muir, a former all-Navy light-heavyweight champion, outweighed Hatch by thirty pounds. The sadistic beating was the result of two "offenses" by Hatch. First, he'd begun hitting the light bag on the first day of class *before* Muir had demonstrated how to do it. Later, Muir had put fourteen-ounce gloves and headgear on Hatch, telling Hatch to spar lightly but matched Hatch against a tough protégé whom he secretly instructed to rip the Eastern kid's head off.

After taking several sharp punches, Hatch got angry and tore into his sparring partner, knocking him flat. At that point, Muir climbed into the ring himself and pounded Hatch to hamburger.

Mormons are strongly encouraged to marry within the faith. Provo, a squeaky-clean town nestled in the foothills of the Rocky Mountains' Wasatch Range, cradled BYU. The school had traditionally played the role of spiritual haven and marriage market for Mormon high school graduates, who comprised 95 percent of its student body. When BYU's 6,325 students completed a survey during Hatch's freshman year, 58 percent said they chose the school because BYU "offers a superior spiritual and religious training." Only 8 percent said it was because "BYU offers superior academic training."

Yet school trustees—all drawn from the hierarchy of the LDS church, headquartered forty-five miles to the north in Salt Lake City—had issued BYU a mandate to become academically excellent. Ernest L. Wilkinson, a prominent LDS attorney, had been chosen in 1951 to effect the change. But the mandate came with a list of off-limits topics: sensitive areas such as church history, evolution, and theology had to conform to the official perspective.

Those in academic circles elsewhere in the nation took a dim view of these restrictions. Wilkinson, who reminded some people of a tough little bulldog, didn't mind the restrictions and imposed a few of his own. A political and theological conservative, he put himself on the school's traditional opening assembly program and lectured the students on school standards—no premarital sex, no tobacco, alcohol, or harmful drugs, no cheating on exams, and no walking on the grass. He always ended by asking students for a standing vote of their willingness to abide by all the standards and help the administration enforce them. The rare student who refused to stand was sent to the treasurer for a tuition refund.

Wilkinson, who prided himself on being a doer, not a thinker, launched BYU into a spiral of increasing enrollments and new construction that would see it become the nation's largest church-sponsored university. But his authoritarian style troubled thoughtful observers. He openly encouraged political conservatism and pressured some "liberal" instructors to resign.

The student body also swung toward conservatism. Hatch's arrival coincided with the 1952 presidential election between Dwight Eisenhower and Adlai Stevenson. In a campus opinion poll a few weeks before the election, 41 percent of the students identified themselves as Republicans, 21 percent as Democrats, and 38 percent independents. Four years later, on the eve of the second Eisenhower-Stevenson vote, 84 percent of students preferred Eisenhower and only 14 percent Stevenson.

But if campus politics had any impact on Hatch, his private writings do not show it. During his first year at BYU he seemed preoccupied instead with intramural basketball and amateur boxing. Even at the college level he was a basketball standout, starring on an intramural squad which took first place out of seventy-three teams. A photo taken immediately after the championship game early in 1953 shows BYU varsity coach Stan Watts presenting team members with first-place certificates. Hatch also fought in about ten three-round boxing matches his freshman year, winning most of them by technical knockouts. He hung up the gloves after walloping one opponent with a Kid Gavilan "bolo" punch, a complete-circle uppercut—to the knee.

Hatch maintained a solid "B" average and, at the end of the school year, returned to Pittsburgh to work as a lather for the summer. As his parents hoped, Hatch found that his world had expanded and his commitment to education had deepened. Although he dated his high school girlfriend occasionally over the summer, he was no longer interested in marrying and settling down just yet.

Returning for his second year in the fall of 1953, Hatch took a job as a lowly janitor. "No one wanted a janitor for a roommate except my friend and fellow janitor, LaVar Steel," he quips.

Steel's family was as poor as Hatch's. They lived in an old army barracks that had been converted into a dormitory and ate frugally. When Steel's family sent home-canned tomato juice, the two students "would scrape enough money together to buy some soda crackers," recalls Hatch, "and have a feast of tomato juice and crackers fit for kings."

Occasionally they got on each other's nerves. Once Steel, who outweighed Hatch by about forty pounds, insisted they go down to the boxing room and have it out. They pulled on gloves and climbed into the ring. The fired-up Steel quickly stunned Hatch with an overhand right. Hands at his side, Steel advanced on his apparently helpless roommate, who was clinging to the ropes. Then Hatch's head cleared. He catapulted off the ropes and hit Steel with a hard right-cross. Steel's knees buckled and he slumped to the canvas, eyes glazed. Hatch helped him up. They threw their arms around each other and never argued again.

Hatch had only two dates during his first two years on campus, both to girl's-choice events. "BYU is known as the marrying school and there were so many beautiful girls there," he mused. "But I couldn't bring myself to ask any of them out. I felt ashamed because I didn't have any money or any good clothes. They all seemed too good for me anyway." It was a painful repeat of his boyhood experiences with poverty. But thanks to alphabetical seating in astronomy class, pretty blonde Elaine Hansen sat next to Hatch. She was pleasant and helpful and they struck up a classroom friendship.

Hatch immersed himself in the religious instruction and activities sponsored by the Latter-day Saint congregations (called "wards" or "branches") into which students were divided according to housing area. "It was exciting to see people living Christian lives, and I really felt at home with them," he remembers warmly. "Most of the students were pretty sincere," but the occasional "classic pious phony really turned me off."

Hatch had held the Mormon priesthood since hands were placed on his head to ordain him a deacon at age twelve. Like most faithful

Mormon males, he was later ordained a "teacher" at fourteen, a "priest" at sixteen, and an "elder"—the first office in the church's higher "Melchizedek Priesthood"—at nineteen.

Many of the young men his age were preparing to go on full-time prose-lyting missions, and Hatch had a deep desire to join them. Most LDS missionaries serve at their own or their family's expense, and Hatch worked extra hours during the summer of 1954 to save the necessary money. He was interviewed by Spencer W. Kimball, a member of the Quorum of Twelve Apostles, who determined that Hatch was living church standards.

Before entering a training center in Salt Lake City, Hatch dropped by Heritage Halls, a girls' dormitory complex at BYU, to say good-bye to Elaine Hansen. He had never seen her outside astronomy class, but she agreed to write. Hatch entered the training center on October 11, 1954, assigned to the Great Lakes Mission.

An intensive week of instruction followed, including practical topics such as personal hygiene and conducting music, along with proselyting tips: what to say at the door, key scriptural references, and teaching methods.

Missionary rules were unequivocal: Keep members of the opposite sex at arm's length. Be with your assigned companion at all times. Males must wear dark suits, white shirts, ties, and a hat, and be called "Elders." Female missionaries, far fewer in number, were "Sisters." Missionaries wouldn't hear their first names again for two years.

English crown hats, with turned-down rims and a crease down the center, were *de rigueur* for elders. Before departing, Elder Hatch stopped at a Salt Lake store and selected a stylish midnight-blue number. Only later did he learn to his chagrin that what he thought was an English crown bowler was actually a homburg, a more formal older man's hat.

His hat wasn't the only thing that set Hatch apart from other Great Lakes missionaries. Mormon lore is filled with stories of particularly zealous or otherwise quirky missionaries who drive their companions nuts. Hatch, with no apologies, was one of those. "My commitment was total. I was going to be the best missionary in the church. Nothing was going to stop me. I had found the Lord at the age of seventeen, the first time I read and prayed about the Book of Mormon, and I was going to find him anew and preach him wherever I went."

Hatch taught the same message as that of church founder Joseph Smith. As a fourteen-year-old boy in upstate New York, Smith in the spring of 1820 went into a grove of trees near his family's farm and prayed to know which church to join. He said that a light descended until it fell upon him, in which he saw God the Father and Jesus Christ standing above him. They instructed him to join none of the existing sects. At that time, Mormons believe, the youthful prophet received his commission to be instrumental in restoring the church that Christ had established when he was on earth, but which had fallen away through an "apostasy"—errors from within the church and persecution from outside it.

Three and a half years later Smith said he was visited by another heavenly messenger named Moroni. In Smith's words, Moroni told him that "God had a work for me to do." In vision, Moroni showed Smith where a set of gold plates which contained "the fulness of the everlasting Gospel" was buried in a hill near his home. The record was an abridged account of God's dealings with peoples of the American continent, including a visit by Christ after his death and resurrection in Jerusalem. The abridgement was made by a prophet named Mormon, whose son, Moroni, had buried the record in the hill. Joseph Smith said that Moroni returned centuries later as a divine messenger to reveal it to him.

Smith said he was allowed to remove the engraved plates from the hill in 1827. He translated the record and published it in 1830 as the Book of Mormon, a new volume of scripture testifying of Christ—not a replacement for the Bible but a companion to it.

From then on, missionaries distributed the Book of Mormon throughout the world, encouraging readers to pray about it and test the following promise given in the book:

> And when ye shall receive these things, I would exhort you that ye would ask God, the Eternal Father, in the name of Christ, if these things are not true; and if ye shall ask with a sincere heart, with real intent, having faith in Christ, he will manifest the truth of it unto you, by the power of the Holy Ghost.
>
> And by the power of the Holy Ghost ye may know the truth of all things. (Moroni 10:4-5)

During the nineteenth century, the church gained converts rapidly, but suffered severe persecution. Joseph Smith and his brother Hyrum were killed by a mob in 1844 in Illinois. Three years later, Smith's successor Brigham Young led the Mormons across the Great Plains and established church headquarters in what is now Utah. The church continuously encouraged its missionaries to "declare the restored gospel."

In 1954 Hatch was among some two thousand full-time missionaries whom the church sent to forty-two missions throughout the world.

His mission president was a Utah dentist named Lorin L. Richards, who, assisted by his wife, Florence, had been "called" by church leaders to preside over the Great Lakes Mission. "When Elder Hatch first got there he told us he was going to fill two missions during the two years— one for himself and one for his brother who was killed in World War II," recalled Florence Richards.

Hatch made a pact with another new elder to determine who was the single best missionary in the Great Lakes Mission, find out how many hours a week he spent tracting door-to-door, and exceed that number. Hatch found his ideal missionary—a former All-American football player—and set his proselyting goal at sixty hours a week—ten to fifteen more than most missionaries were putting in.

His first assignment was to Springfield, Ohio, and his first companion was an experienced elder from St. George, Utah. Much to the impatient Hatch's irritation, he was such a straight arrow he wouldn't even cross a street in the middle of a block. Furthermore, he was "so serious that sometimes he appeared to lack a good sense of humor." Hatch added, without a hint of irony, that "we got along quite well but he did sometimes resent my continual desire to exceed the top record in the mission field."

Missionaries were supposed to follow a rigorous and inflexible schedule: Arise at 6 A.M.; be showered, shaved, and dressed by 7; complete breakfast by 7:30; study scriptures and lesson "discussions" until 8:45; hit the streets at 9; knock on doors and teach all day, return to their apartments by 10 P.M. The desire of Hatch and his companion to be out teaching received impetus from their unappetizing "digs." Hatch described this first missionary apartment as dingy, cold, dimly lit, and infested with bold roaches that ran up the walls and filled the bathtub.

"The Springfield Branch of the church met in the YWCA downtown," Hatch recalls. "They had not had many converts over the prior three years." Hatch and his companion baptized over twenty people before he was rotated to a new assignment six months later.

One door they knocked on was more memorable than most. Inside a potbellied man in a dirty T-shirt was waiting for them, a large revolver in hand.

"I'm going to blow your head off," he growled, aiming the gun in Hatch's face.

Hatch, heart racing, looked coolly at the gunman. "We represent the Lord Jesus Christ," he announced, "and if you pull that trigger, your gun will explode and kill you."

The man slowly lowered his pistol as Hatch and his companion backed away. Reaching the sidewalk, they took off running. "I wasn't about to see if my prediction would come true, and we sure weren't going to give him another chance!" Hatch exclaimed.

Missionary work, Hatch decided, was "a life of opposites—good and evil attacking each other, with us missionaries caught in between." He found laboring among the poor "far more rewarding" than among the self-assured rich, and he took his assignment with the utmost serious-ness. "We had been ordained to the priesthood—the power to preside, heal the sick, administer the ordinances of the church, and teach the gospel through our ministry."

Hatch said he personally witnessed "the blind see, the lame walk, the barren have children, the bitter and disillusioned gain hope, sicknesses of all types healed, the poor gain success, the ignorant become wise, evil transformed into good, boy missionaries become men, young sister missionaries become women, and peace come into troubled lives for the first time."

Mormons are firm believers in healing through priesthood blessings, and some of Hatch's peak memories involve occasions when he invoked his priesthood authority to call down a blessing on the suffering.

One day Hatch and his companion received an urgent phone call from a Sister Hill who, along with her six children, had been learning the Mormon message. One of her young sons had been admitted to the Catholic hospital in Springfield.

"Please come quickly," she begged, "Hybert is terribly sick." Doctors had taken X-rays and found a malignancy on his kidney.

Hatch and his companion sprinted to the hospital and walked swiftly to the boy's room. There, two nuns were physically holding the moaning boy to the bed as he writhed in agony. "We're his ministers," Hatch told the shaken nurses. "Please allow us to have a few minutes alone with him." The nuns agreed and left the room.

In a quiet, dignified ceremony, deeply rooted in Mormon tradition, the two placed their hands on the boy's head and pronounced a blessing. Hatch promised the boy that he would be healed and that the pain would subside so that he could sleep. "As we took our hands off his head," Hatch recalls, "he immediately relaxed and went to sleep."

The next morning, doctors took another set of X-rays and were astounded at what they showed. The malignancy—clearly visible in the first set—was completely gone in the second.

A particularly challenging "investigator" of the faith was a frail woman recluse. She shared a small house with her brother. Missionaries had been meeting with her for a year with no apparent progress toward baptism although she professed a belief in Mormon doctrines. To Hatch and his companion she finally explained why she could not bear the thought of being around other people—in church or elsewhere.

"My late husband was a very cruel man," she began haltingly. "Knowing how much I love animals, he taunted me by doing terrible things to birds and other little creatures. When I became pregnant, I was so ill that I had to spend a lot of time in bed." Her husband would capture birds, break their wings, and throw them onto her bedroom floor. As they flopped around in terror before her eyes, he would summon a cat to kill them.

One day he had another idea. "Look, you don't want this baby anyway," he told her. "And I sure don't want it. I know what to do about it." He urged her into an abortion.

"She was haunted by the memory of his terrible cruelties and racked with guilt over the abortion," recalls Hatch. "It had ruined her life." It was Hatch's first contact with the issue of abortion and he was horrified.

Hatch and his companion patiently counseled the woman, telling her God would forgive her and she must forgive herself. Slowly they helped rebuild her self-esteem but she still refused to leave the house. As they walked out the door after praying with her one day, Hatch said, almost as an afterthought, "We'll be here to walk you to church on Sunday." She started to protest but they were off, pretending not to hear.

Trudging down an icy sidewalk, Hatch's companion lit into him. "Why did you say that? You know we'll have to walk two miles through the snow to get here—and there's no way she's going to go with us."

"That's exactly *why* I said it," answered Hatch. "*She* knows we'll have to go those long cold miles out of our way for her, and I'm betting she won't want to disappoint us." Hatch won the bet. The woman accompanied them to church the following Sunday, the beginning of her reentry into society. Later, after Hatch had been transferred from the area, she was baptized by another missionary, and came to enjoy the companionship of people at church and elsewhere.

While attending a missionary conference in Cleveland, Hatch was strongly impressed to excuse himself before it was over and drive south to Mansfield, some two hours away, to give a priesthood blessing to a sister missionary named Lorraine Miller, so sick with a month-long respiratory infection that the mission president had decided to send her home to recuperate. Also visiting the sister missionaries were the local branch president and Jeremiah Saunders, a church member who worked for the state office of education. Hatch blessed Miller that she would get well and be able to complete her mission.

Then Saunders, a tall man with flaming red hair and a slight Southern accent, said he had been suffering from bleeding peptic ulcers for twenty years and a doctor had recommended surgery. "Would you mind giving me a health blessing too?" he asked. Hatch obliged, blessing Saunders that his ulcers would be healed. Hatch would not learn the results of that blessing until he met Saunders a few years later in an encounter that helped set the stage for Hatch's future in politics.

The following day, Sister Miller was back on her feet proselyting. She credited that blessing with saving her mission.

Hatch also served in Sandusky, Ohio. In addition to routine missionary duties, he became the presiding officer (branch president) of the Sandusky Branch and the first president of their Relief Society —

highly unusual for a man, since Relief Society is the *women's* auxiliary.

Despite Hatch's intensity, he had a good sense of humor and relished the lighter moments of missionary life. Most residents of Sandusky were Catholic. Dressed in dark suits and overcoats, with Hatch in his trademark homburg, the missionaries enjoyed walking city streets. "People would wave to us and say, 'Good morning, Father,'" recalls Hatch. "I would reach my hand out to them and say, 'Bless you.'" In one home, a woman asked Hatch to take her confession. He defused the moment with a Mormon-style joke: "I told her I had graduated from being a priest and I was now an elder."

On another occasion Hatch and his companion were teaching a group of ten women. They expressed interest in what they were learning about the Mormons but seemed bothered by something. Finally a designated spokesperson got to the point.

"The only thing we need to know is: do you have more than one wife?"

Hatch whipped out his wallet and brandished a photo of Elaine Hansen and one of her girlfriends on either side of him. "Here are mine!" he said. It took him three weeks to convince the women that he was kidding and that polygamy had been outlawed by the church more than a half-century earlier.

Elaine, a wholesome farm girl from Newton, Utah, had been writing Hatch weekly throughout his mission, as she had promised. Her encouraging letters, which always seemed to arrive when he needed a lift, had deepened his interest in her.

Hatch was assigned next to Fort Wayne, Indiana, and to a companion who reportedly was the smallest male missionary in the church—an elder who, with his hat on, could walk beneath Hatch's outstretched arm. Elder Barr, fresh off a farm in eastern Idaho, was timid to the point of being terrified. When tracting door-to-door, he tended to melt into Hatch's shadow, so that those answering the door often didn't see him at first.

Although Barr panicked at the prospect of teaching his first lesson, Hatch believed missionaries should jump into the work immediately and insisted Barr take every other lesson. Midway through each memorized discussion, however, Barr invariably stumbled over the introduction to the Book of Mormon, forcing Hatch to finish the lesson.

The routine was repeated over and over during their first two weeks together. Hatch, on edge from doing all the cooking and cleaning so Barr could memorize, finally exploded one morning as his companion practiced aloud.

"Elder Barr," Hatch yelled, "what in the world is wrong with you? Aren't you *ever* going to learn this? I'm doing all the teaching and all the work here and you keep making the same mistakes over and over. Now try it again."

Fuming, Hatch went back to the dishes. Barr silently got up from his chair and left the room. When he hadn't returned ten minutes later, Hatch knew he had hurt his feelings and went looking for him. Barr was sitting on his bed sobbing. Hatch swept him up in his arms, cradling him and apologizing, as the diminutive elder continued to weep.

Putting him down, Hatch, with sudden insight, asked, "Elder Barr, have you ever read the Book of Mormon?"

There was a pause, then a broken, "No."

Hatch was stunned. "How can you possibly teach other people about the gospel when you yourself haven't read the book you're bearing testimony about?"

Hatch struck a deal: He would give all the lessons, start to finish, from now on. Barr was to forget everything else until he had read the Book of Mormon. Barr readily agreed. They shook hands, knelt and prayed, and left the apartment.

Hatch broke their agreement at the very first house when a beautiful, kindly, white-haired lady just Barr's size answered their knock. "It was kind of a dirty thing to do to him," Hatch recalled, "but something told me this was a perfect candidate for him to teach."

After offering the opening prayer, Hatch called upon Elder Barr to teach the lesson. Barr, stunned, looked anxiously at Hatch, then proceeded into the lesson. It was rough and ragged as before, but somehow Barr plowed on to the end for the first time. As he finished and gave an almost audible sigh of relief, the woman smiled broadly.

"My, what a wonderful lesson you have taught me," she said. "You certainly know your scriptures."

Barr sat up straighter and his eyes brightened. Hatch felt a strange lump in his throat at the spark he was seeing for the first time in his companion.

Two weeks later the woman and her husband, dressed all in white, stepped into a baptismal font, one at a time. Waiting there was Elder Barr, now standing very tall in the waist-high water. He raised his hand, intoned the baptismal prayer over each, and immersed his second converts. He himself had been the first.

Later in his mission, Hatch was asked to help supervise other missionaries in the Southern Indiana District. His companion was an Elder Olson, a tall, lanky cowboy from Montana who weighed about ten pounds less than Hatch, who now tipped the scales at about 145 pounds. If Hatch represented one end of the missionary spectrum of zealousness, missionaries in this district were often at the other. The locale was an alternative to sending them home in disgrace for goofing off. Hatch's job: to work with Olson to shape up the slackers.

Olson, however, had served in that district before Hatch arrived and had deep misgivings. Some missionaries had threatened to thrash him if he disturbed their unstressed life.

Hatch proposed a plan: "If I raise one finger, that means we'll show so much love to the missionaries that they'll feel ashamed and will want to do the work with us. Two fingers means that our love approach didn't work and you and I will go out and find such a long list of investigators that, in good conscience, they'll have to go back and teach them. If that doesn't work, I'll put up three fingers and we'll kick the shit out of them."

Elder Hatch's years around tough-talking tradesmen back in Pittsburgh continued to color his language. Hatch never used anything stronger than garden-variety swear words, however, and never blasphemed.

Olson was dubious but had no choice. They picked up two reluctant missionaries in one city and moved them to Washington, Indiana. Most missionaries were between the ages of nineteen and twenty-one, but one of these two was a tall, muscular twenty-seven-year-old convert. "He was one of the great detractors around and had never worked more than twelve hours a week since entering the mission field," recalls Hatch.

When they first met, the twenty-seven-year-old held out his hand in a friendly gesture to Olson. As Olson stuck out his hand, the other missionary hit him hard in the stomach. Olson doubled over in pain. "Oh, Elder, did I hurt you? I was just joking," said Elder "Muscles" with mock concern. That evening, after locating an apartment and stocking it with food, Hatch and Olson asked to have prayer with the other two before going to bed. Elder "Muscles," grinning broadly, reached out his hand to Hatch in agreement. When Hatch automatically responded, "Muscles" hit Hatch in the stomach. Hatch now saw before him not a missionary but an old punching bag hanging from a mulberry tree back in Pittsburgh.

"I wound up and hit him right in the stomach with everything I had," Hatch remembers. "He had been out in the mission field so long and had done so little exercise that his stomach was flabby. I swear my fist went all the way to his backbone."

The missionary's face turned beet-red and he fell to the floor gasping. When he got his wind he started to cry. "Oh Elder, did I hurt you?" Hatch asked. "I was just joking."

The elder lay on the floor for nearly an hour. When he finally pulled himself together, the four missionaries knelt together and prayed. Then Hatch said, "Let's go to bed because we have to get up at six o'clock."

"I'm not getting up at six!" announced the rebellious elder.

"You sure as hell are," promised Hatch.

Hatch slept fitfully that night on a cold concrete floor with no pillow or blanket and only a sheet under him. When the alarm clock went off at six, Elder "Muscles" refused to get up. Hatch, already irritable, threw him out of bed and onto the floor. Squaring off, Hatch announced grimly, "Elder, you're going to get ready, you're going to leave here by nine o'clock, and you're going to work with me all day." Terrified, the elder offered no argument.

As they prepared to leave the apartment—at nine o'clock sharp—Hatch offered to knock on every door, give every prayer, and teach every discussion if his reluctant partner would just accompany him. Olson in turn worked with Elder "Muscles' " companion.

"That week we held sixty-five meetings in homes throughout the city," recalls Hatch. "I believe we did more work in that one week than that missionary had done during his whole mission." By midweek Elder "Muscles" was no longer just going through the motions. He was carrying his share of the load—and continued to do so throughout the balance of his mission. Years later he met Hatch on Temple Square in Salt Lake City. Now a Mormon bishop—head of a local congregation—he thanked Hatch for a lesson taught him long ago in Indiana.

On one swing through a number of cities where missionaries worked, Hatch and a new companion, an Elder Heinz, were baffled by the meals awaiting them. Hatch was not generally a picky eater but he couldn't stand navy bean soup. Yet in city after city, the welcoming missionaries fed them navy bean soup, always laced with purple dye. Finally Hatch and Elder Heinz realized they were the butt of a great joke: Host missionaries would learn their next destination and contact those elders, suggesting a menu.

The two years passed quickly. President Richards was amazed by Hatch's success, and his wife Florence called Elder Hatch "the most wonderful missionary the church ever had." They couldn't clone Hatch, so they cloned his hat instead. When Hatch returned home at the end of two years, scores of Great Lakes missionaries had been forced out of their prized English crowns and into homburgs. And Hatch's own homburg had been bronzed and retired as a traveling trophy for the most successful missionary district. In later years, Lorin Richards often told audiences that Elder Hatch had fulfilled his pledge to serve the equivalent of two missions—one for himself and one for his deceased brother Jess.

Much of that success had come through sheer will. Working past his physical limits to exhaustion, Hatch had endured a headache almost every day during the last eighteen months of his two-year mission. He and his companions averaged sixty-six hours a week proselyting, held thirty-nine meetings a week, and distributed over three thousand copies of the Book of Mormon.

Decades later, as a sitting member of the U.S. Senate, Hatch termed his mission experience, "the most important two years of my life."

3

From Henhouse to Courthouse

E VEN AMONG THE WEATHER-HARDENED farmers of Cache Valley, Utah, Sidney Hansen was known as tough and particular. He coaxed beets, wheat, and hay out of the ground during the valley's short growing season, and farmed a second piece of land to the north in Bancroft, Idaho.

All five of the Hansen children helped in the fields as soon as they were old enough to tell the difference between a boulder and a bullfrog. When it came to work, Sidney made few distinctions between his son, Ramon (pronounced "Raymon") and his four daughters. Elaine, Hatch's mission pen pal, was the oldest child.

For the children it was all hand labor. They thinned beets and picked beans during the summer, then were released from school for "beet vacation" each October, when they used an implement that combined a beaklike hook for yanking the beets out of the ground with blades for whacking off the tops.

Pitchforks were the implements of choice for gathering up the hay. Many farm families were content to simply thresh the weeds growing along with the wheat, but the Hansen children walked the golden fields row by row, keeping a sharp lookout for rye and plucking it out before the combine came behind to harvest the wheat.

Newton was a typical Mormon community, both its social and its religious life revolving around the church. The town became still on the Sabbath. In the morning, most families gathered in Sunday School, where both children and adults received religious instruction, then returned home for big dinners and afternoons together before returning for evening sacrament meetings (preaching services and communion).

For teenagers during the week there was MIA (Mutual Improvement Association), an evening of lessons, games, and other activities with moral overtones. During the school year there was also an hour of religious instruction, called seminary, each weekday for Mormon high school students. Except for the Mormon flavor, Newton was Norman Rockwell's small-town Americana. Elaine and her three younger sisters cheered for their high school teams and learned to cook and sew. Ramon, a handsome six-footer with dark brown hair, was the family's pride: a star basketball player and the football team's quarterback. He married soon after high school and earned two degrees in electrical engineering at nearby Utah State University.

Although the Hansens were a reserved family who seldom expressed affection openly, "we were quietly happy," recalls Elaine. "We worked awfully hard, but it was a great place to grow up. There were only a few hundred people in town, and everybody knew everybody. The older people were always checking up on us; we all felt that we belonged."

The biggest summer holiday was not the Fourth of July but the *Twenty-fourth*, filled with parades, picnics, and fireworks to commemorate the day in 1847 when Brigham Young and the first Mormon wagon train entered Salt Lake Valley.

Elaine, seeking more independence, headed south to BYU in the fall of 1952, while her sisters later followed Ramon to Utah State. She majored in elementary education, stayed in touch with friends at campus parties organized by the Cache Valley Club, and belonged at different times to two social units—BYU's version of sororities and fraternities—the Kappa Debonaires and the Y-Calcares, a service unit.

Her social life was average and adequate, so it was honest friendliness, not connivance, that made Elaine smile and chat with Hatch when alphabetical seating put them side by side in astronomy class during their sophomore year. They had never had a date; but when the intense, slightly built Easterner stopped by her dorm in the fall of 1954 to ask her to write while he was on a mission, she agreed cheerfully and kept her side of the bargain. Her weekly letters contained unfailing warmth, encouragement, and, on occasion, challenge when Hatch expressed discouragement in his own almost-weekly letters.

The letters had moved beyond duty long before Hatch's mission drew to a close. Then in August of 1956, twenty-one-year-old Ramon, a college student and a father of one child with another one on the way, developed a fever, muscular cramps—and then suddenly, paralysis. He had contracted two virulent forms of the dread disease, polio. A year earlier, Jonas E. Salk's vaccine had been declared safe and effective, but Ramon had not yet been inoculated. He spent a full year in an iron lung and afterwards was confined to a wheelchair and a portable breathing apparatus.

Elaine, so used to encouraging Hatch, now turned to him in sorrow and bewilderment, struggling to understand why her younger brother had been stricken down in the prime of life. Hatch's heart ached for Elaine and her family, and he tried to comfort them, writing that somehow Ramon's illness must be God's will and that he would pray for Ramon's recovery.

"I don't remember precisely what Orrin wrote to us, but I do remember it helped us cope with our grief," says Elaine.

Hatch was released from his mission in Cleveland, Ohio, two months later, and reached Pittsburgh on a Sunday in October 1956. On Monday morning, he was hard at work lathing, and grateful for the job. Even though he and Elaine had not formally dated, through their courtship-by-correspondence, by the end of his mission they believed they were in love. She had graduated from BYU in the spring and was teaching elementary school that fall.

At Christmas, Hatch drove from Pittsburgh to Newton, Utah, to meet Elaine's family and discuss the future. Elaine, he concluded, "was everything I expected her to be: decent, clean, intelligent, spiritual, desirous of a big family, and lovely in every way."

Elaine visited Hatch's family in Pittsburgh early the next summer and they set a wedding date for August. He would work for a year before returning to college. Meanwhile, Elder Hatch's reputation from the Great Lakes Mission followed him home, and he was called by the church to direct its missionary work in the Pittsburgh area as a volunteer.

Hatch and his father drove to Utah that summer for his marriage to Elaine. His mother already was in Utah visiting a married daughter. While crossing the country, Jesse belatedly delivered an embarrassed lecture about the facts of life to his equally embarrassed son. Although Hatch was twenty-three, he had never had a sexual relationship or seen a nude woman in the flesh. In fact, he was about to be married without formally courting his new bride—unusual even in straitlaced church circles.

On August 28, 1957, he and Elaine were married in the Salt Lake Temple, a rite of enormous meaning for Mormons, who believe marriages performed in temples potentially bind families together for eternity as well as for mortality.

During the wedding reception, Elaine's friends decorated the honeymoon car with shaving cream letters: "Amateur Night." Hatch says, "Little did they know how true that was. I was embarrassed to death and washed the car before we left Newton."

Ramon and his young family were living in Downey, California, so Orrin and Elaine headed there for the honeymoon. They took Ramon and his wife through the Los Angeles Temple, Hatch carrying his brother-in-law from room to room during the two-hour "endowment" ceremony in which participants make solemn covenants of obedience and righteousness to the Lord, first on their own behalf and then, on subsequent visits, as proxies for deceased individuals.

Hatch returned to BYU that fall, and Elaine taught at a nearby elementary school. It was practical, even necessary, but he didn't like the arrangement much. "One of the greatest difficulties I had was having Elaine support me financially for any length of time," Hatch says. Prior to his mission, Hatch had earned a "B" average. Now he studied harder, taking an oversize load while working full time as a store clerk and making frequent trips to Salt Lake City, nearly an hour's drive away, to help instruct missionaries at the church's training center. He began getting almost straight "A's."

Because of the great satisfaction Hatch found in helping people solve problems, he set the goal of becoming an attorney. He majored in history but his favorite subject was philosophy.

Two professors who especially toughened his intellect both told him they had serious doubts about the authenticity of the LDS church. One taught history and the other was an English professor and dean of the College of Humanities. During a directed readings course from the history instructor, Hatch asked to read the six-volume *Comprehensive History of the Church* by B. H. Roberts, a General Authority and one of the most towering intellectuals the church produced in the nineteenth century. The professor agreed, on one condition: Hatch must spend equal time reading anti-Mormon literature.

Hatch eagerly accepted the challenge. He read tens of thousands of pages of anti-Mormon literature, in print and on microfilm, finding some of it mildly troubling but the great majority of it merely scurrilous. Instead of shaking his faith, the anti-Mormon readings made it steel-hard. Each week he met for a one-hour oral exam with the professor, who tried strenuously but failed to poke holes in Hatch's faith.

For decades to come, Hatch would give seminars to LDS missionaries on "how to answer objections to the gospel"–based in good part on answering his own questions during the voluminous anti-Mormon readings at BYU.

Hatch took literature and creative writing classes from the English professor who also expressed doubts. Hatch considered him one of the best teachers he ever had. The recently returned missionary strengthened his own faith while trying to strengthen the faith of the two professors, but both men later left BYU and reportedly severed their ties with the church.

A surprise diversion in the summer of 1958 foreshadowed Hatch's future in politics. Passing a campus auditorium, he heard a familiar voice with a Southern accent. Hatch stepped in to see middle-aged Jeremiah Saunders giving a rousing speech. Jeremiah was the man with peptic ulcers Hatch had met briefly in Ohio two years earlier during his mission.

Hatch had seen Saunders on campus just that morning for the first time since Ohio. Saunders had explained he was there to take a class and had asked Hatch, "Do you remember administering to me for a bleeding peptic ulcer?" Hatch had remembered. "Well, after twenty years of ulcers, I haven't had one problem since the day of that blessing," Saunders said. They had exchanged pleasantries and parted.

Now Saunders uninhibitedly joined in a student body meeting to nominate candidates for summer student body offices. Saunders' speech was a stemwinder, bringing gales of mirth as his arms pumped and flame-red curls fanned the air. Then Hatch froze. Saunders was shouting: "I don't remember his first name, but nonetheless I place in nomination for student body president the name of the greatest missionary ever to serve in the Great Lakes Mission, Elder Hatch!"

Shouts went up for Hatch. He cowered in the back. When a faculty advisor asked if anyone by that name was in the audience, one of Hatch's friends spotted him and yelled, "There he is!" Hatch, close to fainting from fright, was forced to the front. He protested that he was too busy to get involved. Furthermore, Elaine was pregnant, the baby due in October. The faculty advisor asked him to be a good sport, however, and finally Hatch agreed to leave his name in nomination. "I did it only because I knew I wouldn't win, since I wasn't planning to do any campaigning."

Again Saunders intervened. "My wife and I and our eight kids will run your campaign," he shouted. Laughter again rocked the room.

"I could have killed Saunders," Hatch confessed.

When he arrived on campus the next morning, it was strewn with crudely painted signs announcing "Hatch for President." Saunders and his family had stayed up all night making and posting them. They had even arranged transportation to Hatch's classes: a sign-laden donkey. The unorthodox campaign worked and Hatch was elected BYU's summer student body president.

His most memorable moment as president came during the first event he presided over—a campus dance. He and Elaine attended with Bill and Carol Nixon, who would become lifelong friends. In spite of sweltering heat, Hatch dutifully wore his official new white wool sweater with a block "Y" on the pocket. He was sweating profusely, both from the heat and the apprehension of being on display. The four were seated inside the ballroom, separated from refreshments on the patio by sliding glass doors.

"With a flourish that I thought was expected of a student body president, I stood up and said, 'I'll go get us some pizza,'" recalls Hatch. He stepped briskly toward the patio and walked straight into the floor-to-ceiling glass partition.

"I was so self-conscious and so stunned after smacking my head on the pane, that I still couldn't fathom that this was not an open exit. I backed up a couple of steps, shook my head, thought for a moment that this is only a strange passing experience, and then walked right into the window again."

Other students cheered, thinking their new president was cleverly trying to entertain them. "I just stood there with a silly grin, thinking what a total and complete ass I was."

Orrin and Elaine's first child, Brent, was born in October 1958. Orrin, who had raised his grade point to about 3.4, graduated two months later. They headed east to Pittsburgh with all their worldly belongings in a station wagon, and Hatch immediately began lathing to save money for law school. He and Jesse remodeled the chicken coop behind his parents' house into a tiny two-room cottage, added a toilet and small stove, and Orrin, Elaine, and Brent moved in.

In the summer of 1959, Hatch took the law school entrance exam at the University of Pittsburgh. It was a Saturday, the only day except Sunday he didn't work as a lather. It took determination to go through with the test. "My hands were cracked and sore from lathing. I looked around me and saw well-dressed and very intelligent people. I wondered if I really belonged in this elite group." Again Hatch's feelings of inferiority surfaced.

Hatch then went to the registrar's office, but it was locked for the weekend. Discouraged, he turned to leave, when a professor came around the corner.

"May I help you?" asked the kindly instuctor who introduced himself as Jack Rappeport.

"No, I don't think so," said Hatch, but he explained his problem to this teacher, who opened the office, got Hatch an application form, and then asked, "Where'd you go to school?"

"Brigham Young University."

"Are you a Mormon?"

"Yes."

"You Mormons are really good students. Some of the toughest competitors I had in law school were the Mormons. Why don't you apply for a scholarship?"

"I don't think my grades are that good," Hatch admitted. "I have about a 3.4 overall, although I did get mostly A's my last two years."

"Look," said Rappeport, "I think you can earn a scholarship on that basis. I'm a member of the scholarship committee, and you should apply."

Hatch did apply—and two weeks later received a full honors scholarship to the law school, which paid his tuition for all three years. "I don't know how I would have gone to school otherwise," he said. "Rappeport's intervention was an answer to prayer."

When Hatch began school in the fall of 1960, he anxiously tried to find Rappeport to thank him. But Rappeport, after just one year at the University of Pittsburgh, had moved on to another law school.

Hatch and twenty-seven other would-be lawyers attended classes on the fourteenth floor of the Cathedral of Learning. Hatch found law school difficult at the outset and had a mediocre first semester after one professor graded him low because of poor handwriting. Hatch typed all exams from then on and his grades improved dramatically. Hatch made *Law Review*, the school's legal periodical staffed by top students who were nominated and selected by the faculty, midway through his second year. The next year, he graduated near the top of his class.

Labor law especially interested him. Still a card-carrying union man and sometime lather, he hoped to use legal skills to assist fellow laborers. During a torts class his first year, however, Hatch's mind often went blank under the withering questions on civil law thrown at him by Professor Herbert Sherman, a former Marine top sergeant. Sherman, a national labor arbitrator and noted expert in the field, would describe a hypothetical case, scan the room for a victim, and often bark "Hatch!" who was scared to death of him. Hatch began reading voraciously on the subject, however, and the next semester won the American Jurisprudence Prize in torts. By his third year he was arguing with Sherman and even correcting him in class.

Marcia and Scott were born during Hatch's three years in law school. Now five of them lived in the dank, uninsulated chicken coop cottage whose walls turned black from humidity each winter and were repainted by Orrin and Jesse each spring. During his last year, Hatch worked as a desk attendant at a girls' dormitory from 11 P.M. to 7 A.M. When he got off duty, he ate breakfast at the Pitt Cafeteria and then attended classes until two or three o'clock. Hatch survived on about four hours of sleep most nights and was perpetually tired.

Elaine pitched in to keep the family financially afloat when she was not pregnant. She worked two or three days a week as a substitute teacher, while Helen took care of the children.

Despite school and financial pressures, Hatch scrupulously avoided studying on Sunday, a day he and Elaine devoted to taking the children to church and volunteering their services to the local congregation. "This meant that, while other Law Review members studied as much as eighty hours a week, I could only study about twenty hours a week. So those twenty hours had to be four times as effective as the time put in by my competitors."

Hatch's preceptor, John Chaffo, took a personal interest in the bright, hard-pressed student and hired him at fifty dollars a month to do title searches on weekends. Chaffo also gave Hatch several discarded suits. They didn't fit well—Chaffo outweighed him by nearly fifty pounds—but they were better than anything else in Hatch's closet and he was sincerely grateful.

Years later, as a U.S. senator, Hatch returned to Pitt Law School to deliver a lecture. In the audience were Sherman and Chaffo. When Hatch thanked Chaffo publicly for the generosity that helped him survive law school, the former preceptor's eyes brimmed with tears.

Hatch's political views had changed considerably since he was a youth. He explains: "As a union worker, I heard only one side of things. Almost all the people I knew were working people and Democrats. But I found out later that some of the things I was proud of as a union man were wrong. The Democrats wanted to spend more, raise taxes, and force more government regulations on business. They believed in central control and less personal responsibility. It gradually dawned on me that Democrats were really compassionate, not to the poor, but mainly to union leaders who could help them stay in power." It was a disillusioning realization.

Hatch's political transformation had begun at conservative Brigham Young University and his LDS mission had opened his eyes to exploitation among the poor themselves. "I went on my mission believing that anyone who was poorer than we were in Pittsburgh should have everything given to them. But I saw the difference in the lives of people who counted on handouts to keep them going, and those who struggled to stay independent and maintain their self-respect."

Finally, Hatch says his political views came full circle in law school as he saw how an intrusive government can harm individuals and businesses. In Hatch's turn to the right, however, he developed a healthy suspicion of political extremism and was determined not to turn too far. When several acquaintances tried to recruit him into the recently organized John Birch Society, he refused. "There was something I sensed about that organization that kept me from joining," he wrote. "Those I knew who were interested had an almost rabid fanaticism."

Hatch's first ethical test as a would-be attorney came shortly before graduation in 1962 when he was offered a job with the city's largest defense law firm. There was one stipulation: he must sign an agreement that, if he left the firm, he wouldn't work for any of its clients for five years. Legal jobs were scarce and Hatch desperately needed this one to improve his family's circumstances. But he considered the no-competition agreement unfair and refused to sign it.

"Every lawyer here has signed this agreement," said a white-haired senior partner. "But we respect you and your honesty, and will just take your word for it."

"If I gave my word that would bind me even tighter," answered Hatch, "because I would have to give you every benefit of the doubt if any question ever arose."

"Well, think it over," said the senior partner. Hatch arose, dejected, and left the plush offices.

He walked out onto Grant Street in a daze, wondering what to do next. Before he'd gone a block, he heard the insistent voice of his mentor John Chaffo. "Orrin," yelled Chaffo, "I hope you haven't taken a job yet. The best small firm in town wants to talk to you."

Chaffo, who had recommended Hatch all over Pittsburgh, took him immediately to the Frick Building. There, on the fifteenth floor, he was ushered into the offices of Pringle, Bredin, and Martin, the city's oldest firm. It specialized in defense, and its handful of attorneys—fewer than a dozen—had the reputation of being the toughest but most ethical trial lawyers in Pittsburgh. Hatch could not expect to make as much money as with the much larger firm he had just turned down, but the legal training would be unexcelled. He met with three partners who took an immediate liking to him and told him they wanted him as an associate.

"There's one thing you need to know, though," said one of the three, Bob Grigsby. "No one gets hired here without the approval of Sam Pringle," the firm's principal partner. "And Mr. Pringle hasn't approved anyone we've recommended in years."

With that warning, Hatch was escorted to Samuel W. Pringle's cavernous and sparsely furnished office. After fifteen minutes of grilling, Pringle turned to his three partners and ordered, "Hire this young man. He's just what we need in this office."

Hatch graduated soon afterward and passed the Pennsylvania bar exam, then one of the toughest in the country, in October 1962. He apprenticed by taking small claims cases to county court—sometimes as many as eight in a day, frequently on behalf of insurance companies. Hatch handled hundreds of such nonjury cases during his first two years, settling many out of court and, to his recollection, losing only two.

And the Hatches moved out of the chicken coop. Elaine was ecstatic. Their first home was on Orchard Drive in Mt. Lebanon, a middle-class community several miles south of Pittsburgh. Their fourth child, daughter Kimberly, was born on New Year's Eve in 1964.

As though Hatch weren't busy enough, with his firm's permission, he and an attorney friend named Roy Riehl opened an evening general law practice in Mt. Lebanon. It was located on the second floor deck of a small shopping center where Riehl's wife owned an art gallery. After the years of relentless poverty, it was a luxury verging on indulgence to browse through the gallery. Orrin and Elaine bought a number of pieces from the Riehls.

The law firm gradually began to assign Hatch to more important cases, usually in The Court of Common Pleas, the state's highest trial court. Again his win rate was unusually high.

For all his legal ability, Hatch was occasionally tripped up by his naiveté. On one occasion he represented a plaintiff in a negligence case that was defended by one of the city's more savvy attorneys, Carl Eck.

Hatch's client had slipped and fallen on icy steps—not once but twice, when entering his apartment. The second time the man had fractured a small bone in his left heel, leaving him in constant pain. He was suing his landlord for negligence. The defense claimed Hatch's client was drunk at the time and was carrying a case of beer into the house when he fell.

As the jury trial opened, recalls Hatch, "I thought my client was wearing awfully strong after-shave lotion." Eck also noticed the "after-shave" and promptly invited the man to come to the rail directly in front of the jury to deliver his testimony. As the plaintiff heatedly denied being drunk at the time of the fall, the jurors leaned back in their chairs to escape his odoriferous whiskey breath. Hatch, finally catching on, thought the case was doomed; but after several days of hearing testimony in which Hatch was able to verify the landlord's negligence, the jury awarded a large verdict.

In another case, Hatch faced one of his former professors, a petite, attractive woman who had taught his evidence class at Pitt and who had a reputation as one of the state's toughest and brightest trial lawyers. Her client was a concert pianist whose arms had suffered greenstick fractures when Hatch's client ran a red light and struck him. There was no question of liability, only damages.

The professor sought $150,000 and never offered to settle for less than $100,000, while Hatch, convinced the plaintiff's injuries had healed quickly with no impairment, offered a token $2,500. The plaintiff's attorney apparently operated on the assumption of the longer a case, the larger the settlement.

When it came time to close, Hatch said, "Having tried this case with the professor and hardly having gotten a word in edgewise, I feel like the man who hadn't spoken to his wife for thirty-four years—mainly because he hated to interrupt her." The jury chortled.

Then it was her turn, "I feel like the *woman* who hadn't spoken to her husband for thirty-four years, having tried this case with Mr. Hatch."

Hatch and his client had the last laugh. The jury awarded the young concert pianist $2,500–precisely Hatch's original offer.

Two senior partners retired from the firm and Hatch was made a partner within four years. He was thirty-two. All told, during the nine years he was with the firm, Hatch tried about five hundred cases in court and settled about two thousand others out of court. After practicing five years, he received the highest rating possible for an attorney with that amount of experience for legal ethics and ability–a "bv" rating by Martindale-Hubbell, a national legal organization, based on confidential evaluations by peers. Later, after ten years of practice, including three in Utah, his peers in Utah gave him the "av" rating–again the highest rating possible for an attorney with his length of service. Only about 5 percent of attorneys ever achieve the "av" rating.

The Hatches occasionally went camping or fishing as a family. For one notable summer trip they took Jesse and Helen with them to Georgian Bay, Canada. Almost every summer they drove to Palmyra, New York, to attend a religious pageant held at the hill where Mormons believe Joseph Smith received the record published as the Book of Mormon. In addition, they drove to Utah every other summer to visit Elaine's family–an uncomfortable trek, as Orrin insisted on driving the eighteen hundred miles straight through to save money on lodging.

They were very active in the Pittsburgh Branch, Orrin serving at different times in the branch presidency, district council, and as a teacher in the adult Sunday School. During much of the same time, he also taught non-Mormons about the church as a stake missionary (a part-time local volunteer effort). Elaine, meanwhile, volunteered at different times as a leader in the ward and stake Relief Society, was president of the Young Women's organization, taught in the Primary–the LDS children's organization–and also served as a Cub Scout den leader in the community.

Hatch tended to be a workaholic but usually made it to the children's special activities, including the boys' baseball and football games. He enjoyed roughhousing with the children and had a warm, expressive relationship with each of them. He brought home a ferocious-looking but friendly bulldog that he and the children came to adore. Elaine protested, but to no avail. Like Helen, Elaine also handled most of the discipline in the family.

Hatch's legal success was at last buying the good life. There were hunting and fishing trips with his partners and, early in 1969, a spectacular new home in fashionable Ben Avon Heights in the North Hills section of Pittsburgh. Purchased for a song in a depressed market, the seven-bedroom French Normandy mansion was surrounded by hedges and nestled on an acre and a half of beautifully landscaped grounds.

But Orrin and Elaine never forgot what it was like to survive on bare essentials, and they continued to live frugally. They were practical in even the smallest ways. On Christmas Eve, each child was allowed to open one gift—so long as it was the annual pair of new pajamas, to be worn for pictures around the Christmas tree next morning.

Hatch's youngest sister, Jessica, whose husband was serving in Vietnam, visited for a few days to share the joy of their new home. While there, a Marine officer came to the door and asked for her. Tragedy again visited their family: Jessica's husband had been killed in the war. She took the news stoically; but at night the Hatches could hear Jessica pacing in her room. During the daytime, she sat in a rocking chair, cuddling Orrin and Elaine's newborn daughter, Alysa, silently rocking for hours at a time.

After they had enjoyed the new house only six months, an old friend from BYU invited Hatch to join his Utah company. He was president of an oil and gas drilling firm and offered Hatch a position as senior vice president and general counsel. Hatch had long been drawn toward the Beehive State as a good place to rear their family. Elaine, comfortable and settled in their gorgeous new home, resisted the move at first. Upon reflection, however, the opportunity to be closer to her parents and siblings outweighed other feelings, and she too came to welcome the idea.

Hatch left for Utah in October 1969, but Elaine and the five children stayed six months longer while Elaine tried without success to sell their home. They finally joined Orrin in Utah leaving the home with a realtor who sold it months later for two thousand less than they had paid for it. When Jesse Hatch retired, he and Helen also moved west, purchasing a small house with space for a garden in Midvale, a suburb of Salt Lake City.

Utah was a state of sharp contrasts, partly a result of the LDS emphasis on large families. It had one of the lowest per capita income levels in the country, yet one of the most robust economies; low per capita expenditures on education, yet relatively high academic achievement; high stress on many adults from balancing family, church and professional responsibilities, yet a lifestyle offering a variety of outdoor recreation coveted by outsiders, and the nation's lowest rates of cancer and heart disease. More than two-thirds of Utahns were members of The Church of Jesus Christ of Latter-day Saints, the dominant influence in the state.

Mormonism is not seen as a Sunday-only religion; it is considered by most members a complete way of life. Mormons pride themselves on being a "peculiar people" and follow conservative theological tenets and social mores that are often little changed from those of Mormons a century ago.

Chastity is strongly emphasized. Abortion, homosexuality, and all other sexual relations outside the marriage bond are severely frowned upon. Marriage is considered the ideal way of life, and the church encourages mothers to stay at home and rear the children whenever possible. The church recognizes civil marriages but strongly encourages members to marry in temples.

Faithful Mormons pay a tenth of their income to the church as tithing. They go without food or drink on the first Sunday of each month, giving the equivalent of money saved as a "fast offering" to assist needy members. The church also has a far-reaching welfare plan, available to faithful members. However, it strongly encourages Mormons to be self-sufficient, looking to their own resources first, their families for assistance next, and the church when necessary. Members are discouraged from seeking or becoming dependent upon government welfare.

For Orrin and Elaine, the adjustment to life in Utah was an easy one. They bought a home on the city's fashionable East Bench and quickly made new friends at the local LDS ward. For several years, Hatch was a volunteer guide on Temple Square, where the LDS church has a visitors' center and offers free tours. Elaine was called by local church leaders to assist in leading the Relief Society—the LDS women's auxiliary (the oldest women's organization in the U.S.). Hatch was called to teach an adult Sunday School class in their ward, and later called as one of two "counselors" or assistants to the bishop, Frank Madsen. Hatch later served as a member of another LDS ecclesiastical layer called a "stake high council"—a stake includes six to ten wards—and, in 1973, was called as bishop of his ward. As bishop, he had full responsibility for their congregation of several hundred Mormons but, like other LDS clergy, received no money for his services.

Hatch also made some small lifestyle changes. He began taking vitamin supplements daily and exercising more rigorously to cope with a regimen even more demanding than the one he left behind in Pittsburgh.

In May 1970 Elaine's brother Ramon died. The following month, when the Hatches' last child was born, they named him Jess Ramon in honor of their two late brothers. The Hatches now had six children, ranging from eleven-year-old Brent to baby Jess.

Hatch's rise in his profession in the next few years was marked by change. After nearly two difficult years with the drilling company, which was not going in the direction he desired, he left to form a legal association with V. L. Kesler and Dick Gordon. Less than a year later, he left that firm and, with Lowell Summerhays and Dick Landerman, formed Summerhays, Hatch, and Landerman. Again Hatch found that he had different goals and motivations than his partners. Although they got along well on a personal level—and Hatch remained friends with all his former associates—this partnership also lasted less than two years.

Hatch's most satisfying years as an attorney began in 1975 when he formed a partnership with a bright young lawyer named Walter Plumb who had been an associate at Summerhays, Hatch and Landerman, and stood nearly a foot shorter than Hatch. "Walt was aggressive, intelligent, and always upbeat," says Hatch. Plumb believed in Hatch's abilities even more than Hatch believed in them himself, and with Plumb's enthusiastic encouragement, Hatch blossomed professionally. With Plumb, Hatch at last found the confidence to open a legal practice in which he was the most experienced partner—devoted to the trial work he relished.

With Plumb, Hatch tried cases from tax fraud to personal injuries to contract disputes. But more than anything, he loved fighting for under-dogs and he enjoyed courtroom success in each of his practices.

Hatch's first major Utah case involved a railroader killed after falling under a boxcar when a train had suddenly jerked, knocking him to the rails. In a similar Utah case when a railroader had been killed, his widow and six children were awarded thirty thousand dollars for his wrongful death. That settlement had been considered substantial in a state with one of the lowest per capita income levels in the country.

After one day of no-holds-barred fighting, opposing attorney Clifford Ashton—the dean of Utah's trial lawyers—offered to settle for six thousand. On the second day, he offered twenty thousand. When the trial ended on the fifth day, the offer had risen to sixty thousand. But Hatch advised his client to roll the dice rather than take the offer. The jury awarded ninety-six thousand dollars, almost all of it finally paid after an appeal was filed with the Tenth Circuit Court of Appeals.

Hatch took a rare break for an overseas trip for business purposes in 1975. With an attorney friend named Andrew Grey Nokes and a talk show host for Salt Lake City's KSL Radio-Television, Wes Bowen, he flew to London. In between business obligations, they worked in visits to Parliament, Madame Tussaud's Wax Museum, and the Tower of London. They attended a play at the Royal Shakespearean Theatre, ate rack of lamb in southern England, and slept on feather-ticks. The trip, Hatch decided, was "one of the greatest experiences of my life."

A private two-hour meeting with the influential Lord Thompson, a billionaire who owned newspapers and other enterprises throughout the world, was a significant part of the trip. Although Lord Thompson was ill, he agreed to meet with Hatch in his hospital room.

Noting problems with his country's socialist welfare system, Thompson told Hatch, "We British are very stupid to have allowed this to happen to this great nation. However, you Americans are even more stupid, because you have our bad example before you and are following down the very same pathways we have already walked." The meeting sharpened and focused Hatch's political philosophy.

Early in his Utah legal career, Hatch tried a case before Willis Ritter, chief judge of the U.S. District Court for Utah and one of the most colorful characters in the state's judicial history. Not surprisingly, he was often overturned on appeal by the conservative Tenth Circuit, which he despised. Occasionally, after a ruling, Ritter would say, "Now let's see if those dumb bastards in Denver can overturn this."

Short, barrel-chested, and snowy-haired, the crusty judge was a lapsed Catholic, flamboyantly irascible, conspicuously civil libertarian, staunchly antigovernment, and passionately antiestablishment. A letter to the editor in the *Ogden Standard Examiner* said, only partially tongue-in-cheek: "Before I spent time as an onlooker in [Ritter's] court I believed in only one God. Now I believe there [are] two."

Ritter ruled all aspects of his courtroom with an iron hand. If he caught a TV cameraman filming him, he was known to command U.S. marshals to confiscate the camera. Many attorneys feared or hated him, not without cause.

"Ritter was brutal to any lawyer he thought wasn't good enough to try a lawsuit," recalls Scott Savage, an attorney with VanCott Bagley Cornwall & McCarthy, the state's largest and most prestigious firm. "As a result, he only had to try cases with the best trial lawyers. It was very common for a lawyer to get assigned a case before Ritter, then call some other attorney acceptable to Ritter to take the case to court."

Hatch first stepped into Ritter's courtroom in the early 1970s to represent a man who had lost two fingers in a train coupler. The case was settled after two days of trial for $62,000, one of the highest verdicts of its type. As Hatch was bantering with the courtroom bailiff afterwards, Ritter swept down majestically and announced: "Mr. Hatch, you are one of the finest trial lawyers I have ever had in this courtroom." He added, "I like you and I like the way you try a case. You're welcome in this courtroom any time you want to come back."

Ritter was as good as his word, even when he later learned that Hatch was three things he disliked: a Republican, a conservative, and a Mormon bishop. "One reason Orrin got along well in front of Ritter was that he often represented the little guys that Ritter really liked," says Scott Savage. Hatch saw Ritter's faults but said, "I respected his keen intellect and legal acumen. He was one of the brightest as well as one of the most cantankerous men I have ever known."

Hatch tried another case before Ritter, this one defending a client indicted with others for running a cookie factory in which federal food inspectors had found rodent droppings. The U.S. Supreme Court had recently ruled that such suits were automatic criminal liability cases, even for company executives who had no hands-on responsibility for food processing.

The trial was a donnybrook, and it looked bad for Hatch's client, a Las Vegas businessman. Hatch appealed to the jury to consider the unfairness of holding criminally liable a man who lived nearly five hundred miles away from the Utah factory. But even more effective was Hatch's scorching cross-examination of a Food and Drug Administration witness. Ritter, who also loathed government bureaucracy, suddenly turned on the witness and demanded: "Where's the mouse?"

"The mouse?" stammered the startled witness. "What mouse?"

"You know, the *mouse,* the *mouse,*" Ritter shot back. "I'm sure there has to be a mouse here somewhere for you federal boys to make such a fuss about it."

The agent, of course, couldn't produce the mouse that left his calling cards in the cookie factory. The trial fell into disarray and Ritter called a recess. When the judge returned to the courtroom, Hatch moved for his client's dismissal, which Ritter granted. (They agreed that any law that could send a man to prison because of rodent droppings over which he had no control, in a factory 500 miles from his home, was simply unjust.) Also before Ritter, Hatch represented a Hispanic railroad worker who had slipped and fallen inside a gondola car, injuring his back and neck. In part because the man spoke almost no English, doctors had failed to pinpoint his injuries until months later when he was totally disabled. The Denver & Rio Grande Railroad Company refused to pay the man a dime.

Two lawyers from VanCott Bagley defended the case, bringing in a railroad doctor who said the plaintiff was a malingerer. Cocky from the outset of the take-no-prisoners battle, they offered to settle for fifteen thousand dollars. On Hatch's advice, his client refused. The jury awarded the man $140,000, a very high figure at that time.

Hatch often represented clients who couldn't pay his usual fees. Court records show that one who couldn't pay anything was Thure Carlson, a Swedish immigrant who owned a small dry cleaning shop. The diminutive Carlson and his wife routinely toiled sixteen hours a day, rarely netting more than seven thousand dollars in a year. He had bought cleaning equipment and, instead of depreciating it over time, by mistake had written it off as an expense in one year.

The Internal Revenue Service insisted on its pound of flesh, claiming that Carlson over several years had avoided paying income taxes of about $35,000—five times his annual income. The IRS usually prevailed in such tax fraud cases, but Hatch was tenacious, using Carlson himself as his best weapon.

The trial, an all-out battle, went several days. In one poignant moment on the witness stand, an emotional Carlson turned to the jury and, in his Swedish accent, said simply, "I am an honest man."

Jurors retired to deliberate, then streamed in and announced their verdict: "Not guilty" on all counts. The Carlsons hugged each other, then Carlson and Hatch embraced, tears rolling down both men's cheeks. "I'm proud to be an American," said Carlson. The judge flashed Hatch a smile and gave him a thumbs-up.

"Orrin was a tough competitor," says VanCott Bagley attorney Scott Savage, who tried one case against Hatch and settled about ten others out of court. "He would take advantage when he could get an advantage, but he was fair."

By 1976, Hatch had a lucrative law practice. He had also acquired the rights to some religious family listening tapes—including dramatized Bible stories—and had a growing business on the side selling them to the Mormon market. Hatch saw the cassette business as a way to do well while doing good. He was confident of earning a six-figure income for the rest of his career. But a new challenge was tugging.

Since his years at BYU, Hatch had become increasingly conservative in his political views. He closely followed current events in Utah and the nation and had a list of what he thought Washington was doing wrong. Hatch believed that Utah's liberal senior senator, Frank Moss, who was up for reelection in 1976, was part of the problem rather than the solution.

Hatch's growing sense that something was seriously wrong in Washington hardened into conviction. Sharing and feeding that conviction was his close friend and fellow Salt Lake attorney Grey Nokes. They had discussed politics vigorously while touring England in 1975 and kept the topic hot during numerous lunchtime conversations.

"I was constantly moaning and groaning about what was happening around the world and in Washington," recalls Hatch. "Finally Grey started to say, 'Look, Orrin, you're a good negotiator and one of the smartest guys I know. You'd make a great senator yourself. Why don't you run against Moss?' It was Grey Nokes, more than anyone else, who talked me into running."

At the outset, almost no one else gave Hatch any encouragement. In January 1976, he casually mentioned the idea to his neighbor and fellow church volunteer Frank Madsen, who owned a furniture store.

"I'm thinking about getting in the Senate race and running against Moss," Hatch told him.

"You're crazy!" said Madsen. "Nobody knows you, you're not known as a Republican, and you don't have any money. It's crazy."

Orrin and Elaine took the children to Disneyland over Easter vacation. During the drive to California, Hatch gingerly broached the idea of running for the Senate with Elaine. Elaine was adamantly opposed and didn't want to discuss it further. She and both of his parents regarded politics as nasty business.

Early in April, Hatch again told Madsen he was still toying with the idea of entering the Senate race. Madsen had the same response. But Nokes encouraged Hatch to do it, and challenged him to put up or shut up. "I think you could have a real shot at it," said Nokes. "And if you think you can do better than Moss, go ahead and try."

The idea seemed preposterous. Moss, a Democrat, was solidly entrenched after three terms in which he had risen to chairman of the Senate Space Committee—important to Utah's defense-dependent economy—and majority secretary, the number three position in Senate leadership.

The ranks of Republicans already challenging Moss looked almost as daunting. They included a former four-term U.S. Congressman, a former White House aide and longtime Utah political operative, a Washington lobbyist, and—the odds-on favorite to win the GOP nomination—an impressive former assistant secretary at the U.S. Department of the Interior, Jack Carlson.

In contrast, Hatch's name had yet to even appear in Utah newspapers. With one month to go before the filing deadline, he had no financial reserves and no idea how to raise the substantial amount it would take to run a competitive campaign.

Judge Ritter unwittingly played a key role in aiding Hatch. In mid-April, Hatch, along with dozens of other attorneys, appeared before Ritter to hear his calendar for the next month. The docket had twenty-seven cases on it, including twelve of Hatch's toughest cases. Ritter, the nation's oldest chief judge at seventy-six, smiled disbelievingly as the brash forty-two-year-old Hatch reported "ready" on all twelve.

Ritter knew that no lawyer could possibly be prepared to try a dozen important cases within thirty days. Yet by the time each one was called up, Hatch was ready. Within the month all twelve had been settled, bringing more than a hundred thousand dollars in fees—far more than Hatch had ever earned in a single month. It was enough to keep the law firm going up through the 1976 election.

Ritter didn't know that by burying Hatch in work, he had provided the financial means for climbing a political mountain—and that when Hatch arrived at the summit, he would push one of Ritter's best friends, Frank Moss, over a cliff.

4

Orrin Who?

AMERICANS WERE PENSIVE AS THE political season heated up in 1976. This would be the first presidential election after the United States had been forced to withdraw from Vietnam and after the Watergate scandal compelled President Richard Nixon's resignation—unprecedented events in the nation's history. The country was climbing out of the worst economic slump since World War II but at an erratic pace that left more than 8 percent of workers without jobs and an inflation rate above 5 percent.

Utahns, like most other citizens, were wary of politicians, and had edged toward Democrats in the wake of Nixon administration scandals. Democrat Calvin L. Rampton, the state's first three-term governor, was still riding high but had decided not to run again. Utah's four-member congressional delegation was composed of one Republican—conservative freshman Senator Jake Garn—and three Democrats, including Senator Frank E. "Ted" Moss.

Knowledgeable observers considered Moss one of the nation's few unbeatable incumbent senators running in 1976. By traditional political logic, he was. Moss was a genial man, a superb campaigner, and a powerful figure after three Senate terms.

Many believed that Republicans had, in fact, made hash of things in Washington. Both President Gerald Ford and Vice President Nelson Rockefeller had been appointed—not elected—to their positions after Richard Nixon and Spiro Agnew fell from grace. It was reasonable to think that Democrats had a good shot at the White House, and it was axiomatic that as the nation went, so went Utah. Utahns had cast ballots in twenty previous presidential elections, joining the national tide in voting for seventeen of the winners.

Political incumbents and those hoping to unseat them studied the tea leaves of the nation's discontent for clues to wooing and winning voters. Few searched harder than Hatch.

Once the thought of running for office had taken root in his mind, he began studying the pros and cons with the thoroughness that had brought him success in the courtroom. He knew his entry into the race would be very late. Delegates to the state convention would be chosen at mass meetings throughout Utah in just a few weeks. Other candidates had been working many months to be sure their supporters were at the meetings.

Hatch contacted dozens of citizens prominent in Utah business, government, and LDS church circles for advice. Most told him that, given the lateness of his decision and his lack of political experience, he had little chance of winning the GOP nomination and virtually no chance of beating Moss.

A few weren't so sure. Their champion was former California Governor Ronald Reagan, whose conservative rhetoric was resonating throughout the country, including at the White House where Ford was pressed hard by Reagan's bid for the presidential nomination.

Hatch was enthralled by Reagan. He had never met him, but liked everything he read about him—his clean life-style, traditional values, conservative politics, and willingness to take a stand on tough issues. A bonus was the fact that Reagan, like Hatch, had once been a liberal Democrat. One of Reagan's key Utah supporters was state GOP chairman Richard Richards. Another was Douglas Bischoff, a zealous state chairman for Reagan and head of a committee to recruit Republican candidates. Unlike most others offering advice, Richards and Bischoff encouraged Hatch to throw his hat into the ring, insisting the anti-Washington sentiment sweeping the country would make political virginity a plus, not a minus.

Hatch also won the enthusiastic support of two prominent Utah conservatives, Ernest L. Wilkinson, feisty former president of BYU, and a Wilkinson protégé, W. Cleon Skousen. Their support, along with that of prominent New Right conservatives in Washington, was crucial to Hatch's immediate success—but it would prove to be a Faustian bargain. Thanks to them, he survived the state convention that summer; but eighteen years later Hatch, with considerable frustration, would still be trying to live with the far-right image they helped give him.

Wilkinson had personal as well as political reasons for wanting Moss defeated. A senatorial candidate himself in 1964, he had lost badly to Moss as Utah joined most of the country in electing Democrat Lyndon Johnson over Republican Barry Goldwater. A year after being clobbered by Moss, Wilkinson attended a seminar in Chicago addressed mainly by Robert Welch, head of the John Birch Society, which had found fertile ground in Utah. Although Welch "has almost a Messianic complex," Wilkinson wrote in his diary, "on the whole I think his views were sound." He added, "I decided definitely that the John Birch Society is a real patriotic live and moving organization and that the general bad image it has in this country is not at all justified." Wilkinson did not join the society but resolved "to press forward for more training along this line at the BYU."

To achieve this goal, Wilkinson turned to the services of Skousen, formerly a top aide to FBI Director J. Edgar Hoover. Skousen, a bald, kindly man, had the beatific smile of an undertaker but was a spell-binding speaker and powerful writer. Wilkinson had met Skousen in Washington, D.C., and recruited him to BYU in 1951, where he proceeded to appoint Skousen to a variety of administrative and faculty positions. Over the next two decades, Skousen became widely known in conservative circles as a prolific writer and lecturer, especially on anti-communist and religious topics. His tenure at BYU was interrupted starting in 1956 while he served for several stormy years as Salt Lake City's police chief. After trying his hand at several other things, Skousen returned to BYU in 1967 as a professor of ancient scriptures.

On the Fourth of July, 1971, Skousen launched the Freemen Institute, initially located just off campus. Its mission was to foster "constitution-alist" principles—including a drastic reduction in the size and scope of the federal government. Freemen organized chapters in a number of states and held intensive seminars to educate ordinary citizens and spark their involvement in government. Conservatives flocked to the institute, considered more respectable than the John Birch Society, followed by numerous Utah politicians hoping to win support or at least dampen opposition.

As the deadline for decision drew near, Hatch met with Skousen, outlining his views and seeking support. Skousen seemed impressed and indicated he would help. Days later, on May 10, Hatch filed his candidacy. As he completed the application form and stepped outside to face the media for the first time, he was among a crowded field of Republicans scrambling after Moss. Moss was unopposed in his party in seeking a fourth term, and Hatch described himself as a "nonpolitician." He says he was scared, but he put on a brave front. "The old-line party professionals tell me I have no chance to win—to even come out of the party state convention," said Hatch. "But I'm used to impossible odds. That's the story of my life."

And then the campaign began. As a pleasant surprise to Hatch, Skousen wrote a campaign letter the next day to eight thousand of his

Freemen in Utah, saying Hatch was running for the Senate "for the express purpose of waging a fight to restore Constitutional principles in this country." Skousen added that Hatch "knows how to fight for right without being abrasive," and "I think you will find him a refreshing personality on the political scene."

Hatch's decision was not popular at home. "I cried for three days," confesses Elaine Hatch. "I didn't like politicians and didn't trust them. I wanted nothing to do with it."

Not many took Hatch's challenge to Moss seriously, for a good reason. The contest was strictly Boy Scout vs. Rambo. Hatch had zero name recognition among voters, and the list of qualifications distributed to the press had "amateur" written all over it. His resumé for the U.S. Senate—often called the world's most exclusive club—began:

HIGH SCHOOL

- Voted Most Outstanding Senior Boy
- President, Leaders Club
- Vice President, Senior Class
- Named in "Who's Who in American High Schools"
- Outstanding in Student Activities, Athletics and Fine Arts

COLLEGE

- Summer School Student Body President, Graduating with Bachelor of Science Degree in 1959

The list continued with his good record in law school, said he "Was Partner in One of Pittsburgh's Most Respected Law Firms," and gave his bar and other legal associations. It had no trace of government or political experience in the real world.

Hatch's written statement included a standard litany of conservative complaints against the federal government—too wasteful, too oppressive, too much encroachment on states' rights—plus a few flourishes of his own such as opposition to "the deterioration of morals and ethics in our society" and, inscrutably, "the imbalance caused by the vocal and ill-thinking minority of our society."

"I am here," Hatch told onlookers after filing, "to ask your support by reason of the fact that I believe I have the courage and capability to campaign successfully against Senator Moss."

He had the courage, but he was creating capability on the run. Hatch had little money to hire a campaign staff. He relied largely on old friends who believed strongly in him. His campaign manager was C. McClain ("Mac")

Haddow, twenty-five, whose family had been befriended in Pittsburgh by Hatch's parents, and who had since relocated to Utah. Haddow had joined the Republican Party while a student at BYU in the early 1970s.

Mass meetings were held across Utah a week later to select delegates who would choose party candidates at the state conventions to run in the fall elections. Hatch knew that the number of party delegates had been doubled since the last election, so there would be at least 1,250 new delegates to whom he could appeal.

On the evening of the mass meetings, sixty-nine delegates telephoned Hatch to say they were with him. Many had been Mormon missionaries in the Pittsburgh area and had warm memories of his parents' hospitality. Hatch asked each of the sixty-nine to convert ten other delegates to his camp.

Hatch also counted on doing well in head-to-head meetings with opponents at the twenty-nine county conventions looming between the mass meetings and the state convention in July. He and most others considered native Utahn Jack Carlson his toughest opposition. Carlson, former assistant secretary in the U.S. Department of the Interior and now a full-time campaigner, had moved his wife and seven children to Utah at the start of the campaign. He had visited the state at various times, representing the Ford administration, and had looked good to a sizable number of Republican politicos. Any candidate winning 70 percent of delegate votes at the state convention would be nominated automatically. If Hatch could keep Carlson's lead below 70 percent *and* come in second, then he could force Carlson into a primary runoff in September.

Renee Carlson often accompanied or pinch-hit for her husband at campaign appearances. In a vivid memoir of that campaign she wrote, "[Hatch] hadn't formulated any issues, had laid none of the groundwork, and his main support was obviously the far right who nearly always stubbed their toes on their extreme views."

Carlson, a robust, gregarious man, was a formidable foe. He had been student body president at the University of Utah (arch rival to Hatch's BYU), held two degrees from Harvard, and had one of the longest resumés in Washington, including service as economic advisor to three presidents.

Hatch's three other GOP opponents had Washington experience as well. Desmond Barker had worked in the Nixon White House and had been a longtime political operative in Utah; Sherman Lloyd had previously served several terms in the U.S. House; and far-right conservative Clinton Miller was a Washington lobbyist.

Knowing he could not individually meet all twenty-five hundred delegates in the little time remaining, Hatch hit on a novel idea: he would send his voice instead. He recorded a fourteen-minute cassette tape, glued on a red, white, and blue label with his picture, and mailed the tape to each delegate, accompanied by a parchment bearing the same message.

"For all of Senator Moss's seniority record," Hatch said on the tape, "I have not seen that many of a long list of accomplishments. As a matter of fact, I've seen some things that have been very detrimental to Utah. . . . And if I go back there, I'm going to . . . represent Utah in such a way that no longer are we considered the laughingstock of the country."

The tape, which also included endorsements by several Utahns he had defended in court, dramatically boosted Hatch's name recognition among delegates.

Once Elaine knew her husband was in the race for keeps, she adjusted to the idea of being involved in politics. Later she remembered the campaign as a highlight in their family's life—a time when everyone worked together and the family grew closer. All eight of them drove in a green Ford van to most of the twenty-nine county conventions, which began the first week in June. The children, wearing T-shirts printed with their father's name, passed out campaign literature, and touted him to delegates and others. Meanwhile, Orrin's father, Jesse, put his craftsman's skills to good use, handmaking "Hatch for Senate" campaign signs in his backyard and, with the help of Orrin's sisters and their husbands, posting them across the state.

At county conventions, Senate candidates were allotted three minutes per appearance. Hatch's courtroom experience served him well under the rigidly enforced time constraints. He gave emotional, rapid-fire presentations, blasting Washington and promising reform.

His polished skills and intensity, however, masked inner uncertainties. "Even though I knew I could speak well, I was really lacking in self-confidence, as I had been all my life," recalls Hatch. "I tried to cover it up by acting self-assured, but I was hurting inside all the time. Some people thought I was arrogant because of this. But I didn't feel arrogant; I felt terribly deficient and most of the time felt inferior." And in the cut-throat competition of campaign country, Hatch felt "very much isolated." He knew better than to expect camaraderie from Carlson, Barker, and Lloyd, but it stung to be "sometimes treated . . . not only as an outsider but as an interloper who was an aberration rather than a serious candidate."

And observers weren't quite sure what they were seeing. Renee Carlson described him as "tall, physically attractive . . . and aware of this in an almost sensual way. Sometimes he seemed vain and egocentric; other times he displayed a forced, testimony-bearing humility that left me either awed or disgusted."

Bitter feelings developed quickly between the Hatch and Carlson waffling on whom he supported for President—Reagan, a political demigod in Utah, or Ford, Carlson's personal friend and most recent boss. Hatch also said Carlson falsely branded him a Birch Society member. Carlson accused Hatch of being a dangerous, know-nothing candidate who had no more knowledge of issues than what he was learning from listening to Carlson.

Renee Carlson called Hatch "a quick study" who had "assimilated in a few weeks most of the facts and figures which were a part of Jack's issue discussions. It was a clever campaign tactic from Orrin's point of view, but a rather deceptive one. How could Jack accuse him of being a copy-cat without looking bad?"

Meanwhile, Utah Democrats were holding their own county conventions in early June. Moss largely ignored the political skirmishing in his own backyard to attack the Republican White House and President Ford's GOP opponent Ronald Reagan. The latter, said Moss in a stump speech on June 12, "talks about the national government as though it were a foreign power." The Democratic state convention was in mid-June 1976, with Moss and Rampton, completing his last year as governor, as star attractions. Democrats were generally buoyant over prospects in the fall.

On the night of June 14, however, just after the state party convention, Democratic hopes were shaken severely. Democratic Congressman Allan T. Howe was arrested on the west side of Salt Lake City by two women police officers posing as prostitutes. The forty-eight-year-old father of five was accused of propositioning the decoy prostitutes, and a police report of their alleged salacious dialogue filled local newspapers.

Howe's arrest was political dynamite. Watergate was still a fresh memory. And the stench of other scandals had been wafting from Capitol Hill across the Potomac in recent months: financial misconduct, illegal campaign contributions to dozens of members of Congress, and several other sex-related scandals.

The sleaze in Washington involved a disproportionate number of Democrats, helping to balance the scales with Watergate-tainted Republicans. It largely neutralized the edge that Democrats had counted on as they headed into the fall elections.

Republicans prepared for their own convention, scheduled in the Salt Palace in downtown Salt Lake City on July 16. The preconvention headline: *REAGAN IS COMING!*

By Friday evening of the convention, the Republican candidates had erected a circus-like arena in the Salt Palace. Some running for major offices had spent thousands of dollars on sophisticated campaign booths in a last-ditch effort to attract delegates. One had an imposing tower, topped with a television set; another had a spectacular mirrored display. Jack Carlson created a living room with rug and couches under an

Arabian-style tent. It featured several closed-circuit television monitors set at eye level running slick videos of Jack and Renee Carlson and their seven all-American children.

Then there was Hatch's booth. Later, it would remind him of his foray into BYU politics—when he rode a sign-bedraped donkey to class nearly two decades earlier. Once again, Hatch was in the friendly clutches of an ardent supporter who volunteered to create his display booth. Hatch didn't have the heart to say no and, in any case, didn't have money to hire professionals. The result was a ramshackle booth plastered with bumper stickers and strung with red, white, and blue banners. While other candidates offered tasty *hors d'oeuvres*, Hatch's people handed out popsicles inscribed "Lick Moss, Vote Hatch." Delegates laughed.

Hatch had a lot of enthusiastic volunteers, one of whom turned out to be an unplanned secret weapon: an attractive and well-endowed woman who passed out campaign brochures wearing a "Hatch for Senate" T-shirt and no bra. "More than one male thought our booth was the hit of the conference," recalls Hatch. "But I was mortified. It worried me to death, but she was a nice person and a dear friend, and I didn't want to hurt her feelings."

And Hatch didn't have any time to spare on side issues. Totally focused on the campaign, he stood in front of his booth from opening till closing, pitching anyone who would stop and listen.

Each candidate was to speak the next day, preceded by nominating and seconding speeches. Hatch knew Ernest Wilkinson was both greatly liked and greatly disliked within the party and in Utah generally; but when Wilkinson offered to nominate him, Hatch accepted. Wilkinson said he planned to "slander" Carlson, but Hatch insisted he use the precious few minutes instead to talk of Hatch's good points.

Senator Jake Garn, one of the state's most popular politicians, gave the opening address next morning and was well received—until he mentioned he would continue to support President Ford. Some delegates booed.

Reagan then entered from the rear of the hall, his wife Nancy on his arm. The crowd went wild. Reagan delivered a stemwinder, touching on familiar themes of a less powerful federal government, stronger national defense, and family values.

When a timekeeper tugged on his coattails after some ten minutes, Reagan appealed to delegates: "What do *you* say? I've come all this way to give a speech!" The crowd roared its support, Nancy leaned over and gave the timekeeper a tongue-lashing, and Reagan continued on to the end. He was rewarded by a pledge of Utah's support of his nomination for President at the upcoming national convention.

Among Senate candidates, Hatch spoke first, preceded by Wilkinson who introduced him as one "of our culture"—an attempt to blunt the argument Hatch had lived in Utah only six years. Hatch, in his three-minute speech, said Washington needed new blood and he was the only candidate able to bring a fresh perspective to government. "Give me your support and I *promise* you I'll beat Senator Moss in November," said Hatch. Carlson gave one of his best performances of the campaign, speaking knowledgeably about issues and goals for the country, without bluster or rhetorical flourishes.

When all candidates had finished, delegates voted. Among Senate candidates, Carlson led the pack with 930 votes, followed by Hatch with an amazing 778. Other aspirants were far back. The two forty-two-year-old men would now square off in a campaign ending on primary day in September.

The contest was a classic confrontation between a political novice whose forte was an evangelical appeal to voters and a seasoned veteran steeped in the nuances of government. Both men were vulnerable to charges of "carpetbagging." Carlson had been away from Utah as a military officer for ten years and a federal civilian employee another eight. Hatch had moved to Utah only six years earlier.

Carlson was considered a GOP moderate, Hatch a right-winger. One concerned Republican, in a letter to the editor published just before the convention in the Mormon-owned *Deseret News,* called Hatch "an unelectable conservative" who was "running a slash-em-up campaign" and who would "ruin" the party's chances to dethrone Frank Moss. Hatch doggedly but unsuccessfully insisted that he was not ultra-conservative but rather an "eclectic" who was interested in good ideas whatever their source.

In fact the differences between Carlson and Hatch were more style than substance. Both opposed national health care insurance, the Humphrey-Hawkins full employment bill making the federal government employer of last resort, and a common-site picketing bill—supported by Moss—enabling one striking union to shut down an entire project. Both favored a right-to-life constitutional amendment, Hatch explaining, "I oppose abortions except to save the life of the mother." They also agreed that the Soviet Union had eclipsed the United States in military strength.

And so the summer went—Hatch running against Carlson and challenging him repeatedly to debate, Carlson largely ignoring him and running against Moss.

In mid-July national Democrats met in New York City to crown another political outsider, former Georgia Governor Jimmy Carter, as presidential standard-bearer. Carter chose Senator Walter Mondale of Minnesota as his vice presidential running mate. For Democrats in Utah and other Rocky Mountain states, the ticket was not encouraging.

Neither Carter nor Mondale—one of the Senate's most liberal members—appeared to have much understanding of or affinity with the West.

As Republicans prepared to hold their own national convention, Hatch and a campaign aide, David Fischer, flew to Washington at the invitation of the National Conservative Political Action Committee. NCPAC, in its first full year of operation, was giving moderate and liberal candidates fits by putting political muscle and money behind selected conservatives. Hatch was among the chosen. Committee members escorted him around Washington and introduced him to other conservative PACs. Hatch spoke at a luncheon attended by top New Right conservatives, including Paul Weyrich, head of the Committee for Survival of a Free Congress and regarded as NCPAC's intellectual leader.

"I found this group of people to be outstanding," Hatch wrote for his files. "Some of them were much farther right than they needed to be, but most were dedicated, conscientious people who wanted to do what was right for this country." Perceptively he added, Weyrich "is extremely witty, is very bright, and so long as you don't disagree with him, is very charming."

The conservative groups contacted a number of Republican donors, who sent several thousand dollars to Hatch's campaign—and more later after the primary election in September. Although it was not a huge amount, it was timely and extremely helpful given his lack of resources. Hatch was still running a shoestring operation. He knew that the lack of resources to mount an all-out publicity effort might kill him in the primary.

At the Republican National Convention, held in mid-August in Kansas City, Hatch buttonholed Utah delegates, pressing his case against Carlson. The state delegation included several members of his campaign advisory board, including Wilkinson, prominent businessmen Ken Garff, Ted Jacobsen, and Gerald Smith; Karen Huntsman, wife of industrialist Jon Huntsman; and Douglas Bischoff, a state senator and Reagan's state chairman.

President Ford and Governor Reagan arrived in Kansas City almost dead-even in delegate votes after six months of campaigning. The outcome would largely be decided by ninety-four uncommitted Republicans, and Ford demonstrated the power of incumbency at crunch time, winning a narrow first-ballot victory 1,187 to 1,070. Tears flowed down the faces of many delegates, whose votes were with Ford but whose hearts clearly were with Reagan.

Back in Utah, Wilkinson and Skousen continued to marshal support for Hatch. In late August, Skousen wrote another letter on Hatch's behalf "to the people I know who love the Constitution and want to see it preserved." Skousen said he had spent "many hours" with Hatch and considered him "a Constitutionalist in the tradition of the founding fathers."

Without being abrasive, Orrin is a fighter. He prepares his cases well. He has a reputation among little people of helping when nobody else will. . . . He has an exceptionally sharp mind and expresses himself as well as anyone I have met in a long time. In other words, he is a born advocate. And on the right side. His conservatism is well-balanced and highly responsible. He has never joined any special group but he knows what must be done if the Constitution is to be saved.

Skousen asked recipients of the letter to contribute at least ten dollars to Hatch's campaign, saying he and his wife had each given the legal limit of a thousand.

Now Hatch and Carlson began slugging it out more directly, but usually at long distance. They were well-matched, the advantage seesawed, and neither had delivered a knockout blow as the race entered the final two weeks. But Hatch was ahead by double digits in his own polls and apparently starting to pull ahead.

Carlson, wary of Hatch's speaking skills, was reluctant to share a debate platform. Carlson stressed that Utah had never been represented by a senator who was not a native son. When a letter to the editor of the *Deseret News* made the same point, Hatch's mother flew to his defense in a warm and ingenuous letter:

I feel so badly that I am the culprit—the reason Orrin Hatch was not born in Utah.

His father and I met in Hiawatha, Utah, where I had been living with my father and stepmother. Orrin's father is of old pioneer heritage. His great-grandfather was sent to colonize Ashley Valley near Vernal, Utah. His other great-grandfather marched with the Mormon Battalion in the war with Mexico.

My mother wrote for us to come to Pittsburgh as there was a building boom. Always my husband, a native Utahn, had a deep longing to return to Utah, but by the time Orrin was born we had a large family and the depression was so severe we even lost our home. I am now thinking of Utah's early greats—how they came from New York State, Vermont, Pennsylvania, Canada, and overseas. . . .

Orrin has lived seven years in Utah plus four at Brigham Young University. Orrin has had many hard knocks—he struggled to gain an education. He was a history major and loves this country and Utah very much. I would not wish my boy to win without merit.

On the same page appeared a witty letter that quoted Hatch's gibe: "You know Mr. Carlson has to be a liberal; he has a degree from Harvard." The writer then queried: "Mr. Carlson's opponent seems to think that the better a person's education, the more likely he is to be a 'liberal.' Does that mean he believes the less educated a person is, the more likely he is to be a conservative?"

Brainstorming for an eleventh-hour shot in the arm, Hatch came up with an improbable idea: ask Reagan for his endorsement. It would be almost unprecedented for a Republican of Reagan's stature to take sides in a primary contest, but a Hatch advisor contacted Michael Deaver, Reagan's longtime aide, and Deaver agreed to see what he could do.

Deaver asked Reagan's pollster, Richard Wirthlin—a former Utahn still close to the state's political scene—for advice. Wirthlin had just taken a poll that showed Hatch nine to twelve points ahead and pulling away from Carlson. Wirthlin told Deaver it would be smart for Reagan to endorse Hatch, who was going to win anyway—that by doing so, Reagan would get the credit for Hatch's victory and cement a friendship that could be valuable down the road.

Four days before the September 14 primary election, Hatch returned to his law office to find Mac Haddow almost dancing on the ceiling.

"We've got it!" Haddow shouted.

"What have you got?" Hatch asked.

"We've got Reagan's endorsement!"

"That's great!" said Hatch. "Let me see it."

"Well, it was just a telephone call from Mike Deaver, saying Governor Reagan agreed," explained Haddow. "We've already alerted the press and they're on the way over here now."

Suddenly Hatch was worried instead of enthused, as a lawyer's skepticism replaced a politician's optimism. "Look, we don't have anything until we have something in writing," Hatch lectured his aides. "And I'm sure not going to tell the media I have any endorsement until I have a piece of paper that says it."

Reagan was traveling in Mexico, so Hatch telephoned Deaver in California, urging him to send a telegram immediately confirming Reagan's endorsement. Deaver's telegram arrived just as reporters were trooping into Hatch's office.

On Sunday, two days before the election, the endorsement ran in several daily newspapers:

> . . . THE TIME HAS COME FOR ME TO DO EVERYTHING I CAN TO ENDORSE A MAN OF QUALITY, COURAGE, DISCIPLINE, AND INTEGRITY; A MAN WHO BELIEVES IN INDIVIDUAL FREEDOM AND SELF RELIANCE. WITH THESE QUALITIES IN MIND, I ENTHUSIASTICALLY ENDORSE ORRIN HATCH FOR U.S. SENATOR FROM UTAH. ORRIN HATCH HAS THE QUALITY OF LEADERSHIP, THE FORTHRIGHTNESS OF PURPOSE, AND THE

PERSONAL HONESTY NEEDED TO TURN THIS COUNTRY TO A
PROPER COURSE.
 THIS IS RONALD REAGAN ASKING YOU TO ELECT ORRIN
HATCH TO THE UNITED STATES SENATE. GOOD LUCK.

The endorsement sealed Carlson's political fate. He telephoned the
White House for similar certification from President Ford, but Ford
refused to give it. Utah Republicans went to the polls on Tuesday and
voted almost two to one for Hatch—104,000 to 57,000. Carlson congratulated Hatch—but pointedly refused to endorse him.

Hatch's win focused national attention on the Utah Senate race. Terry
Dolan, the *enfant terrible* of NCPAC, Paul Weyrich, and other New Right
leaders stepped up efforts to channel money to Hatch's campaign. The
possibility that Hatch had a real shot at taking Moss's seat in November titil-
lated conservatives, who ached to be rid of the state's liberal senior senator.

Moss had simply not taken Hatch seriously up to that point. "Hatch
was completely a blank page to me [before the primary]," said Moss. "I
was sure Carlson, who[m] I knew and respected, would win the nomination. When the votes were counted, I just couldn't believe it." He had
not even met Hatch at that point.

Moss's former press secretary, Dale Zabriskie, was with his old boss
on the day of the Utah primary vote. "I told him that Hatch might be
more difficult than he figured, because Carlson had a public record to
run against, but Hatch was an unknown quantity and presented a
different challenge. But Senator Moss just didn't take Hatch seriously."

A public opinion survey one day after the primary vote showed Moss
in trouble among virtually every demographic group except staunch
Democrats. If the vote were taken then, according to Utah pollster Dan
Jones, Hatch would have beaten Moss by about 48 percent to 39 percent.
Other votes were split among "undecided" and two minority candidates.
Still, Moss shrugged it off, believing Hatch's strong showing was the
remaining ripple of the primary's hoopla. "There was just no way I
could be beaten by a carpetbagger who was unknown."

Moss, age sixty-five, was a native Utahn, Mormon, and former judge.
He was right out of central casting, tooling around Washington in a
yellow Mustang convertible, hair slicked back, flashing a million-dollar
smile. Moss chaired the Senate Space Committee and the consumer
subcommittee and held the number three leadership position among
Senate Democrats.

He won his first Senate race in 1958 in a fluke election, taking only 37
percent of the vote in a three-way contest, and had relatively easy races the
next two times. Moss's campaign theme in 1976 was a repeat from past
elections: *"Senator Moss works for you."* Because that was true, most Utahns

had allowed the genial Democrat to vote with the liberal Senate majority on labor and other national issues. He had given good constituent service and had used his political clout to negotiate better land-use policies by the federal government, which owned two-thirds of Utah's real estate.

Moss may have been casual Wednesday morning after the election, but Hatch shoved his own campaign into overdrive. "We immediately started work the next day," reminisced Hatch. "I was so tired I didn't know how I could go on. But I knew that this was an opportunity from the Lord and that I had to give it everything I had, win or lose. In fact," he added, "I couldn't lose because, even should Moss win, I would still be a winner for having come so far."

Wilkinson, who had written letters and made numerous telephone calls on Hatch's behalf, was more impressed than ever with his protégé. Three days after the primary vote, the former BYU president wrote in his diary, "I have tried to get Orrin Hatch today to give him some advice but he didn't call back." Famed for his own work ethic, Wilkinson added admiringly, "One thing I have to concede to him, he certainly gets around everywhere. I have never known anyone who works as hard as he is working."

Hatch planned to hammer Moss's voting record, especially his support of organized labor and its threat to Utah's right-to-work law, Moss's votes for federal funding of abortion, support of federal land use planning and strip-mining legislation, and support of what Republicans considered wasteful government spending.

During the first Hatch-Moss debate, before eight hundred Rotarians at the Hotel Utah, Moss tried to dismiss Hatch as a carpetbagger. "Who is this *young . . . upstart . . . attorney . . .* from Pittsburgh?" he asked rhetorically. The deliberately drawn-out question was calculated to destroy Hatch in as few words as possible. Utahns didn't like young upstarts, were very antagonistic toward attorneys, and had never elected a non-native as U.S. Senator.

Hatch, sitting tensely on the platform, believed that most of the Rotarians were staring at him with disdain. With a sinking feeling, he wondered if he had already lost. By the time it was his turn to respond, however, Hatch had calmed himself and his adrenalin was flowing:

"Senator," he said, nodding politely at Moss, "my great-grandfather, Jeremiah Hatch, founded Vernal and Ashley Valley in Eastern Utah. My great uncle, Lorenzo Hatch, was one of the founders of Logan and Cache Valley in Northern Utah, and my great uncle, Abram Hatch, helped to found Heber City and Heber Valley in Central Utah. They were all three polygamists; and everywhere I go, people come up to me and say, 'You know, I think I'm related to you.' If you keep denigrating my Hatch family background, the Hatch vote alone is going to rise up and bite you in the ass."

The Rotarians roared with laughter, some reeling on their chairs. By the time they were back in order, Moss seemed discombobulated and had difficulty getting back on track. He had taken his best shot and missed.

During a confrontation at BYU, Hatch said Moss voted correctly only during election years. "Now wait a minute, you're attacking my integrity!" responded Moss indignantly.

"That's right!" answered Hatch.

In a traditional luncheon debate before Utah clergy, sponsored by the *Salt Lake Tribune,* Hatch said Congress must clean up its act and return to Judeo-Christian principles so that voters can "look up to our Senators and Representatives." Senator Moss is sincere, conceded Hatch, "but sincerely wrong in his approach to our country."

Moss responded that voters ultimately were responsible for holding members of Congress to account, but meanwhile "we apply fairly high standards of ethics to ourselves." Moss mentioned his Senate seniority several times, pointing out that he wouldn't "be starting at the bottom of the totem pole on the minority side" when the congressional session opened.

Hatch was undaunted: "That's my life, all my life, starting at the bottom."

Utah Democrats were trying desperately to deal with the political problem of Allan Howe, still on the ticket for November. Twice he had gone to trial and twice been convicted, but he stubbornly refused to resign or agree not to run for another term. Moss was inextricably tied to Howe, who had served as his administrative assistant—top aide—in Washington before winning the congressional seat with Moss's help in 1974. The voters were not willing to tolerate Howe, and the Democrats, Moss in particular, had to put some distance between himself and Howe.

Finally things came to a head. Moss asked Howe to meet with him and Gunn McKay, Utah's other Democratic Congressman, at Moss's Washington residence. During that conversation, according to Moss, "Howe acknowledged that he couldn't win in November and asked what he should do about it. We told him he should withdraw from the race and Allan said he'd do it, but he wanted to make the announcement."

Moss took out a pad of paper and wrote down a suggested statement. "Allan finished it, called a secretary at his office from my telephone and dictated the withdrawal announcement, telling her to prepare it for distribution," said Moss. But after leaving Moss's apartment, pursued by reporters, Howe dug in his heels again and refused to withdraw. Moss would later point to Howe's presence on the ticket as the decisive factor in the Senate race, while Hatch would maintain that the issue of most concern by far to voters was Moss's record and not Howe's problems.

Hatch flew to California to cut TV spots with Ronald Reagan for the Utah campaign. Meanwhile, the Hatch children and their friends handed out campaign brochures at shopping malls, and Jesse and Helen, assisted by Orrin's sisters and brothers-in-law, placed campaign posters along major Utah highways—some posted in clusters like the rhyming Burma Shave signs that once lined American highways. Between campaign appearances, Orrin and Elaine knocked on doors across Salt Lake Valley.

One door was answered by Spencer W. Kimball, then president of the LDS church. The diminutive leader, who had interviewed Hatch for his mission two decades earlier, invited him in and listened to Hatch's views for twenty minutes. Hatch left believing he had won another voter. Another Mormon apostle and future president, former Secretary of Agriculture Ezra Taft Benson—a noted political conservative—sent Hatch notes of encouragement throughout the campaign.

Moss's staff compiled an alphabetized briefing book on Hatch, taken largely from newspaper clippings and a dissection of the fourteen-minute recording that Hatch had sent to GOP delegates when first entering the race. Moss ruefully acknowledged the tape as a brilliant stroke and pored over a transcript, pen in hand.

"Now I believe that the only way changes can be made [in Washington]," the transcript said, "is to throw out the old guard that has a low credibility rating, and justifiably so, throw them out and replace them with new, articulate, decent, hard-working people who are willing to give everything they can and who believe in this country, and who believe in this country's ability to be successful. As a matter of fact, I think we are the greatest country in the world."

Under the last sentence, Moss scrawled two large question marks and the words "How come?"

Hatch also said he had been in Utah "the last seven years, and I wouldn't live anywhere else. As a matter of fact, I have real questions whether I want to live in Washington, D.C. But somebody has to go back there and do it."

To this, Moss wrote sarcastically, "Aw shucks, why bother?" But at least—at last—he was starting to take Orrin Hatch more seriously.

Three weeks before the November 2 election, a poll published in the *Tribune* showed the two candidates dead even. Pollster J. Roy Bardsley predicted that "an upset could be in the making" since Hatch led slightly among those considered most likely to vote.

Hatch had staked out positions on a wide range of issues. A position paper on Social Security called the program "almost bankrupt." He had a detailed prescription: "We should choose a blue ribbon panel of five leading insurance experts and give them the power to institute actuarially sound free enterprise principles into the Social Security System."

Moss, whose bedrock support had included senior citizens, pounced. "It is impossible to take this as anything but an incredible proposal," said Moss in a speech on October 11. He pointed out, to considerable effect, that Hatch had represented large insurance companies in his Pittsburgh law practice.

"In one sweeping recommendation, Mr. Hatch has urged that Congress turn over its constitutional power, that is the word he used, to a nonelected 'panel,'" he charged. "This panel would be composed of private insurance company executives, who have an extensive self-interest in any matter having to do with retirement annuities and Social Security. . . . It is difficult to hear of such a proposal without questioning how qualified Mr. Hatch is to be senator."

He continued, "There exists in the country a feeling that, all things being equal, it is better to vote against the incumbent—no matter who he is, no matter what his personal record of service has been, and to support the alternative candidate no matter what his qualifications, no matter who he is. 'Brand X' in other words." Moss implored voters to reject Brand X.

Reagan, who had been stumping for President Ford across the country, made a quick visit to Utah to aid Hatch six days before the election. Appearing before ten thousand wildly cheering partisans in the BYU Marriott Center, Reagan laid out differences between Republicans and Democrats in a series of characteristic one-liners.

"We want to check government spending; they want to spend government checks," charged Reagan. "Jimmy Carter is riding high in the straddle," and "Listening to Walter Mondale talk about inflation is like getting a lesson in fire protection from Mrs. O'Leary's cow." In a pointed reference to the Moss-Hatch race, Reagan said "Don't be fooled by this talk of political experience. . . . What government needs is a new infusion."

Hatch flew with Reagan to Ogden, where he also spoke at Weber State College. On the flight, an awed Hatch wrote later, they had Kentucky Fried Chicken, which the future President "ate with his hands just like the rest of us. . . . Reagan was gracious everywhere we went. He always went out of his way for the young people and would sign autographs and spend time shaking their hands no matter how cold or how difficult it was."

The support of business and conservative groups, coupled with Reagan's personal interest in the outcome, helped fill Hatch's campaign coffers during the crucial last weeks. Money also trickled in through direct-mail appeals orchestrated by Richard Viguerie of Virginia, a godfather among New Right conservatives. Hatch ended up spending about $570,000, most of it on just the costs of soliciting contributions, leaving him less than $100,000 for campaign publicity through radio spots, newspaper ads, brochures, and posters.

According to government records, Hatch outspent Moss. In reality, however, the Moss campaign almost certainly far outspent Hatch. Officially, one-third of Moss's contributions came from organized labor. But Moss also benefitted from tens of thousands of dollars worth of "soft" campaign contributions in union organizing efforts—a huge loophole in campaign finance laws.

As the campaign headed for the wire, Hatch was soaring from the tremendous Reagan boost, while Moss had a trio of albatrosses around his neck: the Carter-Mondale ticket, unpopular throughout the West; the national Democratic platform, almost point-for-point more liberal than the Republican platform; and Allan Howe, still on the ticket. Still, he confessed years later, "I honestly didn't believe Hatch had a chance of winning until the last day before the election when a poll said it was going to be nip and tuck. That was the first time I thought I might lose."

On election day Orrin and Elaine arose early and voted, attended an endowment session in the Salt Lake Temple, and then drove to the Hilton Hotel, where Republicans had rented half the ballroom, to await results. Moss and his campaign workers were in a room next door.

Early returns showed Hatch in the lead. It was a trend that held firm throughout the night. Orrin and Elaine's families were with them, including her father, Sidney Hansen of Newton, who proudly told a reporter that his son-in-law "is all wool and a yard wide, as we say on the farm."

Utah tied with Alaska in giving Gerald Ford—the state's *second* choice for President, after Reagan—his largest popular vote, 64 percent, in a losing battle with Jimmy Carter. Among Utah Democrats, a railroad attorney and political novice named Scott Matheson extended the party's control of the governor's mansion, and Representative Gunn McKay easily retained his seat. Allan Howe was defeated by Republican novice Dan Marriott.

Orrin Hatch got more votes than any other candidate on the Utah ballot, as 287,600 citizens—54 percent—pulled the lever for him. His "unbeatable" opponent Frank Moss won 239,623 votes—45 percent. TV cameras recorded Moss's response: As Matheson embraced him consolingly, Moss dropped his head against Matheson's chest and wept.

5

Settling In

T HE EXHAUSTED AND EXULTANT HATCHES basked in the afterglow of the November election. Elaine and the children, Hatch's sisters, in-laws, and parents had given a full measure of effort, passing out pamphlets and blanketing the state with campaign signs. As it had been a shared family project, now it was a shared family victory. Perhaps Elaine was the least surprised. Time after time she had seen her husband beat impossible odds and achieve what he set his mind to. Now she was resigned to the inevitable changes that would come into their lives.

"We had a wonderful Christmas," remembers Hatch. There was no "bickering" over toys that year. "The kids were just happy to have our family together again now that the election was over." Hatch had planned to continue working part time in his law practice in 1976 but found it impossible to do so and meet the rigorous demands of campaigning. Once he filed for election in June, the active practice of law all but ended for Hatch. He and partner Walt Plumb—and the three associates in their firm—began to reduce their practice after Hatch won the September primary, and Hatch severed ties with it following the November election. Plumb later merged what remained of Hatch and Plumb with a larger law firm. Hatch also sold his cassette tape business after he was elected—but continued to receive several thousand dollars each year in royalties from the new owners.

A few days after Christmas, Hatch flew to Washington to buy a newly built home at the corner of Lawyer's Road and Galloping Way in Vienna, Virginia, a quiet suburb about forty minutes by car from Capitol Hill. He was shocked to pay $130,000 for the four-bedroom red brick house. Their much larger French mansion in Pittsburgh had cost less than half that amount, and they would sell their home in Salt Lake for around $85,000–about double what they paid for it eight years earlier.

Elaine and his parents followed Orrin to Washington several days later in the Hatches' new white Mercedes 240-D for the inauguration and swearing-in. Their belongings arrived in U-Haul trucks and they spent several days furnishing the home. Elaine then returned to Utah to sell their Salt Lake home before she and the children joined Hatch in Virginia near the end of March.

Just before the swearing-in ceremony on January 4, 1977, Oregon Republican Mark Hatfield took Hatch to the corner office of the Vice President, who also is president of the Senate. Inside was Nelson Rockefeller, soon to leave public life.

"Rockefeller was pacing up and down. He seemed dejected and very lonely," recalls Hatch. The former New York governor, never popular with conservative Republicans, now on the ascendancy, had withdrawn from consideration as President Ford's 1976 running mate the previous November. Hatfield introduced the two.

"That was a stunning victory, Senator," said Rockefeller.

"Thank you, sir," answered Hatch.

Hatfield asked the Vice President what he planned to do. Rockefeller responded, "My twelve-year-old son said, 'Dad, we need you at home.'"

"Mr. Vice President," said Hatch, "we also need you here."

Rockefeller's eyes filled with tears and he grasped Hatch's hand tightly. "Thank you," he said. "I really appreciate that." All three walked together to the Senate chamber for the swearing-in. The seventeen new senators marched up the aisle four abreast. (An eighteenth, to replace newly elected Vice President Walter Mondale from Minnesota, had not yet been named.) Hatch, wearing a dark suit, raised his right hand and swore allegiance to the United States and faith to his office in an oath given by Rockefeller, reading from a cue card. As Hatch ended with "so help me God," Elaine and his beaming parents rose in the visitors' gallery and joined in the applause.

It was one of Rockefeller's last official acts after a lifetime of public service. He dropped out of politics and, twenty-five months later, died of a heart attack.

A month after Hatch took office, he and Elaine flew to California, where he had a series of meetings with business groups. He was being interviewed by the editorial board of the *San Diego Union* when the meeting was interrupted by a telephone call from the White House. Jimmy Carter was on the line.

"Senator Hatch, how's the weather out there in California?" asked the new President genially.

"A lot better than in Washington, Mr. President, and maybe even better than Georgia," said Hatch.

"Senator, I need your help with something that's very important for the future of our country and the world. As you know, I have nominated Paul Warnke to be our chief arms control negotiator. He is the best man in America to deal with the Russians and to be sure our interests are protected. Will you support me on this?"

There was a pause. Carter had been in office less than a month and this was his first one-on-one appeal to Hatch, a freshman senator. Hatch wanted to phrase his answer in a way to establish cordial relations with Carter, even though the answer was not the one Carter wanted to hear.

"Mr. President, I think Paul Warnke is very intelligent and is a good man. I could support him in almost any other job in your administration. But I can't vote to confirm him to this one. I just feel that his positions on arms control over the past fifteen years would wreck his credibility as a tough bargainer with the Soviets. I'm sorry."

Another pause. "Senator, I respect your position. And I know it carries some weight with other members. I hope you will be able to support me on other names I'm sending to Capitol Hill."

"Mr. President, I've already been doing that, with the exception of [Secretary of Labor] Ray Marshall. I want to help you be one of the greatest presidents our country has had. I'll support you every time I can in good conscience."

A reporter, excited from overhearing history in the making, cut short their interview and headed for a word processor. The story of Hatch's conversation with the President appeared the next day in the *Union*.

As part of the same visit, Orrin and Elaine boarded an eight-seat corporate jet owned by a large agribusiness company and flew up and down California viewing its reservoirs, disturbingly low after a drought. Water is like gold in the arid West, and its development in California, whose San Joaquin Valley alone fed a quarter of the nation, had been stymied by environmentalists and quixotic Governor Jerry Brown.

Back in San Diego that evening, Orrin and Elaine stayed at the Westgate Plaza Hotel, the most luxurious they had seen, filled with exquisite European antiques and furniture. Their eighteenth-floor suite had a huge living room, marble bath, his-and-her showers, and two television sets.

It was a long way from a chicken coop in Pittsburgh.

Hatch and Carter symbolized the political significance of 1976. Both were outsiders who thumbed their noses at the Washington establishment and won. At Carter's hands, Gerald Ford was the third incumbent President of the twentieth century to be denied a second term by voters, albeit by the thinnest electoral vote margin in sixty years.

At the other end of Pennsylvania Avenue, members of the House of Representatives proved the adage that everyone hates Congress but loves their Congressman. Only 13 incumbents in the 435-member House were defeated, and the party lineup remained almost the same after the elections: 291 Democrats and 144 Republicans.

But on the Senate side of Capitol Hill, a revolution was underway favoring fresh faces over either party. Nine incumbent senators were beaten, more than one-third of those seeking reelection and the most in any year since 1958.

The party lineup in the new Senate remained precisely the same as before the election: 62 Democrats and 38 Republicans. But its freshman class was unusually large. Eighteen of 100 members—nearly one-fifth— took the senatorial oath for the first time.

While party balance was unchanged, noted the *Congressional Quarterly,* "some of the more clearly identifiable Senate voting blocs would be getting some new blood. The 'new right' group, led in the past two Congresses by Republicans such as Jesse A. Helms of North Carolina and James A. McClure of Idaho, would be getting a possible new leader in Orrin G. Hatch."

Congressional Quarterly continued: Hatch "was expected to be one of the most intriguing new figures in the Senate . . . a born campaigner, with unusual stage presence and oratorical skill." It noted that some conservative groups "were even talking about him as a possible presidential candidate in 1980." It was a compliment Hatch didn't want.

To Hatch's surprise and chagrin, the first conservative conference he attended as a senator sold "*Hatch-Simon, 1980*" campaign buttons. Former Treasury Secretary William Simon had just written a book, *A Time to Choose.* Hatch had nothing to do with it, and such early talk was heady but damaging to him. It attracted the enmity of senior members of both parties, gave the impression that he was inappropriately ambitious, and made the press suspicious of his motives.

Immediately after the November election, Hatch named his Utah friend and neighbor Frank Madsen as his administrative assistant, the top position on congressional staffs. After doing volunteer church work together, Hatch trusted him implicitly. Mac Haddow and Mike Hunter also joined his Washington staff. Frank Bailey became director of Hatch's Utah office in Salt Lake City, assisted by Grey Nokes and David Fischer among others, with Carol Nixon as office manager.

Power and perks in the hidebound Congress were tied to seniority, and Hatch began almost at the bottom of the pile—ninety-eighth of 100 senators. Only Republicans Harrison Schmitt, an astronaut from New Mexico, and Malcolm Wallop, a Wyoming rancher, were behind him. Hatch could have started out several notches higher if Frank Moss had followed the lead of more gracious lame-duck members and stepped down weeks or even days earlier, but Moss clung to his seat to the end.

Hatch's ranking landed him in a dingy basement office in the Russell Senate Office Building, among exposed pipes and electrical boxes, with old-fashioned acoustical tile on the walls. Several months later he moved to a more suitable suite in the Senate's other office complex, the Dirksen Building. About three months into the session, Hatch took a quiet hour to record early impressions of some fellow senators:

—Daniel Patrick Moynihan, D-New York, a former U.N. ambassador and Harvard professor. "A stunning character. Very friendly, interesting and intelligent."

—Gary Hart, D-Colorado. "Is sometimes referred to as 'Gorgeous Gary.' The antithesis of the rugged, conservative, pioneer-type western citizen . . . wants things to be liberally so pure that he sometimes votes against liberal programs because of minor liberal impurities." (Hart, who had directed George McGovern's presidential campaign in 1972, would later see philandering charges explode his own bid for the White House.)

—Frank Church, D-Idaho. "Appears to be a creation of the media . . . very affected and not one of the real heavyweights in the Senate."

—Barry Goldwater, R-Arizona. "Was seated behind his desk looking like a wounded old eagle. . . . There are flares of brilliance, but after giving many of us our faith in conservatism, his failure to be a better spokesman for the Republican Party and the conservative movement is pronounced. There is character in his face and eyes and wisdom in his mind. We all love and respect him." (Goldwater, defeated by Johnson in 1964, had fallen into disfavor with many conservatives for supporting the Equal Rights Amendment and liberalized abortion laws.)

—Strom Thurmond, R-South Carolina. "A straight-backed elderly gentleman and one of the truly great men in the Senate. He never fails to stand up and be counted on some of the most important issues facing this country. . . . Has painted himself into a right-wing corner, however, and is predictable on every issue. That seems to be a drawback here. I have great love and respect for him." (Thurmond, a one-time third-party presidential candidate, had married a young beauty queen in 1968, fathering the first of four children with her when he was nearly seventy, and earning the affectionate nickname "Sperm" from Senate colleagues.)

—Jesse Helms, R-North Carolina. "One of the dearest people in the Senate. Has never gotten out of line or been vicious in any way. Does have the reputation of being so conservative that nobody really takes him seriously, except for his parliamentary knowledge."

—Ted Kennedy, D-Mass. "One of the three or four I find basically nothing good to say about. . . ."

Hatch especially liked two of the Senate's most liberal members, Democrat Hubert Humphrey of Minnesota and Republican Jacob Javits of New York. Humphrey, whose long quest for the White House would never be realized, was dying of cancer when he took the Senate oath for the last time as Hatch was sworn in the first time.

"One thing that strikes me," wrote Hatch in May, "is that a number of leading Senate liberals are not as sincerely motivated to help people as they are politically motivated. I do believe, however, that men like Humphrey and Javits are quite sincere in trying to help the overburdened and underprivileged of our society. . . . My inner spirit tells me that Humphrey, for all his faults and deficiencies, is really a great man."

That spring a Utah woman brought her son, also fatally stricken with cancer, to Washington as part of his Boy Scout citizenship merit badge. Hatch shared his chair with the boy in the Joint Economic Committee as Humphrey grilled a witness. Finishing, Humphrey excused himself and joined Hatch in an anteroom to encourage the youngster in his fight against their common enemy. When the mother's camera failed to work, Humphrey and Hatch promised to send photos.

"It's one thing for an older fellow like myself to have this dread disease," Humphrey said in a handwritten note to Hatch. "But what a pity—how sad—to see a 12 year old boy suffering so much and his all too brief life snuffed out—What a pity."

Javits, thirty years Hatch's senior, had been a senator for twenty years. He had a round freckled head, largely hairless except for a back fringe that crept over his collar. Javits was often expressionless and appeared uninterested. But when he spoke others listened carefully.

"Probably the smartest man in the Senate," wrote Hatch. "He is very shrewd, always prepared, very, very articulate, and a prodigious worker. I have deep respect for him, even though we are at opposite poles of the ideological spectrum."

Hatch introduced Javits to friends as "one of the greatest men in the Senate, but one I probably will never vote with." Javits would smile and thank Hatch for his graciousness.

The most caricatured member of Hatch's class was S. I. Hayakawa, at seventy the oldest freshman senator elected in eighteen years. The colorful semanticist had faced down student protesters in the late 1960s as president of San Francisco State College and parlayed that fame into an election victory over liberal Democrat John Tunney, who had been hurt by his playboy image.

Hayakawa had been criticized in the national media for snoozing during meetings. Hatch, asked about his colleague's habit while speaking in San Francisco, quipped that "one Hayakawa asleep is worth two Tunneys awake."

Still, fellow Republicans protected the diminutive Californian's public image. Hayakawa dozed off next to Hatch during a joint session in the House chamber to hear President Ford's last State of the Union address. As a television camera began panning the crowd midway through Ford's speech, the minority whip, Ted Stevens of Alaska, yelled to Hatch in a panic, "Wake him up! Wake him up!"

Hatch forcefully grabbed Hayakawa's arm. "Sam, wake up!"

Hayakawa leaped out of his chair. "I'm awake, I'm awake," he insisted, sheepishly sitting back down. He was, for the rest of the evening.

In March, after the Salt Lake City house was sold, Elaine, Brent, Marcia, Scott, Kimberly, Alysa, and Jess settled into their new home, its acre of property giving them plenty of room to romp. The children enrolled in public schools, and the family received a warm welcome from the local Mormon congregation. Both Orrin and Elaine promptly received assignments to participate: Orrin teaching an adult Sunday School class and Elaine assisting in the women's Relief Society.

Washington is the nation's largest company town; one of every five residents works for the federal government, and tens of thousands are employed in support services. Hatch had not needed to commute in Salt Lake City. In Washington, commuting was a daily necessity, and he maintained a grueling pace. He soon found himself in increasing demand as a speaker, his senatorial duties multiplying. Elaine and the children got less of Hatch's time. There simply was not time to do all his conscience told him he should do with his family.

"One of the things that unnerved me the most yesterday was the realization at 12 midnight that I had failed to call little Alysa on her birthday," Hatch dictated as he drove home to Vienna late one night in April of that first year. "I have got to start thinking more of my family and a little bit less of some of the demands that are being made of me. Those making the demands will forgive me the quickest. My family will remember me the longest."

He had always been busy, but legislation could easily absorb every hour of every day. Hatch generally left home on weekdays by 6 A.M. and returned after 8 P.M. Usually he took Route 123, known locally as Chain Bridge Road, through the lush Virginia countryside, then George Washington Parkway. Curving along the west bank of the Potomac River, it then crossed Theodore Roosevelt Bridge into the District of Columbia. The drive provided a cherished interlude for private thoughts. One morning his heart lifted to the beauty of a Virginia spring: "The greenery is coming on with a fluffy attractiveness that buoys my spirits," he dictated for his files, "Vienna is a nice place to live." Then he added loyally, "I still have a great thrill, however, when I fly over the Wasatch Mountains into Salt Lake City. Our state and desert have a beauty all their own."

Crossing the Potomac and driving east on Constitution Avenue, Hatch daily passed government departments that touch the lives of every citizen—the Federal Reserve, the White House, the IRS, the Justice Department, the Department of Labor, and finally, the U.S. Capitol and the Senate office buildings.

Members of Congress worked in a self-contained Capitol Hill community—with subsidized, on-site meals, haircuts, even medical care — surrounded by a third world they rarely experienced. Washington, D.C.'s inner city was ravaged by the same problems as those of other urban areas: poverty, drugs, high rates of school dropouts, illegitimate births, murder, and untold numbers of lesser crimes. More than two-thirds of D.C.'s residents were black, the highest percentage among major American cities. In sharp contrast, the city suburb's residents were three-fourths white.

Hatch, never comfortable being idle, was a prodigious worker from the outset. He routinely used the daily commute to get a head start on Senate business—dictating correspondence or other work into a tape recorder and, in later years, communicating by cellular telephone with staff workers or colleagues.

During the morning hours at his desk he studied issues and prepared position papers. Committee meetings usually came next, interrupted periodically by bells calling members to the Senate floor for votes. Most work in Congress is done in committees, whose leaders wield great power.

Freshman Senators in 1977 were expected to be seen but not heard. One older Democratic committee chairman patiently explained, "Sonny, we want you to sit back and wait a couple of years before offering your views."

"Thank you, sir," Hatch responded. "I know you're trying to be helpful. But the people of Utah elected me to do a job here, and I owe it to them to get about it."

In his second year, Hatch told a reporter, "I want to be known as a person who fights hard for his beliefs but believes in the institution of the Senate and does not want to win by offending or hurting other Senators and not respecting their ideological perspectives."

Republicans sit on the right side of the Senate chamber facing the presiding officer, Democrats on the left. Hatch was first assigned a desk on the front row. Later he chose one near the rear-center of the chamber, offering a better view of Senate dynamics and, more importantly, a better strategic position from which to be formally recognized during debates—often critical to the outcome of legislative contests.

By tradition Senate desks, made of mahogany and equipped with three-inch-high hinged writing boxes at the top, bear the signatures or carved names of those using them. The drawer of Hatch's permanent desk at the rear had earlier been signed by three men who became presidents— William McKinley, apparently when he served in the House, Harry Truman, and John F. Kennedy.

Hatch was assigned to three committees—Joint Economic, Judiciary, and Labor and Human Resources. The latter two, which handled some of the most controversial issues before Congress, were his first choices. He and Sam Hayakawa replaced Nevada Republican Paul Laxalt on the Labor Committee as its token conservatives. Laxalt candidly described his service on the pro-union panel as "purgatory."

The Senate's new majority leader was Robert Byrd of West Virginia, a no-nonsense legislator who had earned his leadership spurs the hard way: not through charisma, good humor, or rhetorical skills—all of which he lacked—but by mastering the Senate's arcane rules and procedures and by carefully doing favors for his Democratic colleagues.

Byrd had earlier served for several years as the Senate secretary for the Democrats, scheduling meetings and making life easier for his party colleagues by tending to a myriad of housekeeping details. In a party caucus in 1971, Byrd called in the debts from all those favors, succeeded in ousting Ted Kennedy as majority whip, and put himself in line to be the next majority leader. Byrd had defeated Kennedy in secret balloting, even though Kennedy had enough verbal commitments from Democrats to keep his position.

For the next six years, Byrd was a loyal right arm to majority leader Mike Mansfield. When Mansfield retired, Byrd became Democratic leader by acclamation, beginning his tenure just as Hatch's Senate career began in January 1977.

Two other senior Southern Democrats saw an ally in Hatch and trained him to help thwart liberal initiatives. They were James Allen of

Alabama and crusty James Eastland of Mississippi, longtime chairman
of the Judiciary Committee who also presided over the Senate day to day
as president *pro tempore.*

"Senator Allen was one of the most remarkable men I have ever
known," said Hatch of the strapping Alabamian, master of the filibuster
and bane of liberals. "He and Robert Byrd were the most effective
students of the rules in the Senate. Allen took on fellow Democrats
almost every day. His own side hated him. I loved him."

Allen was Hatch's mentor, befriending him and teaching him how
the Senate really operated. "Orrin, spend time on the floor and learn the
rules," Allen advised. "It will give you power and help you stop some of
these things that are ruining our country."

Late one night during a filibuster over a natural gas deregulation bill,
Hatch was standing on the Senate floor when Eastland approached.
"Hatch!" barked the Democratic curmudgeon.

"Yes, sir!" Hatch answered dutifully.

"How about going to dinner with me?"

"I'd be delighted," said Hatch, not about to refuse any invitation
from the powerful head of the Judiciary Committee to which he had just
been appointed.

They caught the members-only elevator and went down one floor to
the Senate dining room. After they ordered, Eastland fell silent. For
twenty minutes, Hatch fidgeted. Then Eastland, a senator for thirty-four
years, boomed again:

"Hatch!"

"Yes, sir!"

"Do you think we can save this country?"

Obviously there was only one right answer. Straightening his shoul-
ders, Hatch looked Eastland firmly in the eye.

"Yes sir, we can!"

Eastland fixed Hatch just as squarely and yelled *"Bullshit!"* Then
Eastland took a sheet of paper from a pocket, on which he had hand-written
"American farm bill—$12 billion, $9 billion of which is for food stamps and
other transfer payments." The Southerner believed farmers were being made
to look like rip-off artists because of the hidden food stamp payments. The
exchange remained one of Hatch's favorite memories. From that day on,
Eastland began to turn often to the Utahn to help manage both liberal
Democrats and conservative Republicans on the Judiciary Committee.

On January 19, 1977, Hatch gave his maiden speech on the Senate
floor, a half-hour address opposing the nomination of F. Ray Marshall as
Labor Secretary. It followed his grilling of Marshall before the Labor

Committee, both events setting a pattern of pointed toughness that would mark Hatch as one of Capitol Hill's most formidable interrogators.

"Mr. President, after a great deal of consideration and thought, I am announcing my intention to cast my vote against the confirmation [of Marshall]," began Hatch. In a style later characterized by one journalist as "the mace and the olive branch," Hatch began with the olive branch. He regarded Marshall as honest, sincere, intelligent, and "quite candid" in responses to difficult questions.

Then came the mace. "My negative vote is hinged upon Mr. Marshall's untenable positions on some of the substantive labor questions with which I do not agree and [with] which a majority of Americans will not agree." Hatch mentioned common-site picketing—which would allow one disgruntled union to shut down an entire construction project, unionism in the military, and especially the repeal of section 14-b of the National Labor Relations Act which allowed twenty states, including Utah, to outlaw compulsory unionism. Right-to-work laws had long been a prime target of organized labor.

". . . It is my general philosophy that a nomination submitted by a President, whether he be Democrat or Republican, should ordinarily be confirmed by the Senate unless there are clear indications that the nominee would not serve the public interest in the furtherance of his office. I find such conditions to exist in the nomination of Ray Marshall." As a freshman's first speech, it was candid, clear, and conspicuous.

Hatch then buttonholed individual senators, urging them to read the committee transcript and oppose Marshall. What had been a slam-dunk for the Carter administration turned into a melée as Marshall retreated from a number of positions taken before the Human Resources Committee, and the White House began to lobby senators.

When the vote came, twenty senators opposed Marshall's confirmation—equalling the number voting against Attorney General Griffin Bell, a far more controversial nominee and the object of a national groundswell of opposition.

President Carter then knew that with Orrin Hatch he was in for a singularly bad headache. But Hatch was only a symptom of Carter's problems in Congress. The first Southerner in the White House since the Civil War, Jimmy Carter was largely unknown and untrusted by establishment Republicans and Democrats alike. His honeymoon with Congress terminated abruptly, after barely a month, when he submitted a revision of President Ford's budget for the 1978 fiscal year, beginning October 1, 1977. It included a tentative "hit list" of nineteen ongoing federal water reclamation projects. Among them was the huge Central Utah Project.

Utah Democratic Representative Gunn McKay spoke for many outraged members. "Regardless of cost, we need the water these projects will supply. In some areas of the West we get only three inches of rain a year. . . . Over $225 million has already been spent on the Central Utah Project, and that would be completely wasted without a dime's return." Ultimately Congress, prodded by Senators Garn and Hatch, shoved most of the water projects, including CUP, down Carter's throat. But other time bombs were already ticking.

Fuses lit in 1977 that would explode later in political fireworks included two Panama Canal treaties, a national energy policy, a proposal to abolish the electoral college and elect the President by direct popular vote, extending the deadline for states to ratify the Equal Rights Amendment, federal funding of abortions, and big labor's ambitious wish list. Overarching them all was a worrisome economy, with inflation and unemployment both at about 7 percent for the year.

The next major confirmation fight was over Paul Warnke. Carter had designated him for two related roles—chief negotiator on the U.S.-Soviet Strategic Arms Limitation Talks (SALT), whose limits had been set in 1972, and as director of the Arms Control and Disarmament Agency. This time senior Democrats on the Armed Services Committee, including Henry Jackson of Washington and Sam Nunn of Georgia, led the opposition.

Hatch attended an evening meeting of a group of conservatives asking him to lead a collateral attack on Warnke. He explained that Carter had called him personally about Warnke; he would join the Senate opposition to the nominee, but he didn't want to slap Carter in the face by mounting an outside attack. The next day Paul Weyrich angrily accused him of letting the President neutralize him.

Hatch explained patiently that it wasn't just the telephone call from Carter. He felt he could be more effective talking individually to fellow senators and, at any rate, as a freshman he didn't want to grandstand. Furthermore, he told Weyrich that he "was slightly offended by [Weyrich's] approach. One thing I am not going to be is a captive of the ultraconservatives in Washington."

Weyrich was a leader of the New Right, a breed of conservative activists that coalesced about 1974. Other leaders included direct-mail wizard Richard Viguerie, John T. Dolan and Charles Black of the National Conservative Political Action Committee, and Howard Phillips of the Conservative Caucus. Conservatives had traditionally focused on defense, foreign policy, federal spending, and states' rights. To these concerns, New Right leaders added an array of social issues like abortion, school prayer, and the Equal Rights Amendment. They unnerved many others, including both the Democratic and Republican parties, with their stridency, rigid ideology, and refusal to compromise.

"We are different from previous generations of conservatives," proclaimed Weyrich. "We are no longer working to preserve the status quo. We are radicals, working to overturn the present power structure in this country."

When the Warnke debate reached the Senate floor, Hatch delayed his own scheduled remarks to allow senior senators time to have their say. Then he acknowledged Warnke's good points—brilliance, negotiating ability, cleverness. However, Warnke's credibility would always be in question because of his consistent opposition to U.S. defense improvements and his record of failing to win concessions from the Soviets.

Major newspapers predicted that the opposition would not get above thirty votes. On the first vote, to make Warnke chief SALT negotiator, the vote was fifty-eight for, forty against. He was also confirmed as head of the arms control agency, seventy to twenty-eight. It was at least a moral victory; and Hubert Humphrey, a floor leader of those supporting Warnke, complimented Hatch for the cogency of his remarks.

Hatch tended to raise a ruckus even when he was supporting Carter's nominees, including Peter Flaherty, the former Democratic mayor of Pittsburgh, an acquaintance of fifteen years and the administration's choice as deputy attorney general. The tall, handsome Irishman was so popular in Hatch's hometown that he once was nominated by *both* political parties for mayor. But a woman from the predominantly black Homewood-Brushton section of Pittsburgh appeared at the Judiciary Committee meeting and, almost screaming, accused Flaherty of racism and called him stupid, incompetent, and a bad attorney to boot. Presiding at the hearing was Senator Howard Metzenbaum of Ohio, a dour liberal, who made no move to rein her in.

Finally Hatch interrupted. He had known Flaherty for fifteen years, he said, and the Irishman was none of the things the woman claimed. On the contrary, Hatch asserted, Flaherty was an excellent attorney and a superb mayor who had done a great deal for Pittsburgh blacks and could not have been elected without their support. As the woman tried to outshout Hatch, he leaned into his microphone and, pointing at her, snapped, "*You* appear to be the racist! *You* appear to be the intolerant one."

The TV cameras were rolling now. She admitted it: "You bet I am intolerant and I'm not going to change for you or anybody else!" Finally, outclassed in the acerbic exchange, she got up and stomped away from the table in a huff.

Also opposing Flaherty was a flamboyant attorney from Pittsburgh,

Allen Brunwasser. He cited four instances of alleged unethical conduct by Flaherty.

Hatch also knew Brunwasser and patiently reasoned, "Allen, don't you think that these instances you have brought out are somewhat picky in the life of any major politician?" Brunwasser admitted they were. Then he expressed fear that, if confirmed to the number two job in the Justice Department, Flaherty would use his power to have an IRS audit thrown at Brunwasser, a prominent civic activist in Pittsburgh.

When Hatch promised, "I am sure Mayor Flaherty will do a very good job and I will personally try to make sure he does," Brunwasser promptly withdrew his opposition.

Brunwasser had said that Flaherty would not shake hands or even look at him when he had entered the room. Hatch urged, "I'm sure he will. Why don't you go over there and shake hands with Mayor Flaherty right now and let him know you are behind him."

Brunwasser, looking tentatively at Flaherty, said, "Mayor, *will* you shake hands with me?" Flaherty, grinning broadly, bounced out of his seat, walked across the hearing room, and shook hands with Brunwasser as the audience burst into applause.

Flaherty called Hatch that afternoon to thank him. The following day every member of the committee except Metzenbaum voted to confirm Flaherty.

Hatch's defense of Flaherty spurred a caustic letter to the editor of the Provo, Utah, *Daily Herald* asking why Utah's "carpetbagger" was fending for one of his friends from Pittsburgh. Hatch noted, "Boy, some of these people can sure make you sick. . . . A number of rank conservatives want you to be such a purist you would become ineffective."

Hatch, though drawing away from radical conservatism, did not find liberalism alluring. In a moment of illuminating introspection, he expressed his amazement that leading liberals could

> embrace a philosophy that has basically bankrupted this country. They know it has. They realize the repercussions that are occurring because of their bad policies, and they continue to maintain [that] their philosophy is the only correct approach. The philosophy of these people is that the federal government owes the obligation, in every case, to right every wrong and to provide every program. There is a total disdain and lack of appreciation for the ability of the various states to handle their own welfare. It is extremely disconcerting to believe that so many intelligent people can be so deceived.

Yet some leading conservatives struck him as "obstructionists to the highest degree." He yearned for "a new type of conservative leadership with a sense of humor. Too many of these people are over-intense over every issue. Many of the issues are clichéd."

Hatch read William Rusher's *The Making of a New Majority Party* and saw himself in Rusher's description of a "social conservative." Hatch defined his emerging political identity as "one who wants economic conservatism but who has a great deal of respect for the rights of people and the sufferings they go through." He added "I am trying to be constructive in my conservative beliefs rather than just finding fault all the time."

It was a self-definition he found comfortable, but others would soon come to regard Hatch as a leading killer of liberal dreams.

6

The Rookie

OLD EPHRAIM WAS REPORTEDLY UTAH'S last grizzly—a monster nearly ten feet tall and weighing perhaps a thousand pounds—that terrorized Cache Valley early in the century.

He met his end in 1922 when he walked into a sheepman's trap fastened to a tree. The sheepman tried to kill him, but Old Ephraim broke the tree and chased the man up a trail before being killed by the last shot from his rifle. Boy Scouts dug up Old Ephraim's skull years later and sent it to the Smithsonian Institution in Washington for a fee. Citizens had tried for years to retrieve the storied bear's skull, but the Smithsonian refused to give it back.

Hatch promised to do what he could.

Colleagues considered Hatch a brainy but brash rookie and knocked him off stride more than once during his early months in the Senate. Intense and unrelenting, Hatch quickly learned the value of defusing a tense situation with humor.

On one occasion, the largely liberal Judiciary Committee had loaded up a bill funding the National Legal Services Corporation, which offered free legal help to the poor. It steamrolled over most attempts to change major provisions or reduce funding to the agency. As the evening session took its toll of participants, Hatch was left alone on the floor to fight for conservatives. Defending the other side as the bill's floor managers were New York Republican Jacob Javits and Wisconsin Democrat Gaylord Nelson. It was 9 P.M., the session had been going on for twelve hours, and they were all dog tired.

Hatch had originally proposed four amendments. During floor debate, he was able to win the adoption of three, but the biggest sticking point remained. He wanted to cut funding for the program from $225 million to $205 million for the coming fiscal year. As the deadlock lurched into its thirteenth hour, the exhausted Hatch proposed a deal: "Come on, fellows. Let me save that $20 million for the taxpayers and we can all go home."

Javits bristled. "Not on your life. It's a matter of principle now. You can filibuster all night but I won't give in."

"Then I'll just have to use my trump card on both of you," said Hatch.

Javits and Nelson grinned, knowing Hatch could not possibly muster more than twenty votes to cut funding. Hands on hips, chin out, Javits took the bait. "And what might that trump card be, Senator Hatch?"

"If you don't immediately give in and let me save the taxpayers that $20 million," answered the Utahn, "I'll send the Mormon missionaries to both of you."

Javits, a Jew, raised his arms in mock horror. "Oh no. Not that!" Then he and Nelson, laughing, agreed to cut the $20 million, and all of them called it a night.

In the swirl of personalities, passions, and principles that make up the stormy vortex of any legislative session, Hatch, a man who stood almost dogmatically for principle, found himself learning a great deal about relationships. One of the tenderest was his relationship with the dying Democrat Hubert Humphrey.

Hatch cherishes a personal note from Humphrey, dated September 26, 1977, calling him "indeed a dear friend." It thanked Orrin and Elaine for a Bible they had sent Humphrey as a gift. "It graces our home and is in fact the centerpiece of my library," wrote Humphrey. "Just this past Sunday I used the Bible . . . to read scripture to my grandchildren who were spending the weekend at our home. I conducted our own Sunday School class."

One month later Hatch joined other senators on the floor to welcome the three-time presidential candidate's return for the first time since learning he had inoperable cancer. "For five emotional minutes the chamber resounded with applause," said a reporter. "Though his body was wasted by the ordeal of sickness, Humphrey spoke of the politics of joy and love and faith."

Humphrey shook hands with the presiding officer, his fellow Minnesotan, Vice President Walter Mondale. Then Humphrey spotted Hatch who was weeping openly. He stepped down from the leadership platform, went to the Utahn, and embraced him.

That evening Hatch wrote soberly, "Although we differ on many political matters, I can't help but say that this man has had a profound impact on my life. He is so optimistic, he is so sincere, he is so loving. . . . I have learned from him. I believe I will have more courage from this day onward. I will not forget him."

Humphrey died the following January, having gained a special place in the nation's heart. Among the eulogies was Mondale's: "[Humphrey] taught us all how to hope and how to love, how to win and how to lose; he taught us how to live, and finally, he taught us how to die."

Hatch's relations remained cool with some colleagues. Ted Kennedy was someone he continued to regard with detached disapproval, even while he began to appreciate Kennedy's strong points. After a hot debate with Kennedy over foreign assistance to Latin America—Kennedy literally screaming his opposition to Argentina and support for left-leaning Jamaica—Hatch walked over to the Massachusetts Democrat as a gesture of goodwill. Kennedy introduced Hatch to his staff, about ten men and women sitting on a couch behind him.

"You folks all owe me," Hatch told them.

"We owe you?" one asked.

"Yes, sir," Hatch explained, "because I'm keeping your boss's blood rushing through his body so that this dissipated sop will probably live longer than he would otherwise, and you fellows will continue to have jobs."

They roared with laughter, joined by Kennedy. That evening Hatch wrote: "I have to admit that I enjoy the guy but believe him to be almost a total demagogue."

Hatch found Ohio Democrat Howard Metzenbaum, elected to the Senate at the same time as Hatch, inordinately liberal and dogmatic. And he had a special category reserved for Idaho's Frank Church, considering him recklessly opportunistic.

Church, one of the Democrats defeated by Carter in 1976 for the presidential nomination, had traveled the globe for the Foreign Relations Committee. In 1975 and 1976 he chaired a special Senate committee investigating alleged CIA abuses and used the publicity to launch his presidential bid. Some intelligence experts blamed Church for crippling the CIA and leaving the U.S. blind and deaf to its enemies in vital parts of the world.

Church returned Hatch's disdain in spades, once remarking on the Senate floor that Hatch reminded him of a bumblebee—larger at birth than at present. Hatch privately prepared a retort for the next time Church insulted him: "Senator Church reminds me of an exquisite butterfly that flits all over the world and finally lands on a big pile of Moose Dung." It was a clever takeoff on a legal case before Church's

Foreign Relations Committee, involving an Indian chief with the colorful name of Moose Dung.

A hard-working senator, Hatch tended his constituents' needs, returning to Utah almost every other weekend. Nobody, not even Hatch's most virulent enemy, called him lazy, unprincipled, or ineffective. But the reviews around Washington were mixed. On one hand, Hatch quickly earned the reputation of being "bright, articulate, unafraid to beard liberal lions in their own dens" and "the most persuasive, tireless defender of the conservative cause to emerge from Utah in several decades." But there was also "a consensus that Hatch has a healthy ego that sometimes comes across as sheer arrogance." A reporter for *Utah Holiday* early in 1978 cited an example: "At the Oakton, Virginia, LDS Ward . . . where Hatch and his family reside, the junior senator from Utah often parks his Mercedes in a No Parking zone directly in front of the church, where he can be seen." It also quoted a secondhand comment by Judiciary Committee Chairman James Eastland. Eastland reportedly told another senator that he enjoyed having Hatch on his panel because he was intelligent, diligent, and articulate, then sighed, "If only he'd quit telling me so."

In his own defense, Hatch conceded, "I may have parked in the ward's No Parking zone a time or two when I couldn't find another space, but definitely didn't make it a practice." Hatch said the magazine's source for the parking lot story apparently was an antagonistic press aide to a fellow senator, and that it was not Eastland but another senator who had made the barbed remark about Hatch's work on the Judiciary Committee.

Back in Utah, actor Robert Redford lashed out at both Garn and Hatch. Speaking to a current affairs class at Brigham Young University, located just down a canyon road from his mountain home, Redford said the "general view" of Utah's delegation in Washington "is one of embarrassment, particularly of Hatch and Garn." He attacked Garn as a "fool" and Hatch as "slippery."

In response, Hatch retorted that Redford had "learned all of his politics from the movie, *The Candidate,* in which he starred." The movie closed with the newly elected candidate looking bemusedly at his staff and asking, "What do we do now?" Charged Hatch, "I guess he never really found out."

Sometimes defensive, sometimes dismissive, Hatch privately did a lot of soul-searching as he felt his way into his new role. His most important Utah colleague was the senior senator from Utah, Jake Garn. "My staff was going crazy when Orrin first arrived in the Senate," recalls the quick-tempered Garn. "He had not held public office before, and was getting a lot of attention in the press. My staff wanted me to change my personality to try to compete with Orrin's exposure on TV and in the newspapers. I told them to relax. His press attention didn't bother me at all."

But Garn didn't approve of other things about Hatch and hauled him into his office where he privately took him to task. Hatch listened with surprising meekness. "You've got to approach things differently if you want to get along back here," warned Garn, who accused Hatch of taking credit for things Garn and other senators had accomplished. Garn advised Hatch not to say "I" so much, to curb his use of an elaborate vocabulary in debates and speeches, and to nip in the bud any talk of running for President. "You may well run for President down the road, Orrin," conceded Garn in a candid compliment, "but it should be after you've proved you can do the job here in the Senate and get reelected in 1982."

The next day Hatch wrote pensively, "Jake was not prepared to listen to any rebuttal, so I just sat there and took it, and am glad I did. I must accept the fact that, although I don't intend to be pushy, aggressive, arrogant or irritating, I apparently am and he is right. . . . I'll try to overcome my bad qualities. I hope that time will heal all wounds."

Another mentor, Paul Laxalt, R-Nevada, one of the Senate's leading figures, recently summed up his 1977 impressions: "Orrin had a save-the-world complex. He wasn't malicious, just very ambitious. He was like other new senators who hadn't held office before . . . He rode pretty roughshod and I was put out with him at first."

Hatch was a quick study, even in humility. A few weeks after Garn lowered the boom, a third conservative senator, James McClure, R-Idaho, told Hatch he had also considered reading him a lecture on the senatorial facts of life but found that Hatch's demeanor had markedly improved in recent weeks, recalls Hatch. "He told me you have to pay a price around here because so many others have been in the Senate a long time and don't want somebody coming right in and trying to take over."

Privately Hatch vowed to earn his colleagues' respect. He saw another new GOP senator, Richard Lugar of Indiana, as a model. "He's basically as conservative as I am," wrote Hatch in a personal memo, "but is perceived as a moderate and liked by everybody. I guess it's because he really doesn't say much and everybody knows what a fine gentleman he is."

Hatch was a hard-hitter, but he played fair and insisted others do the same. He also considered friendship far more valuable than partisanship. Most politicians behave with easy cordiality when they are out of public view. They meet at numerous social functions and share interests that surmount policy differences. For Hatch, a neutral meeting point was a weekly Senate prayer breakfast, coordinated by his friend James Allen and attended by religiously inclined members of both parties. Participants took turns offering inspirational messages, and Hatch quickly felt comfortable in that setting.

Perhaps the private respites made it easier to take up the public cudgels. One protracted and lengthy floor fight that quickly became personal was the contest over two treaties giving the Panama Canal to that country by the year 2000. After the documents were signed by President Carter and Panamanian leader Omar Torrijos in September 1977, the Senate Foreign Relations Committee approved them, and they reached the full Senate early in 1978 to muster the two-thirds vote required for ratification.

Nevada's Laxalt formally led the Senate opposition, but James Allen headed most of the parliamentary maneuvering and much of the opposition floor debate. Allen, an Alabama Democrat, was considered the Senate's master strategist, matched only by majority leader Bob Byrd. Close beside Allen was his protégé Orrin Hatch, offering amendments and arguing against the treaties as the floor debate stretched from days into weeks.

Hatch and several other conservatives made a quick trip to Panama for a firsthand look at the canal and briefings by U.S. and Panamanian officials. Hatch also traveled throughout the United States to speak out against the treaties, telling one group in California: "I feel the same way about the Panama Canal as I do about my car. I bought it. I paid for it. It's mine. And it's not worth the damn trouble it's causing me."

As the battle raged on, it turned uglier and more personal. Six weeks into the floor debate, Senator Daniel Patrick Moynihan, a New York Democrat, called a treaty amendment proposed by Wyoming Republican Malcolm Wallop inane, childish, and stupid. Moynihan later "revised and extended" his actual remarks—a Senate euphemism for "censored"— before they appeared next day in the official *Congressional Record*. Even toned down, Moynihan's words dripped with scorn.

Wallop was not on the floor to defend himself, so Hatch asked Moynihan to yield for a protest. Moynihan refused. When he finally ended, Hatch noted his regard for Moynihan "who I think is very witty at times, but I personally felt he was not very witty today." Moynihan's remarks, added Hatch, offended him personally and were "demeaning to an awfully fine, distinguished man." Days later, the New York Irishman—who others suspected had still been celebrating St. Patrick's Day a week late when he made the intemperate comments—rose in the Senate and apologized to Wallop.

The strongly pro-treaty *Washington Post* weighed in with a vicious editorial attacking another senator, Dennis DeConcini, D-Arizona, who had offered an amendment that outraged Panama's left-leaning strongman Torrijos. The DeConcini amendment, one of the few accepted by President Carter and Senate supporters, specified that the United States could intervene militarily in Panama after the turn of the century if the canal were shut down for any reason.

The *Post* called DeConcini "a 40-year-old freshman senator of no previous renown, of no known international awareness, of little experience of any kind beyond minor administrative posts in Arizona . . . [and] a lightweight whom serious senators should regard as an institutional embarrassment."

Hatch fired off a protest which an aide hand-carried to the *Post*. He called the article "one of the most vicious, irresponsible, and demeaning editorials I have ever read," added that DeConcini "is respected on both sides of the floor," and defended him as "without question, one of the most ethical, decent, fine men in the Senate."

In the end, the two treaties were barely ratified, on identical Senate votes of 68-32, one more than the required two-thirds.

Labor leader George Meany wanted a pen for his eighty-fourth birthday in August 1978. Not just any pen. The pen President Carter would use to sign into law the most sweeping changes in labor union rules in more than forty years.

The crusty leader of the AFL-CIO and his associates had spent tens of millions of dollars as a down payment on that pen. For years big labor had given about 95 percent of its congressional campaign donations to Democratic candidates, and finally helped put a Democrat back in the White House by supporting Jimmy Carter against President Ford in the 1976 election.

The price would be worth it: Labor law "reform" would help reverse a sharp decline for unions, whose membership had gone from 35 percent of nonfarm workers at the end of World War II to less than 25 percent thirty years later. During 1975-77, more than half the union elections held among American workers had resulted in union defeats.

Big labor's solution was not to change itself but to change the rules, amending the National Labor Relations Act of 1935 to protect workers seeking union representation. Also near the top of labor's agenda was strangling the despised Section 14-b of the Taft-Hartley Act, the "right-to-work" provision under which twenty states, including Utah, had outlawed contracts that forced workers to join unions to keep their jobs.

Prodded by threats that future campaign donations would be withheld, representatives in the House overwhelmingly approved Labor Law Reform, 257-163, in October 1977. The bill also sailed through the Senate Human Resources Committee, 16-2. The two committee members voting against it were the rookies: Hatch and Hayakawa.

Hatch took his anti-Labor Law Reform stance after intense analysis. "I had been raised in the union movement but something was going wrong," said Hatch. "Unions seemed to be for every liberal idea, including socialist views such as redistribution of wealth. The unions were principally responsible for the surge of federal social spending which led us to the high budget deficits that were swamping our society. Democrats played workers for chumps, always calling for more taxes on the rich to fund social programs, even though the taxes always hurt their members, including many of the middle class, the most."

Stakes were momentous, as Hatch explained in a recent interview: "If labor law changes were approved by the Senate in the form passed by the House, an estimated 50 percent of all American workers would be forced into unions—double the current rate. More and more money would be poured into welfare-type programs and there would be nothing left over for strengthening America's military. The Soviet Union thus would not be forced to develop a more open society and end the Cold War, and the course of history would be quite different."

He believed laws already on the books stacked the process slightly in favor of unions and reflected privately: "I didn't find that repugnant, having read many books about the terrors of early unionizing attempts by courageous men and women who wanted working people's rights in a society slanted in favor of powerful businesses. However, a delicate balance had emerged which worked quite well and I didn't think it should be upset by slanting the process completely in favor of one side or the other—the unions in this case."

Nothing could stop the proposed changes but a majority vote on the Senate floor. It seemed a hopeless battle. There appeared to be no question that at least the required fifty-one senators would side with big labor when the issue came to a head. Nor was a presidential veto likely. George Meany hadn't taken Carter's support for granted and had been softening him up. The South was the most inhospitable region in the U.S. to organized labor, and Carter was not as responsive to big labor's interests as other Democratic Presidents had been. With the bill already approved by the House, Meany publicly labeled Carter "indecisive" and graded his first-year performance in office "C-minus."

Carter howled with indignation. But Meany's shots across the White House bow accomplished one desired result: Carter vowed that the Labor Law Reform Bill would clear the Senate. Carter believed the labor victory would prove his political ability to myriad doubters and help heal strained relations with Congress.

Ironically, Carter acknowledged that the nation's biggest enemy was inflation, which would average 8 percent for 1978. Studies indicated that, if this bill became law, inflation would soar even higher. Yet politics over-rode logic as the White House dug in for the Senate fight that would leave it and big labor either commandingly stronger or unmasked as losers.

With the canal treaties out of the way, majority leader Bob Byrd announced that Senate Bill 2467, Labor Law Reform, would be taken up by the Senate May 16, 1978.

The bill would require companies to hold "quickie" elections for union representation after employees requested them, without giving employers enough time to defend themselves, give unions the right to come onto company property at the employer's expense before elections to unionize employees during work hours, add two members to the National Labor Relations Board (an invitation to the Democratic White House and Democratic Congress to stack the board with pro-labor members), allow the NLRB to set wage rates for companies refusing to reach an initial contract with workers, and authorize the NLRB to ban such companies from doing business with the federal government.

Unions pointed to a handful of business violators, notably the giant Southern textile manufacturer J. P. Stevens & Company, as justification for labor law overhaul. They accused the NLRB of enforcing the law so rarely and with such light penalties that firms like J. P. Stevens had more incentive to exploit the process and pay the fines than comply.

Businesses were just as adamantly against the changes and had been gearing up for a year in anticipation of an all-out fight. They had formed a coalition that included such giants as the U.S. Chamber of Commerce, the National Association of Manufacturers, and the Associated General Contractors of America. The Labor Law Reform Bill had easily passed the House in October 1977 before the industry coalition was fully revved up.

Carter's point man in the Senate was majority leader Robert Byrd, who had his own political agenda. Like his House counterpart, Speaker Tip O'Neill, Byrd had served as Senate leader just one year and was anxious to prove that the Democrats' future was secure in his hands. Byrd had mastered the Senate's rules through sheer hard work and meticulous attention to detail.

Hard work was not new to Byrd, who had been born in abject poverty to a coal-mining family. He was a meatcutter and welder before rising through the West Virginia and then national political systems. As a young man, Byrd had joined the Ku Klux Klan to win local votes but had quickly left it and apologized. Byrd played a mean fiddle and laced his speeches with quotations from the Bible and the classics. A *U.S. News & World Report* poll in 1978 named him the fourth most influential man in America.

As the date drew near for the labor law battle, all the generals were in place except one: a leader for the Senate opposition. Business representatives, publicly bullish but privately pessimistic about stopping the bill, tried to recruit a number of senior senators. All said no. They were convinced that a significant majority of members would vote for the legislation anyway and did not want to go down on another losing fight just after the Panama Canal treaties.

Finally, almost by default, they turned to the senator who was ninety-eighth in seniority out of 100 members: Hatch. Initially he was reluctant to take the lead because of the recent stinging criticism by senior colleagues that he had been stepping out of line. But there was no one else, and some of Hatch's deepest-felt principles were involved.

Encouraged by promises from other free-enterprise-oriented senators that they would follow if he would lead, Hatch reluctantly agreed on two conditions: "First, that business consolidate and not let anyone break ranks, and second, that they agree to follow and provide the resource support we needed." Several major unionized corporations, believing that the fight was hopeless and fearing union retaliation, were already considering making private labor-management deals on the side. Their defection could have doomed effective opposition from the start. How safe a bet could this rookie senator be? But something gave them hope and they agreed to the conditions.

Hatch asked Senator Richard Lugar to assist him; the Indiana Republican readily agreed. Forty-six years old, a former Rhodes scholar and mayor of Indianapolis, Lugar had beaten a pro-union incumbent Democrat, Vance Hartke, in 1976. Colleagues ribbed Lugar about his dubious distinction of once being tagged by Richard Nixon as his favorite mayor. Unlike Nixon, however, Lugar was open and honest, well regarded by Republicans and Democrats alike.

Hatch's team decided that the only chance to stop the Labor Law Reform Bill was through a filibuster. Such talkathons, while not allowed in the House, had a long if not glorious tradition in the Senate. Filibusters were best remembered as the roadblocks Southern senators had thrown up against civil rights laws decades earlier. South Carolina's Strom Thurmond had set the record on one such bill in 1957, talking for twenty-four hours, eighteen minutes straight.

Cloture—ending debate and proceeding to a vote on the measure at hand—took sixty votes in the Senate. Some senators disliked filibusters and would vote *for* cloture on principle while others, especially Southern senators, almost always voted *against* cloture on principle. But Hatch simply saw the filibuster as a tool in the kit. When Hatch conducted a filibuster, he called it "extended educational dialogue."

Hatch was counting on the support of his good friend James Allen, D-Alabama, as an expert counterweight to Byrd. Allen had an encyclopedic knowledge of Senate rules and procedures and had led more conservative filibusters in recent years than any other senator. He had coached Hatch since his first days in the Senate.

Allen, however, had been exhausted and beaten by the protracted Panama Canal fight. Senate opposition to the treaties had been poorly organized, forcing Allen to stay on the floor with no backup for many hours at a stretch during the ten-week debate and finally breaking his health. On the eve of the labor law fight, Allen, moving slowly, asked Hatch into his office.

"You're going to have to take the baton, Orrin, because I'm not going to be around much longer," said Allen.

Hatch laughed nervously, looking at his robust, six-foot-four friend. "Jim, you just won your last election by 90 percent. You're going to be here for a long time."

Allen looked down and shook his head.

In May 1978, Hatch was on NBC's *Meet the Press*—rare exposure for a freshman senator—facing Human Resources Committee Chairman Harrison Williams, D-New Jersey, who would be Hatch's principal labor law debate opponent on the Senate floor. They cut to the heart of the issue promptly.

> Williams: It is a very simple proposal that we are bringing to the Senate: justice, fairness under law. . . . The timetable of justice should not depend upon those who would avoid justice, and that is exactly what we have in this situation.
>
> Hatch: . . . This certainly isn't justice. I don't think it's justice to crush small business. I don't think it is justice to have punitive remedies such as enlisting the aid of the federal government to blacklist businesses all over America and have federal contract debarment.

Williams, fifty-eight, had been in the House or Senate for a quarter-century. He had the bushiest eyebrows on Capitol Hill, giving him a scowling look that belied his generally good nature. During the nationally televised debate, he lost his cool briefly under Hatch's persistence; but after the session, Hatch and Williams went to lunch together.

Lobbyists on both sides pulled out the stops in one of the heaviest efforts at persuasion ever to hit the Senate. "Up until now the chief casualties in this congressional wrangling are the nation's trees, felled to feed the paper avalanche of letters, speeches and press releases proclaiming and condemning the measure," commented *U.S. News & World Report* in April. "Mail being received in the Senate is beyond counting."

More than a month before the bill was taken up by the full Senate, the National Right to Work Committee had generated some 3 million postcards against it—an average of 30,000 for each of the 100 senators. The AFL-CIO had generated 2 million for it—20,000 per senator, had another 700,000 postcards in reserve, and was ready to put its letter-writing operation into gear again.

Hatch huddled with Lugar and other leaders to sketch out Senate strategy. Key members of his team included Democratic leader Ernest F. (Fritz) Hollings of South Carolina, Senate minority leader Howard Baker of Tennessee, Robert Thompson, a savvy lawyer from South Carolina who was an officer of the U.S. Chamber of Commerce, and business coalition lobbyist Warren Richardson.

Hatch came to rely especially on the tall, heavyset Thompson, forty-eight, who had chaired the U.S. Chamber of Commerce's labor relations committee for five years. A Southerner, he understood why the region was the chief organizing target of union leaders desperate to stop the flow of industry and jobs from the heavily unionized Northeastern "rustbelt" to the right-to-work Southern "sunbelt."

Lugar organized three teams of senators, five to six members to a team, to keep the Senate floor covered throughout the day. When a senator could not be present, Hatch planned to take his place and keep talking until relieved. Hatch also traveled the country during the year before the Senate fight, giving hundreds of speeches, firing up other opponents and helping to coordinate pressure on key senators from their home states.

On May 13, 1978, only days before the fateful Senate showdown began, Hatch and his press aide, Bill Hendrix, boarded a helicopter in Salt Lake City for a flight to Logan. Hendrix carried a large pine box on his lap. The legendary bear, Old Ephraim, was heading home.

At USU, Hatch presented the box to Glen Taggart, Utah State University president, and Lyle Hillyard, the local GOP official who had first urged Hatch to reclaim the huge omnivore. Hatch pried open the box with a pen knife and lifted out the skull. "Old Ephraim didn't have much left," he recalls, "Just the lower part of his skull and upper mandible." Still intact was one tooth nearly two inches long, a reminder of the havoc wreaked by Old Ephraim among the valley's pioneers.

On the return flight to Washington, Hatch mused on Old Ephraim. The bear's last mistake was cornering just a single sheepman. With his aggressive attack on the labor bill, Hatch had cornered half the power brokers in Washington. Would his head be picked as clean as Old Ephraim's?

7

The Labor Law Battle

I n May 1978 the Labor Law Reform Bill reached the Senate floor. Approval was considered inevitable: big labor had lined them all up—the House, Senate, and White House—and had greased the skids well. If the most important labor union bill in four decades passed, the nature of the American workplace and the future of the U.S. economy could change fundamentally. Millions of workers could be forced to join unions and inflation could skyrocket.

Labor interests were a Goliath. The Senate included sixty-two Democrats, most elected with union help, and thirty-eight Republicans, including a number who voted routinely with the Democratic majority on labor issues. Pro-union members were led by majority leader Bob Byrd, floor leader Harrison Williams of New Jersey, Ted Kennedy of Massachusetts, and Howard Metzenbaum of Ohio. Among them, they totaled sixty-seven years of congressional experience.

Facing this Goliath was a youthful David—Orrin Hatch, who had been in the Senate all of sixteen months. At his side was fellow Republican Richard Lugar of Indiana, also a sixteen-month senator. No one doubted that a majority of senators would vote for labor law reform in an up-or-down vote. The only stone in David's sling—and it seemed very small—was to keep pro-union forces from gaining the necessary sixty votes to end the filibuster and proceed to a vote on the bill.

Democrats were so confident of victory that their worst fear was crushing Hatch and Lugar too quickly and arousing public sympathy. Byrd decided to let the two freshmen win the first two cloture votes, then stop the filibuster on the third.

The Senate had voted on cloture only 127 times in history, never more than four times on a single legislative issue, and the outcome this time likely hinged on five undecided Democrats: Lawton Chiles of Florida, Dale Bumpers of Arkansas, John Sparkman of Alabama, Russell Long of Louisiana, and Edward Zorinsky of Nebraska.

May 15, Monday

Hatch takes a study by noted economist Pierre Rinfret to the White House. Rinfret's study warns that "the proposal would hit small business hardest and add as much as 3 percent to the Consumer Price Index and would almost double the base rate of inflation in this country for each 10 percent of unionization."

Hatch tries to go over the Rinfret study with Carter. The President has been "under tremendous stress and his eyes looked almost wild," Hatch recalls. Carter is preoccupied with winning congressional support to sell jet fighters to several Middle East countries. He gives the Rinfret report only cursory attention.

May 16, Tuesday

The battle opens on the Senate floor. The U.S. Chamber of Commerce says "freedom is at stake." George Meany of the AFL-CIO calls it a "holy war."

Meany and President Carter are singing off the same sheet. "We need to have a bill and we'll get it," vows a White House aide. Carter personally will lobby key senators. The aide explains: "It's an important piece of legislation and a top priority of Carter's. You don't give something a White House send-off and then lose."

Byrd announces he will not place the Senate on a two-track system that would allow other business to be conducted during part of each day. Focusing the Senate's entire effort on the Labor Law Reform Bill, he reasons, will maximize pressure on opponents to give up a hopeless fight and let the Senate move to other issues.

The floor fight begins calmly but pointedly. Williams says the bill is simply designed to "end delay and bring an end to the growing number of violations of employee rights" in organizing unions. Senate minority leader Howard Baker calls it an "over-broad solution to an exaggerated problem," and Jesse Helms, R-North Carolina, says its real goal is to "unionize the South by federal force." Hatch holds the floor for two hours in the afternoon.

May 17, Wednesday

Labor Secretary Ray Marshall, in a rally at Lafayette Square, attacks the incipient filibuster and tells 2,500 union supporters that the fight is between "the powerful and the powerless." Those with the most at stake, he says, are the victims of antiunionism, "the men and women at the bottom of the economic ladder."

Hatch swims at the Senate gym. There Democratic senators Sam Nunn of Georgia and Fritz Hollings of South Carolina say they are with him. "It pays to go there," Hatch concludes. The reassurance is heartening.

May 18, Thursday

Byrd announces he will not attempt to end the filibuster until senators return from the Memorial Day recess early in June. Byrd calls it a matter of fairness; opponents believe he wants to avoid more pressure on fence-sitting senators during their visits home.

Hatch delivers floor speeches, helps draft remarks for others, calls for and conducts daily strategy sessions, and pores over Senate rules with James Allen, all while attending to other Senate duties. Issues often have been decided by manipulation of the complex Senate rules, and Hatch counts heavily on Allen to help guide him through the procedural maze.

Hatch continues swimming in the Senate pool to increase his stamina and is up to fifty laps. His workdays now are routinely eighteen hours long, and lunch is often yogurt from an office cooler. Many nights before collapsing into bed, he writes, "I have never been so tired."

May 20, Saturday

Orrin and Elaine take the children to the White House for the annual congressional families' picnic. Last year the fare was hot dogs and hamburgers. This time the picnic basket is filled with cold chicken, cheese, pâté, strawberries, and bread. The evening ends with Tchaikovsky's *1812 Overture*, a spectacular fireworks display supplying percussion.

For Orrin, the memory of the evening that lingers is of a lonely Jimmy Carter. "There was less interest in the President and First Lady than at any time since I had been back there," he recalls. "People didn't flock all around them. Members of the media were there but even they hardly looked at the President."

Power is Washington's aphrodisiac. A perceived lack of it is the capital's great repellent. Washington's politicos have a saying: "If you want a friend, get a dog."

May 24, Wednesday

At the Senate prayer breakfast, Bob Byrd gives the message, then calls on Hatch for one of the responses. Hatch, genuinely moved by Byrd's remarks, compliments him and offers his own thoughts. Hours later they are back in the Senate chamber, locked in verbal combat.

For the White House, it is who-needs-enemies day. GOP leader Baker unveils a poll showing that the labor reform most Americans want is less union power. Stamped "strictly confidential," the poll ironically was conducted by Carter's own pollster, Patrick Caddell.

Then Hatch forces the federal Small Business Administration to release a secret, scathing report of the proposed labor changes. It says parts of the bill are "patently discriminatory" against small businesses. Both the Caddell poll and SBA report make national headlines, increasing labor's pressure on Carter.

New Jersey's Williams says the filibuster is "a total way of life. . . . It restricts your opportunity to do ordinary, routine things." Asked about Hatch's performance, Williams says, "I told him he promises to be a good filibusterer. His speeches are flat, droning, and unemotional." Hatch explained that he and Lugar were indeed trying to "bore them to death" in hopes they would finally give up and pull the bill off the floor.

Walking off the floor exhausted after speaking for four hours, Hatch is confronted by Evelyn Dubrow of the International Ladies Garment Workers Union.

"The other 'labor goon' and I were watching you today," says the labor lobbyist with pointed sarcasm.

"Now, Evelyn, I've never called a union member a goon in my life and I don't intend to start now," says Hatch, feigning wounded innocence. "How come you're picking on me?"

Dubrow admits it doesn't sound like Hatch. "I know you believe in what you're saying," she says. "We just disagree with you."

Spotting another group of union lobbyists in the Senate reception room, who are obviously intent on avoiding him, Hatch approaches and shakes hands with each one.

"How can you guys be for this piece of shit?" asks Hatch.

Disarmed by the familiar salty language from the former Pittsburgh lather, the men start to smile. Steve Paradise, union sympathizer and Senator Williams's top staffer on the labor committee, says, "Don't get mad at the senator personally, guys. He helps us in a lot of other ways."

Two weeks into the filibuster, lobbying on both sides is some of the fiercest ever in Washington. Full-page ads appear in the *Washington Post*, the most widely read newspaper in town, Senate offices are receiving up to a thousand cards and letters a day, plus telegrams and nonstop telephone calls. The National Right to Work Committee estimates that it has mailed 12 million pieces of mail to senators and their constituents since December.

Business interests plan to spend $5 million on their campaign and labor about half that. Small-business owners pour into Washington from across the country to lobby home-state senators, and an AFL-CIO task force imports workers "victimized" under current labor law. The lion's share of pressure is focused on the five uncommitted Democrats — Chiles, Bumpers, Sparkman, Long, and Zorinsky.

June 1, Thursday

Memorial Day recess week. Hatch works in his yard in Vienna until dark. He is summoned to the telephone where an aide delivers devastating news: James Allen has just died of a heart attack in Alabama. That evening Hatch writes:

> I've had very few things hit me as hard as this news did. Senator Allen was not only my best friend in the Senate, but one of the greatest men I've ever known. He was a spiritual man who . . . beat himself into the ground filibustering and stopping so many of the detrimental things that really were hurting the country. . . . I've often said that, if a Republican ran against him, I would go down to Alabama and campaign for Jim Allen because there couldn't be a Republican any better than Jim Allen.

June 2, Friday

Hatch arises early and goes to his office, working until 8:15 P.M. although the Senate is still on holiday recess. He clears his desk of other matters, contemplating a more difficult struggle than ever without Allen at his side.

"None of us knows the rules as well as he did," Hatch writes. ". . . I'm just going to have to get on top of them . . . so that we don't get ruined in the end. I suspect Bob Byrd will do anything within his power to shove the rules down our throats, especially now that Jim is gone."

He turns to Jesse Helms of North Carolina, the best man on rules now that Allen is gone. Helms is optimistic: "We'll have [filibustering senators] on the floor if they have to wear their pajamas and bedroom slippers."

June 5, Monday

Senators start the day by eulogizing Allen. In his tribute, Hatch quotes from two favorite poems: "Thanatopsis," by William Cullen Bryant, ending ". . . approach thy grave like one who wraps the drapery of his couch about him and lies down to pleasant dreams," and "Ode: Intimations of Immortality," by William Wordsworth:

> Our birth is but a sleep and a forgetting:
>> The Soul that rises with us, our life's Star,
> Hath had elsewhere its setting,
>> And cometh from afar:
> Not in entire forgetfulness,
> And not in utter nakedness,
> But trailing clouds of glory do we come
> From God, who is our home.

Then it was back to the filibuster, with Hatch and Helms helping to kill two amendments by pro-labor senators, aimed at softening small business opposition to the bill.

June 6, Tuesday
Orrin and Elaine join other senators flying from Andrews Air Force Base to Gadsden, Alabama, for Allen's funeral at a Methodist church. The Senate chaplain, Rev. Edward L. R. Elson, presides and gives the main sermon. Eulogies are offered by former Senator Sam Ervin of North Carolina and conservative Senator Harry Byrd of Virginia, the Senate's only Independent.

The Hatches console Allen's widow, Maryon, and their children. Orrin tells Allen's staff that his friend gave his life trying to stop the giveaway of the Panama Canal.

June 7, Wednesday
The first cloture vote. Bumpers of Arkansas, one of the five fence-sitting Democrats, tells Hatch half his constituents are for the bill and half against it, so "I will vote my conscience" and support you today. Writes Hatch: "I thanked him greatly. I'm not going to look a gift horse in the mouth, but I thought to myself, why wouldn't you vote your conscience on almost everything?"

The live quorum call comes at 5:00 P.M., followed by the vote at 5:15. Illinois Republican Charles Percy, torn between union and business supporters, votes against cloture. As he walks by, Hatch thanks Percy, who forces a grin and says, "Well, as you know, I'll leave you before it's all over." Percy is promising Illinois businessmen he will oppose labor reform but is clearly planning to vote with big labor when it really counts. "I could have punched him in the mouth," says Hatch, but he has not counted on Percy anyway.

Cloture is easily defeated, forty-two senators voting for it and forty-seven against. The outcome is no surprise—even Bob Byrd had predicted he'd lose on the first one or two votes—but the margin of victory boosts the spirits of Hatch and other bill opponents.

June 8, Thursday
The second cloture vote. Opponents of the Labor Law Reform Bill again defeat it, but this time the numbers have tipped—forty-nine votes for cloture, forty-one against. The votes for cloture are starting to creep up toward the necessary number of sixty.

Byrd announces several revisions to the bill in an attempt to win enough votes to invoke cloture on the third attempt, scheduled for Tuesday. Hatch says the concessions are not enough.

Opponent leaders divide up the five wavering senators, Hatch taking responsibility for Ed Zorinsky of Nebraska who entered the Senate with him in 1976 after switching from Republican to Democrat a year earlier. As the filibuster began, Zorinsky, forty-nine, told Hatch, "I'm with you, but only if you agree to tell me if you are going to lose." Hatch agreed. If the cause becomes hopeless, Zorinsky will cross over and vote with the unions to protect himself politically.

Hatch has earlier suggested to the business coalition that Nebraska newspapers be asked to write editorials about the bill. The tactic works: Zorinsky tells Hatch in wonderment that 90 percent of his constituents invariably ask his position on the Labor Law Reform Bill.

The most problematic of the five Democrats is John Sparkman of Alabama. Now in his late seventies, he is becoming slightly senile and is being exploited by both sides. Hatch and his colleagues plan to have another Southern senator sit with Sparkman during each crucial vote to remind him which way to go.

Maryon Allen has been appointed to fill her late husband's seat for now and Hatch is confident of keeping that vote.

June 9, Friday

Pressure is incredible on the five wavering Democrats—daily calls from the White House, lengthy visits with Byrd and other Senate leaders, threats from union leaders. Southerners need special courage: some of their states are so overwhelmingly Democratic that the only way they can lose their seats is if big labor sponsors other Democrats against them in primary elections. Unions are threatening to do just that.

Hatch works the Senate floor all day, arguing the bill point-by-point with Senator Williams.

Russell Long of Louisiana, one of the five waverers and a master manipulator, meets with Hatch. Long has a proposal: modify the bill, while soothing labor by vesting more power in the international unions to bind local unions, and give labor this victory. That will pacify George Meany and keep President Carter from being embarrassed. Hatch suspects that Byrd and the unions sent Long to try to split the opposition. He is noncommittal.

Hatch goes off the Senate floor to answer a telephone call from Neal A. Maxwell, a top LDS official. The church has just issued a statement that "every faithful, worthy man" in the church will henceforth be given the priesthood. It means that black men are no longer denied the Mormon priesthood. Hatch's personal notes rejoice: "This is really, really wonderful. I had been praying for a long time for this change. I was so excited and so buoyed up by this event that I floated all day long. I think I could have stood losing labor reform today."

In the evening he and Jacob Javits—leader of Republicans favoring Labor Law Reform—debate the bill hotly on public television's MacNeil/Lehrer Report. Javits gets angry but afterwards they embrace.

June 12, Monday

Russell Long, under intense pressure from union leaders in Louisiana, again buttonholes Hatch with his proposal. Hesitant to tell Long "no" outright and lose him for sure, Hatch puts him off.

Labor's forces get to John Sparkman, who is sitting in the manager's chair for the majority during today's debate. Hatch approaches him and the aging senator, who once ran for Vice President with Adlai Stevenson in 1952, confirms that he's going to vote for cloture "because of all these good amendments."

Hatch doesn't mince words. "You come from a right-to-work state, John, and most of your people oppose this bill. If you vote for cloture, it will be a terrible black mark against your long and distinguished career in the Senate." Sparkman looks as if he's been punched in the face.

Hatch's coleaders believe Sparkman will vote for cloture. Hatch thinks they still have a chance with him.

June 13, Tuesday

The third cloture vote. Hatch drives to the office in a downpour, arriving late at 7:30 A.M., and is on the floor throughout the day, carrying some of the debate. His side beats the third cloture vote, but pro-labor forces pick up five votes, 54-43. Byrd and the White House predict victory tomorrow.

A low point comes when fellow Republican Ted Stevens of Alaska, a heavily unionized state, tells Hatch that his commitment to vote with him ended with the third cloture vote. South Carolina's Fritz Hollings tells Hatch he will threaten to oppose Stevens on an important Alaska lands bill if Stevens switches sides.

All five wavering Democrats vote with Hatch, including Long and Sparkman. Hatch anticipates that Byrd will try to change Sparkman's mind and plans to have another Southerner sit by Sparkman tomorrow. Byrd tries a carrot-and-stick approach with senators, warning that if the filibuster is not defeated soon they may have to return to work right after the November elections to complete Senate business that has languished during the protracted filibuster.

June 14, Wednesday

The fourth cloture vote. Both sides call it "crucial." As the 4 P.M. vote nears, Hollings sits with Sparkman. Byrd approaches Sparkman's desk. The old man, greatly agitated, barks, "Get away from me!" and shoves Byrd. Sparkman will hold.

Stevens, however, jumps to the other side, along with three other Republicans—John Heinz of Pennsylvania, Lowell Weicker of Connecticut, and Charles Percy of Illinois. Percy reportedly tells the head of Nabisco that Baker says his side doesn't need Percy. Baker nearly goes ballistic.

Labor Secretary Ray Marshall, expecting victory, makes an unusual appearance in the visitors' gallery to be on hand for the celebration. But the final vote is 58-41 —two short of the magical 60.

"I think that was their high-water mark," Hatch tells the *Washington Post*. He is outwardly confident but inwardly apprehensive.

June 15, Thursday

The fifth cloture vote. Hatch tosses all night, waking at 3:30 A.M. and going over every contingency in his mind. He reaches the office at seven o'clock and goes to Baker's office at nine for a strategy session. If they win today, they believe, Byrd will be forced to withdraw the bill.

Senators are assigned to keep track of Sparkman, Chiles, and Bumpers. Hatch continues to take Zorinsky.

Hatch gives Maryon Allen a tape of the last speech Jim made on the Senate floor. She tells him that Bob Byrd, trying to peel her away from labor law opponents, has threatened to remove her from her late husband's committees.

Hatch learns that three supporters will miss the afternoon vote: Pete Domenici, R-New Mexico, is attending his daughter's graduation; John Stennis, D-Mississippi, is visiting his wife's doctor; and Paul Laxalt, R-Nevada, is going to Idaho, apparently for a speech. Baker calls Laxalt and urges him to stay but Laxalt says no. The vote begins at 1:45 and ends at 2:30. Hatch's team wins again, 58-39.

The fifth cloture vote beats the old Senate record of four cloture votes on a legislative issue. The Senate has conducted almost no other business since the filibuster began May 16. Nonetheless Bob Byrd, outwardly calm, schedules a sixth vote for Tuesday.

June 20, Tuesday

Byrd postpones the cloture vote until Thursday. He can't get his forces lined up.

Lugar writes in the *New York Times*: "To say that there is no public enthusiasm for the bill is to understate the matter. In poll after poll, fewer than one in four Americans endorses any change that would ease the job of union organizers . . . . Thus, it should come as no surprise that our filibuster has displayed such resilience."

Lugar adds, "The majority leader's duty to the Senate, its rules, its traditions and to the country was to withdraw this bill last Friday, secure in the knowledge that he had done his best for the President and for George Meany. Regrettably he has chosen to proceed."

In the evening, Byrd, Chiles, and Long meet with Zorinsky, all of them browbeating him for four hours. At one point, Byrd says of Hatch and Lugar, "We've got to defeat these guys. If we allow these two crazy freshman senators to win this battle, we're going to have all kinds of kookie freshmen trying to do the same thing in the future." The words slip out before Byrd remembers Zorinsky is also a freshman.

Before retiring at 11:30 P.M., Hatch writes, "I sense that we have had extra help from the Lord. There is no other way we could have held out this long against Bob Byrd with all his power. The only way we can beat them is if the Lord is kind enough to continue to help us. I think He will be. If He does, although we will have to praise all of those who worked with us, I will give God the full credit."

June 22, Thursday

The sixth cloture vote. Tossing fitfully all night, getting even less than his usual four to five hours of sleep, Hatch arrives early at his office, then attends a Western Coalition breakfast. He doesn't eat. He is fasting—abstaining from food and drink—and praying through both breakfast and lunch.

This week's *Kiplinger Washington Letter* arrives in Hatch's office. "In all our years covering Congress this is one of the most effective jobs of business lobbying we have seen," it says. But ABC's *Good Morning America* predicts Hatch's side will lose today.

Opponent leaders meet in Hatch's office. Later Hatch goes to Baker's office. Hatch has a nagging worry that Baker—who wants to run for President—will compromise rather than risk a permanent rupture with big labor. Louisiana's Long, blood in his eye, is leaving Baker's office as Hatch arrives.

"Orrin, you know you're going to lose today?" says Baker.

"Not if we can hold onto those five votes," answers Hatch.

"Well, they now have Long and all they need is one more vote and we're whipped," says Baker. "They want to give you a partial victory by sending the bill back to committee, change it enough to void all your amendments, then report it forthwith as the pending business. If you object, Byrd will claim it's a procedural vote and his people will feel that they have to vote with him procedurally. They'll have enough votes to win."

Hatch faces a no-win choice. He has prepared some five hundred amendments as a back-up for a postcloture filibuster if necessary. But Byrd hopes to take the bill off the floor and rearrange how it is written, so that the amendments won't match it and therefore it will be valueless to Hatch. If Hatch objects, Democrats will feel obliged to support Byrd, and the filibuster will be defeated. If Hatch doesn't object, the bill will go to committee and be changed just enough to win a couple of wavering votes. Byrd will have cloture. The filibuster will be dead and the bill passed into law.

"Let me know what you want to do," says Baker. "I'll back you—but I think you ought to take the offer."

Hatch calls Zorinsky and says he must have his vote today. Zorinsky sounds haunted. Hatch guesses that Byrd worked him over last night. Zorinsky confirms it: "They promised me everything."

"Ed, you didn't give in, did you?"

"No, but you can only count me as a mushy no," says Zorinsky, meaning he's still with Hatch—barely. "If I change my mind, I'll call you."

Hatch tries to phone him two hours later. Zorinsky refuses to take the call.

Dimly Hatch recalls that Jim Allen once faced a similar challenge. How did he handle it? Hatch digs into Senate records and strikes gold. During an earlier filibuster, Allen made sure the Senate adopted a rule that a procedural vote to stop a filibuster could be amended, if the amendments were introduced *before* the vote was called for. If Byrd won on a procedural vote, Hatch and Lugar would force the Senate to vote on amendments to that motion—*seven hundred* amendments—in a post-cloture filibuster.

Hatch swings into gear. All his staff members, and all those of a key ally, South Carolina business lawyer Bob Thompson, become instant amendment-writers. They write two hundred new amendments and alter the language on the five hundred already waiting as a second line of defense, changing the language slightly so they can now be used to help thwart Byrd's call for a procedural vote.

Five minutes before the 3 P.M. vote, Hatch enters the Senate chamber, clutching the amendments, and deposits them with a clerk. Byrd nearly has apoplexy. He has been fairly warned of the latest Allen-Hatch nightmare that awaits him if he pushes the procedural vote. The Senate has already been brought to a standstill for five solid weeks on one bill. How long will it be tied up voting on seven hundred amendments to the bill?

But Hatch's immediate concern is to make sure the amendments are never needed. He and Thompson, the labor lawyer, retire to Baker's inner office. Thompson, a beefy man with boundless energy, leans on the fireplace mantle. "Maybe they've got us, Orrin," he says. "What do we do? It's up to you."

"I would rather lose it straight up and go down fighting, so that all America could see who did it to them, than cave in to these guys," answers Hatch.

"I agree," says Thompson.

They join Baker in his outer office. "Howard, we've come too far to give in now," says Hatch. "Let's beat 'em today."

Baker looks sick, perhaps seeing his political dreams vanishing up the fireplace flue. But he is true to his word. "I'm with you. Let's do it."

They go to the Senate chamber where Fritz Hollings of South Carolina approaches Hatch. "Orrin, I don't know if we can win. Russell Long is gone. You know what he's trying to do, but what are we going to do?"

"Can you hold onto Chiles, Sparkman, and Bumpers?" asks Hatch.

"Don't worry about them," answers Hollings, a handsome, white-haired Democrat, highly popular with his colleagues. "But what about Zorinsky?"

"Zorinsky was a mushy 'no,' the last time I checked," sighs Hatch.

"Are you going to object to Byrd's motion?" asks Hollings.

"If I object to it as a Republican, there's no doubt your fellow Democrats will feel it necessary to follow Byrd on a procedural vote," says Hatch. "A Democrat has to object."

"Who?" asks Hollings.

"You!" says Hatch.

Hollings pauses. The personal political costs could be enormous. "What about Zorinsky?" he asks again.

"Let me handle Zorinsky," says Hatch.

Just then—three minutes before the vote—Zorinsky walks onto the Democratic side of the chamber. Hatch, sitting in the minority leader's chair, catches Zorinsky's eye and raises his brows questioningly. Zorinsky nods "yes."

Hatch hurries back to Hollings. "Zorinsky's with us!"

"Then *I'm* going to *object!*" says Hollings with a big grin.

With a confident flourish, Byrd makes the motion to recommit the Labor Law Reform Bill to committee. He glances toward Hatch, waiting for him to object. Instead, a big booming Carolinian drawl fills the chamber from the other side of the aisle: "I object!"

Caught totally unaware, Byrd explodes. Russell Long, maneuvering for weeks for an excuse to cross over, jumps up from his desk and joins in Byrd's barely controlled tirade, raging about how unfairly opponents are preventing an up-or-down vote on the Labor Law Reform Bill. Long announces he is going to vote for cloture. He is obviously angling for at least one more senator to cross with him, giving Byrd and big labor the votes to kill the filibuster.

But Hollings, in a brilliant stroke of psychology, says, "Well, the distinguished senator from Louisiana has always been the *fifty-ninth* vote for cloture and we have always known it."

Everyone fills in the blank. The next crossover will be the *sixtieth* vote—carrying the onus of killing the filibuster and foisting the Labor

Law Reform Bill on America. The chamber is momentarily silent as Hollings's words sink in.

Then Republican Ted Stevens of Alaska, who deserted Hatch's team after the third cloture vote, rises. "If Senator Long is going to cross over and vote for cloture, I am going to cross back and vote *against* it."

Pandemonium breaks out in the chamber. Bob Byrd knows that he, President Carter, and the union leaders are sunk.

Byrd's last maneuver is an attempt not to save the bill, but to save face. Suddenly he announces that he, too, is going to vote against cloture – hoping to trick history into believing the vote is meaningless–and advises other senators to do the same. No one is listening to Bob Byrd any longer. Fifty-three senators vote for cloture with forty-five against.

The Labor Law Reform Bill is dead.

The hoopla on the floor is surprisingly muted. Earlier today, Hatch told his team, "If we win today my union friends are going to be devastated. Let's not shove it down their throats. Let's not cheer or go out of our way to talk to the press. Let's just quietly walk off the floor and thank God we've won."

That is exactly what they do. The three TV networks and other media clamor for interviews. Hatch and other opponent leaders are cordial but reserved.

Then, as celebrations break out across Washington, Hatch returns to his office to work on the business that has languished during the five-week filibuster.

Lugar's staff has kept track of the actual number of lines the historic debate has taken in the *Congressional Record*—8,515 lines from Lugar, third highest, 15,789 lines from Williams of New Jersey, floor leader for big labor, and 24,485, the highest number, from Hatch.

This evening, though physically and emotionally drained, Hatch keeps a social engagement in Georgetown at the home of former Kentucky senator John Sherman Cooper. As Hatch walks into Cooper's living room, he sees a familiar figure in dark glasses sitting glumly in a cushioned chair, cane at his side. It is George Meany, known only to Hatch until this moment in newspaper photographs.

Hatch groans inside, not wanting yet another confrontation on this very long day. He swallows hard and steps up.

"Hello, Mr. Meany, I'm—"

"I *know* who you are!" roars Meany in a voice so loud that a woman leaning against a nearby wall jumps in alarm.

Then Meany quiets down. "Orrin, we never expected to lose. All I can say is that I wish we had had you on our side." Hatch has pictured

Meany as eight feet tall, but he comes only to Hatch's chin. He is courteous and, to Hatch's surprise, even likeable. But very tough.

"We've suffered other defeats, and we'll live with this one," says
Meany. "We underestimated the whole situation. We respect you, Orrin,
and no hard feelings, but we're going to get rid of you in 1982 if it costs
us $4 million."

Hatch laughs. "Mr. Meany, if you spend that much money to get rid
of me in Utah, you'll double our gross state product and make me a
great hero." Meany laughs, too, in spite of himself.

They remain on good personal terms until Meany's death in 1980—
even though Hatch has cost him the pen President Carter never used to
sign labor reform into law.

Accolades pour in from across the country and from Hatch's Senate
colleagues. Fellow Utahn Jake Garn, in a handwritten note, says,
"Congratulations on a job well done. I'm very proud to serve in the
Senate with you." Richard Lugar writes, "The satisfaction of the past six
weeks has come from fighting for a good cause with men I respect. Your
knowledge, enthusiasm, stamina, and humor made the whole experience especially enjoyable."

Then there is this letter: "To the leader of the important fight against
the legislation which would enhance the power of the national labor
union leaders. . . . You did a *great* job, Orrin. The American people are
indebted to you."

It was signed by Senator Byrd. Harry Byrd, the Independent from
Virginia.

Big brother Jess with Orrin.

Jesse and Helen Hatch and their growing family, 1934: *(from left)* baby Orrin, Nancy, Jess, and Marilyn ("Nubs").

Family home in Pittsburgh, built with used lumber.

Orrin, with his white locks and perpetual worried look, Marilyn, and Nancy.

Playing baseball at home.

An all-American boy.

Jess Hatch *(standing third from right)* with B-24 crew. The glass over this portrait was shattered shortly before the crew was shot down over Europe in 1945.

Front row (*from left*) Siblings Chloe, Frances, Marilyn, and Orrin. Second row: family friend, Jesse and Helen Hatch, and more family friends.

Hatch's first campaign speech in high school.

Senior yearbook photo, 1952. The white streak in his hair was a constant reminder of his brother's death.

BYU intramural basketball champs, including a bespectacled Hatch, receive awards from varsity coach Stan Watts, 1953.

Elaine Hansen as a BYU freshman, 1952–53.   Hatch as an underclassman at BYU.

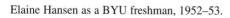

Elder Hatch (*kneeling second from left*) with other new LDS missionaries in Ohio, 1954.

Preparing to serve as a missionary for the LDS church, 1954.

Helping to train other missionaries.

Campaigning for BYU summer student body president, 1958.

Wedding day, August 28, 1957.

Elaine, pregnant with first child Brent, as Orrin picks the tune.

As a new attorney in Pittsburgh.

Young family in Pittsburgh. Orrin and Elaine with children (*from left*) Brent, Scott, Kimberly, and Marcia.

The Hatches' dream home in Ben Avon Heights, Pittsburgh, left behind to move to Utah in 1969.

Jesse and Helen Hatch (on 60th wedding anniversary in 1983) with surviving children (*from left*): Nancy, Marilyn, Orrin, Fran, and Jessica. (Photo by: Dave Updike, JayLynn Studios. Used by permission.)

Hatch children and cousins
campaigning for Dad in 1976.

Family home in Vienna, Virginia.

Utah's new U.S. Senator and Elaine with their children: (*from left*) Kimberly,
Scott, Marcia, Brent, Alysa, and Jess.

8

Encounter
with a Feminist

O N AUGUST 18, 1978, HATCH received a mailgram:

SINCE YOU HAVE ANNOUNCED YOUR INTENTION TO FILIBUSTER
WHEN THE ERA EXTENSION BILL COMES BEFORE THE SENATE, I
AM ANNOUNCING MY INTENTION TO BEGIN FASTING ON THE
CAPITOL GROUNDS IN WASHINGTON AS SOON AS THE FILI-
BUSTER BEGINS—A GENUINE MORMON FAST, WITHOUT FOOD OR
LIQUID—AND TO CONTINUE UNTIL YOU STOP TALKING OR I DIE.
—SONIA JOHNSON
STERLING, VA.

Hatch had tangled with the Mormon feminist two weeks earlier in a
Senate hearing on the Equal Rights Amendment and was still nursing
the bruises.

Hatch seemed more at ease dealing with men than women. But his
private writings showed that he considered women his intellectual
equals, and Hatch's lifestyle and attitude toward women set him apart
from many colleagues. He treated women with dignity on both a
personal and professional level.

The U.S. Senate—"the world's most exclusive club"—was a 98 percent
male bastion. Its only two women, Muriel Humphrey and Maryon Allen,
had been appointed to complete the terms of their deceased husbands.
Not until November 1978 would a woman enter the Senate in her own
right without suceeding a male relative. Even then, Kansas Republican

Nancy Kassebaum would benefit politically from the prominence of her father, 1936 presidential nominee Alf Landon.

As Hatch considered running for chairman of the GOP Senatorial Campaign Committee, a supporter, Roger Stone, approached Nevada's Paul Laxalt on his behalf. Laxalt said he preferred someone else because "Orrin is not a member of the club." When Stone reported this comment, Hatch was puzzled. "He meant you don't drink and carouse with them," Stone explained. "Then I'll never be a member of the club, because I'll never do that," said Hatch flatly.

Even before the start of his Senate service in January 1977, women's groups were wary of Hatch because of the ultraconservative reputation that preceded him to Washington. Their concern was reinforced that year when Hatch tried to water down a bill to stop employers from discriminating against pregnant workers—although in later years, as a power on the Labor and Human Resources Committee, Hatch would become a leading sponsor of legislation specifically to benefit women.

Feminist antipathy toward Hatch had been deepened by his successful leadership against the Labor Law Reform Bill. Unions, civil rights groups, and women's groups often worked in tandem to increase their political clout. Eleanor Smeal, president of the National Organization for Women (NOW) explained that the purpose of these different groups was identical: to redistribute power and resources in America.

Ironically, feminists labeled Hatch unsympathetic while touting another western Republican, Bob Packwood of Oregon, as their ideal senator. During the 1970s Packwood was a strong supporter of the Equal Rights Amendment, the Senate's leading advocate of zero population growth, and its firmest proponent of nonrestrictive abortion. Packwood's reelection in 1980 would be the top political priority of women's rights groups, who contributed more money to his campaign than any other bloc. The money flowed even as rumors spread that Packwood's intense interest in women went far beyond their causes. By 1993 Packwood would stand publicly accused by more than two dozen women of having sexually harassed them.

Another feminist favorite was Senator Ted Kennedy, whose alleged womanizing was legendary. An informal survey by a Washington writer found that "those who thought the question of [Kennedy's] philandering is irrelevant tended to be women who were deeply involved in the political aspects of the feminist cause. For them the important matter was getting feminist positions into the party platform, or getting the ERA passed, and so forth."

No credible report suggests that either Orrin or Elaine was ever less than a strictly faithful spouse. Their philosophy mirrored that of their church, which holds adultery second only to murder as a grievous sin. Such views were scorned by the Washington establishment, which defined morality in purely political or societal terms, not in terms of sexual relationships.

Hatch lived in a different world. He actively tried to pass his and Elaine's values on to their six children and encouraged a single standard for both sons and daughters. In August 1978, as their oldest daughter Marcia prepared to leave home for college, Hatch took her to lunch and—not for the first time—gave her some fatherly plain talk:

> Young men are not evil because they desire to physically touch girls and to have physical contact with them. The girl should not turn them off by saying, "Don't touch me, keep your filthy hands off of me," but by saying, "Look, I have some similar feelings . . . but I set certain standards for myself a while back and I intend to live up to those standards or I'd never forgive myself, and I don't think you would respect me either."

Because of his squeaky clean lifestyle, his Senate colleagues saved their bawdier jokes for times when Hatch wasn't around, occasionally stopping themselves in mid-sentence—half-joking, half-apologizing—saying, "Whoops, I can't tell that one; Orrin is here." While Hatch didn't appreciate off-color jokes, he enjoyed being around those adept at using humor in public and on occasion he tried his hand at telling jokes, usually relying on those with surefire punchlines. During a Senate breakfast, Hatch explained the Mormon practice of holding "testimony" meetings on the first Sunday of each month, when individual members of the congregation spontaneously express their feelings.

"Out in Sanpete County, Utah, one old Danish convert stood in testimony meeting and said, 'I haff to confess my sins," explained Hatch. "The brother then said, 'I haff committed adultery with Sister Petersen over there.'"

"Sister Petersen was shocked and yelled, 'Oh, no! Oh, no!' But the old Dane said, 'Oh, yes! Oh, yes! Sister Petersen, because the good book says that if a man looketh upon a woman to lust after her, he hath committed adultery with her already in his heart!'"

The story was a beloved staple among Danish converts to Mormonism in Utah, and a favorite of Hatch's, who was upright but not prudish. It was about as close as he ever came to telling a "dirty joke."

Although Hatch often seemed to prefer the daytime company of political liberals for intellectual stimulation, for after-hours social relationships he sought out others who held similar moral convictions, including fellow Mormons. There were approximately twenty thousand members of his faith scattered throughout the greater capital area among a population of several million. Hatch also met occasionally with LDS church officials about various public issues, encouraging them to build strategic alliances with other religions.

When Pope Paul VI died in August during the fifteenth year of his tenure, Hatch praised the late pontiff in his private writings: He had been "an excellent Pope of tranquility, peace and stability. . . . I think the Catholic Church has been a bulwark for honor, dignity, and what is right." Mormons and Catholics held similar views on the importance of families, and those views were the prism through which Hatch saw many women's issues.

He recognized that women faced discrimination. "I feel so strongly that women are not treated fairly in our society, especially at the workplace," he wrote privately on July 24, 1978, "but to lock into the Constitution that there can be no discrimination based on sex may well lead to disastrous, unchangeable Supreme Court and lower court rulings. The statutory route is better."

He wrote and copyrighted a brochure called "An Intelligent Guide to the Equal Rights Amendment," entered in the *Congressional Record* on October 3 as "The Intelligent *Woman's* Guide . . ."

"When it is not necessary to adopt a constitutional amendment, it is necessary not to adopt an amendment," the brochure argued. Hatch insisted there was no provision in the Constitution nor in any Supreme Court decision preventing American women from enjoying the same rights as American men. In fact, Section 1 of the Fourteenth Amendment specifically prohibited any state from denying any person "the equal protection of the laws."

"In order to end all discriminations against women, it is not necessary to abolish all legal distinctions between men and women," Hatch wrote. ". . . There are laws which tend to discriminate against women, as the opponents of ERA freely admit. These laws should be abolished, and can be abolished simply by repealing them."

Most Americans disagreed. In 1972 two-thirds of both houses of Congress had passed the Equal Rights Amendment to the Constitution. The amendment read succinctly, "Equality of rights under the law shall not be denied or abridged by the United States or by any State on account of sex," and gave Congress the power to enforce it.

Now, six years later, polls indicated a majority of citizens still supported the ERA. But ratification required the approval of three-fourths of the states—thirty-eight—and the number of ratifying states was stuck at thirty-five. The seven-year ratification deadline was approaching in March 1979. Furthermore, four of the thirty-five state legislatures had since voted to rescind their approval, further complicating the issue.

No amendment to the Constitution had taken even four years to ratify. But Congress was under tremendous pressure in 1978 to extend the deadline. Opponents said extending the deadline would be changing the rules in the middle of the game. Proponents echoed Senator Birch Bayh, D-Indiana, a leading ERA sponsor: "We must place no time limit on the pursuit of equality and justice in America today."

Hatch's heart was against the extension; but fresh from leading the stunning victory over the Labor Law Reform Bill, he preferred to work behind the scenes on this issue. Strongly advising him in that direction was Betty Southard Murphy, a member of the National Labor Relations Board and a feminist friend. They disagreed on the ERA, but he took her counsel not to go out of his way to wave a red flag before women's groups.

This time the field marshal was fellow Utahn Jake Garn. On August 15, as the House of Representatives voted to extend the ERA deadline, Hatch accurately foresaw how the issue would haunt him anyway:

> It's all going to come down to the Senate. I just hate that battle. There's no political margin in it for us, but it is something that we just have to do out of principle. It's going to give me troubles the rest of my life with some of these recalcitrant and obnoxious feminists. I suppose everywhere I go I'll have them all over me.

Sonia Johnson was Hatch's worst nightmare come true. She was a mother of four and the organist for her congregation in Sterling, Virginia, a Washington suburb, but otherwise did not fit the Mormon mold. She had a doctorate from Rutgers University, had taught school in several Third World countries, and in 1977 broke sharply with her church over its active opposition to the Equal Rights Amendment.

Johnson and a few friends formed "Mormons for ERA" and began marching in parades, attracting curious attention because their position stood in such marked contrast to their church's conservative stand. A telephone call during the last week in July—which the little band came to consider providential—was the beginning of their ascent to visibility as a feminist force. The call was from Senator Bayh's office, asking if Johnson would join a panel of citizens testifying for the ERA extension.

Three days of hearings before the Senate subcommittee on the Constitution were scheduled, starting August 2, chaired by Bayh. The panel included four Democrats and two Republicans—Hatch and Virginia's William Scott.

As time approached for the hearings, even leading liberal voices—

including the *New York Times, Washington Post, Baltimore Sun,* the *Chicago Sun Times,* and the *New Republic*—had come out against extending the deadline without also giving states a chance to rescind their earlier votes for the ERA during the extension period.

Garn was among nine witnesses testifying on opening day, Wednesday. He insisted that while he personally opposed the ERA the real issue was constitutional. He urged the committee to recommend extension of the time limit *only* if it also allowed states to rescind during the same period. It was a position widely held by ERA opponents, including Hatch, but hotly opposed by feminists.

While acknowledging that national polls showed most citizens supporting the ERA, Garn cited a survey by a California polling firm suggesting that citizens strongly opposed specific changes that could flow from the amendment, including sending draft-age women into combat, transferring matters of marriage, divorce, and child custody from the states to the federal government, and giving homosexuals the right to marry and teach in schools.

Witnesses on Thursday included Ruth Bader Ginsburg, a Columbia University law professor and pioneer in securing women's legal rights before the Supreme Court. In 1993 Ginsburg would be appointed to the Supreme Court by President Bill Clinton.

"Based on experience since 1972," said Ginsburg, "I believe Congress not only has the authority, it has the responsibility to extend the deadline. It would be the bitterest of ironies if the Equal Rights Amendment were to become the first proposed amendment in this nation's history to die because a procedural time bar . . . ran out."

Also testifying on Thursday was former North Carolina Senator Sam Ervin, who had once chaired the Judiciary Committee and was widely considered a foremost expert on the Constitution.

Borrowing a phrase from Oliver Wendell Holmes, Ervin said those favoring extension of the ERA time limit were committing "first-degree verbicide" on the Constitution, specifically on Article 5 which outlines the amending process. "Nothing can be found in Article Five or any other provision of the Constitution which confers on Congress by express words or by necessary implication the power to extend by seven years the deadline for State action respecting the ERA," said Ervin.

"It is an interesting fact that all of the ratifications of the ERA were obtained during 1972, the year of the submission, and the following year, 1973, except five. They were adopted before the people of this nation learned what the ERA really means and what the ERA will really do."

Since 1973, he noted, only five additional states had ratified the ERA, while four had voted to rescind approval. The reason, said Ervin, is that the ERA is "unnecessary, unrealistic, and destructive of the system of government the Constitution was ordained to establish."

Early on the morning of August 4, 1978, two cars crossed the Potomac River from Virginia, headed for Capitol Hill. Behind the wheel of one was Sonia Johnson, forty-two, erect and brisk, her curly brown hair close-cropped. The other was driven by Orrin Hatch.

Traffic was surprisingly light. Many residents had already fled the city for a three-day weekend at Atlantic Ocean beaches to escape Washington's oppressive summer heat and humidity. Johnson arrived an hour early, found a shady place to park near the Capitol, curled up in the back seat of her car with a "Mormons for ERA" banner, and went to sleep.

Hatch arrived at his air-conditioned office in the Dirksen Senate Office Building to await the third and final day of subcommittee hearings. He was a little frustrated. Because of the hearing he couldn't attend a GOP breakfast meeting and hear Henry Kissinger skewer President Carter's foreign policy from the fascinating perspective of a former Secretary of State.

Waking with a start, Johnson blotted her face and, using the car's rearview mirror, picked through her flattened brown curls. She pinned on a homemade "Mormons for ERA" button, and headed for the huge hearing room on the third floor of the Russell Building.

When she arrived, Room 318 was already filled with hundreds of pro- and anti-ERA spectators, and others lined the walls outside, clamoring to get in. Johnson, familiar with the routine after following the previous two days of hearings on TV, was seated and ready to join a panel with three other witnesses when Hatch entered. She made a mental note that Hatch was "flanked by two young male assistants," while committee chairman Bayh's assistants were "both young women."

The panelists were called to the long wooden table, located in the center-front of the hearing room facing the senators, who were seated on a raised platform behind a matching wooden barrier.

Senator Bayh, boyishly handsome with wavy brown hair and dimples, brought the hearing to order and welcomed the four witnesses, all of whom supported an extension for the ERA ratification. They included Rev. Joan M. Martin, a Presbyterian minister; Judith Hertz, representing a Jewish women's group; Rev. William R. Callahan, a Catholic priest representing Priests for Equality; and Johnson. Martin and Hertz testified first.

Then Johnson read a prepared statement, asking rhetorically how was it possible to remain a member of the Mormon church—a leading force against the Equal Rights Amendment—and still support the ERA?

Early Mormon feminists demonstrated that the movement for equal rights could be compatible with Mormon doctrine. . . . Joseph Smith, the founder of the church, once remarked that his method of governing the members was to teach them correct principles and let them govern themselves. In doing so, he was acting in accord with one of the most profound doctrines of the church–the human right to, and necessity for, free agency . . . [Today's church leaders] have chosen instead to tamper with our agency, to attempt to compel us to do what they believe is right through the use of fear and of their considerable authority. Unlike the Lord, they are afraid now, having taught us correct principles, to let us govern ourselves.

Applause erupted as Johnson finished. Bayh said the other side would also get one chance to applaud. Otherwise, he cautioned spectators not to react openly.

Johnson was followed by Father Callahan, who injected a note of levity into the proceedings when Bayh asked if he believed in abortion.

"I do not."

"Do you believe it is possible to oppose abortion and still support the ERA?" Bayh then asked.

"I have no difficulty distinguishing abortion from the Equal Rights Amendment," answered Callahan. "I think I will have no trouble until men are eligible to have abortions and would come under the equal rights provision."

There was laughter and Hatch quipped, "Heaven forbid." Hatch questioned witnesses, beginning with Callahan and then moving to Johnson, who was testy from the start.

> Hatch: Ms. Johnson, . . . do you not believe it is basically fair to recognize that if we are going to extend, which clearly is of benefit to the pro-ERA people, that we should recognize sovereign State rescissions?
>
> Johnson: I believe you are asking a rhetorical question and you do not want to hear the answer.
>
> Hatch: No, I want to hear your answer. But it is not a rhetorical question. It is a very profound question and it involves huge constitutional implications. You can make a decision in your mind whether it is fair or not fair. You can say so.
>
> Johnson: I do not think there is any unfairness. I do not think you are hearing that, because it seems to be throughout the hearings you keep saying this over and over again. No matter what anyone says, you would continue to say it. So I cannot add anything to what

I have heard other people say very well.

Hatch: What you seem to be saying is that I have a closed mind because I believe differently from you.

Johnson: No. You may have a closed mind because you do not seem to be hearing what anyone is saying. . . .

Hatch: How about fundamental fairness? You seem to be awfully irritated that I am asking you this question.

Johnson: I would like to have you stop addressing me because I have said all I can. I do not personally think that it is unfair. . . . I have said all that I can say.

After questioning other panelists for about fifteen minutes, Hatch returned to his fellow Mormon for the exchange that made national headlines.

Hatch: Ms. Johnson, how many people do you represent in the Mormons for ERA? How many women do you represent?

Johnson: I have no idea how many. We have not taken a poll.

Hatch: Is it a large number?

Johnson: It is a steadily growing number of women. I think—I am sure there are more than we have any idea about. I think the numbers are growing.

Hatch: I think that you would have to admit that in the Mormon Church, almost 100 percent of the women are against the Equal Rights Amendment, right?

Johnson: Oh, my goodness. [Applause.]

Bayh: I did not realize there were that many Mormons here to clap. Please keep the applause down. . . .

Johnson: I do not have to admit that. It simply is not true.

Hatch: I think it is true.

Johnson: You say it is true and I say it is not. . . .

Hatch: Let me say this to you. I have had some very wonderful Mormon women, as you apparently are, come into my office who are very much for the ERA. They are very much the exception, however, and the mail that we get is overwhelmingly against the ERA. . . . I would be surprised if the Mormon women who are for the ERA would comprise one-tenth of one percent. I think you would be surprised.

Johnson: The point here is that numbers of adherents have never proven an issue true or false.

Hatch: That is a good point. . . . I notice you are very self-confident that you are right and everybody else is wrong. I would have to admit that the majority can be wrong but on the other hand I have also seen the minority wrong many times. You may very well be wrong here, as confident as you are.

Johnson: You may very well be wrong, as confident as you are. . . .

Hatch: That is true and I am very confident. As a matter of fact, I am very confident that I am right.

Johnson: And so am I.

At this point, with temperatures and decibels rising, Bayh verbally stepped between them, admonishing: "Now, let's calm down."

Hatch lapsed into several meandering monologues. He accused Johnson of implying that most Mormon women were not as intelligent as she and defensively stated, "I have met an awful lot of Mormon women who are brilliant. My wife is one of them."

A few minutes later, he lectured panelists again on the fairness of allowing states to rescind their ERA votes during any extension period granted by Congress, citing a previous Supreme Court case to prove his point. Finally Bayh interjected:

> Bayh: I do not want to cut this off, Senator, but you are a distinguished lawyer. You are in tune with the Constitution. . . . If we are talking about fairness, I wonder if it is fair to put a sharp constitutional lawyer on one side and four very concerned lay citizens on the other side who are not as familiar as any of us are with the Constitution. You proceed as you think is fair.
>
> Hatch: Let me put it this way. I think it is fair when the only consideration before us is whether or not we should rescind and not all of the emotional arguments which have been given today.
>
> Bayh: Senator Hatch, we know what you think. We are trying to find out what these witnesses think.

After several more sharp exchanges between Bayh and Hatch, Bayh called the next group of witnesses. The group included Jane O'Grady. She read the statement of her boss, AFL-CIO president George Meany, who had been unable to attend at the last minute. Meany wrote that the ERA had been stopped short of the needed thirty-eight ratifying states "because of a vicious campaign against it by such right-wing groups as the Stop ERA movement of Phyllis Schlafly, the John Birch Society, and the Conservative Caucus." The statement accused opponents of "misinformation, emotional rhetoric, and distortion."

Even Bayh took umbrage at the harsh broadside, telling O'Grady: "This type of statement, I think, does not actually help your cause any. I feel compelled to say that." Hatch's questioning was succinct and pointed:

Hatch: I would think that the federation would want to make the best case it could that it does not discriminate against women and has not in the past. The statement is such a strong statement here today. How many women are on the governing board of the federation?

O'Grady: There are 33 vice presidents of the AFL-CIO.

Hatch: How many of them are women?

O'Grady: I think you know the answer to that, Senator. There are no women on the executive council of the AFL-CIO.

Hatch: Yes, I did know the answer. . . . I have no further questions.

Hatch won the last round. But by tangling with Sonia Johnson, he lost the match. What otherwise would have been a footnote in history became headlines across the country the next day: "Utah Senator, Mormon Woman Clash at Hearings on ERA." The handful of Mormons for the ERA got a publicity windfall that money couldn't buy.

Leaving the hearing room, Hatch approached pro-ERA women, including Eleanor Smeal of NOW, who greeted him cordially. Johnson was surrounded by anti-ERA women, including a number of Mormons who called her to repentance.

Johnson, elated, fired off a letter to Bayh a couple of days later: "After watching you in the hearings, I have decided to nominate you for the first man to be cloned–quickly, and by the hundreds of thousands. If this sounds like a love letter, it's because it is. Gratefully, Sonia Johnson, A Mormon for the ERA."

Hatch tried with only limited success to line up opposition to defeat the ERA extension in the Senate. In a private note, he vented his frustration: "The gutless wonders just don't seem to want to take on the women." Even his most conservative colleagues–Helms, McClure, Lugar, and Wyoming's Clifford Hansen–shrank from the prospect of taking a high profile, leaving Jake Garn, assisted by Hatch, to lead a lonely fight in the Senate against the extension.

At the end of August, Hatch returned to Salt Lake City and met with LDS church president Spencer W. Kimball. Kimball, in his early eighties, was a much-loved church figure who had closely followed Hatch's rise to prominence since first approving him for a church mission when Hatch was a teenager. Gentle and self-effacing, Kimball had spoken in a whispery rasp since undergoing surgery for throat cancer several years earlier. Small in stature but large of heart, he was revered as a prophet of God by his followers.

"He was full of questions," recalls Hatch. The senator briefed Kimball on developments in Washington, including his recent confrontation with Sonia Johnson. Kimball listened patiently, never suggesting what course Hatch should take next. In fact, Hatch had yet to be told by church officials what action to take on an issue. The LDS church wielded great influence on Utah's politicians, not by telling them what to do, but by making its views known publicly and then relying on those who shared its spiritual and moral beliefs to consider those beliefs in their decision making.

After an hour, Hatch rose to leave. "We hugged. He only came up to about my middle chest. He raised up and kissed me on the right cheek. I'd never been kissed by a man before. I leaned over and kissed him on his right cheek. It was a very moving and poignant experience."

During the hectic closing days of the session, with members more focused on the 1978 fall election than on legislative issues, majority leader Bob Byrd pulled a sleight of hand and scheduled the ERA for a vote.

Senate Republican leader Howard Baker called his troops together and angrily suggested they mount a filibuster and all vote against cloture to teach Byrd a lesson. Several liberals, however, including Oregon's Packwood and Connecticut's Lowell Weicker, said such a move would be interpreted by women as a unanimous Republican vote against the ERA itself and would cost the party dearly in the elections. Baker dropped the suggestion, and the threatened filibuster never materialized—saving Sonia Johnson from her fast on the Capitol grounds.

On October 6, 1978, the Senate voted on extending the ERA ratification deadline by three years and three months—with no provision that states could also rescind votes. Fifty-three senators told Garn they would vote with him against the extension. Thirty-six kept their word. The ERA extension passed 60-36 and was signed by President Carter, moving the deadline for ratification to June 30, 1982.

Both sides renewed the tug of war, but now many felt that pro-ERA forces had surrendered the moral high ground by steamrolling the extension into law while refusing to grant ratifying states an equal chance to change their minds under the new rules. Conservatives were by no means alone in echoing the reaction of Phyllis Schlafly, head of Stop ERA, who said the extension "is a fraud and will have no legal effect when tested in the courts."

A week after losing the ERA fight, Hatch accepted the Senate chaplain's invitation to replace him in opening that day's proceedings with prayer. As the Senate convened at 9 A.M., Hatch, using no notes, prayed:

We are grateful for this great land and the freedoms we have under this constitutional form of government. We are grateful to be here to have the opportunity to do what is right for this country. We pray thy spirit to be with us this day and to guide us that we may put our country first and do the things that are best for the people. Imbue us with decency, integrity, and strength that we might be able to fulfill our noble cause as Senators.

As ERA proponents stepped up their lobbying efforts to gain approval by three more state legislatures, one of the most powerful forces they faced was the Mormon church with its legendary organizational ability. The church had been criticized in the past—by its own members and others—for meddling in politics. In recent years it had retreated to a more restricted position of remaining silent on strictly political questions while reserving the right to announce and argue for its position on "moral issues."

The church formally opposed the Equal Rights Amendment in 1976 and explained its opposition again in 1978 as Congress breathed new life into the ERA. The proposal, said the church, would strike at the family, encourage homosexuality, and fail to recognize biological differences between men and women. "Because of our serious concern," said the church's governing First Presidency, "we urge our people to join actively with other citizens who share our concerns and who are engaged in working to reject this measure on the basis of its threat to the moral climate of the future."

The church gave marching orders and supplied foot soldiers in a number of states that hadn't ratified the ERA, including the key battlegrounds of Virginia, Florida, Nevada, North and South Carolina, Missouri, Illinois, and Arizona. LDS officials encouraged members to lobby as private citizens rather than as church members, both to magnify their effectiveness and to obscure the church's imprint on the effort.

Sonia Johnson and her band of rebels would have none of the behind-the-scenes tactics, however, and forced the church into the open in a number of states as a sort of self-styled "truth squad." Their numbers and influence still relatively small but growing since Johnson's clash with Hatch at the Senate hearing, Mormons for the ERA adopted an aggressive, in-your-face approach (including airplane-towed pro-ERA banners flown over church conferences) that frustrated and angered some church officials.

In answer to persistent questions, LDS leaders emphasized that open support of the ERA by itself was not grounds for excommunication but that "when those of its members publicly deride [the church], demean its leaders, and openly encourage others to interfere with its mission, then it may exercise its right to disassociate itself from them."

Despite being a thorn in the church's side, Johnson might have remained a member if she had confined her activities to promoting the ERA. Instead she grew increasingly radical, sharply criticizing church leaders and encouraging citizens supporting the ERA to tell church representatives: "'If the missionaries ever come to my door, I wouldn't consider letting them in.'"

Finally church leaders had had enough. Her bishop, Jeffrey Willis, summoned Johnson to a church court at the Sterling Park Ward in Virginia, held November 17, 1979. The LDS church considers such proceedings strictly confidential, but Johnson milked the court for maximum publicity, and the chapel that night was surrounded by a contingent of reporters and singing, chanting pro-ERA activists.

Johnson's plight was grist for largely sympathetic national news stories. *Time* and *Newsweek* both covered the excommunication. *People* magazine said:

> Her appearance before a congressional committee infuriated Utah's arch-conservative Sen. Orrin Hatch, a Mormon elder. "He really lit into me," Johnson remembers. "Aides were tugging at each arm and passing him notes to cool it." Though startled by the outburst, she was grateful for the publicity that followed. "Orrin Hatch is really responsible for our group becoming a national organization," she says.

Hatch, angered by the *People* piece, fired off a letter. Almost immediately he had second thoughts, but it was already in the mail and appeared in print three weeks later:

> I was pleased to see in your entertaining magazine that pro-ERA Mormon feminist Sonia Johnson credits her national prominence to a clash with me at a Senate subcommittee hearing. We politicians like to help each other out, even if neither my memory nor the official transcript supports her version of what happened. It is true that I sometimes have to be restrained by aides, and occasionally even foam at the mouth. But this is invariably only when confronted with reporters who don't bother to check their stories.

Hatch's feminist friend Betty Murphy also wrote to *People:* "Although [Hatch] opposes the ERA as written, he is a tireless worker for equal rights for women and has a proven track record." *People* declined to print Murphy's letter.

Witnesses to the Hatch-Johnson exchange differ as widely in their interpretations of it as Hatch and Johnson differed. UPI's veteran Capitol Hill reporter Cheryl Arvidson—whose story on the hearing was carried in newspapers across the country—said, "He never did really get loud, but he got mean and personal. He denigrated her. It was more his tone. There was a point where I thought he was really losing control."

However, there is no indication in the hearing transcript that Hatch was ever in danger of "losing control." The transcript, as well as the recollection of committee staffers, suggests that Hatch was more irritated at Bayh for repeatedly interrupting him than at Johnson for differing with him.

Although Johnson conjectured to *People* magazine that Hatch's aides were "passing him notes to cool it," in fact they were doing precisely the opposite. "We had some 'zinger' questions we wanted him to ask her," explains Randy Rader, one of those at Hatch's side, and a federal judge when asked about the hearing. "We were trying to get him to be tougher than he wanted to be." Rader recalls the Hatch-Johnson exchange as "very normal for a hearing like that; obviously they disagreed, but they were civil to each other."

Another former committee aide, Steve Markman, likewise agrees that Arvidson's UPI story and *People* missed the mark. Markman, later U.S. attorney for Detroit, was in the committee room for only a portion of the hearing but recalls asking other staff members who were there throughout for their reactions. "They just didn't see it as the senator trying to engage in argument," says Markman. "I've seen him in a lot of heated situations, but I have never seen him discourteous with either witnesses or his fellow senators."

At any rate, even some Mormons in good standing criticized Hatch's handling of Johnson, one writing that the senator had "focused the media attention on her in a way that was to have debilitating consequences for the church's public image."

On December 5, 1979, two men from the Sterling Park Ward appeared at Johnson's door with a letter bearing the court's decision: excommunication. She gave a series of emotional interviews responding to the decision and generating more sympathy. Two days before her excommunication, Johnson had said, "I think I'll always be a Mormon, no matter what. . . . I'm Mormon down to my toenails." But in the preface to the 1989 edition of her book, *From Housewife to Heretic,* Johnson repudiated both the Mormon church and the ERA.

Johnson and her husband were divorced soon after her excommunication, though not over ERA which he also supported. Her general mindset and direction became clearer when she explained a decade later that:

Marriage also ceased to engage my attention. The idea went from distasteful to repugnant as I saw more and more clearly how it subordinated and oppressed women. I smiled when I discovered in *Housewife to Heretic* how convinced I had been that I was "hopelessly heterosexual." I am amused and bemused at my ignorance about myself . . . Now, having taught *myself* to love women in every possible way, I know that *no* woman is "hopelessly heterosexual," and that to think so is to mistake conditioning for destiny.

The day after the excommunication, Hatch wrote privately: "I viewed her on television, and she is really a very good actress. It's a shame that she has done this to herself and her family. Had she just advocated her social conscience for the Equal Rights Amendment, this would not have happened to her."

But there were personal consequences for Hatch as well. The confrontation with Johnson generated a level of animosity toward the senator that startled him, and it branded him an implacable enemy in the eyes of many feminists.

9

Gentlemen
of the Senate

HATCH, NOW WITH A NATIONAL reputation, campaigned throughout the country in 1978 to help keep incumbent Republicans in the Senate and elect new ones. He was a key member of the Republican Senatorial Campaign Committee, headed by Oregon's Packwood, which raised funds for candidates.

At one point, Hatch talked the committee into borrowing $300,000 to prevent Packwood from finding an excuse not to energize the campaigns of GOP conservative challengers Gordon Humphrey in New Hampshire and Roger Jepsen in Iowa. Some supporters urged Hatch to move into position to succeed Packwood as Campaign Committee chair when Republican senators chose new leadership early in 1979. It was an idea that appealed to Hatch.

Over dinner at a downtown restaurant in August 1978, Hatch discussed the idea with Packwood, who was noncommittal. "He's trying to get me to blunt my conservatism, but I don't think I will," wrote Hatch afterwards. "I'm not that interested in political prestige to not vote for principle. . . . [But] I know that I will be very ineffective if I allow myself to become simply an idealogue at all costs."

Hatch then met with minority leader Howard Baker and got the same response. "He indicated he thought the one difficulty I would have would be the possibility that I would just try to build the conservative ranks. I told him I would help the liberals every bit as much as the conservatives and that we would be evenhanded across the board."

At the same time, Hatch clearly hoped to strengthen the ranks of Senate conservatives, believing they usually voted more often than liberals in the national interest. "There are only about 25 men, plus Mrs. Allen, in the whole United States Senate who really consistently stand up for principle," he wrote privately. "That's a sad indictment for the greatest and most powerful legislative body in the world." After one Senate decision that disgusted him, Hatch quickly agreed with a colleague who quipped, "It's one of those votes where the Senate rises above principle."

An acid test of whether Hatch would work for liberal as well as conservative GOP incumbents came in September when he joined others in signing this telegram endorsing liberal incumbent Edward Brooke of Massachusetts, the Senate's only black, who faced a primary election against a GOP conservative:

DEAR ED:
WE WANT YOU TO KNOW THAT YOU HAVE OUR STRONGEST, MOST ENTHUSIASTIC SUPPORT IN THE PRIMARY ELECTION ON TUESDAY.

Brooke won the primary in a close race and sent Hatch a note saying, "Your endorsement was perfectly timed and politically potent. . . I'll always be grateful." Other liberal and moderate Republican senators, and even some fellow conservatives, were pleased with Hatch. But New Right leaders were appalled.

Paul Weyrich, who had backed Brooke's primary opponent, telephoned Hatch's administrative assistant Frank Madsen with this message for his boss: "I have permitted aberrations by Hatch in the past, but this is one I cannot forget and will not forget because it is more than an aberration."

Privately Hatch mused that even though he and Brooke rarely voted alike, it would have been hypocritical not to support him after assuring liberals that he was committed to help all GOP senators. "Besides, Ed Brooke is the only black in the U.S. Senate, and a friend, and I would hate to have him lose. And the only way we can retain that seat is for Brooke to win the primary because he is the only Republican who could probably win in the general election."

Although some critics suggested that Hatch's endorsement was an attempt to buy Brooke's vote for campaign chairman, Hatch strongly suspected Brooke would not support him for the position anyway.

On September 29 Hatch attended a luncheon sponsored by Weyrich's organization, the Committee for the Survival of a Free Congress. Paul Laxalt led the discussion, focused on raising money for Republican candidates. At one point, Hatch spoke up, affirming, "Paul is our leader in the Senate." Then, glancing at Weyrich, he added wryly, "I mean Paul *Laxalt*, not Paul *Weyrich*. . . . Paul Weyrich just *thinks* he's our leader in the Senate."

Everyone laughed—except Weyrich. Weyrich's open, quizzical baby face belied his humorless approach to politics. No shades of gray confused his world. Weyrich was a straitlaced Catholic who took absolutist positions on both people and public issues. To deviate was to assure his wrath.

"I'll never forget the fact that he helped me in the 1976 campaign," said Hatch in a recent interview. "But he claims a little too much credit for what he did." Federal records show the Committee for Survival of a Free Congress contributed $8,000—less than 2 percent of the more than $500,000 cost of Hatch's campaign.

Hatch's backing of Brooke brought unexpected rewards along with the criticism. Wrote Hatch:

> It's interesting how friendly many of the Senators have been since my endorsement. Even the conservatives have been kind. . . . Jim McClure kids me about it, but unless we can get the [GOP Senate] numbers up there, we're never going to control the committees and the budget. . . . It's going to take people of all political philosophies to help us solve these problems. However, if I can get that Campaign Committee Chairmanship, we are going to certainly get the majority to be conservatives. And then we're going to find us a leader and lead this party the way it should be led. I believe we can get the liberals to move more to the right as we control the Senate. This has to happen.

Laxalt, who had kept Hatch at arm's length, likewise warmed to him after the Brooke endorsement. "I must admit I was offended by you when you first came to the Senate," Laxalt confided. "I thought you had a Messianic complex and were willing to walk on other people to get to the top. I now know I was wrong."

Laxalt and Hatch worried about current Republican leaders. Both personally liked national chairman William Brock, House minority leader John Rhodes of Arizona, and Senator Baker, but questioned whether they had the vision or drive to lift Republicans from their decades-long minority status in Congress.

"We've got to have the presidency to turn this whole thing around," said Laxalt, Ronald Reagan's closest friend in the Senate.

"Who else do we have that we can bring along?" asked Hatch.

"*You!*" answered Laxalt. "Orrin, you're one of the few guys we have who is aggressive enough and who has the guts to lead out."

Laxalt apparently communicated his new opinion of Hatch to Reagan and his political aides, who asked Hatch to be a surrogate for Reagan in appearances around the country. Hatch, a strong Reagan supporter already, did so with relish, even as various political observers speculated that Hatch himself might seek the presidential nomination in 1980.

Illinois Representative Phillip Crane, a young, conservative, darkly handsome former college professor, was first out of the starting gate in the GOP presidential sweepstakes, declaring his candidacy in the summer of 1978. Some Republicans were unhappy at Crane, believing he would steal the thunder from Reagan, who had yet to announce his intentions. Hatch, however, believed that Crane's entry "is the best thing that could happen to Governor Reagan. Phil will be branded as the ultraconservative, and Reagan will look more moderate."

Noted political analyst Kevin Phillips wrote in August that "Crane wants exposure to establish his primacy among a group of possible Reagan heirs including [New York Representative Jack] Kemp, Paul Laxalt, Bob Dole and Orrin Hatch (by this scenario, he could drop out if Reagan actually launches a solid bid in 1979)."

Despite periodic rumor-floating of Hatch's presidential aspirations, Hatch's private writings suggest that he didn't seriously entertain the prospect. In fact, it tended to cause him more trouble than satisfaction as the Utah media magnified such reports to suggest that Hatch's main drive was his political ambition, not his state's interests.

The early jockeying for position for 1980 reflected President Carter's continued weakness. During the first half of 1978 his approval ratings dipped abysmally to the 30 percent range. According to Kevin Phillips, polls "suggest that Carter is already unlikely to recover politically," short of a national or international crisis.

The media continually frustrated Hatch, who was convinced journalists had a double standard—generally treating liberals well and conservatives poorly. Among members of Congress, he was particularly open and responsive to reporters, but their coverage of him was colored by Hatch's reputation as overly conservative and unseemly ambitious. In some newsrooms, a reporter writing favorably about Hatch risked being put on the defensive by the reporter's colleagues.

Washington Post editor Ben Bradley, the epitome of the liberal establishment press, could not bring himself to be cordial to Hatch in public. One evening in December 1978, Orrin ran into the Bradleys as they all left Duke Zeibert's restaurant, a favorite eatery of the rich and powerful.

"They did not even acknowledge me or return my greeting," Hatch recorded with some indignation. "They abruptly walked on by. As we both walked in the same turnstile at the next-door parking lot, Bradley quickly went ahead of me and paid his bill without so much as saying a gruff 'hello.' They both seemed about as friendly as tarantulas."

National newspapers and magazines were forced to report on Hatch's efforts, which were integral to such stories as defeat of the Labor Law Reform Bill. However, Utah newspapers barely mentioned them. "As I traveled around Utah, everybody was saying, 'Why don't you get more press out here? We see it everywhere else but in Utah,'" Hatch commented. "I didn't know how to solve that problem. I think it was so difficult for the Utah media to believe that we [he and his staff] could have that dramatic an impact that early in my Senate career."

Although other Utah media also had correspondents in Washington, two stood out because of their many years of covering the capital: Gordon White of the *Deseret News* and Frank Hewlett of the *Salt Lake Tribune,* Utah's two statewide dailies.

Hewlett was friendlier than White toward Hatch. A chunky, balding man who had covered the Pacific theater in World War II, Hewlett was gruff but compliant. Each weekday he grazed through the offices of Utah's congressional delegation and invariably was rewarded with a feeding of news releases which the *Tribune* usually ran, with little editing, in the next day or two. The day's "work" accomplished, Hewlett spun out most of his creativity in war stories around the National Press Club bar, where he was an afternoon fixture.

White was more enterprising and independent, less likely to take a politician's word at face value. He wore heavy black-framed glasses and bore a slight resemblance to Woody Allen. Hatch was continually frustrated by what he regarded as White's lack of interest or respect for his accomplishments. But he genuinely enjoyed Hewlett, who welcomed Hatch to Washington early on and proceeded to offer advice on how to get along in the capital—advice Hatch often took. Hatch saw Hewlett as a good-old-boy newsman who didn't take himself too seriously.

White, Hewlett, and other regional correspondents in the capital were influenced by the opinions of their peers on national publications. In the early years especially, while conservative publications gave Hatch high marks, mainstream newspapers and journals that tended to set the tone for smaller publications were more skeptical.

One particularly damaging phrase showed up in a lengthy profile on Hatch by Robert Kaiser of the *Washington Post.* After a generally favorable analysis, Kaiser ended the piece by saying, "Hatch's rhetoric has earned him the nickname 'Borin' Orrin' in the halls of the Capitol." Kaiser actually got the phrase from Hatch himself, who explained to the reporter that his intent in a filibuster was to "bore the other side to death" in the hope that opponents would give up on the bill in question. "Borin' Orrin" stuck like glue, and for years it was a staple when conversation among reporters turned to Hatch.

At the end of 1978 a private poll showed that Hatch's approval rating in crucial Salt Lake County was far lower than that of other major Utah officials. Second District Congressman Dan Marriott scored 62 percent, Governor Scott Matheson 61, Garn 58, and Hatch 46. Some respondents raised the by-now-tired accusation that an arrogant Hatch was using Utah for his national ambitions.

Although the tag of arrogance continued to follow Hatch, he was in fact unusually deferential to those around him. He had masterminded the defeat of the Labor Law Reform Bill, for example, but *Time* magazine's coverage used a sizeable photograph of Richard Lugar—who played a significant but secondary role—and barely mentioned Hatch.

"That's fine with me," Hatch wrote privately upon seeing the article, "because Lugar is such a fine guy that I don't care what kind of credit he gets. He deserves it. . . . Anytime I can push Lugar's career, I am going to because he is one of the premier people. I really think the world of him."

An issue that occupied Hatch in mid-1978 was a proposal to give the District of Columbia full voting rights in Congress. The district had a nonvoting delegate, Rev. Walter Fauntroy, who had the same status in the House of Representatives as delegates from Puerto Rico, Guam, and the Virgin Islands. Proponents wanted the district treated as though it were a state, complete with two voting senators and voting representation in the House.

The *Washington Post* called the proposal "an issue of elementary human rights" and said the district's nonvoting status was "an inadvertent exclusion" by the Founding Fathers when they carved off pieces of Virginia and Maryland and moved the seat of government there from Philadelphia in the last quarter of the 18th century."

Leading proponent Ted Kennedy said those opposing the idea did so because the district's senators would be too black, too urban, too liberal, and too Democratic. By injecting racism as an issue, Kennedy and others put additional pressure on opponents. Hatch saw the issue both in political and constitutional terms, and resented Kennedy's attempt to brand opponents racist.

There is no evidence in Hatch's public or private life that he was ever racially prejudiced, though some of his political allies may have been. During a Senate-House conference the previous year, held to write guidelines for selecting federal judges, Hatch had a protracted discussion with Congresswoman Barbara Jordan of Texas, an impressively articulate black woman who had keynoted the 1976 Democratic National Convention.

Hatch and Jordan finally agreed on language for a key part of the judicial merit selection bill. As the conference was adjourning, Mississippi's James Eastland leaned over to another Southern senator, out of Jordan's earshot—but not out of Hatch's—and murmured, "That Hatch, he just wrapped that nigger around his little finger."

That evening, Hatch wrote that he had been "shocked and hurt by Eastland's racist remark." Although he disagreed with Jordan on many issues, Hatch felt she was "a truly regal lady . . . decent, gracious, and bright. I can easily see why she charms so many people. She charmed me today."

While there was no doubt that district senators would in fact be liberal Democrats, Hatch's primary opposition to the D.C. voting rights act was constitutional. He argued that the District of Columbia—just ten square miles—was never intended to be a state, that its economy was almost wholly dependent on the federal government, and that it had a unique status as the seat of government.

As the day of the D.C. vote approached, Hatch walked off the Senate floor and into a group of prominent blacks lobbying for passage. Jesse Jackson, winking at Hatch, said, "We're going to encircle you in prayer and maybe you'll see the light." Walter Fauntroy asked, "Orrin, can't I get you to go play tennis with me during the votes?"

Hatch responded: "I know how much this means to all of you, and I really hate to oppose you on it. But I'm convinced it goes against the Constitution, so I have no choice. And I'll really resent it if you make it a black-white issue."

"Well, when you Mormons make up your minds to do what you feel is right, you do what's right," said Jackson.

"That's for sure," said Hatch. "We're pretty tough."

The key vote came August 22, with the proposal squeaking through the Senate 67-32—only one more vote than the two-thirds needed for constitutional amendments.

Despite the loss, which he took hard otherwise, Hatch immediately went to Fauntroy, who was a guest on the Senate floor, and hugged him. He then walked out into the foyer and hugged or shook hands with many others on the winning side, including Benjamin Hooks, head of the NAACP, and Rev. Martin Luther King, Sr. "They were ecstatic," he recalls. "It almost made you want to ignore the Constitution to help them."

Hatch did ignore protests of other conservatives to back a bill to protect the constitutional rights of the mentally ill, prisoners, and other institutionalized citizens. Hatch said such citizens are "unique in their inability" to assert their own rights and are "people that society has basically ignored." Conservatives said the legislation would infringe on states' rights, but Hatch succeeded in amending the final bill to require that the U.S. Attorney General warn individual states to clear up abuses before instituting action against them.

Senator Birch Bayh, the bill's sponsor, wrote Hatch to thank him for "the spirit of compromise and fairness which marked your treatment" of the bill. "Without your help this important piece of legislation might not have been reported [by the Judiciary Committee]. It most certainly would not have received the overwhelming[ly] favorable vote that it did." The bill passed the Senate by a single vote, Hatch providing the margin of difference.

In the closing days of the ninety-fifth Congress, labor unions tried to salvage something from their disastrous year by securing passage of the Humphrey-Hawkins full-employment bill. Once more, Hatch was the chief hurdle, introducing a hundred amendments and threatening to tie the Senate in knots with another filibuster.

Proponents of the measure, under which the government would provide "last resort" jobs to the unemployed, conceded that there would be no bill without Hatch's approval. During a meeting with him, he negotiated them into so many changes—including elimination of the last-resort provision—that some called the final version the Humphrey-Hawkins-Hatch bill.

The original goal of reducing unemployment to 4 percent by 1983 – unemployment in 1978 was around 6 percent—remained intact, but the bill was stripped of its massive federal jobs and economic planning provisions. Added at Hatch's insistence were new goals of reducing the inflation rate to 3 percent by 1983 and to zero by 1988. Civil rights and labor leaders gave the final bill mixed reviews. Coretta Scott King called it "a major victory" despite its deficiencies, while Ken Young of the AFL-CIO said it represented only "a small symbolic step forward" and charged that "the Senate weakened it severely."

Hatch, generally pleased with the bill he had helped deliver, was sorely tempted to vote for it as a goodwill gesture to civil rights and labor groups. However, it had become a symbol of a welfare mentality; and in the end, Hatch decided that voting for it would be misunderstood in Utah. When the Senate passed the compromise version 70-19 on October 13, Hatch was still among the opposing minority.

Hatch campaigned for Republicans across the country as the midterm elections drew near in 1978. October 22 found him in Illinois stumping for Senator Percy, who, polls indicated, was trailing his

Democratic challenger by seventeen points. Local businessmen told Hatch they couldn't support Percy because he had taken a powder on labor law reform and "doesn't stand for anything." Hatch bit his tongue and encouraged them to vote for Percy anyway, noting Percy's support for such things as regulatory and civil service reform.

In the following days, Hatch campaigned for GOP Senate challenger Gordon Humphrey in New Hampshire, as well as for candidates in Massachusetts, Idaho, New Jersey, California, and Washington State.

On Saturday, November 4–three days before the election–he got an urgent call from Percy's office begging him to return to Illinois to help save Percy's seat. Hatch dutifully flew to Illinois, where a haggard Percy was throwing $450,000 of his own money into TV spots in which he acknowledged mistakes, assured voters, "I got your message," and promised to help cut wasteful spending and reduce taxes if they would give him another chance.

On November 7, Orrin and Elaine voted straight Republican tickets in Utah, going to the polls along with 57 million other Americans. The turnout was only 37 percent of eligible voters–the lowest in thirty-five years–and reflected a national mood of caution and retrenchment. The GOP picked up three seats in the Senate, eleven in the House, and six governorships. Democrats retained large majorities in the Senate (59-41), House (276-157), and among governors (32-18).

The Senate results, however, were a small disaster for liberals. Five liberal Democrats were defeated by more conservative challengers. Ed Brooke, the Massachusetts Republican endorsed by Hatch in the primary, was ousted by another liberal, youthful Democrat Paul Tsongas.

Other than Brooke's loss, Hatch's own batting average for the election was quite respectable. He had fought successfully to have the Senate Campaign Committee borrow money that helped assure victories for conservatives Roger Jepsen in Iowa and Gordon Humphrey in New Hampshire. And Charles Percy won in Illinois. Percy dictated a warm letter to Hatch on December 1: "Your presence was a turning point and did more good than I can ever describe to you. . . . Your two appearances in Illinois were really well beyond the call of duty."

Notable new senators included Nancy Kassebaum, R-Kansas, the only woman in the new Senate, and John Warner, R-Virginia, former Navy Secretary and latest husband of Elizabeth Taylor.

Labor was left weaker by the election: the new Congress had twenty-five fewer Representatives and five fewer senators endorsed by the AFL-CIO. "I think our chances [of passing pro-union legislation] were diminished by the election," acknowledged a grim George Meany.

Jimmy Carter had just reached the apex of his presidency in September by engineering a historic peace accord between Israel and Egypt but was unable to turn the rare public acclaim into political capital. Carter campaigned for challengers to three of the staunchest Senate conservatives from his native South—Helms of North Carolina, Thurmond of South Carolina, and John Tower of Texas—but failed to dislodge any of them. Carter's weakness suggested that the 1980 presidential contest could be wide open in both parties. Disillusioned Democrats were determined never again to allow their party's banner to fall to a figure from a small Southern state who was nationally untested.

But ironically, another winner in 1978 was the nation's youngest governor in forty years. The thirty-two-year-old former boy wonder had already lost a bid for Congress and had been his state's attorney general. An Arkansas newspaper dubbed him "a living monument to the god 'Charisma.'" His name was Bill Clinton.

Within days of the elections, Hatch began to campaign in earnest to replace Bob Packwood—who had his eye on a higher post—as leader of the GOP Senatorial Campaign Committee for 1979-80. The committee raised funds for incumbent and prospective Republican senators, and the chairmanship was a possible springboard to higher office. Barry Goldwater had held it before winning his party's presidential nomination in 1964. Two other candidates began campaigning also—John Heinz of Pennsylvania and Pete Domenici of New Mexico—but Domenici dropped out, leaving Hatch and Heinz to go head-to-head.

Both had been born in Pittsburgh and entered the Senate at the same time, but they had little else in common. In contrast to Hatch's humble roots, Heinz was heir to the H. J. Heinz food fortune and was one of the Senate's richest members. After serving five years in the House, he spent $2.9 million of his own money in 1976 to win a Senate seat. Heinz was a true blueblood—degrees from Yale and Harvard, a mansion in the pricey Georgetown section of Washington, and an air of superiority that some colleagues found distasteful.

Hatch's relations with Heinz, proper but cool, weren't helped in August 1978 when he told *Congressional Quarterly*—the most widely read periodical on Capitol Hill—"If you look at the soft heads in Congress, most of them are inheritors of wealth." The politics of Hatch and Heinz were also dissimilar: a conservative group, Americans for Constitutional Action, rated Hatch's 1978 voting record 96 percent "correct" but gave Heinz a meager 18 percent. On the flip side, the liberal Americans for Democratic Action gave Hatch a 5 percent rating and Heinz 60 percent.

In July 1978, New Right activists Paul Weyrich, Charles Black, and Roger Stone had urged Hatch to seek the post, which would be filled in

January 1979. Now some Republicans worried that if they elected Hatch they would also get his New Right friends.

One of Hatch's first calls after the November election was to Senator Percy. Despite Hatch's pivotal role in his reelection, Percy indicated he probably would vote instead for fellow millionaire John Heinz.

Hatch also put in an early call to Bob Packwood. "I know you're not *for* me, but at least I want to tell the new senators that you're also not *against* me," Hatch told Packwood.

"Orrin, you can't do that," answered Packwood.

"Well, does that mean you *are* against me?" asked Hatch.

After pirouetting around the question, Packwood finally said, "Yes."

"Why?"

"Because I think you're too conservative."

Hatch reminded Packwood that he had kept his word to campaign hard for Republicans of every political stripe and had promised to continue doing so. The reminder fell on deaf ears, and the conversation ended abruptly on a sour note. Hatch seethed for an hour, then called Packwood back. "I feel bad about how we ended and don't want to have ill feelings between us," said Hatch. "I still am amazed that you think I'm too conservative, and want to ask you something. Aren't you too *liberal?*"

"No," answered Packwood.

"Well, Bob, almost all of your votes this past year have been in favor of liberal causes. But we still supported you and gave you all the backing you needed. Now, don't you think I can be trusted to be honest with you when I say I'll do a good job for all of our candidates even though I'm a conservative?"

Packwood apologized then but continued to criticize Hatch to journalists and others. Days later, influential columnists Jack Germond and Jules Witcover wrote: "[Packwood] is so determined to block Sen. Orrin Hatch as his successor in the campaign committee that he is threatening to bypass any election that might give the post to the Utah conservative and appoint someone else instead." They quoted a Packwood aide as saying that Packwood feared Hatch would give preferential treatment to right-wing candidates and that electing the Utahn to head the committee would "put him on the informal escalator through which many campaign committee chairmen move up in the Senate GOP leadership." The column concluded: "So much for Republican unity."

Hatch was more determined than ever. He contacted other senators, including those whose recent victories resulted in part from his personal efforts in campaign appearances or fund raising. Among them were Jepsen, Humphrey, Tower, Warner, Simpson, and Pressler.

Alliances were being formed for other party leadership posts as well. Of particular note was the ambition of Hatch's fellow Utahn Jake Garn to be secretary of the Republican conference. Given possible concern over regional balance, some observers wondered if Garn's desire to be secretary might scuttle Hatch's chances to head the campaign committee.

Hatch assembled the last pieces of his campaign organization and set about methodically wooing fellow senators. "We have 40 people across the country helping me," he recorded with satisfaction. "Packwood is finding that everywhere he goes we already have been there."

In mid-December 1978, one month before the leadership elections, Orrin and Elaine went to a dinner at Howard Baker's home honoring newly elected GOP senators. Most were very friendly to the Hatches—Mrs. John Warner, aka Elizabeth Taylor, planted a memorable kiss on Orrin's cheek—and even Packwood went out of his way to be cordial. Packwood's demeanor led Hatch to believe that his nemesis thought Hatch had a good shot at winning the campaign leadership post.

"We have twenty-three committed votes," wrote Hatch—enough for victory among the forty-one Republicans who would cast secret ballots in a month. But he had seen such numbers melt away before. "It's a shame but it is incredible that we can't trust the word of people who are elected to the United States Senate." He continued to campaign hard.

Conservative columnist Pat Buchanan contrasted Heinz's "leftist voting record" to that of Hatch, who had "not only conservative convictions, but also the industry and energy to see them translated into policy." Customarily, added Buchanan, "one would anticipate a Hatch-Heinz contest to be settled in straight sets, with Heinz graciously bowing out before the votes were counted."

Presidential politics also affected the contest. Paul Laxalt initially told Hatch he couldn't support him openly for fear of hurting "Ron's chances" among their colleagues. Laxalt wanted to add other Republican senators to the three formally supporting Reagan for President in 1980: himself, Hatch, and Jesse Helms. Others who had worked alongside Hatch in Senate battles were not so reticent. Two weeks before the vote, Richard Lugar answered an appeal from Heinz with a letter. "I know that you would do a good job," Lugar told Heinz, "but I believe that Orrin Hatch will do a better job in this particular responsibility."

Hatch told Charles Bartlett of the *Washington Star:* "One of my goals is to bind up [the divisions in] the Republican Party, which must appeal across a broad spectrum and cannot be ideologically pure if it is to succeed nationally."

Christmas brought a welcome respite. On Christmas Eve the Hatches—except for missionary Brent—gathered around their decorated tree and read the Bible account of Jesus' nativity. "It was one of the nicest, most pleasant Christmases we have had," wrote Hatch. "The children appreciated what they got." He was especially pleased with his gift from son Scott: a camel's hair dart board. Hatch took it to his office to help relieve stress.

"We feel so blessed this yuletide season," wrote Hatch, then added presciently, "I hope it is not a prelude to a lot of bad things."

Thursday, January 11

Party elections are four days away. In an interview with Mary McGrory of the *Washington Star,* Hatch compliments all his colleagues, including Packwood, frustrating McGrory who wants dirt. Hatch also defends campaign aide Roger Stone, telling McGrory that Stone was a nineteen-year-old idealist at the time of Watergate and should no longer be vilified by the media for his minor role in the scandal. In the evening Hatch, confident of victory but weary of the time and effort it is exacting, writes:

> I was pretty naïve to think they would naturally vote for me because I had raised so much money and campaigned so hard for various people. I did not realize that these prima donnas really require an awfully lot of stroking in order to even consider voting for anybody. It comes down to politics, politics, politics. That's a shame. That's a terrible shame.

Friday, January 12

McGrory's highly complimentary interview appears in the *Star.* She also calls Heinz a "lightweight."

Hatch lines up those who will formally put his name in contention. Laxalt agrees to nominate Hatch. Barry Goldwater of Arizona and New Mexico's Pete Domenici, a popular moderate, will second the nomination.

Hatch talks with South Dakota's Larry Pressler. The boyish Pressler, considered by veteran observers as more image-conscious than issue-conscious, acknowledges that Hatch raised over $100,000 for his recent campaign—a quarter of Pressler's total expenditure. But Pressler is supporting Heinz.

"The most wonderful thing that happened to me all day," Hatch writes, "is that Bill Roth [Delaware] called and told me that he will be voting with me, but didn't want anyone else to know about it." Roth's gesture touches Hatch for a good reason: Roth himself is running against Jake Garn for conference secretary and promises Hatch his support despite Hatch's explanation that, out of loyalty and friendship, he must vote for his fellow Utahn.

Saturday, January 13

Orrin and Elaine arise early and attend a two-hour session at the Mormon temple in nearby Kensington, Maryland. They go shopping and return to Vienna where Hatch takes a rare nap.

Sunday, January 14

Hatch attends church for an hour, then goes to his office for a meet-the-candidates session with six new GOP senators. Candidates for all other offices make their pitches first, then he meets alone with the six newcomers for a spirited give-and-take.

Roger Stone reports to Hatch that he will get twenty-four votes. Paul Manafort, another key Hatch operative, says it will be twenty-five. Hatch believes the number will be about twenty-three—still enough for victory. Nagging at Hatch, however, is the memory of the voting for the minority leader two years ago. Michigan senator Bob Griffin went into the balloting with twenty-three "solid" pledges and lost to Howard Baker 19-18—a loss some believe contributed to Griffin's defeat by Michigan voters the following year.

Monday, January 15

Election day. Hatch arrives at his office at 6:30 and huddles with Stone and Manafort. They again assure him he will receive twenty-four to twenty-five votes. "I think it will be twenty-one," Hatch jokes, convinced it will actually be at least twenty-three and, at any rate, secure in the knowledge that twenty-two of his colleagues looked him in the face and vowed they would never desert him.

The GOP caucus convenes at 9 A.M. Voting will be by secret ballot. Vermont's Robert Stafford cannot attend and has submitted a letter asking to vote by proxy. Hatch knows Stafford is against him but doesn't object for fear it will cost him other support.

The conference chairman is selected first. Bob Packwood and Idaho's Jim McClure are nominated, with Packwood winning the post 22-19—closer than expected. One knowledgeable source says that, after nominating his fellow Oregonian, Mark Hatfield, whose life-style was quite opposite Packwood's, voted against him.

Conference secretary is next. Roth, Garn, and John Chafee of Rhode Island are all nominated. Roth is eliminated on the first ballot. Garn wins the run-off, also 22-19. Howard Baker, Ted Stevens of Alaska, and John Tower of Texas are accepted by acclamation as minority leader, assistant minority leader, and policy committee chairman, respectively.

It is now the Hatch-Heinz contest for Campaign Committee chairman. Heinz is nominated by Henry Bellmon of Oklahoma and seconded by two of the Senate's most liberal Republicans—Jacob Javits of New York and Charles Mathias of Maryland. They note that most of those already selected are from the West and call for regional balance.

It is the first time all morning that such an argument has been raised, and Hatch is momentarily concerned. But he recalls the pledged word of twenty-two of these men and shrugs off his apprehension. Hatch is nominated by Laxalt and seconded by Domenici and Goldwater—an all-Western team that plays into the hands of Heinz's call for regional balance. The three wax eloquent, noting Hatch's record of winning fights against great odds and his recent role in increasing the number of GOP senators by campaigning and raising millions of dollars for candidates.

Then the voting begins. It ends 21-20. Hatch has lost.

Hatch congratulated the winners graciously, but he did not linger longer than necessary. In the following days, he tried to swallow his hurt but it ate at him. Deep down he knew he had been betrayed by some he had considered his best friends.

Others didn't take Hatch's loss so graciously. Roger Stone, Paul Manafort, and Charles Black, who had run his campaign, were angry, vowed to find out what had happened, and started sleuthing. They felt certain that those who had been playing it coy had voted against Hatch. Hatch had hoped for better, but they were never in his hard count of twenty-two. The real question was which two of the twenty-two senators who had given Hatch rock-solid pledges had betrayed him.

Stone and Manafort came up with a startling candidate: Jake Garn. They suggested Garn had thrown support to Heinz in return for Packwood's delivering some of Chafee's votes to Garn. Although relations between the two Utahns occasionally were strained, Hatch liked Garn personally and refused to believe the report. Perhaps the disappointed aides were just speculating or deliberately trying to cause trouble. Garn went to Hatch and assured him he had not betrayed him. Hatch considered Garn an honorable man and took him at his word.

Others suggested Paul Laxalt or Pete Domenici—who had nominated and seconded Hatch—had secretly gone against him. But Hatch considered the speculation pointless and tried to wipe the whole affair from his mind. In the end, he would never know who had done him in.

Ronald Reagan telephoned Hatch on the evening of the vote to offer condolences. Hatch's unwavering commitment to Reagan for President had complicated his own campaign. Hatch also received a letter from San Clemente, California, which said in part: "After a disappointing defeat what is most important is not to be bitter or discouraged but to work for victory the next time around." It was signed "Richard Nixon."

On January 17—two days after party elections—Senator Henry Jackson of Washington was chairing the year's first session of the Senate Energy Committee. He welcomed new member Paul Tsongas of Massachusetts, but mispronounced his name, calling him "ton-gas" instead of "son-gas." Tsongas let it slide.

Later in the same hearing, Idaho's Frank Church noted that Tsongas, who previously had served in the House, was continuing the "habit of the House of addressing colleagues as 'gentlemen.'" On this side of Capitol Hill, explained Church, we call each other "Senator."

Tsongas was speechless, then had an answer. "I'm not likely to make *that* mistake again." As many of the Senators had shown in their leadership elections, they were not necessarily gentlemen.

10

Bouncing Back

Y EARS LATER HATCH WOULD LOOK back in genuine gratitude for his loss
of the Campaign Committee chair. It freed him to be more independent and to pick his issues. But in the weeks after the letdown,
he had difficulty getting it off his mind and tried various distractions to
assuage his disappointment.

A voracious reader of both fiction and nonfiction, Hatch buried
himself in *The Glory and the Dream,* William Manchester's social
history of the Kennedy presidency. It didn't help his mood. Hatch
found the history absorbing but depressing in its negative portrayal of
American conservatism. He also changed offices, moving from the
Dirksen Building into the more historic and rustic Russell Building.
His office was three floors above the Senate gymnasium. Hatch began a
stiff exercise regimen, determined to shed ten pounds and trim his
weight to 165.

Still restless, Hatch flew to Utah where he went shopping at his
favorite clothing store, Mr. Mac's, whose proprietor Mac Christensen
was a personal friend. Hatch purchased a very bright sport coat/slacks
combination and a light blue suit flecked with tan. "I don't know why I
did it," wrote Hatch, usually reluctant to buy personal items. "I guess it
was because I was discouraged. When I get discouraged, I feel like
buying some clothes and changing my image."

At the end of January 1979, Hatch wrote a memo to himself: "I must
now concentrate more on my family and on my own personal goals and

134

achievements rather than worry so much about the overall Republican Party."

Despite the setback from his GOP colleagues, Hatch was gaining in stature among independent analysts. Early in 1979, *National Journal* chose Hatch as one of five first-term Republican senators "most often named as leaders of the future." The article said, "Orrin Hatch does his homework—and then some. He set a new model for Senate advocacy when he led the battle against labor law reform legislation." The periodical quoted a Democratic aide as saying, "There's no question he is at the top of the list of conservatives. He's brighter and harder, and he won't cave."

Opportunities for committee leadership in the ninety-sixth Congress were unusually bright for a young senator in a system based on seniority. There were twenty newly elected senators—ten had won open seats when incumbents retired—representing the largest freshman class since 1946 when twenty-three had been elected. Coupled with Hatch's eighteen new-member class in 1977, more than a third of the Senate had now served two years or less.

With behind-the-scenes help from his good friend Strom Thurmond of South Carolina, ranking Republican on the Judiciary Committee, Hatch became ranking Republican on the Constitution Subcommittee. The subcommittee, still chaired by Birch Bayh of Indiana, would shortly face one of the most important constitutional battles of the century—the longstanding drive to abolish the electoral college and choose U.S. presidents by direct popular vote.

In February Hatch had lunch with Tom Korologos, a former Utah sports reporter and one of the most powerful lobbyists in Washington. Korologos had been a Capitol Hill lobbyist for President Richard Nixon, survived Watergate with his reputation intact, and was well liked by both Republicans and Democrats.

Korologos now offered his peacemaking skills to calm the waters between his longtime friend Jake Garn and Hatch. Korologos suggested the two senators meet weekly to iron out differences and coordinate their work for Utah. Both Garn and Hatch readily agreed, and the two began to get together each Wednesday morning before the Senate prayer breakfast.

The proposal to abolish the electoral college, which had been simmering on the Senate's stove, was shoved to the front burner early in 1979. "One-man, one-vote," was the persuasive battle cry of proponents, led for more than a decade by Senator Bayh, who had staked his reputation on changing the Constitution.

The electoral college gives each state voting power equal to the size of its congressional delegation. Like Congress itself, with its intricate system of checks and balances, the electoral college was devised by the Founding Fathers to help assure that the interests of smaller states were not automatically crushed by more populous states when choosing a president.

It may have served the nation well in its early years, argued Bayh and others, but it no longer was adequate. The system constantly threatened to send someone to the White House who had won the most electoral votes but not the most popular votes. Should that happen, they warned, the United States could face a constitutional crisis.

Changing the system, often proposed in the past, received fresh impetus in the wake of the whisker-close 1976 election. A shift of fewer than 10,000 votes in Ohio and Hawaii from Jimmy Carter to Gerald Ford could have left Carter with 268 electoral votes and Ford with 270. Ford would have stayed in the White House despite Carter's popular majority of nearly 1.7 million votes.

Abolishing the electoral college had the bipartisan backing of Carter, Ford, Nixon, most Senate leaders, including Majority Leader Byrd and Minority Leader Baker, and an impressive array of national organizations ranging from the American Bar Association and AFL-CIO to the U.S. Chamber of Commerce and League of Women Voters.

But it was not backed by Orrin Hatch, who considered it one of the most important constitutional questions in history. Underlying Hatch's public philosophy was a reverence for the Constitution, a document he considered divinely inspired, and a corresponding caution in altering it.

"The electoral college is *not* an archaic remnant of eighteenth-century nonmajority rule in our Constitution," said Hatch. "Rather, it is one of the political institutions created by the Founding Fathers that are representative of the popular will yet are careful to check excesses in that will."

Hatch feared that abolishing the electoral college could unhinge the Constitution's delicate system of representative government. "I felt that the amendment would strike at the very foundations of the American Republic by subordinating to the single principle of one-man, one-vote equally important notions of federalism, checks and balances, separation of powers, geographical balance, minority rights, and states' rights."

Hatch also believed that small states would be ignored in a direct-election system, with voters in a dozen or so of the largest states—swayed to an unhealthy degree by the media—determining the outcome. Bayh's amendment proposed that presidents be chosen by direct popular vote, with a candidate needing at least 40 percent to win. If no one reached that threshold, a runoff would be held between the two top vote-getters.

Hatch believed Bayh's proposal in reality would be a big step *away* from majority rule rather than toward it. "The nation would have a Boston Marathon of candidates, and regularly elect someone supported by a minority of voters," he argued. Hatch painted a perilous scenario of a presidential candidate receiving, say, 39 percent in the first balloting, followed by someone else with 25 percent. But in a runoff election, the second candidate makes a populist appeal and wins the election—giving the nation a president originally supported by only 25 percent of voters.

Bayh, however, said that abolishing the electoral college was "a simple question and you're either for it or you're against it."

"That is where we disagreed the most," said Hatch. "Our country's political institutions are not simple and were never meant to be. Proposals to radically restructure those institutions are not simple. As eloquently stated in the past, 'For every problem, there is a single solution—neat, simple, and wrong.'"

But most observers, including the media, believed that the surface logic of Bayh's amendment would assure its passage. Minority Leader Howard Baker bet Hatch he'd lose this one. Supporters of the amendment, brushing off Hatch's concerns, asked what could be wrong with assuring that the presidential candidate supported by most citizens would take office? At least once in history—some say twice more—a candidate won the most individual votes but was denied the presidency by losing in the electoral college. The clearest case was in 1888 when Benjamin Harrison was declared president even though Grover Cleveland received nearly 1 percent more of the popular vote. And even in that election there was widespread fraud as Cleveland had conducted only a regional, not national campaign.

"The electoral college is a product of its time—America in 1787," argued Ted Kennedy on the floor. "A major reason for its adoption stemmed from a distrust of the electorate: The lack of available information would, supposedly, prevent the electorate from making an informed decision on the candidates . . . Clearly, the Founding Fathers were dealing with a much different society. We should not let the political realities of 1787, . . . dictate the course of presidential elections in 1980, let alone in the 21st century."

Journalist Edwin Yoder summarized the other side of the issue:

The main argument for the electoral college system is the oldest argument of all. *It works.* It works to reinforce popular majorities; it buttresses the two-party system; it draws the attention of candidates, in the winner-take-all system, to states that would otherwise be easy to ignore; it affords politically sensitive minorities (blacks, labor, ethnics, southerners) a crucial role in closely fought states; and it is very nearly the last fixture of dual federalism in the national political picture–giving the states a role that would vanish in a national popular vote.

Bayh decided he couldn't get his amendment through the Judiciary Committee, which included two staunch foes–Hatch and ranking Republican Strom Thurmond of South Carolina. Instead Bayh used a rare procedural ploy to bypass the committee and put his proposal directly on the Senate calendar for floor consideration in March.

"What is the rush on this amendment?" Hatch demanded in a floor speech. "Where is the emergency? Our country has nicely survived its first forty-seven presidential elections under the present procedures."

Bayh answered that the idea had been talked to death over the years, in forty-three days of hearings since 1966. Hatch was unmoved. There were twenty new senators and six new members on the Judiciary Committee who had not heard the arguments, he noted. Furthermore, Hatch believed that bypassing normal review on such a momentous issue would set a terrible precedent.

Hatch huddled with Thurmond and another senior Senate lion, Democrat Howard Cannon of Nevada, to plot strategy. Both veterans had participated in a successful filibuster against direct election early in the 1970s, and proposed another filibuster this time. Hatch disagreed. He feared a filibuster might divide their fragile coalition, which included the NAACP and other civil rights groups, who were concerned that their people would lose power in a direct-election system. That fear might be outweighed by their animosity toward the filibuster, a tool used historically to deny African Americans their rights.

There was a more practical reason not to filibuster, he reasoned: To approve direct election as a constitutional amendment, proponents needed two-thirds of the Senate–sixty-seven votes if all of the members voted. Opponents would need only thirty-four votes to defeat the amendment itself, but would need over forty votes to defeat cloture and sustain a filibuster. Thurmond and Cannon agreed to Hatch's no-filibuster strategy.

Thurmond and Hatch pressed Bayh to pull the bill from the floor and agree to committee hearings. Keeping his side's strategy close to his chest, Hatch made a veiled threat of a filibuster if Bayh refused. Finally Bayh relented. He agreed to four days of committee hearings in exchange for a promise from Hatch, Thurmond, and others that they would not filibuster the amendment when it reappeared on the floor after the first of June.

Most senators from sparsely populated states like Utah believed that abolishing the electoral college would hurt their states politically. But that case was not clear-cut, and Hatch—though agreeing that the current system gave small states a slight advantage—based his arguments largely on other issues.

For Hatch, there was another complicating factor: Jake Garn, a co-sponsor of the direct election amendment, wanted it both ways—to push for abolishing the electoral college in Washington but not to suffer political fallout in Utah during his reelection the following year.

During debate in March 1979, Garn rose on the Senate floor and said the electoral college system was "grossly unfair; it seems un-American to me that it even exists." He added: "As a small state Senator, I am not going to defend a system that will allow a president to be elected by 10 or 11 large states and where the people in my state are told, 'Your vote is worthless, it does not even count.' I cannot condone it, and I am probably going to get into trouble, because the theory of the small-state advantage still exists."

Garn then left the floor, returned to his office, and telephoned Hatch in an attempt to control the political damage. He asked Hatch to soft-pedal his opposition to the amendment to minimize publicity back in Utah. Specifically, Garn asked Hatch not to press for new hearings. Hatch replied that, because of the overriding importance of the issue, he had to lead the fight and go all-out. But he agreed to not emphasize his differences with Garn over the issue to the Utah media.

Hatch buttonholed senators one by one, pressing the case for retaining the electoral college. By the third week in June the coalition Hatch had helped form and hold together—including blacks, Jewish groups, and other powerful special interests—was making inroads among the Northern senators whom Bayh had counted on for support.

On July 9, 1979, the issue reached the Senate floor. By that afternoon, Democrat Paul Sarbanes of Maryland and Republican Richard Schweiker of Pennsylvania both declared their opposition to the Bayh amendment. To Hatch, Bayh looked panicked.

July 10 was D-Day. In a floor speech, Democrat Bill Bradley of New Jersey said the vote later that day would be "perhaps the most important one members of the Senate will cast this year. . . . In a very real way, the responsibility placed on me and on every other senator is the same as that placed on the members of the Constitutional Convention 200 years ago."

Hatch arrived at his office early and was on the floor to help lead the final battle. Spotting Howard Baker he asked, "Haven't we convinced you yet?"

"You may have convinced me, but I'm going to have to vote against you," answered Baker, who would announce his candidacy for president four months later. He hesitated, then acknowledged, "Orrin, you're going to win this vote today."

"I know," said Hatch softly.

Baker held out his hand in congratulations. "What a victory! I never thought you could pull it off."

Hatch was now confident of victory but continued to press hard, hoping for a margin that would discourage opponents of the electoral college from raising the issue again for a long time.

At a luncheon that day, Hatch lobbied Percy of Illinois, still undecided. Three weeks earlier, Percy had taken the floor to thank Hatch for helping educate him on the issue. This time Percy went further, rising on the Senate floor in midafternoon to commit himself: "I see no compelling reason for us to amend the Constitution to provide for direct election of the president."

Momentum was now moving swiftly against the amendment. As the bell rang, signifying the final vote, Hatch walked toward the cloak room to make several last-minute calls. Jesse Helms, normally one of the Senate's better vote-counters, grabbed Hatch's hand. His eyes were soulful and his voice full of resigned sadness, convinced they could not defeat the direct-election bill. Hatch vividly remembers Helms saying:

"Orrin, do you think we can get at least thirty-three votes?" It was one *less* than they needed to stop direct election.

"Jesse," answered Hatch, "mark my words. We're going to get forty-five or better."

"That's impossible!" Helms shot back. "No way you can do that."

Hatch smiled and walked on into the cloak room.

The final vote was fifty-one for the amendment and forty-eight against. Opponents had defeated direct election with an astonishing fourteen votes to spare.

As senators were shuffling away amid back-slapping from one side and head-shaking from the other, Birch Bayh, tears in his eyes, approached Hatch. "I never thought you would be able to do this," said Bayh, holding out his hand.

"You handled this very intelligently, Birch," responded Hatch consolingly, "but you were on the wrong side of the issue. I think the debate woke a lot of people up to the many difficulties in this proposal."

They parted friends and remained friends. The following year Bayh lost his Senate seat to a youngster named Dan Quayle.

The victory was good for Hatch's morale. Two political polls early in the year had startled him. The first showed his approval rating among

Utah voters at only 57 percent. Worse still, his *disapproval* rating was 26 percent. Polling experts believed that an incumbent whose latter number was higher than 20 percent was vulnerable to defeat. In a second poll, three-fourths of Utah respondents said they didn't know what Hatch stood for or what he had accomplished.

Hatch brooded about the findings as Garn offered advice.

"Your problem is not substance but style," said Garn, whose own record reinforced that view. Garn often voted more conservatively than Hatch, yet Hatch was the one tagged "ultraconservative." Hatch and Garn were both considered men of high personal integrity. But unlike many of their colleagues, neither was wealthy, and both gave numerous two thousand dollar speeches to make ends meet. Some critics frowned on such honoraria, believing it was an open invitation to buy unwarranted influence.

Hatch considered honoraria an unfortunate necessity. The evidence is strong that he was motivated by need and not greed. During one of his trips to Utah early in 1979, a multi-millionaire friend tried to give Hatch a five thousand dollar Rolex watch, "no strings attached." Hatch turned it down. Then, as Hatch admired the man's new Cadillac Eldorado, the owner pressed Hatch to take it back to Washington with him. Again Hatch declined.

A few months later he made a note to himself to have the fenders repaired on an old Buick that he and Elaine used as a second car and added: "Once we get it fixed up it ought to last us another 30,000 or 40,000 miles without any major overhauls."

Democrats had their own headaches as they looked ahead. Their party had controlled both houses of Congress for a quarter-century, and there was little hope of changing Democratic domination of the House in next year's elections. The Senate, however, was a different matter and it provided Republicans a tantalizing opportunity. While only seventeen of the thirty-five seats up for grabs in 1978 had been held by Democrats, twenty-four of the seats up in 1980 were Democratic. If the GOP could make a net gain of ten seats in 1980, it would control the Senate for the first time since 1952.

The word around Washington was that Bob Byrd, the Senate's autocratic majority leader, wanted to avoid particularly contentious issues during the ninety-sixth Congress that could make Democrats unnecessarily vulnerable. He began 1979 by meeting with an ad hoc group of Senate leaders from both parties to change Senate rules. Notably Byrd wanted to weaken the rule that had given him the most fits: the filibuster.

Republican leader Howard Baker asked Hatch, one of the most feared practitioners of the filibuster, to accompany him as they met with Byrd and nine others in Byrd's office. Midway through the meeting, as

Byrd pressed for a hundred-hour limit on all further debate once cloture had been invoked, Hatch objected.

"I didn't invite *you* here!" Byrd said icily.

"Oh, I thought I *had* been invited," answered Hatch, starting to get up to leave.

Then Byrd relented: "Well, you're welcome to stay."

Hatch was unhappy with his Republican colleagues, including Baker and Minority Whip Ted Stevens, who agreed with Byrd's move to weaken the filibuster. But for the moment he was unhappier with Byrd's rudeness. As senators left the meeting, Hatch turned to several Democrats and sharply told them to convey his disgust to Byrd. In recording this event for his private files, Hatch wrote, "I had gone through too much to put up with bullies."

Jimmy Carter felt the same way. He was having his worst year yet at 1600 Pennsylvania Avenue. Runaway inflation, maulings by Congress, and trouble brewing abroad—notably in revolutionary Iran—all spelled desperation for the administration. An ABC-TV news poll in July 1979 rated Carter's acceptance at 25 percent—lowest of any surveyed president in history. A Gallup poll among Democrats indicated by a whopping two-to-one margin that they wanted to dump Carter and run Ted Kennedy instead in 1980.

In mid-June, a frustrated Carter finally responded to persistent reporter questions about what he would do if Kennedy ran: "If he does, I'll whip his ass."

Later that day, in a committee hearing chaired by Kennedy, Hatch could not resist commenting, "Mr. Chairman, in spite of what the president said about his modest—or, should I say, immodest—approach to you, I don't believe he can beat you." The hearing room audience laughed as Kennedy grinned, his face reddening.

Ted Kennedy had long been expected to run for president at some point. With "draft Kennedy" movements springing up around the country and Carter at the nadir of his presidency, the summer of 1979 was a logical time for a Kennedy announcement. Except for one problem: it was also the tenth anniversary of Kennedy's car plunging off a bridge on Chappaquiddick Island, Massachusetts. He swam, then walked away. Passenger Mary Jo Kopechne drowned.

"What happened that night and the senator's attitude toward it and conduct thereafter represent a legitimate subject of interest and anxiety over his candidacy," noted liberal columnist Meg Greenfield. "It emerges as a failure of personal and public responsibility so large and deep as to overwhelm much of the undeniable goodness and strength of the man."

There was an avalanche of publicity on the anniversary of the tragedy, none of it complimentary to Kennedy. "This has been one of the roughest weeks of my life," he confided to Hatch. But when one prominent Democrat advised him not to challenge Carter, Kennedy said, "Thanks, but my father always said, 'If it's on the table, eat it.'"

As Kennedy bided his time, Carter tried to seize the initiative, replacing five members of his cabinet in July. The shakeup failed to revive his presidency, and by September Carter still had the lowest job rating of any president in thirty years. The general consensus was that he had no more than two months to somehow rescue his reelection hopes.

Then Ayatollah Khomeini, Iran's new leader, accomplished for Carter what he couldn't do for himself. On November 4, 1979, other U.S. problems suddenly took a back seat as Iranian militants seized some fifty Americans at the U.S. Embassy in Tehran and held them hostage. They demanded that Washington turn over the Shah, who was then in the U.S. for medical treatment. Carter refused, and a long nightmare began for the hostages, their families, and the nation.

Three days after the embassy was overrun, Kennedy gave a speech attacking Carter's stewardship and announcing that he would seek the presidential nomination. But his move came too late. Americans traditionally rally around their president in the face of threats from abroad, and the Iranian crisis was no exception. Five weeks after it began, Carter had skyrocketed thirty points in the polls. By the first week in December, a nationwide Gallup poll among Democrats showed him leading Kennedy as their preferred candidate for the first time in nearly two years—48 to 40 percent.

As Kennedy prepared his candidacy late in 1979, Hatch took new stock of him. Hatch's views had changed substantially since, as a new senator, he had found nothing good to say about Kennedy. The two were still at opposite ends of the political spectrum, but after facing each other almost daily on two standing committees—Judiciary and Labor and Human Resources—Hatch had come to respect Kennedy for his work ethic, legislative skill, and humor.

"He has great ability to motivate the masses," wrote Hatch in an introspective note. "If he became president he could change things in this country for twenty or thirty years because of his great charisma, desire for hard work, and outstanding liberal staff. . . . It will be most interesting to watch history unfold as we move into the '80s and '90s and see what really happens to Kennedy."

During a hearing before the Judiciary Committee on a Kennedy-backed proposal to prevent the merger of large corporations, Hatch had questioned a witness excessively in Chairman Kennedy's view. A bell rang, summoning them to the floor for a vote, but Hatch droned on, prompting a gibe from Kennedy: "Go ahead, we'll listen to you as long as you want to talk. I could listen to you all day."

Returning to the hearing room after the vote, Hatch continued his questioning of a feisty mayor, who said no oil company president ever retired without being a millionaire.

"Yes," responded Hatch, "and do you realize that we have forty-six millionaires here in the United States Senate, a couple of whom are responsible for this legislation which is going to require even more regulation and more control of our free enterprise system?"

"Do you have *that* many?" asked the mayor.

Kennedy quickly tried to gavel the questions to an end, saying, "Well, we've got to get on to other meetings."

"Oh, no," Hatch interjected. "I could sit and listen to this man all day."

Kennedy was visibly flustered as the hearing room erupted in laughter. Exiting, another colleague said to Hatch, "You can get to Kennedy more than any other man in the Senate."

Hatch used his generally good relationship with Kennedy to press for public hearings in St. George, Utah, to investigate an abnormally high rate of cancer that coincided with atomic tests in Nevada during the 1950s and 1960s. He also proposed establishing a southern Utah clinic to study radiation.

Kennedy approached Hatch on the Senate floor in midyear with his own list of requests, including Hatch's support for a drug regulatory reform bill and an overhaul of the federal criminal code. In turn, he agreed to help push for the radiation clinic. "In fact," said Kennedy, "after we've done that, I suppose you'll want to see about moving all of NIH [National Institutes of Health] out to Utah."

"You know, Ted, when I came back here, people indicated to me that you were probably pretty dumb," Hatch needled him. "But it's so pleasant to find that you're not so dumb after all."

"Orrin," responded Kennedy expansively, "that goes both ways. As a matter of fact, when I run for president, I want you to run as my Vice President." Kennedy had been imbibing and was, of course, kidding.

Republican ranks also began to swell with presidential hopefuls, lured by Carter's weakness. Former Texas Governor John Connally announced his candidacy on January 24, 1979. The following day he asked Hatch to meet with him at the Mayflower Hotel. During the one-hour session, Hatch expressed great admiration for the Texan but said he had to continue supporting Reagan out of loyalty to the man who had helped put him in the Senate. Hatch's compliments were sincere; he believed Connally had an excellent shot at the nomination should Reagan stumble.

Other Republicans entering the sweepstakes in 1979 included Reagan—the last to formally announce but immediately the front-runner; George Bush, a former congressman who had held several high-level federal posts; Senators Howard Baker and Robert Dole; and Representative John Anderson of Illinois. Conservative Philip Crane, another Illinois congressman, had announced in 1978.

Iowa and New Hampshire would be the first formal tests of strength early in 1980. But New Hampshire's political curmudgeon William Loeb couldn't wait for the fun to begin. A strong Reaganite, Loeb took dead aim at Crane. The longtime publisher of the *Manchester Union Leader,* New Hampshire's largest daily newspaper, had issued a withering attack on both Crane and his wife, Arlene, in March 1979. The scurrilous coverage included a front-page Loeb editorial headlined "The Two Faces of Congressman Crane" and cited mostly anonymous sources to charge both Crane and Arlene with heavy drinking and sexual misconduct.

Crane blamed Reagan's camp for the vilification, but Reagan professed innocence. Hatch appealed to Loeb the next day by phone to halt such stories. But Loeb was adamant and later widened the attacks to include Crane's children. Crane remained in the race into 1980 but was politically wounded and never came close to winning the GOP nomination.

One of the first beauty contests for the Republicans was on April 7, 1979, in Concord, New Hampshire. Reagan, who wouldn't formally become a candidate until November, telephoned Hatch, asking him to appear with his wife Nancy and speak in his place. The Utahn agreed.

Hatch, the only presidential stand-in, participated in a joint press conference with GOP candidates. Nancy Reagan arrived just before show time that evening, accompanied by a campaign aide. She was perfectly coiffed, wore a flowing, white-on-white silk gown, and received sustained applause as she walked from a holding area into the banquet room with Hatch.

Participants had up to five minutes each to make their pitches, and Hatch followed Bush and Dole. He concentrated on Reagan's work as governor of California, delivering a speech written by Reagan press aide Lyn Nofziger. Hatch received enthusiastic applause and Nancy's compliments but felt he would have been more effective if he'd been free to use his own words.

The short speech for Reagan whetted Hatch's appetite for the campaign trail, which he would hit often in 1980, playing a vital role in putting Ronald Reagan in the White House.

11

Reagan and Other Rebels

JIMMY CARTER OWED THE WEST almost nothing—and he paid what he owed. After his first three years in office, opinion polls showed that the West had replaced the South in feeling most alienated from Washington. The West had led the nation in voting against Carter in 1976 and would do so again in 1980.

Over 90 percent of all land owned by the federal government is in the West, including two-thirds of Hatch's Utah. The Carter administration's insensitivity to the region galvanized the West's historic distrust of Washington, leading in 1979 to the Sagebrush Rebellion—a quixotic threat by western states to take ownership of millions of federal acres within their borders.

Westerners were angry at their "absentee landlord" for locking up land from multiple use; overregulating ranchers, miners, and timber interests; and restricting water and energy development. Many Westerners never forgave Carter for trying to kill ongoing water reclamation projects upon taking office in 1977.

Hatch led the Sagebrush Rebellion in Congress and helped organize a grassroots effort across the West. In a recent interview, he called the effort "sort of a punch in the mouth to let the Carter administration know we weren't going to take it any more." Hatch denied that Westerners were "rapacious, money-grubbing philistines." States were best equipped to care for lands within their borders and were "unlikely to repeat such federal mistakes as telling our ranchers to delay their lambing season."

In June 1979, Hatch drafted a bill boldly declaring that, within five years, 400 million acres managed by the U.S. Forest Service and Bureau of Land Management in thirteen states "west of the 100th meridian" would be transferred to state ownership.

The odds of Uncle Sam moving gracefully aside were about as good as the British standing down at Lexington and Concord two centuries earlier. But to defenders of public lands, the Sagebrush Rebellion was no joke. "It's not the first attempted land grab," warned an editor of *Field & Stream*, "but it may be the most dangerous."

Hatch's bill, in the view of many observers, was flawed. It would not have prevented hard-pressed states from selling their lands to the highest bidder. But the real reason his Senate colleagues met his initiative with stony silence was protocol: Hatch had acted without consulting them on an issue crucial to their states and, possibly, their own political futures.

When Hatch distributed copies of his proposed bill in late June, his Western colleagues refused to a man to sign on. In fact, Garn, McClure of Idaho, and Laxalt of Nevada promptly issued a joint news release calling for hearings throughout the West. By July 12, Hatch realized, "They're all putting me off . . . I have been very bitterly disappointed with my colleagues."

They accused Hatch of jumping out of line again in response to aroused westerners. "Back then, Orrin was a lot like Ronald Reagan," says Laxalt. "He . . . just didn't know how to say 'no.' It was a damn good thing he was a man—otherwise he would have been pregnant all the time."

Finally Hatch introduced his bill anyway, while the others later introduced their own lands-transfer bill. Legislatures in five western states, led by Nevada and including Utah, passed bills claiming ownership of federal lands; another five rejected such bills. The two most intriguing self-described sagebrush rebels were Reagan and a bald, bespectacled conservative activist in Colorado named James Watt, who would come to personify much of what critics found wrong with the Sagebrush Rebellion.

In addition to filling the Senate chamber with far more than his share of rhetoric, Hatch was a prolific writer. While other senators doodled or daydreamed through meetings, Hatch often outlined his next article for a professional journal or the opinion pages of major newspapers. His articles appeared in the *New York Times, Washington Post, Chicago Tribune,* and *Barron's,* among other major general-circulation publications. Longer scholarly pieces were published by the *Harvard Journal of Law and Public Policy* and the *Fordham Law Journal.* Subjects ranged from such social issues as abortion and the Equal Rights Amendment, to the mood of conservatives, Soviet persecution of Jews (Hatch personally adopted several refusenik families and helped them emigrate to Israel), and radioactive fallout in southern Utah.

Late in 1979, a Utah political reporter, Rod Decker, sifted through a thick packet of Hatch's writings from his first two years in office. "Hatch writes well," Decker concluded. "He is clear and smooth. He marshals arguments well, and makes engaging jokes." Both as a writer and a speaker, however, Hatch "too often seems determined to overpower rather than persuade. One rarely gets the sense that Hatch appreciates the other fellow's side, except as a target."

Hatch also wrote—mostly for his own eyes—poetry. Robert Frost he wasn't. But it was rare that he failed to convey a point. Once, when he felt surrounded by critics, Hatch wrote:

> I've brought it on myself,
> I haven't played the game as well
> As I know I can.
> However, I'm not sure it's worth it,
> I'm not sure that being political—
> Is politics to me.
>
> Like a wounded deer
> Hiding in the thicket,
> With dark and frightened eyes,
> Watching all around me, I see it all,
> With sharpened eyesight
> Only wounded animals have,
> And pray for safety
> From those who kill,
> Because they like to destroy.
>
> Unlike the deer,
> Though wounded,
> I will fight back,
> I won't go down easily.
> I won't go down at all.

During 1979 Hatch compiled one of the most conservative voting records in the Senate. Based on twenty-seven votes selected by the Americans for Constitutional Action, only Garn, Jesse Helms, and Bill Armstrong of Colorado scored 100 percent "correct" voting. Next came Hatch at 96 percent. He still served on the Judiciary and Labor and Human Resources committees and had added the influential Budget Committee to his schedule.

But the forty-five-year-old Hatch was paying a price for the frenetic pace. Several minor health problems had been worsening under stress and, as 1980 got underway, demanded his attention. On January 28 he complained of feeling "plain lousy. . . . It's as though my eyes are too tired to stay open but must. It's as though my chest is filled with congestion but isn't. I am totally exhausted but yet still have to continue pushing forward." He suffered almost constant lower back pain, aggravated by several traffic accidents over the years beginning in 1976. The pain contributed to his sleeplessness. "I'm working myself to death," he admitted to himself.

He had slept fitfully for years, and resorted to sleeping pills one weekend to get three nights of solid rest in a row. But two months went by with little improvement. "I was actually shaking today," he wrote on March 31. "I wonder if I am not close to some very serious problems. . . . Have had short cough for two months. Also very difficult time with my voice. I wonder if I haven't permanently damaged it." Hatch's physical problems, however, proved chronic rather than acute or crippling.

He was traveling frequently, campaigning for GOP candidates during the year and fund-raising for Garn's 1980 reelection effort. And he was worried about his own campaign needs for 1982.

One well-connected friend anxious to help Hatch was Anna Chennault, chair of the National Republican Heritage Groups Council. Her deceased husband, Claire Chennault, had led the famed Flying Tigers, a small group of American aviators who fought for China against Japan before the United States entered World War II.

Chennault told Hatch he should run for president some day, an idea he apparently did nothing to encourage. "Anna," Hatch told her, "I might not even be elected to a second term in 1982 if I don't start raising money now for my campaign."

"How much will you need?" she asked.

"Probably about $1.2 million."

"You let me be in charge and I will raise it," said Chennault.

Much of Hatch's work in 1980 was devoted to putting Reagan in the White House. When Reagan, the tenth and final Republican to throw his hat into the ring, announced his candidacy on November 13, 1979, he was by far the GOP front-runner in national polls.

Reagan's campaign aides coveted Hatch's services. They saw in him a talented tactician, energetic campaigner, and an unusually effective stump speaker. Unlike such surrogates as Congressman Jack Kemp, Hatch exhibited a highly desired quality: it appeared that his sole interest was to advance Reagan's presidential ambitions, not his own.

Reagan campaign manager John Sears, concerned about his candidate's age—he would turn sixty-nine on February 6—and mental agility, counseled Reagan to sit on his lead. Reagan accordingly rejected a debate appearance with other GOP candidates in Iowa, where precinct caucuses would be the first important test of the campaign, and otherwise did little but make "cameo appearances" in the state.

On January 16, Hatch received an urgent call from Reagan headquarters in Los Angeles. Nancy was supposed to speak in Iowa but had a 103-degree temperature. The caucuses were five days later. Would Hatch go? He would, but only once: Iowa was looking shaky, warned an old friend, Reagan campaign coordinator Richard Richards. He advised Hatch to protect himself from blame should Reagan lose.

Richards' warning was both timely and prophetic. By staying above the fray in Iowa, Reagan had unwittingly allowed George Bush to out-hustle him. On election eve, Bush could tell Iowans that he had spent more days campaigning there than Reagan had spent hours. Bush's tortoise overtook Reagan's hare in a stunning victory.

Hatch stayed up late on the night of January 21 to watch the returns from Iowa. "I frankly thought the loss was a good thing for the Reagan campaign, because they really had been taking it too easy," he recalls. "I had to hand it to Bush, but did think he came across as very cocky and arrogant. I doubted seriously that he could sustain the momentum."

Hatch called the Reagans on their private line the next day.

"I'm *so* glad you called," Nancy said.

"Well, I just wanted to let you and Ron know how bad I feel about Iowa," said Hatch. "Don't be discouraged."

Worried about intruding, Hatch tried to hang up quickly but Reagan picked up the phone. "Orrin, it's so good to hear from you. Where do we go from here?"

"Ron, I honestly feel this isn't the worst thing that could have happened. Better here than later. I do think it tells us that the campaign team has got to work harder, and that you personally have got to be more involved." Hatch also suggested he overhaul his campaign organization.

"We're looking at everything, including our people," said Reagan. "There'll be some changes. I can promise you we won't be caught asleep at the switch again."

All eyes were now on presidential bellwether New Hampshire, considered critical for Reagan. The nation's first primary, barely more than a month away, was suddenly up for grabs. Only four years earlier, dark horse Jimmy Carter had, like Bush, done better than predicted in Iowa. Carter rode that momentum to victory in New Hampshire, and ultimately claimed the White House.

Laxalt found Hatch on the Senate floor January 24. "We've reworked Ron's schedule," said Laxalt. "He's going to spend a lot of time up in New Hampshire. You, [Pennsylvania Senator] Dick Schweiker, and I have got to get together and do some planning, because we're going to have to spend a lot of time up there, too."

"I'll do whatever you need me to do," said Hatch.

The next day Hatch got a panic call from Reagan headquarters. In the worry over New Hampshire, they had forgotten one detail: Arkansas. The small Southern state was about to hold its own caucuses; and Bush, strongly backed by popular Congressman John Paul Hammerschmidt, was poised to walk away with the prize. While the delegate votes were few, a second Bush victory would make huge headlines and perhaps cripple Reagan's chances in New Hampshire. Would Hatch represent Reagan in the Arkansas caucuses?

Hatch flew to Little Rock, arriving the night before the caucuses. He crashed a Republican event where candidates were pitching for support. Over Bush's objections, Hammerschmidt agreed to let Hatch have five minutes, like the other candidates. Instead he took ten, delivering an off-the-cuff stemwinder and urging delegates to vote for Reagan. The audience roared its approval. Bush, steaming, refused to shake hands with Hatch.

Bush had even more reason to be angry the next day. Operatives for Reagan and Howard Baker quietly joined forces and threw support to each other at the state's four caucuses—Hatch speaking for Reagan at each of them. By day's end, the maneuvering had cost Bush his predicted victory. In fact, Bush didn't even come in second. Reagan won Arkansas, followed by Baker. Bush was livid. But there was nothing he could do about it.

While Reagan came in second in Iowa, several insiders said Hatch came in first—among surrogates. Dick Richards called two days after the Iowa caucus, asking Hatch to head for South Dakota. "By the way," added Richards, "our people are all saying you did the best job of all those speaking for Ron in Iowa. You were less self-serving and didn't talk people to death."

Cindy Tapscott, a campaign advance person, told Hatch the same thing. "I spent almost a full day with Nancy, and all she could talk about was how much you have done to help both her and the Governor."

Hatch came to believe Reagan faced two main foes: George Bush and the media. He wrote:

> Almost all the media are giving Reagan an awful time. The media control too much of the election process. It's pathetic when a Jack Germond can determine who's going to be President of the United

States. . . . We must come to an effective solution to the problem. However, most politicians are not going to do anything about it legislatively because they are so afraid of the media. I believe a man could become a hero if he would take the media on.

Hatch did not specify what "effective solution" he had in mind, or how he would square attempts to curb a free press with First Amendment guarantees in his revered Constitution.

After Reagan was blasted in the media for telling an ethnic joke, Hatch acknowledged that Reagan shouldn't have used it, but jotted a note to himself: "Don't joke with the media. They simply are not on our side. Conservatives will never be able to be treated fairly by the liberal media. . . . I'm sick of the media and the way they treat good people."

In truth, the media were unhappy with most of the presidential choices in 1980. But once Reagan had secured the nomination, he ended up with far more endorsements than Carter. On the eve of the general election, a poll by *Editor and Publisher* showed that 443 daily newspapers had endorsed Reagan, 126 had endorsed Carter, and 40 had endorsed Anderson. But a whopping 439 were uncommitted—more than double the number that had stayed neutral when Carter beat Ford in 1976.

Hatch seemed less concerned about New Hampshire's pro-Reagan publisher William Loeb, who now had George Bush in his crosshairs. The *Manchester Union Leader* trumpeted every conservative concern about Bush—that he belonged to the Trilateral Commission and the Council on Foreign Relations, supported the Equal Rights Amendment, and allegedly favored gun control laws and abortion.

Bush, in Hatch's estimation, had not handled such questions well while campaigning in Arkansas. "He got mad and said . . . right-wing kooks and Birch Society members [were] raising those issues," recalls Hatch. "The fact is that there were a lot of reasonable Republicans concerned about the international organizations controlled by the David Rockefeller crowd who were financing Bush's campaign."

On February 14, Hatch received a warm note:

Reports from the field tell me you knocked 'em dead in Arkansas and Union County, New Jersey, as well as the many stops in between. Charlie Black has told me how extensively you've hit the road on my behalf, and I want you to know how much I appreciate all you do. Friends like you make this entire effort worthwhile.

Ron

After Iowa, Reagan followed his gut instinct, as well as advice from Laxalt, Hatch, and others. He waded into the adoring crowds that had waited fifteen years—ever since Reagan's heroic though futile attempt to salvage Barry Goldwater's campaign in 1964. Their overwhelming response now renewed his spirit and put the campaign back on track. Reagan parked his campaign jet and bused through the back roads of New England, campaigning for twenty-one days straight at one point. In the grueling process, he erased age as a campaign issue.

But the momentum generated by Bush's win in Iowa—he called it the "Big Mo" ad nauseam—was still paying big dividends. Once far behind Reagan, Bush had pulled ahead in New Hampshire 41-37 by the end of January, according to Reagan's own polls.

Reagan needed a strong finish—and got it in two debates the week before the February 26 primary. After refusing to debate in Iowa, Reagan met his Republican competitors head-to-head, first in Manchester and then in Nashua. He came out a winner both times.

Monday, February 25, found Hatch back in New Hampshire with a dozen other members of Congress for an election-eve blitz of the state for Reagan. He returned to Washington the following morning to help pass the Institutional Civil Rights Bill on the Senate floor. In the afternoon he flew back to Manchester to await primary election results. David Fischer, a former Hatch staff aide and now Reagan's personal assistant, took Hatch to the Reagans' suite where Nancy gave him a welcoming hug. Both she and her husband insisted he stay for the evening.

Reagan then told Hatch he had fired campaign manager John Sears, Hatch's friend Charlie Black, and press secretary Jim Lake earlier that afternoon in the same room, with Nancy and the new campaign manager, William Casey, looking on. Hatch, who respected Sears's abilities, was shocked. But Laxalt and other conservatives had cried for his hide, blaming Sears for the slip in Iowa and for not letting "Reagan be Reagan." Kindly Reagan might have let it slide, but Nancy, determined that her husband needed new campaign leadership, stiffened his resolve.

They watched the New Hampshire returns on three television monitors. It was apparent early that Reagan was going to win overwhelmingly. He ended up with 51 percent in the seven-candidate race, followed by Bush with 22 percent, and Baker with 13 percent.

"I was so proud of Ron and Nancy," said Hatch. "They handled it all with grace and dignity." Hatch accompanied the Reagans everywhere that evening. "I couldn't have been happier."

New campaign chairman William Casey was a tall, older, enigmatic man who had headed the Securities and Exchange Commission. He tended to mumble but had a brilliant mind and a huge capacity for work. Casey managed the campaign, while Ed Meese, an attorney and longtime Reagan confidant, was personal staff director. Hatch telephoned Casey with several staffing suggestions and, two weeks later, was delighted to learn that he had followed through on every one.

Meanwhile, in the Democratic primary, Carter and Kennedy were slugging it out. Carter had demonstrated admirable personal qualities during his presidency—honesty and hard work among them—but most Americans also perceived him as vacillating and weak.

As Carter's campaign swung into high gear, the nation faced multiple crises: at home, a devastated economy and no coherent energy program; abroad, the continuing hostage situation in Iran, a flood of Cuban and Haitian refugees, turmoil in the Middle East, and the Russian invasion of Afghanistan during the last week in December 1979.

Hatch was brutal in his assessment of Carter, telling a Utah audience, "If we had not let ourselves be bullied all over the Middle East, the Iran crisis would never have happened." After Russian troops poured into Afghanistan in December, Hatch wrote privately, "The whole world is in an uproar and [Carter] is sitting in the White House, calm and collected as though nothing is happening."

Carter used the crisis in Iran—where some fifty Americans were held hostage throughout 1980—as his excuse for not debating Kennedy. The "Rose Garden strategy" worked politically for about three months. Then in February, his ratings tipped down, bottoming out at an abysmal 21 percent in July as Republicans were whooping it up at their national convention.

Democrats ached for a change; but as the campaign season dragged on, it became evident that Kennedy was not what they wanted after all. Befuddled by the international crisis, Kennedy seemed tepid and rambling, the liberal fire that endeared him to followers extinguished. The albatross of Chappaquiddick and revelations of discord with his wife, Joan, eclipsed Kennedy's star during the first few weeks of 1980.

A brief revival came when he reclaimed the liberal banner on January 28 at Georgetown University. He rehearsed campaign themes that would take him through the rest of the primary season and called for economic constraints to tame inflation. Hatch read Kennedy's speech as staking "his reputation as a pure socialist."

But it was too late. The early floundering proved fatal, even though he proceeded through the campaign season respectably enough, given Carter's enormous advantage of incumbency. Kennedy ended up winning ten primaries and losing twenty-four. He would arrive at the Democratic National Convention with 37 percent of delegate votes while Carter had 59 percent.

In early March, Hatch attended a luncheon where John Wayne's family received a medal in honor of the recently deceased actor. As

Hatch entered, the host, John Warner of Virginia, asked him to say a few words. "Two of my greatest heroes have been Barry Goldwater and John Wayne," Hatch told the audience.

Like his heroes, Hatch was wearing boots that same week when he took yet another urgent call from Reagan. Connally, Bush, and Baker were all speaking to 2,000 people at an important event that evening in South Carolina, four days before that state's primary. The election looked tight. Reagan couldn't make it. Could Hatch fly immediately to Charleston?

Hatch gulped. He had pulled unusually casual clothes out of the closet that morning: a brown herringbone sports jacket, double-knit slacks, and cowboy boots. He had no personal grooming items at the office, but he wouldn't refuse. Hatch caught the flight, and a Reagan campaign aide met him in Charleston with a razor and toiletries.

When Hatch got to the hall for the event, he ran into Howard Baker. "He looked like a beaten man," Hatch recalls. "I asked what I could do to help and he just laughed. It was apparent he was just going through the motions." The candidates and Hatch spoke that evening. When the results were in, Reagan had scored another triumph with 54 percent of the vote, trailed by Connally with 30 percent, and Bush with 15. Baker had withdrawn from contention even before the vote. During the next ten days, Connally and Dole also folded their campaigns.

With candidate ranks thinning fast, Hatch was aghast to learn that Senator Charles Percy was pushing John Anderson, still in the race, as a candidate for *vice* president. Anderson, a twenty-year House veteran from Illinois, had an unpredictable voting record and was widely distrusted by Republicans. "The idea was revolting," Hatch recorded with private candor.

The important Illinois primary loomed only six days away when, on March 12, Hatch urged Percy not to publicly endorse Anderson, saying it could cost Reagan two to five percentage points. Percy protested that he had been openly supporting Anderson but agreed to mull it over. That afternoon Percy telephoned Hatch: he wouldn't formally endorse Anderson. Reagan won again with 547,000 Illinois voters supporting him and 415,000 backing Anderson. Carter won among Democrats, more than doubling Kennedy's votes.

Anderson dropped out of the Republican primary and, on April 24, announced he would run for president as an independent. A month later Reagan had accumulated enough delegates to clinch the nomination. His last opponent, Bush, gave up the chase. Bush had won six primaries. Reagan won all twenty-eight of the others.

Hatch had already campaigned in twenty-four states for Reagan when Republicans gathered in Detroit on July 14, 1980, for their four-day national convention. The delegates were largely conservative, and they adopted a platform that echoed most of Reagan's campaign themes: lower taxes, military superiority, and a solution to the nation's energy problems. The document also dropped support of the Equal Rights Amendment—a staple of GOP platforms since 1940—and called for a constitutional ban on abortion.

Despite the sharp conservatism, Reagan was determined to avoid Goldwater's 1964 mistake of allowing ideology to split the party. Republican strategists looked for a moderate vice president. Hatch publicly suggested Connally, privately saying he did so to help widen Reagan's options as sentiment swelled for two other possibilities: former President Ford and Bush.

The most intriguing idea was putting together a Reagan-Ford combination. The deal came close, but in the end Ford's people, including go-between Henry Kissinger, bargained too hard and sought what would have amounted to a copresidency.

Hatch, scheduled to pronounce the benediction as the session meandered toward a close that night, was standing in the hallway on the ramp leading to the microphone when the Reagans came up the stairs.

"Orrin, I have decided to choose George Bush," Reagan said.

"That's fine, Ron," answered a disappointed Hatch. "I'll support you."

Nancy grabbed both of Hatch's arms and looked directly into his eyes. "Orrin, we *hope* you'll support us," she said.

"Of course I will," said Hatch. But he wanted to know why the Ford deal had fallen through.

"Well, Orrin," she said, *"Ronnie* is going to be the president."

Then the Reagans, along with Paul Laxalt, walked down to the microphone, where Reagan announced that Bush would be running with him. The whoops of Bush partisans largely disguised the stunned silence of many other delegates.

Although it was already after midnight in Michigan, and no such announcement had been expected, the convention switchboard lit up like a Christmas tree, as listeners all over the country called to register disagreement. Finally the exasperated switchboard operator, also upset with the choice, threw up her hands and abandoned her post.

Hatch, a jumble of emotions, closed the session with an unscripted prayer. He hoped to soften this bitter blow for conservatives by reconfirming the principles for which they had struggled so long. He besought the Almighty, "Help us to stamp out discrimination, but not by discriminating." It was a statement against affirmative action programs, which he believed created reverse discrimination and were splitting the country.

Early the next morning on the last day of the convention, Hatch drove across a bridge connecting Detroit to Canada. Conservative activists in

Windsor had called a major meeting to oppose the Bush decision. Participants were spoiling for a fight, and there was talk of embarrassing both Reagan and Bush by disrupting the convention.

Hatch held his tongue for some time, then intervened. "Look, I'm not thrilled with the turn of events either, but the question is what makes sense now," he began. "Our major goal must be to elect Ronald Reagan. He can help turn Congress around, will put at least one new justice on the Supreme Court, if not two or three, and will give us a conservative in the White House for the first time in many, many years."

Bush's selection, Hatch reminded them, was a *fait accompli*. "The Democrats would love nothing more than to see us divided over this," he said. "We can't let that happen. What we really should do is get a good conservative to second Bush's nomination tonight." Hatch suggested Jesse Helms. However, Helms's aide, Carter Wrenn declined, saying his boss was "just a country boy" who "doesn't understand all these problems. All he's interested in is right and wrong."

Hatch then reminded conservatives of the Carter alternative: "See pro-abortion justices put on the Supreme Court . . . see another 200 liberal federal judges appointed . . . see all the federal agencies loaded up with anti-free enterprise people . . . and see our country continue to deteriorate." He summarized, "It would be just plain wrong."

Across the river in Detroit, word spread around the convention that Hatch had quelled a rebellion. At 3:30 P.M. Bush telephoned Hatch. "I've asked Bob Dole to give my nominating speech this evening," explained Bush. "Will you give one of the seconding speeches?"

"I'd be honored," said Hatch.

That evening Hatch was given two paragraphs of comments about Bush that he was to read. Hatch, one of seven nominating speakers, in a further effort to unify Republicans, complimented other potential Republican vice presidential candidates by name.

Reagan's speech ended the evening and the convention. He made a bid for minorities to join the Republican fold, saying they were the main victims of the disastrous national economy and promising to help create inner city job skills and opportunities.

Flaunting his sagebrush rebel credentials, Reagan called for a pro-growth energy policy and a 30 percent cut in federal income tax rates over the next three years to stimulate the sagging economy, and lambasted Democratic weakness in military and foreign affairs. He ended with a silent prayer and the words, "God bless America."

To Hatch, the feeling on the convention floor was "almost spiritual. . . . We knew that the Republican Party was the party that stood for the family, for decency, for good government, and for morality in government."

The Democratic National Convention a month later was like a photographic negative of the Republican convention: Delegates were deeply divided, the platform was as liberal as its GOP counterpart was conservative, and, according to Jimmy Carter, the nation's economic mess and military deficiencies were because of previous *Republican* administrations.

Carter arrived in New York with 1,981 delegate votes—some 300 more than needed for the nomination—to 1,226 for Kennedy. Congressman Morris Udall of Arizona keynoted the convention. Citing the GOP platform, Udall pointed out what many more would soon conclude: "You can't have $140 billion in tax cuts, $100 billion in new defense spending over three years, and a balanced budget."

Despite Carter's control, Kennedy cast a giant shadow over his coronation. The well-orchestrated demonstration following Carter's speech ran out of steam after about ten minutes. In contrast, Kennedy's spellbinding speech two days earlier had brought an emotional thirty-five-minute demonstration.

Many considered it Kennedy's best speech ever, and it was easily the highlight of the convention—delivered not as a political candidate but as keeper of the liberal flame. "Programs may sometimes become obsolete, but the ideal of fairness will never wear out." Kennedy skirted differences with Carter and attacked Reagan head-on, calling the Republican's proposed tax cuts "a wonderfully Republican idea that would redistribute income in the wrong direction." At a pinnacle likely never to be reached again, Kennedy electrified Madison Square Garden with his closing declaration: "For all those whose cares have been our concern, the work goes on, the cause endures, the hope still lives, and the dream shall never die."

Hatch was openly skeptical of the Democratic proceedings. Senate Budget Committee figures showed that its platform contained seventy proposals for new spending which would add up to "an astounding $600 billion" over the next five years. Hatch instead repeated Reagan's supply-side economic mantra, calling for "a balanced program of spending restraint, productivity-oriented tax cuts, a stable monetary policy and elimination of burdensome federal regulations to encourage economic growth and reduce inflation."

Almost simultaneously, *U.S. News & World Report* turned the tables, accusing *Hatch* of wasting taxpayer money. Its "Whispers" section on September 29 reported that Hatch had inserted three long speeches in the *Congressional Record* that month—112 pages on affirmative action vs. equal protection, and 33 on antitrust divestiture and ancillary restraints in the petroleum industry.

"Some members of the Senate are squirming," wrote *U.S. News.* "It's not the content of the statements that bothers the lawmakers, but fear that the entire Senate would suffer when news of the printing costs — more than $60,000—was made public."

Hatch said the 112-page statement was the most thorough analysis of racial quotas ever included in the *Record* and that its cost was justified by having it readily accessible to scholars and others. He blamed the negative publicity on "liberal Democratic friends trying to give me a hard time."

He continued to carry Reagan's colors across the country, right to Carter's doorstep in Plains, Georgia. Just two weeks before the general election, about seven hundred people—many bused in (Plains's entire population was less than a thousand)—gathered in the rain for a symbolic Reagan rally. Hatch, actor Robert Conrad, and a former prisoner of war in Vietnam spoke, and a telephone call from Nancy Reagan was broadcast to the crowd.

"If we have a war," Hatch told the crowd, "it is not going to be because of how strong we are but because of how weak we are . . . . Ronald Reagan will bring us back to number one."

Reagan first had to get past Jimmy Carter. Though weighed down by the Iranian crisis and an economy in shambles, Carter began to narrow the gap with Reagan soon after the Democratic convention, and ran neck-and-neck from about Labor Day.

The pivotal event of the campaign was the single debate between Carter and Reagan on October 28, memorable for Reagan's carefully rehearsed rejoinder which sounded perfectly spontaneous and disarmed Carter: "There you go again." Reagan charged Carter with weakening the U.S. military and devastating the economy. Carter in effect labeled Reagan a warmonger, and, on the economy, simply quoted George Bush's earlier characterization of Reagan's tax-cut plan as "voodoo economics."

During the final days leading to the November 4 election, the ground moved beneath the campaign. Reagan's pollster Richard Wirthlin found the numbers swinging their way so totally that he hesitated to use them for fear of causing overconfidence. Meanwhile, independent public opinion polls on election eve reported, almost without exception, that the race was too close to call.

On October 28, Hatch was back in Washington. He had campaigned in thirty-two states for Reagan and privately predicted a Reagan win, including a sweep of the West, with the possible exception of Hawaii.

Sagebrush country was only the beginning of Reagan's stunning victory a week later. Except for Hawaii, he won in every western state and every other region as well, including Carter's native South. When the ground stopped shaking, Carter had only his home state and five others, plus the District of Columbia, for 49 electoral votes. Reagan won 489 electoral votes and crushed Carter 51 to 41 percent in the popular count. The Democratic coalition was in shreds.

During his nomination acceptance speech, Reagan had said, "I ask you not simply to 'Trust me,' but to trust your values—our values—and to hold me responsible for living up to them." As the Reagan era dawned, yet to be answered was who would define those values—and, at a time of turmoil abroad and at home, how they could be transformed into law.

12

The Republicans
Take Charge

REPUBLICAN GAINS WERE ENORMOUS in 1980. The party made strides at every level, picking up thirty-three House seats—its best showing since 1966—and four governorships, along with about two hundred state legislative seats around the country. But the real prize lay on the other side of Capitol Hill, where the GOP captured the Senate for the first time since 1952.

Carter's vote total was lower in every state than it had been in 1976—at least 10 percent lower in nearly half. While Carter lost every region of the country decisively, his worst showing by far was in the West, where he received just 35 percent of the popular vote. Utahns led everyone in pulling the lever for Reagan—giving him 73 percent of their votes, followed by neighboring Idahoans at 67 percent.

Blacks were the only major group of Democratic loyalists who held firm for Carter, more than 80 percent voting for him in 1980 as they had in 1976. They paid a high price for their loyalty. Reagan had promised inner-city renewal; but in the face of other national priorities, the cities seemed to become to Reagan what the West had been to Carter: politically expendable.

The election outcome probably reflected more anti-Carter than pro-Reagan sentiment. Clearly the eight-hundred-pound gorilla was the economy, especially double-digit inflation. Citizens were fed up with the stalemate in Washington, where Carter's relations with the Democratic establishment remained poisonous to the end. Fifty-two hostage Americans in Iran and the unimpeded Soviet march into Afghanistan underscored Reagan's message of U.S. weakness. Voters demanded change. But change to what?

It was one thing to define the problems and quite another to begin solving them. Whatever factors led to his landslide, Reagan had every right to act as though he had a mandate to take new approaches, following four years of drift under Carter and the Democratic control of Congress. With the Senate in GOP hands for the first time in a quarter-century, Reagan had a historic opportunity to show what conservative principles could accomplish.

Orrin Hatch had devoted 1980 to getting Reagan elected. The investment would pay enormous dividends for the next twelve years: Many of Hatch's accomplishments might have been canceled if Democrats, instead of Republicans, had controlled the White House.

Hatch was point man for much of what the Reagan administration hoped to change. The *New Republic,* in a tough profile on Hatch in mid-1980, had written: "If the Republicans take control of the Senate . . . Hatch will become chairman of the Senate Committee on Labor and Human Resources, a chilling thought not only for labor but for the social service advocates frequently subjected to his perorations on the evils of the welfare state."

For the *New Republic* and other liberal bastions, the nightmare had become reality. The enemy had breached their ramparts and was within the castle walls. And Orrin Hatch was in the front line.

Hatch, suddenly a powerful Senate chairman, was delighted with the election outcome. Back home in Utah, Republicans swept almost everything, with one big exception. Popular Governor Scott Matheson bucked the tide to win a second term. Matheson was part of a fascinating pattern among Rocky Mountain states, which usually sent conservative Republicans to Washington but left moderate Democrats in the governors' mansions during the Reagan years.

Early in January 1981, two thousand Utahns filled a high school auditorium to hear Hatch's fourth annual "Report to Utah." Wearing a gray suit, cowboy boots, and an "I Love Utah" button, Hatch said Iran and other potential adversaries had good reason to fear Reagan because "he's tough as nails." Iran, in fact, would release the hostages as Reagan was sworn into office less than two weeks later.

Hatch vowed to help reduce the "gang of four million"—the federal bureaucracy—which he and Reagan charged were a serious drag on the nation's productivity. Reagan would peel tens of thousands of bureaucrats from the public payroll, and much of the money they parceled out would be consolidated into "block grants" for states themselves to administer.

Republicans had captured the Senate by picking up a net twelve seats, the largest net gain for either party since 1958 when Democrats had won fifteen. The GOP margin would be 53-47 during the ninety-seventh

Congress, with the Senate significantly more conservative and more Republican. Four liberal Democratic pillars toppled: Birch Bayh of Indiana, George McGovern of South Dakota, Frank Church of Idaho, and John Culver of Iowa. Conservative Republicans replaced some liberal Republican senators, notably Jacob Javits of New York who lost to Alfonse D'Amato.

Bayh was among those calling on Hatch and other former colleagues, wearing a new hat: attorney-lobbyist. Scores of defeated legislators filled Washington's law firms, trade associations, and corporations, working *on* Congress instead of in it. One of every four defeated members from the ninety-fifth Congress, inflicted with a malady known locally as "Potomac fever," had remained in Washington to sell their contacts and influence.

The Senate that convened in January 1981 was unusually inexperienced as well as conservative: eighteen freshman senators—an overwhelming sixteen of them Republican—would rival other recent large classes, including the eighteen elected in 1976 and twenty in 1978. Twenty-seven Republicans—a majority of GOP senators—had now been elected in either 1978 or 1980.

Although Hatch had been in Congress only four years, he was a senior Republican. The status gave Hatch unusual opportunities, unusual challenges, and one of the busiest portfolios in Washington. He sat on five committees and ten subcommittees, chaired the Labor and Human Resources Committee, and also chaired the Constitution Subcommittee. He had important responsibilities on the Judiciary Committee, the Budget Committee, and the Select Small Business Committee, and energetically picked up other irresistible causes. As a committee chairman, he helped the new majority leader Howard Baker set policy for the entire Senate.

Even given Hatch's enormous energy, spreading himself too thin was a perpetual problem. "Despite a first-class intellect," wrote Al Hunt of the *Wall Street Journal*, "[Hatch] often shows a lack of intellectual discipline. Senator Hatch talks knowledgeably about an array of subjects, but tends to get carried away by fringe activities."

Commanding Hatch's first attention was the most ideologically split panel in the Senate—the fourteen-member Labor Committee. Kennedy underscored the committee's significance by opting to become its ranking Democrat, over the same position on the Judiciary Committee, now chaired by Strom Thurmond. His presidential ambitions blasted, Kennedy concentrated on putting his stamp on the nation's labor and social laws. Lined up against Kennedy's six solidly pro-union Democrats were six staunchly conservative Republicans on Hatch's side of the table. Five had just been elected in November. "We were like a bunch of rookies up against the New York Yankees," said Hatch. "But it didn't bother us. We looked forward to taking them on."

Two liberal Republicans held many swing votes. Lowell Weicker of Connecticut and Robert Stafford of Vermont, both serving second terms, often voted with the Democrats, giving Kennedy a nine-seven ideological edge over Hatch on the committee

For unions, the 1977 labor law defeat was still a painful memory, and organized labor welcomed Hatch's rise to committee chair about as enthusiastically as Europe welcomed Napoleon's escape from Elba in 1815. To labor leaders, wrote the *Boston Globe,* "Hatch's assumption of control over labor legislation . . . is the worst thing that happened during the election. To them it is worse than the election of Ronald Reagan as President."

Hatch, however, emphasized that he himself had been a card-carrying union lather in Pittsburgh and said he genuinely wanted to help American workers, as opposed to helping their unions achieve unwarranted advantages at the expense of the rest of the nation. Early in 1981 Hatch tried to reach out to labor leaders. "I've been taking them to lunch, and I've really liked them," he said. "My door is open—but in their eyes it's very difficult to find areas where we can agree."

Civil rights leaders likewise worried over Hatch's sudden power. While professing concern for minorities who historically had suffered injustice, Hatch was a firm foe of quota-laden affirmative-action remedies aimed at helping them secure a foothold in the American mainstream. Hatch favored outreach, job training, and other nonquota programs.

"I believe in equality of opportunity, but not equality of condition or result," explained Hatch in a recent interview. "Preferences and quotas favoring one group virtually always hurt another. There is no such thing as reverse discrimination. There is only discrimination, pure and simple, whether it runs forward or in reverse"—hence his prayer at the Republican National Convention, "Help us to stamp out discrimination, but not by discriminating."

In December 1980 he led a filibuster that killed a fair-housing bill, insisting on evidence that alleged violators directly or indirectly *intended* to discriminate. Kennedy said Hatch's provision amounted to "rolling back" existing civil rights laws, while Hatch in a private outburst accused Democrats—operating as the Reagan era was about to dawn—of a "last-gasp ultraliberal effort to impose the federal government on the lives of people."

Following that effort, Hatch left the floor and shook hands with every black civil rights leader present, saying he empathized with them and promised to support a different approach to help wipe out housing discrimination.

"Senator Hatch, because he is so personable, makes you feel that he has your best interests at heart," said Althea Simmons, head of the

Washington office of the NAACP. "He is opposed to the social programs we favor. The fact that he is so personable about it doesn't make it more palatable. It just makes him more difficult to perceive as a staunch foe."

During 1981, Hatch also: led an effort to abolish the Legal Services Corporation—saying it was more involved in "lawyer activism" than in helping the poor; sought to outlaw all busing for racial balance; and introduced a proposed constitutional amendment to prohibit quotas, goals, timetables, or preferential treatment on the basis of race or sex.

At the same time, however, he led efforts to get Congress to pass a youth minimum wage, lower than the national minimum for other workers, to encourage businesses to create more jobs for young people. Hotly opposed by unions, who feared youths would take away their jobs, Hatch's approach would have assisted unemployed teenagers—a great proportion of whom were black—to begin productive lives in the work force.

"While I oppose quotas, which always discriminate against someone, we need to recognize the worth of voluntary recruitment and job-training programs to assist the less fortunate," said Hatch in a recent interview. "This kind of affirmative action is truly affirmative, while quotas are not."

Committee decisions in 1981 were made more difficult by the economy, already extremely worrisome and headed into recession. Inflation—tagged the nation's number one problem by both Reagan and Carter—was in double digits for 1980, when most wage earners lost about 4 percent of their purchasing power.

The prime interest rate—the rate at which banks lend to their best customers—had hit a record 20 percent on April 18, 1980, then another record, 21.5 percent, on December 20. Eight million men and women were unemployed, and—perhaps the most ominous sign of all—more than 40 percent of black teenagers couldn't find jobs.

Reagan's cure was supply-side economics, an approach many economists regarded as hogwash. Its centerpiece was a schedule of steep tax cuts which theoretically would lead to new investment, an expanded economy, and more jobs—which in turn would produce more tax revenue. By reducing government costs and unharnessing the nation's economic engine, Reagan had said during the campaign, federal coffers would fill and the budget deficit disappear by 1984.

"You and I, as individuals," Reagan said in his inaugural address on January 20, 1981 "can, by borrowing, live beyond our means, but for only a limited period of time. Why, then, should we think that collectively, as a nation, we're not bound by that same limitation?"

Why, indeed? True, in 1981 inflation slowed to about 9 percent and the prime rate dropped to 16 percent. But Reagan had not counted on an ever-increasing expansion of Great Society and other entitlement programs, nor the pressure on the budget caused by his military buildup. These factors, combined with his tax cuts and a looming recession, soon killed any hope of a balanced budget. After first projecting a budget deficit of $42.3 billion for the fiscal year beginning in October 1981, the president admitted it would be more than $100 billion—and gave up the idea of a balanced budget by 1984.

Instead of the worrisome eight-figure deficits Reagan had decried throughout his campaign, the nation was headed into an unprecedented era of nine-figure deficits. Democrats and many economists would call Reagan's program delusive from the start. Reagan and his supporters in turn would blame Congress for not cutting spending more steeply. And caught in the middle would be millions of hapless citizens, neither independent nor wealthy enough to escape the inevitable vagaries resulting from conflicts between the Republican and Democratic economic approaches.

As the ninety-seventh Congress convened in January 1981, few jobs were more daunting than that facing Hatch's Labor and Human Resources Committee. The administration's budget priorities meant a smaller share of the pie for basic human needs. Wrenching decisions had to be made, pitting groups of citizens least able to care for themselves against each other—children, the handicapped, those afflicted with AIDS and other deadly diseases, the elderly, and citizens trapped in poverty.

"Asked about his priorities," wrote Hunt of the *Wall Street Journal,* "the new Labor Committee chairman talks first about combatting sex discrimination; he is an opponent of the Equal Rights Amendment, but he believes tougher enforcement of existing laws can correct some inequities." Two months later, Hatch held one of the nation's first hearings on sex discrimination. But the media and social activists showed little interest; Hatch believed that was because they stereotyped conservatives as people who didn't really care about such issues.

Hatch invited the head of the Equal Employment Opportunity Commission to report on new guidelines under which women could file complaints of discrimination. "Sexual harassment in the workplace is not a figment of the imagination," J. Clay Smith, Jr., the EEOC's acting commissioner, told a subcommittee, also chaired by Hatch. "It is a real problem." Smith cited a survey in which 42 percent of federally employed women said they had been victims of sexual harassment.

Testifying against the guidelines was Phyllis Schlafly, who said they "penalize the innocent bystander, the employer, for acts over which he has no control." Feminists in the packed hearing room hissed Schlafly when she added, "The most cruel and damaging sexual harassment taking place today is the harassment by feminists and their federal government allies against the role of motherhood and the role of the dependent wife."

Schlafly, fifty-seven, was head of the Eagle Forum and the nation's leading opponent of the Equal Rights Amendment. Largely thanks to her, the Republicans had dropped their forty-year support of the ERA from their 1980 platform. In testimony denounced by many others as a model of insensitivity, Schlafly said the "virtuous woman" need not fear harassment except in the "rarest of cases." She added: "When a woman walks across the room, she speaks with a universal body language that most men intuitively understand. Men hardly ever ask sexual favors of women from whom the certain answer is 'No.'"

Schlafly and other ultraconservatives would increasingly be a thorn in Hatch's side as he sought to balance competing interests and make headway on labor, health, and other national problems. While Jesse Helms's strategy was to put his colleagues on the spot and use their votes against them at the next election, Hatch was determined not just to tear apart but to build. That meant compromise, however, and compromise was anathema to extremists.

"I believed in doing the best we could within the framework of what we had to work with," explained Hatch in a recent interview. "All too often conservatives had fought great battles only to go down in flames of glory. I wanted to win. I wanted to be on the offensive and not perpetually on the defensive. I wanted to turn excesses around and, if I couldn't get 100 percent of what we wanted, I would get whatever we could." However, Hatch continually refused to compromise on matters he defined as representing a key principle.

Hatch had been at Reagan's beck and call throughout the Californian's climb to the presidency. But any notion that he would automatically be in Reagan's pocket as they assumed their new roles at opposite ends of Pennsylvania Avenue was dispelled after the White House announced its nominee for Secretary of Labor.

Raymond J. Donovan, fifty, was executive vice president of a New Jersey construction company. His nomination ran into a buzz saw when allegations of links to organized crime and illegal payoffs to corrupt union and political officials surfaced. The FBI launched an intensive investigation; Hatch, Kennedy, and their chief aides also dived into Donovan's past. As the White House screamed, Hatch allowed the committee investigation to run for two weeks.

"The investigation showed that Hatch and Kennedy, despite their ideological differences, could work together on a contentious issue," said *Congressional Quarterly*. "Hatch pursued the investigation vigorously and allowed Kennedy time, up to a point, to do his own looking."

In the end, neither the FBI nor the committee proved the charges, although the FBI said it could not disprove all of them either. The committee reported Donovan favorably to the full Senate, which confirmed him by a vote of 80-17 on February 3. The seventeen votes were all Democrats.

Hatch's Labor and Human Resources Committee and its various subcommittees could now focus on a myriad of social issues: health, education, child abuse, family planning, employment and training programs, legal services for the poor, a subminimum wage for youth, and alleged union corruption. The powerful committee also oversaw three cabinet-level departments—Labor, Education, and Health and Human Services—and nearly two thousand federal programs.

On June 18, 1981, Justice Potter Stewart announced his retirement. Three weeks later Reagan kept a campaign promise and broke a Supreme Court barrier by nominating a woman, Sandra Day O'Connor of Arizona, to fill the vacancy.

Hatch was about to embark on what would arguably be his most enduring domestic achievement: helping to decide the makeup of the high court for decades to come. As a member of the Judiciary Committee, Hatch met privately with O'Connor, then sat on the panel that confirmed her. In both cases he liked what he heard and was the first non-Arizona senator to publicly endorse her. "She was conservative but not inflexibly so, and—most important—she was not a judicial activist," he summed her up privately. "I believed she would try to strictly interpret the Constitution."

O'Connor, fifty-one, held undergraduate and law degrees from Stanford University, graduating third in her class the same year she married her classmate-husband, John J. O'Connor III. She had served in the Arizona state senate and county and state court systems.

When some conservatives raised questions about her views on abortion, Delaware's Joseph Biden, ranking Democrat on the Judiciary Committee, said, "It troubles me that we would require of a judge something beyond a profound sense of the law," and "I am a little concerned that in effect we try to get commitments from a judge on how he or she is going to vote in the future." In later years, when *liberals* raised the abortion question, Biden's attitude would be quite different.

Hatch's early endorsement of O'Connor stopped an incipient movement by the far right to oppose her nomination. In the end, she was confirmed 99-0 by the full Senate on September 21.

Future Supreme Court nominees would not have it so easy.

Hatch soon proposed two more amendments to the Constitution, using his power as chairman of the Constitution Subcommittee to press for passage. One dealt with budget deficits and the other abortion.

The budget amendment, introduced in 1980 and again in 1981, would have required Congress to balance the budget each year, except in times of war or other national emergencies when it could spend into the red by a simple majority vote. All other exceptions would take a three-fifths vote in each house. It was not a new idea. Thirty state legislatures—four short of the number required—had passed resolutions over the previous six years calling on Congress to convene a constitutional convention on the issue.

While most members of Congress deplored deficits, it was mostly lip service. Only five budgets had been in balance since 1950, and members were deeply divided on how to cure the problem. The GOP itself was split, with some leaders calling the constitutional approach "gimmickry" and saying the real answer was for Congress to grow a backbone. Hatch regarded that attitude as an excuse to do nothing. Reagan also supported the amendment approach; and with his help, in 1982 the Senate passed Hatch's amendment 69-31, only to see it die in the House. It was a very long way from becoming part of the Constitution.

The Constitution can be amended two ways: (1) by two-thirds vote of each house of Congress, ratified by three-fourths of the state legislatures, or (2) by a constitutional convention convened by Congress upon request by two-thirds of the states, with amendment approval still required by three-fourths of the states.

The Constitution had been amended twenty-six times but never by the second method. Some worried that a convention could invite all kinds of mischief by individuals intent on adding their pet concerns to the nation's governing document. Legal scholars were split over whether a convention could be limited to a single issue—with Hatch taking the position that it could be, and thus supporting the drive for a constitutional convention. But the effort remained stalled despite the favorable Senate vote.

Hatch's abortion amendment was even more controversial. "Pro-life" forces had tried in vain to push a strict anti-abortion amendment through Congress ever since the Supreme Court's *Roe v. Wade* decision in January 1973 had legalized abortion. The nation was polarized between those who insisted abortion was a woman's decision alone and those who considered it murder. Hatch found the practice abhorrent but stood on what middle ground existed. He believed, as his church taught, that abortion could be justified if the pregnancy endangered the woman's life or resulted from rape or incest.

Late in 1981, Hatch introduced an amendment opposed by both sides. It didn't attempt to outlaw all abortions but would have given Congress and states joint power to "restrict and prohibit" abortion in the various states, with federal law prevailing except in states that were more restrictive. Some considered the approach ingenious.

"There are two things that are for sure," said Karen Mulhauser, executive director of the National Abortion Rights Action League. "Senator Hatch is determined to find language that will get a two-thirds majority. The other thing is that Congress wants very much to get rid of this issue, and even members who have said in the past they don't want to outlaw abortion may put their names on this one."

An alarmed Planned Parenthood took out full-page ads in the *New York Times* showing a woman behind bars and charging: "If this amendment becomes law, all abortions will be outlawed. Overnight." Hatch insisted that was nonsense: "Nothing at all would happen overnight other than the fact that the people's elected representatives would once again possess the authority to take some kind of action with respect to abortion."

Although most anti-abortion groups took an absolutist position and were cool to Hatch's approach, others—this time including New Right leader Paul Weyrich—came to believe it was the only realistic hope of overturning *Roe v. Wade.* Two of the major organizations backing Hatch's amendment were the National Conference of Catholic Bishops and the National Right to Life Committee.

Hatch's Constitution Subcommittee approved his amendment, followed on March 10, 1982, by the full Judiciary Committee, which voted 10-7. After numerous previous attempts, it was the first time since *Roe v. Wade* nine years earlier that any committee of Congress—the people's representatives rather than unelected judges—had approved anti-abortion legislation.

Hatch's proposal, along with one by Jesse Helms that would have outlawed virtually all abortions, languished in the Senate for six months. Then, in a surprise move, Hatch withdrew his from further consideration on September 15—two months before facing reelection—acknowledging that he couldn't muster the votes.

Ray Donovan's confirmation as labor secretary completed Reagan's cabinet. Along with other top-level appointments, overall it was an experienced, mainstream group that suggested the imprint of Vice President Bush more than Reagan. The "takeover" of Reagan's presidency by Bush insiders, in fact, was a source of considerable bitterness by many conservative Reaganites, who felt betrayed.

Also grating on the New Right was Reagan's selection—strongly endorsed by Hatch—of Richard Richards as national party chair, replacing William Brock. The former head of the Republican Party in Utah was one of Hatch's earliest political supporters. His goal in 1981 was to lead the GOP to a long era of political dominance, including control of the

House—a goal never attained—to go along with the Senate. Richards bluntly told the Moral Majority and other elements of the New Right that they were welcome to come along for the ride but that Reagan would chart the course.

Reagan's cabinet was generally well received. A big exception was Secretary of the Interior James Watt, forty-two, who, like Reagan, had been a sagebrush rebel. As head of the Denver-based Mountain States Legal Foundation, Watt had spent the past several years challenging the Interior Department's administration of public lands. He had fought attempts to limit grazing on public land, to designate new wilderness areas, and to limit access to the oil, gas, mining, and timber industries which helped fund his organization.

Interior traditionally had been led by individuals more committed to conserving the land in its natural state than exploiting it for commercial purposes. Watt's selection, in the view of environmentalists, was inviting the fox into the henhouse. But Reagan labeled Watt's detractors "environmental extremists," and Wyoming Senator Alan Simpson added: "You're either with them 100 percent of the time or they'll cut your bicycle tire."

After the election, Reagan reaffirmed his support for the rebellion, sending a message to six hundred westerners meeting in Salt Lake City. "Please convey my best wishes to all my fellow 'Sagebrush Rebels,'" said Reagan. "I renew my pledge to work toward a 'sagebrush solution.' My administration will work to insure that the states have an equitable share of public lands and their natural resources."

In May 1981, Hatch threw a revised version of his federal lands bill into the Senate hopper, this time with the support of fifteen colleagues, including Garn, Laxalt and Cannon of Nevada, and Wallop and Simpson of Wyoming. The 1981 bill, Hatch explained, included additional safeguards against states taking the proposed 460 million acres of land received from the federal government and simply disposing of it to private developers. Nevada Democrat Jim Santini introduced a companion bill in the House. Hatch insisted that a transfer was necessary to correct injustices. Unlike states in the East, he pointed out privately, those in the West had no choice but to give up huge tracts of land to enter the Union.

Many Americans had pulled up stakes in recent decades and moved to the Mountain West seeking fresh opportunity, giving the region the nation's youngest population. The shift of people into the South and West was accompanied by a parallel shift of power in Washington, where westerners began in 1981 chairing a number of the most important Senate committees.

Changing demographics also heightened national concern over the protection and controlled disposition of the area's natural resources. But for those living in the Mountain West, a growing population also meant increasing difficulty in eking out a living on lands controlled by a federal landlord two thousand miles away.

Environmentalist groups such as the Sierra Club, National Audubon Society, and National Wildlife Federation strongly opposed the proposed lands transfer. Their objections were echoed by some influential western lawmakers, notably two Arizona Democrats, Representative Morris Udall, who chaired the powerful House Interior Committee, and Governor Bruce Babbitt.

Although from an old Arizona family, Babbitt, forty-three, was not a mainstream westerner. He had been educated at Notre Dame, Harvard, and in England, and was an ardent environmentalist and political liberal. Serving his first term in 1981, the boyish Babbitt was less sympathetic than most western governors to the problems facing those trying to live off public lands.

The Sagebrush Rebellion, he said, was in fact an attempted "land grab" by commercial interests, and those promoting it were "the same crowd of ranchers who have been trying for 70 years" to take over federal lands. Babbitt alleged that rebellion leaders like Hatch were saying, "It's time to dismantle the parks and send the conservation officers back where they came from."

Babbitt would learn a dozen years later that, especially in politics, what goes around comes around. He would stand at the gate of the opportunity of a lifetime in Washington—and Orrin Hatch would hold the key.

If the utopia described by the Sagebrush Rebellion had ever been possible, it should have materialized after the 1980 election. With Reagan in the White House, Jim Watt at Interior, and conservative Republicans controlling the Senate for the first time in a generation, the time was ripe for a massive lands transfer.

But utopia was never possible. It was, in the baldest terms, a huge huff and a bluff.

"We knew it wasn't going to happen," Hatch acknowledged years later. "Our thirteen western states had only twenty-six of the hundred senators. There was never a chance that the others were going to fork over hundreds of millions of acres. But we had to make this fight, and we were trying to rock the Carter administration back on its heels and get their attention. And we succeeded."

When Nevada started the whole thing in 1979 by passing the original Sagebrush Rebellion Act, lost in the small print was the large fact that the legislature appropriated not a cent to administer the lands and a measly $250,000 to finance anticipated litigation. Nevada didn't even attempt to defend the law when the Interior Department offered to challenge it in court.

Rebels talked tough, like their barroom gunslinger forebears, but they were not about to walk out into the street at high noon. The cost of properly administering some 400 million acres of public lands would have bankrupted some state treasuries, especially if they couldn't sell off parcels of land. In the end, no federal administration, however conservative its instincts, could withstand the withering criticism that would follow a genuine attempt to dispose of such national treasure.

Jim Watt's bluster dissolved with his nomination as Interior Secretary. Otherwise the Senate never would have confirmed him. Suddenly gone—to the consternation of true believers—was any talk of a massive lands transfer. Instead, Watt said meekly, the answer is "a good neighbor attitude calling for balanced use."

In the fall of 1981, Watt returned to his native Wyoming for a powwow with eleven western governors. "The President continues to be a Sagebrush Rebel and so does Jim Watt," he assured them. "But while I continue to be a rebel, I hope to be a rebel without a cause."

Wholesale transfer of lands became a dead issue after the Jackson Hole conference. Watt deserved much of the credit for defusing the issue and the West's anger. He staffed his department with officials more committed to supporting development of public lands, reversed a Carter administration policy that allowed Washington to preempt state water rights, and began transferring selected small parcels of federal land to individual communities.

"While we believe in the multiple use, the preservation and the development of the lands for America and Americans," Watt wrote, "our critics want a centralized, bureaucratic control of the use of land. . . . We intend to restore the parks, to improve wildlife habitat, to develop the energy that is needed for the American people. . . . The question is not whether we develop these resources, but when and how."

Hatch's high polish marked him as more of an urban cowboy than one with saddle sores, despite the boots and string tie he occasionally wore when tramping Utah. He looked far more natural carrying a golf putter than a deer rifle. But political observers gave him high marks for pushing western issues close to the hearts of constituents. One such issue was guns. No longer needed as tools to help tame a frontier, guns remained powerfully entwined with the West's psyche.

The National Rifle Association had long since harnessed the sentiment, fascination, and paranoia of millions of gun owners to create one of Washington's most powerful lobbies. "Guns don't kill people, *people* kill people," it said. No gun-related tragedy or carnage was too horrendous not to be explained away by the NRA–including the attempted assassination of President Reagan and critical wounding of press secretary James Brady in March 1981.

Later that year Hatch co-sponsored a bill introduced by Jim McClure of Idaho to loosen the 1968 gun control law to stop alleged harassment of gun owners and dealers by federal agents. Hatch was a powerful ally for honest western gun owners and the NRA. While advocating tough penalties for those using guns to commit crimes, Hatch also used his legislative skills and knowledge of the Constitution to fashion ever more intricate arguments for almost unlimited access to sporting weapons and other guns sought by honest collectors.

In a hearing before the Judiciary Committee, in fact, Hatch elevated the sanctity of guns above the Constitution. The right of citizens to keep and bear arms is recognized by the Second Amendment, he testified. "I say 'recognized,' not 'created,' because in my view that right . . . is a gift of the Creator, not of the first Congress."

Life, liberty, the pursuit of happiness–and guns.

On other occasions he deadpanned a line that tickled westerners but appalled many others: "The only kind of gun control I believe in is a steady aim."However, after the shooting and violent death of the son of one of his friends a decade later, Hatch dropped that line.

Hatch's most politically potent special interest group by far was the LDS church. About two-thirds of Utahns belonged; and while Mormons had been reasonably divided between political parties in earlier times, more recently a majority had moved into the Republican camp.

The natural conservative bent of Hatch and most other members of the state's congressional delegation was usually sufficient to keep the goodwill of church officials. But on very rare occasions, LDS leaders made pronouncements on national issues which they deemed moral in nature even though most others considered them political. It was highly risky– though not necessarily fatal–for Utah politicians not to accommodate themselves to the church's views. One such issue was the Equal Rights Amendment; and in 1981, another was the deployment of the MX missile.

A pillar of Reagan's campaign had been to strengthen the military, many experts believing it had eroded dangerously during the Carter years. The nation's strategic forces rested on three legs of a nuclear triad–air, sea, and land-based missiles capable of striking the Soviet Union. Defense experts had become especially alarmed over a supposed inferiority in land-based weapons and, under Carter, had been developing a blockbuster ten-warhead missile called the MX.

The key question was how to hide the MX, so that the Soviets would always face the certainty of U.S. retaliation should they launch a first strike. Fantastic schemes had been devised, including one by the Carter administration—another "gift" to the West—to disguise and continually move 200 of the missiles among 4,600 shelters in barren regions of Utah and Nevada. It would be a colossal shell game, forcing the Soviets to guess which shelters to strike.

During the first week in May, 1981, the LDS church's three-member First Presidency unexpectedly opposed MX deployment in the Great Basin on "moral" grounds. The church historically had been fervently patriotic, encouraging members to fight in the country's wars and frowning on those who claimed to be conscientious objectors. For the church itself to object to a vital weapons system seemed highly out of character and set heads spinning at the White House and Pentagon.

The written statement explained that Mormon pioneers had chosen Utah as a "base from which to carry the gospel of peace to the people of the earth." It was "ironic, and a denial of the very essence of that gospel, that in this same general area there should be constructed a mammoth weapons system potentially capable of destroying much of civilization." Concentrating the system in a single restricted area, said the church, meant that "one segment of the population would bear a highly disproportionate share of the burden, in lives lost and property destroyed, in case of an attack. . . . Such concentration, we are informed, may even invite attack under a first-strike strategy on the part of an aggressor."

Church leaders pointedly did not object to the MX itself, however, inviting criticism that the church was practicing a morality of convenience. The Mormon statement, said General Richard Ellis, head of the Strategic Air Command, "did not discuss the responsibility of its members as citizens pledged to defend our nation."

A week after the First Presidency statement, the *Salt Lake Tribune* editorial page carried a political cartoon depicting the Mormon Tabernacle Choir singing "Farther, MX, from Me," next to a withering syndicated column by Carl Rowan, who asked:

> Does a Mormon in Utah have a greater exemption from the problems and perils of national defense than a Methodist in Michigan or a Catholic in Maine? . . . There are a lot of Lutherans in the Dakotas who think they represent the gospel of peace, and yet they have in their midst a lot of Minuteman missiles targeted at the Soviet Union.
>
> We, and our government, must remember that in God's eyes, life is as precious on the arid stretches of North Dakota and the scrubby farmlands of Arkansas as it is in Utah, or California, or New York, or the nation's capital.

Utah's four-member congressional delegation had all supported the MX concept but had reservations on deployment. Both Hatch and Garn said they would weigh the church's position carefully but would have to reach their own conclusions, based also on classified information not available to church leaders.

In July, Hatch reported that before the church's statement in May, his mail had been running about 50-50 for and against basing the MX in Utah. After the pronouncement, his mail shifted to 75 percent against it. On August 17, Hatch finally came out solidly against "shell-game" deployment, citing possible "ecological and socio-economic impacts" on the area. He suggested instead that the MX be placed in existing, upgraded Minuteman III missile silos and possibly in an air-launched system.

Before the end of the year, Reagan announced he was deferring a decision on permanent MX deployment until 1994. Meanwhile he called on Congress to fund production of a hundred missiles, the first thirty-six to be placed in silos then being used by aging Titan missiles.

Hatch received generally good marks for his first year as a Senate chairman. Whenever controversial social issues surface, wrote Steven Roberts of the *New York Times,* "Mr. Hatch—an aggressive, ambitious man who, as much as anything, resembles a minister making his rounds—is certain to be in the middle of the fray, carrying the flag. . . . Since assuming his two chairmanships, Mr. Hatch seems to have made a determined effort to soften his image."

Nadine Cohodas of *Congressional Quarterly* observed, "The main ingredients of Hatch's senatorial style seem to be his willingness to work hard, his intelligence, and his outwardly sincere manner."

Hatch told Cohodas, "I think that I've been a little too blunt on occasion. I've not been as understanding of the political problems of my colleagues, in part because I had never been in politics before coming to the Senate." But he disagreed that his orientation had shifted: "I think if you look at my voting record, I've never been far right. I never deserved the 'ultraconservative' label."

The New Right's Paul Weyrich ruefully came to the same conclusion, calling Hatch "definitely not as predictable as many of his conservative colleagues."

13

Winning a Second Term

ATCH HAD CUT A LARGE SWATH in Washington and was a major player as he neared the end of his first term. In a city known for two kinds of steeds—workhorses and show horses—he was the rarest of breeds: both. But among Utah voters Hatch enjoyed only grudging respect and even less love. He continued to be tagged by critics with unflattering labels—aloof, arrogant, far-right, stubborn, sanctimonious.

Hatch still was largely an unknown quantity to his 1.5 million constituents, some of whom would have endorsed a blue-covered book: *The Political Wit and Wisdom of Orrin G. Hatch and His Protege C. McLain "Mac" Haddow.* The book, by "Trickle Down Productions," has seventy totally blank pages.

Early in 1982 a poll showed that 65 percent of Utahns approved of Hatch and 35 percent—a stunningly large figure—disapproved. "It's pretty pathetic that I have this kind of problem after how well I have served for these last five years," wrote Hatch privately, then added a familiar refrain: "Of course we've done nothing but taken a beating from the media."

Democrats and others who wished Orrin Hatch ill were licking their chops as 1982 dawned. The chance to legally knock off a senator comes but once every six years, and the line forming to help slay Hatch had grown long: organized labor, feminists, civil rights leaders, both far ends of the abortion issue, and various others who plain didn't like him.

Vulnerable as Hatch appeared, he was still a powerful incumbent with all the built-in advantages incumbency bestowed, especially in

177

raising money, the mother's milk of campaigns. Democrats knew they couldn't beat a somebody with a nobody and searched for the ideal candidate. He should match Hatch's strengths but have the engaging personality Hatch was accused of lacking. The ideal profile: young and energetic, Mormon, solid family man, some but not too much government experience, intelligent, attractive, and charismatic with a touch for the common man.

One man fit the profile perfectly: Ted Wilson, Salt Lake City's mayor for six years. Wilson, forty-two, had been gearing up for nearly a year to take on Hatch. The former high school social studies teacher seemed to be liked by everyone, including Hatch, despite their differences. Wilson's disapproval rating early in the year was 7 percent—one-fifth of Hatch's.

"Ted Wilson announced for the Senate against me today," Hatch wrote on January 21, 1982. "He called me on the phone and he was very cocky. . . . His announcement speech was irritating. I've always thought he would be the most dangerous to run against because he's a very handsome and believable populist."

One minute into his announcement speech—delivered first in Salt Lake with wife Kathy and infant son Joey at his side—Wilson threw down the same gauntlet that Frank Moss had used: you're not one of us.

"My candidacy brings an opportunity for our state to elect a senator who was born and raised in Utah, knows Utah, and would represent Utah first in the United States Senate," said Wilson, summarizing the themes on which he would base his challenge. In one sentence, Wilson had neatly accused Hatch of carpetbagging and neglecting Utah to become a national figure.

Although Wilson had a background in the liberal wing of the party, "liberal" is a relative term in Utah. His speech carefully put him on the conservative side of key issues dear to the hearts of Utahns: support for a strong U.S. defense, economic growth and balanced budgets, opposition to abortion and gun control. Then Wilson returned to exploiting the most negative perceptions of Hatch.

> As we review these critical issues, one overriding theme begins to emerge. That theme is confrontation, stridency and fear. Issue after issue pits labor against management, rich against poor, educators against legislators, oil companies against consumers, developers against environmentalists. . . . Isn't it time for a change nationwide, and in Utah, to elect some diplomacy? . . . My candidacy gives Utahns an opportunity to select a style of representation which will lead to real solutions, not just spectacular headlines.

Weeks after Wilson's announcement, Hatch appeared on successive days at BYU, his invariably friendly alma mater in Provo, and its arch-rival, the University of Utah in Salt Lake, often a hostile environment for him. He answered Wilson's charges without naming or even referring to him—a nonrecognition strategy he followed throughout most of the campaign.

Speaking at the Y on "Conservatism with a Human Face" on Tuesday, February 16, Hatch said conservatism was essentially "the commitment to conserve the freedom that is unique to America. . . . We seek to preserve these values not because they are old, but because history has proven that they are the best."

Hatch also defended Reagan's economic program. "In 1981 the national debt crossed the $1 trillion mark. . . . The trillion-dollar legacy of debt that my generation will leave yours is not a monument to compassion. It is a monument to government programs under the guise of compassion that threaten us with economic bankruptcy if the trend is not reversed. . . . [That] is what President Reagan and today's conserva-tives are trying to do."

The next day, Hatch spoke at the U in the "Last Lecture" series, a forum which invited public figures to give their most essential philoso-phies. Paraphrasing Robert Frost, Hatch said he hoped that upon his last lecture people "would not find me changed . . . only more sure of myself," adding, "The strongest and sharpest blade is the flexible blade that can bend with the times."

In 1981 the United States had been bent to Ronald Reagan. But the strength and sharpness he had promised upon taking office were in serious doubt a year later.

The country was well on its way to becoming the greatest military power in history, leaving the USSR in its wake. But the economy was still in trouble, in part because of the enormous cost of the military buildup. That cost included a defense budget of $189 billion for the fiscal year beginning October 1, 1981—$27 billion more than the previous year—*plus* an additional $180 billion sought by Reagan, to be spread over six years, for a sweeping overhaul of the nation's strategic nuclear forces. The weapons were needed, he said, to close "a window of vulnerability."

Rather than seeking additional tax revenues to pay for the military increases, Reagan, with Hatch's help, pushed through Congress a 25 percent across-the-board cut in personal income taxes over three years. Whatever their consequences for other citizens, the cuts were a bonanza for those in the middle and upper income brackets. Reagan's supporters publicly claimed that the tax cuts would stimulate enough investment and economic growth to more than make up the shortfall to the Treasury. Privately, however, some were doing a lot of soul-searching.

"I hope Reagan wins on his tax program tomorrow," Hatch wrote on July 28, 1981, the evening before both houses of Congress voted to approve the package. "However, I am worried about the 710 million dollars in tax cuts over the next number of years. . . . It does seem excessive and I'm not so sure that it's a good situation."

Reagan entered office promising to balance the budget in 1984. The first budget he submitted in 1981 included a projected deficit of $45 billion—if Congress gave him his desired budget cuts in health, social, and education programs. Congress came close. But as the combination of higher defense costs, lower revenue projections, and a worsening recession threw cold water on optimistic White House estimates, Reagan asked for even deeper cuts in domestic programs. His eight-year tug-of-war with Congress was on.

Near the end of 1981, the promised economic magic was nowhere in sight, and Reagan admitted that the federal deficit for 1984 might be, not $45 billion, but a record $109 billion. The supply-side concepts known as Reaganomics—and derided by George Bush during the 1980 campaign as "voodoo economics"—had been sold to the president by a clique of economists headed by a man with the unfortunate name of Laffer. Early in 1982, forty-one-year-old Arthur Laffer, an economics professor at the University of Southern California, submitted to what should have been an embarrassing interview with editors of *U.S. News & World Report*. When they asked what went wrong, Laffer blamed everyone but his pet theories: incompetent White House officials, doubting Democrats, reluctant Republicans, and the Federal Reserve.

"There is one supply-side 'mole' in the White House," said Laffer. "It's the President. He's the only guy who wants it." Laffer urged Reagan and Congress to pour on the steam—to cut taxes more steeply and faster. Projections of deficits as high as $182 billion were strictly "scare tactics" by bureaucrats who were "trying to unelect Reagan," said Laffer.

The federal deficit was in fact a record $111 billion for Reagan's first budget year. For his second year, ending September 30, 1983, it was almost a hundred billion higher: $207 billion. The nation's national debt—to be balanced on the backs of future generations—was heading for trillion-dollar heights that were the stuff of nightmares.

Reagan was simply unwilling to tackle the most politically difficult problems facing the budget. During his presidency the states were saddled with more and more federal mandates without the funds to pay for them, new regulations were clamped on businesses, and—most glaring of all—the cost of entitlement programs continued to soar. The cost of interest on the national debt, coupled with Social Security and other entitlements, ate more than 60 percent of the federal budget pie. The Pentagon devoured the lion's share of what remained, leaving precious little to feed the rest of the nation. But Reagan was determined to stay the course, whatever the cost in human terms to his countrymen and to a world looking vainly to the United States for fiscal stability and leadership.

At the start of 1982, most challengers running against incumbent members of Congress voting for Reaganomics had a ready arsenal of issues. Although inflation and interest rates had gone down from the historic levels Jimmy Carter left behind, deficits were heading into the stratosphere and unemployment had increased to nearly 9 percent for the nation as a whole and substantially higher for minorities, including 40 to 50 percent for black teenagers.

On January 26, Reagan, in his State of the Union address, unveiled another concept designed to whittle Washington down to size: "new federalism." He proposed to shift forty-four domestic programs to state and local governments, starting in 1984, with the federal government in return taking over Medicaid.

Hatch was disappointed in Reagan's speech, which, among other things, did not endorse Hatch's constitutional amendment to require a balanced budget. Typically, however, Hatch blamed the omission not on Reagan but on his top aides: "I am so sick and tired of his disserving staff. I think they're wrecking this country. They're certainly wrecking this President. . . . I feel badly for him because I know that he's a good man and would not do these things except for the bad advice he's getting from these very rapaciously Machiavellian staff members."

Ted Wilson was one of the mayors struggling to serve his city in the recession. Although Utah's economy was better than most, it was not exempt from the ripple effects of Reaganomics. Reagan, in fact, presented Wilson with a political as well as economic problem. Wilson hoped to hang resentment of Reagan's policies around Hatch's neck. But that was risky business in Utah, which had given Reagan a higher percentage of votes than any other state, and where Reagan remained personally popular. And Wilson had a more immediate concern: not being drowned by the flood of money already filling Hatch's campaign coffers.

At the same time Wilson's candidacy was making headlines, a fund-raising letter for Hatch was arriving in mailboxes of known contributors to conservative causes around the country. Dated January 15, 1982, and signed by Paul Laxalt, it called Hatch "a true leader in the United States

Senate" who "played a major role in helping to elect Ronald Reagan, President of the United States."

Laxalt called Hatch the number one target of "many major unions and liberal political action committees" who might spend $4 million to defeat him. The letter asked for a political donation of from $25 to $100 "to build a war chest of $200,000, $300,000—as much as $400,000—to commit toward Senator Hatch's campaign. This is not extra money. . . . This is a *must* budget that we *must* reach within the next sixty to ninety days. Senator Hatch must plan his campaign."

Hatch, of course, had been planning his campaign for many months. The letter offered no hint that in 1981 he already had raised $865,000 for his reelection effort, spent $354,000, and still had a half-million dollars in the bank when the Laxalt letter was mailed.

Three well-placed Washingtonians had helped spearhead efforts to build Hatch's campaign war chest, freeing him to concentrate on Senate duties. They were Betty Murphy, former chairman of the National Labor Relations Board; Anna Chennault, a conservative Republican, and Tommy Corcoran, a former FDR New Deal brain-truster. The three had done a spectacular job. A single event—a $500-per-head reception and dinner in Washington in October 1981, featuring the likes of Vice President Bush and various cabinet officers—had raised a cool half-million.

Hatch's first major fund-raiser of the campaign season, a dinner at Hotel Utah the previous May, likewise was a tremendous success. Eight hundred patrons paid between $125 and $1,000 each, raising a state record of nearly $200,000.

As the huge infusions came in, opponents bitterly cried "Foul!" Mike Miller, Democratic state chairman, was the party's pit bull terrier: Hatch couldn't make a move without Miller biting his ankle. Miller filed a string of complaints with the Federal Election Commission. Although the FEC dismissed them as meritless, some thought Miller was closer to the mark in complaining about the extraordinary amount of Political Action Committee money flowing to Hatch's campaign—$276,000 in 1981 alone—and how it distorted the election process.

During a debate with Utah Republican Chairman Charles Akerlow in October, Miller alleged that nearly 95 percent of Hatch's money to date had come from outside Utah. Akerlow questioned the figure but justified a substantial campaign fund because of George Meany's threat to raise $4 million to defeat Hatch for his role in quashing the 1977 Labor Law Reform Bill.

When Miller charged that Hatch would "buy" the election by spending between $3 million and $4 million on his campaign, an amount unheard of in Utah politics, Akerlow countered that the campaign budget was about $1.5 million.

Other critics accused Hatch of making himself vulnerable to unwarranted influence from corporations by accepting campaign donations from their political action committees (PACs). Hatch was deaf to such arguments. One of his press aides, Gina Savoca, told United Press International–in UPI's words–that "no one donates to him expecting favors because they would not receive them." Whether they received favors might be reasonably questioned; that they expected them could not be.

Common Cause, the citizens' lobbying group, took Hatch and others to task for voting to remove the $25,000 annual limit on outside earned income, principally speech honoraria. Hatch and Garn's votes had provided the margin of victory as the Senate passed the measure 45-43. Common Cause labeled the votes "expedient, self-interested and extraordinarily damaging to the integrity of the institution."

Garn said that money from honoraria did not come from taxpayers. While wealthy senators didn't need it to supplement their $60,000 salaries, he did. Hatch agreed, noting that he had always exceeded the limit in honoraria, but had disclosed it all and had donated the excess each year to charity. For all of 1981, Hatch earned $46,330 in honoraria, keeping $29,700 and donating $16,630 to charity. Garn earned $48,000 and kept all of it.

Critics said fairness had taken flight before Reaganomics and a self-indulgent Congress, replaced by old-fashioned greed. But apologists were nonplussed. Instead of seeking shared sacrifice, they defended politics as usual, saying all that mattered was that *your* ox didn't get gored.

The *Washington Post* ran an article on "Pork Barrel Politics," noting that Hatch issued a press release praising Reagan's proposed cuts of $40 billion in domestic programs, and–on the same day–a second press release calling for full annual funding of the Central Utah Project, a multi-billion-dollar water reclamation system. Carter Clews, director of communications for the Senate Republican Conference, sent the *Post* article and a cover letter to other newspapers, insisting that such priorities were a *virtue:*

> "Economy," wrote the great fiscal conservative Edmund Burke, "is a distributive virtue, and consists not in saving but selection. Mere parsimony is not economy." As the enclosed article . . . points out, modern fiscal conservatives like Senator Orrin Hatch are putting Burke's principles to work for the American people. While cutting

the waste from the federal budget, Majority senators continue to fulfill their primary duty—the protection of the interests of their constituencies.

Chairing Hatch's 1982 campaign was a bright, earnest, young insurance executive named Mike Leavitt, who would be elected Utah's governor in ten years. He was the son of one of Utah's best-known state legislators, Dixie Leavitt of Cedar City, and anxious to do well in his own venture into the political arena.

Given the widespread perception that Wilson was a nice guy, Leavitt strongly counseled Hatch not to provoke public sympathy by getting rough. Periodically Hatch told Leavitt, "I'm going to kill the wimp." It always elicited a frustrated groan from Leavitt—until he finally caught on that Hatch was joking to get a rise out of him. Hatch, in fact, liked Wilson and privately admitted that he did not relish running against him.

Wilson had a reputation as an honest mayor of Salt Lake City, and the city treasury enjoyed a budget surplus. While Wilson matched Hatch on most issues of special interest to Utahns, he supported the Equal Rights Amendment, affirmative action programs to help minorities, and union organizing rights for city workers.

Wilson also believed Reagan and Congress should have cut the taxes of industry rather than individuals, to provide quicker job creation. The average citizen "took it right in the teeth" with the tax package, which Wilson believed favored the rich. "And it's not doing anything to stimulate the economy." History would prove Wilson wrong on the latter score. Reagan's economic program in fact resulted in almost nine years of economic growth—the longest peacetime expansion in U.S. history.

Early in January, a poll commissioned by the *Salt Lake Tribune* showed Hatch leading Wilson 51-40 percent, with 9 percent undecided. Both candidates were strong in their own parties; the election would likely be decided among independent voters, who were split evenly between them.

During the first half of the year, most of the Hatch-Wilson sparring was at long distance. Hatch made frequent forays to the state but was still busy in Washington. Wilson also journeyed to the capital, garnering nearly $100,000 at a two-hundred-dollar-a-head fund-raiser in May. Among the guests were actor Robert Redford, also a Utahn and strong Wilson supporter, and a number of Hatch's Senate colleagues including Ted Kennedy, Gary Hart, and Robert Byrd, now minority leader.

Wilson had powerful Democratic backers in the state, notably Governor Scott Matheson, popular former governor Calvin Rampton, who chaired Wilson's campaign, and former Senator Frank Moss, still smarting from Hatch's licking six years earlier.

Moss's return to the campaign trail for another Utahn was bitter-sweet. He had remained in Washington and joined a law firm, but his history of championing consumer-oriented federal agencies was not the sort of background most lobby firms wanted. "I can't say I was stampeded by people . . . looking for my services," Moss acknowledged. While many former members found life after Congress less stressful and far more rewarding financially, Moss was not among them. "You never get over missing it," he said. "Time just sort of hangs heavy."

A sprinkling of outside Democrats visited Utah in Wilson's behalf, but most big-name Democrats were liberals who would have turned off Utah voters. Wilson could not begin to match the political firepower parading through the Beehive State for Hatch. Just a week after Wilson announced in January 1982, Vice President Bush told a Salt Lake reception that Hatch was one of the five or ten most influential senators. "Along with his adherence to principle, he has the ability to get the job done."

Secretary of the Interior James Watt spoke in Utah at least three times, once saying the "Eastern elite" regarded the West as their private "vacation land" and wanted to prevent development of its resources. "The wealth of a people comes from the land, and our Eastern friends don't realize that," said Watt.

Various other cabinet officers and Republican senators also visited Utah to help GOP candidates. But by far the biggest gun in Hatch's arsenal was the same one that had helped pulverize his opponents in 1976: Ronald Reagan. The president made two stops in Utah during the campaign.

Although the parade of outsiders played to the charge that Hatch was more concerned about national issues than Utah issues, their marquee value was enormous, reinforcing the campaign's portrayal of Hatch as an indispensable part of the Reagan revolution.

The Evans-Novak Political Report for April 13, 1982, said Hatch was "in big trouble" against Wilson. It cited the anger of some right-to-life groups over Hatch's constitutional amendment on abortion, considered a "sellout" which would put the issue in the hands of state and federal legislators rather than banning abortion outright. However, despite Utah's general conservatism, the issue did not resonate as strongly in the state as outsiders assumed. Because the dominant LDS church saw abortion as permissible in cases of rape, incest, or a threat to the mother's life, the position of most Utahns on the issue was more equivocal than that held by many pro-lifers.

During their state convention on July 10, Democrats slugged away at GOP economic policies that were costing people their jobs, businesses, and the opportunity to purchase homes. "My Republican opponent," said Wilson, "has voted right down the line for every unfair tax cut and loophole—the greatest transfer of wealth to the rich in the history of the United States."

Wilson failed to slow Hatch's juggernaut. The senator was campaigning in Utah on weekends and still benefitting from favorable headlines out of Washington, notably Senate passage of his constitutional amendment to balance the federal budget. The amendment passed the Senate August 4 by 69-31, but died when it fell short of the necessary two-thirds vote in the House.

When the Equal Rights Amendment finally expired on June 30, three states short of the thirty-eight needed for ratification, Hatch again grabbed headlines. "Most everybody in Utah is for equal rights for women," explained Hatch, but not for a constitutional amendment "that would convey massive power to the federal government over everybody's lives." He promised to work for such rights "within the framework of the Constitution."

Near the end of August, Wilson's campaign began running a series of harder-hitting radio ads than before, which threatened to tarnish Wilson's nice-guy image. The ads suggested improbably that Hatch cared more for the federal government than for Utah.

Hatch had raised nearly $1.9 million from January through June 1982 and spent 81 percent of it during that time, according to an analysis by *Congressional Quarterly*. Wilson had raised $316,000 during the first six months and spent 78 percent of it. Incumbents like Hatch who spent most of their money early, said *Congressional Quarterly*, could "prevent a challenger from developing momentum or even discourage the challenge altogether."

Some of Hatch's money had been used to soften his image. A series of TV ads showed him at home in Vienna, playing with the dog, Sir Reginald, in the yard and talking with his children in the kitchen. After mid-year, Hatch also started taking off the gloves, mentioning Wilson by name for the first time in the campaign.

"Let's assume that Ted goes back to Washington and he really means to be a moderate, as he says he is," Hatch told an interviewer. "He walks into the Democratic caucus, which is 80 percent left-wing liberal. Where do you think he's going to end up?" Democratic members must "play ball" with the Democratic majority or "you're dead. You won't be on the committees you need and you won't get anything you need on the [Senate] floor or anywhere else."

As fall arrived in Utah, Wilson's last chance to overtake Hatch appeared to be a series of face-to-face debates that began September 25 in Park City.

Hatch stressed that Utahns had a big investment in him and that he had kept his 1976 campaign pledges: "You paid a price to educate me, and I've done what I said I'd do." Hatch mentioned his support of fiscal conservatism, a balanced budget, and a strong national defense among other issues.

Wilson countered: "We need a workhorse for a change; get rid of the show horse." Hatch's accomplishments proved that Hatch had a "national agenda," he charged, and not a Utah agenda. Hatch had shown little interest in Senate committees dealing with energy and natural resources—issues vital to a state that was two-thirds owned by the federal government.

Hatch defended Reagan's economic plan, saying it needed more time to work. Electing Wilson and other Democrats, he added, would return the United States to a system of "tax tax, spend spend, and promise promise." Wilson pointed out that Hatch had voted for the Reagan budget with its record deficit. What was the difference between "a big-spending conservative and a big-spending liberal"?

On October 11 they squared off in Logan, just days after news that the nation's unemployment rate had hit 10.1 percent. Students booed during Hatch's entrance and cheered Wilson. "That was a little unnerving," recalled Hatch, "but otherwise I felt good throughout the debate."

Wilson again called Hatch a "show horse" and not a workhorse. Hatch pounced. "*Nobody's* outworked me in six years, not one senator," said Hatch, steaming. "I have authored and supported legislation that has cut taxes, reduced federal spending, decreased government fraud and waste, strengthened the nation's economy, and encouraged American industry." Hatch noted that labor leaders and the Democratic National Committee had designated him their number one target for defeat, "so I must be doing something right."

Hatch also defended his record for Utah: "My behind-the-scenes efforts may not have landed me on the headlines of every Utah newspaper, but they did put me at the forefront of every battle." Hatch had opposed basing the MX in Utah, resisted establishing a nuclear waste dump in southern Utah, and helped lead the Sagebrush Rebellion, resulting in more favorable policies by the Bureau of Land Management.

Other debates followed over the next nine days. Both sides predictably claimed victory, but clearly Wilson had failed to deliver a knockout blow. Then, with victory seemingly within his grasp, Hatch seemed intent on throwing it away in their final bout.

The event was on Hatch's home turf, the BYU campus, on October 20. Hatch had only to protect his lead to win the election, now less than two weeks away. Throughout 1982 he had heeded warnings from campaign chairman Mike Leavitt not to get rough with Wilson and not to try to "win" debates, but simply to hold his own. Although restive with the restraint, Hatch agreed the strategy was necessary to counter an image fostered by critics that he was mean-spirited. Then Hatch threw caution to the wind at BYU–and paid dearly for it.

Defending Reaganomics, Hatch insisted the president was a compassionate man: "He has my support and I can tell you this. If you want a future let's not go to socialism. Let's not risk redistributing the wealth." When some audience members booed, Hatch added, "Sorry if I've offended some of our Democrats." Wilson took the comment personally, charging that Hatch had labelled his economic proposals socialist.

More damagingly, Hatch offended teachers and their largest union, the National Education Association, which numbered 13,000 in its Utah Education Association. He did so while defending tuition tax credits for parents whose children attend private schools–a proposal pushed by Reagan but hotly opposed by the NEA and by Wilson, a former teacher, because of what they claimed would be its impact on funding for public schools.

"I can tell you what we are concerned about [in Washington] is that the teachers have been organized into the largest white collar union in the country, maybe in the world, in the National Education Association," said Hatch, opening his mouth wide and preparing to insert his foot. "And they are more concerned about wages and fringe benefits, which I think have to be part of their concern, than I think they are really about education."

That evening Hatch acknowledged privately that he had "made some inarticulate comments" about the NEA. Most of the BYU audience had given him a standing ovation at the end of his wrap-up, but Hatch wrote, "I felt I had won the debate but maybe lost the war."

The president of the Utah Education Association, Hurley Hansen, heatedly said the senator owed teachers an apology for his "ill-informed remarks about teachers and their concern about education." If Hatch really believed teachers were more concerned about wages and fringe benefits than educating children, said Hurley, "then he doesn't know teachers."

Hatch immediately issued a formal statement saying his criticism was aimed at NEA lobbyists, not at individual teachers. "I did not, in any way, mean to suggest that public school teachers believe wages and benefits come first. I am sorry I was misunderstood. I wholeheartedly stand behind our public school teachers." Hatch's campaign also sent out letters of explanation to every public school teacher in Utah.

A majority of teachers probably were with Wilson no matter what

Hatch did, but the last thing he wanted was to galvanize them into frenzied activity in the crucial closing days.

On Wednesday, October 27, six days before the election, Democrats rallied in the lobby of the Rio Grande Station for a get-out-the-vote drive. Governor Matheson chided Hatch's technique of having prominent politicians "slip into our state on a turnstile basis," forcing Wilson to fight a good part of the national Republican power structure as well as Hatch.

On Friday, October 29, right on cue, Air Force One landed at Salt Lake International Airport. Down the ramp came President Reagan—for the second time in the Utah campaign—as part of a five-state swing through the Mountain West.

To twelve thousand partisans at the Salt Palace, Reagan vowed that the United States "will lead the way out of this worldwide recession." Standing before a huge American flag, with thousands of small flags being waved by audience members, Reagan added that critics "say our economy is on its knees. Well, you know something: If the economy is on its knees, that's quite an improvement, because two years ago it was flat on its back." Without Hatch and other Utah delegation members, said Reagan, "we could not have made the progress we have."

His speech was followed by a long rendition of "The Battle Hymn of the Republic" by a 240-voice chorale and Utah's own Osmond Brothers. Outside the Salt Palace, a hastily assembled protest demonstration was underway. One man, dressed in depression-era garb, held aloft a sign: "Earth to Reagan: All is not well."

Hatch had introduced the president. When Reagan reached the podium, he grabbed Hatch's left hand and raised it in the air. The scene became Hatch's final campaign television spot.

The last poll by Hatch's organization probably summarized the entire campaign: Hatch had started out with a 35 percent disapproval rating and Wilson with 7 percent. At the end of the campaign, Hatch's negative rating was 31 percent—and Wilson's had shot past him to 34 percent.

"The biggest single factor was the economy," said one of Hatch's pollsters, Dan Jones. Wilson had tried to make the election a referendum on Reagan as much as on Hatch. In Utah it was a losing strategy. Voters had faith that better times were ahead, as Reagan and Hatch promised.

Although Wilson apparently had difficulty coping with Hatch's money, he later acknowledged to Hatch that funding had not been a problem. Millions of dollars in "soft" money from unions had gushed into Wilson's campaign, paying the salaries of dozens if not scores of full-time political operatives and underwriting phone banks, graphics and signs, door-to-door canvassing, and driving voters to the polls. However, because of a loophole in federal election law—which clearly favored Democrats, who routinely got over 95 percent of union donations—none of it had to be reported.

Meanwhile, Hatch received so much money from out-of-state PACs that *Newsweek* magazine dubbed him "Foreign Orrin." At one point, Hatch wrote privately, the money was coming in so fast he was "having trouble turning off the spigot."

In addition to the massive union efforts, Wilson officially spent $2.3 million on the campaign, a huge sum for Utah and about $4.35 for every voter. But Hatch nearly doubled it, spending $4.3 million—$8.13 for every vote cast and over $13 for every vote received. Hatch's money included nearly $1 million from PACs, mostly representing businesses. Hatch's was the eighth most expensive congressional campaign in 1982 and the single most expensive per capita. It was also the most costly political campaign Utah had seen to that point.

On election day, Orrin and Elaine voted, then went to the Jordan River Temple. In the afternoon Hatch drove around Salt Lake Valley to thank volunteers staffing get-out-the-vote phone banks in a dozen locations. Early in the evening, the day was marred by a telephoned death threat against Hatch. Two Salt Lake detectives hovered over him for the rest of the evening, frustrated as Hatch waded into crowds of well-wishers at the Hotel Utah.

Soon after the polls closed it was apparent Hatch was headed for a big win. The final result was a landslide: 58-41. Wilson conceded just before 10 P.M., with only a small portion of the vote counted, praising Hatch for running an honorable campaign. Hatch was a gracious winner, saying Wilson belonged on "the first string" and had run a tough and good campaign. Hatch also held a sleeping granddaughter aloft for cameras and praised his father Jesse, now seventy-eight, who had hand-made campaign lawn signs.

The Hatches left the hotel in separate cars, twelve-year-old Jess riding with a group of young people. When Orrin and Elaine arrived home at 1:15 A.M., Jess wasn't there. With the death threat still fresh on their minds, they waited an increasingly anxious half hour, then called the police. Fifteen minutes later Jess walked in. He had gone for a late-night snack.

Three weeks later Hatch was playing basketball with Jess on a blacktop court next to their garage in Vienna. "We played a number of one-on-one games and he is getting better," wrote Hatch. "But I made sure I beat him each game."

Suddenly Hatch felt an excruciating pain about four inches above his right ankle, as though someone had slugged him with a baseball bat. He hobbled into the house and elevated the leg for the rest of the day with ice on it. He had severed his Achilles tendon and would still be in a cast and on crutches when Vice President Bush swore him in for his second term in January.

Among numerous get-well wishes was a hand-written note on Salt Lake City letterhead from Wilson, dated December 8.

Dear Orrin,

Sorry to hear of your basketball injury! I'll have to admit my own physical condition was not improved in the long campaign. I hope you are recovering quickly.

I would like to express my best to you and your family, thank you for your graciousness on election night, and wish you a joyous Christmas.

Sincerely,
Ted

14

Family Matters

FIFTEEN-YEAR-OLD SCOTT HATCH was in the kitchen with his mother when the phone rang. Another teenager was on the line. "Are you ready for the fathers and sons camp-out?" came the excited question. "Nah," answered Scott. "My father can't go."

Hanging up, he turned to Elaine and said softly, "I don't *have* a father—really."

More than a decade later, Elaine vividly remembered how helpless she felt then, and tears came again.

"When Orrin went to law school, someone remarked that 'the law is a jealous mistress.' The Senate is the same," said Elaine. "The first time Orrin ran, he said, 'When I win we'll have every weekend off to go see the historic sites in the East. Five years later I asked him, 'When are those weekend outings going to start?'"

Hatch's hectic schedule—traveling back and forth to Utah, fronting for Reagan, spearheading floor fights on important issues, speaking throughout the United States on behalf of GOP candidates and other causes, all the while attending to heavy Senate duties—meant that his family, though unquestionably first in his heart, did not come first in his schedule. Hatch, who cared passionately about his children, struggled constantly with the challenging reality of being at best a weekend father when he really wanted daily continuity. He was never completely successful at juggling fast enough or hard enough to give his children the kind of time he longed to give them—and they longed to have. But he never pretended, even to himself, that it wasn't important or that his limitations didn't hurt deeply.

Returning to Vienna late one night when Alysa was nine, he found a misspelled but heartfelt note on his dresser from her:

DEAR DAD, THANK YOU VERY MUCH FOR THE STAMPS. I LOVE YOU VERY MUCH, I'M SO GLAD THAT YOUR MY DAD . . . I WISH YOU WOULD SEND MORE TIME WITH US. . . . LOVE, ALYSA

Hatch recalled a familiar Mormon aphorism, "No other success can compensate for failure in the home," and his conscience tugged at him.

That year, 1978, Hatch soberly took stock of his children. Brent, then twenty, had given them sleepless nights as a rebellious teenager but had worked through that stage, attended Brigham Young University for one year, and was serving a Mormon mission in New York. Eighteen-year-old Marcia had graduated from both high school and seminary—daily religious instruction for LDS adolescents—and was attending college at BYU.

Scott, a handsome and well-built sixteen-year-old, was finding new identification with his father by taking up amateur boxing. Elaine, concerned lest Scott struggle with the same issues as Brent had, let Orrin know when intervention was timely.

The three younger children—Kimberly (thirteen), Alysa (nine), and Jess (eight)—all seemed well-adjusted and happy.

Hatch had grown adept at including the children in activities, such as golfing, whenever he could. Occasionally he took a child with him when he spoke out of town, rotating the privilege to give each child one-on-one time. Hatch also tried hard to attend the boys' ball games and the girls' musical events.

Following the grueling 1976 campaign, Orrin and Elaine flew to Hawaii for recuperation. Later that year they went again and took Brent and Marcia—their two oldest—with them. The other Hatch children got their Hawaii trips with Hatch alone when he returned to the islands to speak. Although Elaine enjoyed traveling, she seldom went on trips with Orrin because she felt her absence was too disruptive to the children.

Politicians' children are sometimes pressured to maintain a picture-perfect image. In contrast, the Hatches encouraged candor in their youngsters, despite its occasional backlash. Arriving home late one evening after winning a Senate battle, Hatch, oblivious that he was interrupting, began recounting his day. An exasperated son cut him off in mid-sentence. "Look, Dad, being a United States Senator doesn't cut any mustard around here!"

"He *says* he listens to us," said Elaine. "But the kids and I would like to have more of his time. Sometimes, to make sure we've really got his attention, we say, 'Look me in the eye.' The Senate is just *part* of Orrin's life," Elaine continued. "I want him to remember he has a life here too."

Looking back on the teenage-intensive years she confessed candidly: "It was hard not having Orrin around more, and the children and I really resented it at times. But we never doubted his love for us."

Elaine cheerfully managed the chores of the house and yard in Hatch's absence, acknowledging, "I'd really like him to be more energetic at home," but settling for what she could get—an occasional Saturday morning when Orrin would bake bread, even grinding the wheat in an electric grinder.

With Hatch frequently on the road, Elaine made the six children her top priority, dealing creatively and energetically with their needs, deftly maintaining schedules, tracking schoolwork, cheering their efforts, and meting out needed discipline with a usually sure hand. Hatch frequently praises Elaine, calling her a "pioneer" who always kept their family productive and happy despite his absence. He attributes her homemaking skills and pioneer spirit to her early upbringing.

Growing up in a Utah farm family, Elaine learned habits of frugality that never left her. When one guest started to throw away a plastic gallon milk container, Elaine gently reminded, "It still has milk in it." It did—about two tablespoons worth. During Washington's suffocating summers, most residents who had air conditioning ran it full-tilt. But given the faintest breeze or break in a heat wave, and the air conditioning went off at the Hatch house, windows went up, and room fans went on.

Hatch's frugal background showed up in different ways. Sensitive about clothes as a youth when family money was scarce, he became known as one of the sharpest dressers in Congress. However, his crisp, high-collar shirts didn't get that way at the corner laundry. Elaine ironed them by hand on a board set up in their second-floor master bedroom.

Hatch purchased his clothes for a fraction of the amount spent by most senators. In Salt Lake City he shopped at Mr. Mac's, one of Utah's least exclusive men's store, with locations across the valley and a proprietor who hawked his suits on TV with frequent two-for-one specials. Mac Christensen kept Hatch supplied with the latest designer ties, dozens of which bulged out of his crammed walk-in closet. Hatch occasionally ordered relatively inexpensive, handmade shirts from the Orient—size 15-by-35—to fit his unusual combination of slender neck and long arms.

Utah's restaurant equivalent of Mr. Mac's was a chain of eateries called Chuck-A-Rama. Adults could get a bounteous buffet dinner there for $6.99—the best bargain in town. Chuck-A-Rama, not surprisingly, was one of Hatch's favorite Utah restaurants.

One evening the family invited a reporter for dinner at their home in Vienna. As the salad dressing was being passed around the table, Hatch requested nonfat French dressing. That brought a quip from Elaine: "I've told Orrin he can have nonfat milk, nonfat margarine, and nonfat salad dressing. But he cannot have a nonfat wife."

Secure and self-possessed, Elaine led the laughter. Her weight went up and down as she tried various diets and other regimens. "I have another favorite saying," Elaine offered. "Can you imagine a world without men? No crime—and a lot of happy fat women."

Elaine was intelligent, well-read, and highly popular with peers and had been a leader of the LDS women's auxiliary everywhere they lived. In Vienna, she belonged to a neighborhood Bible study group.

She also set an example of reaching out to those in need, taking meals to neighbors and church members and encouraging the downcast. Though warmhearted and loving, Elaine has always been less demonstrative than Orrin, who is noted for saying "I love you" and offering reassuring hugs to family, friends, and even casual acquaintances needing a morale boost.

Most members of Congress considered Washington's social scene part of the job, but Hatch usually spent free evenings at home in Vienna, studying issues or reading for pleasure.

One reporter astutely observed that guest-lists in "Embassy Row functions or stuffy Georgetown dinner parties" rarely included the names of Tip O'Neill, Orrin Hatch, business lobbyist Charls Walker, or AFL-CIO executive Kenneth Young. All four, he wrote, "appreciate the use of power here and all exercise their influence while shunning the social circuit."

Elaine, on the other hand, enjoyed such events. They provided pleasant moments that helped compensate for a lifestyle that was notoriously hard on marriages and families. In December 1979 they attended the annual White House Christmas party for members of Congress and their partners, dancing to the Peter Duchin orchestra.

"I have to admit," Hatch wrote afterwards, "I really don't enjoy the social scene and whirl [as others do]. . . . I don't know whether there's something wrong with me or something wrong with them."

As Hatch's power and prominence grew, however, he found himself hosting Hollywood celebrities lobbying for favorite causes. Among them were such stars as Elizabeth Taylor, Linda Evans, and Victoria Principal.

Principal, whose father had osteoarthritis, chaired the National Arthritis Foundation. She was then starring in the TV series Dallas. She met with Hatch several times on Capitol Hill and sent him a pair of monogrammed handkerchiefs for his birthday.

"She is extraordinarily beautiful," he wrote after one visit. "Being around her gave me a little insight as to how David could fall for Bathsheba. . . . Personally, I'm glad I have Elaine."

Elaine was, in fact, Hatch's perfect complement. No Nancy Reagan, she concentrated her considerable talents and energies not on overtly furthering her husband's career, but on eliminating as many obstacles and distractions as possible so he could pour his full energies into achieving his professional goals.

Elaine remembered advice she had received as a bride: "Make your home as comfortable and peaceful as possible, so that your husband will want to be there." She created wholesome cheeriness throughout the house. The ranch-style kitchen was decorated with favorite aphorisms and quotations, such as one by Alexis de Tocqueville, a perceptive Frenchman who visited America when it was still a young Republic:

> I sought for the greatness and genius of America in her commodious harbors and her ample rivers, and it was not there; in her fertile fields and boundless prairies, and it was not there; in her rich gold mines and her vast world commerce, and it was not there. Not until I went to the churches of America and heard her pulpits aflame with righteousness did I understand the secret of her genius and power. America is great because she is good, and if America ever ceases to be good, America will cease to be great.

Given Hatch's passionate commitment to his family but very real time constraints, his peace of mind and productivity required a strong, willing partner tending the home fires while he was off slaying dragons. There was nothing phony or forced about his frequent tributes, in public and private, to his wife and children.

For Hatch, Elaine was the ideal wife: content to forego an outside career; skilled and fulfilled in the home arts; a model of compassionate service to her family, church, and neighbors; and wise and tough enough to maintain a home and rear six healthy children with only sporadic help from her peripatetic husband.

Two dogs were important members of the household at different times while the children were growing up. In Pittsburgh the family included a ferocious-looking but extremely gentle bulldog named Mahonri Moriancumer. A decade later, during the summer of 1979, a friend came to Hatch's Washington office with a special delivery: a schnauzer puppy. When Hatch arrived home at 8:15 P.M. with the furry surprise, the children were thrilled. Elaine was not. She felt like the family's anchor, and now her itinerant husband had brought home one more barnacle to weigh her down.

"Elaine said she was going to leave home if I kept him," Hatch recorded, hoping her unhappiness would pass. "I felt bad, but the kids were just overjoyed with the pup. I think every little boy and girl should have a dog. I really want Jess to have this one." The puppy was royally uncooperative the first night, whimpering and barking without letup from its exile in the basement.

"I've made it clear to the children that they're going to have to clean up after it, train it, and do everything they possibly can to make it more acceptable to their mother. I believe they will," Hatch added optimistically, then admitted, "Elaine is mad at me because she knows that I would do that if I was home, but I will never be home at the right time."

The schnauzer stayed—and so did Elaine. They named him Sir Reginald and soon he was accompanying the family on jogs around the neighborhood.

During the summer of 1986 when Sir Reginald was seven, he achieved the dubious family distinction of being named one of five finalists out of seventy congressional canines in a benefit contest sponsored by Purina Dog Chow to choose the "Top Dog on Capitol Hill." Reggie won a certificate for five hundred pounds of dog food, which Hatch sent to the humane society.

Reggie's application said, "I know I'm a member of the Capitol Hill family because my master lives a dog's life. His staff keeps him on a tight leash, he's collared by lobbyists, the press howls over controversial votes, and he's had some real bowwows for opponents."

Hatch was torn as the older children matured in his absence and reached milestones in their lives, reminding him of too many memories forfeited. His poetry is sprinkled with joy over each son and daughter. In 1981, he wrote: "Last evening I realized how wonderful my family really is—Brent through Jess, one and all, dear to me. I owe [Jess] more than I am giving. He needs me and I am seldom there. The Senate engulfs . . ."

As a junior senator, still paying his dues and fighting for his place in the sun, Hatch had made some tough choices about giving his profession top priority and nearly all his time. But as the youngest son, Jess, irrevocably left childhood behind, Hatch had a little more control over his schedule, and he deliberately pulled away from the "engulfing" Senate for some precious times with this last child.

At the end of January 1979, just after Hatch had lost his election for GOP Senatorial Campaign Committee chair, he resolved to concentrate more on his family and immediately followed up on that resolve. On February 1, he left Capitol Hill while the Senate was still in session—a rarity for him. He was bound for the Flint Hill School in Vienna with eight-year-old Jess. The event was one relished by some fathers and dreaded by others: the annual Cub Scout Pinewood Derby.

Fathers were supposed to "guide" Cubs in carving and constructing their five-ounce race cars, but in reality, fathers were notorious for taking over the job. Hatch had become involved late on Jess's project, rationalizing that Jess would learn more by doing it himself anyway. The boy had whittled away at his chunk of wood until it weighed a mere two ounces—less than half the prescribed weight. Hatch drilled holes and filled them with lead to get the car to regulation weight. But there was little he could do to improve its appearance. The box-shaped Hatch entry was painted a sludgy black with wavy, uneven racing stripes. Even the wheels were gobbed with paint, raising serious doubts whether the car would make it to the bottom of the inclined racetrack at any speed.

"Jess was so upset with the final result that he didn't even want to enter," recalls Hatch. "I felt so sorry for him. Jess didn't know what to do."

But Hatch did. He contacted a man known as a pinewood derby expert. The man promptly came up with an unusual set of wheels, lathe-turned and shaved until there was only one-sixteenth of an inch of tread on the tires. The design cut friction to a bare minimum.

When Hatch and Jess arrived at Flint Hill, they endured knowing smirks from other fathers and sons as they weighed in. Their entry looked like a Model-T in a lot full of Ferraris and Porsches. Jess was in the third heat. Shortly before it began, Hatch carefully sprayed graphite on all four custom wheels. The cars raced two at a time, and most finished within a half-foot of each other.

Then it was Jess's turn. His car began precisely at the same time as a sleek, beautifully crafted silver racer—and beat it by more than two feet, to considerable oohing and aahing from the crowd—and astonishment from Jess, who hadn't comprehended the meaning of the wheels. In race after race, the result was the same, as Jess's eyes grew bigger and bigger.

Finally two cars were left in competition: the boxy Hatch entry and a flashy red car belonging to an engineer and his son who had won the derby several years running. Jess's car won—by about six inches—and he walked away with the grand prize.

"That was one of the greatest nights of Jess's life—and of my life," says Hatch. "There are very few experiences I'd trade for the thrill of watching Jess win that derby."

Then Hatch's pressing schedule took over again. By March 31 the next year, Hatch was writing, abashed, that the previous weekend was his first at home in almost four months.

But Hatch never gave up struggling for balance. Sundays at home—rare in election seasons—always included a three-hour block of church meetings followed by a family dinner and, often, watching football or basketball on television with his sons.

When Jess was thirteen, he accompanied his father to Cape Canaveral on a Morton Thiokol corporate jet to watch the blast-off of the orbiter Columbia carrying a research laboratory into space. Afterwards they walked the Atlantic beach and swam in the hotel pool.

Hatch—realizing with each year how fast the time with his older children had flown—attended Jess's high school basketball games whenever he was in town, just as his father Jesse had always attended *his* games. During Jess's senior year, he stood six-foot-three, played guard, and was captain of his team at James Madison High School.

On one particular night near year-end, Madison was playing Theodore Roosevelt High School. Jess poured in twenty-two points toward his team's win of 71-56. He found his picture in the *Washington Post* sports section the next morning.

Hatch was proudest, not of his son's shooting but of his son's self-control. "The kid guarding Jess was a terrific player, clearly their best," recalled Hatch. "However, he kept kicking, elbowing, hitting, and shoving Jess all night. After the game, the referee said he was amazed Jess hadn't punched the kid in the face. But Jess really stayed cool and never struck back. He basically answered the kid by scoring twenty-two points. I was really proud of my son."

Senators had a generous travel allowance and Hatch visited Utah nearly every other weekend, invariably returning to Washington feeling renewed. Whenever possible, he stayed at his parents' little home in Midvale. They kept a special bedroom furnished for Hatch, complete with a large formal photograph of him, arms folded and looking as though he had just conquered the world.

On one flight home, Hatch's gratitude welled up for his parents' unfailing emotional support, and he penned a poetic tribute to his mother:

> This saintly one, now wrinkled, with white hair,
> But sparkling with wit and humor and good grace,
> With so much love.
>
> . . .
>
> Throughout the years, and right into eternity
> Where loved ones meet again
> And further love is shown—forevermore.

Hatch is a frequent source for Washington journalists. . .

—Behind a forest of microphones.

With fellow columists (*from left*) Pat Buchanan, Robert Novak, Hatch, Al Hunt, and Mark Shields.

—Being interviewed by Lee Davidson, Washington, D.C., correspondent of the *Deseret News.*

—Appearing with Leslie Stahl on CBS's *Face the Nation.*

—With others, including NPR's Nina Totenberg, who later broke the Anita Hill story, and moderator Marvin Kalb on NBC's *Meet the Press.*

1981 Family photo: (*from left*) Alysa, Scott, Marcia, Orrin, Jess, Elaine, Brent, Mia, and Kimberly.

Anna Chennault spurs Hatch's fund-raising for 1982 campaign. Fellow Utah
Senator Jake Garn and Elaine join reception line.

President Reagan, in Utah days before the 1982 election, helped to ensure
Hatch's victory.

A political rally on the eve of winning a second Senate term—with a little help from a friend.

After a basketball injury Hatch limps into 1983, taking the oath for his second term from Vice President Bush.

Wayne LaPierre of the National Rifle Association presents Hatch with a token of appreciation for leadership in fighting gun-control measures.

Reagan signs a bill, watched by: (*from left*) Senators Thurmond, Hatch, Helms, Rep. Conable, Vice President Bush, Senators DeConcini, and Baker.

Hatch with his aging parents, ca. 1990.

Baking bread on a Saturday morning—the closest Hatch came to doing household chores.

Cartoonist Pat Bagley's takeoff on just one of the labels given Hatch by the media. (Used by permission.)

Actress Victoria Principal, prepared to testify before Hatch's committee as chair of the National Arthritis Foundation.

Touring an industrial site in Utah. (Photo by Thiokol Photographic Section. Used by permission.)

Hatch joins in welcoming President Reagan at a joint session of Congress in 1986.

Hatch and Sir Reginald agree that the Senate can be a dog's life.

15

Tackling
Women's Issues

THE NINETY-EIGHTH CONGRESS BEGAN in January 1983. Republican hopes for broadening the Reagan revolution had been blasted in the November elections. Reagan's active campaigning could not overcome recession and high unemployment. The GOP kept its 54-46 majority in the Senate but lost twenty-six seats in the House, more than double the average for midterm elections since World War II.

With the House solidly Democratic, the administration looked to Congress's "conservative coalition"—Republicans aligned with southern Democrats—to win approval for Reagan's initiatives.

But the coalition was weakening in 1982 and occasionally Hatch was blindsided by his own team when carrying the ball for the White House on Capitol Hill—by Reagan aides who refused to share responsibility for initiatives that proved unpopular.

Hatch was determined to be more independent during his second term. "I have to lead my own life and do my own things," he wrote privately. "I have to be the senator I need to be."

During 1983, Hatch crossed swords with the White House and Senate GOP leaders on a number of occasions. As the federal deficit headed for new heights, members of Congress had the choice of raising the statutory ceiling on the debt limit or watching the federal government grind to a halt.

When Hatch and some others said they wouldn't support lifting the debt ceiling, Majority Leader Baker said, "Boys, be prepared to stay here till Christmas."

"I *am* prepared," wrote Hatch in a memo to himself. "I think it's time we started to face these problems. I believe that Congress is institutionally incapable, without a balanced budget amendment, to really solve the financial problems of this country. We are creators of financial problems, not solvers of them."

Hatch became convinced that the Reagan defense budget was weighted too heavily in favor of strategic weapons. When Georgia Democrat Sam Nunn offered an amendment to defer production of twelve B-1 bombers in favor of upgrading conventional weapons, Hatch supported him even though Baker threatened to tell Utahns that Hatch's move could cost the state 4,500 defense-related jobs.

During the year, Hatch's fellow sagebrush rebel James Watt bit the dust. The embattled Interior chief already had made many enemies with his insensitive comments before he shot himself in the foot for the last time on September 21. Watt said a five-member commission had "every kind of mix you can have. I have a black, . . . a woman, two Jews, and a cripple. And we have talent."

"I have to admit his comments were tasteless," wrote Hatch. "But I hope this isn't the end of Jim Watt at Interior. He has been the best Secretary of Interior we have ever had." Reagan tried to help him ride out the storm, but Watt finally resigned on October 9.

Overseas, 1983 was also a difficult year for the United States. In September, the Soviet Union shot down a South Korean airliner that had strayed off course, killing 269 passengers and crew, including 61 Americans. In October, 241 Marines on a peacekeeping mission were killed in Beirut when a suicide terrorist drove a truckload of explosives into their headquarters as many slept.

Barely two days after the terrorist bombing in Beirut, six thousand U.S. Marines and Army rangers invaded the tiny Caribbean island of Grenada after a Cuban-backed junta seized power. Eighteen American soldiers were killed and another 115 wounded. Reagan said he had acted to protect the lives of a thousand Americans on the island.

The following month, violence struck much closer to home for Hatch and his colleagues. On November 7, a Monday, the Senate was scheduled to be in late session. During most of the evening, Hatch and other senatorial football fans would have been sitting in the second-floor cloakroom watching Monday Night NFL Football between votes. But a schedule change sent them home early.

That night a powerful bomb exploded right where the senators would have been sitting. A group calling itself the Armed Resistance Unit claimed responsibility, saying the bombing was to protest U.S. military actions in Lebanon and Grenada.

Hatch surveyed the damage the next day and was shocked at the force of the blast. "It blew out all the windows in the cloakroom as well as damaging the nearby archway," he said. "Had we been in session, I believe a number of us would have been killed. All the young clerks at the desk certainly would have been murdered. It was very sobering."

Waiting for Hatch as he began his second term was the constitutional proposal from the black lagoon: the Equal Rights Amendment. Killed many times, the ERA just wouldn't stay in its coffin. In ten years of coaxing—three times longer than any amendment ever added to the Constitution—the required thirty-eight states had refused to follow Congress's lead and ratify the ERA. But its proponents were back again.

During the ERA's last incarnation before the Senate, Constitution Subcommittee chairman Birch Bayh helped breathe three more years of life into the ERA, extending the state ratification deadline to June 1982. As Bayh's replacement, Hatch was expected to try to smother the reintroduced proposal. Instead he did just the opposite, giving the ERA its most extensive congressional airing, in a series of eleven hearings featuring expert witnesses on all sides of the issue.

Hatch also contributed personally to the dialogue by publishing a book, *The Equal Rights Amendment: Myths and Realities*. In 103 pages, he argued that "the burden properly lies with proponents of the Equal Rights Amendment to demonstrate what precisely the amendment means and why the 'parade of horrors' raised by opponents is not likely to occur."

The first congressional hearing in more than a decade on the potential impact of the ERA came before Hatch's subcommittee on May 26, 1983, and resulted in a dreadfully embarrassing public performance by Senator Paul Tsongas of Massachusetts. The freshman Democrat was a principal sponsor of the resurrected amendment and, in later years, a major contender for the presidency.

Tsongas arrived at the hearing prepared for more show than substance. Then he compounded that mistake in his opening remarks by arrogantly lecturing Chairman Hatch and his allies, saying "there is something unseemly about the male members of this body" deciding an issue of such import to women. "History does not treat well those who stand at the courthouse door. They are remembered by history as not part of the hope and solution of America, but [as] part of the fear and the darkness that reside in all of us."

Hatch felt his pulse quicken. He had planned to let Tsongas off easily. But, aroused by the challenge, he decided on the spot to use Tsongas as a foil to unmask what Hatch saw as the real intent behind the ERA: to force issue after issue to a liberal, unelected Supreme Court, where the ERA's backers had to convince only five justices at a time—as opposed to trying to persuade a majority of the people's 535 elected representatives in Congress. Tsongas, a forty-two-year-old Greek-American, had defeated Senator Edward Brooke in 1978 with the help of Ted Kennedy, who now squirmed helplessly on the panel as Hatch deftly dissected his protégé.

> Hatch: [Commentators] have stated that veterans preference programs would be unconstitutional under the Equal Rights Amendment. Would you agree with that?
>
> Tsongas: . . . Well, I do not think that that is for you or I to say. I mean, we have what is called the Supreme Court, which is in a position to resolve those particular matters. . . .
>
> Hatch: So, therefore, you would feel that [ERA] would overrule the Hyde amendment which would prohibit federal funding of abortion?
>
> Tsongas: I am telling you, Mr. Chairman, as I said before, that that issue would be resolved in the courts. . . .
>
> Hatch: Would you agree, then, that the ERA would certainly outlaw single-sex public schools and universities? . . .
>
> Tsongas: I do not know. I mean, I can see the arguments that would be made, and again you would have this resolved in the courts.

Tsongas, obviously feeling cornered, ironically pointed out over and over that complicated legal issues often have to be decided by the courts, the very point Hatch was trying to make.

After a colloquy on abortion and various other tangential issues, Hatch dragged Tsongas back to the ERA, leading him through more problem areas, including sex-based rates on insurance policies, fair housing laws, pregnancy leave (would new fathers also be given time off?), and sex education in public schools (would it be illegal to segregate classes by sex for such courses?). Again Tsongas was noncommittal.

Finally Tsongas began to get testy: "Mr. Chairman, why do we not call a spade a spade here?"

"Yes?" answered Hatch.

"What you are trying to do is to suggest that there are a whole host of questions which may go to the courts."

Hatch brightened:

> Exactly right, exactly right! . . . These are questions that are real; these are questions that are going to affect every American. These are questions that you need to answer as the chief sponsor of the Equal Rights Amendment. Look, I will skip over most of them. Let me just go to one . . .

Tsongas: If the Chairman was really serious about having—

Hatch: I am really serious.

Tsongas:—particularly detailed answers to these questions, the Chairman would have provided them to myself and to [the other main sponsor] Senator Packwood before the hearing. You knew damned well that these were specific issues—

Hatch: That is right.

Tsongas:—that no one coming here unprepared could answer. . . .

Hatch: Let me go to the military issue . . . again, not to embarrass you, Senator, but just to get your viewpoint. First, would the Equal Rights —

Tsongas:—If the Chairman was so interested in my viewpoint, why were these questions not submitted when we would have had a chance to review them and give you detailed answers?

Hatch: Well, in all the hearings I have ever held, we have never submitted questions to the witnesses in advance. . . . These are not difficult questions.

Tsongas: But I would be glad to get back to you—

Hatch: Senator, my gosh, this has been debated for 12 years—50 years, some people say. This is not something that is incomprehensible.

Tsongas continued to dance around the rest of Hatch's questions, each time saying he would supply a written answer. Near the end of Tsongas's ordeal, Hatch asked if the ERA meant women in the military would have to be assigned to combat units, the same as men. Tsongas said he had feelings about it but again demurred.

"Well, tell me your feelings," said Hatch. "That is all I want. You know, I am not going to hold you to it." As the audience laughed again, Hatch added, "Maybe the public will, but I will not."

A new word had been added to Capitol Hill's vocabulary: to be *Tsongasized* meant to have your ignorance paraded out for all to see.

After the Senate exchange, House Speaker Tip O'Neill appeared before the Civil and Constitutional Rights Subcommittee, House counterpart to Hatch's panel, to testify for the ERA. But when ranking Republican James Sensenbrenner of Wisconsin tried to lead O'Neill through a series of Hatchlike questions, O'Neill stood up and stomped out.

Representative Don Edwards of California, a leading ERA booster and House subcommittee chairman, announced that he too would hold a series of ERA hearings. "Who do you want to call as your witness?" Edwards asked Sensenbrenner.

"Paul Tsongas!" the feisty Sensenbrenner shot back.

Edwards slumped in his chair, looking stricken.

William F. Buckley called the Hatch-Tsongas exchange "marvelous," noting at one point Tsongas said he would prefer to talk instead about *Hatch's* constitutional amendment. "At that point," said Buckley, "Sen. Tsongas, to tell the truth, would have preferred changing the subject to the Falkland Islands crisis, the probable date of the end of the world, or the beautiful violet eyes of Elizabeth Taylor."

George F. Will said Hatch "simply asked Tsongas what the amendment means. This question caused Tsongas to show that he does not know and does not deeply care." Will said Tsongas's testimony "shows how persons preening themselves on their love of 'equality' play judicial roulette with sensitive social policies."

Many observers, including some of the ERA's feminist intellectual sponsors, believed that Hatch unmasked the paucity of the ERA's position as never before—in hearings as well as in writings and debate. His concern ranged over a multitude of issues. In an appendix to his book, Hatch listed fifty-eight varieties of federal, state, and local laws likely to be affected by the ERA. In the book's conclusion, Hatch wrote:

> One can only reasonably conclude that [the ERA's] words mean what they seem to mean—that no law establishing disparate treatment for men and women will be constitutional. . . . I do not believe that the American people are as cynical as some would suggest about the structure of traditional values that has evolved in our culture over a period of centuries relating to the roles of men and women, and the family, in our society. It is far from a perfect structure, but it is one in which our civilization has flourished and in which hundreds of millions of Americans, male and female, have found personal satisfaction and fulfillment. Its defects can and ought to be addressed, but with the scalpel of statutory revision, not the meat cleaver of the Equal Rights Amendment.

Finally, after ten years of trench warfare, many of Hatch's colleagues agreed enough was enough. On November 15, 1983, the House—traditionally the friendliest body toward the ERA—failed to pass the reintroduced amendment by six votes. The coffin lid slammed down again.

Hatch continued to be embroiled in the issue of abortion. Some right-to-life critics accused him of not being fervent enough in opposition, but in fact Hatch had always been horrified by abortion. Few issues in history had divided the nation so sharply, however, and Hatch was sure Congress would never pass a blanket prohibition. Instead he sought support for an approach that would at least substantially reduce the number of abortions.

The depth of Hatch's commitment no doubt was suspect to some critics because his moral philosophy was rooted in the LDS church, which opposed the Supreme Court's 1973 *Roe v. Wade* decision but was not in the front ranks of those fighting to overturn it.

Mormons believe every person lived in a premortal existence as a separate, intelligent being with a spirit body. The church teaches that human life—as opposed to *biological* life—begins when the spirit joins the physical body. But it is silent on exactly when the spirit and body come together. Thus, in the church's eyes, while abortion in most cases is a serious sin, it may not always be the willful taking of human life.

Hatch's first encounter with abortion came long before it was a burning national issue. He remembered the woman he had counseled when he was an impressionable young Mormon missionary in Ohio in the early 1950s. Talked into having an abortion and racked with guilt, she had been a recluse for many years. (See Chapter 2.)

Now, three decades later, he was powerfully moved by the testimony before Congress of the founder of a support group called WEBA — Women Exploited by Abortion. One of its founders, Nancyjo Mann, had also been talked into having an abortion, five and a half months into a normal pregnancy, after her husband deserted her and their two children. She said a leading OB-GYN in the Midwest cavalierly drew amniotic fluid from her and injected a saline solution through her abdomen. As soon as the needle went in, she said, "I hated myself."

"Once they put in the saline there's no way to reverse it. And for the next hour and a half I felt my daughter thrash around violently while she was being choked, poisoned, burned, and suffocated to death. I didn't know any of that was going to happen. And I remember talking to her and I remember telling her I didn't want to do this, I wished she could live. And yet she was dying and I remember her very last kick. . . ."

Mann, grief-stricken, left the hospital determined to warn others. She and another woman organized WEBA and, in ten months, ten thousand women in thirty-four states had joined their crusade.

"One psychological effect we see almost all the time is guilt," said Mann. "Others are suicidal impulses, a sense of loss, of unfulfillment. Mourning, regret and remorse. Withdrawal, loss of confidence in decision-making capabilities, . . . lowering of self-esteem. Preoccupation with death."

Two years before conducting abortion hearings, Hatch was brought up short on the subject by Kathryn Crosby, widow of singer Bing Crosby. They and several other prominent Republicans were meeting in New York City to plan a series of GOP fund-raising events across the country.

Over dinner at Trader Vic's, Crosby talked about her volunteer work with the Sisters of the Immaculate Conception. Hatch, trying to be conversational, said, "I'm probably the only Mormon endorsed by the National Council of Catholic Bishops, because of my stand on abortion." It was the wrong thing to say: Crosby was a convert to Catholicism and strongly disagreed with her church's position.

Crosby explained how she and Bing used to visit Baja, California, a vacation paradise where she spent her time working with poor Mexicans instead of socializing. She told of the horrors of watching innocent Mexican children being battered and neglected by parents who didn't want them to begin with. Crosby provided appointments with her own gynecologist for some of the women to get interuterine contraceptive devices.

Hatch listened and did not argue. He left Crosby with a stronger belief that all views should be heard and a better appreciation that there were well-intentioned arguments on both sides of the abortion issue.

In January 1981, Jesse Helms and fellow North Carolina Republican Senator John East had introduced a simple statute stating that human life exists from the moment of conception and merits the full protection of the law. Legal scholars, including Hatch, questioned the constitutionality of the bill, for a logical reason: Its passage would have nullified a Supreme Court ruling, *Roe v. Wade,* by a simple majority vote in Congress. When hearings were held in April, Hatch refused to cosponsor them because they were blatantly stacked in favor of the legislation: six of seven physicians invited to testify supported the bill's definition.

Instead, several months later, Hatch used his anti-abortion constitutional amendment as a vehicle to hold an exhaustive set of hearings, similar to his ERA hearings, with nearly seventy-five expert witnesses testifying in nine days. The hearings, chaired by Hatch in the Constitution Subcommittee, were praised by both pro-life and pro-choice forces for fairness. The Judiciary Committee approved Hatch's constitutional amendment early in 1982—the first time a committee of Congress had approved legislation to overturn *Roe v. Wade*—but the full Senate didn't vote on the measure before the ninety-seventh Congress adjourned.

Hatch reintroduced his proposed constitutional amendment in January 1983, the same month the ninety-eighth Congress convened. Its key clause: "A right to abortion is not secured by the Constitution. The Congress and the several States shall have concurrent power to restrict and prohibit abortion: *Provided,* That a provision of a law of a State which is more restrictive than a conflicting provision of a law of Congress shall govern."

In February, Hatch held two more days of hearings. In opening remarks, Charles Grassley, an Iowa Republican, noted earlier committee approval of the measure and told Hatch, "We all know that it would not have been possible without your leadership." Oregon's Packwood, the Senate's leading pro-choice figure, also testified, thanking Hatch for "the fairness with which you have conducted these hearings in the last Congress and in this Congress."

Packwood noted that most public opinion polls showed that a majority of Americans favored a woman's right to choose whether to have an abortion. "There is no . . . consensus in this country for a constitutional amendment to reverse *Roe v. Wade*," said Packwood, who also rehearsed familiar arguments about the suffering caused by illegal back-alley abortions when the practice was restricted.

Professor Laurence Tribe of the Harvard Law School, a frequent witness before Congress, testified that Hatch's states-rights approach was "profoundly misguided." Tribe said, given the politics of abortion, states in reality would have only one option: to impede it. More affluent women would simply go to less restrictive states if necessary, while some poor women wouldn't have that option.

Among those flatly opposing curbs on abortion was the American Medical Association, which testified that "women could potentially be denied a necessary medical procedure." The AMA said, "A woman who has determined that she cannot carry a pregnancy to term will still seek an abortion even if abortions are prohibited by law."

In the end, efforts by Hatch and other pro-life members of Congress to overturn *Roe v. Wade* came to naught. But Hatch, ever the optimist, gave the effort one more shot in 1984, hoping against hope that others would join the struggle to stop abortion if only they understood it as he did. This time he used the power of his pen instead of public hearings.

Hatch authored a sixteen-page booklet distilling what he had learned from the nation's leading experts. The publication, entitled "The Value of Life," was published and distributed by the National Committee for a Human Life Amendment. Its purpose was "to contrast some of the myths with the facts, to scrutinize the emptiness of pro-abortion slogans when exposed to the truth."

Some "myths" Hatch addressed in his booklet included:

Freedom of Choice: "The real question is not the freedom to choose, but freedom to choose *what?*" wrote Hatch. "If freedom of choice were itself a justification for choice, then individuals could justify stealing, or pushing drugs, selling pornography, or even killing another human, on the basis that they were free to choose to do so. . . . If we value freedom of choice, shouldn't we respect the choice the unborn child would obviously make—the choice to live?"

Supreme Court Error: Roe v. Wade overturned state laws and instituted "a more permissive policy than exists, or had ever existed, in any other nation except Communist China. . . . Even during the last months of pregnancy, after the child is capable of surviving outside the womb, the mother may obtain an abortion by simply alleging any impediment to her 'physical, emotional, or psychological . . . well-being.'" The Constitution is silent on abortion. Therefore the Supreme Court decision had no basis whatsoever in law, and states should have been left to regulate abortion.

Protecting the Mother's Life: "Every state prior to 1973 protected the life of the mother by law. Protecting the life of the mother has little or nothing to do with today's indulgent regime of abortion." Hatch said expert testimony showed that not more than 3 percent of all abortions were medically necessary, and 97 percent were in fact for reasons of convenience. In leading U.S. cities, including the nation's capital, there were more abortions than live births.

Unwanted Children: "What does 'unwanted' really mean? In this context it apparently means that whether one person 'wants' another is sufficient to decide whether or not the other shall live. This is absurd. Each individual has his own inestimable worth, regardless of whether another person 'wants' him or not."

Fetal Pain: "The neurological developments necessary for feeling pain are complete by the 13th week after conception and perhaps earlier. . . . It is a wrenching nightmare to see in the mind's eye the delicate little hand of an unborn infant reaching out playfully to touch the very [suction] curette that is poised to rip him apart. We must ask again, 'Freedom to choose what?'"

Eleven years after the 1973 Supreme Court decision, said Hatch, 15 million children had been aborted—more than ten times the number of American lives lost in all of America's wars combined. Nearly one in every three pregnancies in 1984 ended in abortion.

"I realize that not every child is greeted with the joy Elaine and I felt over the arrival of our six unique, challenging, and rewarding children," said Hatch in a recent interview. "But every child is special and capable of making a contribution to their family, community, and nation that no other individual can make. Many thousands of couples pray every day that they will be able to adopt children. Those contemplating killing their unborn infants instead could help answer such prayers."

In coming years much of Hatch's anti-abortion effort would be focused on the Supreme Court itself rather than Congress. Perhaps a new set of justices, which Hatch would be pivotal in confirming, would vote to overturn *Roe v. Wade*.

He vowed not to give up the struggle. The stakes were too great. Wrote Hatch: "No human being should exercise the power which God has reserved to Himself—the power to determine when men and women shall be born and when they shall die, the 'bounds of their habitation' (Acts 17:26)."

Near the end of 1983, Hatch's office sent Christmas cards, including a family photo, to eighteen thousand Utahns. Then Orrin, Elaine, and the four younger children flew to Utah and borrowed a four-wheel-drive Suburban to drive to a large old house up Ogden Canyon for Christmas. Hatch was part owner of the house, which he and his former law partner Walt Plumb had purchased as an investment, adding to the value of the limited partnership that Plumb had directed ever since Hatch was elected to the Senate in 1976.

Joining in the celebration were Hatch's parents, Orrin and Elaine's married daughter, Marcia, with her husband and son, and Kimberly's fiancé. Oldest son Brent, attending Columbia Law School, spent Christmas in New York with his wife and baby daughter.

"Everything in the woods was snow-covered and perfectly peaceful," recalled Hatch, "It was wonderful to just relax and enjoy each other."

They watched television, played games, opened gifts, read scriptural accounts of the Nativity, and gathered around the piano and sang— Hatch taking his turn at the keyboard. The family "just plain had the best Christmas I think we'd ever had."

A few days later, they attended Kimberly's wedding in the Jordan River Temple, and Hatch accompanied their second oldest son, Scott, as he picked out an engagement ring for his fiancée.

Hatch had been injured in a series of accidents over the years when his car had been struck from behind, and he had chronic neck and lower back pain. Now the year ended with yet another impact. As he drove on ice-covered I-15, the main north-south artery through Utah, a woman struck him from behind, again causing him to worry about neck and back problems.

Excited when she saw it was her senator in the Suburban, the woman had a request: "Would you mind if I tell people that I hit you?"

"Be my guest," sighed Hatch, rubbing his neck. He knew that he would shortly be back in Washington, where many others would be lining up to claim similar bragging rights.

16

Against the Tide

I N MAY 1981, NEW JERSEY DEMOCRAT Harrison A. (Pete) Williams was convicted of bribery and conspiracy in an FBI sting operation known as Abscam. Williams, organized labor's leading Senate supporter, was accused of selling his influence to a U.S. agent posing as an Arab sheik.

Early in 1984, having exhausted legal appeals, Williams learned through the media that he was about to be sent to a federal penitentiary in Danbury, Connecticut. That night, January 8, his wife, Jeanette, telephoned for help—not to Williams's fellow Democrats and liberals, but to Orrin Hatch, a Republican at the opposite end of the political spectrum.

"Orrin, do you have a few minutes to talk to Pete?" asked Jeanette Williams.

"Of course," said Hatch.

Williams asked a favor: Would Hatch ask the Justice Department to imprison him at Allenwood, Pennsylvania, closer to home, so his family could visit more easily? Hatch contacted the Justice Department the next day and urged the change of venue. Two weeks after Hatch's intercession, Williams reported to prison in Allenwood.

"I just couldn't express how my heart swelled up for him," said Hatch in a recent interview. He had found Williams, his predecessor as chairman of the Labor and Human Resources Committee, a tough but honorable opponent. "Can you imagine spending more than twenty-four years in the United States Senate and winding up in a federal penitentiary? What made it especially offensive was that I didn't think he ever offered to accept a bribe."

211

Six members of the House had been convicted earlier in Abscam. A videotape clearly showed Williams, unlike the others, refusing twenty thousand dollars in cash to help the "sheik" become a U.S. citizen. But Williams had also played along with the scam for nearly a year and accepted shares in a titanium mine that he said he believed was worthless. The mine was owned by a group of friends and Williams encouraged the Arabs to invest millions of dollars in it. An FBI informer had carefully coached him on how to impress the Arabs. Williams conceded it was "foolish" but pled that he had done nothing illegal.

Hatch, who read the trial transcript and Senate Ethics Committee report, believed Williams had not broken the law and that the FBI had entrapped him. "The government committed outrageous violations of due process of law," Hatch reflected privately. "He was convicted because of the actions of many others, because of the politics involved, because it did look sleazy, and because he let it go on for so long. My own belief was that it could happen to any Senator who had a superabundance of zeal to help his constituents." Early in 1982 when the Senate voted overwhelmingly to expel Williams, Hatch voted no.

Hatch's files contain a handwritten note on blue card stock from Jeannette Williams, addressed to both Orrin and Elaine:

> February 13, 1984
>
> Only critical events have prevented my writing you sooner to express my profound gratitude for your kindness to Pete and me. I only hope and pray somewhere, somehow, someone with a conscience will recognize the evil that has been done to a great man.
>
> Orrin, your words to me in 1982 still torment me. You believed in Pete's innocence but other considerations in his colleagues in the Senate made them turn their backs. How tragic.
>
> Please accept my thanks as well as [those of] Pete's children for your help.
>
> Sincerely,
> Jeanette

The next month, Hatch again went against the tide in the highest-pressure place of all: President Reagan's private living quarters, face to face with the President and his top aides.

The issue was prayer in the schools, which Reagan strongly supported. Hatch supported it, too, but as with the abortion issue, felt extreme care was necessary before overturning a Supreme Court decision by legislation. For two decades Congress had unsuccessfully tried to "put God back in the schools" by reversing Supreme Court rulings in the early 1960s against organized prayer and daily Bible readings in public schools.

Now, in 1984, there were two proposed constitutional amendments on prayer before the Senate. The first, strongly supported by Reagan and fundamentalist religious groups, called for organized, vocal prayer in school. The second, sponsored by Hatch, would have permitted silent prayer or reflection. Either would have overruled the Supreme Court's 1962 anti-school prayer decision in *Engel v. Vitale.*

Hatch, uncanny at counting votes, was certain that the vocal prayer amendment could never muster a two-thirds majority in each house; but he was confident that two-thirds would support silent prayer and, in the process, finally begin to reverse high court rulings that, in the words of former North Carolina Senator Sam Ervin, had "made God unconstitutional."

"The Supreme Court had erred in its interpretation of the Constitution," Hatch believed. "The purpose of the First Amendment's 'establishment' clause was to prevent the federal government from establishing a preferred, official religion, not to create an unbreachable 'wall of separation' between the government and all expressions of religious values."

On March 1, Hatch, Strom Thurmond, and Jesse Helms met with Howard Baker in the majority leader's office before a scheduled meeting at the White House. Everyone, including Hatch, supported vocal prayer in concept, but Hatch believed only the silent prayer amendment could pass Congress. And the important thing, he argued, was not the form of prayer (vocal or silent) but the overruling of a series of unjustified Supreme Court decisions.

"The President wants an up or down vote on his bill," said Baker, fixing his eyes squarely on Hatch.

"That's fine," responded Hatch. "But I want silent prayer or reflection brought up back to back with it." Baker agreed to bring up Hatch's bill if the President's bill first failed to pass. "But you can't tell anybody I'm going to do that," he added.

Baker, Thurmond, and Helms apparently believed Senators would vote for vocal prayer—*if* they didn't know that its defeat would let them vote for the more widely acceptable alternative of silent prayer or reflection. Hatch was willing to compromise, but he wasn't happy about it.

"Orrin, this is a historic opportunity and you don't want to stop this from happening," said Baker, supported by the others.

"You're right, it's a historic opportunity," answered Hatch, "and what you're going to do is maybe pass it in the Senate and then the House will do nothing with it, and we'll end up with nothing. Or we could all get behind silent prayer or reflection, which is much more likely to be accepted both by the Senate and House as well as the states. I won't kid you, I'm very upset about it. But, of course, I'll give the President his vote."

Hatch and Thurmond then rode to the White House together and were immediately ushered into the Reagans' second-floor living quarters. There waited the President, aide Michael Deaver, Chief of Staff James Baker, Counselor Ed Meese, Attorney General William French Smith, and Vice President Bush, along with Howard Baker.

The purpose of the meeting quickly became clear: shove Hatch into line. All the others were chanting the same mantra, praising the vocal prayer amendment which, among other things, had become a mainstay of Reagan's campaign for a second term. Hatch defended his position without wavering: Silent prayer was much more likely than vocal prayer to become the twenty-seventh amendment. "I'm sorry, but vocal prayer will not get more than fifty-seven votes," Hatch said. Baker insisted it would do better than that in an election year.

Hatch shook his head but said, "Mr. President, I still believe fifty-seven votes is all it will get. But if it weren't for you we wouldn't even be here with an opportunity to talk about it, so I'll do the very best I can for your vocal prayer amendment." Hatch asked something in return: that his silent prayer amendment be brought up immediately afterward if vocal prayer was defeated as he predicted. The others agreed.

Hatch then mentioned the possibility that another supporter of silent prayer might move on the floor to substitute a silent prayer bill for the President's vocal prayer bill.

"Well, if he does, will you support a motion to table it?" Hatch was asked. Tabling it meant to kill it.

"I probably would not," answered Hatch.

The others looked stunned.

"Well, can't you abstain from voting?" asked Jim Baker.

"Probably not," answered Hatch.

The others all started talking at once, even Reagan becoming uncharacteristically hostile. "Orrin, we haven't come this far just to wind up with a silent prayer amendment," said Reagan. Hatch wondered if Reagan really understood what was going on as the President spouted clichés. But he bit his tongue.

Thurmond echoed Reagan's opinion that silent prayer meant nothing because schoolchildren could already exercise that option whenever they chose.

"It's a lot more important than that," Hatch patiently explained again. "This amendment not only could pass the Senate and House, but it would knock down this false wall of separation between church and state that has existed for so many years. It would open the door to the recognition of religious rights all over the country. Even if your amendment passes, a lot of state and local school districts are not going to opt for the vocal prayer approach. And by the time a set vocal prayer is decided on, it will be so watered down that it'll be meaningless."

Hatch's arguments fell on deaf ears. Two weeks later, on 15 March 1984, the issue reached the Senate floor. When another senator introduced silent prayer ahead of the vocal prayer bill, silent prayer was tabled and killed. Five days later the Senate voted 56-44 for vocal prayer—eleven votes short of the two-thirds necessary for constitutional amendments, and just one vote off Hatch's prediction.

Organized prayer of any kind in the nation's public schools remained illegal, and the political makeup in succeeding Congresses would make it increasingly difficult to pass any kind of prayer amendment.

"This is a very trying and tiring job," a discouraged Hatch wrote that night. "It's really a dog's life, and getting worse all the time. The work has almost doubled in intensity since I arrived in 1977."

A staff aide tried to cheer him up with this note: "Remember what the Reverend Gerald Mann said when opening a session of the Texas legislature with prayer: 'Lord, help these senators to remember that making laws is like a love affair: If it's easy, it's sleazy. Amen.'"

Three weeks later, Hatch recorded, "My eyes are killing me tonight. I just don't know what to do. Have been so tired lately. Most of the time I don't sleep well even if I do get to bed early enough to get six to eight hours sleep." His lower back hurt most of the time.

Hatch exercised hard, at home or at the Senate gym, and monitored his weight carefully. At midyear he recorded it with precision: 161¼ pounds, about five pounds more than when he and Elaine were married twenty-seven years earlier. "It feels good to be able to control my weight," he wrote. Later in the year an electrocardiogram confirmed his usual low blood pressure: 110/60 on the first reading and, ten minutes later, 90/60. Hatch's persistence in sticking to an exercise program paid off in increased endurance. Two years later, during the sweltering summer of 1986, he and four aides ran in a three-mile race at East Potomac Park, all wearing light blue T-shirts stenciled with "The Orrin Legion." Hatch finished in just under twenty-five minutes, a time others considered amazing for one who hadn't run seriously in some twenty years.

Still, Hatch was reluctant to stop long enough to get a thorough physical exam. "When I do slow down, I feel guilty because I'm not doing more." Finally Elaine conspired with his doctor and made an appointment on another pretext. Waiting for Hatch when he entered the office were two doctors—his own physician and a stranger.

"Is he the speech therapist?" asked Hatch.

"No, he's a proctologist," said Hatch's doctor.

"Oh, no!" said Hatch, bolting for the door—now blocked by both doctors.

"You're not getting out of here without this exam," said his doctor.

Hatch submitted. The proctologist reported that his system seemed fine. "It certainly was a humbling experience," said Hatch.

Hatch was not always helped by his staff. Staff members shoulder many of the daily details of a senator's life, and it is axiomatic that the most influential members of Congress also have the most competent aides. Hatch had many excellent staffers—some of whom went on to other important positions in government, often with Hatch's help, and were known collectively as "Hatchlings." But a few embarrassed him badly, and Hatch had only himself to blame for maintaining close associations against the advice of others.

He had an almost unshakable faith in those around him, and friends and associates tended to take advantage of Hatch because of his trusting, generous nature and reluctance to retaliate. Some observers believed that Hatch—so tough on issues—ironically lacked discernment when it came to people. Hatch himself insists that he did not have an inherent blind spot but was willing to risk problems with unconventional aides who had unique strengths that complemented his own abilities. Those who know him well also say Hatch simply loves people and is extremely loath to give up on anyone.

One aide who caused Hatch considerable grief was C. McClain (Mac) Haddow. Mac and his brother John, who also worked for the senator early on, had become like second sons to Hatch's father, Jesse, when he was a leader in the Mormon church back in Pittsburgh. They had moved with their mother to Utah, where Mac managed Hatch's first campaign in 1976 and thereafter became a key political operative for him in Washington and Utah. Haddow, who had excellent political instincts, was bright, hardworking, and street smart.

However, there were clues that Haddow seemed to lack an ethical compass. He was a champion debater at Brigham Young University, for example, but one debate opponent recalls that, when stuck, Haddow sometimes would simply invent a fantastic quote, author and all, to win his point.

After the 1976 election, Haddow served briefly on Hatch's Washington staff. When Haddow found the capital not to his liking, Hatch sent him back to Utah to run his state office in 1977. But Haddow's brashness offended some constituents and party officials and as early as 1979, political consultants urged Hatch to get rid of him. Hatch considered reassigning Haddow to his Washington office, then gave some thought to discharging him. In the end, Hatch did nothing. Haddow had believed in him when he first ran for the Senate and had worked hard and loyally. Hatch prized those qualities and would tolerate the rest.

In 1980, Haddow resigned as head of Hatch's Utah staff to start his own political consulting and fund-raising firm and he became a spark-plug for the Sagebrush Rebellion. He also was elected to the state legis-lature that year and served one term in the Utah House where he was twice investigated—and cleared—by a state legislative committee for alleged ethics violations.

Haddow worked briefly for the Department of Housing and Urban Development at HUD's regional office in Denver in 1983—initally over the strong objection of Jake Garn—but reportedly became bored and again set his sights on Washington. He turned to Hatch, who telephoned Health and Human Services Secretary Margaret Heckler on Haddow's behalf. In the fall of 1983, Heckler appointed Haddow as her executive administrative assistant. His native ability took over from there, and by the end of 1984, Heckler had appointed Haddow as her chief of staff.

At HHS, Haddow started the T. Bear Foundation, an apparently altruistic effort to remind children and those attending them to wash their hands to prevent the spread of infections. Toy bears were distrib-uted to children's hospitals. The program blossomed beginning in 1984, with the department spending $300,000 in federal funds to promote the idea and raising another $350,000 from major health-related private companies. Haddow continued to serve as Heckler's chief of staff and became the nonprofit foundation's vice president.

Hatch, whose committee oversaw Heckler's department, cooperated with publicity efforts in 1985 by posing for photos with a huge stuffed T. Bear. But he refused Haddow's insistent requests to be a member of the foundation's board of directors. Prompted by an uneasy feeling and Haddow's persistence, Hatch even put his refusal in writing. After Heckler lost her position at HHS, Haddow left the department in February 1986 to open a Washington consulting firm, immediately picking up hospital clients he had dealt with at the department. He also remained an unpaid vice president of the T. Bear Foundation.

Four months later, Hatch picked the *Washington Post* off his doorstep and immediately was grateful for having not joined T. Bear's board. There, on the bottom-left corner of the front page, was Haddow's photo and a headline: "$30,000 Routed to Wife of Ex-HHS Official."

While at HHS, according to the *Post,* Haddow had secretly channeled foundation money to his wife through a woman allegedly hired to raise funds. The other woman acknowledged she did not earn the money and said she turned 90 percent of it over to Alice Haddow. Mac Haddow later admitted that, as Heckler's top aide, he had also arranged $25,000 in speech-writing contracts for two friends—with nearly $22,000 of it likewise going to his wife.

Ironically, Alice Haddow was in fact an accomplished writer and almost certainly had the ability to perform the services in question for both the foundation and Heckler. Had Mac hired her openly and honestly, he may have been criticized for nepotism, but there would have been no charge of criminal conduct. But that was too simple. The Haddows claimed Heckler had in fact signed a waiver allowing Alice to write speeches for her; but Heckler, a master at self-preservation, pleaded ignorance, and the Haddows were stuck with the appearance of corruption.

A federal grand jury handed down a seven-count indictment against Mac Haddow in April 1987. Five counts were dismissed in a plea bargain, with Haddow pleading guilty to two counts of conflict of interest. The judge sentenced him to one year in prison—with good behavior, only ninety days to be served. Haddow reported to prison in Petersburg, Virginia, in January 1988.

There was heavy press coverage of the Haddow affair, and most accounts identified him as Hatch's former aide and campaign manager. Hatch, who for years had refused to sever ties with Haddow, now said flatly that his friend "got himself into this mess and he'll have to get himself out of it." Although Hatch, out of compassion, visited Haddow in prison, their professional relationship was over. But the political damage to Hatch already was palpable.

Another problematic aide was foreign policy specialist Michael Pillsbury, first hired by Hatch in 1979. Supporters and detractors alike considered Pillsbury brilliant but, like Haddow, someone who also had a penchant for cutting corners and ruffling feathers.

After Senate conservatives organized themselves into a "steering committee" to monitor Carter administration policies, Hatch in 1979 was assigned to the Strategic Arms Limitation Talks (SALT) in Europe. He took Pillsbury on as a special assistant, persuading a handful of senators to help pay his salary. Thus began a long and sometimes rocky relationship—and, for Hatch, a fascinating tutorial in world affairs.

"I knew Pillsbury was not easy for some others to get along with," explains Hatch. "But I also knew he was a brilliant strategist. I was willing to put up with the challenges of working with him because I cared for Mike as an individual and because of his remarkable ability in foreign policy."

Ten years younger than Hatch, the blond, balding Stanford graduate held a doctorate from Columbia University in Chinese studies and spoke Mandarin without a trace of accent. Pillsbury began his career as an analyst at the Rand Corporation, a leading think tank. His writings reportedly were a key influence on President Nixon in his decision to play the "China card," visiting that country in 1972 as a start toward normalized diplomatic relations. Pillsbury also suggested that the U.S. should cultivate a military relationship with China to counter Soviet influence in Asia. He sent a paper outlining his ideas to Ronald Reagan who, upon becoming President, adopted it as U.S. policy.

Pillsbury's government career was a stormy cycle of high-level appointments followed by noisy departures over policy disagreements. Like Hatch, he was an activist who had little patience with bureaucratic red tape. But while Hatch had mellowed somewhat over the years and had excellent people skills, Pillsbury invariably alienated colleagues and officials whose cooperation was essential to turn his ideas into national policy.

Pillsbury and Hatch developed a symbiotic relationship: Pillsbury had taken the lead in formulating some foreign policy plans, and Hatch had taken the lead in working with others to give them life. In midyear 1979, over the strong objections of some other Senators, Hatch had taken Pillsbury to Europe for a firsthand look at progress toward a SALT treaty. Three years later, just weeks after his 1982 reelection and once more against the advice of Senate colleagues, Hatch again was off to Europe with Pillsbury in tow, this time to visit the sites of four sets of arms-control talks in which the U.S. was engaged.

In 1984, Hatch personally met with Defense Secretary Caspar Weinberger at the Pentagon on Pillsbury's behalf, and Weinberger hired Pillsbury as a policy advisor. The following year, after Hatch was appointed to the Senate Intelligence Committee, Pillsbury wanted to return to Capitol Hill as a senior staffer to the committee. But committee chair David Durenberger, R-Minnesota, vetoed him. Although some members of the nation's national security inner circle also continued to rebuff him, Pillsbury had an uncanny knack for bouncing back. He was one of about two dozen subcabinet operatives who actually decided U.S. foreign policy, including covert actions. Also in the group was an earnest Marine officer named Oliver North.

Pillsbury continued to be a world guide for Hatch. Almost immediately after being named to the Intelligence Committee in January 1985, Hatch was off to Central America for a firsthand look at the troubled region, including a tough session with Nicaragua's leftist president Daniel Ortega and his brother, Humberto, the country's defense minister.

Four months later, Pillsbury accompanied Hatch and a handful of

others to southern Asia on Air Force Two—the Vice President's plane—
on a secret mission that would have historic consequences. (See Chapter
19.) But even that eventual shining triumph would be tarnished for
Pillsbury as his career blew up in allegations of professional misconduct
the following spring.

Most of Hatch's other staff members were team players who were a
credit to their boss and fiercely loyal to him. They were typically bright,
capable, hardworking, and honest. They also seemed to genuinely like
Hatch and agreed he was caring and solicitous about their well-being on
and off the job, even long after they had left his employ.

For his part, Hatch reciprocated with respect and trust. Occasionally
he complained when they made mistakes in using his name with others
or jammed his schedule too full to leave time for creative thinking or to
consult adequately with them.

"I've never known a person who's more misunderstood," said Bill
Loos, Haddow's replacement as state director. "A lot of people see him
as very intense, uncaring and narrow-minded, and really, the antithesis
is true. He's almost too caring. If I had to fault him, I'd say it's his
propensity for trying to help too many people."

Ronald Madsen (no relation to Frank) had been a business lawyer
for twenty-five years when he went to work for Hatch in 1981. He
replaced Loos as state director in 1984 and still held that position ten
years later. "I don't know anyone easier to work for than Orrin Hatch,"
said Madsen. "I've never met anyone as influential and powerful, yet as
humble. He really is very teachable."

Hatch credits Wendy Higginbotham with being the advisor who
finally persuaded him, for his own protection, to keep at arm's length
individuals who tended to have private agendas contrary to the public
interest. Higginbotham joined Hatch's staff in 1985 as director of
women's issues for his Washington office. "She hasn't got a lot of experience in government or politics," wrote Hatch in recording his decision.
"However, the great value she has to offer to our office is good judgment. Wendy is extremely intelligent. She is willing to tell me the way it
is no matter how much it hurts and no matter how bluntly she has to. I
respect that."

Higginbotham rose to become Hatch's top aide—administrative assistant—in 1992 and still held that position two years later. She followed in
the footsteps of an impressive galaxy of earlier "A.A.s," including Frank
Madsen, Tom Parry, Stan Parrish, Dee Benson, and Kevin McGuiness.

Another key staff change came in January 1981 when Hatch
switched press secretary Ed Darrell to a similar role on the Labor and
Human Resources Committee and hired veteran Utah newsman Paul

Smith in Darrell's place. The easygoing Smith was a popular choice with reporters and would still be serving Hatch well in 1994.

Early in 1984, the Senate Judiciary Committee took up legislation to overturn the 1968 gun control law, enacted after the assassinations of Martin Luther King and Robert Kennedy. The new law would release the ban on mail-order or interstate shipment of firearms and ammunition and, Hatch believed, correct injustices to law-abiding sportsmen. He led advocates for the relaxed law on the Judiciary Committee.

Ted Kennedy, who had lost two older brothers to gunmen, was the Senate's leading opponent. But the struggle was more difficult each year against the National Rifle Association and other powerful lobbies. When Hatch brought up Congress's main anti-gun-control measure—the McClure-Volkmer bill—in the Judiciary Committee in March 1984, Kennedy vowed to filibuster, then posed a series of technical questions about the bill's provisions which Hatch was unprepared to answer.

Hatch turned to a staff aide, who gave Hatch a written answer to a particular question. As Hatch began to read it, Kennedy cut him off: "Let's not read the material; let's tell me what *you* know about it." Kennedy then made the point that many members did not know much about the bill, suggesting they supported it because of gun lobby pressure and without much regard for what it said.

When Hatch protested that he had not had time to study the bill in detail, Kennedy delivered the *coup de grâce:* "Well, I remember when Senator Tsongas was before *your* committee."

Forcing a smile, Hatch said, "Senator, just ask the questions. I'll try to answer them to the best of my ability. I'm prepared to sit here all day, and get here at 7:30 in the morning, and to work all day and all night and on weekends to try and accommodate the Senator and resolve this problem."

That afternoon, a gorgeous basket of flowers arrived on Hatch's desk for his fiftieth birthday, a note from Kennedy attached.

Still later that day, Hatch ran into Kennedy again. "Ted," scolded Hatch jokingly, "you were your usual rude self today." Kennedy laughed, but blanched as Hatch added: "You know, two can play that game. I hope you know every detail of the twenty amendments you intend to bring up on gun control."

Hatch and Kennedy also sparred most of the year over the Civil Rights Act of 1984. It was introduced after the Supreme Court ruled in February (*Grove City College v. Bell*) that a federal ban on sex discrimination applied only to specific programs receiving federal funds, not to all activities of a recipient institution.

Grove City, a college in Pennsylvania, had refused to accept government aid in order to maintain its independence. But about a quarter of its students had received federal grants or loans, bringing the full weight of federal regulations down on the school anyway.

After the Supreme Court ruled that federal bureaucrats had erred, legislation was introduced to overturn *Grove City*. While they were at it, sponsors included three other federal statutes. The House bill passed in June by an overwhelming vote of 375-32; and the companion bill in the Senate, introduced by Kennedy, was now before the Labor and Human Resources Committee chaired by Hatch.

Proponents said the legislation would merely return the law to its intended status prior to the court decision. But Hatch and the Reagan administration believed it would in fact substantially broaden the sweep of federal law into areas it had never reached before. "This is the most massive shift of power . . . [that] the U.S. Congress . . . will make to the federal bureaucracy and the federal courts in your lifetime," warned Senator East, who chaired the Separation of Powers Subcommittee.

Hatch scheduled eight hearings over several months in an attempt to focus public attention on the bill's provisions. But Kennedy and his allies stalled each time, repeatedly asking for a postponement or absenting themselves to leave the committee without a quorum. Finally, when November elections were just weeks away, assuring maximum pressure on individual members, Kennedy and his chief GOP ally Bob Packwood made their move.

They knew it would be virtually unprecedented for Congress not to pass a major civil rights bill under such circumstances. To paint Hatch further into a corner, Kennedy, Packwood, and Senate rules wizard Bob Byrd took two other steps: They attached the civil rights bill as a rider to a must-pass appropriations bill needed to keep government agencies running. Then, blocking Hatch's last escape route, they got the Senate to invoke cloture by an overwhelming vote of 92-4, presumably choking off floor debate.

Before cloture was voted, Hatch was able to quickly muster enough support to attach three amendments to the bill—on school busing, anti-gun control, and tuition tax credits—that dulled its luster for advocates.

On September 29, 1984, the day cloture was invoked, Hatch pleaded with his colleagues not to pass the intrusive bill. "I feel deeply about civil rights," he said on the floor. "It is not easy to confront an issue like the Civil Rights Act of 1984 regardless of how many ways this act will actually *frustrate* civil rights. And I venture to say there probably have not been more than two or three Senators in this whole chamber who have read that bill and analyzed it."

What happened next was so complex that even veteran parliamentarians shake their heads trying to describe it. In essence, Hatch stretched Senate rules to the breaking point, introducing a record 1,600 individual amendments to the bill, including Amendment Number 1412, which read in its entirety: ".".

Hatch, surviving on two to three hours of sleep a night, forced a record seventy-three hours of post-cloture debate, during which there was also a record number of additional cloture petitions filed to shut him up. Despite pleadings from both sides of the aisle, however, Hatch refused to submit.

Finally, on October 2, the other side blinked. Packwood threw in the towel, saying the civil rights bill had to be sacrificed for that year "so that we might get on with the public's business, but also so that we can get on with the procedures by which we govern ourselves." By that time, Hatch had tied the Senate so tightly in knots that the parliamentary motion to kill the bill was a bewildering, pretzel-like single sentence of over 250 words.

Against all odds, the Civil Rights Act of 1984 was dead.

Kennedy roared with indignation—"Shame on this body! Shame on this body!"—as accolades rained on Hatch, even from opposing Senators who, on the Senate floor, acknowledged his "complete and total victory."

The liberal *New Republic* on November 26, 1984, conceded that Hatch's objections "to the bill's ambiguous language were legitimate. . . . Taken to its logical extreme, the bill implied that groups such as grocery store owners accepting food stamps, small farmers taking crop subsidies, and landlords receiving rent vouchers could all be defined as 'recipients' of federal aid."

A staff aide, in a hand-written letter to Hatch, said, "Your performances on the floor and your protracted efforts behind the scenes showed the skill of a seasoned trial lawyer and the cunning of a desert fox."

The U.S. Chamber of Commerce, in a news release the day after the final vote, called it "a major victory for small business over big government." It added, "Senator Hatch's floor effort was one of the finest examples of truly outstanding Senate leadership in the past decade."

Two of Hatch's old allies in his first great battle against the Labor Law Reform Bill also sent letters. Richard Lugar wrote, "The result of the debate was clearly governed by your intelligence combined with remarkable stamina." And business attorney Robert Thompson added that "the so-called Civil Rights Act of 1984 victory is the pinnacle of your career. . . . I would put this ahead of Labor Law Reform in terms of your accomplishments."

While Hatch continued to oppose much of organized labor's legislative agenda, he strongly supported its role as a bulwark against world communism. He considered Irving Brown, international vice president of the AFL-CIO, based in Europe, the world's leading anticommunist. Hatch also respected and personally liked Lane Kirkland, who succeeded George Meany as head of the labor federation upon Meany's death in 1980.

One arena that brought Hatch and Kirkland together was the National Endowment for Democracy, a partially federal-funded umbrella organization that included national labor and business leaders and both political parties, which received operating funds from the endowment. Its aim was to compete against the Communist bloc, led by the USSR, in the global competition for hearts and minds using ideas instead of weapons. Many did not realize that the Soviets were spending $3 billion annually on their disinformation campaign, while the NED would have only $14 million with which to help counter them—and it did.

Hatch strongly supported the NED, but some other citizens, including liberal Connecticut Republican Lowell Weicker, believed it was either superfluous or had too much potential for mischief.

"The Soviets are deathly afraid of the competition the NED will bring to their strategy for global conquest," said Hatch in floor debate over NED funding. ". . . They would like to see the NED, which they term an 'anti-socialist orgy,' derailed as quickly as possible. The biggest sigh of relief, if we do what the distinguished Senator from Connecticut wants to do on this matter, will come from the Soviet Union. I'm convinced of that."

At that, the burly, bespectacled Weicker shot out of his seat. "Would the distinguished Senator from Utah yield?"

"Yes," said Hatch.

"Would you clarify that remark? Is there, in other words, some sort of implication as to the purpose of the Senator's remark?"

Hatch assured Weicker he was not implying that he *purposely* was trying to aid the Soviet Union. "But I am saying this: that the Soviets understand what the NED has been set up for. They are afraid of it. They do not want it to continue. They do not want this competition in the world of ideas. . . . But there was no implication whatsoever."

Later that evening, Hatch approached Weicker on the Senate floor. "Lowell, I would really feel bad if you thought I was implying anything deleterious about you."

But Weicker was in a fighting mood: "I'm going to invoke Rule 19 and you're going to have to apologize to me in front of the whole Senate."

"Oh, bullshit," answered Hatch. "Do whatever you want."

Just then Majority Whip Ted Stevens walked by. "Party unity, party unity," he said with a grin. Hatch started to laugh but Weicker stomped off in anger.

NED funding was saved in the Senate, with union leaders crediting Hatch and reportedly softening their view of him as an implacable foe. Unions were well aware that their Democratic allies had to go through Hatch as head of the Labor Committee and that Hatch had personally led a number of fights for labor, including saving the Railroad Retirement Act and passing a black-lung bill to protect coal miners.

Hatch was tenacious on principle but exceptionally softhearted with people. He went to bat for two other controversial figures in 1984: Sun Myung Moon, head of the Unification Church, and George Hansen, Republican Congressman from Idaho. Both were in trouble—Moon imprisoned for income tax evasion, and Hansen sentenced to prison for filing false personal income disclosure forms in the House.

Hatch believed both men were being unjustly punished. Moon, who moved to the United States from Korea in 1972, had been convicted of evading federal income taxes and filing false tax returns. He reminded Hatch of other immigrants he had defended as an attorney years ago who had technically but not willfully broken U.S. tax laws. Hatch believed prejudice was at the bottom of Moon's indictment and conviction.

"I really believed that religious freedom was the issue," explained Hatch in a later interview. "I think the young assistant U.S. Attorney handling the case was trying to build his reputation at the expense of Reverend Moon, who hardly spoke English when he was indicted and convicted, yet was accused of intentionally violating our income tax laws. It really was an injustice."

For his interest in their plight, Hatch received two letters of thanks—along with some ginseng tea—from Hak Ja Han Moon, Reverend Moon's wife and the mother of their twelve children, who had briefly met Hatch during a subcommittee hearing on religious freedom. One letter read in part: "All of my children join with me in expressing to you my heartfelt gratitude. Especially my second daughter, In Jin, felt so close to you when she met you . . . and when you kissed her on the way out, she said she felt the warm loving embrace of her father."

Toward the end of the year, Hatch personally appealed to President Reagan, after failing to get the Justice Department to reconsider Moon's case. Hatch's goal was to win clemency for both Moon and Pete Williams so they could go home for Christmas. Jeanette Williams, who had recently been in a serious car accident, had sent Orrin and Elaine a note, thanking them for sending flowers, "a constant reminder of two extraordinary people that I feel privileged to call friends."

But White House Chief of Staff Jim Baker continued to fend off Hatch's repeated requests to intervene with Reagan, saying he didn't want to "put the President on the spot." Finally, on the evening of December 22 while Hatch was in his bedroom reading *The Hunt for Red October,* Reagan telephoned.

They talked for nearly a half hour. Hatch laid out the case for

granting Moon clemency, emphasizing he had nothing to gain personally, was not a close personal friend of Moon's, and did not endorse his
theology. "You've made a number of points I hadn't heard before," the
President told him. But Hatch hung up convinced that Reagan would
not intervene.

On Christmas Eve, White House counsel Fred Fielding telephoned
Hatch to say Pete Williams was furloughed for Christmas and Moon
would receive a similar furlough from New Year's Eve to January 4.
Neither received clemency.

Hatch was deeply disappointed. "If I were in the White House," he
wrote, "I would certainly try to find a number of reasonable cases for
clemency at the end of each year."

Idaho's George Hansen was one of a kind. Like Hatch, he was also a
maverick and a Mormon who frequently intervened in problems no one
else wanted to touch. He had great native ability and, at least for other
ultraconservatives, great charisma. But many people felt he didn't have
great common sense.

The friendly six-foot-six giant was always on the side of the little guy
in his struggle against Big Brother on the Potomac. Hansen was hostile
to the IRS and other government agencies, and persistently bent or
broke their rules—filing late income tax returns, violating campaign
finance laws, and failing to disclose sources of income as required by
House rules.

Hansen had represented Idaho's largely Mormon Second District off
and on since 1964 and had been sentenced to jail for two months in
1975 after pleading guilty to violating campaign finance laws. The judge
changed the sentence to a fine after Hansen's attorney argued successfully that Hansen had been "stupid" but not "evil."

By 1984 Hansen had been in various other legal scrapes and his luck
was running out. Earlier in the year he had been convicted of filing false
financial disclosure statements and was sentenced to five to fifteen
months in prison. Yet the Justice Department was clearly acting selec-
tively. Immediately after Hansen's conviction, more than a hundred
other members of the House reportedly were allowed to revise their own
disclosure statements with no penalty.

Hansen, free while appealing his conviction, said he was a victim of
government persecution and ran for reelection against Democrat
Richard Stallings, a history professor at Mormon-owned Ricks College.
Although Hansen was a pariah among many Idahoans and fellow
Mormons in Utah, Hatch saw him as a friend in need and campaigned
in Idaho for Hansen, passing out copies of a legal brief on his behalf to

the media. Despite Hansen's pending jail term, Stallings beat him by fewer than two hundred votes.

But Hatch paid a political price. Governor Scott Matheson and Utah Democratic official Patrick Shea, both attorneys, said Hatch was a poor member of the bar and blasted him for publicly supporting a "convicted felon." Hatch's pollster Dan Jones told him the Hansen furor had cost Hatch 10 points in the polls and that his negative rating had climbed to 30 percent. Hatch was taken aback by the public reaction. "Nonetheless," he wrote to himself, "we have to do what we believe is right."

In 1986 Hansen reported to prison in Petersburg, Virginia.

Hatch had less compassion for another Idahoan. Former Senator Frank Church was one of the few with whom Hatch never developed a good relationship. In January 1984, when Church entered the Sloan-Kettering Cancer Institute, Hatch wrote, "I have my differences with Frank Church but I certainly feel sorry for him and hope he will be all right."

But when Church died three months later, Hatch was not so sensitive. On April 9, a memorial service was held for Church at the National Cathedral in northwest Washington. Hatch was scheduled to chair a committee hearing at the same time, with witnesses assembled from across the country.

Nearly an hour after the session began at 9:30, Arizona's Dennis DeConcini asked Hatch if he would postpone the hearing for about an hour so he and others could attend Church's memorial service. Hatch, citing inconvenience to witnesses, said no.

When the afternoon session was ready to begin, an outraged Joseph Biden, D-Delaware, pulled Hatch aside in the committee room and tongue-lashed him for not postponing the hearing. "And I want to tell the rest of the committee how I feel," Biden said sharply.

Hatch agreed and called the committee to order. "Senator Biden wants to make a statement," he said.

Biden lit into Hatch, repeating what he had said in private.

When Biden had ended, Hatch said, "Senator, you're right. In retrospect I have to admit it would have been better to have recessed. . . . I'm very sorry and I hope you'll accept my apology." Biden did.

That evening, Hatch wrote, "I just felt terrible the rest of the day. I made a terribly insensitive mistake."

Hatch had far less involvement in the presidential election of 1984 than in 1980. Reagan didn't need him: by the end of 1984, the economy had finally rebounded, with strong growth, low inflation, and a sharp drop in unemployment. But one cloud remained on the horizon: The federal deficit was $175 billion for the most recent fiscal year and slower growth in 1984 promised to push it back over the $200 billion mark. Reagan and Bush were renominated in Dallas, with Republicans passing a staunchly conservative platform despite warnings from moderates that the party needed to broaden its base.

Former Vice President Walter Mondale captured the Democratic nomination and named New York Congresswoman Geraldine Ferraro as his vice presidential running mate. It was the first time a major political party had nominated a woman for that office. A controversy over Ferraro's family finances soon dulled her sheen, however, and the ticket trailed Reagan-Bush throughout the fall.

On November 6, Reagan won the biggest electoral landslide in U.S. history. Mondale carried only his home state of Minnesota and the District of Columbia for thirteen electoral votes, as Reagan walked off with the other 525 electoral votes and 59 percent of the popular vote. It was a personal triumph for Reagan, but the long-range forecast was ominous. The GOP picked up only fourteen House seats and, although it still controlled the Senate 53-47, suffered a net loss of two members.

"This has been a very heartrending day," Hatch wrote that evening. "We lost some tremendously good people." Republican Senators Charles Percy of Illinois and Roger Jepsen of Iowa were defeated, replaced by Democratic liberals Paul Simon and Tom Harkin. After Majority Leader Howard Baker stepped down, his seat in Tennessee was won by Democratic Representative Albert Gore, Jr.

Hatch sent condolences to defeated candidates in both parties. Mondale responded early in December:

"Thank you for your kind and thoughtful note. . . . It is always disappointing to lose an election, but it takes a little sting out of the defeat when members of the opposing party write, as you did, with such warmth and generosity. Thanks again for your letter.."

Mondale added a hand-written postscript: "Your letter was a very kind act. This old Democrat appreciates it."

17

Friends and Foes

AMONG THE HUNDRED SENATORS WHO came together in committees and coalitions, Hatch occupied an anchor role on the conservative side of the aisle. But his approach was constructively different from that of other leading conservatives.

Ted Kennedy, Hatch's most frequent sparring partner, had studied Hatch up close for years. "There is a blind ideological aspect to some politicians, whether on the left or the right," said Kennedy, acknowledging that some people put him in that category. Ideologues "add fuel to the fire" by introducing bills, then refuse to defend their ideas in debate or meet with other members of Congress to try to find workable solutions.

"But Orrin is not of that ilk. He pursues his agenda and viewpoint, but with genuine respect for your position. The problems stay, the values don't change. And values can be shared. People have different approaches to how best to deal with the issues. If you have respect for people and a commitment to values, that's an important start for finding common ground."

Independent observers were likewise struck by the difference between Hatch and some other conservatives. After helping to defeat one civil rights bill he considered extreme, Hatch immediately circulated among disappointed proponents, promising to come up with an approach he could support.

"That took gall, guts, and an awful lot of sense," a labor lobbyist commented to the press. "If Jesse Helms could do that, he'd pass a lot more legislation."

Hatch, nonetheless, came to occupy a special place on the liberal blacklist—and not without reason. He had been singularly effective in

229

thwarting some of liberalism's most cherished goals: forced unionism, various civil rights initiatives he considered extreme, the ERA, and taxpayer-financed abortions. He had also steered many Reagan adminis-tration nominees to confirmation and helped implement much of the administration's domestic agenda.

At a 1984 dinner sponsored by the American Legal Foundation, Hatch entered the ballroom to be greeted by Roger Craver, direct-mail king for liberal causes. In more than two hundred tough fund-raising letters over the years, Craver had invoked Hatch's name to raise liberal hackles and open checkbooks. "You have really made me a lot of money," Craver told Hatch in a left-handed compliment.

Conservatives also invoked Hatch's name—usually with his permis-sion—for attacks on liberal colleagues. In addition, he had a tendency, when speaking outside Washington, to paint liberals with a broad, black brush. Yet he had ethical lines he seldom knowingly crossed. In 1986 Hatch received a handwritten note from a Senate colleague: "I enclose a piece of direct mail that is going out under your name to people in my state," wrote Christopher Dodd of Connecticut. ". . . When a colleague, particularly one I happen to like and respect, suggests as this letter does that I am not patriotic, nor care about America, and worse am sympa-thetic to Marxism, [it] goes way beyond the bounds of decency."

The offending, four-page, mass-mailed letter, sent by a conservative group called the Council for Inter-American Security, sought donations and asked: "How can elected officials be so blind to the danger threatening our Nation? And how can key liberal leaders in the U.S. Congress PROMOTE Soviet propaganda? Senator Christopher Dodd (D-Conn.) gave a nationally tele-vised response to President Reagan's Central American speech that was so radical—A SOVIET DIPLOMAT *PRAISED* IT AS A "PERFECT MARXIST-LENINIST ANALYSIS OF THE EVENTS ON OUR SOUTHERN BORDERS!"

Dodd ended his letter: "Frankly, Orrin, I'm very disappointed. This is not the Orrin Hatch I know."

Hatch wrote a prompt reply:

Dear Chris,

Frankly, I am embarrassed. Apparently, one of my former staff members may have approved the use of my signature on this. He, if he did so, did so without my approval. When I saw this letter, I had my administrative assistant immediately call the Council and tell them to not send any more of these letters with my signature. I apologize. I would not have approved this letter had I reviewed it. I hope you can accept my apology. You are a fine man, and although we disagree on many matters, I have great respect for you.

Orrin

Hatch also became increasingly concerned over the New Right's "constant sniping" at the President and other mainstream conservatives. Greed was the motivator, he concluded. "I believe the reason they are doing so much of it is because of their insatiable desire for money, knowing that they do much better with negative campaigns than with positive campaigns," he wrote privately. "They always have to find something they are against."

In addition, Hatch had second thoughts about his association with some politicos whose guiding principle seemed to be victory at any cost. Notably they included Roger Stone, a political *wunderkind* who had led Hatch's unsuccessful bid in 1979 to chair the Senate GOP Campaign Committee. "The Rise and Gall of Roger Stone" headlined a long profile in the *Washington Post* about the thirty-three-year-old power monger who reportedly was making $450,000 a year telling others how to gain and keep power.

Paul Weyrich called Stone "one of the all-time frauds of American politics" according to the *Post* reporter. "Every meeting I've had with the guy, I wanted to wash my hands three times afterwards."

Stone, who had also helped run campaigns for such Republican stars as President Reagan and Congressman Jack Kemp, called himself "the Prince of Darkness," named his dog Milhous, and arrived at meetings in his chauffeur-driven Mercedes. When the *New Republic* ran a cover story on him, headlined "The State-of-the-Art Washington Sleazeball," Stone made photocopies and sent it to important friends to show he had arrived.

Hatch was disliked and feared by many special-interest groups, but the unkindest cuts of all, in his view, came from women's groups. Hatch had led out in introducing and passing legislation of special interest to women and families, but he had been demonized by militant feminists, notably for opposing ERA and abortion on demand.

During the ninety-eighth Congress alone (1983-84), Hatch had sponsored at least seventeen initiatives of special benefit to women and families. Among those signed into law by President Reagan—sometimes after Hatch personally lobbied him—were such things as:

- child support enforcement.
- a block grant to states to establish dependent care resource and referral programs.
- funds for alcoholism and drug abuse treatment, prevention, and research programs for women.
- the Missing Children's Act, first sponsored by Hatch in 1981, creating a federal-state effort to list missing children in a national information bank.

- expanding child abuse statutes to prohibit the withholding of medical treatment except under certain limited circumstances—hailed as a major civil rights victory for handicapped children.
- the first bill in a quarter-century to encourage the pharmaceutical industry to develop new and better drugs, leading to lower costs for brand-name drugs, and the manufacture of generic drugs.

Hatch also added $100 million for women's programs to a vocational education bill sponsored by Republican Dan Quayle of Indiana. When Quayle proposed a flexibility amendment, allowing the $100 million to be used for other programs as well, Hatch was adamantly opposed. "I am not about to let the $100 million women's package go down the drain because of Dan Quayle," wrote Hatch. Quayle got angry but Hatch prevailed, and the funding remained intact.

Hatch had a high opinion of women in general and was known for showing them uncommon respect. At the same time, he was at a disadvantage in understanding feminism. He and Elaine followed the same traditional pattern as his income-earning father and homemaking mother. The Mormon church insistently taught that this arrangement was ideal for all concerned—women themselves, their husbands, children, and society as a whole.

But Hatch also knew the roles of American women had changed dramatically, even in conservative Utah where over 50 percent of mothers worked outside the home. Trying to sensitize himself on such issues, Hatch hired female assistants in both Utah and Washington specifically to work on family and women's issues. Without condescension, he listened to them, engaged them in meaningful debate, turned them loose with important projects, and stood behind them on important issues.

"I remember when legislation was pending to remove funding under Title IX for women in athletics," said Jan Bennett, a longtime aide who began working in Hatch's Salt Lake office in 1979. "He got to work and saved the funding."

"He was open and he gave me professional challenges I wasn't sure I could do," said Bennett. "Certainly I disagreed with the senator occasionally. But he listened and sometimes he changed his mind. I respected him enough that I wasn't going to flatter him. I would always tell him the truth. At times he took a deep breath, but he was great about it."

Hatch extended this regard to women who were his opponents. Sana Shtasel, a staunch feminist on Packwood's staff, had guided Packwood's fight against Hatch on the ERA, abortion, and civil rights. When Shtasel announced she was leaving Packwood's staff, Hatch dropped by the office to tell her good-bye, leaving a letter and this poem:

The sharp eyes blazing, the fulgent mind churning,
The fire shooting out, with fierce determination . . .
This one believes and lives her scenario
[As] very few others do who really make a difference,
Or count for something in the end.

Shtasel sent Hatch a note of thanks for his "incredible kindness,"
writing, "That you would take the time to be so thoughtful speaks to
what I believe is ultimately important and enduring: caring for others
regardless of any philosophical differences."

He found it harder to find common ground with Eleanor Smeal, who,
for the second time, had been elected president of the National
Organization for Women in a bitter contest with Judy Goldsmith.
Goldsmith had been criticized for relying on negotiation rather than
confrontation, and Smeal had promised to "raise hell."

Her first speech after taking office in September 1985 was at the
National Press Club. The feminist agenda, said Smeal, included legalized
abortion, homosexual rights, an Equal Rights Amendment, and pay
scales guaranteeing women the same wages as men for comparable
work. Although NOW was $1 million in debt and losing members,
Smeal promised a recruiting campaign on campuses and among business and professional women.

"Right-wing bigotry" threatened to erase the "human rights gains of
the past 30 years" in such areas as civil rights, birth control, and abortion, she said. "The fight to outlaw abortion, and make no mistake about
it, is an attack on birth control," said Smeal. "We must recognize bigotry
when it raises its ugly head," she added. "We must wrap it around the
neck of the right wing as we fight for liberty and justice for all. We don't
take our right-wing fascist opponents seriously enough."

Asked to name these "fascists," Smeal listed Jesse Helms, Orrin
Hatch, direct-mail fund-raiser Richard Viguerie, and Paul Weyrich.
"When they stop calling us leftists and communists and pinkos, I'll stop
calling them fascists," she said.

Hatch issued a press release that afternoon:

I can't speak for the others she mentioned, but I have never
referred to Ms. Smeal as a Communist or a "pinko." Ms. Smeal and I
have had occasional differences on some issues . . . [but] I believe I've
given her, or her associates, every opportunity to air her views at my
hearings. And although we haven't agreed on every issue, I hope
never to resort to name calling.

Hatch and his staff were simultaneously finalizing plans for the first of what would become an annual women's conference in Salt Lake City. Held in October 1985, the conference was keynoted by Jeane Kirkpatrick, former U.S. Ambassador to the United Nations. Keynoters in future years would range from Henry Kissinger to humorist Erma Bombeck to Jihan Sadat, widow of slain Egyptian leader Anwar el-Sadat. An unexpected fourteen hundred women jammed into the Hotel Utah for the one-day conference in 1985. Several hundred others were turned away.

The conferences were an outgrowth of another Hatch innovation: his own women's advisory group, established shortly before the first conference. The group included some thirty Utah women leaders representing a wide range of the political spectrum. "I wanted all views represented," explained Hatch, "so I made certain that Democrats and independents—some of whom would never vote for me and probably hated me—were included on the committee." Hatch met with the group regularly and implemented many of their ideas—including the annual conferences.

"He started these women's conferences long before such things were fashionable," said Jan Bennett, who cochaired the event. "He was thinking about the broad range of women's needs and genuinely wanted to find the best solutions."

Workshops included such topics as legal rights; opportunities for women in the 1980s; training, education, and employment; home-based/cottage industries; homemaking as a career choice; combatting stress with healthy lifestyles; and women as policymakers.

Conservatives threatened to picket because one workshop discussed child care. The need was as urgent in Utah as elsewhere, but the dominant culture hadn't yet got the message. Panelists, including a national child care authority, Edward Zigler of Yale University, called child care services the number one problem facing women.

The women's conference helped open Hatch's eyes. He realized that the concerns of women appearing before his committee in Washington were also major issues in Utah, despite the state's strong emphasis on traditional family patterns and lifestyles. Divorce ended half of all marriages; 53 percent of Utah women worked outside the home, including 45 percent of mothers with preschool children. Hundreds of thousands of Utah children needed care. And Utah was not well represented by women in political jobs: 55 percent of Utahns were female, but only 7 percent of elected officials were women.

Hatch introduced Elaine and his mother Helen to attendees, saying, "Together [they] are the strength and inspiration of my life" and pledged himself "to a partnership of men and women striving together for a better society."

Following the 1984 elections, Republican senators chose their leaders for the ninety-ninth Congress on November 28. The process once more was a parade of broken promises, reminding Hatch afresh why he had vowed not to run again for party leadership after his abortive attempt six years earlier.

Choosing a replacement for the retired Howard Baker led the agenda, and five men were candidates: McClure, Lugar, Domenici, Dole, and Stevens. McClure had seventeen look-in-the-face promises of support going into the secret balloting. On the first ballot he got just eight. On the final vote, Bob Dole was elected over Ted Stevens 28-25. Wyoming's popular Alan Simpson was elected assistant majority leader.

Two candidates vied for chairman of the Republican conference: John Chafee of Rhode Island and Jake Garn. During the 1982 election, Garn had worked effectively for Hatch, and Hatch seconded Garn's nomination, warmly praising him as a man of integrity, guts, candor, and common sense. Garn had twenty-nine personal pledges of support in his pocket. He lost 28-25.

For Hatch, the last race was *déjà vu*. To head the senatorial Campaign Committee, Hatch's old vanquisher John Heinz faced off against conservative Malcolm Wallop of Wyoming, Hatch's preference. Wallop had thirty promises of support. He lost 27-26.

During the process, as the outlook for conservatives became clear, Hatch penned a poem of telegraphic phrases, ending:

> Conservative losses stupendous,
> Some thought impossible,
> Unity was not tremendous,
> Jealousy's cup so full.
>
> This President's next four years,
> Endangered by what has been done,
> Explicating all our fears,
> Neutralizing all that's been won.

Later Hatch learned that the "gang of six"—six Republican liberals— had agreed to bloc-vote to move those of similar political persuasion into key positions. Some believed they had cut a deal: in return for the six votes, Dole and Simpson would accept Chafee instead of Garn.

Hatch's view of fellow conservatives was so dim that he verbally disassociated himself. "I think the conservatives deserve what they're getting," he wrote privately the day after the election. "They never band together. They never get together. They never work for each other."

Paul Laxalt was equally fed up, telling Hatch the same day he was going to retire in 1986. Hatch guessed that Laxalt might ask Reagan to appoint him to the Supreme Court. "If you get on the court, pull me in with you," Hatch said with a wink. "I'll do all the work for both of us."

Hatch was only half joking. Others, including White House personnel director John Harrington, had suggested the possibility of his selection. "You would really make a good appointment for that," Hatch recorded Harrington's comment in late 1983. "You're just the right age and you have the right philosophy. And you know the Constitution very well. However, you're almost too valuable to us in the Senate to leave there."

"I'd have at least thirty years on the court," Hatch agreed, "and I could do an awful lot of good for the Reagan legacy." But although he was flattered and too canny to foreclose options prematurely, Hatch did not see himself spending the rest of his career in the cloistered atmosphere of the Supreme Court.

Hatch, meanwhile, had serious misgivings about part of the Reagan legacy: the federal deficit. The budget package Reagan submitted to Congress in 1985 for the fiscal year beginning October 1 was, Hatch believed, "just a fake, phony budget." Among other things, it included unrealistically low farm subsidy estimates and user fees for currently free federal programs—something Congress in the past had refused to approve.

"It was just pathetic," he wrote privately. He planned to vote against it and publicly charged in a floor speech: "We have raised taxes a great deal in the last few years, and we are still facing a 220 billion dollar deficit for fiscal year 1986. . . . Raising taxes has only tempted Congress to spend more money."

Echoes of Vietnam could still be heard in Utah in 1984. The state's congressional delegation and Governor Matheson held a meeting in October to present medals to the parents or spouses of thirteen Utahns missing in action. As one serviceman's name was called, a rough-hewn old rancher and his wife stood to receive a medal, the rancher sobbing uncontrollably.

Each official spoke for about three minutes. When Hatch's turn came, his own eyes frequently filled with tears. He said in part:

> While a man can have no greater love than to be willing to lay down his life for his friends, . . . the pain of losing a family member who has so laid down his life sometimes seems unbearable.
>
> I have never hurt so badly as when I, as a boy, learned of my older brother's death in World War II. Not a day passes but that I

reflect upon the loss of my brother. These melancholy moments are filled with so many emotions—anger that he was taken from me; pride that he died honorably for his country; sadness, for I miss him still; solace, in that I will be with him again someday.

But as piercing as my own pain has been, I realize full well that your own sorrow has been augmented by uncertainty. . . . In closing, I am compelled to mention that truth of which I hope you are all aware: These men are not missing in the eyes of God. The God who rules the universe watches over these young men—wherever they might be. And surely He wants each of us to feel His love and comfort just as deeply as we long to extend our love and comfort to those whose absence we remember today.

As the meeting broke up, Hatch embraced the ranch couple, telling them he understood what they had gone through. "It almost tore my heart to shreds," he summarized privately that night.

Earlier, with time on his hands between flights at an airport, Hatch had put other thoughts about his dead brother on paper.

> Almost forty years ago my only brother died,
> We know not how, but it must have been badly,
> For one member of his crew returned, unspeaking,
> Never to talk again about the awful end
> Which laid my brother down, till brought home again,
> Encased in metal, no longer to be seen,
> Or touched, or loved, except in absentia
> For such future time God provides,
> To those who hope, who pray,
> Who never go away, in spite of death.

Demands on Hatch were unceasing. Especially debilitating for him and most other members of Congress was the constant need to raise funds for the next election campaign while fulfilling promises made in the last one. Although senatorial terms were three times longer than those in the House, senators had to campaign statewide—a costlier proposition.

Elected to a second term in November 1982, Hatch began fundraising for the 1988 campaign less than a year later in September 1983. A successful reception by the Committee for Republican Leadership "should have raised thirty to fifty thousand dollars for my PAC," he wrote privately on September 21. "That's a good start."

Anna Chennault organized a fund-raising birthday party for him the following March, netting another $35,000. Also helping Hatch raise funds were motion picture industry lobbyist Jack Valenti, a strong supporter, and corporate leader—some said raider—T. Boone Pickens, Jr., who promised to raise $100,000 and did.

Incumbents already had such built-in advantages as free mailing privileges, called "franking." Most used it to distribute newsletters and other mass mailings to constituents, in addition to other correspondence. Ostensibly the newsletters were to keep home folks aware of issues in Washington and to solicit their ideas. But the mailings also had the distinct political utility of keeping a member's name before voters in a light of his or her own choosing.

In December 1985 the Senate, under pressure, revealed for the first time how many taxpayer dollars each member spent on mass mailings for the previous quarter. Not surprisingly, all but two of the top mailers were up for reelection the following year. While twenty-one senators had spent nothing, seventy-nine others spent a total of $10.95 million, led by California Democrat Alan Cranston at $1.63 million—more than double the next closest senator.

Hatch had spent $135,819 during the quarter to send 969,350 pieces of mass mail to a state with a population of less than two million. The cost for Hatch, based on total state population, was about eight cents per resident, putting him tenth among senators.

One reason for the intensive mailings was to bypass what Hatch continued to regard as a generally hostile mainstream media. Another successful approach was through the more than forty weekly newspapers in Utah. Hatch's office began sending them Washington columns carrying Hatch's byline, which many of the short-staffed weeklies ran unedited.

Speaking to the state's association of weekly newspaper publishers in February 1986, Hatch thanked them for the support and acknowledged continuing challenges with the state's major dailies. "They continue to write 'moving' editorials about me," quipped Hatch. "The *Salt Lake Tribune* wants me to move more to the left, the *Deseret News* wants me to move more to the right, and the *Ogden Standard Examiner* wants me to just move back to Pennsylvania."

On the national scene, Hatch was mentioned often in newspapers and periodicals, but seldom in detail. He was also a favorite utility player for television networks because of his ability to speak knowledgeably at short notice on a wide range of topics. Between fall 1985 and June 1986, Hatch and his liberal nemesis Howard Metzenbaum squared off weekly in a debate on CNN, aired during "Take Two," the TV network's midday magazine-style program.

Hatch usually felt guilty if he took time for a genuine vacation, but he sometimes managed to work in recreation between other duties.

During the August 1985 congressional recess, Hatch had what he called "one of the best days I have ever spent."

Virginia Senator John Warner and his son teamed up with a group including Hatch, his son Jess, and a son-in-law for a trip down the Colorado River in inflated rafts and then on Utah's Lake Powell by speedboats. Warner, former Navy Secretary and now divorced from Elizabeth Taylor who complained that he was dull, was anything but dull on the Colorado.

"He was a hoot," recalls Hatch. "He kept going skinny-dipping every time we'd stop." At one stop, Hatch returned from a hike to see a ghostly chocolate-colored apparition at the campsite. It was Warner, stark naked and plastered from head to toe with pumice mud. "They had formed a mud hole near the river and he was diving in and out of it," said Hatch. "Warner was in his glory." The pumice supposedly was good for the skin.

They stayed overnight at Bullfrog Marina on Lake Powell and fished the next day, catching sixty striped bass. Warner was so taken with one of Hatch's catches, an eight-pounder, that he asked to keep it whole. That evening they arrived by plane just in time for a tourism reception up north. With no time to change, Hatch and Warner, still dressed in fishing jeans, strode into fancy Deer Valley Lodge and waded into the coat-and-tie crowd, Warner proudly carrying the huge bass.

Hatch also enjoyed attending college football and basketball games in Utah. After Brigham Young University won the national football championship, Hatch accompanied coach LaVell Edwards to the White House in January 1985 to receive congratulations from another football fan and former collegiate player, President Reagan.

Hatch continued to read whenever he had a spare minute, often alternating among several books at once. As he finished a volume, he would add it to a bedside stack that sometimes got several feet deep before Elaine found another corner for their unwieldy library. "I now have an excellent light and a comfortable chair for reading," wrote Hatch. "What more could a man ask for?"

Recently he had been reading *Decision,* a novel by Alan Drury about a Supreme Court case; *The Constitution* by Edward Samuel Corwin; and two books by John Fowles, *The Magus* and *The French Lieutenant's Woman.* Hatch kept a dictionary beside him, noting that *The Magus* had 148 words new to him.

He bought an anthology of modern poetry and made a half-dozen pages of notes on favorite thoughts, including a quote from Coleridge, "Prose equals words in their best order; poetry equals the best words in the best order," and thoughts from Aristotle: "Poetry is something more philosophical and more worthy of serious attention than history," and "Plato is dear to me, but dearer still is the truth."

Hatch also liked Jean Cocteau's enigmatic epigram: "Victor Hugo—a madman who thought he was Victor Hugo."

Stanzas of a Robert Frost poem had personal significance to him:

> The woods are lovely, dark and deep,
> But I have promises to keep,
> And miles to go before I sleep.

Already immersed in domestic issues, Hatch was increasingly drawn toward foreign affairs. In 1985 he considered taking a seat on the Foreign Relations Committee, chaired by his friend Richard Lugar, but was appointed instead by Majority Leader Bob Dole to the Intelligence Committee, equally important at that time.

The committee was changing hands. Minnesota's David Durenberger was named as chair, with Vermont Democrat Patrick Leahy as vice chair. Hatch worried about both choices. Durenberger was separated from his wife, and there were rumors he was drinking excessively. Leahy, a liberal dove, also seemed out of place helping to lead the sensitive committee.

Hatch's concerns were realized in spades: During the two years they led the committee, Durenberger and Leahy attacked CIA Director William Casey, hotly opposed U.S. covert actions in Nicaragua and else-where, and—totally beyond the pale for Hatch—reportedly leaked national security secrets to the media.

Late in 1985 Hatch openly criticized Durenberger, bringing a stinging rebuke from the Minnesotan, scrawled in half-inch-high black letters on committee stationery:

> Dear "disgusted,"
> A Republican President once said "you can disagree publicly with your colleagues, but to attack them thusly, is to defeat your purpose."
> If you want to be a productive member of this committee you might keep that in mind. . . .

Some members of Congress disliked Hatch, but he had long since opted for respect over popularity. Respect he had. Hatch was among those who could slug it out in hearings and floor debate, then walk into the cloakroom or Senate restaurant to banter and joke with no after-taste. Most senators understood that a political foe on one issue may be a crucial ally on another.

Despite his reputation for intensity, Hatch saw how the most influential senators used humor and obvious goodwill to defuse tense situations with their colleagues. The Senate combined some of the worst aspects of both pressure cooker and fishbowl, so comic moments were welcome when they came—even when the joke was on a member of the club.

During an all-night debate on a tax bill in April 1984, some of the senators began swapping stories between votes. One of the funniest involved Larry Pressler, the young South Dakota Republican lampooned by the media for being overly image-conscious. Pressler, it seems, had returned to his apartment at the Watergate one night and was asleep when a buzzer went off, signaling a vote on Capitol Hill. Pressler raced to his car and drove to the hill, trying to call the cloakroom on his cellular phone to make sure the vote was kept open until he arrived. But he could not get through.

Hair disheveled, he burst through the Senate door just after Majority Leader Baker had called an end to the vote. Beside himself with anger and frustration, Pressler asked Baker who was handling the cloakroom. "George is," answered Baker.

Steam shooting from his ears, Pressler stormed off the floor and into the cloakroom. Seated inside were two clerks—George and a petite, pretty blond woman named Ann. Pressler stomped up to the two and, firmly planting both feet, said, "Okay, which one of you is George?"

Many funny stories were told about former Virginia Republican William Scott. Shortly after his single term began in 1973, *New Times* magazine named Scott the dumbest member of Congress. Scott called a press conference to refute the charge—proving the magazine right.

Scott reportedly was once at a Pentagon briefing when an officer began discussing missile silos. "I didn't come here to talk about agriculture," insisted the Virginian.

Executives often personalize letters by crossing through impersonal salutations typed by a secretary. But Garn got a letter from Scott that was typed "Dear Jake." Scott had crossed out the "Jake" and, above it, written "Colleague."

When Edwin Meese, Reagan confidant and White House counsel, was nominated Attorney General in 1984, Democrats, led by Kennedy and especially Ohio's Howard Metzenbaum, put him through an extraordinarily long and bitter confirmation fight before the Judiciary Committee.

Early on, with Thurmond and Hatch momentarily away, Wyoming Republican Al Simpson wielded the gavel. He got into a tussle over how to proceed with Metzenbaum, a wealthy liberal and the bane of White House nominees. Finally Metzenbaum nodded to Meese, saying "Look, if you want to give me a signal, put up one finger."

Simpson quickly jumped in: "No, I won't permit that. Knowing how he feels about you, he might put up the wrong finger."

Rejoining the hearing, Hatch led Meese through a recitation of the financial sacrifices made by the Meese family in leaving California to work in government, including tens of thousands in interest costs on homes, along with transportation and moving costs to Washington.

"This has really been a disaster for you financially to make this change, hasn't it?" asked Hatch. "I know you're not a wealthy man."

"My testimony proves that," answered Meese.

"Well," said Hatch, "I find it very refreshing that somebody like you is willing to make this kind of sacrifice for your country and your President. It's apparent that you're not one of the millionaire senators asking questions."

The audience burst into laughter as Metzenbaum leaned into his microphone: "I didn't hear that."

Hatch cheerfully repeated it.

Meese was left to twist in limbo throughout 1984, as committee members charged that he had helped get federal jobs for individuals who had given him financial assistance. It would be thirteen months—longest for a cabinet nominee in recent history—before Meese was confirmed by the committee and then the full Senate in February 1985.

On the day the Judiciary Committee voted 12-6 to confirm, Meese telephoned Hatch. "Without you, Orrin, I never would have made it through," Meese told him. "My wife and children really love you."

"Tell them I love them, too," responded Hatch. "This has been a tough year for all of you. But brighter days are ahead." Several weeks later the full Senate voted 63-31 to confirm Meese, Democrats casting all the negative votes. Again Meese phoned Hatch: "I fully know I could not have made this without you."

Meese's year-long torment foreshadowed other titanic struggles to come before the Judiciary Committee.

18

The Rehnquisition

I T WAS A BEAUTIFUL SPRING MORNING in Washington as the dark blue Lincoln glided toward the Supreme Court. In the back seat were two men who could have been father and son—white-haired Chief Justice Warren Burger and Associate Justice William Rehnquist.

As they reached the corner of Second and East Capitol streets, Burger suddenly pointed disbelievingly out the window and shouted for their driver to stop. Standing on the corner was a life-size cardboard cutout of him in his flowing judicial robes next to a photographer and this sign: "HAVE YOUR PICTURE TAKEN WITH THE CHIEF JUSTICE. ONLY $1."

Burger, not known for his sense of humor, sputtered as Rehnquist howled with laughter. When Rehnquist had regained his composure, he had two words for his senior colleague: "April Fools'!"

Now Orrin Hatch chortled as Rehnquist retold the story in Hatch's office. Rehnquist's photographer-accomplice in the practical joke was Hatch's son Brent, now a graduate of Columbia Law School and climbing his way up the legal ladder in Washington.

On June 17, 1986, President Reagan announced the retirement of Burger, seventy-eight, and the elevation of Rehnquist, sixty-one, to take his place as Chief Justice, with Antonin Scalia nominated to become an associate justice. "Nino" Scalia, fifty, a judge on the U.S. Court of Appeals in Washington, would be the first person of Italian descent to serve on the high court.

A week after his nomination, Rehnquist met with Hatch, the White House's designated point man to lead Rehnquist and Scalia through the

Judiciary Committee maze and on to confirmation. Strom Thurmond chaired the committee. While Thurmond was solid and predictable, at eighty-three he lacked the all-around stamina for which Hatch, fifty-two, was acclaimed. It was a foregone conclusion that Democrats would give Rehnquist, the Court's leading conservative, a rough time.

As they laughed and talked in his office, Rehnquist reminded Hatch of a caricature by satirical French artist Honoré Daumier. "Rehnquist's hair hung straight down over his eyebrows, and he had thick glasses that accented his huge head," recalled Hatch. "While everyone else in Washington wore spit-shined dress shoes, he wore desert boots or sandals around town." Hatch liked him a lot and assured the judge he would support him "as hard as I can."

The following day Scalia came in. He had been named to the appeals court in 1982 by President Reagan, who admired Scalia's outspoken conservatism as a former Justice Department official and more recently as a teacher at the University of Chicago. Scalia was gregarious and artic-ulate—traits Hatch believed would help make him a consensus-builder on the high court.

"We hope you'll be on the bench for at least thirty years," Hatch told Scalia, a heavy smoker, "so it's important that you take care of your health." He nodded toward the cigarettes in Scalia's pocket. "You ought to quit those."

Immediately Scalia pulled the pack from his pocket and cheerfully handed it to Hatch. "I quit as of this moment."

"You mean that?" asked Hatch.

"I really do." Then Scalia caught himself. "But you don't include pipe smoking, do you?"

"Sure I do."

"Well, that will take a little bit longer."

Both men laughed heartily.

January 1986 had begun with Hatch standing on the Capitol steps and belting out the Ohio State University fight song, carried coast-to-coast on National Public Radio. Hatch was paying off a bet against Metzenbaum that BYU would beat Metzenbaum's alma mater in the Florida Citrus Bowl. Ohio won 10-7.

That same week, Hatch dived into a more urgent task: Eight-month-old Keile Burrell of Roy, Utah, was dying of biliary atresia, a malfunction of the bile duct, at Salt Lake City's famed Primary Children's Hospital. Keile (pronounced "Key-lee") urgently needed a liver transplant to survive. The University of Nebraska Medical Center agreed to attempt the operation—but only with a guarantee of full payment.

With Keile sinking fast, Primary Children's called Hatch for help on Friday, January 16. Hatch immediately called President Reagan, who ordered a medical jet from Utah's Hill Air Force Base to stand by to transport the tiny girl to Omaha. The President also guaranteed that the money would be made available to cover costs, probably through Medicaid.

That evening Keile went into a coma. By the next afternoon a donor had been found and Keile was flying to Omaha. She was still comatose and was the hospital's youngest transplant patient. Doctors were dubious but operated anyway.

Four months later, Hatch entered an anteroom in the west wing of the White House. Waiting to enter the Oval Office with him and greet the President were Wayne and Rochelle Burrell holding their daughter, now a healthy one-year-old.

When Thurmond, DeConcini, and Hatch's 1982 constitutional amendment to balance the federal budget passed the Senate but died in the House, he didn't give up. In March 1986 he worked out a slightly revised version with several other senators.

"Already we face a $170 billion bill each year just to pay the interest on the national debt," said Hatch in floor debate. "Our children face even greater burdens in the future.... The opponents of [the amendment] suggest that the answer to this moral dilemma is that Congress should simply exert its will to balance the budget. Congress has exerted its will, yet we have had deficits for 25 of the last 26 years and 48 of the last 56.... We have run up nearly half of our national debt in just the last nine years. This Congress and its predecessors simply cannot overcome the spending bias without a constitutional tool."

In 1985, Congress had passed the Gramm-Rudman-Hollings antideficit act, supposedly setting strict deficit targets over the next five years that would result in a balanced budget by 1991. Opponents of Hatch's amendment argued that Gramm-Rudman-Hollings would take care of the problem. Hatch and his supporters agreed that the measure was the best vehicle presently available, but argued that Congress would slip around it.

Republican Senator Daniel Evans of Washington led the opposition, calling the amendment "completely unworkable" because the federal budget was too complex and didn't lend itself to simple accounting rules. Special interest groups, including organized labor and the powerful American Association of Retired Persons, also lobbied hard against it. The final vote was 66-34, one short of the two-thirds necessary for constitutional amendments.

Hatch was disappointed with two members of the Republican leadership, Heinz of Pennsylvania and Chafee of Rhode Island, who had voted against the amendment. He was also frustrated with Delaware Democrat Joseph Biden, preparing to run for President in two years, who feigned support for the amendment, then voted against it. "I like Joe Biden," Hatch wrote in his private notes, "but he has great ambition. It's not bad to have great ambition, but it is bad if you don't rise above it when the national interest is at stake."

As an example of what he meant, he cited Ted Kennedy. True, "Kennedy takes cheap shots and is a demagogue. However, Kennedy is more than a politician. I will never forget the time we were able to resolve the railroad strike. Kennedy easily could have played politics with it, but he agreed with me that something needed to be done. There have been other cases of this as well."

Despite the outcome, accolades poured into Hatch's office. "You were really superb," wrote Paul Simon on March 27. "You are a *good legislator* in the finest sense of that term. I'm proud to be associated with you."

Another Democrat, DeConcini of Arizona, wrote on the same day: "Orrin, as I said on the floor, and have repeated many times, you are absolutely a model for a Senate leader. Your in-depth understanding of and eloquence in describing the amendment put us all in awe. You have my admiration—I look forward to many future fights we can wage together."

James Davidson, chairman of the National Taxpayers Union, a major force behind the amendment, told Hatch, "We fell one vote short. But without your leadership we would have had no chance to reach 66 votes. It is regrettable that American children cannot comprehend what your efforts mean for their future. If they could look into the future, the letters of thanks would come spilling forth."

But all the plaudits didn't balance the budget nor lessen the sting for Hatch of losing so valuable an opportunity by a single vote.

Testing both the power of the presidency and the perils of partisanship for Hatch and his colleagues were Reagan's appointments to the federal judiciary—perhaps his most enduring domestic legacy.

By the end of 1986 Reagan had appointed nearly 30 percent of active federal judges, all with lifetime tenures. Democrats on the Judiciary Committee, alarmed over the changing complexion of the federal bench, began to scrutinize White House nominees more thoroughly—an effort Hatch called "a foot-dragging ideological exercise" to screen the political views of nominees.

Congress had long been controlled by Democrats except for the short-lived GOP breakthrough in the Senate. But voters had a habit of putting

Republicans in the White House, with Democrat Jimmy Carter's single term being the lone exception since 1968. With the Executive Branch usually out of reach, liberal special interest groups—labor unions, feminists, civil rights organizations—exerted enormous pressure on Democrats to help control the courts, where they had won victories unattainable through the legislative process. The Democratic choke-point on the courts was the Senate Judiciary Committee, which approved federal judges.

Victories on Capitol Hill were coming harder for Reagan, a lame-duck President and, at seventy-five, the oldest chief executive in U.S. history. Although his administration usually got the judicial appointees it wanted, exceptions were becoming more frequent, especially for high-profile positions. William Bradford Reynolds was turned down to head the Justice Department's civil rights division, and the committee also turned thumbs-down on several conservative nominees for judgeships.

Hatch, angry at the rejections, accused several Democrats of turning the committee into a "star chamber" reminiscent of the English court in the 1600s which passed judgment without trial by jury and finally resorted to torturing confessions out of victims.

Leverage was greatest at the Supreme Court level, where only nine unelected individuals ruled on the nation's laws—compared to the 535 members of Congress who wrote them at the federal level. Nominees Scalia and, especially, Rehnquist were ultimate targets for special-interest groups. Their confirmations could decide a host of vital issues to be tested before the high court, including continuing efforts to erode or overturn *Roe v. Wade*.

In Hatch's view, confirmation of the two solid conservatives was vital because Reagan's first appointee to the Supreme Court, Sandra Day O'Connor, had been "waffling" on a variety of issues. She and her husband had become fixtures on the Washington social scene, and Hatch felt she was in danger of being compromised by the Washington establishment. The *Washington Post* and *New York Times* nudged O'Connor toward the left, often praising her as "maturing" when she voted more liberally than expected.

Reagan had taken a chance in nominating Rehnquist as chief justice. Rehnquist had a well-defined record as the high court's leading conservative—a record certain to be attacked by opponents during confirmation. Considered extremely bright by all sides, he held a law degree with highest honors from Stanford University, had practiced law in Phoenix, and had been appointed to the Supreme Court in 1971 by President Nixon.

July 29, Tuesday
Justice Rehnquist, with his wife, Natalie, and other family members sitting behind him, takes his seat at the witness table.

Wyoming Republican Alan Simpson advises: Hang on tight. A bird of prey known as "a bug-eyed zealot" is out to get you. Expect "loose facts, nastiness, hype, hoorah, maybe a little hysteria," and be prepared to hear yourself described as "a racist, extremist, trampler of the poor, assassin of the First Amendment . . . and a crazed young law clerk who was about two tacos short of a combination plate."41

Rehnquist faces a daunting Democratic lineup including ranking Democrat Joseph Biden, ambitious, brash, and utterly partisan despite a pleasant outward demeanor; Howard Metzenbaum, a liberal ideologue as far to the left end of the political spectrum as Jesse Helms is to the right; and the irrepressible Ted Kennedy.

Kennedy admits that his mind is already made up. "Mainstream or too extreme—that is the question," he says. "By his own record of massive isolated dissent, Justice Rehnquist answers that question. He is too extreme on race, too extreme on women's rights, too extreme on freedom of speech, too extreme on separation of church and state, too extreme to be chief justice."

Metzenbaum seconds Kennedy's objection, prompting the observation by columnist George Will that the two senators "are not exactly [the] Lewis and Clark team you would send exploring to locate the American mainstream."

Hatch counters, "When it comes to competence, when it comes to integrity, when it comes to faithfulness to the law, I believe you get an A-plus in those areas." Opposition to Rehnquist, he adds, is nothing more than "character assassination. . . . It's time that we quit hacking at everybody who comes before this committee."

July 30, Wednesday

Vermont Democrat Patrick Leahy asks about a clause in the deed to Rehnquist's summer home in Vermont that bars sales to Jews.

Rehnquist says he wasn't aware of the provision until Senate aides recently brought it to his attention. Certainly the language is "obnoxious," but it is also "meaningless" since the Supreme Court has declared such covenants illegal. At any rate, he agrees to have it removed.

Democratic senators say witnesses are standing by to testify that Rehnquist, as a Republican activist in Arizona some twenty years ago, harassed minority voters at the polls, asking blacks to read excerpts from the Arizona Constitution.

Rehnquist denies the charges. The witnesses are simply "mistaken. I just can't offer any other explanation."

What about a memo he wrote thirty-three years ago as a clerk for the late Supreme Court Justice Robert Jackson? It defended the Court's historic position that "separate, but equal" facilities for blacks were constitutional. Rehnquist says that, as Jackson's clerk, he was summarizing Jackson's views more than his own.

Representatives of the American Bar Association testify that, after numerous interviews and a review of Rehnquist's cases, he is "well qualified"—the ABA's highest rating—to be chief justice.

July 31, Thursday

Hatch is working nearly twenty-hour days, keeping Rehnquist's nomination on track while tending to other duties. Behind the scenes, he teams with Ted Kennedy on a very sensitive matter: Rehnquist's health, including earlier episodes of alleged overmedication. The committee agrees to have Hatch and Kennedy choose a doctor to review the medical records fully and testify about Rehnquist's current fitness.

They turn to Dr. William Pollin, former head of the National Institute on Drug Abuse. His confidential report concludes that Rehnquist has no unresolved health problems. Committee member Paul Simon, D-Illinois, however, says the public is "entitled" to see the full report, while conceding there is nothing in it that would "impair his ability to serve effectively as chief justice."

But Hatch objects, telling the *New York Times*, "Frankly, the only significant thing in the report is that Justice Rehnquist is well today." In a pattern to be repeated in future Supreme Court confirmation struggles, however, portions of the report are leaked to the media anyway, beginning with the *Washington Post*, which reports on August 13 that Rehnquist "was seriously 'dependent' on a powerful hypnotic drug from 1977 to 1981, frequently using up a three-month prescription in a single month and going back for another supply, according to informed sources."

The *Post* says the drug Placidyl was prescribed in 1971 by Dr. Freeman Cary, the Capitol physician, "to help [Rehnquist] sleep despite severe back pains." It quotes Simon as saying there was "no question" Rehnquist had become "dependent" on the drug well before entering a hospital in 1981 to break its usage. Left ambiguous in the media accounts was whether Rehnquist had simply followed doctor's orders—as Hatch maintains—or whether he exceeded the recommended dosage, as Cary reportedly told the FBI.

"As soon as he was informed it was a bad drug, he stopped using it," says Hatch. "Rehnquist followed his physician's directions in all respects, and, at any rate, that was all in the past and he was found physically and emotionally fit to serve as chief justice."

Kennedy also leads Rehnquist into another thicket about a restrictive covenant on a former home in Arizona that Rehnquist bought in 1961 and sold eight years later. Kennedy reads the 1928 deed, which says the home shall not be "sold, transferred or leased to . . . [nor] inhabited by or occupied by any person not of the white or Caucasian race."

> Kennedy: Were you familiar with that particular provision?
> Rehnquist: I certainly don't recall it, no. . . .
> Kennedy: Would you now examine the warranty if you purchased property today?
> Rehnquist: Well, if a lawyer were handling the thing for me—or any sort of a complicated warranty—I think I would tend to rely on the lawyer. . . .
> Kennedy: . . . Would you care if you joined a country club or something like that that restricted women or Jews?
> Rehnquist: No, certainly [I wouldn't join].
> Kennedy: Or blacks?
> Rehnquist: No.
> Kennedy: Well, you'd know about that then. You would find out about that before you made application I assume.
> Rehnquist: Yes, I would. . . .
> Kennedy: Well. . . . You didn't in 1961.
> Rehnquist: It simply hadn't occurred to me.

Kennedy continues to press the issue, but Hatch explodes: "This is the biggest red herring I've seen in the whole hearing, and there are a number of them. He didn't know about it, he found out about it through this process. . . . It is ridiculous. . . . You know it's ridiculous, I know it's ridiculous. It isn't enforceable. *Come on.*"

Several senators speak at once and Chairman Thurmond bangs the gavel to restore order. Thurmond and DeConcini note that property owners often don't read every word of their titles. But Kennedy still won't drop it. The point, he insists, "is the real question of the sensitivity of this nominee. The issue of civil rights."

A few days later, the tables turn neatly. *U.S. News & World Report* produces a deed to a Georgetown house that John F. Kennedy purchased in 1957 as a senator. The deed specifies that no part of the land "shall ever be used or occupied by or sold, conveyed, leased, rented or given to Negroes or any person or persons of the Negro race or blood."

Asked to comment, Ted Kennedy brazens it out. He has "no knowledge of any covenant on the former home of President Kennedy" and his late brother couldn't have known about the "deplorable" clause.

August 1, Friday
The Arizona witnesses materialize. Four Democrats testify that they

saw Rehnquist challenge black and Hispanic voters during statewide elections between 1958 and 1964. A fifth witness, former federal prosecutor James J. Brosnahan says he went to a precinct where minority voters pointed out Rehnquist as the Republican challenger who had been harassing them.

Hatch tries to shake Brosnahan's testimony, suggesting he has Rehnquist mixed up with someone else. "I didn't get Bill Rehnquist mixed up with anybody," says Brosnahan, now a San Francisco trial lawyer and prominent Democrat. "I knew him then. And I could spot him now. And there's no question about that."

The Republicans, however, consider Brosnahan unreliably partisan. Years later, as an assistant to independent counsel Lawrence E. Walsh, observers would point to Brosnahan as the source of damaging revelations about President George Bush's alleged involvement in the Iran-contra affair — leaked to the media just four days before the 1992 election that Bush lost.

Six former Arizona Republican officials and party workers deny seeing Rehnquist harass anyone. Phoenix attorney Jim Bush, who worked directly with Rehnquist, says "no lawyer, including Mr. Rehnquist, acted as a challenger."

Judge Scalia appeared before the committee for a comparatively painless one-day hearing in August. Like Rehnquist, Scalia had been brought to Washington initially by President Nixon, to serve as an assistant attorney general. A Harvard law graduate, Scalia then taught at the University of Chicago, where his outspoken conservatism attracted Reagan, who appointed him to the D.C. Court of Appeals in 1982.

"I assure you I have no agenda," he told the Judiciary Committee. "I am not going onto the court with a list of things I want to do."

Kennedy said, "The nomination of Judge Scalia presents none of the troubling issues with respect to truthfulness, candor, judicial ethics, and full disclosure that have marred the nomination of Justice Rehnquist." On most issues, said Kennedy, "it is difficult to maintain that Judge Scalia is outside the mainstream."

But politics made the difference between Democratic support of Scalia and opposition to Rehnquist. Ironically, Scalia's judicial record was as conservative as Rehnquist's. But as the first Italian-American to be nominated to the Supreme Court, he was a key to continued Democratic domination of the Italian-American vote.

In mid-August, the Judiciary Committee voted 13-5 to recommend Rehnquist's appointment and 18-0 for Scalia's. The five against Rehnquist were all Democrats: Kennedy, Biden, Metzenbaum, Leahy, and Simon.

Senator Laxalt said Rehnquist "had everything but the kitchen sink thrown at him," and Simpson added that Rehnquist was the victim of "harassment and hearsay that would never be admitted in any court in the world and would never be used against the most wretched felon."

The anti-Rehnquist fight went to the Senate floor during the second week in September 1986. The full Senate debated the Rehnquist and Scalia nominations for five days, scheduling a vote for September 17.

Hatch defended Rehnquist in numerous media interviews and TV news-talk programs. In a final floor speech the day of the vote, Hatch attacked Rehnquist's opponents as extremists:

> The Rehnquisition is nearly over. The nation has watched in horror as the grand inquisitors have turned the Senate chamber into a star chamber. The inquisitors have dragged out their racks and stretched the truth..... [Rehnquist] has written more majority opinions over the last four terms—73 to be exact—than any other justice.... Just like the real Inquisition, these inquisitors were not interested in Justice Rehnquist's faithfulness to the Constitution; they were interested in whether he agreed with their narrow dogmas.... [The inquisitors] have searched in vain for any inconsistency, crack, or break that they might use to justify their foreordained verdict—guilty, guilty, guilty....
> It is time for the Senate to end the Rehnquisition and proceed to a fair vote.

That evening the Senate voted 65-33 to confirm Rehnquist as the nation's sixteenth chief justice, and 98-0 to confirm Scalia. Hatch watched with relish as Metzenbaum walked to the marble counter at the front of the Senate chamber as his name was called on the Scalia vote. As a Democrat, Metzenbaum felt duty-bound to support Italian-American Scalia, despite the judge's solid conservatism. But the liberal Metzenbaum was so reluctant that he could barely croak, "Yee-aaa."

The thirty-three negative votes were the greatest number cast in the twentieth century against a Supreme Court nominee who was confirmed. Eleanor Smeal of NOW, who had campaigned hard against Rehnquist, called the negative votes a "moral defeat" for the Reagan administration. Reagan himself predicted Rehnquist "will prove to be a Chief Justice of historic stature."

One *New York Times* summary of the Rehnquist hearings was an article headlined "Defender of the Justice," accompanied by a photo of Hatch. "Now the fierce partisan, now the student of the Constitution," began the piece, "with biting sarcasm or gentler gibes, Senator Orrin G.

Hatch emerged from the Supreme Court confirmation hearings this week as the principal defender of the Reagan administration and its nominee for Chief Justice, William H. Rehnquist."

Although Hatch was "only fourth in seniority among the Republicans on the Judiciary Committee, . . . it was he, rather than Senator Strom Thurmond, who took the lead in trying to guide Justice Rehnquist through the traps the committee's Democrats had laid."

Rehnquist sent Hatch a hand-written note: "You have been a tower of strength on the Judiciary Committee during a rather grueling ordeal for me. Thank you from the bottom of my heart."

President Reagan also sent a warm letter: "Your comments during the committee hearings and your skilled negotiations with your colleagues were key to the committee's approval of my nominees, and I thank you."

A third letter came from Senator Dan Quayle:

September 18, 1986

Dear Orrin:

Just a note to say you did a terrific job on the Supreme Court nominations.

"Rehnquistition" was a master stroke! . . .

Dan

Quayle misspelled "Rehnquisition," adding an extra *t*, but his heart was in the right place.

Hatch's stock rocketed after his skillful defense of Rehnquist. "Washington is already fluttering with rumors about the court's *next* vacancy," said *Newsweek,* days after Rehnquist was confirmed. "Sources in the Reagan administration and the Senate say the nominee could be Sen. Orrin Hatch." *Newsweek* added that "Hatch himself seems eager: colleagues observe that he is prepping for the nation's highest court by reading official reports of recent cases as he pedals an exercise cycle in the Senate gymnasium."

The *Baltimore Sun's* respected legal reporter Lyle Denniston called Hatch "a tall, superbly dressed senator with a made-for-television face, the real leader of the pro-Rehnquist forces and a senator with a conservative record entirely pleasing to Ronald Reagan." He reported that "among the Reagan administration's judge-makers, the Utah senator has been on various 'short lists' for a Supreme Court nomination for some time, insiders say. . . . [Hatch] has been teased about it by colleagues, but the idea now apparently is being taken more seriously."

And the *Legal Times* said, "The 52-year-old Hatch . . . has been in the thick of virtually every constitutional battle waged during his decade in the Senate" and "does not try too hard to squelch such speculation. 'It's nice to have people think of me in that light,' he admits. 'I suppose if any President asked any of us to be on the Supreme Court, it would be a great honor that you would have to consider.'"

One reason for the flurry of media attention was a general belief that senators would not oppose a colleague for the high court. Democrats, however, put out the word that they wouldn't go easy on Hatch or any other conservative nominated to the court.

19

The Stingers

S TARTING IN 1985, HATCH BECAME a catalyst for action in the international arena, much as he had been domestically. He had tested international waters earlier and found them to his liking. Just two weeks after his reelection in November 1982, Hatch and an aide were off to Europe for ten days, visiting the sites of four different arms-control talks in which the United States was then engaged. Hatch helped monitor foreign policy for the Republican senatorial Steering Committee.

Hatch seemed to handle himself with the aplomb of a seasoned diplomat on that trip. His only nervous moments came when he missed a connecting flight in Frankfurt and drove to Bonn on the autobahn. He was traveling 115 miles an hour in his rented Mercedes-280 as other drivers whizzed past going 130 to 160. "I was scared to death," confessed Hatch in a private note.

One of Hatch's meetings was in Madrid with the Commission for Security and Cooperation in Europe. After a breakfast briefing with Max Kampelman, head of the U.S. team, Hatch had a session with a group of Russians including a senior official named Dubinin. He was handsome, with unusually thick, wavy hair that stood perhaps five inches off his head—in sharp contrast to most other members of the Soviet delegation, who were bald. "We made absolutely no headway in expressing American concerns," recalled Hatch. "The Russians were very serious and noncommittal."

As Hatch and Kampelman stood at the door to leave, Hatch suddenly turned to the head of the delegation: "I would like to get some of the vitamin pills that Yuri Vladimirovich Dubinin used to get all that hair." When it was translated, the other Russians howled with laughter as Dubinin smiled. Then Hatch added: "And it looks like the rest of your delegation could use some of those vitamin pills, too." This time Dubinin doubled over laughing.

Once the ice was broken, it continued to melt. Several years later Dubinin was assigned as Soviet ambassador to Washington, where he and Hatch renewed their acquaintance and where Dubinin helped guide his country into the post-Cold War era.

During 1985 and 1986, Hatch took an active role in shaping U.S. foreign policy. He championed freedom fighters on three continents and insisted that the United States should not just help them survive against vastly superior forces. They should also assist them in punishing, and if possible, defeating the oppressors. The key tool in Hatch's diplomatic bag was the Stinger—a five-foot-long, thirty-five-pound, heat-seeking missile, fired from the shoulder by one man. Its specialty: to destroy low-flying enemy aircraft.

Two months after Hatch was appointed to the Senate Intelligence Committee in January 1985, Soviet leadership changed hands for the third time in four years. Konstantin Chernenko, general secretary of the Soviet Communist Party, died. His successor was Mikhail Gorbachev, a relative youngster at fifty-four with a tantalizing reputation of being potentially moderate and perhaps willing to bargain.

Reagan early on had denounced the USSR as an "evil empire." Relations between the two countries had been frozen ever since. The United States had embarked on an unprecedented arms build-up, aimed primarily at checking Soviet expansionism and diminishing the threat of a Soviet nuclear strike.

For their part, the Soviets were sponsoring and arming client regimes and insurgents around the world, including Cuba and Nicaragua in this hemisphere, Angola in Africa, and Afghanistan in southern Asia. The Soviets had broken off arms reduction talks with Washington in late 1983 when NATO began installing a new generation of missiles in Europe.

With Gorbachev newly in power, Reagan called for a "fresh start." The two nations resumed arms talks in Geneva early in 1985. Reagan and Gorbachev held a two-day summit there in November. But Afghanistan, which the Soviets had invaded in December 1979 and occupied, ostensibly at the invitation of its Communist government, remained a sticking point.

Both leaders secretly heated up the stalemated war in early 1985. Gorbachev, bowing to hard-liners, reassigned General Mikhail Zaitsev from the prestigious command of Soviet forces in Germany to command in Afghanistan, along with two thousand elite Spetsnaz paratroops, new battlefield equipment, and an aggressive campaign aimed at winning the war within two years. They joined an estimated 115,000 Soviet troops already in Afghanistan.

In an intelligence coup, the new Soviet war plan fell into U.S. hands. Almost as Zaitsev headed for Afghanistan, Reagan signed a national security directive overriding Carter's 1980 authorization of aid to Afghan guerrillas to "harass" Soviet occupation forces. Thousands of tons of routine small-arms, many purchased from China, had since been channeled through neighboring Pakistan to Afghan guerrillas, the mujahedin.

Reagan, through National Security Advisor Robert McFarlane, beefed up assistance to Afghan resistance, setting the goal of expelling the Soviets from Afghanistan. But how?

On May 26, 1985, a small group boarded Air Force Two at Andrews Air Force Base, Maryland. The blue and white plane, emblazoned with "UNITED STATES OF AMERICA," was assigned to Vice President Bush—an unmistakable signal of the importance of the mission.

Orrin Hatch was head of the CODEL (congressional delegation). Dressed in a dark blue sweatsuit and carrying several books, including one entitled *India,* he led the delegation aboard. Three other members of the Senate Intelligence Committee were with him—Republican Chic Hecht of Nevada, and Democrats Bill Bradley of New Jersey and David Boren of Oklahoma. Top national security experts included Norm Gardner from the CIA; Vincent Cannistraro, CIA operations officer posted at the National Security Council; Mike Pillsbury from the Pentagon; and Morton Abramowitz from the State Department.

Although their round-the-world itinerary included stops in Greece, Turkey, India, and Thailand, the real point of the trip was talks in Pakistan about how to aid Afghan insurgents.

"Our goal was to influence the more moderate Gorbachev to withdraw rather than siding with his hard-line advisors to prolong their occupation," explained Hatch in a recent interview. "Gorbachev had just come to power and we needed to move quickly. We didn't want a Vietnam syndrome to develop, with the Soviets pouring in ever more resources to prosecute the war. We also wanted to show that the KGB and the Red Army were not invincible."

Hatch noted, "Some critics said I was trying to escalate Soviet-U.S. frictions or 'fight to the last Afghan.' That was completely false. I wanted an early end to the war before it became 'Gorbachev's war,' so we had to move fast after he took over in March."

They met with Pakistan's president, Mohammed Zia ul-Haq, in Peshawar, a northwestern city near the famed Khyber Pass. Peshawar was headquarters for leaders of the major mujahedin factions fighting the Russians across the border, and the U.S. delegation met with the top dozen mujahedin leaders. The groups were fiercely independent but, as Muslims, shared the goal of driving the atheistic Russians from their homeland.

Zia was worried about increasing Soviet incursions across Pakistan's border. He feared if they were not stopped, the Soviets would overrun Pakistan to acquire a long-desired warm-water port. Hatch suggested to Zia, a strong U.S. ally, that he needed Stingers for his own army to stop Afghan and Soviet planes which had been raiding inside Pakistan's border. Zia agreed and added that he supported arming the mujahedin with the Stingers.

Hatch and the administration representatives returned to Washington with their recommendations. About six months later, the United States rushed Stinger and Sidewinder air-to-air missiles to Pakistan.

But providing Stingers for the mujahedin was a far more complicated issue. Other conservatives in Congress and the intelligence community were already pushing for the weapons. But it was unprecedented to give such sophisticated technology to loosely organized Third World groups. Stingers were notoriously complicated to operate, and trainers would have to accompany them. Furthermore, the specter of a Stinger being used by a terrorist to bring down a civilian airliner haunted U.S. officials.

The CIA had a policy of "plausible deniability" for its covert operations. Once Stingers were introduced into Afghanistan, it would be virtually impossible to disavow U.S. involvement. "The CIA believed they had to handle this as if they were wearing a condom," quipped Cannistraro, a pro-support advocate. With the Soviets dramatically escalating the conflict in 1985 and Washington encouraging the mujahedin but hesitating on support, Cannistraro believed that U.S. aid was "just enough to get a very brave people killed."

Hatch and a number of colleagues, including Senator Gordon Humphrey, R-New Hampshire, who earlier had talked and traveled with the mujahedin, lined up such key allies within the administration as Fred Ikle and Mike Pillsbury at the Pentagon and Morton Abramowitz at the State Department.

While Washington argued, the Soviets and their puppet Afghan government continued a reign of terror, destroying crops, bombing villages, and executing civilians. Nothing could stop the high-tech Mi-25 helicopter gunships, which were massacring the mujahedin. In a Senate speech, Hatch explained:

> The Soviet strategy in Afghanistan is not aimed at winning a military victory per se, but at cutting off the mujahedin from their base of support by terrorizing the Afghan people. . . . A former officer of the security police has described the following types of torture: giving electric shocks; tearing out fingernails, . . . plucking out the beards of some prisoners—especially elderly men or religious freedom fighters, . . . setting police dogs on detainees, [and] raping women in front of family members. Soviet atrocities against the Afghan people are too horrific to be described as mere "human rights violations." The only appropriate term is genocide.

An estimated million Afghans—one of every sixteen—had been executed or starved since the Soviet invasion, said Hatch; another half-million were on the point of death from starvation. Some 4 million refugees, more than a quarter of the country's population, had fled to neighboring Pakistan and Iran. "The mujahedin have two fundamental strengths," said Hatch. "Their steadfast support by the overwhelming majority of the Afghan people, and their own personal determination and courage."

Hatch called for more military hardware and expanded funding for the U.S. Information Agency so it could tell the world what was happening in Afghanistan. Hatch also met with representatives of the mujahedin journeying to Washington. After one such session, he received a letter from M. Nabi Salehi, their emissary in the capital: "Your courage, honesty and frankness are highly appreciated by the Afghan resistance. . . . The people of Afghanistan are determined to continue their rightful struggle until they will free their country from the Soviet occupation."

Following Reagan's directive early in 1985, an interagency committee coordinated the shipment of thousands of additional tons of routine arms and ammunition to the guerrillas. The National Security Council, CIA, Pentagon, and State Department all were represented on the committee.

But the additional war matériel failed to halt Russia's aggressive new tactics, which now included devastatingly effective night fighting by the Spetsnaz. Finally, Hatch received a green light near the end of 1985 to lead another delegation to Asia. Its mission: sound out key power brokers in the region, secure support for more lethal U.S. assistance, and suggest specific Soviet targets to Pakistani and mujahedin leaders.

In January 1986, days before the group left Washington, Under

Secretary of State Michael Armacost wrote Hatch, "I consider it very important for your [mission] to meet its objectives during your stay in Peshawar. . . . The year 1986 will be important in the development of our policy approaches to both Afghanistan and Pakistan, and we look forward to working closely with the Congress in our effort to get the Soviets out of Afghanistan."

This time the delegation included several members of the House Intelligence Committee along with Senators Hatch and Hecht, and U.S. intelligence experts Pillsbury, Cannistraro, Abramowitz, and Norm Gardner of the CIA.

Although some details of their mission remain classified, the group flew to Beijing, where Hatch huddled with the chief of China's intelligence. Hatch was accompanied by two senior CIA operations officers. Concerned about Soviet hegemony, China from the start had strongly encouraged the United States to help drive the USSR from Afghanistan. Many of the covert weapons flowing to the mujahedin were paid for by the United States but made in China.

Hatch now posed careful questions to China's top spy master: Would China support greater U.S. involvement, including helping Pakistan destroy strategic targets?

"Yes."

Would China—Hatch held his breath—also support the United States in supplying the guerrillas with the Stinger? Some U.S. analysts believed the spy chief would refuse, but again the answer was "yes." The Chinese official agreed to communicate his support directly to President Zia in Pakistan.

The group then flew to Peshawar and again met with Zia to affirm his support for arming the Afghans with Stingers. Again Zia concurred.

Hatch and Zia agreed that the Stingers were not enough. They studied satellite photographs of key Soviet facilities and drew up a list of specific targets. The classified list likely included Soviet military headquarters in Kabul, the bridge from the USSR into Afghanistan over which the bulk of supplies was transported, Soviet air bases, electronic command and control centers, the airport where helicopter gunships and fixed-wing aircraft were stationed, and a vulnerable pipeline carrying natural gas from Afghanistan to the Soviet Union.

As Hatch said in a recent interview, the ultimate goal was "to increase the cost of the war to the Soviets, help discredit hard-liners in Moscow, and influence Gorbachev to withdraw from Afghanistan."

Members of the delegation also visited a refugee camp, where Hatch addressed about 500 tribal fathers seated on the ground under a huge tentlike structure. Dee Benson, Hatch's aide, watched the refugees brighten with hope as Hatch's encouraging words were translated, calling it "one of the most significant experiences I have ever had."

The jubilant delegation returned to Washington near the end of January 1986 and reported their findings to senior Reagan administration officials. But their enthusiasm dashed against the wall of CIA and army warnings that giving Stingers to the Afghans was too risky. Reagan's desire to help the rebels wavered when he listened to Secretary of State George Shultz, who had the larger goal of improving overall relations with Moscow. How could the United States send more lethal aid to insurgents and still plausibly deny responsibility for its results?

That concern heightened in late March when the *Washington Post,* in a startling front-page story, reported that the United States had in fact decided to send Stingers to rebels in both Angola and Afghanistan. "The decision, which has been closely held among the President's national security affairs advisers since it was made earlier this month, marks a major shift in U.S. policy," said the piece.

Reagan exploded. Columnists Rowland Evans and Robert Novak reported that Reagan asked national security aide John Poindexter how such an outrageous leak could have been permitted, risking destruction of the whole effort to shore up freedom fighters. "The Stingers-for-[Angola's Jonas] Savimbi entered a gray area of doubt," they said.

Mike Pillsbury's career also entered a gray area. In a stormy meeting, Poindexter accused Pillsbury of being the source of the leak. Pillsbury denied it but reportedly failed two lie-detector tests given by apparently inexperienced polygraphers in the Defense Investigative Service (he passed two more by the FBI the next year). The Pentagon did not prosecute Pillsbury but fired him.

As Pillsbury continued to assert his innocence, Hatch conducted his own investigation. An aide telephoned Patrick Tyler, one of the two *Post* reporters who broke the story. A memorandum prepared for Hatch said, "Tyler repeated in no uncertain terms that Pillsbury was not his source and that he was certain that Adm. Poindexter knew this." Tyler also told the aide, "Somebody was 'out to get' Pillsbury, and they succeeded."

Because Pillsbury had great difficulty getting along with others, he may have been a convenient scapegoat for the administration. Yet it seemed illogical to finger him as the source of the leak, since he was a strong Stinger advocate. Why would he torpedo the operation? On the other hand, independent observers thought they recognized the *modus operandi* as Pillsbury's. *Time* magazine later did a profile on him and another national security activist, titled "Washington's Master Leakers: How Two Crusaders Use Secret Information to Manipulate Policy."

Hatch retained faith in Pillsbury and arranged a soft landing for him on Capitol Hill as his foreign policy advisor, sharing the cost of Pillsbury's salary with three other conservative senators: Hecht, Humphrey, and Helms. Secretary of State Shultz was appalled, saying an alleged "leaker" shouldn't have access to the top-secret information supplied to the Intelligence Committee.

Debate continued to rage over the Stingers, now compromised by the embarrassing publicity. As Washington talked, Hatch kept seeing the faces of the women, children, and old men huddling in the Pakistani refugee camps, waiting to return to their Afghan homes. And he remembered the mujahedin in Peshawar whose lives were on the line every time they crossed the border. What was Washington's risk compared to theirs?

In August 1986, Hatch delivered a frustrated speech to the congressional task force on Afghanistan: "The State Department continues to divert attention from the problem by praising the willpower of the mujahedin, as if willpower will somehow protect them from Soviet tanks and helicopter gunships," stormed Hatch. ". . . The 120,000 Soviet forces in Afghanistan have willpower–and massive firepower too."

"To understand the military effectiveness of the resistance," said Hatch, "you have to use Sherlock Holmes's famous technique of noticing the dog that did *not* bark. What hasn't happened is sometimes as important as what has. . . . What hasn't happened in Afghanistan is a very long list." Major strategic targets remained untouched, recent battles were really Soviet initiatives to close down rebel supply lines from Pakistan, and the number of Soviet defectors had dwindled.

> Kabul remains a dependent-accompanied tour. In other words, Soviet officers in Kabul bring their wives and children along, so safe is the city from the resistance. . . . The next time you hear the Soviets may be about to withdraw from Afghanistan because of the terrible pounding they have been taking, perhaps you ought to be thinking instead about what happened to the Soviets when they increased their forces by 50 percent to 120,000 and brought in the elite Spetsnaz commandos and began to fly reconnaissance patrols along the Pakistan border to catch and kill resistance supply caravans– remember what happened? All the sanctions put on by Jimmy Carter were removed. In fact, just four months ago, Aeroflot landing rights were restored.

That same month, August 1986, Hatch and several aides–Pillsbury among them–boarded a plane for yet another flight to the other side of the world. Destination: southern Africa.

The *Washington Post* later said that Hatch, "who helped persuade the Reagan administration to send Stinger anti-aircraft missiles to Angolan rebel leader Jonas Savimbi, spent his summer vacation becoming the first senator to make the clandestine journey into–and out of–the rebel headquarters at Jamba, a feat that requires flying at treetop level and a gut-splitting off-road ride."

Savimbi led a rebel faction called the National Union for the Total Independence of Angola (UNITA), which controlled about a third of the country, with strong backing from South Africa. Some observers believed the moral case for aid to Savimbi's freedom fighters was not nearly as clear-cut as aid to the Afghans. Critics called him an opportunist and said the Angolan conflict was a civil war in which the United States had no stake, and that UNITA had no chance of winning.

In 1975 Savimbi helped Angola gain independence from Portugal after two decades of rebellion. But a rival faction to UNITA called the Popular Movement for the Liberation of Angola (MPLA), backed by thousands of Cuban troops, gained control of most of the country in 1976 and established a Marxist-Leninist dictatorship. Also in 1976, after the disclosure of covert CIA aid to Savimbi's group, Congress passed the Clark Amendment banning further assistance to UNITA.

Following nine more years of war, Congress in 1985 repealed the Clark Amendment, opening the door to major U.S. assistance to UNITA. Hatch had helped persuade the Reagan administration to send Stingers to UNITA, as well as to the Afghans, and was determined to help speed the assistance to Savimbi.

"Savimbi captures two-thirds of his weapons from the MPLA, so overall, UNITA is doing well in terms of weapons and supplies," wrote Hatch in an article printed in a number of U.S. newspapers. "However, like the Afghan mujahedin and the Nicaraguan contras, Savimbi's freedom fighters desperately need anti-aircraft weapons to defend themselves against Soviet Hind helicopter gunships."

"The battle for Angola is . . . a battle over ideologies," continued Hatch. "Soviet totalitarianism vs. freedom, self-determination and democracy. U.S. aid to UNITA will send a strong signal to the world that the Reagan Doctrine is not mere words, that we are determined to help freedom fighters resist Communist hegemony."

Hatch's efforts to assist Savimbi were encouraged by several private groups, including the American Security Council and friends who had formed the lobbying firm of Black Manafort Stone & Kelly—which Savimbi had hired to help secure U.S. military aid.

Now, in August 1986, months after Stingers and other promised help had arrived at rebel headquarters in Jamba, Hatch and his party were arriving by helicopter at the jungle outpost, after a stopover in Namibia, for a firsthand look at the war.

The party, including a South African intelligence officer, was met by Savimbi, a friendly but fierce-looking, barrel-chested man with full beard, green uniform, and beret. Earlier in the year, Hatch had introduced Savimbi at a dinner in Washington as "a true revolutionary hero" and pledged "to do everything in my power to make your dreams of a truly free and independent Angola become a reality."

At Jamba, Savimbi thanked Hatch profusely for the weapons and, according to another source, showed him evidence of their effectiveness, including burned-out Russian aircraft. There was considerable other evidence near the jungle outpost of Soviet involvement in the "civil war," including captured artillery and a truck-mounted rocket launcher—the latter with a door full of bullet holes. All bore identification plates in Russia's Cyrillic alphabet.

Hatch helped secure weapons for UNITA which played a role in persuading the Cubans to leave Angola in 1991. Angola became a small dot on the geopolitical landscape as communism collapsed in the USSR. In 1993, Savimbi and his followers agreed to join a coalition government; but unsuccessful in national elections, Savimbi returned to the battlefield.

When not traveling to meet with freedom fighters in 1986, Hatch used his powerful pen in their various causes. As the faces of starving Ethiopians stared hauntingly from newspapers, magazines, and TV screens, Hatch noted that the devastation in northeastern Africa was man-made as well as a result of drought.

"Ever since Mengistu seized power in 1977, he has conducted a Stalinlike reign of terror," Hatch wrote in an article for the opinion/editorial page of the *Los Angeles Times*. "His forced resettlement program, collectivization of agriculture and disregard for human rights have wreaked economic and social havoc throughout the country, imposing suffering on millions."

At least 100,000 deaths were caused during transport alone while forcibly relocating peasants away from their traditional lands where two Marxist resistance groups were based, said Hatch. Congress had passed sanctions against Ethiopia, but the State Department had vetoed them. Hatch now called for more forceful U.S. action. "We should support a little-known democratic resistance group, the Ethiopian People's Democratic Alliance . . . [whose leader] claims that with political and financial support from the United States, the group could mobilize 50,000 men in a matter of months."

Hatch was also a strong supporter of the contra rebels fighting the Sandinista regime. He helped push through the Senate a $100 million contra aid package early in the year, but feared that the Ortega brothers and their Marxist comrades would pretend to mend their ways just long enough to keep the U.S. House from also approving the aid.

While the Sandinistas portray the contras as intransigent warmongers, wrote Hatch in the *Washington Times,* "in truth, Nicaragua's democratic resistance is a genuine, spontaneous opposition to the Sandinistas. . . . It is clear that the Sandinistas will not institute *any* reforms . . . except under pressure.

". . . The United States has a very clear-cut choice: either support the resistance forces now or end up making a military commitment ourselves later. Unlike the Sandinistas, who rely on Cuban troops and Soviet-bloc 'advisers' to fight their war, the 'contras' are not asking for a commitment of outside forces. They are only asking for military assistance. It would be unconscionable not to respond to their cry for help."

While the impact of Hatch's assistance to some other freedom fighters may have been ambiguous, his impact on the war in Afghanistan was not. As Hatch was criticizing the sluggish Reagan response to Afghanistan in the summer of 1986, a shipment of 150 Stingers arrived in Pakistan. A missile at a time, they were distributed to four-man mujahedin units who had been trained for six to eight weeks. The Stingers reportedly entered rebel arsenals for the first time in October.

Two months later the State Department reported that rebels had been shooting down an average of one Soviet or Afghan government aircraft each day since October. By the following spring, Pentagon sources said the Soviets had stopped flying both helicopters and fixed-wing aircraft over some parts of Afghanistan because of the Stingers. And each surface-to-air missile which turned a Soviet aircraft into scrap metal arrived compliments of Orrin Hatch.

"The fighting is going much better this year," one guerrilla told a correspondent in Pakistan in October 1987. "The Stinger has caused the Soviets to change strategy," said another. "Mostly they stay in their garrisons now. Their strategy is to hold on, since they don't have air cover all the time."

Although other weapons were also used, "the Stinger, numerous sources say, has had the sharpest impact on Soviet tactics," wrote the correspondent. "The Soviets have diminished sharply their close air support of ground troops and use of helicopter gunships. Soviet bombing by Su25 jet attack planes now must be done at high altitudes where bombing is less accurate, sources say. The ability to strafe more accurately by flying slower also has been cut way back because of vulnerability to Stingers."

Shocked by the turn of events, the Soviets at first stepped up bombings of border villages inside Pakistan, trying to pressure Zia's government to stop aiding rebels. The mujahedin in turn struck Soviet villages near the Afghan border, bringing retaliatory Soviet raids in nearby areas of Afghanistan but raising fears in the Kremlin that the war could spread to Soviet peoples religiously and ethnically close to the Afghans.

Finally a white flag went up the Soviet pole. With Washington holding out the carrot of better relations, Gorbachev in February 1988 announced that the USSR would withdraw from Afghanistan. Soviet troops began leaving in May, the same month Reagan arrived in Moscow for a summit in which he praised Gorbachev's reforms and signed a major nuclear arms-control treaty.

By the following February, all Soviet troops were out of Afghanistan. An estimated million Afghans had been killed, and more than half the country's people had either been displaced within Afghanistan or were refugees abroad. For the Soviets, their Vietnam had cost $75 billion with some 14,000 dead, 35,000 wounded. Soviet Foreign Minister Eduard Shevardnadze acknowledged in 1989 that the invasion had violated both Soviet law and "international norms of behavior."

By every account, introducing the Stinger was a key factor in forcing the USSR to abandon its war of aggression in Afghanistan.

Hatch's pivotal role in getting the Stinger into the hands of the mujahedin remained concealed until the *Washington Post* broke the story in 1992. Its investigative reporter concluded, "In retrospect, many senior U.S. officials involved see the decision as a turning point in the war and acknowledge that Hatch's clandestine lobbying played a significant role."

A time-line accompanying the *Post* series carried the photos of just four key figures in the Stinger saga: President Mikhail Gorbachev, General Mikhail Zaitsev, CIA Director William Casey, and Hatch. The chart spelled out his role in 1986: "In January, Sen. Orrin G. Hatch (R-Utah) goes to China and Pakistan, wins their support for supply of Stinger anti-aircraft missiles. Stingers arrive in the summer and begin downing the assault helicopters key to Soviet strategy."

"Today, some involved in the Afghan program say they believe the Soviet defeat was one of several decisive factors that helped discredit Soviet hardliners and encourage Mikhail Gorbachev's reforms," summarized the *Post*. "And there is little doubt that defeat in Afghanistan had a profound impact on Soviet society in the late 1980s, as the Soviet empire unraveled."

The story represented a significant departure for the liberal *Post,* which routinely eliminated Hatch from its news coverage when possible. This time it apparently wasn't possible.

In coming years, analysts would credit the end of the Cold War to at least four factors: Reagan's military buildup, the deployment by NATO of Pershing II nuclear missiles in Europe, America's pursuit of the "star wars" Space Defense Initiative (SDI), and the Stinger decision which led to the Soviet defeat in Afghanistan, unmasking the USSR's vulnerability to its Eastern bloc allies.

20

Democrats
Retake the Senate

ND THEN IT WAS OVER FOR Senate Republicans. After six years of
Senate control for the first time in three decades, the 1986 elections put that body solidly back in Democratic hands.

But voters on November 4 sent mixed signals on the Reagan presidency, now limping into the last two of its eight years. The GOP held its
own in House elections, though Democrats retained an overwhelming
258-177 majority. And Republicans picked up an impressive eight governorships, now trailing Democrats by just 26-24, compared with the
previous margin of 34-16.

But the Senate elections were an unmitigated disaster for the GOP.
The Republicans went into the elections holding an edge of 53-47 over
the Democrats and emerged from the elections on the short end of a 55-
45 Democratic majority.

"The outcome was much worse than I expected," wrote a dismayed
Hatch. "It was just terrible, just awful." Senate losers included two of his
strong Republican allies: Paula Hawkins of Florida–a fellow Mormon
and good friend–and Jeremiah Denton of Alabama. Six strong Senators
had retired instead of seeking reelection: Republicans Laxalt, Goldwater,
and Mathias, and Democrats Hart, Long, and Eagleton.

Reagan's presidency had peaked and was heading downhill, already
seriously distracted by revelations over secret U.S. arms sales to Iran and
assistance to rebels fighting the Marxist government in Nicaragua.
Reagan's growing political impotence was underscored in the fall elections: He campaigned in sixteen states after Labor Day but Republican
Senate candidates prevailed in only four.

Loss of the Senate meant that the administration would have a more

267

difficult time than ever persuading Congress to pass significant White House initiatives over the next two years.

On the eve of the elections, Hatch had demonstrated the kind of grit that would be required often in the years ahead if he were to make his mark in a Senate run by Democrats.

Literally in the closing minutes of the ninety-ninth Congress, Hatch pulled off another feat of legislative wizardry, this time for a major health bill. Working with him to secure passage in the House was a fellow wizard: Representative Henry Waxman of California, chair of the House Health Subcommittee.

Waxman and Hatch seemed opposites: Waxman, a liberal Jew and Democrat, stood a head shorter than Hatch, was bald, and had a thick mustache. But like Hatch, Waxman was bright, hardworking, and a master of House rules and procedures—all of which he exploited to become one of Congress's most productive legislators.

Now, as colleagues clamored for adjournment to go home and campaign, Hatch was determined to keep them just long enough to win approval for the omnibus health measure. Seven bills were involved, including a major one to permit pharmaceutical firms to export drugs not yet approved for use in the United States. This bill enabled U.S. pharmaceutical companies to maintain jobs in the U.S.

On October 17, 1986, Waxman got House approval by a voice vote. The next day, with the Senate scheduled to adjourn in the evening, Hatch lobbied senators to pass it. But the White House registered strong opposition because Waxman had added a provision to have the federal government compensate families whose children suffered adverse reactions to major childhood vaccines.

Hatch wanted to appeal to Attorney General Ed Meese, but Meese was attending a wedding in Philadelphia and Hatch couldn't find him until just twenty minutes before adjournment. Over the phone, Hatch made his pitch. Meese reluctantly gave the bill a green light but warned that Reagan would veto it anyway.

Hatch raced onto the Senate floor and announced Meese's approval. The Senate passed the bill just minutes before adjourning.

Over the next month, Hatch lobbied the White House not to veto the bill, explaining that at least two of the three companies producing vaccines might go out of business if the government didn't assume their liability. Finally the administration backed down. In a very private Oval Office ceremony, Reagan signed the bill into law. Hatch was the only member of Congress looking over his shoulder.

On January 17, 1987, as the 100th Congress was getting revved up, Hatch returned briefly to Utah, joining fifteen other senators in Park

City for the Ski Cup Classic, an annual charity benefit hosted by Jake Garn. Hatch had skied fewer than ten hours in his life but determinedly signed up for the slalom run.

Turning too sharply, he wiped out the first pole, its flag tumbling into the snow. Only fifty-five gates to go. Carefully he aced the next dozen poles and, gaining confidence, picked up speed. Three poles later Hatch was really flying. Then he hit a steep mogul, his skis crossed, and Hatch was suddenly airborne upside down. As he tumbled down the mountain, one ski flew off. Sliding to an ungainly halt, Hatch gingerly checked his neck and breathed a sigh of relief: nothing injured but his pride. Hatch crawled to his missing ski, clamped it on, and resumed his run.

He finished in just over two minutes—slower than all the other senators except for his fishing buddy John Warner. Most of the others were veteran skiers and were amazed that Hatch would even attempt the slalom. Garn, nowadays a good friend, came up to him at the bottom of the hill, Elaine at his side.

"Orrin," said Garn solemnly, "what you just did took more courage than it took for me to donate the kidney to Susan."

"Sure," answered Hatch, laughing.

Garn's kidney had been implanted in his diabetic daughter just months earlier. Both were doing fine.

The Senate was in transition, with the Democrats assuming control of major committees. West Virginia's Bob Byrd cracked the whip again as majority leader, with Bob Dole now minority leader, assisted by Wyoming's Alan Simpson, Hatch's friend and ally.

Hatch relinquished the chairmanship of the Labor and Human Resources Committee to Ted Kennedy, and Strom Thurmond lost the reins of Hatch's other major panel, the Judiciary Committee, to Joseph Biden. Hatch was now ranking Republican on the labor panel and number two behind Thurmond on judiciary.

Byrd took charge with a vengeance, kicking Republicans out of Room S-207 in the Capitol where they had held their weekly policy luncheons and letting them drift for weeks before allowing them to use the Lyndon Johnson Room, just off the Senate floor. Kennedy initially was more considerate, offering Hatch extra funds to help with the Labor Committee transition. But as the months wore on, he too became more partisan.

At one point, Hatch asked Kennedy for the courtesy of a delayed markup of an important civil rights bill. Hatch needed to finish another major assignment before he could attend the writing of the bill. Kennedy refused. On the day Kennedy scheduled the markup, the Senate was in session until midnight, so his hearing didn't begin until about 12:15 A.M.

When Hatch got to the hearing room, it was packed with Kennedy partisans, including NOW President Eleanor Smeal, who led cheers each time another Democrat arrived. Everything was orchestrated to intimidate Hatch and his GOP colleagues. When a quorum finally assembled, Kennedy called the meeting to order. Immediately Hatch grabbed the floor.

"Mr. Chairman," said Hatch, "speaking for the Republican side, I am angry. And we're not going to mark up any bill tonight."

Hatch castigated Kennedy for his heavy-handedness toward other GOP committee members and discourtesy for not honoring Hatch's own request to delay the markup. He challenged Kennedy to cite a single instance when Hatch had not been courteous to him during the six years of Hatch's chairmanship. Hatch ended by calling Kennedy a "bully" and threatening to filibuster every bill that came before the panel if Kennedy didn't mend his ways. The audience was stunned, but even Democrats sided with Hatch. Metzenbaum leaned over to his fellow liberal and, as Kennedy reddened in anger, said, "You know, Orrin is right. Why not let us go home?"

After an hour of give and take, Kennedy agreed to delay the bill for at least two weeks and not to schedule other bills for markup again after Hatch requested a delay. The meeting ended on that note at 1:30 A.M.

In February, Hatch returned to his alma mater, the University of Pittsburgh School of Law, to deliver the 1987 Louis Caplan Lecture. His topic: "The Role of the Senate in Appointments to the Federal Bench." Hatch began with a question reportedly once asked of former Senate chaplain Edward Hale: "Do you pray for the senators, Dr. Hale?"

"No," Hale reportedly answered, "I look at the senators and pray for the country."

Hatch recalled the treaty John Jay negotiated with England to settle boundary and trade disputes with England after the Revolutionary War. "Jay was the original Colonel [Oliver] North," said Hatch, and the Jay treaty was not popular among Americans who believed he had conceded too much.

"In fact," said Hatch, "on one fence were chalked the words: 'Damn John Jay! Damn every one that won't damn John Jay! Damn every one that won't put lights in his windows and sit up all night damning John Jay!' Sounds very much like a recent newscast about the Iran situation. Senator Metzenbaum must have had an ancestor with chalk on his hands."

Hatch, still sharply critical of the media, called for both Congress and the White House to "avoid negotiating a conflict in the national media. . . . One of the primary reasons for the constitutional division of powers was to slow the pace of deliberations and prevent precipitous decisions based on the passions of the moment. Appeal to the media often defeats these benefits . . . and prevents the quiet, systematic resolution of confrontations in a reasoned atmosphere."

Congress sometimes "gets so carried away with prolonging a crisis for political advantage that it forgets that its real job is to end the crisis," said Hatch. He urged restraint from all three branches of government.

One of Hatch's personal heroes in Washington was Dr. C. Everett Koop, a world-renowned pediatrician and U.S. Surgeon General since 1981. Liberals had originally delayed Koop's appointment for months because of his age—then sixty-five—and his opposition to abortion and homosexuality. More recently, *conservatives* had called for Koop's head because of his aggressive campaign against AIDS, including easy access to condoms. But Hatch, noting Koop's trailblazing efforts across a broad range of health issues, including smoking and diet, continued to regard him as "a remarkable human being."

A Washington dinner honoring Koop was planned for spring 1987, with Hatch among congressional sponsors. Paul Weyrich and Phyllis Schlafly wrote Hatch and others, asking them to withdraw as sponsors. Hatch refused but a number of others caved in, including Senator Dole, Congressman Jack Kemp, and several other Presidential aspirants. Vice President Bush said he couldn't attend but sent a letter praising Koop.

On the evening of the banquet, only two members of Congress showed up—Henry Waxman and Hatch. Hatch gave a glowing tribute to Koop, who looked, as always, like Captain Ahab with his trademark beard and Public Health Service uniform.

"Dr. Koop exhibits all the qualities that we want in our nation's top doctor," praised Hatch as Koop, in a rare moment of vulnerability, dabbed at his eyes with a napkin, "compassion, skill, leadership, and dedication to preserving human life." He added that Koop "has helped focus the debate regarding a new group that needs our compassion—citizens dying from AIDS. . . . Dr. Koop and I have not always seen eye-to-eye. And I understand that I might not be in total agreement with all the people in this room. But by working together, we can develop effective solutions."

Privately, Hatch was angered that some government workers were "very frightened" to be at the dinner. One man told Hatch he might be fired if his photo got into the newspaper. "This type of mind control really bothers me," wrote Hatch that evening. "This is where the conservatives really hurt themselves. Some of them are not broad-minded. I am known as one of the strongest conservatives in Washington but I wouldn't have missed this meeting for anything."

Koop wrote warmly to Hatch, saying it was "so like" the Utahn "to come and speak to that gathering on my behalf that it didn't surprise me nearly as much as it pleased me. You have always been my strongest supporter in the Senate and Betty and I will be forever grateful to you for that."

The New Right wasn't about to forgive Hatch's latest display of independence. Weyrich's monthly *Family Protection Report* castigated him in a long article entitled "Senator Hatch: Only a Fair-Weather Friend?" After cataloguing grievances, the newsletter charged:

> Perhaps the most insulting slap in the face to his conservative allies has been Hatch's performance in the matter of AIDS. . . . This dinner was generally perceived to be an insult to the conservative community, which Koop at the time was belittling at every opportunity. . . . What accounts for this catering to the liberal establishment? The most obvious explanation advanced is that the name of Orrin Hatch is sometimes advanced as a candidate for the next Supreme Court vacancy. . . . He is setting his sights for the next seat on the court, and to that end is very carefully not antagonizing even his most liberal fellow Senators.

The newsletter conveniently overlooked Hatch's continuing clashes with such liberal powers as Kennedy and Metzenbaum and his history of independent actions that sometimes angered the New Right years before there was any talk of a Supreme Court appointment.

Hatch attended other dinners in 1987, where contributors shelled out hundreds and sometimes thousands of dollars each toward his reelection in 1988. Typically the events raised $30,000 to $75,000 at a time, but one noteworthy bash at Washington's Sheraton Grand Hotel in June netted a cool half-million dollars.

Elaine and most of their children proudly listened with other patrons who paid a thousand dollars apiece to hear President Reagan call Hatch "Mr. Balanced Budget" for his efforts to pass a constitutional amendment. "If every member of the Senate were like Orrin Hatch, we'd be arguing over how to deal with a federal surplus," said Reagan. He called for structural changes, including a line-item veto to allow a President to object to one or more items in a bill without having to veto the entire measure.

"The United States has been strong enough to deter aggression and maintain the peace, in no small degree due to the efforts of Orrin Hatch," said Reagan. "He has been a champion of those who fight for freedom in Afghanistan, Nicaragua, Angola, and other Third World countries. . . . If I could ask the people of Utah, my fellow Westerners . . . to stand with me one last time, it would be in support of Orrin Hatch's reelection to the United States Senate."

Hatch, in introducing the President, reminisced about the political campaigns they had waged together starting in 1976 and said, "Our support of one another was not born out of political expediency but of a deeply felt philosophy that we share about the proper role of government."

He also noted "Many have said that 'money is the mother's milk of politics.' Well, that may be true, but I have always thought of fund-raisers as the 'listerine' of politics—nobody likes doing them but they have to be done. . . . Your willingness to come here to one big event rather than insisting on a hundred little breakfasts or lunches will allow me to spend my time doing the work I was elected to do."

One who hadn't made it to the event was Alan Simpson, Hatch's seat-mate on the Judiciary Committee. He sent a colorful apology:

> You may come to my office at S-243 at which location upon the mantel is a whip which you may remove, uncoil and [use to] administer six lashes! Of course, I shall be clutching at your bony hand while you try this exercise! I'm sorry to have missed it, my friend. . . . You are a superb colleague in this arena and we desperately need your good services and your sharp and incisive intellect. Oh, what the hell, just list me as a fan! I always have been and I always will be.

That summer, Hatch's constituents were powerfully reminded of what his influence meant to Utah. Following the longest steel strike in America's history, its largest steel manufacturer, USX—formerly U.S. Steel—announced it was shutting down a marginally profitable plant in Utah Valley called Geneva Steel.

While the plant was small potatoes to USX, it was one of the state's biggest employers, and more than a thousand families faced bleak futures. The announcement triggered a barrage of angry press releases from other Utah politicians. Senator Garn and the district's Republican Congressman, Howard Nielson, were among the voices blasting USX.

When Hatch said nothing, a Washington correspondent for the *Daily Herald* in Provo, Utah, blistered him for not rallying round the state. Hatch promptly invited the correspondent to his office and for an hour explained that he was holding his fire so that he would have a stronger position from which to persuade USX officials to change their mind.

Meanwhile a young man named Joe Cannon, a former Utahn and top official at the Environmental Protection Agency, was trying to pull off a miracle. Although Cannon knew nothing about making steel, he and a handful of relatives and friends tried to talk USX into selling them the plant rather than closing it.

Cannon succeeded in winning wage concessions from local steel workers and even lined up financing with a Texas investment bank. At the end of July, however, the bank suddenly reneged on the deal. Desperate, Cannon asked Hatch to intercede for an extension on the financing.

Hatch went to bat for Geneva Steel. On August 3, a Monday, he met with two USX officials in Washington. They told him that the plant was costing $100,000 a day just to pay utilities and keep on idle and that there was virtually no hope USX would keep it open beyond the end of that week. Once closed, the plant would be prohibitively expensive to restart because of shut-down damage to the ovens.

Hatch reminded them of his pro-industry efforts in Congress and told the two men in no uncertain terms they owed him one. "I don't want that plant shut down until after I meet with David Roderick," said Hatch. Two days later Roderick, USX's chairman, and a vice president flew to Hatch's Washington office from Pittsburgh.

Roderick had come in person to tell Hatch "no." But Hatch wasn't listening. He reminded Roderick of his fight against the Labor Law Reform Bill, his battles on behalf of the steel industry, and other free-enterprise scuffles that had saved USX millions of dollars. He pointed out that USX would continue to need Hatch's help on various government-related problems. Then he made his pitch: would Roderick take $15 million up front, with more coming later?

"Orrin," said Roderick, "you know as well as I do that all we are ever going to see out of this transaction is the up-front money." In 1987 there was a worldwide slump in the steel industry, and Roderick was convinced Cannon and his fellow novices couldn't keep the plant going even if they owned it.

"In that case," said Hatch, "why don't you just sell them the plant for a total of $25 million?"

Roderick sprang out of his chair. "We'd never do that. It's much too low. We won't be taken in like that."

"All right," countered Hatch, "then tell us what you'll take up front and make it somewhere between $25 million and $33 million. I want you to know that I want it to be less than $33 million." Hatch also told Roderick he wanted until August 20 to raise the money. "If we don't have it by then, you can shut Geneva down immediately," said Hatch.

Roderick gave Hatch no encouragement but agreed to think it over and call him back. Next day the USX chairman phoned Hatch with an even better deal: $30 million up front and another $10 million to be paid out of net profits —*if* there ever were any. It was about half the price of the original terms, and the Cannon group had until August 31 to put the financing together.

Hatch hung up the phone, let out a war whoop, and called Cannon. He outlined the deal to his disbelieving friend.

"Tell him we'll accept it," said Cannon.

"I already did," said Hatch.

Hatch continued to work with Cannon to keep the deal on track with both USX and financiers—which took right up to the last of August.

"There's no question that Senator Hatch saved the deal by interceding with USX," said Cannon. "The whole thing was threatening to come apart, but he stepped in and used his clout to hold it together. Without Senator Hatch, Geneva Steel and all those jobs probably would have been lost."

On Saturday, October 3, 1987, thirteen railcars loaded with steel coil rolled out of the Geneva yard, on their way to a manufacturing company in Texas. Geneva Steel was back in business after fourteen months—forty days faster than USX said it could get it up and running.

Hatch, wearing a hard hat, helped cut the ribbon.

Later, Hatch stepped in again. Although the plant was producing handsomely, the Cannon brothers fought among themselves, reaching an impasse that threatened to destroy the plant. Once again, they turned to Hatch, who mediated their dispute in marathon bargaining sessions that helped save the plant a second time.

To unwind during his occasional free evenings in 1987, Hatch read a number of novels, including a new best-seller by Tom Wolfe, *Bonfire of the Vanities,* which he greatly enjoyed, and Frederick Forsyth's *The Fourth Protocol.*

But he continued to make only duty calls on the social circuit. One exception was the National Kidney Foundation dinner honoring Jake Garn for donating a kidney to his daughter the previous year. At one point during the evening, Garn was on one side of Senator Simpson and his daughter Susan was on the other side. Quipped Garn: "Alan, I want you to know you are sitting between my two kidneys."

Hatch's third annual women's conference in Salt Lake City in October featured Henry Kissinger as keynote speaker. Hatch and Kissinger alone represented their gender. The conference was largely planned and executed by women, with panels on such topics as property laws and women, surviving in a male-dominated work force, intimacy in marriage, women's health concerns, building self-esteem in children, and, for employed women, "simplifying" a hectic schedule.

In welcoming remarks, Hatch said as a "direct result" of what he learned at his first women's conference two years earlier, he recently introduced a new bill, the Child Care Services Improvement Act, to provide incentives for private groups to develop programs "to assure good, reliable, affordable child care."

During the conference, held in the Salt Palace, Hatch's mother, Helen, now age eighty, went to the restroom. Inside was a big, husky man dressed as a woman. She quickly exited and security guards raced to the room, locked it from the outside, and summoned the police. As officers removed the transvestite, Helen remained perfectly calm at her son's side. "Well," she said, with utterly typical kindness, "he certainly had on a beautiful pink dress."

The 1988 Presidential sweepstakes were in full swing in 1987. One Democratic candidate, former Colorado Senator Gary Hart, dropped out of the race after reports of womanizing sapped his popularity, then dismayed Democrats by jumping back in during December, saying he had a "set of new ideas" that "no one else represents."

Republican hopefuls sought Hatch's support during the year, starting with Congressman Jack Kemp and followed by Vice President Bush and Senators Dole and Laxalt. Hatch had declined to endorse anyone until, out of loyalty, he went to the National Press Club with Laxalt as the Nevadan announced his exploratory effort.

When Laxalt's bid faded months later, he wrote a note to Hatch. "When I needed you, you were there," said Laxalt, "even though you knew it was a 'long shot' situation. What that translates to me is that you committed to a belief without first putting your finger to the 'political wind.' In this rather different business of politics, I've come to value your type of person more and more."

21

The Iran-contra Affair

D EMOCRATIC CONTROL OF THE SENATE was not all that made 1987 a
particularly taxing year for Hatch and his GOP colleagues. The
foreign-policy fiasco known as the Iran-contra affair kept
Republicans off balance throughout the year—especially those like Hatch
who helped conduct a public investigation of how the Reagan administration had erred, while still trying to protect the nation's vital secrets.

In October 1986, an American-owned cargo plane loaded with
weapons destined for the contras—rebels fighting to overthrow the
Sandinista government in Nicaragua—was shot down over that country.
Thus began the public unraveling of a complex scheme to sell arms to
America's arch-enemy Iran and use some of the proceeds to secretly
assist the contras at a time when Congress had barred such aid.

Washington braced against a paroxysm of charges and counter-
charges that rapidly grew far out of proportion to either the intent or
result of wrongdoing. Iran-contra sapped much of the energy from
Reagan's last two years in office.

The President addressed the nation twice in November 1986, trying in
vain to stamp out the spreading fire. By then it was public knowledge that
there had been a series of secret weapons shipments to Iran over a four-
teen-month period that coincided closely with the release of three
Americans held hostage by pro-Iranian militants in Lebanon. Reagan called
the operation a "high-risk gamble" to gain "access and influence" with
Iranian moderates, bring the six-year Iran-Iraq war to an end, and curb
terrorism. He insisted it was not simply an arms-for-hostages swap.

Reagan also claimed he was not "fully informed" about the diversion of funds to the contras. Attorney General Meese acknowledged that between $10 million and $30 million in profits from the weapons sales to Iran had been deposited in Swiss bank accounts and "made available to the forces in Central America" despite a congressional prohibition on such assistance at the time.

Reagan accepted the resignation of his national security advisor, John Poindexter, and fired Poindexter's deputy, Marine Lieutenant Colonel Oliver North. Meese identified North as the only person in government with "precise knowledge" of the cash transfers—a claim immediately derided as ludicrous by Democrats and Republicans alike.

By the end of 1986, polls showed that most Americans believed Reagan was lying about his lack of knowledge of the operations. His approval rating plummeted some twenty points in a single month to 46 percent in one poll, with his disapproval rating a virtually identical 45 percent. Donald Regan, the President's autocratic chief of staff, was forced to resign the following February, replaced by former Senate Republican leader Howard Baker.

On May 5, 1987, twenty-six members of Congress, including Hatch, entered the hallowed Senate Caucus Room and sat in two tiers of leather armchairs to begin the public phase of inquiry into the Iran-contra affair. The joint select investigating committees included fifteen congressmen and eleven senators.

The magnificent chamber above Hatch's office in the Russell Senate Office Building echoed with history. If its twelve Corinthian columns rising from the marble floor to the thirty-five-foot ceiling could speak, they would report other senatorial investigations: the sinking of the *Titanic,* the 1929 stock market crash, Joseph McCarthy's witch-hunt for Communists, and Watergate.

The question now, after months of quiet investigation by intelligence committees in the Senate and House, was how much more the nation would learn of the mysterious deals arranged in the basement of the White House by President Reagan's National Security Council in 1985 and 1986.

"These hearings will examine what happens when the trust which is the lubricant of our system is breached by high officials in the government," said Hawaii Democrat Daniel Inouye, Senate committee chairman. ". . . The story is one, not of covert activity alone, but of covert foreign policy. Not secret diplomacy, which Congress has always accepted, but secret policy-making, which the Constitution has always rejected."

Senate vice chairman Warren Rudman, a New Hampshire Republican, acknowledged, "The story that will be told is a sad one. There will be evidence of illegal behavior and contempt for our democratic form of government." He also promised that "by the time these hearings are concluded, the American people will learn the answers to the five final questions: who, what, when, why, and how."

Hatch interjected a less melodramatic note. While he, too, wanted "to finally get to the bottom of the crucial facts," he added, "I think, frankly, we have overdone it. . . . Whereas a measure of public self-flagellation may be constructive, we seem to have turned it into an art form." There were two key questions to answer, said Hatch: "What did the President know? And where did the money go? . . . I hope after we have heard all of the facts, we will examine them carefully and take whatever corrective action is necessary. . . . We need to take constructive action while looking ahead, not destructive action while looking back."

High administration officials continued to circle their wagons, protecting the President at all costs, content to let a uniformed Marine officer take the heat for what others had also known and done. CIA director William Casey took the ultimate vow of silence, dying of pneumonia on the second day of hearings at age seventy-four.

The lead-off witness at the televised hearings was retired Air Force Major General Richard Secord, who had established the arms airlift to the contras at Oliver North's request. The United States had realized about $18 million in profits from the sale of weapons to Iran; $3.5 million went to fund the airlift of arms to the contras. Millions remained in various foreign bank accounts, linked to a business partner named Albert Hakim, said Secord.

Pressed by Senate counsel Arthur Liman, Secord admitted that another $520,000 had been transferred from the Swiss accounts to a Virginia-based company in which he had a major financial interest. Although Secord characterized the money as a loan, he acknowledged that he had made no repayments and paid no interest.

The smell of graft further complicated attempts by Hatch and a few other panelists to focus the hearings on motives and U.S. strategic interests rather than on scapegoats and the incessant questions of Watergate: What did the President know, and when did he know it?

Robert McFarlane, who had preceded Poindexter as National Security Advisor, was up next. He had been a Marine officer with two combat tours of Vietnam, military assistant to then-National Security Advisor Henry Kissinger, and a counselor at the State Department. McFarlane said that throughout the congressional ban on aid to the contras, Reagan had instructed his top aides to help rebels "hold body and soul together" and that Reagan had helped arrange funding for them from additional countries as well.

Hatch led McFarlane through a series of questions designed to high-light foreign policy goals of the Iran-contra operations: Was opening a channel to Iranian moderates one objective? Was weaning Iran away from terrorism another? Did you hope to lessen Soviet influence in Iran? Does the Cuban-supported Sandinista regime in Nicaragua also pose a serious threat to U.S. strategic interests? What might happen over the next twenty years if we ignore this threat?

"And isn't it a fact," asked Hatch, "that President Reagan, as the Commander-in-Chief of our Armed Forces, and as the sole person to whom our Constitution gives the responsibility for conducting foreign relations, was sincerely committed to a position in Nicaragua that would ultimately lead to peace and stability in our region of the world?"

Hatch also put on public record the strange history of Congress's on-again, off-again assistance to the contras: in December 1982 the so-called Boland Amendment prohibited funding; in late 1983, in a complete reversal, Congress appropriated $24 million; in October 1984, it slammed the lid shut again; in July 1985 it opened the lid a crack and voted $27 million for humanitarian assistance; in October 1986 it voted $100 million in unrestricted aid. It was in the teeth of such micromanagement of foreign policy that the Reagan administration was attempting to stop the spread of Marxism from Nicaragua throughout Central America.

That same week, a correspondent for the *Wall Street Journal* reported from Honduras that "observers throughout Latin America worry that Washington still isn't focusing on the vital question" of what happens next if Congress again cuts off military aid. "Many see an outright Sandinista victory as a harbinger of greater instability in Central America, with guer-rilla movements in El Salvador and Guatemala gaining new momentum."

The *Journal* quoted a Latin American expert at the Council on Foreign Relations: "If Americans are chafing now at having to spend $100 million a year to support the contras, wait till they see what they'll have to spend to contain the Sandinistas after the contras are disbanded."

Hatch was sharply criticized in the media and back in Utah for his leading, "softball" questions to McFarlane and other witnesses. A typical reaction came from Ross Peterson, Utah State University history professor and a former county Democratic chairman, who said Hatch "is not asking hard questions, but in fact is posing questions in a sympathetic manner that tends to justify the whole scandal."

A political cartoon by Herbert Block ("Herblock") in the *Washington Post* depicted Hatch and Congressman Henry Hyde of Illinois, Hatch's soul mate on the committee, doing a song and dance routine wearing "Reagan" hats. Their act was billed "Hatch and Hyde: The Apologists," and Hatch also wore a button that said "The witnesses are all noble people."

But Hatch defended his attempts to have policy motives behind the actions brought to light. "The fact of the matter is [the hearings are] slanted against the President," he said. Democrats outnumbered Republicans on the joint committee and controlled most of the questioning. Furthermore, both Senate counsel Arthur Liman and his House counterpart John Nields were also Democrats, although personally liked by Hatch.

Following his appearance at the hearings, McFarlane and his wife Jonny took a two-week trip to Japan and China. Upon their return, McFarlane wrote to Hatch expressing "desperation" that the ongoing joint hearings were not considering such vital issues as: "How *are* we going to deal with Soviet efforts to subvert and establish control over developing countries ever closer to vital U.S. interests?"

> Throughout our trip. . . . Jonny and I kept coming back to your courage in going against the tide of unrelieved negativism and superficiality. Neither were you soporific, playing on people's sympathy for me or anyone else. You pounded home several fundamental truths—that Iran is important, that stopping the [Iran-Iraq] war is important, that sharing such an initiative broadly is infeasible, and that losing in Nicaragua holds untold costs for us as a nation. But you sure were alone. . . . Someday it will be my responsibility to write about this period. . . . When it comes, Orrin Hatch will have a place of distinction as one who, when principle was involved, was deaf to expediency.

The Iran-contra hearings dragged on. During the first six weeks, eighteen witnesses appeared before the joint committees for 110 hours. They testified that:

- An elaborate private network had been set up to carry out U.S. foreign policy.

- Reagan had approved payments to terrorists to win the release of American hostages in Lebanon.

- High government officials had lied to Congress about the operations.

- National Security Council officials had secretly raised money and purchased arms for the contras when the Boland Amendment prohibited official involvement with the contras.

- Oliver North had carried out highly sensitive negotiations to secure release of the hostages, helped others alter critical documents about the operations, and organized a "shredding party" to destroy documents.

"What the committees have heard is a depressing story," said House chairman Lee Hamilton, an Indiana Democrat, as he closed the first phase of the hearings on June 9. "It is a story of not telling the truth to the Congress and the American people. It is also a story of remarkable confusion in the processes of government. Those involved, whether public official or private citizen, had no doubt they were acting on the authority of the President of the United States."

Other administration witnesses followed Reagan and Meese, blaming everything on North. The attempt to throw the hounds off Reagan's trail might have worked if the White House had sicced them on someone less appealing. Instead they helped create, in the minds of some people, an American hero.

Early in July, in a long-awaited appearance, North testified for six days before the committees, dressed in his green Marine uniform with a chest full of decorations. As the morning session ended on the first day, he was walking alone down a hallway outside the hearing room, head down and looking dejected.

Suddenly North looked up and spotted Hatch coming from the other direction. North rushed to him and held out his hand.

"God bless you, Senator Hatch," said North.

"God bless *you*, son," answered Hatch, shaking hands warmly. "Keep it up and hang in there. You're doing a great job."

Although the administration had gone to some lengths to distance itself from North, they could not erase a record of service suggested in a letter Reagan had written North a year before he summarily dismissed him.

"You are a man who has devoted your life in the most unselfish manner to building our nation," Reagan's letter said in part. "As a heroic soldier in the field, as a military planner and as an aide to me on some of the most important issues of our time, you have proven yourself to be an outstanding American patriot. . . . I am proud to have Lt. Col. Oliver North, United States Marine Corps, on my team."

North, forty-four was born in San Antonio and had been an infantry platoon commander in Vietnam, winning the Silver Star and Bronze Star for bravery, and two Purple Hearts after being wounded twice in action. He and his wife, Betsy, whom he described as his "best friend," had been married for nineteen years and had four children. North had taught military tactics to other officers and in 1981 joined the National Security Council, spending much of his time secretly trying to secure the release of the American hostages in Lebanon.

North began to win public sympathy. "Lying does not come easy to me," said North. "But we all had to weigh in the balance the difference between lives [lost if Congress divulged the operations] and lies." Insisting he did nothing without being authorized, he said, "If the commander in chief tells this lieutenant colonel to go stand in the corner and sit on his head, I will do so."

Hatch opened his questioning of North with the stern statement: "I don't want you to get the impression that I believe there weren't some mistakes made here. There were. . . . I think that trading arms for hostages is wrong. . . . I also don't feel that misleading or lying to Congress can ever be condoned."

Then the senator led North through a series of questions similar to those used with McFarlane, again trying to establish motives and bring to light U.S. strategic interests.

> Hatch: Now, Colonel North, if you had achieved that objective [helping to end the Iran-Iraq war], the Iran initiative probably would have been considered a great success?
> North: I am sure it would have.
> Hatch: That was quite an objective. That was quite a desire, right?
> North: Yes, it was. . . .
> Hatch: Was one of those goals to wean Iran away from its support of terrorism?
> North: It was.
> Hatch: By opening a second channel to moderates who believed it was not in Iran's best long-term interest to foster and support terrorism?
> North: Yes. And for 18 months it worked, sir.
>
> . . .
>
> Hatch: . . . Do you think these hearings might achieve some success if they result in Congress recognizing that the President needs to be given some latitude to carry out his foreign policy objectives without 535 members of Congress, mini-Secretaries of State, second-guessing everything the President is trying to do?
> North: Yes, sir.
> Hatch: . . . I believe that, too.

Many of Hatch's colleagues on the committees did a slow burn as he called the hearings a "public media show" that was helping America's enemies by publicizing U.S. documents, methods, and secret plans. "Mistakes have been made," Hatch repeated to North. "But . . . we don't have to beat our country into submission, or people like you, just because mistakes have been made." He concluded, "I don't want you prosecuted. . . . And I think there's going to be one lot of hell raised if you are."

Some committee members were unnerved, but should not have been surprised, by Hatch's refusal to march in lock-step with them.

Warren Rudman, Senate vice chairman, was concerned about what Hatch might say about him. He scratched a note on a pad of paper bearing committee letterhead and slipped it to Hatch. "Orrin," he said, "You are going to meet Jay Merwin today, a reporter for the *Concord Monitor,* our state's 2nd major paper. He is doing a story on me and the hearings. Please see me first! Warren."

When Bill McCollum, a Florida Republican and House committee member, finally expressed unhappiness with North after strongly supporting him, Democratic Senator George Mitchell of Maine wrote another note on committee paper, folded it twice, and passed it along to Hatch.

"Orrin," it said, "McCullum [sic] just got off the North Express. You're the last one on board, but there's still a chance to get off! Move Fast! George Mitchell."

Hatch was disappointed that North had accepted an expensive home security system from General Secord, then tried to disguise the transaction. The system had been installed at his Virginia home after North expressed concern that foreign terrorists might strike at his family. He acknowledged that trying to hide how it was paid for was a "terrible mistake."

Otherwise Hatch held firm, writing privately at the end of North's six-day ordeal that his testimony was "magnificent. They threw everything they could at North and he came back with more. He admitted mistakes but he also said he believed in what he was doing. He thought taking monies from the Ayatollah and transferring them to the contras was a 'neat idea.' So did I. I do not believe there should have been a diversion of funds but I do believe that this still was a neat idea."

A lot of others agreed, as North succeeded, at least temporarily, in turning the hearings from a hanging party into a one-man rout of the committees. "Ollie Takes the Hill," said *Newsweek's* cover on July 20. Its subhead read: "The Fall Guy Becomes a Folk Hero." *Time* magazine's lead story on the same date was headlined "Charging Up Capitol Hill: How Oliver North Captured the Imagination of America."

Forty-four percent of those responding to a Gallup Poll after North testified called him a "patriot and hero"; 48 percent disagreed. The largest majority in the poll—70 percent—said North had authorization from superiors for everything he did and "should not be indicted and tried on criminal charges."

By early September, Hatch's office had received some eight thousand letters on the hearings, fewer than a thousand of them from Utah. Letters expressing definite opinions included: 528 pro-North, 295 anti-North, 4,202 pro-Hatch, 2,536 anti-Hatch. Letters from Utah were far more pro-North and somewhat more pro-Hatch than those from outside the state.

The committee's long knives continued to seek Reagan's scalp but were all but sheathed by the man who followed North to the witness table: former National Security Advisor John Poindexter. "The buck stops here, with me," said Poindexter. He insisted that he alone had authorized the secret diversion of profits from arms sales to Iran to assist the contras in Nicaragua and likewise insisted that Reagan was never told about the arms deal to protect the presidency. Late CIA Director Bill Casey reportedly had warned Poindexter that he would have to take the fall for the operation if it became public knowledge.

"I felt that I had the authority," said Poindexter. "I was convinced that the President would . . . think it was a good idea." Poindexter then repeated variations of "I cannot recall" 184 times during five days of testimony.

Although committee members and many other citizens remained skeptical about the President's claimed lack of knowledge, Poindexter had protected Reagan and apparently ended the search for another smoking gun.

In November, after ten months of work, the joint Iran-contra committees released a stinging, highly politicized 450-page report. All six Republican House members on the committee and two of five Republican senators, including Hatch, refused to sign it. The report scored Reagan's lax management style and concluded, "The ultimate responsibility for the events in the Iran-contra affair must rest with the President."

Hatch and the other Republican dissenters issued a 150-page report of their own, calling the investigation a "witch hunt" and maintaining that the President and his aides were guilty, not of criminality, but only of errors of judgment. Their conclusion: "The President himself has already taken the hard step of acknowledging his mistake and reacting precisely to correct what went wrong."

In retrospect, while Oliver North would continue to be verbally pummeled by critics, many authorities believe that the $3.5 million he transferred to the contras kept them alive as a viable force and resulted ultimately in democracy in Nicaragua with the election of President Violeta Chamorro.

22

To Hang a Judge

O N June 26, 1987, Justice Lewis F. Powell, Jr. announced his retirement, giving Reagan a rare opportunity to place a third justice on the Supreme Court—O'Connor and Scalia were his first two — and likely set the court's direction for decades to come.

"Reagan and a few top aides immediately began discussing names," said *Time* magazine in its July 6 issue. "The two leading candidates were Robert Bork, a federal appeals court judge in the District of Columbia, and Republican Senator Orrin Hatch of Utah." The nation's two other leading news magazines—*U.S. News & World Report* and *Newsweek*—likewise reported Bork and Hatch as the top candidates.

Bork, sixty, was a brilliant conservative jurist, a former Yale law professor who had published widely, and a former solicitor general at the U.S. Justice Department. He had a reputation on the bench of strictly interpreting the intent of the Constitution.

The mannerly, soft-spoken Powell, seventy-nine, had been the court's most unpredictable member, though usually siding with its liberal wing. For fifteen years he had been the pivotal justice in numerous 5-4 decisions, including a June 1986 ruling reaffirming the original *Roe v. Wade* abortion decision of 1973. The prospect of losing him to a Reagan appointee jolted abortion-rights activists and other special interests.

White House Chief of Staff Howard Baker had a short list of potential nominees that, in addition to Bork and Hatch, included J. Clifford Wallace, a San Diego appeals court judge, close friend of Meese, and, like Hatch, a Mormon; and Anthony Kennedy, a circuit court judge in Sacramento. Reagan postponed discussion until Attorney General Ed Meese, who was out of Washington the weekend of Powell's announcement, returned on Monday.

Baker and Meese reportedly had the most influence on Reagan in choosing the candidates. Meese had reasons to be pro-Hatch. He was a conservative ally who owed his confirmation as attorney general to Hatch. But Baker was likely to be unenthusiastic. As Senate Republican leader, he had often found Hatch hard to control, particularly when Baker was giving away more to the Democrats than Hatch could support.

"I was honored to be mentioned as a possible candidate," said Hatch, "but it honestly was not something I really wanted. I think I would have found the Supreme Court too confining. . . . What was a big deal to me was believing that I was good enough to be considered for it."

As Washington buzzed with speculation and liberal special-interest groups mobilized to oppose any conservative nominee, someone observed that Hatch might be ineligible. Article I, section 6 states that no member of Congress can accept another federal position that was voted a salary increase during his term. Congress had approved a pay raise for Supreme Court justices the previous February. Although some legal scholars believed there were ways around the provision, clearly it was a hurdle.

On Wednesday morning, July 1, Meese telephoned Hatch with apologies. The White House was engaged in too many battles already to invite a confirmation fight over Article I. Reagan would announce Bork as his nominee.

Hatch, who insisted his feelings were not hurt, told Meese that Bork was a superb choice. He believed the nomination could have been his—and a way found around the constitutional issue—if he had actively sought it. But Hatch was ambivalent about the prospect of being on the court and did not pursue it. "I would have [had] to accept it, if Reagan [had] asked," wrote Hatch privately, "but I do not think I would enjoy spending the rest of my life in a cloister."

The day Hatch and thirteen other members of the Senate Judiciary Committee began hearings on Bork's nomination, this headline appeared in full-page advertisements in major newspapers: "Robert Bork vs. The People."

Reagan's selection of Bork "has caused a lot of controversy," said the ad, "And has a lot of people worried." A list of his "extremist legal views" followed in bold subheads, suggesting that Bork, among other things, believed in: "Sterilizing workers" and allowing "No privacy," even for married couples to use contraceptives, "No day in court" for some types of cases, and "Big business is always right." The ad demanded whether America really wanted to "Turn back the clock on civil rights?"

"Judge Bork has consistently ruled against the interests of people," the ad text continued. "Against our Constitutional rights. And in favor of his extremist philosophy. . . . We're fighting back. We're People for the American Way, 270,000 Americans . . . committed to protecting American values. Those values have never faced a tougher challenge than Robert Bork."

"Robert Bork's America," said a demagogic Ted Kennedy, "is a land in which women would be forced into back-alley abortions, blacks would sit at segregated lunch counters, rogue police could break down citizens' doors in midnight raids. . . . No Justice would be better than this injustice."

"We will fight Bork all the way until hell freezes over," said the NAACP, "and then we'll skate across on the ice."

Molly Yard, aging feminist and president-elect of NOW, called Bork "a Neanderthal."

Bork, born sixty years earlier in Pittsburgh, had been an unusually inquisitive youth and a voracious reader. As a teenager, he shocked his predominantly Republican suburb by declaring himself a socialist—but his odyssey had just begun.

He earned a B.A. degree at the University of Chicago in less than two years, being named to Phi Beta Kappa in the process, then enrolled in Chicago's law school where his views shifted first to New Deal liberalism, and finally to free-market conservatism.

Bork also had peculiar notions about public service. World War II was raging when he graduated from high school in 1944. Over his parents' protests, he enlisted in the Marines, but the war ended before he got out of boot camp. Later, after two years of law school, as classmates were deciding which lucrative firms to join, Bork dropped out of school and trained as a Marine tank commander. Why? Bork said he liked the discipline and "thought you should serve."

Bork returned to law school for his final year in 1952, married a Chicago undergraduate, and fathered three children. By 1962 Bork was a junior partner in Chicago's largest law firm, earning $40,000 annually, when he abruptly resigned to accept a $15,000 teaching job at Yale Law School. A friend recalled, "He told me he didn't want to spend his life practicing law and cash in at the end, leaving nothing but a trail of depositions, briefs and money. He wanted to leave something enduring."

Bork had earned the right to exercise his fertile mind and did so energetically, writing provocatively in both academic and popular journals on a variety of legal questions. Frequently he would come down on one side of an issue, watch its dissection by others, consider it further, and in the end arrive at an opposite conclusion.

It was a classic and legitimate intellectual exercise that would have brought only compliments had he remained in academia. But Bork's brilliance, ability, and integrity moved him up the judicial career ladder. Now at the top, his writings were like time bombs.

To critics, Bork's primary sin was in being a leading intellectual force against judicial activism that had led to such rulings as the *Roe v. Wade* abortion decision. Even many pro-abortion-rights legal scholars acknowledged that *Roe v. Wade* was not well-grounded in the Constitution. Bork had not taken a public stand on abortion itself, but his belief that the ruling was not justified by the Constitution terrified pro-choice forces and spurred their scare tactics.

He wrote and, as a lower court judge, ruled against the right of judges to go beyond the intent of the Constitution in inventing legal privilege. Society's problems outside the scope of established or reasonably inferred law should be settled by the people's elected representatives in state legislative bodies and in Congress, Bork believed.

From 1973 to 1977, Bork was solicitor general in the U.S. Justice Department. He returned to Yale, but in 1980 his wife died of cancer and in part to escape the memories, Bork went back to Washington. He later left a law practice worth $400,000 annually to accept a Reagan administration appointment to the U.S. Court of Appeals for the District of Columbia. In 1982 he remarried.

Early in July 1987, a week after being nominated by President Reagan, Bork paid a courtesy call on Hatch, who found him warm and witty as they discussed their common roots in Pittsburgh and the confirmation battle ahead. Outwardly they were opposites—Bork smoked two packs of cigarettes a day, had curly, scraggly hair and a beard, and was portly—but in judicial philosophy they were soul mates.

"Judges are no better equipped than anyone else to decide the needs of society," Hatch reminisced recently. "In fact, a good argument can be made that they are probably less so because they usually deliberate in secret and do not have frequent contact with the electorate. The function of the judge is to interpret the law, not to make it."

Hatch believed, "When unelected judges seek instead to impose their own policies on the people, or disregard the intent of the Constitution, then neither democratic nor constitutional government can long survive. Judicial activism may sometimes produce good policies but it takes us down a road of being ruled not by the steady anchor of law but the changing whims of men." While Supreme Court nominees routinely reflected political considerations, for a century their confirmations had rarely been decided on politics. Fifty-three justices had been confirmed since 1894, thirty-six of them unanimously. Four had been rejected, but only one—J. J. Parker, nominated by President Hoover in 1930—primarily because of his views on public issues.

One supposedly objective measure of a candidate's fitness was the opinion of the American Bar Association. In 1982, the ABA's judicial selection committee had unanimously given Bork its highest recommendation for the D.C. court of appeals. Now, just five years later, in what appeared to be a politically motivated shift, four members of the same committee judged him "not qualified" and a fifth member abstained from voting—though a majority again gave him the highest rating.

In the fall of 1986, committee chairman Joseph Biden told the *Philadelphia Inquirer* that if Reagan nominated Bork, "I'd have to vote for him, and if the [special-interest] groups tear me apart, that's the medicine I'll have to take." But in 1987 Biden, who desperately wanted the 1988 Democratic Presidential nomination, anxiously began wooing special interests. Within twenty-four hours of Bork's nomination, Biden announced that in light of retiring Justice Powell's "special role" as a swing vote on the court, someone with an "open mind," not Bork, was needed. A week later Biden acknowledged the "overwhelming prospect" that he would vote against Bork. It was tantamount to a judge handing down a verdict before hearing the evidence.

Other Democratic Presidential hopefuls quickly climbed aboard the anti-Bork bandwagon—Congressman Richard Gephardt of Missouri, former Arizona Governor Bruce Babbitt, and Governor Michael Dukakis of Massachusetts. Democrats and their supporters had failed to scuttle Rehnquist's nomination the year before. They were determined not to fail again and proceeded in a political exercise that imperiled the integrity and independence of the court itself.

Virtually overnight, being anti-Bork became a litmus test for political correctness. The capital had seen propaganda barrages before, but the anti-Bork effort was almost unprecedented in size and intensity. Over the objections of committee Republicans, Biden delayed hearings until September 15, giving Bork's opponents two and a half months to destroy him.

Millions were spent on media advertising and direct-mail campaigns by People for the American Way, founded by Hollywood producer Norman Lear, and other lobbying organizations including Planned Parenthood, the National Abortion Rights Action League (NARAL), the American Civil Liberties Union, and the AFL-CIO.

Hatch denounced this campaign to "mischaracterize, misconstrue, and mislead." The September 15 advertisement by People for the American Way had sixty-two falsehoods, charged Hatch. A Planned Parenthood ad about women's rights had ninety-nine, and a NARAL ad had eighty-four. "When I pointed out the falsehoods, the sponsors of the scurrilous ads didn't even try to rebut them," recalls Hatch.

The White House, still reeling from the Iran-contra hearings, failed to mobilize an effective defense, signaled conservatives to lie low, and, in effect, abandoned the field of battle to the liberal activists.

Bork's critics could not base their opposition solely on his judicial record for a good reason: Less than a year earlier, senators had voted *unanimously* to put Antonin Scalia on the Supreme Court; and during the five years that Bork and Scalia served together on the D.C. Court of Appeals, they voted together an overwhelming 98 percent of the time.

Critics instead resorted to name-calling, finding "extremist" especially effective. They went through Bork's voluminous academic writings, which by their nature were written provocatively, and lambasted him for carrying out his legal duty in 1973 as acting attorney general during Watergate when he fired special prosecutor Archibald Cox.

As the televised hearings opened on September 15, 1987, Democrats were determined to avoid the tactical mistakes that had helped Oliver North win the public opinion battle, at least temporarily, during Iran-contra. Senators wouldn't risk arousing sympathy by badgering Bork, and even members' chairs were lowered to the same level as Bork's, to avoid the impression of talking down to him. Democrats would carve up the judge with scalpels instead of cleavers.

Biden planned to use the hearings as a springboard to his party's presidential nomination in a year and feared that Hatch might tarnish the statesmanlike image Biden hoped to project. As the hearings began on September 15, Biden scrawled a misspelled note to Hatch. "Orin, are you going to go easy on me?"

All eyes were on three Judiciary Committee members who appeared genuinely undecided: Democrats DeConcini of Arizona and Heflin of Alabama and Republican Arlen Specter of Pennsylvania. The other six Democrats had already announced their opposition or leaned strongly that way: Biden and fellow presidential candidate Paul Simon of Illinois, Kennedy, Majority Leader Byrd, Metzenbaum, and Leahy. Four committee Republicans were strongly pro-Bork—Thurmond, Hatch, Simpson, and Humphrey—and a fifth GOP member, Charles Grassley of Iowa, leaned that way.

Bork's supporters believed he would dazzle the committee with his erudition and counted on Bork to save himself. However, while Bork was unexcelled in the realm of ideas, he had been neither a politician nor a courtroom lawyer. He was ill prepared by training and temperament to answer in tight "sound bites" that would clarify his views to senators and to the larger audience watching on television. Instead he resorted to rambling legal lectures that failed to clearly explain his judicial reasoning.

His basic position he did state clearly: "My philosophy of judging is neither liberal nor conservative," said Bork. "It is simply a philosophy [that] where the Constitution is silent, the policy struggles [are left] to Congress, the President . . . and to the American people."

On the defensive much of the time, Bork faced a no-win situation: if he refused to comment on controversial views, he was "closed-minded." If he engaged the issues, Democrats accused him of undergoing a "confirmation conversion." Bork in fact modified or retracted some scholarly positions taken up to two decades earlier.

Biden was pleased. "Every time I could get him to recant, I won," said Biden. "People don't believe in recantations."

Veteran lobbyist and former Utahn Tom Korologos had been brought in to shape White House confirmation strategy. "The communication level," said the dismayed Korologos, "was zero."

On the fifth and final day of Bork's testimony, September 19, with the three swing senators still uncommitted, Korologos slipped Hatch a note before he delivered his summary statement: "Praise Specter's Questions & Brilliance!!"

Hatch took the strategist's advice and praised both Specter and Heflin, hoping to help nudge them into the pro-Bork column. Then Hatch turned to Bork, by now a bewildered man, pointed out that he had spent some thirty hours in the witness chair, and praised him: "You have answered every question, dispelled every doubt, risen above every insult or indignity, and disposed of every complaint."

Hatch was overreaching: clearly Bork had *not* dispelled every doubt. "Unfortunately, as I said at the outset of this trial," Hatch continued, "the standard for judgment has been political. You have not been judged by your faithfulness to the law, but by your critics' fidelity to a political agenda."

In two critical areas—women's rights and privacy—Hatch insisted that Bork's record was good. For women, said Hatch, Bork "would grant as much or more protection as the Supreme Court does, with more fidelity to the words of the Constitution, which favors no special groups but guarantees any person equal protection of the laws." On privacy, said Hatch, looking at Bork, "you would enforce all privacy rights in the Constitution and strengthen the ability of Congress and the President to enforce any others they take time to define."

Hatch summarized his case for Bork this way:

> By any standard of fairness, the judgment must be rendered in your favor. If this body could rise above political measurements and be half as fair as you have been as a judge, the verdict would be unquestionably delivered in your favor. . . . [But special-interest critics] are afraid. They fear that you would let legislatures legislate. . . . Judge Bork would make Congress, which is accountable to the voters, make the tough decisions. Many Senators do not want to

make those tough choices. . . . What [special interests] fear is that the people will once again rule America and it might not bring the results they want. They fear that their results-oriented activism may not win in a Court ruled by law, not politics.

Prior to delivering his summary, Hatch had penned a note at the end of his typed text. It gave his remarks a fiery finish, but perhaps cost as much goodwill among colleagues as his conciliatory words at the start had gained.

These lawmakers ought to learn one critical lesson from this great jurist—the lesson of fairness. . . . Every person is entitled to his or her own opinion, but not to his or her own facts. The so-called facts used against you are totally manufactured by people who have made up their own facts out of the vacuum of their closed minds.

A political bombshell competed with Bork's testimony for headlines: Joe Biden, Bork's smilingly merciless chief inquisitor, was himself in steaming-hot water. The issue went beyond Biden's views to the heart of his character as he campaigned for the Democratic presidential nomination.

Biden, it seemed, had been liberally appropriating the words of others for his public speeches, while pretending they were his own. He had lifted generous chunks of rhetoric from the likes of John and Robert Kennedy and Martin Luther King, Jr.

He had even stolen someone else's ancestry. A videotape circulated by the camp of presidential rival Michael Dukakis showed Biden mouthing, almost word for word, a speech by British Labor Party leader Neil Kinnock. During a debate the previous month, Biden movingly told an Iowa audience of his ancestors who had worked in the coal mines, also saying he was the first in his family to go to college. While an accurate description of Kinnock's lineage, none of Biden's ancestors had been miners, though one grandfather had been a mining engineer. And at least one Biden ancestor had also gone to college.

Another videotape surfaced, including a Biden speech in New Hampshire in which he claimed to have been a good law school student. In fact, Biden had finished 506th out of 688 students at the University of Delaware, then seventy-sixth in a class of eighty-five at Syracuse Law School, where he had to repeat three classes and had also been caught plagiarizing five pages of a published law-review article. "Please, I implore you," Biden had written the Syracuse law faculty, "don't take my honor. If your decision is that I may not remain . . . please allow me to resign, but don't label me a cheat."

The irony of Biden's predicament was lost on no one. On September 23 he ended his campaign for the presidency.

On September 22, 1987, the intellectual godfather of anti-Bork forces testified before the committee. Preparing for the hearing, Laurence Tribe of the Harvard Law School had consulted privately with Kennedy and Biden, playing Bork's role as Biden peppered him with questions.

Tribe had often jousted with Hatch, an ideological opposite, as an expert witness before the Judiciary Committee and once in a debate on Tribe's turf at Harvard. Tribe had written a book in 1985 which provided a philosophical foundation for anti-Bork forces. In *God Save This Honorable Court,* Tribe argued that it was not only the right but also the duty of senators to weigh a nominee's political views when judging his or her fitness to sit on the high court. Merit, as measured by temperament, intellect, and integrity, were not enough, said Tribe.

Hatch strongly disagreed. Reviewing Tribe's book for the *Harvard Law Review,* Hatch warned, "Political involvement in the selection of justices is a two-edged sword whose backswing has the potential to injure the prestige and independence of the Court. *Save This Court* disregards the potential costs of political vendettas."

During the hearings, Hatch tried but failed to get Tribe to admit that much of his criticism of Bork stemmed from Bork's writings as a legal scholar—not his work as a judge.

> Tribe: I am concerned about a very simple 200-year-old tradition of liberty. I am concerned about—
>
> Hatch: As you interpret it. See, that is the difference. [Bork] interprets it rather broadly, too, if you listen carefully to his statements. . . .
>
> Tribe: I guess I am relying on statements —
>
> Hatch: On his writings as a professor.
>
> Tribe: No. I am relying on statements [by other Justices] . . . that liberty is not limited to the specifics in the Bill of Rights. And I am saying that someone who does not believe that is making a fundamental error with respect to what our revolution and our Constitution was all about.

Witnesses the following day included former Chief Justice Warren Burger. Hatch asked, "What is your opinion with regard to whether or not Judge Bork is in or out of the mainstream of American judicial thought?"

Burger answered, "Senator, if Judge Bork is not in the mainstream, neither am I, and neither have I been. . . . I simply do not understand the suggestion that he is not in the mainstream of American constitutional doctrine."

Bork's nomination began to come apart on October 1 when committee Republican Arlen Specter announced he would vote "no." Specter's decision opened the floodgates, and Bork's last real hope—Southern senators—swam through.

Bork also lost the committee's swing Democrats, DeConcini and Heflin, as the Judiciary Committee on October 6 voted 9-5 against his nomination. White House officials hoped Bork would gracefully withdraw at that point, but Bork insisted on a full Senate vote.

Speculation surged over the White House's next choice. Again Hatch was prominently mentioned. Connecticut Republican Lowell Weicker, who often voted with the Democrats, was asked on October 7 whom he would support as the nominee. Weicker, up for reelection the next year, pointedly replied that if Hatch were chosen, he would vote against him.

That evening Weicker held a campaign fund-raiser. Among those showing up to support him was Hatch, who wrote in his private notes, "I decided to go to his fund-raiser to show that I am a better man than he is."

Hatch had even more reason for offense days later when he and four other GOP senators met with White House Chief of Staff Howard Baker to help prepare a list of Supreme Court candidates in the all-but-certain case that the Senate voted Bork down. Baker had thirteen names on his list; Hatch and his colleagues struck four and added two others.

Hatch's name was not on Baker's sheet—a glaring omission after reportedly being on White House lists for other Supreme Court vacancies under Reagan. A revealing colloquy about J. Clifford Wallace, another Mormon who had previously been on the short list, helped explain why. Hatch suggested that Wallace's name be added to the present list, but Baker objected, saying Wallace's religion was a problem.

"How's that?" asked Hatch.

"Well, Wallace made a statement that everything he does is motivated by his religious beliefs."

"What's wrong with that?" asked Hatch, feeling his pulse quicken but staying outwardly calm.

"Well, I agree with that," said Baker, "but it could cause some trouble."

"That's precisely the type of person we ought to have on the bench," said Hatch. "Is there anything else?"

"Wallace has also stated that there is no wall of separation between church and state," answered Baker.

"What's wrong with that?" repeated Hatch, explaining that most of the Founding Fathers held the same view, that the "wall of separation" theory came from a Thomas Jefferson letter, and that even Jefferson would not agree with the current distancing of religion from schools and other government-supported institutions.

Baker shrugged off Hatch's explanation, and Wallace stayed off the list. By inference, Hatch, too, was no longer a viable Supreme Court candidate. However, Hatch agreed with the top two choices on the final list—each of whom would shortly surface as nominees in the protracted effort to fill the high court vacancy.

Fifty-four senators—a majority—had already declared against Bork by the time the full Senate formally took up his nomination.

On October 23, after several days of speech-making, Bork's wife, Mary Ellen, a former Catholic nun, was in the visitors' gallery with Bork's two sons. At one point, she could no longer stand the misinformation about her husband and left the room. Seeing her in an outer hallway looking dejected, Hatch came up, gave her a bear hug, and told her she had been "magnificent" throughout Bork's three-and-a-half-month ordeal.

Within hours, the Senate voted to defeat the nomination 42-58. The margin of defeat was the largest for any Supreme Court nominee in history. Only two Democrats—Boren of Oklahoma and Hollings of South Carolina—had voted for Bork. Six Republicans had voted against him: Chafee, Packwood, Specter, Stafford, Warner, and Weicker.

Before the corpse was even cold, Senate Majority Leader Byrd announced: "It is time to start the healing. I urge the President to back away from a policy of defiance."

Bork refused comment on the outcome until he gave a speech at a closed meeting in Chicago early in December. Some members of the Judiciary Committee "did not care if the legal methodology was legitimate—only if the results were politically expedient," Bork reportedly said. "If viewers, listeners and readers believed 10 percent of what was falsely said, they would have been right to be horrified. If I believed 10 percent of it, I would have had at least to consider ritual hari-kari."

Ten days later, Bork sent Hatch a hand-written note "to express both my gratitude and my admiration for the masterful way you supported my nomination. . . . You made the whole trial much easier for me than it otherwise would have been. Your destruction of the opposition's newspaper ads in the Senate debate was a delightful masterpiece and Mary Ellen, the children, and I are glad your analysis is on the record."

Six days after Bork was defeated and over Baker's strong objection, President Reagan nominated Douglas Ginsburg, forty-one, a conservative judge on the same U.S. appeals court as Bork. Attorney General Meese apparently was the key influence on Reagan's decision, after Hatch had lobbied Meese hard and organized several other Senate conservatives to do the same.

Ginsburg, a bearded former professor at Harvard Law School, had only a fraction of Bork's experience and stature; but Hatch liked him, as he explained privately, because "like many of us former liberal Democrats, he had seen the error of his ways and realized the honesty and integrity of conservative thinking."

Almost immediately he ran into trouble. The right-to-life community became alarmed when they learned that Ginsburg's wife, as a young resident doctor, had once performed abortions. Hatch, worried about the trouble that anti-abortion supporters might cause, telephoned her for the facts. She explained that she disliked performing abortions at the time and had since become very anti-abortion.

But the bombshell that blew Ginsburg's nomination out of the water was his admission that he had smoked marijuana, as recently as 1979 while on the Harvard faculty.

Support for Ginsburg melted. Nine days after his nomination, under intense pressure from Reagan's aides, Ginsburg asked Reagan to withdraw his nomination. Hatch urged him to hold on. "At the first sign of trouble, [White House officials] cut and run," charged Hatch. "Yes, [Ginsburg] made some mistakes, but I believe in the principle of repentance and forgiveness." Irritated by the administration, he called the White House staff "gutless wonders" and insisted Ginsburg "would have gone on to the Supreme Court had he had support from the White House."

The White House stepped up to bat for the third time on November 11, 1987, when Reagan nominated Anthony Kennedy, a judge for eleven years on the Ninth Circuit Court of Appeals in Sacramento.

Judge Kennedy had been Baker's strong choice ahead of Ginsburg, after Baker reviewed his list with Ted Kennedy and Biden. The two Democrats expressed approval of the California judge, who had a generally conservative record but a reputation for compromising.

Hatch, initially dubious, warmed up to Judge Kennedy during his hearing before the Judiciary Committee. "He is a very articulate, interesting spokesman," wrote Hatch in his private notes. "He weighs his words carefully and intelligently. I am impressed."

Other senators were, too, and Kennedy sailed through the Judiciary Committee, was approved unanimously by the full Senate, and took his seat on the Supreme Court on February 18, 1988. The court had spent the first four months of its term operating with eight members.

Ironically, many observers came to believe that Judge Kennedy voted more conservatively on the high court than Bork would have.

The ferocious opposition to Bork had been a backhanded tribute. Hatch believed if Bork had been nominated before Judge Scalia, he would

have been confirmed; and if *Scalia* had been the second conservative
nominee, he, too, would likely have been confirmed, because Democrats
from the Northeast who scuttled Bork would not have dared oppose the
court's first Italian-American. But with Scalia already on the high court by
1987, liberal activists were free to go all-out to stop Bork. Scalia did give
them added incentive: with two exceptional conservative intellects already
on the bench—Rehnquist and Scalia—liberals were desperate to stop a
third, believing the trio would have been too devastating to their goals of
winning at the high court what they could not force through Congress.

Hatch continued to regard the "DeBorkle" with dismay: "The potential damage to the independence and integrity of the judiciary is a cost
yet to be fully counted. Smear tactics are familiar to almost anyone who
has run for office," he told an interviewer. "The sad truth is that the
debate over Judge Bork was consumed with issuing and responding to
red-herring questions. . . . His judicial record was practically ignored.
This was the tragedy—and the danger. Federal judges are not politicians
and ought not to be judged like politicians."

Hatch feared conservative reprisals when "liberal" nominees came
before the Judiciary Committee. He vowed not to be party to "an endless
cycle of revenge and retribution" which would "damage the institutional
standing of both the Senate and the judiciary."

Explained Hatch:

> Judging a judge by political, rather than legal, criteria strips the
> judicial office of all that makes it a distinct separate power. The
> framers of the Constitution gave judges life tenure and insulated
> them from the political branches for a crucial reason. Judges must
> protect our lives, liberties, and property against impassioned politi-
> cians who at times are convinced that economic or social conditions
> justify extreme measures. . . . No American would wish his life,
> liberty, or property to rest in the hands of a judge who is most
> concerned about what a newspaper headline might say or what some
> senator might say in a future confirmation debate.

Foreign policy guru Henry Kissinger befriended Hatch and briefed him periodically on the state of the world.

Hatch and Mike Pillsbury on Air Force Two, heading for Pakistan in 1985.

Pakistan's president, Mohammed Zia ul-Haq, in 1985 welcomes Hatch and two other members of the Senate Intelligence Committee, Bill Bradley of New Jersey (*left*) and David Boren of Oklahoma, on a secret mission that would have historic consequences.

Chinese leader Deng Xiaoping welcomes Hatch to Beijing in 1986. Hatch headed a U.S. delegation that won China's support for giving high-tech weapons to guerrillas fighting the Soviets in Afghanistan.

Hatch and Angolan rebel leader Jonas Savimbi point to a plate bearing Cyrillic letters, on a Soviet rocket launcher captured from Cuban troops during Angola's "civil" war.

Hatch welcomes Angolan freedom fighter Jonas Savimbi to Washington. Behind Hatch, in glasses, is New Right leader Paul Weyrich.

Hatch and Democratic Congressman Henry Waxman of California teamed up to pass health-related legislation.

Comparing notes with Joe Cannon who, with vital help from Hatch, purchased and saved Utah's Geneva Steel plant.

Reagan signs an omnibus health bill rammed through the Senate by Hatch just minutes before adjournment in 1986.

Grilling—critics said coddling—a witness during the Iran-contra hearings in 1987.

Marine Lieutenant Colonel Oliver North, aided by Hatch's leading questions, temporarily puts the Iran-contra committees to rout.

Washington Post cartoonist Herbert Block's view of GOP panelists Hatch and Congressman Henry Hyde of Illinois.

"Now again that famous team—" (From *Herblock at Large* [Pantheon Books, 1987] Used by permission.)

Preparing to run the slalom in the annual Ski Cup Classic in Park City, Utah.

Running the Nike Capital Challenge in 1986.

Hatch and fellow senator John Warner of Virginia on duty...

and off . . . a rare vacation day, fishing for bass on Utah's Lake Powell.

With Ohio
Democrat Howard
Metzenbaum, a
frequent Senate
foe.

With Mother Teresa at a national right-to-life convention.

The Gipper congratulates BYU football coach LaVell Edwards and Hatch after the Cougars win the national championship in 1984.

With former Senate Majority Leader Robert Byrd (D-West Virginia).

23

Float like a Butterfly

THERE WAS A STIR IN THE HALLWAY of the Russell Building as Hatch's secretary, Ruth Carroll, called her boss on the intercom. "You've got a surprise visitor."

Hatch emerged from his private office to find a legend standing almost shyly outside. No introduction was needed. After months of talking by telephone to one of the most famous men in the world, Hatch was finally meeting Muhammad Ali.

"Ali looked in fighting shape," recalls Hatch. "It was just a thrill to shake hands with him." Carroll said, "He impressed me as one of the sweetest-natured men I had ever met. He was extremely handsome—almost beautiful. He was very quiet, but made a big impression on everyone. He kissed me on the cheek, then pretended to faint."

Hatch, a former amateur boxer, had followed Ali's career closely. Still vivid was the thrill of listening to the radio with his father as Ali—then Cassius Clay—crumpled the menacing Sonny Liston in 1964 to first win the heavyweight crown. That same year, Clay converted to Islam and changed his name to Ali. He lost and regained the title several times, then finally hung up the gloves in 1980. Ali remained an enigmatic character, derided by many citizens and nearly worshipped by others.

Now, as he stood in Hatch's office, the forty-six-year-old poet laureate of boxing was using his fame for causes more important than beating other men senseless. Ali often appeared in foreign capitals, especially in the Islamic world, where he was revered, to help mediate disputes. He was a dedicated missionary for Islam, distributing tracts wherever he went. And he got involved in national issues, working through a handful

299

of public figures he had learned to trust, Democrats and Republicans alike. Hatch was one of those few.

"Welcome, champ!" said Hatch. He gripped Ali's shoulder with one hand as his other hand disappeared into Ali's large fist.

"Got time for me?" asked Ali in a voice so soft that it was barely above a whisper.

"Are you kidding?" answered Hatch, as staff members, aroused by the hubbub, came pouring in. Hatch introduced several aides and pointed to the light punching bag hanging on a wall. Ali's former manager Jimmy Jacobs had given it to Ali, who in turn sent it to Hatch weeks earlier. The inscription read: "To Orrin Hatch, From one Champion to another, with friendship and thanks, Muhammad Ali, 4-26-88."

Ali suffered from Parkinson's syndrome, apparently brought on by boxing. Similar to Parkinson's disease but without its degenerative pattern, Ali's speech was soft and occasionally slurred. Also his movements were sometimes labored, but his mind was unquestionably alert.

The Ali visiting Hatch's office was not the same brash youngster who won an Olympic gold medal and mesmerized the sporting world by declaring himself "the Greatest." His friends insisted there was a "real Ali" unknown to the public. This Ali no longer talked about his glory days. Instead he read the Koran and prayed four times daily, facing toward Mecca: *"Allahu akbar"*–God is great. He told Hatch, "God gave me this condition to remind me always that I am human and that only He is the greatest."

Ali had dropped by to thank the Utahn for his help in landing a federal job for a friend, Stephen Saltzburg, a law professor at the University of Virginia, who had just been named an assistant to Attorney General Ed Meese.

It was June 7, 1988. Before the year was through, Hatch and Ali would team up repeatedly.

The association with Ali was only one part of what would be a particularly satisfying year for Hatch. It was, in fact, a year filled with pleasant surprises for the United States and much of the rest of the world as well.

Bitterness over Iran-contra and filling the Supreme Court seat were fading. For the first time since the Cold War began, there was genuine hope that it was ending. In February, Mikhail Gorbachev called for a "complete overhaul" of the Soviet political system, then began to push through the breathtaking changes of *perestroika*–political and economic restructuring–and *glasnost*–openness in the flow of information.

In mid-May 1988, Soviet troops began to pull out of Afghanistan. Two weeks later Reagan arrived in Moscow for his fourth summit with Gorbachev. The two leaders exchanged treaty documents, newly ratified by the Senate, to eliminate all intermediate-range nuclear missiles. It was the first superpower agreement to destroy an entire class of missiles.

As East-West tensions eased, Iran and Iraq ended their brutal eight-year war; the Palestine Liberation Organization (PLO) renounced terrorism and recognized Israel's right to exist; Angola, Cuba, and South Africa signed a treaty calling for the independence of Namibia and a troop withdrawal from Angola.

While Washington's shenanigans had left many citizens disgusted with both major political parties, Americans were generally pleased with the economy, then enjoying its sixth consecutive year of growth—the longest peacetime expansion in U.S. history. As a result, Reagan's personal popularity was high. Huge budget and trade deficits were worrisome, but inflation for 1988 was 4.4 percent and unemployment, which had declined for five years in a row, was 5.3 percent. In 1980, Jimmy Carter's last full year in office, those figures were about 13 percent and 8 percent, respectively.

Vice President Bush benefitted both from the economy and Reagan's popularity to win the GOP's presidential nomination in August. He'd begun shakily by losing the Iowa caucuses in February to Bob Dole and TV evangelist Marion G. (Pat) Robertson. But Bush rebounded to win the New Hampshire primary and went on to sweep all sixteen primaries on "Super Tuesday"—March 8. He wrapped up the nomination when Dole folded his campaign at the end of March.

Democrats fielded seven presidential aspirants who generated little enthusiasm among voters and were tagged by the media as the "Seven Dwarfs." Congressman Richard Gephardt of Missouri won the Iowa caucuses, with Senator Paul Simon coming in second, then Massachusetts governor Michael Dukakis, civil rights leader Jesse Jackson, former Arizona governor Bruce Babbitt, former Colorado senator Gary Hart, and Senator Albert Gore of Tennessee.

No clear front-runner emerged in the early primaries, but the biggest surprise was the strength of Jesse Jackson, who won five Super Tuesday states and smashed everyone in Michigan, with Dukakis finishing a distant second. It remained a two-man race until Dukakis wrapped up the nomination early in June.

Back in Utah, Hatch looked so invulnerable heading into his third-term campaign in 1988 that Democrats had great difficulty finding someone willing to run against him.

Scott Matheson, a highly popular two-term Democratic governor, had decided against running in mid-1987, leaving a frustrated state party chairman, Randy Horiuchi, scratching his head for a candidate. "There is a moral imperative to running against Hatch," said Horiuchi, known for colorful overstatement.

The sacrificial lamb selected was Brian Moss, forty-three, son of former Senator Frank Moss, whom Hatch had beaten in 1976. Brian Moss, a stocky, amiable economics graduate of the University of Utah, was the father of four and the owner of sandwich shop franchises. A former federal and state government bureaucrat, he had run unsuccessfully for Utah treasurer in 1984 in his only bid for elective office.

On March 11, 1988, Moss formally announced his candidacy. "I think the difference between the incumbent and myself is hope," said Moss. He listed world problems ranging from hunger to war and concluded, "I have hope."

Moss didn't have much else. Hatch already had more than $1 million in his campaign war chest when Moss announced, and Moss estimated he would need at least that much himself to mount a serious challenge. Furthermore, opinion polls showed Hatch leading Moss by an enormous 40 percent. Democratic Party officials in Washington looked cold-bloodedly at the figures and slammed their wallets shut, abandoning the Utah Senate race as unwinnable and leaving Moss stranded.

Moss's weakness left Hatch unusually free to pursue Senate duties despite his upcoming election, and he spent much of 1988 on legislation before the Labor and Human Resources Committee. As ranking Republican, Hatch worked *with* the chair, Ted Kennedy, to reach compromises when possible and *against* him when compromise was impossible.

Hatch and Kennedy remained political opposites, yet learned to cooperate out of sheer necessity while serving together on both the labor and judiciary committees throughout Hatch's first twelve years in the Senate. Each man had uncommon ability to assist or thwart the passage of the other's legislation. The choice was simple: to seek common solutions to the nation's problems or face perpetual stalemate.

Kennedy, when he chose to, could usually muster Democratic support for Hatch's bills. Hatch, in turn, could bring along his Republican Senate colleagues. In addition, Hatch could usually persuade Reagan to sign Kennedy legislation that Hatch had amended to match administration goals more closely.

"Kennedy and I fought each other on 95 percent of the issues," explained Hatch. "But when we worked together on the other 5 percent, people tended to get out of the way. We were very hard to stop."

Kennedy's staff, one of the most talented in Washington, generated one proposal after another to help America's poor and downtrodden, usually at taxpayer expense. Hatch sat through the same hearings and saw the same problems, but sought solutions based more on local initiative and less on federal initiatives. "The linchpin of my philosophy," he said in a recent interview, "is that when people can't help themselves, government may step in. Too many people have become dependent on the government, but there is a legitimate need for public help for the handicapped, the aged, the emotionally disturbed, and others who cannot fend for themselves."

Hatch's determination to pass important social legislation increasingly put him at odds with some of his most conservative colleagues. During the 100th Congress, he and Kennedy negotiated a wide-ranging health bill that included the first important federal policy steps for combatting AIDS. Although they saw the deadly epidemic as a public-health disaster, Jesse Helms and other ultraconservatives saw AIDS as a moral issue. By funding education, treatment, and research programs, they argued, it would encourage male homosexuals and intravenous drug users. They discounted people who had contracted AIDS through contaminated blood and heterosexual relations.

In a dramatic encounter during floor debate, as Helms sought to attach a killer amendment to the AIDS bill, Hatch challenged, "Let us quit judging and let us start doing what is right. This bill is not a homosexual rights bill, but a public health bill. It is to help people who need help, and that includes homosexuals."

Helms countered, "The point is, we should not allow the homosexual crowd to use the AIDS issue to promote and legitimize their lifestyle in American society. And that is what is going on."

Hatch answered: "I do not agree with [homosexuals'] sexual preferences. But that does not mean I do not have compassion for them; that I am just going to write them off and tell them to forget it, go ahead and die, because they differ from me. . . . We have to tell homosexuals more than simply to become heterosexuals."

Most of the bill remained intact, providing nearly $700 million for AIDS education, anonymous blood testing, counseling, and home- and community-based health services. Reagan was unhappy with portions of the bill but Hatch lobbied him hard to sign it. On November 4, 1988, the President did.

In 1988 the Senate also passed—and Reagan reluctantly signed—a Kennedy-Hatch bill to ban private employers from using lie detectors with workers and job applicants. The bill, pushed for years by unions and civil-liberties groups, outlawed about 85 percent of current use of polygraphs, which Kennedy likened to twentieth-century witchcraft.

"An altar boy would probably fail a polygraph test," said Kennedy. "But who passes it? The psychopaths, the deceptive ones."

An estimated 2 million Americans annually, most seeking jobs, were required to take lie-detector tests. According to experts, a great majority of the tests took about fifteen minutes and gave false results as often as 50 percent of the time.

"Some 320,000 honest Americans are branded as liars every single year," explained Hatch. "That's a stigma they have to wear every day for the rest of their lives and careers."

The law allowed exemptions for special circumstances or sensitive industries, but some conservatives were livid. Dan Quayle claimed that outlawing the use of lie detectors would stop businesses from screening out dishonest employees.

It was not the first time Quayle and Hatch had disagreed. They had served together for years on the Labor Committee but were not close. "Their differences were less philosophical than personal, political, and practical," noted Richard Fenno, Jr., in a biography of Quayle. "Dan Quayle is an exuberant, expansive young man. He is a 'kidder,' with a spontaneous, hyperbolic, golf course, locker room brand of humor. . . . Orrin Hatch is a very serious, self-contained person. He is not naturally gregarious, and he has to work at a sense of humor. . . . They are both very kind human beings. But . . . Dan Quayle skates along the edge of brashness, Orrin Hatch skates along the edge of solemnity."

Early in 1988, Hatch again led the opposition to the reintroduced "Grove City" civil rights bill he had defeated in 1984. Chiefly sponsored by Kennedy, the bill passed this time, and Reagan's veto was overridden by Congress.

However, Hatch successfully filibustered against two other Kennedy bills, one attempting to increase the federal minimum wage for the first time since 1981. Hatch opposed raising the minimum wage without a youth-opportunity subminimum training wage to encourage companies to hire first-time workers. But unions adamantly opposed a training wage, fearing that their members would be displaced by lower-paid youths.

Kennedy also introduced a fair housing bill in 1988—similar to a civil rights bill defeated by a Hatch-led filibuster eight years earlier. Hatch planned to fight this one as well—before a telephone call gave him second thoughts. The call was from Muhammad Ali, asking Hatch's position.

"I told him I was probably going to lead the fight against it unless there were appropriate changes made," recalled Hatch. Ali then called Kennedy, with whom he had also struck up a friendly relationship, and pressed Kennedy to make the changes Hatch wanted.

After negotiating amendments with Kennedy and Arlen Specter, Hatch returned Ali's call several days later. "You've won another fight, champ," said Hatch. When he explained that both he and President Reagan now supported the legislation, Ali was "thrilled."

The Kennedy-Specter-Hatch substitute became the landmark Fair Housing Bill of 1988. When it reached the Senate floor, most conservatives, including Strom Thurmond, were set to filibuster it. But when Hatch surprised his colleagues by announcing he supported the amended version, Thurmond immediately announced that he, too, would vote for the bill. It sailed through the Senate on August 2 by an overwhelming margin, 94-3.

"I really felt good about the outcome," said Hatch, "because I believe in civil rights, but I want these bills to accomplish their intended goals without trampling on the legitimate rights of other citizens."

As soon as the vote was over, Kennedy walked over to Hatch on the floor. "I have really done you a favor," said Kennedy in a low, conspiratorial voice. "The *New York Times* wants a picture of us in the President's Room. I suggested you should be there, rather than Strom, because you were the one who made it possible to pass this bill."

Kennedy, Specter, and Hatch stole from the Senate chamber. As they entered the ceremonial room, there was eighty-five-year-old Senator Thurmond.

Kennedy, resigned, arranged the group for the photographer: Hatch on Kennedy's right, Specter on his left, and Thurmond on the other side of Specter. Just as the *Times* photographer started to snap the picture, Thurmond's face suddenly appeared between Kennedy and Specter.

"Strom, what are you *doing?*" asked an exasperated Kennedy.

"I'm the ranking minority floor manager of the bill," explained Thurmond, "and I thought I ought to be able to stand next to the majority floor manager." Thurmond had, in fact, deferred to Hatch, who managed the bill on the floor.

With that, Thurmond put a shoulder into Specter and muscled him out of position. Hatch and Kennedy burst out laughing, but Specter muscled his way back in. The tussle between the octogenarian and fifty-eight-year-old Specter continued until Thurmond stopped and looked at Kennedy.

"Well," he said, "then I'll get on the *other* side of you." Thurmond started to nudge Hatch, who good-naturedly stepped aside.

Next morning, the *New York Times* carried an article on the fair housing bill, accompanied by a picture of the four senators laughing. Left to right: Hatch, Thurmond, Kennedy, and Specter.

Hatch felt great affection and respect for his senior colleague. He had called Thurmond

> A man of inestimable charm
> And physical strength, with cleverness instilled
> Through long years of battling for the truth as he sees it,
> And also, much native intellect,
> Refined through the tumultuous years,
> During which he has served the people as he . . . saw fit,
> Which fact is doubted by none who know this great man.

Democrats gathered in Atlanta in July 1988 for their national convention, Michael Dukakis choosing Texas Senator Lloyd Bentsen as his vice presidential running mate. Brian Moss also attended, trying to raise money for his contest against Hatch.

In a convention interview, Moss trotted out tired campaign themes that hadn't worked for either Senator Moss or Ted Wilson in their Senate races against Hatch. Prior to defeating his father in 1976, said Moss, Hatch "had been a resident of Utah less time than my six-year-old son. . . . Hatch has worked to maintain a national presence, not one in Utah, at the same time our state has suffered unprecedented decline" under Reagan's economic program. "Orrin Hatch does not care for the working man of this country," added Moss. "Not many people think he has more than an ounce of compassion in him."

Democrats, whose internecine warfare had regularly cost them in national elections, succeeded in getting their most polemical factions—including gays and feminists—to mute their demands in Atlanta in order to present the image of a moderate, united party to American voters. "We're not going to blow it this time," Pennsylvania's Peter Kostmayer told a theoretically closed liberal gathering at the convention. "Just shut up—gays, women, environmentalists. Just shut up. You'll get everything you want after the election."

Dukakis was ahead of Bush in opinion polls as he left Atlanta, but Bush had the healthy economy and the Cold War thaw going for him. Democrats also failed to realize the power in Bush's gut-level campaign themes in time to stem the damage. Bush accused Dukakis—who opposed the death penalty—of being soft on crime, soft on national defense. Furthermore, Bush hinted he was unpatriotic, since, as governor of Massachusetts, Dukakis had vetoed a bill requiring teachers to lead their students in the Pledge of Allegiance.

Muhammad Ali and Hatch conferred often by telephone and Ali continued to drop by Hatch's office in 1988, sometimes with his wife of two years, Lonnie, and often with his lawyer, Richard Hirschfeld. Hatch found Ali intelligent and unpretentious. A warm friendship developed.

"He is probably the most electrifying, charismatic man I have ever been around," wrote Hatch. "The man has the softest, gentlest, kindest eyes of anybody I've ever seen. He also has a magnificent way with children." Hatch watched as Ali picked up a crying child and put his face close to the little boy's. When the child turned his face the other way, so did Ali. After a couple of minutes of what Ali had made into a game, the tot started laughing.

Ali and Hatch talked about religion, history, politics, and literature. One day Ali said to Hatch, "Senator, I feel like a very intelligent man who is trying to break out of this body so I can speak."

In July, Ali sent a pair of Everlast boxing gloves to Kennedy, inscribed:

"Senator Ted, I hope this glove helps you knock out injustice. Your friend, Muhammad Ali." Kennedy hung the gloves on his reception room wall, under a photograph of him and Ali.

One day Hatch told Ali he, too, would like to have a pair of autographed boxing gloves. Ali sent autographed light gloves to each of Hatch's three sons. Then, early in August, he showed up at Hatch's door, carrying a display in a glass box. The display included a two-page article from *Insight* magazine, based on an interview with Ali, and one of Ali's world championship belt buckles.

Insight noted that Ali had friends in both political parties, including Democrats Kennedy and former Governor Charles Robb of Virginia, where Ali had a farm.

"His favorite is the deeply conservative Hatch," said *Insight*. "This summer and fall Ali will be campaigning for [Hatch's] reelection to the Senate." Ali told the reporter, "I like Orrin. He's a nice fella. He's a capable man and he's an honest man. And he fights for what he believes in."

Ali told the magazine he had first been impressed with Hatch when he listened to his comments during the Iran-contra and Bork hearings. He told the magazine:

> So I went up to Washington and met him in his office, and he was such a gentleman. He was so polite and courteous. And I could tell he wasn't patronizing me like some people do. He was sincere. You meet as many people as I do and you learn who the phonies are. . . . People don't see him that way, they don't understand. He's conservative, but that doesn't prevent him from recognizing the rights of the individual. I don't think he's got a prejudiced bone in his body. . . . He makes an attractive appearance, too. You know, he's pretty. Not as pretty as I am, but he's still pretty.

Ali felt a kinship with Hatch for another reason. Ali had grown up in Louisville, Kentucky, seeing awful cruelties to blacks, including lynchings. As a child of eleven, he decided, "I'm gonna be a boxer and I'm gonna get famous so I can help my people." But now that his fighting days were over, he said, "I never talk about boxing. It's just something I did."

Hatch, too, had fought his way up from poverty and anonymity, using the law and politics as his fists. "I admire [the fact that Hatch] came up the hard way," said Ali. "He was born on the wrong side of the tracks, and he worked as a laborer—a union man, as strange as that may sound—and it's always difficult to outgrow your environment."

The framed display was inscribed, "To my dear friend Orrin Hatch, the man who *should* be President of the United States. With the highest respect and the deepest affection—From one champion to another. Love, Muhammad Ali." It was dated August 1, 1988.

Hatch was stunned. "I can't accept your championship buckle," he told Ali. When Ali insisted, Hatch said, "Then I'll hold it in trust for your children."

"No," Ali answered with finality. "It's yours."

Ali also showed Hatch his massive gold ring, similar to those given to players on championship teams, with a crown on the stone and three diamonds.

"I had this custom-made, and I'm going to have one made for you," said Ali. Hatch, embarrassed at the generosity, hoped he would forget about the ring but could not conceal how touched and honored he felt. "He is a remarkable human being," wrote Hatch. "I really like him."

As the Hatch-Ali relationship became public, civil rights leaders and Democratic Party officials—who had long held that America's blacks belong to them alone—were unnerved and tried to talk Ali out of the unholy alliance. But Ali was undeterred. When Hatch suggested he attend the Republican National Convention and, further, that he endorse Bush for President, Ali agreed.

As Republicans gathered in New Orleans in August 1988, Ali was there as Hatch's guest, staying in a suite of rooms high up in the Marriott Hotel. Ali and Richie Hirschfeld walked onto the convention floor wearing campaign buttons they had designed—with no encouragement from Hatch. The red, white, and blue buttons said "Bush in '88, Hatch in '96."

Ali and Lonnie attended a reception for Utah delegates with Orrin and Elaine, Ali smiling patiently for photos. "I want you to welcome a new friend, who has become one of my best friends in the world," Hatch told the delegates. "I call him Ali." While Ali's voice was weak that night from his medical condition, he refused to be patronized. When a reporter asked if he was supporting Bush for President—obvious enough from the button on his lapel—Ali leaned over deadpan and whispered into the reporter's ear: "That's what I'm here for."

Nor had Ali's sense of humor deserted him. Alex Hurtado, a diminutive, popular GOP figure in Utah, posed with his two daughters and Ali for a photo. Ali, who stood more than a head taller than Hurtado, leaned over and whispered: "They look better than you."

Hatch was still in excellent political shape. A recent poll showed him an amazing 50 points ahead of Moss. Rumors floated that Bush might choose Hatch as his vice presidential running mate. Hatch was flattered but didn't seem to take such talk seriously.

The question of the Vice President was on everyone's lips at the convention. Political experts believed a wise selection wouldn't necessarily help Bush, but that a poor choice could hurt him.

On Tuesday afternoon of convention week, Bush introduced Dan

Quayle as his vice presidential choice, calling the forty-one-year-old Indiana conservative "a man of the future." Quayle, showing the youthful exuberance that would be endlessly mocked on late-night TV talk shows, responded, "Let's go get 'em!" Quayle was not well known nationally, and reaction at first was muted. But Hatch confessed privately, "I became almost instantly depressed. I had worked with Dan for the past eight years, and although he was a nice man, he seemed to be so self-interested that I wasn't sure he'd be a good team player."

However, as the media began attacking Quayle mercilessly in the following days, Hatch wrote approvingly, "He weathered the vitriolic media and hung in there. Dan is attractive, hard working, and basically intelligent. I think he will probably be an asset in the end."

Hatch's reputation for being straight but not narrow took a body blow soon after the convention. On a campaign swing through southern Utah, in impromptu remarks, Hatch remarked that Democrats, among other things, were "the party of homosexuals."

When a local newspaper reported his comment, Hatch compounded the problem by denying it. A one-day embarrassment mushroomed into a *cause célèbre* for Democrats as well as gays in both parties. A local radio station had recorded Hatch's speech, and the Associated Press filed a story that appeared throughout the country.

The Democratic Party, unlike the Republican Party, Hatch had said, was the "party of big government, anti-defense, continual failure to support freedom fighters all over the world, weak foreign policy. . . . And of course they love—they are the party of homosexuals, they are the party of abortion, they're the party that has fought school prayer every step of the way." For good measure, Hatch added, "They're the party that has basically, I think, denigrated a lot of the values that have made this country the greatest country in the world."

Hatch's inarticulate comments left some with the erroneous impression that he was branding all Democrats as homosexuals. Hatch said he would never do that—nor, he added in a futile attempt to defuse the situation with humor, would he "denigrate all gays by calling them Democrats."

State Democratic chairman Randy Horiuchi, hoping to breathe life into Brian Moss's moribund campaign, told a press conference that Hatch had shown a "streak of venom" and should apologize for "name-calling and stereotyping." Hate mail and obscene phone calls poured into Hatch's office. His life was threatened.

"The thing I feel worst about is that I have a great deal of compassion for people who are homosexual, even though I despise their lifestyle. It was a stupid thing to say," acknowledged Hatch, "but it certainly was not meant the way the media twisted it." He noted that the eight offending words were taken from an impromptu speech lasting about twenty-five minutes, and wrongly implied—despite his recent defense of the AIDS bill—that he had no empathy for homosexuals.

What Hatch meant to convey was that the national Democratic platform—out of step with Utah Democrats who tended to be more conservative—favored expanding gay rights. Also that presidential candidate Michael Dukakis supported passage of a gay-lesbian civil rights bill, and that the National Gay and Lesbian Task Force was a strong supporter of the Democratic Party.

Returning to Washington, Hatch faced a mixed reception among Senate colleagues. Kennedy was consoling: "I know what being quoted out of context is like." Another leading Democrat told him, "When I read the eight words by themselves, I wondered what my friend Orrin Hatch was doing. Then I looked at the words in context, and I have to say I agree with everything you said."

In contrast, Howard Metzenbaum was acerbic: "Orrin, you have offended all of us Democrats. You'd better make an apology on the floor of the Senate."

"The hell I will," answered Hatch, who had reached the limits of his contrition.

A number of people conceded that Hatch's remark, though imprudent, was not inaccurate. Congressman Peter Kostmayer had admitted that the Democrats counted on gays in the fall elections and had promised them "everything" they wanted—if they would lay low until Democrats had won.

For Hatch, the disheartening episode in southern Utah was made easier by what came immediately afterward on September 1, 1988: an upbeat political rally in Salt Lake City, featuring his friend Muhammad Ali, accompanied by Ali's wife, lawyer, and photographer.

Ali was at his wisecracking best, gracious and reasonably strong of voice. They met with reporters in the State Capitol, Ali telling them he campaigned only for politicians whom "I feel I could have my fans trust."

Brian Moss had sent Ali a telegram, welcoming him to Utah but telling him he shouldn't be supporting Hatch because of the senator's voting record on social issues. A reporter asked Ali about the telegram, which he apparently hadn't seen.

"Who is he?" Ali asked about Moss.

Hatch explained that Moss was his election opponent.

"Tell Moss you're the boss!" said Ali in vintage rhyme.

They adjourned to the Capitol lawn, where about two hundred Utahns waited to greet Ali and Hatch. Ali hugged each youngster and many elderly guests, and posed smiling for numerous photos.

Ali also went with Hatch to the Primary Children's Medical Center, to a martial-arts gymnasium where Ali drew oohs and aahs hitting a speed bag, then to Temple Square to hear the famed Mormon Tabernacle Choir. Hatch later took him to services at a local black congregation.

Ali was enthralled with the choir but didn't hesitate to assert his own beliefs. Everywhere they went, he passed out pre-autographed pamphlets that explained Muslim beliefs: Jesus wasn't God but was a prophet, like their founder Muhammad, who lived about six hundred years after Christ.

Missionary zeal for their respective religions was another tie between Hatch and Ali. They enjoyed the similarities between their faiths: Muslims and Mormons each have health codes, including a prohibition on alcohol. Each religion also teaches that life on earth is a period of preparation and testing to determine opportunity in the life to come.

The highlight of the weekend for Hatch—and perhaps Ali—was a family dinner at his parents' little home in Midvale. Hatch told his mother to call his Salt Lake office for help in preparing the dinner, but Helen insisted on doing it all herself, and turned out a fried chicken dinner that Ali devoured in huge helpings that amazed other guests.

"The whole neighborhood came over to meet Ali and his darling wife," recalled Helen. "He was so dear. . . . One neighbor who had said he didn't like blacks stayed the whole time and had to admit they were wonderful. I think it opened his eyes."

The main reason Hatch took Ali home was to meet his father, now eighty-two and suffering from diabetes. For Jesse, hosting one of his all-time heroes was a thrill of a lifetime, bringing back poignant memories of listening to fights on the radio in Pittsburgh with Orrin.

Late in the 1988 campaign, Hatch took a principled stand on behalf of a Democrat. It was typical for him but caused consternation among Republicans. Dennis DeConcini, running for reelection in Arizona, was receiving negative fallout because his brother, apparently handling the family partnership properties, invested in land along the Central Arizona (water reclamation) Project, then sold it to the government at a profit.

Although DeConcini said he had no knowledge of the government's interest, he was pilloried in the media. Steve Benson drew a political cartoon for the *Arizona Republic* in Phoenix, depicting the senator and his next residence: a jail. DeConcini, formerly a shoo-in for reelection, dropped like a rock in the polls. Republicans couldn't contain their glee, and DeConcini's opponent ran campaign ads accusing him of being unethical and dishonest.

Hatch spoke by telephone to DeConcini to determine the facts, then issued a press release saying he had served with DeConcini for twelve years and knew him to be a man of impeccable integrity. Former Senator

Paul Laxalt did the same, explaining privately to Hatch, "I was not going to let you hang out to dry by yourself."

Senate Republican leader Bob Dole was bitter about Hatch's "defection" and so was Senator Rudy Boschwitz of Minnesota, head of the GOP Senate Campaign Committee. "I probably won't ever hear the end of it," wrote Hatch privately, "but it was the right thing to do. Dennis is a good person. Although we disagree on some things, and I would like to see more Republicans in the Senate, I couldn't stand by and see him treated so unfairly."

Arizona newspapers, in banner headlines, erroneously said Hatch and Laxalt had endorsed DeConcini for reelection. They had in fact merely attested to his honesty. DeConcini steadied his campaign and went on to win with a 57-41 percent margin.

In Utah, the media tried to spice up the Hatch-Moss campaign by playing it as a "grudge match," but Moss could never mount a serious challenge. Early on, Moss said, "I believe the Moss name has a great deal of credibility in this state," and "It's certainly one of my biggest assets." In truth, the Moss name stood for old-fashioned liberalism that had long since lost its luster in the Beehive State.

Hatch and Moss went through the motions, holding several low-key debates in which Moss accused the incumbent of voting against education, of not caring about the hungry because Hatch opposed a bill to buy surplus food for the poor and elderly, and of opposing civil rights legislation. Elaine signed a fund-raising letter that said, "I have never seen Orrin so mad" and accused Moss of "misrepresent[ing] Orrin's position on education, on domestic programs, even on jobs Orrin helped bring to Utah."

Hatch's campaign manager, Bud Scruggs, was a chunky young man with political savvy and a rapier-sharp wit. When Hatch stayed in Washington on Senate business, Scruggs took his place in facing Moss. Like Hatch's previous campaign manager, Scruggs cautioned Hatch not to get mean. Hatch complied, privately vowing to "bore" listeners in the debates.

In October, a public opinion poll showed Hatch leading Moss by a stunning 70 percent to 23 percent. Moss complained bitterly that Hatch was outspending him 25 to 1, prompting a rejoinder from Hatch that other Democrats running against Republican incumbents were raising sufficient funds, so the problem must lie with Moss himself.

"The greatest thing about being [in Washington] and representing my state is that I am able to help people," said Hatch in a wide-ranging interview a week before the election. "I think that even those people who don't support me, and who really don't even like me, have found that when they come to me, I pull all stops for them. . . . If you need help, I don't care if you love me, hate me, or whatever." Representing Utah in the Senate, he summarized, is "the highlight of my life."

By the election on November 8, Hatch had indeed officially outspent Moss nearly 25 to 1–$3.7 million to $153,000–though labor unions probably poured far more unaccounted "soft" money into Moss's campaign than his official amount. Hatch could have won the election by spending a tiny fraction of his total, given the advantages of incumbency. But the contributions process proved difficult to impede, even as almost-certain victory loomed. In addition, seasoned candidates like Hatch followed a political rule of thumb: always run scared.

On election night, Orrin and Elaine, some of their children and grandchildren, and his parents, gathered at the Little America Hotel to watch the returns. Hatch crushed Moss 67 to 32 percent. During the celebration, a familiar figure suddenly appeared, wearing a Bush-Hatch button. Muhammad Ali had come to surprise his friend. "I knew you'd win," beamed Ali.

Hatch called Brian Moss to commiserate, and Moss was gracious in return. Hatch also tried to call–but couldn't reach–Ted Wilson, his 1982 Senate opponent, who was demoralized after losing a close race, this time for governor. Days later, Wilson told Bill Loos, a fellow university staff member and Hatch's former state director, that Hatch was "a very fine senator" who had always treated him with respect. Wilson added: "I know my political career is over. The next time Orrin runs, I would be honored to head the Democrats for Hatch organization."

Bush won the presidency, rolling over Dukakis 426-111 in electoral votes, where it counted, but only 53 to 46 percent in the popular vote. Bush-Quayle did better in Utah than in any other state, taking 66.2 percent of the vote. But their victory was no mandate. Voters were disgusted by the negative tone of the Presidential race, and a record number stayed away from the polls–breaking a forty-year-old mark for low turnout. Exit polls taken by ABC indicated that 50 percent of Dukakis voters were mainly interested in beating Bush, while 49 percent of Bush's voters were mainly interested in beating Dukakis. Exit polls also indicated that Quayle had cost the ticket about 2 percent of the vote.

Further dulling the sheen on Bush-Quayle was a poor showing by congressional Republicans. Democrats made a net gain of one seat in the Senate and five in the House. It was the first time since 1960 that the party winning the presidency didn't also gain seats in the House.

Republican maverick Lowell Weicker, who had publicly stated he couldn't support Hatch for the Supreme Court, and had alienated many of his fellow Republicans, narrowly lost his Senate seat to Democrat Joseph Lieberman in Connecticut. When Lieberman's victory was assured on election night, a cheer went up from the *Republican* victory party in Washington. But Hatch didn't cheer. Instead he telephoned Weicker to say he'd miss him.

"Lowell and I differed on almost everything," wrote Hatch privately, "but I liked him. I will feel a great personal sense of loss, because Lowell really believed in what he was doing. I can never really hold it against somebody who is really a believer."

Hatch had one final request of Ronald Reagan before the President left office in January 1989: pardon Oliver North and John Poindexter. Special prosecutor Lawrence Walsh, assembling a small army of lawyers and other investigators, had already spent millions of dollars preparing cases against them and other Iran-contra figures.

Hatch had been the most persistent voice in Congress in pressing for a full pardon for North, arguing that such a move would not be placing him above the law, because, as he wrote privately, "it is lawful to forgive as well as punish." Hatch was also concerned lest national security secrets be revealed in open court. Days before the Reagans were due to vacate the White House, Hatch tried repeatedly to meet with the President, but aides blocked his access.

Instead Hatch prepared almost identical letters to the President and to the person who had the most influence on him—First Lady Nancy Reagan. The letter to Mrs. Reagan said, in part:

> I have not asked for anything [for myself] over the last eight years, but I am asking, as your close friend, for these pardons to be granted. . . . Do not permit this matter to haunt the new Bush Administration over the next two years as it did your Administration in the past two years. . . . North and Poindexter never meant to hurt you. They are the most loyal and courageous soldiers of this Administration, right or wrong. To leave them fighting a rear-guard action in Washington, D.C., is unbecoming of the Commander-in-Chief.

In a hand-written postscript, Hatch emphasized again, "Nancy—This is the right thing to do. It will save your husband much pain. Please help! Love, Orrin."

Reagan was unmoved, however, and left office with North, Poindexter, and others facing prosecution. Both North and Poindexter were convicted of obstructing justice, though both convictions were overturned on appeal.

As Hatch warned, Iran-contra continued to haunt the Bush-Quayle presidency, and the fishing expedition led by Lawrence Walsh cost taxpayers officially nearly $40 million. Unofficially, including the inordinate amount of time spent by other federal agencies responding to Walsh's office, the probe probably cost in excess of $100 million. For their money, taxpayers got a final Iran-contra report in January 1994 that revealed little of significance that congressional investigators hadn't learned some six years earlier.

Orrin and Elaine had made his parents' guest room their home on numerous trips to Utah for twelve years, but in 1988, they finally purchased a condominium in a large complex called Zion's Summit, which overlooked Temple Square in downtown Salt Lake. Hatch went shopping for a piano to help him relax in the city and made a note to visit Helen and Jesse often now that he would no longer be sleeping there.

In December, Hatch was honored at a dinner by the National Kidney Foundation of Utah for his health-related work. Celebrities participating in the event included actress Lynda Carter, considered one of the world's most beautiful women and formerly "Wonder Woman" on the TV series of the same name. Accompanying her to Salt Lake was her attorney-husband, Robert Altman, one of Washington's superlawyers and a partner of Clark Clifford, a storied political figure.

Muhammad Ali, who had planned to come, had just returned from the Sudan and was ill. Ali's attorney, Richie Hirschfeld, represented him at the dinner, bringing a gift from the champ: a replica of Ali's gold championship ring, specially made for Hatch.

Among other Christmas socials, Orrin and Elaine attended a lavish party at the home of Sargent and Eunice Shriver in Potomac, Maryland. Numerous Hollywood stars attended, including Danny DeVito and Arnold Schwarzenegger.

Only a few other members of Congress were there. Hatch, who was personally fond of the Shrivers, was dazzled by their house and hospitality but wrote introspectively about the gala: "Personally, I can stand one of those evenings about every two or three years. There really are a lot of people who love this type of life. I'm not one of them. . . . Perhaps I'm just a strange person, but I felt completely alone in that large crowd of about 1,000 people."

Crossing Hatch's path again that evening were Robert Altman and Lynda Carter, neighbors of the Shrivers. Hatch thanked them again for going to Utah earlier in the month, not knowing that soon enough Altman would call on him to return the favor—and that by doing so Hatch would jeopardize his good name and his career.

24

The Odd Couple

THE WIND WHIPPED FIERCELY ACROSS Boston, and the temperature shivered well below freezing. Residents wrapped in scarves and buried in winter coats struggled across the square outside historic Faneuil Hall. It was Thursday morning, January 5, 1989.

Heat from the basement's boiler had thawed the first two floors of this chilly "Cradle of Liberty," but the third floor was still icy. Two hundred fifty Mormon missionaries and local church leaders sat bundled in their overcoats. Filling the back rows were reporters and camera crews from TV stations.

Shortly after 9 A.M., Frank Madsen, Jr., president of the Massachusetts Boston Mission and Hatch's former top assistant in Washington, arose, energetically whipped off his topcoat, and began speaking, ignoring the fact that every word turned into a puff of vapor.

"We're in for a treat this morning that I'm sure will warm us up," Madsen assured his missionaries, mostly young men and women in their early twenties. "We're honored to have Utah Senator Orrin Hatch and his wife Elaine with us, and we will be joined shortly by Senator Edward Kennedy."

Madsen, middle-aged with dark hair, a pleasant face, and calm demeanor, continued, "Senator Kennedy is not a member of our faith. But he arranged for us to use Faneuil Hall this morning and has agreed to share some thoughts with us and to answer questions. We'll give the time to him as soon as he arrives. Let me suggest that you keep your comments general and don't ask any personal questions of the senator."

Madsen called on an elder to offer an opening prayer, then bantered with the group until a rear door opened. In strode Kennedy, impeccably dressed in a blue pin-striped suit and red tie. Barely nodding at the media, he walked briskly to the front, shook hands with Hatch and Madsen, and took the podium as invited.

"I'm not sure if it's colder outside or inside the hall," quipped Kennedy. "When we made the arrangements, they forgot to tell us it cost extra if we wanted a little heat."

Kennedy, attending at the invitation of Madsen and "my good friend Senator Hatch," gave a thumbnail sketch of his state's history and put the Mormon missionary program in the same tradition as the Peace Corps, begun by his late brother, President John F. Kennedy, in 1961.

"Many say that America's young people are not interested in the issues because you are caught up in a 'me' psychology that cares little about others and that is unwilling to make the private sacrifices needed to advance the public good," said Kennedy. "I reject that pessimistic view. In many parts of America today, young men and women are directing their talents to meet the challenges of the future. And your mission and dedication here is witness to that truth.

"Sometimes, the sheer size of these challenges can seem over-whelming," he wound up. "Often they call for the commitment of a life-time and there is no guarantee they will meet success. But you, above all, . . . understand the need for sacrifice. You, above all, know the impor-tance of service. And one thing is certain—if the rest of your generation truly commits itself as you do, we shall surely succeed."

The cold audience gave Kennedy warm applause, then Madsen called for questions. A reporter immediately asked about a bill pending in Congress.

"I didn't come here to talk about that," said Kennedy, politely but firmly. "I'm here to discuss what's on the minds of these young people."

Camera tripods clicked shut, accompanied by a low chorus of disgruntled moaning. Within minutes every reporter and photographer had trooped out.

Kennedy answered questions for about half an hour. One elder asked the senator if he had a copy of the Book of Mormon.

"No," said Kennedy. Glancing at Hatch with a grin, he added, "But I bet there's a copy on my desk Monday morning."

Hatch grinned back. "It'll be there this afternoon."

After Kennedy left, Hatch spoke for an hour about his experiences in the Great Lakes Mission. He described working eighteen-hour days and memorizing five hundred scriptures during his two-year mission, then offered suggestions on how to answer specific church-related questions. "The best advice I can give you is to read and reread the scriptures."

Hatch also praised a new guideline for Mormon missionaries— contributing four hours of community service each week in health care, education, and helping the poor. "Sometimes it isn't enough to know the gospel," he counseled. "Sometimes how you perform your daily chores as a member of the human race makes the difference in those you want to teach. Be humble and be ever prayerful. You are doing the work of the Lord. No one can ask more."

Orrin and Elaine met Kennedy for a lunch of Atlantic sole, oyster stew, and Boston clam chowder. Kennedy had been impressed with the young missionaries. "You know," he said, "I'd consider becoming a Mormon and going on a mission myself, except for one problem."

"What's that?" asked Hatch.

"I wouldn't be able to date for two years."

The Senate was under new leadership as the 101st Congress got underway in January 1989. After twelve years of leading the Democrats — six as majority leader–Bob Byrd stepped down to chair the powerful Appropriations Committee. At a thank-you luncheon in his honor, the single-minded Byrd launched into a speech describing his austere life as a senator the past thirty years that graphically showed why he had such difficulty relating to his colleagues:

"I have been to only one football game in the whole time I have been here . . . if you've seen one football game you've seen them all. . . . I have attended one movie in the last forty years. . . . What does Bob Byrd do? I read and improve myself. In this last year alone, I have read all thirty-seven of Shakespeare's plays—twice. I have read *The Iliad*, *The Odyssey*, and Plato's *Republic*. . . . I have also read the dictionary."

As they left the luncheon, Hatch saw George Mitchell of Maine who was taking up the reins. "Well, George," said Hatch, "when you become majority leader, you certainly have your reading list all laid out for you."

Mitchell just shook his head.

In secret-ballot elections as full of intrigue as a shake-up in the Kremlin, Mitchell had beaten out two other Democratic contenders, Daniel Inouye of Hawaii and Bennett Johnston of Louisiana. Mitchell was a strongly partisan liberal, but his soft-spoken manner and genial temperament had won respect on both sides of the aisle.

The forty-five Senate Republicans unanimously retained strongly partisan Bob Dole as their leader, with Alan Simpson as second in command and William Armstrong of Colorado as head of the Republican Policy Committee.

For the first time since 1977, Hatch owed no political favors to the White House and was even freer to follow his own drummer. His relations with George Bush had been proper but lacked the warmth he had felt for Reagan. Moreover, Vice President Quayle's relations with Hatch had been cool, and

White House Chief of Staff John Sununu had an imperious personality that didn't sit well with congressional Democrats or Republicans.

There would be no rumors of a Supreme Court appointment for Hatch from this administration. And Hatch had long ago lost interest in Senate GOP leadership. His focus was simply being the best senator he could be—for Utah and the nation.

Issues interested him even more, partisan politics less. He compared politics to silverfish, wingless insects "flitting over a stagnant pond / In which nothing grows, / Nothing lives . . . Politics exhilarates, / When one has won, . . . But wins are transient / In the never-ceasing changeover / From one person to another, / From one regime to yet one more. . . .

Kennedy's presidential flame had flickered and died in 1980, when Americans signaled that, no matter how much they wanted new national leadership, they didn't want his. In losing the Democratic nomination to Carter, Kennedy learned that no merit would overcome the dark questions that surrounded the death of a young woman on July 19, 1969.

Now, on the twentieth anniversary of the date when Kennedy's car plunged into a pond on Chappaquiddick Island, drowning Mary Jo Kopechne, the fresh rush of publicity made it more obvious than ever that Kennedy would never sit in the Oval Office. To casual observers, Kennedy was a caricature—either a jaded remnant of a storied American family or a cheap staple for tabloids and trash-talk shows.

His outrageous personal life reinforced two decades of doubts. Recently he had been photographed atop a shapely brunette on a boat in St. Tropez after being caught in similar repose with a woman in La Brasserie restaurant. Kennedy drank alcohol copiously but handled it surprisingly well, thanks to his considerable bulk and an annual diet-drink fast. Instead of making him surly or depressed, liquor loosened his tongue and stirred his Irish sense of humor. During drinking bouts, Kennedy could regale listeners with uproarious tales for hours.

However, Hatch, his colleagues, and serious students of government knew another Kennedy—a consummate legislator and public advocate. While heroic visions of his late brothers John and Bobby were etched into the hearts of America, those visions were a good part myth, enhanced by their early deaths as martyrs. Neither had ever been the senator that the youngest brother had become during nearly three decades in Washington.

John F. Kennedy especially loomed far larger in public image than he had in reality. But Ted's reality dwarfed his image. Backed by a large, talented, aggressive staff that was the envy of his colleagues, many recognized Kennedy as a serious legislator of historic stature. He was relentless and hard working, taking a battered black briefcase full of work home each night. Daytime found him on the Hill where he would corner and cajole other senators on his current piece of legislation, using charm if possible, and intimidation and shameless demagoguery if not.

Although Kennedy was notorious for awkward syntax and verbless sentences, when he got wound up on the Senate floor, his meaning was never in doubt. Fired sufficiently during floor debate, his decibel level often rose until he was screaming. Occasionally a nervous staff member would slip him a note: "Sir, you're shouting."

Kennedy's approach worked in the clubby Senate, and he had introduced a stunning array of social legislation. However, not a lot of it had become law until recent years. The catalyst who, more than anyone, had helped move Kennedy's bills into law was Orrin Hatch.

During the 100th Congress alone, 1987-88, thirty-nine bills which had gone through the Labor and Human Resources Committee (alternately headed by Kennedy and Hatch since 1980) were now the law of the land. During the current 101st Congress, more than a dozen Kennedy-Hatch bills would be introduced. Nothing could have seemed more improbable in Hatch's early Senate years, when the two had consistently blocked each other's initiatives.

Kennedy had come to appreciate the importance of working with Hatch, even at the cost of compromise, and consulted him regularly on issues coming before the committee. Although Kennedy, as new chair of the Labor Committee in 1987, had tried to run roughshod over Hatch, he now went out of his way to be conciliatory. "He has reached out and tried to be friendly," wrote Hatch. "I feel good about that because I personally like the man and think he has many redeemable qualities."

On issues like Bork's confirmation, however, the two senators remained opposing field generals, giving no quarter.

"Orrin is well prepared and very persevering," said Kennedy, explaining what has also made Hatch an effective legislator. "He's tough but he's very kind."

Kennedy recalled working with Hatch on a bill to encourage the development of "orphan" drugs, needed by people with rare diseases but expensive to develop because of slight demand. "I can remember that Orrin said, 'Let's go over [to the House] and talk to old Henry [Waxman].'

"I said, 'Orrin, we've already been over talking to Henry about this thing, and were unable to work out differences.' But Orrin and I went over, just the two of us, and sat down with Henry. And in just the way Orrin articulated his position, he really changed the mood and the atmosphere in a very important way, so that significant progress could be made. Those are moments that don't make the front page, but do make the difference."

Kennedy had periodic dinners with Labor Committee members to discuss the legislative agenda. At the end of one recent dinner, he recalled that Hatch said, "Quite frankly, I can't support any of these matters. But I notice you're doing something on summer programs for children. Let me work with you on that." Kennedy accepted. "And with Orrin's help we changed that 'weed and seed' program for children, and we passed it in the Senate. We had a program that next summer for needy children that was more generous than the one it replaced."

Answering a question others were starting to ask, Kennedy said, "Orrin has not changed his philosophy in the years I've known him. Orrin has a defined political philosophy, which is a rudder that guides his political actions. It suits him temperamentally and in his soul. That's impressive at a time when many put their finger to the wind to find out which way the winds are blowing, and sort of adjust accordingly."

At the same time, added Kennedy, "We've been able to make important progress in some areas because he has a very strong sense of justice, particularly regarding children and children's issues, and in terms of a number of different health issues. . . . He looks for ways to find common ground, and doesn't let strong philosophical differences interfere with the opportunity to work toward common purpose.

"He understands and I think is fundamentally committed to the concept of civility, which is an essential element to be an effective legislator."

In December 1988 Hatch was working out in the Senate gym when Kennedy came in. "Are you coming to my party tonight?" asked Kennedy. "We have a special entertainer."

It was the first Hatch had heard about Kennedy's annual staff Christmas party, but he promptly accepted the invitation.

That evening, Hatch and scores of others jammed the Labor Committee hearing room. Lights dimmed as a Kennedy staffer introduced "the king." Music blared, and from offstage came a familiar stout figure in a body-hugging white suit open almost to the navel. He sported black sideburns, a wig, and dark glasses, and carried a guitar.

The audience roared with laughter as the senior senator from Massachusetts, aka Elvis past his prime, cavorted to a rock song, cape fanning the air. Then Kennedy and a legislative aide put on a hilarious skit, lampooning Bush, Reagan, Quayle—and themselves.

The previous year, Kennedy had worn a blond wig and dressed as Fawn Hall, Oliver North's former secretary, Iran-contra "documents" stuffed down the back of his pantyhose. Masquerading as North was Joseph Kennedy, Robert's oldest son, who had won Tip O'Neill's seat in the House when O'Neill retired in 1986. Another year Kennedy was Batman—reminding the audience, "That's *Batman*, not *Fatman*."

While Hatch would have been mortified in an Elvis outfit, he thoroughly enjoyed Kennedy's satiric humor and often found his own wit sharpened in Kennedy's company. Hatch had even invented the mock-pompous nickname of "Theodoe" for Kennedy.

When Hatch and other just-elected or reelected senators took the oath of office in January 1989, Kennedy was in Rhode Island for the swearing-in of his son Patrick, the youngest legislator in the state House of Representatives. He was sworn in later by Bob Byrd. Kennedy invited Hatch to attend the ceremony in the old Senate chamber; and Hatch showed up, along with family members and a half-dozen other senators. The Kennedy family Bible was being used for the occasion—an 1850 Douai edition about ten inches thick, with the family genealogy in the middle.

Kennedy thanked everyone for coming, then, nodding at Hatch, said, "I think I'll ask my Mormon bishop friend to come up here and explain why this Bible is so thick."

"I'll be glad to," Hatch shot back.

Grinning impishly as the audience laughed, Kennedy had second thoughts. "Maybe we could put that off until another time."

Quite often Hatch dined at Kennedy's house in McLean, Virginia. Hatch's office reception room was adorned with a lithograph of a seascape by Kennedy, an amateur painter.

After Hatch ribbed Kennedy about the "Republican" tie he was wearing, which sported tiny elephants, Kennedy gave it to Hatch, instructing him to "wear this at the Republican Convention when you are giving the left-wing Democrats hell."

In Kennedy's reception office were black and white photos of the Boston birthplaces of his mother, Rose Fitzgerald Kennedy, and her father, John F. Fitzgerald, onetime mayor of Boston. On an adjacent wall was a large pencil sketch of Bobby Kennedy and a photo of John F. Kennedy.

If Ted Kennedy bore the difficult legacy of his late, larger-than-life brothers, his focus was very much on the next generation of Kennedys, who were starting to make their own marks. The devotion of Hatch and Kennedy to their children was another bond between them.

Ted Kennedy's father, Joseph P. Kennedy, for all his fabled faults, was known as a conscientious father. And his gracious and stoic mother, Rose, who turned 100 in 1990, instilled a fierce commitment to family in her children. Kennedy's three children—Kara Ann, Edward Moore, and Patrick Joseph—were his delight, and their memorabilia filled his office. One photo showed father and children with Pope John II. A framed copy of the *Providence Journal* announced Patrick's House win. Headlined ". . . Kennedy Triumphs," it featured a tender hand-written inscription: "To Dad, my father and my hero, Love, Patrick."

Kennedy was an open-handed uncle, watching over the children of his late brothers. The family spent its vacations in world trouble spots giving volunteer service, and birthday gifts to family members were created by the giver. The children had also been taught proper manners. When Patrick had an operation in the spring of 1988, Hatch sent him flowers, receiving back a gracious note of thanks that was signed, "Love, Patrick."

For his father's fifty-seventh birthday on February 22, 1989, Patrick, then twenty-one, offered a toast at a family celebration. He said, in part:

> Tonight we celebrate your birthday, and it's my turn to toast.
> For I as your son have good reason to boast.
> In retrospect, Dad, you had one hell of a year.
> And while my race for state office was your biggest fear
> My election last November proves that now I'm your peer.
> . . . Let's rise for a toast to my father and my friend.

The friendship developing between Hatch and Kennedy did not lure either away from his philosophical moorings. And Hatch had no illusion that their personal relationship lessened partisan differences. "Ted would cut my gizzard out in a minute over a political issue and never think twice about it," said Hatch.

Hatch also remained wary of Kennedy's mercurial temperament. "He has a very infectious personality and can show a lot of friendship," recalled Hatch. "Then there is that ruthless side to him. He can turn on you at a moment's notice. Having been through that experience a number of times, I am somewhat cautious."

A study of Senate voting for 1989 showed that, among the ninety-nine other members, Hatch agreed most—87 percent of the time—with conservative Republicans William Armstrong of Colorado and Trent Lott of Mississippi. He agreed least—53 percent—with liberal Democrats Paul Sarbanes of Maryland, Paul Simon of Illinois, and Kennedy.

Early in 1990, Kennedy said of their friendship, "I think my people are finally accepting it." Hatch said, "My people are still having a hard time believing it. . . . They see it in the legislation that passes and I tell them that we are friends, but it used to be that [the name of] Ted Kennedy was my best fund-raiser."

"Orrin and I like to say that when we sponsor the same bill, one of us hasn't read it," quipped Kennedy.

Some staunch conservatives wouldn't even consider ideas advanced by Kennedy. But Hatch refused to build a career on simply opposing "liberalism" to score debating points, when so many urgent needs were pressing. He was a principled pragmatist.

"I don't know why we so often let the labels of 'liberal' and 'conservative' get in the way," Hatch told one reporter. "Sure, most of my voting is conservative, but that doesn't mean that conservatives should have a corner on the marketplace of ideas. If a liberal has a good idea, I'm not going to kick him in the teeth, just because he's liberal or a Democrat."

Once the children were grown, Hatch felt more free to pursue personal interests. He took a WordPerfect software course in 1989 and launched a new project: writing a thriller, set primarily in the Middle East. The plot involved psychiatric intelligence, inspired in part by the gripping *Silence of the Lambs,* and involving the United States and USSR. He worked sporadically on his home computer over the next two years, eventually finishing a manuscript. Writer friends told Hatch it needed major revisions, but Hatch hadn't found time for a rewrite as of early 1994.

During the year Hatch read *Russia House* by John LeCarre, *The Negotiator* by Frederick Forsyth, and *Clear and Present Danger* by Tom Clancy. Nonfiction books read included two on the Supreme Court, one by William Rehnquist and another by Archibald Cox; a biography of James Madison, Nancy Reagan's memoirs, and *The Tempting of America,* by Robert Bork, which he reviewed for *National Review.*

One of Hatch's favorite television shows was *Murphy Brown,* with Candice Bergen in the title role. One night Murphy had a dartboard in her fictional newsroom office, with a bumper sticker above it that said "I love Orrin Hatch." In response, Hatch mounted an "I Love Murphy Brown" inscription above *his* office dartboard and sent Bergen a black and white photo of him throwing darts at it. Four years later, Hatch accepted Bergen's invitation to be a guest performer in a sequence on November 8, 1993.

Hatch also was an ardent fan of Gary Trudeau's "Doonesbury," even though Trudeau occasionally lampooned him. "It is too liberal but it is always funny," he explained. After Trudeau's wife, TV journalist Jane Pauley, lost her longtime spot on NBC's *Today* show, Hatch was among a handful of senators honoring her and Trudeau at a luncheon hosted by Howard Metzenbaum.

During the August 1989 recess, Hatch took his father fishing at Flaming Gorge Reservoir in Utah. When a huge lake trout won a ten-minute battle by tangling the line and escaping, Hatch recorded, "I felt bad because this would have been the highlight of Dad's fishing life."

Next morning on the Wyoming side of Flaming Gorge, Jesse Hatch caught seven nice kokanee salmon. "We had a terrific time," Hatch reported, "Dad was in his glory and hated to leave."

Back in Washington, Kennedy and Hatch teamed up shoulder-to-shoulder in pushing a major AIDS bill through their committee and the Senate, with Henry Waxman leading the charge in the House.

The two senators unveiled their bill at a news conference, accompanied by actress and anti-AIDS crusader Elizabeth Taylor. The Associated Press photo had Taylor positioned between Kennedy and Hatch, looking at Kennedy. Kennedy clipped a copy from the *Boston Globe* and sent it to Hatch, writing in the margin: "Here's looking at you, kid! I'm sure she'll be facing the other way on page one of the *Deseret News!*"

The Kennedy-Hatch bill authorized $600 million in new anti-AIDS funding, half to go to the thirteen U.S. cities hardest hit by the disease and the other half to states to expand noninstitutional care for patients. Many cities offered AIDS patients no alternative but hospitalization, even when they needed less intensive and less expensive care.

Hatch was particularly concerned about the 2,050 children reported with AIDS. According to chilling estimates, up to ten times that many had not yet been diagnosed. He authored a number of provisions, including one honoring Ryan White, the eighteen-year-old infected by contaminated blood who had touched the nation's heart with his battle against discrimination aimed at AIDS victims. The amendment required states to spend at least 15 percent of their $300 million to treat children and mothers with AIDS.

Kennedy warned that unless the U.S. expanded hospital and home health care for AIDS patients, both costs and chaos would continue to increase. He indicated that in terms of pain, suffering and cost, AIDS is a disaster as severe as any earthquake, hurricane or drought.

Jesse Helms opposed the bill, saying taxpayer dollars were being used "to proselytize a dangerous lifestyle." Hatch said: "I do not condone homosexual activity, but that does not have a thing to do with this bill. AIDS is a public health problem."

Although Bush had threatened to veto the legislation, he signed it into law in August 1990.

Hatch was the prime cosponsor and helped write a bill introduced by Paul Simon of Illinois, requiring the FBI to gather data on "hate crimes"–those motivated by prejudice based on race, religion, ethnic origin, or sexual orientation.

"For persons who are members of minority groups with a history of mistreatment or persecution," said Hatch, "these crimes cause anxiety, unease and concern about their security, a security others may take for granted."

Also during the session, Hatch played a crucial role in passing a landmark civil rights measure, the Americans with Disabilities Act (ADA). It barred discrimination against the estimated 43 million Americans who were physically or mentally impaired, giving them the same civil rights protections in jobs, housing, and services already given minorities.

He had refused to cosponsor an earlier version introduced by Democrat Tom Harkin of Iowa, calling it "left-wing and excessive." The bill required businesses and other organizations to provide facilities and make special accommodations enabling handicapped workers to do a wider range of jobs. But Hatch agreed to work toward some agreement to protect the handicapped.

In August 1989, Hatch, Harkin, Kennedy, and Durenberger, along with several staffers, met in Republican leader Dole's office to try to reach an agreement with the Bush administration on ADA. Representing the White House were Chief of Staff Sununu, Secretary of Transportation Samuel Skinner, Attorney General Richard Thornburgh, and domestic affairs advisor Roger Porter.

Sununu had a visceral dislike of Kennedy's Massachusetts, and a no-love-lost history with Kennedy himself. Still, negotiators were shocked when Sununu looked at Kennedy and sneered, "Are we going to have to provide wheelchair service on our ski lifts?" Teddy, Jr., who had lost a leg to cancer, was an avid skier.

Kennedy counterattacked, and the intensifying argument went over the edge into a shouting match when a Harkin staffer tried to defend the legislation to Sununu. Glaring, Sununu began a tirade that rose in volume until he was screaming.

Kennedy, enraged, cut Sununu off. "You can't talk to our staff members like that," he yelled back. "You have to talk to us big boys."

When Kennedy paused to catch his breath, Hatch jumped in: "Let's *all* calm down here." Turning to Kennedy and Harkin, he pointed out that the administration had sent its top people to discuss ADA. Obviously the White House was serious about supporting a bill. Placating Sununu, Hatch added that it was "highly inappropriate" for a Senate aide to lecture the White House Chief of Staff, then invited: "It's ridiculous for us to nitpick this thing to death. We can solve every one of these problems if we just sit down in good faith and do it."

Hatch's peacemaking worked. Everyone calmed down, worked more constructively for the rest of the meeting, and parted on a reasonably good note. Sununu was visibly relieved and several White House officials thanked Hatch for defusing the tense situation.

Hatch also met with Justin Dart, a friend, prominent GOP fund-raiser, and strong advocate for the handicapped. Dart, who was crippled and in a wheelchair, urged Hatch to help pass an ADA bill. Hatch began to work out differences and became the bill's cosponsor. He prepared an amendment to exempt businesses with fifteen or fewer employees from ADA's more costly provisions, so that Mom-and-Pop operations would not be put out of business.

However, during crucial negotiations, Sununu, apparently miffed at Hatch over other issues, cut him out of the loop and worked out an ADA bill directly with Kennedy. His spite cost the administration and American business dearly. Sununu had a genius-level IQ, but was no match for Kennedy when it came to negotiations. Kennedy genially ate Sununu's lunch, persuading him to swallow a bill far tougher on small businesses than Hatch would have accepted, and marveling to Hatch that the White House had "caved in" so completely. Hatch considered dropping his support for ADA but reluctantly decided it still had more pluses than minuses.

The final bill reached the Senate floor in July 1990, almost a year after the hot-tempered meeting. In an emotionally intense and moving final debate, Harkin delivered part of his floor speech simultaneously in sign language, to honor a deaf brother. Kennedy spoke of his mentally retarded sister, Rosemary, and Teddy, Jr., after the amputation. Hatch dedicated his effort "to my brother-in-law, who contracted both types of polio as a college student undergraduate." Then he faltered, tears stinging his eyes as he recounted Ramon's courageous fight to provide for his young family while fighting the disease. "Other than my own brother who was killed in World War II, he was without question, the greatest inspiration of dogged determination to do what is right and make his life worthwhile of anybody in my life," Hatch said.

The Senate passed the bill overwhelmingly by a vote of 91 to 6 on July 13, 1990. Hatch stepped into a side room filled with handicapped citizens who had been listening to the debate. He embraced a weeping Justin Dart as the crowd exploded with cheers and applause. Hatch tried to speak but couldn't.

Reactionaries Paul Weyrich and Phyllis Schlafly did not applaud. For them, Hatch's support of ADA and his friendship with Kennedy were more deviations from conservative dogma.

Hatch "came here as a very committed and brilliant conservative with grit, ideals and principles," said Weyrich. "But today, I couldn't tell you what they are" —or what his philosophy is, "because he doesn't have one."

Schlafly blamed Hatch's "feminist staff . . . That's all he hears." Actually, Hatch's top aide was Kevin McGuiness, though Wendy Higginbotham, now his legislative director, tutored Hatch on how to deal more sensitively with women's groups.

Hatch insisted: "When I believe something is right I will fight for it. But one thing I will never do is compromise on principle."

Other conservatives agreed. "This is not someone who has seen the liberal light," said Thomas Winter, editor of the conservative journal *Human Events.* An executive of the National Right to Work Committee, Karl Gallant, called Hatch one of the group's "most consistent supporters." ·Hatch's votes during all his years in the Senate were rated 93 percent "correct" by the American Conservative Union and had risen to 96 percent for 1988.

But Weyrich and Schlafly were 100-percent people. While 93 percent qualified Hatch for an "A" on the report cards of most conservatives, it fell short of the mark for them.

A firestorm of criticism came from another direction in October 1990 when a letter over Hatch's signature asked Attorney General Dick Thornburgh to "investigate" Randall Robinson, a prominent black who headed a group called TransAfrica.

Robinson recently had said he wanted to "build a fire" against U.S. military aid to Jonas Savimbi and his rebels in Angola, who, he accused, were murdering other blacks. Robinson "should not be permitted to propagate Marxist propaganda," insisted the letter.

Scathing columns denouncing Hatch appeared in the *Washington Post* and *New York Times,* with Courtland Milloy of the *Post* saying Hatch "lied" about Robinson and was "staunchly anti-human rights," as evidenced by his support of South Africa.

"When Hatch smears Robinson as a 'foreign agent,' as he did in his letter to the attorney general," said Milloy, "it amounts to more than a threat to Robinson. It is an incendiary attempt to keep blacks out of so-called white folk business."

Hatch, as it turned out, had not written the letter. An overzealous staff member whose girlfriend worked for a lobbying firm with an interest in the issue had drafted it and signed it by "autopen," a mechanical device imitating Hatch's signature. Although Hatch had been a strong supporter of Savimbi's, he said it was a "stupid letter" and that he had, in fact, championed human rights throughout the world, including in South Africa where he had urged its leaders to eliminate apartheid.

"I'm a little offended that people would think I'm dumb enough to write that letter," said Hatch. However, the letter did bear his autopenned signature. Hatch also met personally with Robinson—who graciously accepted Hatch's explanation and apology—reprimanded the staff member severely, and instituted tighter office procedures.

Privately Hatch commented, "Conservatives will probably be upset that I didn't allow the maligning of the man, but I felt we were wrong."

Hatch tried to get the Bush administration to take advantage of Muhammad Ali's talents, suggesting he could help open America's ghettos to the message of antidrug czar William Bennett or assist the President's Council on Physical Fitness and Sports. Bush was strangely unresponsive, despite Ali's endorsement at the GOP convention. Bush did not ask Ali to campaign for the GOP ticket, and in the end the Republicans won only 11 percent of the black vote. Hatch and others had repeatedly urged the party to broaden its base, but to no avail.

Bush may have been concerned that the controversial Ali would further cool his already tepid support among conservatives. Although Hatch didn't want to face it, Bush may have also wanted distance from the energetic little man at Ali's side—Richie Hirschfeld, forty-four, Ali's attorney, financial advisor, and almost constant companion.

Questions concerning Hirschfeld's relationship to Ali had been raised by Dave Kindred, a sports columnist for the *Atlanta Constitution,* in a series of articles in December 1988. Kindred charged that someone impersonating Ali had made numerous calls to a half-dozen senators, various congressional aides, and assorted journalists. Three voice experts who analyzed taped conversations couldn't agree but couldn't rule out imposture either. Kindred pointed out that presently Ali in person spoke slowly, often haltingly, while the "Ali voice" was voluble, animated, and teasing—more like the float-like-a-butterfly Ali of the 1960s. Also, the "Ali voice" spoke knowledgeably about politics and current affairs, while Ali in person said little on such matters. Kindred concluded that someone was pretending to be Ali and that all evidence pointed at Hirschfeld.

"The Ali voice" had asked Hatch and other senators for three favors—to pass a bill allowing Ali to sue the government for income lost during his prime boxing years after he had been improperly convicted of draft-dodging; to get a high-ranking job at the Justice Department for Virginia law professor Stephen Saltzburg; and to have the Justice Department determine whether an on-going criminal investigation of Hirschfeld was motivated by spite. Saltzburg was much closer to Hirschfeld than Ali, as Kindred pointed out, so at least two of the three favors obviously bene-fitted Hirschfeld more than Ali.

Although several public figures had received numerous calls from the "Ali voice," none had developed as close a personal relationship with the former boxer as Hatch. When Kindred's stories made national headlines, Hatch told reporters he was convinced he had "always been dealing" with Ali himself on the telephone.

Ali held his own news conference on the steps of the U.S. Capitol, saying "there's no truth" to Kindred's claim, and insisting that he personally had made all the telephone calls. That evening, Hatch issued a written statement, repeating, "I've had hours and days of discussions with Ali and have no doubt that my conversations on the phone were with him."

But the plot thickened. Although Ali's admiration for Hatch was undeniable and they continued to see each other on occasion, Hirschfeld had also carefully cultivated Hatch's friendship. The three men occasionally attended boxing matches together, and in May 1989 Hirschfeld drove his 1965 white Rolls Royce from his farm in Charlottesville, Virginia, picked Hatch up and took him to a speaking engagement in suburban Virginia.

Also that spring, Rick Shenkman, a correspondent for KUTV, the NBC affiliate in Salt Lake City, alleged that the championship ring Ali had given Hatch was a payoff for favors. Hatch had properly reported the gift on his annual government ethics report, estimating its materials at about $1,000 and its intrinsic worth at $6,500. Shenkman's story was full of holes and not credible, given Hatch's record of integrity; but apparently he shared it with *Time* since the magazine, using statements Hatch had given only to Shenkman, spread the story nationally, not even bothering to contact Hatch. Hatch had done nothing wrong; but to avoid even the appearance of impropriety, he later returned the ring to Ali.

On March 5, 1991, Hirschfeld was convicted of filing a false income tax return and found guilty of tax and securities conspiracies, by a federal court in Norfolk. "The United States is prepared to prove that Mr. Hirschfeld has imitated Ali's voice in the past," said Assistant U.S. Attorney David Barger. "Further, Mr. Ali and [his manager] Herbert Muhammad have advised the government that the defendant asked Mr. Ali to have a press conference and claim responsibility for the calls, even though he had not made them, noting that if he (Ali) did not, Mr. Hirschfeld could get in trouble."

Although Hirschfeld may have fooled dozens of prominent people—and it would never be known with certainty just which calls Ali himself had made—no one was taken in more completely than Hatch. The exposure of Hirschfeld's apparent duplicity and brilliant mimicry was a betrayal of Hatch's trust. In good faith, Hatch and other senators had required a self-examination by the Justice Department of its handling of Hirschfeld's case, perhaps delaying his trial.

"Senator Hatch, the government respectfully submits," wrote Barger, "has been a victim of the defendant's manipulation." Hirschfeld received a maximum sentence of thirteen years and was fined $600,000 for several offenses, including complicated financial deals unrelated to the "Ali voice."

Years later, Hatch was still reluctant to acknowledge that some "Ali" calls may have come from someone other than Ali—and was even more reluctant to accuse Hirschfeld. "I had many very intelligent conversations with Ali in person as well as on the telephone," he explains. At any rate, Hatch's conversations with Ali—to Hatch's disappointment—largely ended after the Hirschfeld episode, perhaps as Ali's advisors encouraged him to make a clean break with a cloudy saga.

In the fall of 1989, *Dossier,* a slick Washington society magazine, asked Hatch to be a celebrity model for a cover photo and inside spread. With some hesitation, he agreed, wearing a bolo tie and double-breasted tuxedo from a local retail merchant. He was photographed with a tall brunette model in an evening gown on his arm.

At the end of the early-afternoon shoot, however, a vote was called in the Senate, and Hatch had to race back to the Capitol without changing clothes. Colleagues ribbed him considerably as he walked onto the Senate floor, more than one suggesting their straight-arrow colleague hadn't made it to bed the night before.

"Actually," Hatch responded, "this is a terrible time for a vote because it's interfering with my second job as a maitre d'."

There were other signs that Hatch had learned to take himself a little less seriously. He spoke at a luncheon for AFL-CIO president Lane Kirkland and the leaders of several affiliate unions, soon after the media quoted an underworld figure as saying Jimmy Hoffa, the controversial Teamsters Union president who disappeared in 1975, had been cut up and buried near the end zone of New York's Giants Stadium.

"There is only one thing I want from you unions," Hatch began solemnly. "I want you to pay the costs of excavating Giants Stadium in the Meadowlands, to find our dear friend, Jimmy Hoffa, so that we can give him a proper burial." The union brass, disarmed by Hatch's humor, roared with laughter.

At year's end, Utahns liked what they were seeing in Hatch. A December survey by his pollster, Dan Jones, showed that 75 percent of Utahns approved of Hatch's performance, which, for the first time, edged ahead of Jake Garn's rating, 73 percent.

25

Kinder and Gentler

PRESIDENT BUSH CALLED FOR A "kinder, gentler nation" in his inaugural address, speaking for those children "who have nothing—no love, no normalcy." The new President assured them that "democracy belongs to us all and freedom is like a beautiful kite that can go higher and higher with the breeze."

That same January day in 1989, a ten-year-old boy from Wyandanch, Long Island, appeared in court, charged with selling crack cocaine from a bicycle. One of six children living with a single mother, he was led away in handcuffs, carrying a comic book.

Three days later, in a neighborhood across the Potomac River from the White House, an eight-year-old boy shot his six-year-old sister to death with a .38-caliber handgun as they played at home alone after school.

For too many of the nation's children, there was no breeze to lift their kites. As the baby boom generation came of age, an unprecedented share of married women with children joined their husbands and single mothers in the work force, often leaving children at home to fend for themselves. At the same time, a soaring percentage of inner-city families were headed by single women living in poverty.

Many children had day-care supervision, but too often it was inadequate. "We are cannibalizing our children," said Dr. Edward Zigler, a noted child psychologist. "I know that sounds awful, but when you see 13 babies in cribs and one adult caretaker who can do nothing but change diapers and pop bottles, you see children who are being destroyed right after birth."

And yet, as one child advocate remarked, "The future is in very small hands."

Zigler, fifty-nine, a professor at Yale, had participated in Hatch's women's conferences in Utah. The biggest influence on Hatch, however, was his Utah women's advisory group. Repeatedly they told him that child care was the leading social problem in the state and nation.

The thirty-five-member group included "people who will never support me but who have good ideas," said Hatch. Although Utah overall was a traditional, family-oriented state, it had a relatively high divorce rate and the youngest median age in the country, including a hundred and fifty thousand children under age thirteen who needed day care, with only thirty thousand slots available in licensed facilities.

Child care, however, was perhaps the hottest of the hot-button issues among conservatives, and Hatch faced formidable opposition in even approaching the subject. "Some conservative [politicians] predict that Sen. Orrin Hatch of Utah will need a neck transplant before the year is over, to replace the one he's sticking out on the issue of day care," wrote one columnist.

The last time Washington had considered a child-care program was in 1971, with the blessing of President Nixon and under the leadership of Zigler, then director of the White House Office of Child Development. In 1971, one of every four women with children under age three worked outside the home. Most Americans recognized the need to care properly for children in their parents' absence, but conservatives campaigned fiercely against a national program, charging it was patterned after the Soviet model and would lead to a state takeover of parental responsibility. Congress approved child-care legislation; but Nixon, shaken by opposition from evangelicals and his party's right wing, vetoed the bill.

Now, a generation later, one of every two women with children under three worked outside the home—double the number a generation ago—and the costs of the nation's neglect had become staggering. A huge underclass had grown up with little adult guidance or care. They filled the nation's prisons, slept and shot up in city alleys, and, with no dreams and no hope of their own, haunted the future of all citizens.

"I believe it is far preferable for parents to care for their own children," said Hatch, introducing his child-care bill in September 1987. "But I have been persuaded by the facts. . . ." The trend toward two working parents and single-parent families would continue, and "whether these changes are good or bad is not the issue. It is time to face reality."

Hatch's involvement turned heads. "Since the 1950s, when the conservative movement coalesced out of many exasperations," wrote columnist George Will, "conservatism has been on a long march, transforming itself from an ideology of protest to a philosophy of governance. Another small step in that direction is Sen. Orrin Hatch's decision to act on the fact that Ozzie and Harriet are as gone as tail fins."

Hatch credits his involvement in child care and similar issues in part to Wendy Higginbotham, his new legislative director—and later his administrative assistant—who brought his staff together and helped Hatch understand the special needs and interests of women.

The Hatch bill modestly proposed providing $250 million in block grants to states for developing community child-care programs and setting child-care standards. Other Republicans cosponsored Hatch's bill, and alternative proposals sprouted on Capitol Hill. Most Democrats lined up behind the Act for Better Child Care Services (ABC), a far more comprehensive and expensive approach, chiefly sponsored by Senator Christopher Dodd of Connecticut.

Dodd, like his close friend Kennedy, could scarcely have been more opposite from Hatch in most ways. He was best known nationally for his views on Central America, including sympathy for the Marxist Sandinista regime in Nicaragua—which Hatch wanted to help topple with the help of the contras. Now Hatch's interest in child care piqued Dodd's interest in Hatch. Democrats needed an influential Republican to make ABC at least *look* bipartisan. Otherwise, conservatives might strangle child care as they had in 1971.

Hatch had become one of the Senate's premier power brokers on tough issues, sought by both Republicans and Democrats. He was coveted for a trait many lacked: He would not break his word, whatever the consequences. Dodd, aided by Kennedy, began lobbying Hatch to cosponsor ABC.

Because the Democrats controlled both houses, Hatch knew no bill could be passed that did not meet their approval. He weighed the high personal cost of supporting the Democrats against the likelihood that, if he remained politically pristine, Congress would once again sacrifice the nation's children to political expediency.

He decided for the children.

Hatch negotiated for months with Dodd and another member of the Labor Committee, Maryland Democrat Barbara Mikulski, to create what he called "son of ABC." He insisted on greater state and local control in setting minimum health and safety standards for day care and added $100 million to create a liability insurance pool to help day-care providers purchase affordable insurance. "Son of ABC" stated that grandparents and adult aunts and uncles caring for relatives up to age fifteen would also be eligible for state-administered direct subsidies.

Given these changes, Hatch, in January 1989, formally became ABC's cosponsor. Then he braced for the storm. His usual allies—Republicans, the Bush administration, and conservatives—compared him to Karl Marx,

Benedict Arnold, and Brutus. Phyllis Schlafly sent a scathing letter, which she also released to the media:

> Dear Orrin:
>
> To echo the famous cry of one who was betrayed by a man thought to be a friend, *"Et tu, Orrin!"* Why have you disillusioned your friends and abandoned the pro-family cause? ... It is, indeed, "the unkindest cut of all" for mothers to be betrayed by Orrin Hatch.... The Dodd bill is unjust ... because it discriminates against mothers who take care of their own children and taxes them in order to subsidize those who use stranger care ... and because it encourages and subsidizes institutional care of babies....
>
> Why have you abandoned us by co-sponsoring such a thoroughly bad bill?

Bush had promised a child-care proposal, probably based on tax credits for low-income working parents. But months went by with no movement from the White House. Then on March 15, the very day the Labor Committee voted 11-5 to approve ABC, Bush—hoping to steal the bill's thunder—finally sent his own proposal to Congress.

Hatch was under intense pressure to rejoin the Republican fold to support the long-awaited Bush alternative. But he was already committed, writing privately: "Dodd has been so good to work with, and has tried hard to compromise with everyone. I'm not going to desert him now." Hatch took Dodd to the White House in a last attempt at reconciliation but failed to move Bush and his aides.

As child care headed for a Senate vote in June, the far right and Hatch's fellow Republicans spread what he called "downright deliberate deceit" about the bill. Senate GOP leader Dole, hoping to derail ABC, introduced Bush's measure, still centered on tax credits, as a substitute.

Showing the streak of cynicism that has hurt his long public career from time to time, Dole compared Hatch to Donald Trump because "anything you put in front of him, he'll buy."

"I'd rather be the Donald Trump of child care than the Ebenezer Scrooge," answered Hatch.

The full Senate debated child-care alternatives for several days, voting on June 23, 1989. Hatch made the final argument on behalf of ABC, which had been newly revised with a tax-credit provision introduced by Texas Democrat Lloyd Bentsen, along the lines of the Bush proposal.

When the roll was called on Bush's plan, voting "nay" were Hatch and two other Republicans—John Chafee of Rhode Island and James Jeffords of Vermont. It was defeated 56-44.

In final debate on ABC Dodd paid glowing tribute to Hatch, noting that "[we] do not share a similar political philosophy in many areas, but Orrin Hatch cares about this country deeply. He cares about its children deeply. He was willing to put aside ideological or partisan differences." Dodd continued:

> He reached his hand out across the aisle . . . and said: let us do something about the one out of every four Americans who is a child . . . living in poverty. We can do it if we work together. If we do not bring excess baggage and luggage that has nothing to do with this debate, we can accomplish what had not been accomplished for 46 years. . . . I had [great respect for Hatch] even before this debate. What has grown is my friendship for this individual, for his humor, his joy in the political process, for his heart and his soul.

Majority Leader Mitchell also praised Hatch for "the remarkable independence of judgment and political courage that have marked his political career. . . . Often [we] find ourselves on different sides of an issue. But as always, he has conducted himself with intelligence, with dignity, with vigor and genuine courage."

As Dole saw the writing on the wall, he asked Hatch to keep ABC from being a roll-call vote, so that opponents wouldn't be politically embarrassed. Then Democrats smelled blood and wanted a recorded vote to use against Republicans. But Hatch, for his friend Dole and other Republicans, persuaded Democrats to back off, and helped pass ABC on a voice vote.

Child care then bogged down in the House for more than a full year. Over that time, Hatch continued to mediate between the Senate and White House, fine-tuning ABC to give states a greater say in setting standards and distributing funds, and, in the process, winning Bush's support. An important first step had been taken toward salvaging the future of young Americans.

In October 1990, the *Los Angeles Times* editorialized, "The sleeper accomplishment of the 101st Congress—with all its showcase whining, combativeness, petulance and guile—is that, despite everything that went wrong, the federal government for the first time emerged with legislation to help working families pay for child care."

Washington Post columnist Judy Mann called child-care legislation "the big prize" for American families, awarded only after Hatch, "one of the Senate's staunchest conservatives, made child care his top legislative priority."

His support of child care alienated Hatch from the far right as never before. Out in Utah where it really counted, however, he got support from realists, including subtle but timely and crucial encouragement from an unlikely establishment venue: the pulpit of the Mormon Tabernacle.

Each April and October, the LDS church holds a two-day general

conference, broadcast live in the intermountain area and by radio and satellite television to members throughout the world. Mormons are encouraged
to listen carefully and read the texts in their monthly magazine, the *Ensign*.

A key sermon delivered on October 1, 1989, was by Thomas S.
Monson, one of two counselors to LDS church president Ezra Taft Benson,
and a man with whom Hatch had discussed national affairs. Monson told
of touring a computer manufacturing plant built in a poor area. "I was
impressed with the employment provided—but more impressed with the
company nursery, which occupied a wing of the building," said Monson.
He avoided the term "day care" but praised its achievement: "The chain of
poverty was broken."

Hatch, who usually attended conference, was in the audience. As the
session ended, several general authorities approached Hatch, making
sure he read Monson correctly. The church had just sanctioned child
care as a topic for discussion and action.

Hatch alienated other conservatives in 1990 by supporting an effort
to loosen restrictions on the National Endowment for the Arts, still
under a cloud because it had funded some exhibits in 1989 that Jesse
Helms and others deemed obscene. At issue were about twenty out of
85,000 visual and performing works of art funded with the NEA's help.

Hatch was strongly influenced by many hours spent as a poor youth
in Pittsburgh galleries. He knew the power of art to inspire and ennoble,
and he and Elaine had accumulated a modest collection themselves,
including a number of works by Valoy Eaton of Vernal, Utah, a
renowned landscape artist and Hatch's second cousin.

He agreed with Helms that Robert Mapplethorpe's homoerotic
photographs were "disgusting" and cheered when the NEA restricted
funding for those whose work, in Hatch's view, had little or no
redeeming social value. He supported the right of artists and museums
to prepare and display their works freely—but not at taxpayer expense.

Yet he found the crackdown on the NEA excessive. "Some of these
fundamentalists wouldn't have allowed the Sistine Chapel to be
painted," said Hatch.

Crippling the NEA, Hatch believed, would threaten too many legitimate artists and arts groups, including Utah's acclaimed symphony
orchestra and Ballet West. He helped craft a compromise to continue
funding the NEA, based on the agency's closer scrutiny of grant
proposals for "general standards of decency and respect for the diverse
beliefs and values of the American public." Congress passed the
compromise in October 1990.

Again Hatch was attacked. Donald Wildmon, head of the American

Family Association, informed his members "with deep regret" that Hatch "supports government funding of pornography and anti-Christian 'art.'" Wildmon's improbable conclusion came from Phyllis Schlafly, head of Hatch's "fan" club.

Hatch patiently explained again: "I endorse freedom of expression under the First Amendment. At the same time, I do not condone the use of taxpayers' dollars for the use of obscene or pornographic or irreligious work."

Robert Bork's seat on the U.S. Court of Appeals for the Washington, D.C., circuit had been vacant since shortly after Reagan's abortive attempt to send him to the Supreme Court. The twelve-member appellate court, important as a stepping-stone to the Supreme Court, had provided three of Reagan's nominees—Scalia, Bork, and Ginsburg.

In October 1989, Bush nominated Clarence Thomas to fill the vacancy. It was not a popular choice with Democrats and their anti-Bork allies. Thomas was a rare combination: a conservative black intellectual. The last person they wanted a step away from the Supreme Court was a conservative black judge—especially a potential role model who had risen by his bootstraps from discrimination and abject poverty. What if he influenced other blacks to question their bloc allegiance to the Democratic Party?

Thomas, forty-one, was born in a sharecropper's cabin in Pin Point, Georgia, and had been reared by grandparents who were dirt-poor but were hard-working and had high ideals. They set high standards for him.

In August 1989, Judiciary Committee Democrats had defeated the nomination of another black, William Lucas, former executive of Wayne County, Michigan, to head the Civil Rights Division at the Justice Department. Democrats said Lucas lacked experience, but Hatch and others charged it was because he was too conservative.

Hatch was close to Thomas. As chairman of the Labor Committee, he had presided over three Thomas confirmations: for a position at the Education Department in 1981 and twice to head the Equal Employment Opportunity Commission—in 1982 and for reconfirmation in 1986. During the 1986 EEOC hearing, Kennedy and Metzenbaum, prodded by civil rights groups, had raked Thomas over the coals for disagreeing with recent Supreme Court rulings allowing racial timetables in hiring. Thomas said he would enforce the law regardless of personal feelings and was reconfirmed.

In another Thomas hearing, Kennedy had upbraided him at length over the same kinds of issues. Thomas had responded by rehearsing his humble roots, noting that his illiterate grandparents were so poor that he didn't always have shoes. He said only three pictures had adorned the walls of their home—Martin Luther King, Jr., Jesus Christ, and John F. Kennedy.

As Hatch remembered the exchange, Thomas looked squarely at Ted Kennedy and said with dignity, "If President Kennedy is watching these proceedings today, he can't be very well pleased." With that, Kennedy wilted: "I think that's all the questions I have."

In addition to Thomas's confirmations, Hatch had conducted a number of oversight hearings on Thomas's work.

"Even after he knew me and liked me, he always asked tough questions," said Thomas. "The Senator gave us goals to meet and held us to account." Thomas continued: "At some point he became a close friend—someone you call on and trust, and who loves you. He insisted I call him 'Orrin.' He wasn't obsequious. We didn't want anything from each other; we just thoroughly enjoyed each other. We talked often by telephone and occasionally went to lunch."

Hatch was elated with Thomas's nomination to the D.C. court. But within forty-eight hours of the nomination, twenty-three groups had sent a letter to the Judiciary Committee suggesting that Thomas wasn't committed to equal justice and wasn't qualified. Fourteen House members had already urged Bush not to nominate Thomas.

The American Bar Association grudgingly gave Thomas a "qualified" rating, meaning he met the necessary standard, though not the highest standard, for satisfactory performance as a judge.

Hatch made a private judgment. "He is a natural choice to some day be on the Supreme Court of the United States."

As the Judiciary Committee prepared for hearings early in 1990, attention focused on Thomas's seven-year tenure as head of the EEOC. There were questions of bias against Hispanic employees and delay in handling age-discrimination cases. Chairman Biden—who had survived a brush with death after a post-Bork brain aneurysm that took him away from the Senate for seven months—made Thomas produce thousands of EEOC documents, and his aides pored over them in what critics called a "fishing expedition."

Wyoming's Alan Simpson said of the document search: "The staff people get together and say, 'How do we do a number on this guy, and still not have any glue on us and no blood on our hands, and we'll just drive him crazy with 17 metric tons of crap?'"

Hatch foresaw another "character assassination" in the offing, and warned Democrats that conservatives would not allow this nominee to be crucified. Finally, Biden conceded that the EEOC documents failed to produce any evidence and that the accusations were "totally meritless." The actual hearing on February 6 was quite staid.

Thomas shared Hatch's stand: equal opportunity for everyone but not through racial hiring quotas and timetables. Liberals questioned his empathy for minorities who hadn't succeeded in lifting themselves as he had.

"The reason I became a lawyer," responded Thomas, "was to make sure that minorities . . . gain access in society. Now, I may differ from others on how best to do that, but the objective has always been to include those who have been excluded."

Kennedy simply said, "I don't think anyone can ask for any better assurances." Only Metzenbaum opposed Thomas in committee; but the panel, followed almost unanimously by the full Senate, voted to confirm him to the U.S. circuit court. Eighteen months later Thomas would be back before the Judiciary Committee for perhaps the most sensational hearings in Senate history.

In July 1990, only six months after Thomas was confirmed, Justice William J. Brennan, Jr., announced his retirement from the Supreme Court. Eighty-four and in ill health, he was the court's longest-serving member and one of its vanishing liberals. Two others were in their eighties, including Thurgood Marshall, the court's only black, for whose seat Democrats feared Thomas was being groomed.

Bush, hoping to avoid another bruising Supreme Court fight, nominated a little-known moderate, David Souter. He was fifty, a Harvard Law graduate, and a former member of the New Hampshire Supreme Court, who had been appointed to the First Circuit Court of Appeals just two months before Brennan's announcement. Unlike Rehnquist and Bork, Souter had published almost nothing, and his views on most controversial issues were unknown. Opponents had little ammunition to fire back at him in confirmation hearings.

"Even the conservatives were upset during the hearings, because he gave quite liberal responses to the liberal senators' questions," explained Hatch. "However, after what happened to Bork, I don't know what else he could say. Souter pretty well had to please them or face possible rejection of his nomination."

The committee approved Souter, and the full Senate confirmed him in October on a vote of 90 to 9.

Many observers, including Hatch, were concerned by a lack of direction and drive in the Bush administration. Reagan had entered office with specific goals and set about accomplishing them, but Bush seemed to be a president largely without purpose.

Reagan had aggressively created a more conservative judiciary by appointing forty-two judges during his first year in office. While the nation's overworked courts were staggering under their caseloads, Bush, in his first year, appointed just fifteen judges—the fewest of any President since 1963—and ended 1989 with fifty-nine vacancies. Scores of executive branch positions also languished.

"It's like a paralysis," said Sheldon Goldman, a political scientist at the University of Massachusetts. He compared Bush to Hamlet, pointed out the administration's "lack of focus," and hypothesized that it was "torn between different imperatives."

Biden repeatedly lamented the lack of judicial nominations from the White House to his colleagues on the Judiciary Committee, adding, "I am not casting aspersions."

"I *will* cast aspersions," said a frustrated Hatch. "I think it is abominable, because we can't handle the caseloads in most of the areas now."

The one "read-my-lips" promise Bush had made during his 1988 campaign was not to raise taxes. In mid-1990, however, he broke that promise and was stunned when a majority of Republicans in both houses voted against his tax and deficit-reduction package, leaving the President relying on Democrats to enact the agreement.

"He has listened to the wrong staff," wrote Hatch privately. "I think all of us would consider increasing taxes if we knew that every nickel would go to pay off the deficit. But just like Reagan, Bush will find that the Democrat-controlled Congress will spend every nickel on new programs."

Meanwhile the federal deficit soared to a near-record $220 billion for the fiscal year ending in September 1990, and to an absolute record of $268 billion the following year. The national debt by the end of 1991 was $3.6 trillion—more than triple the amount when Reagan/Bush took office ten years earlier with a promise to *eliminate* the national debt by 1984.

Bush bolstered his image briefly during Desert Storm, a U.S.-led assault that drove Iraq out of Kuwait early in 1991. But Iraq's brutal leader, Saddam Hussein, was left in power, a further sign to critics of Bush's reluctance to finish a nasty job.

Hatch and Garn backed Bush's war plans, bringing them into conflict with pacifists who swarmed over Capitol Hill voicing displeasure. After the final vote supporting Bush, correspondents for Utah newspapers and TV stations interviewed Hatch and Garn in a corridor. A group of pacifists formed behind them. One man, dressed in an expensive suit and tie, kept stepping into the camera frame and yelling. He was a Jew, he shouted. His relatives in Europe died because of World War II.

Garn, a former Navy pilot, suddenly turned to face him. "It was because of assholes like you that six million Jews were lost in World War II."

Still the man would not shut up: "You guys have no compassion for anyone. You're warmongers!"

Hatch saw red. He clenched a fist and said coldly, "I lost my only brother in World War II, a brother-in-law in Vietnam, and another brother-in-law was shot up badly in Korea. And if you come one step closer, I'll knock your block off!"

The Capitol police, sensing trouble, arrived and quieted the trouble-makers. The interview continued peaceably.

Hatch's customary good nature obviously had limits. But he was far more in character as a healer and was known as one of the Senate's peacemakers. Even those who disagreed with him on other matters had to acknowledge his personal decency.

In February 1991, Hatch took Jack Carlson—whom he had defeated in the Utah Republican primary fifteen years earlier—to see Education Secretary Lamar Alexander about a position. Carlson's wife had written *The Best Man Doesn't Always Win*, suggesting that the Carlsons had considerable contempt for Hatch. Still Hatch wrote privately, "I thought I would do every-thing in my power to get [Carlson] back into government. He has a really outstanding background and is a good man." Hatch had assisted Carlson in various other ways through the years but was not successful this time.

When Carlson died suddenly of cardiac arrest in December 1992, Hatch wrote, "I enjoyed knowing him both before, during, and after the 1976 elec-tion. I grieve for his wife and family." He and Elaine sent flowers. Renee Carlson responded with thanks, especially for "your kind note, Orrin."

Another private act of compassion came when Spencer Kinard, one of Utah's best-known personalities, toppled from power and visibility late in 1990. For nearly two decades, Kinard had been news director at KSL-TV as well as the man introducing the Mormon Tabernacle Choir and giving a sermonette to a nationwide CBS radio audience each Sunday morning.

When Kinard became romantically involved with one of KSL's woman anchors, he became something of a pariah; but Hatch telephoned Kinard weeks after he lost his positions, offering reassurance at a time when Kinard and his wife had hit bottom. Hatch's timely concern helped mend their lives and relationship. Kinard refused to slink away and in early 1993 was made general manager of a local television station.

Another compassionate phone call went to White House Chief of Staff John Sununu, after an April 1991 story in the *Washington Post* revealed that he had flown military jets on some sixty trips in a two-year period, many for personal or political reasons. Taxpayers had footed a bill of tens of thousands of dollars. Capital comedian Mark Russell wrote and sang, to the tune of "The Army Air Corps Song":

> Off we go carrying John Sununu
> Whatever the cost—a minor detail.
> We're on the alert—taking him to the dentist
> And then off again—for skiing at Vail.

Hatch had plenty of personal reasons to savor the arrogant aide's plight; but instead of gloating, he promptly called Sununu.

"Hang in there John," he told him.

"I don't know, Orrin," said a despondent Sununu. "This is really hard on my family."

"I know it is, but you can't let them get to you. . . . A lot of us are pulling for you."

Hatch spent the next weekend drafting an opinion-editorial article supporting Sununu, but in December 1991, the embattled chief resigned.

Hatch occasionally drove the round trip of 350 miles to visit Richie Hirschfeld in the federal penitentiary at Petersburg, Virginia, and telephoned Hirschfeld's wife and children to offer encouragement. Although many others believed Muhammad Ali's former attorney had deceived and exploited Hatch, the senator was more concerned that, as a first-time offender, Hirschfeld had been sentenced too severely.

In July 1991, Nancy Taylor, a Labor Committee staff member, told Hatch that Terry Beirn, one of Kennedy's top assistants, was in a New York hospital with AIDS and a probable melanoma on the brain. Expecting to die, he had asked to talk to Hatch before the surgery. Hatch called immediately. Beirn thanked Hatch for his compassion and work on behalf of AIDS patients and asked for his prayers. Hatch promised.

When Beirn died days later, Hatch, against the wishes of his political advisors, joined Kennedy in speaking at a memorial service held in the Labor Committee room for Beirn.

Ted Kennedy was Hatch's toughest rehabilitation project. During the 1988 Democratic National Convention, Kennedy had led a chorus in "Where was George?"—a repeated taunt suggesting GOP presidential candidate George Bush had been a do-nothing Vice President. At a political rally a month later, Republican Congressman Harold Rogers answered: "I'll tell Teddy Kennedy where George is. He's home sober with his wife."

It was a telling riposte. Kennedy hadn't been home sober with his wife since at least 1981 when he and Joan Bennett Kennedy ended their marriage of twenty-three years. Kennedy's probity was questionable even before then; and in the past decade, one bachelor escapade had followed another.

For those who hated the very name "Kennedy"—and they were legion—the senator's reputation was tarnished whatever he did. But his admirers, also legion, along with a majority of Massachusetts constituents, cut Kennedy slack for after-hours womanizing and boozing as long as he voted right during the day.

Publicly brazen, Kennedy privately confided to Hatch that he wasn't proud of his lifestyle. In January 1991, his sister Eunice Shriver was hospitalized after a serious auto accident. Kennedy had just returned from visiting her when Hatch spotted him in a Russell Building hallway.

"You know," Kennedy told Hatch somberly, "Eunice is . . . really a saint—pure and noble. To think that something like this could happen to her." Then Kennedy paused and shook his head. "If Eunice has to go through something like that, as pure and good as she is, what the hell is going to happen to *me?*"

"Theodoe," agreed Hatch, as Kennedy started to laugh, "you are *really* going to be in trouble."

In March 1991, Hatch drew Kennedy into a project to teach values in public elementary schools. In addition to the social good, Hatch hoped Kennedy would reassess his own values. He wrote privately, "I'm also going to . . . tell Ted that he has got to quit being such a partisan senator and start becoming the statesman he has the capacity to become. . . . I don't have any illusions; he will be a very difficult nut to crack. However, unlike so many others who believe he is totally evil, I believe there is a very good side to him which can be appealed to."

On Friday morning, March 22, Kennedy asked Hatch to go with him to the Labor Department for a working luncheon with newly installed Secretary Lynn Martin. Kennedy drove, taking along a huge leather portfolio.

"Don't tell me you're bringing charts to educate the secretary," said Hatch.

"Of course," smiled Kennedy.

As the luncheon began, Kennedy unzipped the case and withdrew a lithograph of a painting he had done of the Kennedy family compound in Hyannis Port. "Happy birthday, Orrin!" he said. Hatch was fifty-seven. Across the bottom of the picture was written:

"To Orrin—Handle with care, if the paint comes off the numbers will show! We'll leave the light at the compound on for you anytime. Ted Kennedy '91."

Lynn Martin produced a birthday cake, and Kennedy pulled out a bottle of Heinz 57 sauce, with the label altered to read "Hatch 57." "This is a little of the blood you have squeezed out of me in all our battles, Orrin," said Kennedy. "Happy birthday, fella."

A week later, on Good Friday evening, 1991, Kennedy was at the family compound in Palm Beach, Florida. Feeling restless, at about 11:30 P.M. he awoke his twenty-three-year-old son Patrick and a nephew, William Kennedy Smith, age thirty, a medical student at Georgetown University, and suggested they go have a few beers. They drove to a trendy watering hole called Au Bar. Patrick paired off with a twenty-seven-year-old woman, Michele Cassone, and Willy found twenty-nine-year-old Patricia Bowman.

When the bar closed around 3:00 A.M., Ted and Patrick Kennedy returned to the estate, Cassone going with them. Smith hitched a ride back with Bowman.

What happened next depends on who you believe. Ted disappeared, and Patrick showed Cassone around the mansion and grounds. Around 4 A.M., she said, she was with Patrick in his room when Ted wandered in—wearing an Oxford-cloth shirt and no pants. Startled, Cassone suddenly remembered it was past her bedtime and hightailed it out of there.

Bowman was not so prompt. She and Smith walked along the beach and shared a few kisses. Then Smith, according to Bowman, stripped off his pants and suggested they go swimming. Uneasy, Bowman started up the stairs leading to the house, calling that it was late and she was leaving.

She said Smith pursued her as she ran across the lawn, threw her to the ground, and raped her. Smith admitted they had sex but said Bowman had consented.

Bowman telephoned a friend, who picked her up. She went home first, then to the police to charge Willie Smith with rape.

Ted Kennedy's actions were already blameworthy. He had roused two young men from sleep to go drinking, on a religious holiday, no less, and let them bring women back. Then he played cat-and-mouse for two days with law officers, quietly returning to Washington as the police tried in vain to talk with him.

It stirred memories of Chappaquiddick. No one claimed that Kennedy had done anything illegal at Palm Beach; but in 1969, he had malingered for perhaps eleven hours while Mary Jo Kopechne's body lay underwater in his car. Now, in 1991, pundits and stand-up comedians had a field day, and the line was soon blurred between the tabloids and the mainstream press.

"Teddy Sighted on Mars!" screamed one headline—not in the National Enquirer but in the Washington Post. An accompanying photo showed a volcanic formation on Mars that looked like a face with a heavy lock of hair and fat jowls that resembled the senator. Talk-show host Jay Leno quipped, "Ted Kennedy has the 1992 Democratic nomination in his pocket . . . if he could only find his pants."

During the week after Palm Beach, Kennedy and Hatch joined mourners at the funeral of Senator John Heinz, killed in a plane crash in Philadelphia. As they left, Hatch put a hand on Kennedy's shoulder.

"How are you doing, Ted?"

"I'm getting by, Orrin. Thanks."

"I want you to know I've been thinking of you, and Elaine and I are praying for you."

Kennedy nodded.

"You know, Ted," added Hatch, "if you keep getting into trouble, I'm going to . . . send the Mormon missionaries after you."

"Orrin," answered Kennedy wistfully, "I'm just about ready for them."

The media feeding frenzy continued unabated. Reporters and photographers, never far from Kennedy anyway, were relentless. They pressed on him everywhere he went, insistent for any new scrap of information, gesture, or throw-away line they could use to sell a few more newspapers.

The Kennedy mystique had worn thin over the years, especially as revelations of John F. Kennedy's insatiable womanizing shattered the image of Camelot. Even the long-supportive *Boston Globe* published a column early in April 1991, predicting an end to Ted Kennedy's career because "people have grown tired of a man who is out of control."

Several weeks after Palm Beach, Kennedy telephoned Hatch at his office. "Can I come see you?"

"Of course," answered Hatch.

Kennedy arrived at Hatch's door minutes later, looking harried and depressed, and sank into an easy chair next to Hatch's desk. "Orrin, would you mind if I referred the media to you on this matter?"

"No problem, Ted, that would be fine." Then Hatch took advantage of the moment to offer some unsolicited advice. "Ted, you know it's time to grow up," Hatch began. "You could go down as one of the all-time great senators, if you would just quit being such an ideological jerk."

Kennedy winced but Hatch continued, "You know what you really need to do, don't you?"

"What?"

"You've got to stop drinking."

Kennedy's face reddened at Hatch's impertinence. There was a story on Capitol Hill that another close friend—former Democratic Senator John Culver of Iowa—had made the same suggestion, and that Kennedy hadn't talked to him for years afterwards.

Kennedy stared at his hands. There was a long silence, then Kennedy slumped and looked up sadly. "I know."

Citing the pending legal case, Kennedy maintained a public silence, as Hatch became his spokesman. When *Newsday,* the *New York Times,* the Associated Press, and others asked for interviews, Hatch unhesitatingly agreed. The interviews took many hours of Hatch's time for weeks.

Kennedy would have to give his own account of Palm Beach events, Hatch told them, but he described the Kennedy he had come to know — the devoted father who had reared three fine children alone in recent years, the guardian for assorted nieces and nephews of his departed siblings, the consummate legislator who was willing to compromise, the liberal partisan who could ease tensions with his infectious Irish humor.

Hatch pointed out that when Kennedy's sister Eunice had her recent auto accident, Kennedy went to her side immediately. When she was moved to Johns Hopkins Hospital in Baltimore, Kennedy was there. And when she returned home, Kennedy was with her again.

Kennedy and Hatch also had a number of joint newspaper and television interviews.

"He is very appreciative that I always say something nice about him," wrote Hatch privately. "I choose to look for the good in Ted Kennedy. . . . There is at least one side of him that is absolutely excellent. The other side leaves a little bit to be desired, and I have been making that clear to Ted as well."

At the end of April, as Hatch and Kennedy left the White House together, Hatch reported a forty-five-minute interview with *Time* magazine. "She asked me if you were an alcoholic."

"What did you say?"

"I told her you were not—that I have watched you go on lengthy liquid diets where you went without any alcoholic beverages for extended periods of time. I said it's really unlikely you could be that disciplined if you were an alcoholic."

"That's right," Kennedy quickly responded. "I couldn't do those liquid diets and be an alcoholic."

"Ted," said Hatch, turning solemn. "You are still going to have to quit drinking."

"I know," said a somber Kennedy once again.

On May 9, 1991, William Kennedy Smith was officially charged with second-degree sexual battery—the equivalent of rape in Florida—and misdemeanor battery. In a hastily called press conference, Ted Kennedy denied that he had received a message to call the police on Easter weekend or that he had been told then that Willy might be charged.

The strain was showing on Kennedy. He looked perpetually haggard and his appearance was becoming slovenly. One day he and Hatch ran a gauntlet of photographers into a committee room. Once seated, Hatch leaned over to his friend. "Ted, take my word on it—go get a haircut. And get it cut shorter than usual."

Hatch believed that most liberals wouldn't like seeing Kennedy sheared but was convinced it would be a start in cleaning up his image. Later Hatch reconsidered his nagging and started to apologize. Kennedy held up a hand to silence him.

"I already took your advice, Orrin. I've got an appointment with my barber."

26

Clarence and Anita

S OME MEMBERS OF CONGRESS WHO came to Washington as devout
religionists departed from their traditional faiths. Hatch was not
among them.

He continued to be a faithful Mormon who paid tithing, prayed daily,
and was in church every Sunday he wasn't on the road. For fourteen
consecutive years—ever since arriving in Washington—he had also achieved
a 100 percent record as a "home teacher"—a church assignment to visit
several assigned families each month to offer encouragement and assistance in both spiritual and temporal matters.

Also after fourteen years, Hatch still taught the adult Sunday School
class in their Vienna ward, where Elaine had served in many roles,
including president of the women's auxiliary. More recently, she had
begun to volunteer each week in the local temple, located in Kensington,
Maryland. Periodically Orrin also attended one of its daily sessions.

In July 1989, when he and Elaine went to Israel, he wrote reverently
in a private memo from Jerusalem: "It is such a privilege to be in the
Holy Land, where Jesus walked and talked, and also where the great and
holy prophets were."

Hatch's first love in the church remained missionary work. He eagerly
shared his religious beliefs with non-Mormons. In February 1991, for
example, he gave an evening address at the visitors' center adjacent to the
temple on "Why I Believe." To the capacity crowd, he related his experiences as a young missionary and testified that he had seen Christ's
promise fulfilled that "all things are possible to them that believeth"
(Mark 9:23).

In Indiana, Hatch recalled, he and his companion visited an elderly blind woman and explained the priesthood's power to bless and to heal. The woman said, "I believe you young men really do have the power of God with you. . . . I have not wanted much in this life, but I do so want to see light again. Would you bless me so I can see the light?"

Hatch and three missionaries with him glanced nervously at each other, then he said all of them would combine their faith; and if it were the Lord's will, her desire would be granted. Another elder anointed her head with oil, and Hatch gave the blessing, feeling prompted to promise her she would indeed see light again.

The room was lighted by a single bulb hanging from the ceiling. As the missionaries removed their hands from her head, the woman stood, walked to the center of the room, reached up, and touched the bulb. Her face grew radiant. "I can see light for the first time in thirty-two years!" she said.

Hatch also told the story of how young Hybert Hill was relieved of his agony and healed of his kidney tumor after a similar blessing. (See Chapter 2.) Among those who thronged Hatch after his remarks was a handsome man, choked with emotion as he shook Hatch's hand. Swallowing hard, he said, "I'm Hybert Hill." Hatch, who had not seen Hill since that day in the Springfield hospital, embraced him, eyes misting.

The following month, Hill, who lived in nearby North Potomac, sent Hatch a letter. Dated March 28, 1991, it said, in part:

Dear Orrin:

. . . I was very touched to realize that after all these years you remembered that moment when the mother of a very sick little boy asked you and your companion to come to the hospital and administer to him.

I still remember the soothing calm that came over me and how later, in the operating room, the doctors were confounded over the restoration of renal function to my kidneys. I remember, too, how the Catholic Nuns treated me and how they knew something miraculous had occurred.

. . . Words cannot truly express how grateful I've always been for that blessing and the immediate healing I received. Years later as I stood on the field of combat in Viet Nam I remembered the feelings of that day and the Spirit continually whispered to me have faith in the Lord. I have since been blessed to raise a family in the Church and have a son on a Mission. . . .

With Warmest Regards and Eternal Thanks,
Hybert M. Hill

Yet another miracle would be needed after Bush, on July 1, 1991, nominated Clarence Thomas to the Supreme Court. Thomas would be cast into a fiery furnace and only Hatch could keep him from being consumed.

On June 27, Justice Thurgood Marshall announced his retirement. Marshall, nearly eighty-three, had been one of the nation's leading civil rights lawyers and the first black on the high court, appointed by Lyndon Johnson in 1967. In recent years he had become a bitter voice of dissent as the court turned increasingly to the right.

It was one thing to slice up Robert Bork, whose upward path at least began on level ground. It was quite another to attack Thomas, who epitomized the American dream that anyone, however humble their start, can aspire to greatness.

Thomas was a toddler in tiny Pin Point, Georgia, when his father walked away, leaving a pregnant wife, a daughter, and little Clarence. Leola Thomas shelled crab at five cents a pound, living with relatives in a small house with no indoor plumbing. When the house burned down, the Thomases moved to Savannah. Leola worked while her parents, Myers and Christine Anderson, cared for the children. When Clarence was eight, he and his younger brother moved in with their grandparents, and his sister went to live with an aunt.

Thomas attended a segregated Catholic school. After school he helped his grandfather deliver ice, coal, fuel oil, and wood. Anderson became the dominant influence in Thomas's life, giving him stability and discipline. Anderson, a devout Catholic and strong Democrat, opposed welfare in most circumstances, believing it robbed a person of both independence and self-worth.

"My household . . . was strong, stable, and conservative," said Thomas years later. "In fact, it was far more conservative than many who fashion themselves conservative today. God was central. School, discipline, and hard work, and knowing right from wrong, were of the highest priority" and "marked the path of survival and escape from squalor." Crime, welfare, laziness and alcohol were "enemies."

Thomas hungered for learning and thrived under the rigors of his grandfather at home and the Catholic nuns at school. He was the only black in his high school class and began college at the Immaculate Conception Seminary in Missouri. But Thomas abandoned plans to become a priest in 1968 after hearing a white seminarian cheer when he learned that Martin Luther King, Jr., had been shot. He transferred to Holy Cross College in Worcester, Massachusetts, graduating with honors in 1971. A day later Thomas married his first wife, Kathy, and headed for Yale Law School. They had one son, Jamal, awarded to Thomas after he and Kathy divorced in 1984.

At Yale, Thomas discovered that quota-based programs intended to help minority students were not targeted for people like him, but rather for blacks already in the middle class. He strenuously questioned the assumptions of civil rights leaders. Wouldn't blacks do better in a truly color-blind society, he asked, competing strictly on merit and not relying on a white-controlled power structure for favors that could be taken away as well as granted? "Racial quotas and other race-conscious legal devices only further and deepen the original problem," said Thomas. "I firmly insist that the Constitution be interpreted in a colorblind fashion. . . . I emphasize black self-help as opposed to racial quotas."

Such unorthodoxy spelled calamity to the civil rights community, including Democrats, who depended on minorities' reliance on them to safeguard and expand racial preferences. Thomas as a visible role model, as an articulate spokesman, and as a powerful jurist was to them, in a word, dangerous.

Within days of Thomas's nomination, the campaign began. Barbara Reynolds, an editor at *USA Today*, wrote viciously, "Judge Thomas strikes me as a man who would get a note from his boss before singing 'We Shall Overcome.'" Reynolds sneered at Thomas's second wife, Virginia, as "a white conservative who lobbied against comparable pay for women." Calling attention to Virginia's race was a crass appeal to racism, especially in the South, whose senators would be key in deciding Thomas's fate.

The tactic foreshadowed the ugliness that lay ahead. "We're going to Bork him," said Patricia Ireland, president of NOW, vowing a character assassination by political correctness. Another feminist leader, Flo Kennedy, agreed, "We have to Bork him. We don't wait for questions, we don't wait for the senators, and we kick ass and take names. . . . We're going to kill him politically. This little creep, where did he come from?"

The Congressional Black Caucus fell into line July 18, calling Thomas a "dangerous thinker" and voting 24-1 against confirmation. The monolithic opposition hoped for by liberal Democrats and most civil rights leaders did not materialize, however. A CNN poll showed that 57 percent of blacks supported Thomas. The NAACP hesitated. Finally its board, under pressure from organized labor, an important source of funding, voted 49-1 against Thomas.

However, Margaret Bush Wilson, former chair of the NAACP's national board for nine years, published a powerful rebuttal in the *Washington Post*. As a new Yale graduate, Thomas had stayed with Wilson, a St. Louis attorney, in 1974 while studying for the Missouri bar. "I don't recall seeing another young person as disciplined as Clarence

Thomas," wrote Wilson, who let him use her son's room and fixed dinner for him each evening.

> We didn't always agree . . . but I was impressed continually with one so young whose reasoning was so sound. . . . The Clarence Thomas I have been reading about often bears little resemblance to the thoughtful and caring man I have known over these years. . . . His views are not nearly as radical as his critics suggest. . . . Let the record show that the NAACP's former national board chair respectfully disagrees with its position.

Hatch was angered by the anti-Thomas barrage. He had known Thomas for more than a decade, knew of his integrity, admired him, and considered him a friend.

"He is a wonderful choice," Hatch wrote privately when he was informed by the White House three hours before the public announcement. "Clarence is a truly good person."

Hatch's support was much more than ideological. "I expect he will be more of a centrist than a conservative," wrote Hatch privately, "but I think he will lean to the right. That will be a wonderful thing. He could become the prime role model for young African Americans all over this country. What a pleasant change over some of their current role models."

Thomas had served in state government in the Missouri attorney general's office and in all three branches of the federal government: as a legislative assistant to Senator John Danforth, a Missouri Republican; as assistant secretary in charge of civil rights at the Department of Education, as chairman of the Equal Employment Opportunity Commission (EEOC), and now as a circuit court judge.

Hatch identified with Thomas's rise from poverty to prominence, his independence, and his refusal to worship at the throne of political orthodoxy. The Utahn was grimly determined to block the "Borking" of Thomas.

In mid-July with controversy already swirling, Thomas paid a courtesy call at Hatch's office. The two embraced in greeting and again in parting. A huge throng of reporters pressed in, one asking Hatch if it bothered him that Thomas had said he *may* have smoked marijuana a couple of times in college. "I judge people by what they are now, not what they were," answered Hatch.

The Thomas hearings began Tuesday, September 10, 1991. Sitting behind Thomas were his wife, Virginia ("Ginny"), who also held a law degree, his son, mother, sister, and several friends and advisors, including his mentor Senator Danforth and White House strategist Kenneth Duberstein. When Danforth was attorney general in Missouri, he had hired Thomas fresh out of law school and would defend him ferociously in the unfolding contest of the next month.

The fourteen-member Judiciary Committee—eight Democrats, six Republicans—had had two changes since the Bork hearings: Wisconsin Democrat Herbert Kohl had replaced Bob Byrd, and Colorado Republican Hank Brown had replaced Gordon Humphrey.

In formally welcoming Thomas, Hatch called him a man of "fierce independence" and said some special interest groups "fear Judge Thomas will be faithful to the Constitution and federal laws as enacted, instead of to their political agenda."

Concern over Thomas's civil rights record at the EEOC was a "smokescreen," accused Hatch. "These liberal critics really object to Judge Thomas having spoken out against what is popularly called reverse discrimination. . . . The overwhelming majority of the American people favor equal opportunity—not equal results."

After his formal statement, Hatch ad-libbed some personal observations, reminiscing that he, too, had lived in a house without indoor facilities. *Newsweek* lampooned Hatch's walk along memory lane, saying he had elevated outhouses over log cabins and had praised Thomas so effusively he had "Orrinated" all over him. "I had to laugh at that," Hatch recalled. "It was pretty clever."

Then the grilling began. Thomas had written about "natural law" as an underpinning for the Constitution, and committee members asked what he meant. When Thomas's response was less than articulate, Chairman Biden bored in. Hatch then helped Thomas express his thoughts. Biden slipped Hatch a note: "Orrin, what would witnesses do without your rehabilitation—from now on you are *Doctor* Hatch."

Liberal critics wrote that because Thomas was educated by Catholic nuns, he would oppose abortion. Democrats now insisted on knowing Thomas's views on *Roe v. Wade*. When Leahy of Vermont asked if he had ever discussed the case, Thomas carefully responded he had never *debated* it. Leahy and Kennedy began spreading the falsehood that Thomas said he had never "discussed" *Roe v. Wade*—a highly unlikely proposition for a law school graduate. The implication was that Thomas was lying. Hatch corrected the record. When Kennedy repeated it again on the Senate floor, Hatch challenged him, reading from the actual transcript, and finally silenced Kennedy.

Thomas declined to offer his views on abortion, saying it was improper to discuss issues that might come before the court. Kennedy and other Democrats accused him of evasion, and in a sort of Chinese water-torture, asked him questions about abortion no less than seventy times during the first three days alone of his five-day appearance.

As the repetition continued, radio talk-show host Rush Limbaugh, the bane of liberals, began playing a tape over and over, heard on some four hundred radio stations that carried his show, including WMAL-AM in Washington, D.C. The voice was Ted Kennedy's: "We will have to respect that any nominee . . . will have to defer any comments on any matters which are either before the court or [are] very likely to appear before the court. This has been a procedure which has been followed in the past and is one which I think is based upon sound legal precedent."

The 1967 tape, retrieved from a New York archive, was a Kennedy comment about Thurgood Marshall, a very liberal *Democratic* nominee to the high court.

Thomas refused to hand Democrats ammunition with which to execute him. After Thomas's third day of testimony, a *Washington Post* analyst observed that Thomas, in addition to alarming liberals, had also expressed many views "contrary to conservative ideology." He criticized conservative plans to limit access to the courts, expressing deep humanitarian concern for criminal defendants. He questioned a recent ruling by the Rehnquist-led court that liberals believed would make it too easy for states to interfere with religious practices. Thomas even told the panel of rabid Washington Redskins fans that he was a longtime booster of the football team's arch rival, the Dallas Cowboys.

Bork had spelled out his judicial philosophy in great detail, and his critics wove his words into a noose and hanged him. Souter had used a "stealth" approach and been confirmed, and Thomas had learned from his example. When Democrats complained bitterly that they could not get enough information from Thomas, Hatch noted, "They have made the process into the process it has become." When Democrats criticized Thomas for "being outside the mainstream," Hatch retorted that liberals "couldn't find the mainstream if they paddled for weeks and months."

Biden accused Thomas of "inartfully" dodging the issues, and Kennedy ended his questioning with a broadside: "The vanishing views of Judge Thomas have become a major issue in these hearings," and "I continue to have major concerns about your commitment to the fundamental rights and liberties at the heart of the Constitution and our democracy."

Thomas's mother sadly told Hatch: "I expected Senator Metzenbaum to do that to my boy, but I did not expect Senator Kennedy to do so."

In his own summary, Hatch chastised Democrats for basing their opposition to Thomas on the single issue of abortion while ignoring the breakdown of the family, restricted job opportunities, drugs, crime, single-parent households, and a lack of education incentives. "Unless [minorities] work on and are part of the liberal plantation," he added, "your ideas, your thoughts, your abilities, your experience, your pain, and your history of growth mean nothing."

After Thomas's testimony, some seventy-five witnesses testified. They included Kate Michelman, executive director of the National Abortion

Rights Action League (NARAL), who urged the committee to reject Thomas. She said of abortion rights: "No issue—none—has a greater impact on the lives and futures of American women and their families."

Committee members began to announce their positions. Heflin of Alabama, offering typically tortured logic, would not vote to confirm, he said. Biden told Hatch he was "very close" to voting for Thomas but obviously didn't want to end up to the right of Heflin. In the end he sided with the committee's ideological liberals—Kennedy, Metzenbaum, Leahy, and Simon. Democrat Herb Kohl also opposed Thomas when the committee voted on September 27, 1991. DeConcini of Arizona was the only Democrat voting for him, joining six committee Republicans—Hatch, Thurmond, Simpson, Grassley, Specter, and Brown—to give Thomas a 7-7 tie. The panel would make no recommendation to the full Senate.

All committee members except one—Paul Simon—then voted to send the nomination on to the full Senate for final action.

Hatch, in Utah the day after the vote, telephoned Thomas. "You did fine during the hearings," Hatch told him. "Don't be discouraged at this point." Both were aware that opponents, having failed to kill his nomination in committee, were now engaged in a vicious campaign of slurs against him.

"Orrin," said Thomas, "I hope it is over soon because this has really hurt my family and me." What lay ahead would eclipse all other pain.

Despite the committee tie, a comfortable majority of senators were ready to vote for Thomas. Hatch and others pressed to have the floor vote in time for him to be seated for the court's next session, beginning October 7, 1991.

Democrats, however, made veiled threats of a filibuster. Metzenbaum and others invoked technicalities to stall. A compromise was reached: the debate would begin Thursday, October 3, with the vote coming the following Tuesday, October 8.

As the floor debate opened, Metzenbaum conceded that there was only a "very slim chance" of defeating Thomas. Hatch's headcount indicated that forty-one of the forty-three Senate Republicans would vote for Thomas. Twelve Democrats had already pledged support, giving Thomas at least fifty-three votes.

"His success is guaranteed unless something happens between now and next Tuesday," wrote Hatch on Friday, October 4.

Something happened. On Saturday, October 5, National Public Radio and *Newsday* reported that a woman named Anita Hill had accused Thomas of sexual harassment. The stories cited a confidential FBI report, leaked by a committee member or staffer. All of the Judiciary

Committee Democrats and half of its Republicans, including Hatch, knew about Hill's allegations *before* the committee vote. Both sides agreed they were not relevant. Any concerned member could have pursued Hill's charges further; none did and none could since Hill did not want her name used and did not want to come forth as a witness.

Even after the charges were leaked to the press and became public on October 5, both Biden and Senate Majority Leader George Mitchell argued against postponing the scheduled floor vote three days later. But a firestorm of opposition swept the nation, fanned by feminists and other activists already after Thomas's scalp.

Suddenly Thomas's near-certain confirmation changed to calls for a full investigation. The Senate vote was postponed to October 15, and the nation braced for the spectacle.

Who was Anita Hill? The portrait offered the world during the hearing and the one uncovered later were significantly different. Hill created the impression that, like Thomas, she was conservative, though basically apolitical, and religious. Hence, an inappropriate motive on her part seemed lacking.

In reality, by the time of her appearance before the Judiciary Committee, Hill was a dedicated—some say shrill—feminist. Investigative journalist David Brock detailed a history of bizarre behavior regarding men and sex sixteen months later in his powerful, controversial book, *The Real Anita Hill: The Untold Story* (New York: Free Press, 1993).

Born into a large Oklahoma farm family, Hill graduated from Oklahoma State University, received her law degree from Yale in 1980, and was teaching law at the University of Oklahoma when Thomas was nominated to the Supreme Court. In the fall of 1981, Hill, twenty-five, began working for Thomas at the Department of Education where the alleged harassment began. She followed him to the Equal Employment Opportunity Commission the following year—*after* the alleged harassment.

A decade later, Hill strongly resisted going public, preventing timely and thorough Senate deliberation. Anti-Thomas Senate staffers led Hill to believe her allegations alone could help destroy Thomas behind the scenes and get him to withdraw. When that proved impossible, someone double-crossed Hill, leaking her FBI statement to the media. It is unlikely Hill's allegations would have ever reached the Senate without considerable prodding from Thomas's enemies.

Kate Michelman reportedly told another pro-abortion woman in Washington days before Hill's charges hit the media that NARAL's leaders were "very excited because we have Anita Hill." When the woman asked who Hill was, Michelman said, "She's going to come forward with a claim of sexual harassment against Clarence Thomas. We've been working on her since July."

Vague information about Hill's allegations was also given in July—the month Thomas was nominated—to Timothy Phelps of *Newsday* and Nina Totenberg of National Public Radio, the reporters who later broke the story. They sat on it until October when someone leaked them additional details from the FBI report.

Thomas had an impeccable record of personal integrity and deportment toward female coworkers and had already passed four FBI background checks for other positions. His critics were clearly desperate for something—anything—to halt his advance toward the high court.

Juan Williams, a reporter at the *Washington Post* who had known and written about Thomas for ten years, began a column: "The phone calls came throughout September. Did Clarence Thomas ever take money from the South African government? Was he under orders from the Reagan White House when he criticized civil rights leaders? Did he beat his first wife? . . . And finally, one exasperated voice said: 'Have you got anything on your tapes we can use to stop Thomas?'"

Liberals, charged Williams, have been "mindlessly led into mob action against one man by the Leadership Conference on Civil Rights," and now with Anita Hill, Senate staffers "have found their speck of mud to fling at Clarence Thomas."

Thomas first learned of Hill's charges when two FBI agents came to his Virginia home and outlined Hill's allegations. Thomas was incredulous. "Anita Hill said that?" he asked. "That's impossible!"

Hatch learned of the charges several days later, before the committee vote, and telephoned Thomas. The nominee told Hatch the cost to his family was too great and he might withdraw. Hatch urged him not to.

"Senator, do you think I can still make it?"

"Clarence, you're not only going to make it, but you're going to end up being one of the finest Supreme Court justices in history." Hatch called Thomas several more times in the following days to buoy his spirits, telling him to "hang in there."

Thomas absolutely denied Hill's charges, telling Hatch they had always enjoyed a cordial relationship and that he had boosted Hill's career from the day she began working for him at Education.

"*Think,* Clarence, *think,*" urged Hatch. "Is there anything at all that might provide the slightest reason for her to say this?"

Thomas answered that Hill had once been passed over for a leadership job on his EEOC staff in favor of a woman named Allyson Duncan, who was more analytical and a better attorney. But he and Hill had maintained cordial professional relations even after she left EEOC to teach at Oral Roberts University in Tulsa in 1983. Hill had telephoned him on a number of occasions, and was always friendly.

"That would certainly show your real relationship with her. Are there telephone logs to back up those calls?" asked hatch.

"I assume so," answered Thomas.

The logbook kept by Thomas's secretary showed at least twelve calls from Hill between 1983 to 1990.

Hill would later call the logs "garbage" and claim she was returning Thomas's calls, but the secretary's notes made it clear that almost all the calls *originated* with Hill. Some examples:

> January 31, 1984, 11:50: "just called to say hello. Sorry she didn't get to see you last week."
>
> August 29, 1984, 3:59: "Needs your advice on getting research grants."
>
> January 3, 1985, 3:40: "Pls call tonight."
>
> October 8, 1986, 12:25: "Pls call."
>
> August 4, 1987, 4:00: "in town til 8/15 . . . wanted to congratulate you on marriage."

Friday, October 11, 1991 was the first day of the second round of hearings. The historic Senate Caucus Room was packed, and thousands more spilled into the halls and outside the Capitol hoping to get into the nationally televised hearings.

Hatch arrived early, waiting outside the main entrance to welcome Thomas and his wife. As they ascended the marble staircase with Senator Thurmond, scores of well-wishers, many conservative to moderate blacks, lustily cheered Thomas. Outside the caucus room, Hatch and Thomas shook hands, then hugged.

"Ready?" asked Hatch.

"Ready!" said Thomas.

The fourteen committee members were sitting in one long line behind a green-draped table, level with Thomas, who sat alone behind a matching table facing them.

Chairman Biden and ranking Republican Thurmond offered opening statements, then it was Thomas's turn. Reading from a prepared text of sixteen double-spaced pages, he stated:

> The fact that I feel so very strongly about sex harassment and spoke loudly about it at EEOC has made these allegations doubly hard on me. . . . I have not said or done the things that Anita Hill has alleged. God has gotten me through the days since September 25 and

He is my judge. . . . No job is worth what I have been through, no job. No horror in my life has been so debilitating. Confirm me if you want, don't confirm me if you are so led, but let this process end.

Biden said Thomas would testify first, then Hill, but Hill had asked the committee to keep her statement confidential until she testified. Hatch vigorously objected, noting that Hill's statement was already in the national media: "It is a matter of fairness."

Simpson, Thurmond, and DeConcini agreed with Hatch. Hill had been on television and portions of her statement had appeared in print. Thomas should be allowed to point out discrepancies in them. When Biden still insisted on keeping the FBI report confidential, Hatch exploded: "I think it is time to be fair to the nominee. . . . They have the burden of showing that he is not telling the truth here, and he has a right to face the accuser and everything that accuser says, and if he does not, then I am going to resign from this committee today."

Biden called a recess, during which Danforth brought word that Thomas had offered to let Hill testify immediately as long as he could testify the same day. He didn't want the weekend to begin with only Hill's version available to the media.

The hearing reconvened, and Hill began. A mutual friend had introduced her to Thomas in 1981 while she was working at a Washington law firm. Hill accepted a job as Thomas's assistant after he was appointed Assistant Secretary of Education for Civil Rights. Three months later, she said, he began to ask her out socially, but she declined, believing it unwise to have a social relationship with a supervisor. She continued:

> My working relationship became even more strained when Judge Thomas began to use work situations to discuss sex. . . . His conversations were very vivid.
>
> He spoke about acts that he had seen in pornographic films involving such matters as women having sex with animals, and films showing group sex or rape scenes. He talked about pornographic materials depicting individuals with large penises, or large breasts involved in various sex acts. On several occasions Thomas told me graphically of his own sexual prowess. . . . My efforts to change the subject were rarely successful. . . .
>
> When Judge Thomas was made chair of the EEOC, I needed to face the question of whether to go with him. I was asked to do so and I did. The work itself was interesting, and at that time, it appeared that the sexual overtures . . . had ended. . . . However, during the fall and winter of 1982 these began again. . . .

One of the oddest episodes I remember was an occasion in which Thomas was drinking a coke in his office, he got up from the table, at which we were working, went over to his desk to get the coke, looked at the can and asked, "Who has put pubic hair on my coke?" On other occasions he referred to the size of his own penis as being larger than normal and he also spoke on some occasions of the pleasures he had given to women with oral sex. . . .

In the spring of 1983, an opportunity to teach at Oral Roberts University opened up. . . . I agreed to take the job, in large part, because of my desire to escape the pressures I felt at the EEOC due to Judge Thomas. . . . In July 1983, I left the Washington, D.C. area, and have had minimal contacts with Judge Clarence Thomas since.

Biden probed for other incidents as specific as the Coke can. Hill testified that Thomas had described a man with "a very large penis" called "Long Dong Silver."

The committee accepted Hatch's suggestion that each side have one main questioner for Hill and one for Thomas. Although Republicans wanted Hatch to question Hill, he instead suggested Arlen Specter of Pennsylvania, who had voted against Bork and was both pro-ERA and pro-abortion rights. Hatch agreed to question Thomas for the GOP side. Kennedy's Easter weekend escapade meant that he was not a possibility for the Democrats, and they chose Patrick Leahy of Vermont, a solid liberal. Questioners would take turns in thirty-minute segments.

Specter, a former district attorney in Philadelphia, was brainy and persevering. He methodically took Hill's story apart; but she remained cool, conceded almost nothing, and calmly changed parts of her story as necessary.

For example, Carlton Stewart, an attorney, had told the Judiciary Committee that he had run into Hill two months earlier at an American Bar Association convention. Hill had said " 'how great Clarence's nomination was, and how much he deserved it.' "

When Specter quoted Stewart, Hill corrected him: "I was very passive. . . . I did say that it is a great thing for Clarence Thomas. I did not say that he deserved it."

Specter read a statement from Roger Tuttle, former dean of Oral Roberts Law School, where Hill had taught for three years. Tuttle quoted Hill as saying Thomas "is a fine man and an excellent legal scholar." Hill demurred: the school's founding dean, Charles Kothe, liked Thomas, so "I did not risk talking in disparaging ways about Clarence Thomas at that time."

Phyllis Berry, who had worked at the EEOC, had told the *New York Times* that Hill's charges "were the result of Ms. Hill's disappointment and frustration that Mr. Thomas did not show any sexual interest in her." Asked about Berry's statement, Hill said, "Well, I don't know Phyllis Berry and she doesn't know me." Specter challenged this statement, and Hill modified it: "We were not close friends. . . . She has no basis for making a comment about my social interests."

Specter asked Hill why she hadn't mentioned either the Coke can or "Long Dong Silver" in her extensive interview with the FBI. Hill said the two agents told her she could omit material that was "too embarrassing" and that it was "regular procedure to come back and ask for more specifics if it was necessary."

The two agents in Oklahoma, John B. Luton and Jolene Smith Jameson, filed separate affidavits that very day. Luton said he had told Hill "to provide the specifics of all incidents" and that the mention of follow-up interviews came "at the end of the interview." In the hearing, Hill acknowledged that Democratic staffers had called, urging her to come forward. Luton said Hill had told the agents nothing about these calls, naming only telephone conversations with Susan Hoerchner, a friend and former Yale classmate. Luton also swore that Hill had not mentioned a Coke can or "Long Dong Silver."

Jameson's affidavit focused on discrepancies in Hill's interview and her testimony. Yes, Luton had "apologized for the sensitivity of the matter" and even offered to let her speak alone to Jameson "if the questions were too embarrassing," but he had definitely told her to "be as specific as possible and give details." Yes, Luton had mentioned a possible follow-up interview, but only when they were finished. Hill had said Thomas described "pornographic incidents involving people in sex acts with each other and with animals" but did not say Thomas had mentioned his own physique, "Long Dong Silver," or a Coke can.

As Hatch left the hearing room at lunchtime, a network anchor stuck a microphone in his face. "It's all over, isn't it? How could anyone not believe her testimony?"

"Well," answered Hatch, "I've been in many trials where you might have thought it was over after listening to the first witness. I suggest you wait until you've heard [Thomas]."

Based on Hill's testimony, Nina Totenberg was already reading Thomas's obituary to her National Public Radio audience.

When the committee reassembled, Leahy questioned Hill for the Democrats. The testimony focused on Hill's claim that she had told Susan Hoerchner about the alleged incidents when they occurred.

Hoerchner's role was pivotal. Apparently she was the first person to contact Hill in July when Thomas was nominated to the Supreme Court, urging that Hill try to stop him. In her phone call, Hoerchner reportedly reminded Hill how Hill had told her a decade earlier that Thomas was guilty of sexual harassment. A month before the Thomas-Hill hearings, however, Hoerchner told a Biden staffer—and later told Senate lawyers in a deposition—that Hill's complaint about sexual harassment had occurred before September 1981 —*before* Hill had started to work with Thomas. When a lawyer pointed out the discrepancy, Hoerchner quickly huddled with one of Hill's attorneys—Janet Napolitano, a feminist activist—and then said she no longer was sure when it happened.

It was possible Hoerchner had the date wrong. It was also possible she had it right, and the harassment took place instead at the law firm where Hill was then working. A third possibility was that the harassment never took place at all but that Hill had invented it when senior attorneys at her firm—Wald, Harkrader & Ross—told her, as they later verified, that her performance was not adequate and that she should look for work elsewhere. Democratic staff members kept Hoerchner's damaging affidavit out of the official record, however, and she waltzed through the hearing without ever being confronted with it directly.

Specter returned as Republican questioner in the afternoon, pointing out that the statute of limitations for filing a case on sexual harassment was relatively short, 180 days, because of the difficulty of defending against such a charge. Was it fair to ask Thomas to respond ten years after the fact? Hill replied coolly, "I don't believe it is unfair."

Specter also asked about a 1987 occasion when Thomas spoke in Tulsa. Why had Hill "voluntarily agree[d] to drive Judge Thomas to the airport?" Hill remembered it differently: "I think the dean suggested that I drive him to the airport, and that I said that I would." Dean Charles Kothe, however, later told the committee that Hill and Thomas had breakfasted at his house "in a setting of conviviality or joy" and that Hill *asked* to drive Thomas to the airport to show off her new car.

And the inconsistencies continued: Hill said she went with Thomas from Education to EEOC despite the harassment because she didn't know his replacement and didn't know she still had a secure job. In fact, Thomas's replacement, Harry Singleton, had arrived four weeks before Thomas left and wanted Hill to stay on as one of his advisors. Furthermore, Hill was a Class A attorney under the civil service rules with a guaranteed job in the department.

Had Democratic staffers told Hill that her statement might force Thomas to withdraw without her going public? At first, she denied it.

But later she admitted that James Brudney, an aide to the rabidly anti-Thomas Metzenbaum, had said just that.

In exasperation, Hill finally told Specter: "Well, I think if you start to look at each individual problem with this statement, then you're not going to be satisfied that it's true, but I think the statement has to be taken as a whole."

Hatch said almost nothing to Hill during the hearing, except to apologize on behalf of the committee for the unethical leak of the FBI report. "I wish you well," he told Hill.

Hill's lengthy testimony ended at 7:40 P.M. As she finished, media commentators were already speculating that Thomas was as good as dead. Despite numerous inconsistencies, she had come across as sincere and believable to many viewers. Others, including courtroom-experienced Hatch, found her lack of emotion in relating such traumatic experiences incongruent.

Hatch hurried out of the hearing room and down a flight of stairs to Clarence and Virginia Thomas in Danforth's office. Although most Americans were riveted to their television sets, Thomas, who was furious, had refused to watch Hill's testimony. In little more than an hour he would be back before the committee.

Virginia and others had briefed Thomas on Hill's testimony, and he was upset, strained, and exhausted. "Clarence, get a half hour's rest before the next session," Hatch urged. Thomas agreed to do so.

Hatch reminded Thomas of how he had silenced Kennedy years earlier by describing John F. Kennedy's picture on the wall of his childhood home. "Clarence, just be yourself," advised Hatch.

"Don't worry," said Thomas.

"And don't take any crap from anybody out there—including me."

"Don't worry!" Thomas repeated with emphasis.

Hatch had overheard a conversation between two black men. One commented, "This woman is trying to demonize us." The remark stuck with Hatch, who realized Hill was accusing Thomas of using language in describing sexual material with which racists stereotyped blacks. It was not the kind of language an intelligent, professional African American was likely to use.

"Clarence, I'm going to ask you about negative, antiblack, white-racist stereotype language, the kind she is accusing you of using," said Hatch.

"I hope you do!" Thomas responded fervently.

Hatch then returned to his office. Something tugged at him. Hill had offered four versions: a four-page single-spaced legal-size statement to the FBI, an edited version of that statement, the extensive oral interview with the FBI, and a three-page statement to the committee. The Coke can incident hadn't shown up until the last document, and Hill had mentioned Long Dong Silver—which sounded slick and contrived to many listeners—only when Biden asked a question.

Hatch called his staff together. "I've heard that Coke can thing somewhere else," said Hatch. "Let's find it." Hatch, a voracious reader with an unusually keen memory, thought it had come from a book.

His staff dug in. Several aides turned on computer terminals at their desks and began researching data banks, notably Lexis/Nexis, a broad-based information system covering both legal and general topics. Others called the Congressional Research Service at the Library of Congress and spread the word to the White House and friends both inside and outside government. Leads began pouring in from across the country.

Within an hour, a female aide hung up the phone and yelled: "I think we've got it!" She quickly instructed her young male assistant, who raced out of the Russell Building, dodged traffic across Constitution Avenue, darted into the Capitol, and ran up another flight of stairs to the Senate Library on the third floor. The young man located the library's only copy of *The Exorcist,* a 1971 best-seller by William Blatty, quickly turned to page 70, ran his finger down the page, suppressed a triumphant shout, slammed the book shut, and shot back out of the library.

"You did it!" yelled Hatch, ten minutes later when his assistant returned, grinning and gasping. Rather than use it in the Friday night session, however, he spurred on the search for the reference to Long Dong Silver. Scores of Thomas supporters throughout the country joined the search.

Thomas did not nap before the committee reconvened, yet Hatch perceived a substantial change. He was no longer a battered victim but an energized man, intent on reclaiming his honor.

Thomas's opening statement was a categorical denial of all allegations:

> I think that this today is a travesty. . . . This hearing should never occur in America. . . . This dirt was searched for by staffers of members of this committee, was then leaked to the media, and this committee, and this body validated it and displayed it in prime time over our entire nation.
>
> The Supreme Court is not worth it. No job is worth it. I am not here for that. I am here for my name, my family, my life and my integrity. . . . [This] is a high-tech lynching for uppity blacks who in any way deign to think for themselves. . . . Unless you kow-tow to an old order, this is what will happen to you, you will be lynched, destroyed, caricatured by a committee of the U.S. Senate, rather than hung from a tree.

Heflin, designated questioner for the Democrats, missed the mark badly by asking Thomas about an obscure issue at EEOC that had absolutely nothing to do with Anita Hill. After learning that Thomas had not watched Hill's appearance, Heflin turned the floor over to Hatch, the Republicans' official questioner.

Hatch led Thomas point by point through Hill's allegations. Thomas emphatically denied each. Hatch noted the irony that Hill dated the charges to her work at the Equal Employment Opportunity Commission, the very agency that adjudicates such job-related grievances. Why had Hill, an attorney herself, not filed a grievance about the harassment?

> Thomas: It never occurred. That is why there was no charge.
>
> Hatch: You see, one of the problems that has bothered me from the front of this thing is, these are gross. Cumulative, I don't understand why anybody would put up with them or why anybody would respect or work with any other person who would do that . . .
>
> Thomas: I agree.
>
> Hatch: Furthermore, I don't know why they would have gone to a different position with you, even if they did think that maybe it had stopped. . . . And then when they finally got out into the private sector, wouldn't [they] somehow or other confront these problems in [your] three successive confirmation proceedings. Does that bother you?
>
> Thomas: This whole affair bothers me. I am witnessing the destruction of my integrity.

Hatch quoted a statement on the Senate floor three days earlier by Democrat Joseph Lieberman, who had interviewed women associates of Thomas at the Department of Education and EEOC: "There has been universal support for Judge Thomas. . . . All of the women we spoke to [agreed] that there was never, certainly not a case of sexual harassment, and not even a hint of impropriety." Hatch again reminded the committee that the American system of justice puts the burden of proof on the accuser.

Biden, who was fair to both Hill and Thomas in his conduct of the hearings, agreed the benefit of the doubt should go to Thomas. "Judge," he told Thomas, "just because we take harassment seriously doesn't mean we take the charges at face value."

The session ended at 10:34 P.M., to reconvene with Thomas the next morning at 10. As Hatch left the hearing room, NPR's Nina Totenberg stopped him.

"Senator, you just saved his ass."

"No, Nina, *he* just saved his ass."

Friends at the EEOC—the very agency Thomas had once headed— telephoned Hatch's office the next morning, Saturday, October 12, in triumph with the "Long Dong Silver" reference. Hatch went into the session armed and angry.

Thomas seemed forceful and in command that morning. He said he had always treated Hill respectfully, mentoring her career as he had mentored his other assistants. Leahy asked the logical question: Then why would Hill do this?

> Thomas: Senator, . . . I have asked myself that question. . . . I have not slept very much in the last two and a half weeks. I have thought unceasingly about this, and my wife simply said, 'Stop torturing yourself.' . . . I do not have the answer.

Hatch again represented Republicans. "Do you think . . . any . . . intelligent male, regardless of race, would use this kind of language to try and start a relationship with an intelligent, attractive woman?" he asked Thomas. Thomas didn't.

Hatch then asked about black male stereotype language.

> Thomas: Senator, the language throughout the history of this country . . . about the sexual prowess of black men, language about the sex organs of black men, and the sizes, etc., that kind of language has been used about black men as long as I have been on the face of this Earth. [Hill's] are charges that play into racist, bigoted stereotypes and these are the kind of charges that are impossible to wash off. . . .
>
> Hatch: There is an interesting case that I found called *Carter v. Sedgwick County, Kansas,* a 1988 case. . . . It is a District Court case within the Tenth Circuit [Court of Appeals]. Do you know which circuit Oklahoma is in?
>
> Thomas: My guess would be the Tenth Circuit. . . .
>
> Hatch: . . . Oklahoma is in the Tenth Circuit. I know because Utah is also.

Hatch read the case's explanatory note: "Black female brought suit against county and county officials, contending she suffered sexual harassment and was unlawfully terminated from her employment with county on the basis of her race and sex."

He then read from the case: "Plaintiff further testified that on one occasion Defendant Brand presented her with a picture of Long Dong Silver—a photo of a black male with an elongated penis." As a professor of law in the Tenth Circuit, Hatch noted, Hill almost certainly was familiar with *Carter v. Sedgwick County* and the reference to Long Dong Silver.

Hatch then turned to the alleged Coke can incident. Holding a copy of *The Exorcist,* he asked if Thomas had read it or seen the movie based on it. Thomas said he had not read the book and only remembered "the scene with the bed flapping" in the film.

Hatch read from page 70: "'Oh, Burk,' sighed Sharon. In a guarded tone, she described an encounter between the Senator and the director. 'Dennings had remarked to him, in passing,' said Sharon, that 'there appeared to be an alien pubic hair floating around in my gin.'"

As Hatch read the passage, and suggested the court case as the source of Hill's other bizarre charge, the hearing room fell dead quiet. A number of reporters nodded knowingly at Hatch. Then the room came alive with a din as it sunk in: Apparently Hatch had found the smoking guns of the Thomas-Hill hearings.

"These two FBI agents told her to be as specific as she could possibly be," he noted, "and yet she never said anything about Long Dong Silver or pubic hair to them. She didn't say it in her . . . four-page statement, which is extensive, single-spaced, four pages. But she said it yesterday."

Toward the end, there was this exchange:

> Hatch: . . . Sexual harassment is ugly, it is unforgivable, it is wrong. It is extremely destructive, especially to women, but to men, too. . . . Describe . . . what it is like to be accused of sexual harassment.
>
> Thomas: . . . The last two and a half weeks have been a living hell. . . . I think it's hurt me and I think it's hurt the country. . . . I will never be able to get my name back . . .
>
> Hatch: Some people have been spreading the rumor that perhaps you are going to withdraw. . . .
>
> Thomas: I would rather die than withdraw. If they are going to kill me, they are going to kill me.

When Anita Hill had finished testifying the previous day, Friday, public opinion seemed strongly in her favor. Thomas's Friday night testimony had begun to turn that around. Then his Saturday in the witness chair put Hill's public persona to rout.

Wittingly or unwittingly, Hill had been an accomplice to a character assassination, not only smearing Thomas but marshaling the ugliest instincts of white racism against him.

Thomas was whisked out of the caucus room at 6:15 P.M. at the end of his exhausting ordeal. He was mobbed by joyous well-wishers who had never lost faith in him—officials from the White House, Justice Department, and EEOC, along with family and personal friends. When Thomas spotted Hatch coming, he broke free and went to him, embracing him with an exuberant bear hug. Virginia Thomas then hugged Hatch.

"You're my hero," added Danforth, an independent-minded Republican like Hatch and the Senate's only ordained minister.

Hatch was exhausted, too. In addition to the grueling hearings, Hatch had responded to more than four hundred media requests for interviews in recent weeks regarding Thomas. Yet concerned about the emotional letdown Thomas would likely feel, he insisted, "I want to take you and Virginia to dinner tonight." Thomas accepted. Jack and Sally Danforth agreed to join them.

Hatch picked up Elaine in Vienna and drove to Morton's of Chicago, an upscale restaurant in Tyson's Corner shopping center, not far from the Hatch or Thomas homes. Because Hatch was a friend of one of the owners and an occasional VIP patron, Morton's kept a special wine cabinet bearing Hatch's name on a brass plate. It was stocked with alcohol-free Martinelli's sparkling cider.

The restaurant was packed with a Saturday-evening crowd. As the Hatches and Thomases waited for the Danforths at their table, another familiar couple came in by total happenstance: Robert and Mary Ellen Bork.

The Borks rushed to them and unabashedly exchanged hugs all around—the man whose Supreme Court bid was destroyed by mob action, the man the mob still hoped to destroy, and the senator who had fought to keep the mob at bay. It was like a dispensation of grace: There were hundreds of fine restaurants in the area, but Bork that night chose Morton's, arriving just when Clarence Thomas needed a lift from the one man in all of Washington who knew exactly how he felt.

Patrons streamed by throughout the evening, offering encouragement. Five young white women from a nearby booth were the first. "We believe everything you said, Judge Thomas." Thomas beamed.

It was a leisurely three-hour meal that passed through the many moods of celebration, decompression, anger, bewilderment, solidarity, and affection. When they rose to leave, other diners throughout the restaurant jumped to their feet spontaneously, giving Thomas a standing ovation. Thomas walked on air out of the restaurant.

Sunday, the last day of hearings, featured panels of witnesses for each side. That night, two liberal committee Democrats—Biden and Leahy—told Hatch they believed Thomas. Two days later, the Senate voted 52-48 to confirm Thomas, with Biden and Leahy among those voting against him. It was one of the closest margins ever for a Supreme Court nominee. Between Thomas's first set of hearings and the Hill-Thomas hearings, he lost an estimated ten votes. Every committee Democrat except DeConcini voted against him. Only two Senate Republicans did so—Jeffords of Vermont and Packwood of Oregon.

Most of the eleven Senate Democrats who voted for Thomas were from the South. The attempt to swamp Thomas with racist sentiment had failed, both because of his eloquent and credible defense—guided by Hatch—and because blacks throughout the South and the nation were outraged at the attempt to destroy him.

"How important was Senator Hatch to my confirmation?" Thomas asked rhetorically in a recent interview. "That's easy. I never would have made it without him. . . . He was the one person on the committee who knew me very well, both professionally and as a friend."

Most polls soon after the hearings showed Americans believed Thomas by a margin of two-to-one (a poll by *U.S. News & World Report* showed three-to-one). Columnist George Will later noted that "to believe that Hill told the truth you must believe that dozens of people, with no common or even apparent motive to lie, did so. . . . Thomas's ordeal was a manifestation of the politics of character assassination."

But memories are short, and the incident took on a life of its own, becoming a generalized issue of men versus women. A clever slogan was coined—"They just don't get it"—and feminist organizations boasted that the Hill case, within a year, was filling their coffers with millions of dollars. The media, with rare exception, treated Hill with velvet gloves. Thomas was at a disadvantage. As a sitting justice he felt it inappropriate to discuss the situation further or defend himself publicly. Hill was meanwhile wined and dined by feminists all over the country. Although no new facts emerged, by October 1992, the first anniversary of the hearings, the drumbeat of propaganda had paid off: A poll for *U.S. News & World Report* showed Thomas and Hill tied in credibility, a Gallup Poll gave Hill a four-point lead, and the *Wall Street Journal* showed her ten points ahead of Thomas.

Hill returned to the University of Oklahoma as feminism's new icon, commanding fees of up to $12,000 for speeches on legal issues, including women's rights, that exploited her fame while carefully avoiding specifics from the hearings. She refused media requests for interviews and also refused to be interviewed for this book.

Thomas—determined to prove himself—hit the court running, writing twenty-two opinions during his first term and voting with fellow conservative Antonin Scalia 87 percent of the time. In comparison, David Souter wrote twelve opinions during his first year. Thomas participated in a press reception a month after his confirmation in 1991, and then, like Hill, adopted a blanket policy against media interviews. He made an exception for this book, however, over dinner in the summer of 1993, and again in a wide-ranging interview late that year.

"No Klansman ever did anything that bad to me," he says of the hearing. "I lived forty-three years before then. . . . That surreal moment had nothing to do with my real life. I really don't look back on it." He emphasized: "I drew a line in the sand of time and moved forward. . . . The next forty-three years will be my answer to what happened."

Thomas's view of the world late in 1993 was coming from conservative sources: the *Washington Times* and talk-show host Rush Limbaugh, whose radio tapes he listened to while exercising several times a week at a gym. Baffled by liberal bias in the mainstream media, he refused to read the *Washington Post* or *New York Times*. "They can say absolutely anything they want about me. I will never read them again to see it. I have no desire for accolades. . . . Maybe some generation down the line a hundred years from now will believe I did something worth emulating. That will be reward enough."

Reflecting back, Thomas says, "I never wanted to be on the Supreme Court before President Bush came to me. In fact, I never wanted to be a judge before I became one. Ideally, I'd like to be a truck driver or have a small business." Once on the bench, however, "I found that I loved it. I'm not a flamboyant person, and being a judge suited my personality. It's a monastic life, and I like that. It's hard work but a wonderful job. You feel that the people of the country have entrusted something special to you. . . . It's a secular but a sacred trust."

Thomas laughs easily and often now, including at himself. It is a trademark, two-pitched laugh ("uh-HUH, uh-HUH, uh-HUH"), accented on the second syllable. During dinner, Thomas had already devoured a plate full of fresh fruit when someone suggested he be brought more watermelon. "Oh no, don't do that," he said in mock alarm. "We don't want any of these black stereotypes."

He and Virginia, an aide to a Republican congressman, live in seclusion in a semirural area of Fairfax County, Virginia, an hour's drive from Capitol Hill. "Life is not bad—in fact, it's a wonderful life," says Thomas. "If it got any better I think I'd be doing something illegal."

When Thomas went to the White House to take the federal oath of office in mid-October 1991, the crowd gathered nearby was so great that Hatch and his aides parked and walked the last several blocks. As they neared the iron gates, a woman tried to spit on Hatch.

Bush thanked Hatch for helping Thomas through to confirmation and warmly welcomed Clarence, Virginia, and Jamal Thomas, special guests, and 150 friends from Pin Point, Georgia. His mother, Leola, was recuperating at a nearby hospital from the stress of recent days. Two weeks later, on November 1, 1991, Thomas took his seat on the Supreme Court. Hatch, Dole, Specter, and Danforth attended the short ceremony.

"A good, kind, gentle human being was destroyed, and that person came back to life," Danforth told an interviewer. "I am convinced that when a human being is destroyed and comes back to life, that is an act of God."

"How so?" he was asked.

Danforth reflected for a long moment. "I believe in Easter."

27

BCCI and Other Trials

F OR HATCH, THE PERSONAL COST of defending Clarence Thomas was about to pale in comparison to the cost of defending a shadowy financial institution called the Bank of Credit and Commerce International (BCCI).

But first it was payback time for helping Thomas.

Hatch was invited to speak at the University of Chicago in January 1992, three months after the Thomas-Hill hearings. He walked into the law school past placards from a warm-up rally reading "Down the Hatch" and "We Believe Anita."

Some five hundred students jammed the auditorium for Hatch's lecture on civil rights legislation. When he was introduced, about fifty students – apparently from the sponsoring Federalist Society, a conservative legal group–stood and applauded. But fifty others booed and hissed with gusto.

As Hatch began to speak, protestors interrupted repeatedly. Trying to ignore them, he plowed on, paying tribute to the university's intellectual contributions while students shouted "Hatch, you're a pig!" and "Was that in *The Exorcist?*" Hatch gamely maintained his composure, occasionally answering the taunts with a joke or self-deprecating comment.

"You gave Anita Hill an unfair trial," yelled one student in front.

"Young woman," answered the senator coolly, "you must not be a very good law student if you don't know the difference between a congressional hearing and a trial."

Near the end of his remarks, members of the audience began to stamp in unison, trying to drown Hatch out. They failed but laughed derisively at his conclusion—that the family was the best transmitter of traditional moral values.

Meanwhile, some University of Utah professors and students bought a page in the University of Oklahoma's school paper, apologizing for Hatch. However, the University of Utah's black student editor changed the ad's language to support Hatch and ran it full page in the student *Chronicle*.

Anti-Hatch letters appeared in Utah papers for weeks. Most Utahns, however, were supportive. Polled a month after the hearings, 56 percent rated Hatch's role "excellent" or "good." Another 18 percent said "fair." Only 19 percent said "poor." Asked who was telling the truth, 48 percent said Thomas and 19 percent said Hill. Utah women believed Thomas two-to-one.

The entire all-male Judiciary Committee was blamed for not taking Hill's charges seriously enough soon enough. But feminist anger was directed especially at three Republicans: Simpson, Specter, and Hatch.

Simpson had gone too far during the hearings by referring to Hill's "proclivities"—widely considered code for "lesbianism," though he did not mean it that way. Simpson said many Oklahomans who knew Hill warned him to watch out for her, "but nobody has got the guts to say that because it gets all tangled up in this sexual harassment crap." Simpson later apologized publicly. Specter was blasted for his "ruthless" interrogation, but in fact he had failed to follow up on several key points. For instance, he should have insisted on reviewing records at a hospital that Hill claimed she entered for stress related to Thomas's alleged harassment. If the records existed, Hill's critics believed, her entourage would have introduced them during the hearings.

Feminists were angry at Hatch both for leading Thomas safely through a minefield and for providing sources for Hill's Coke can and Long Dong Silver stories. *Glamour* published "Men of the Moment: Citations and Awards for Notable Knavery and Bravery." Awards included: Clarence Thomas ("there is no Justice"), and Hatch, Specter, and Simpson ("hatchet men of the year").

Specter's reelection was jeopardized. In November 1992, a woman who had decided to run because of the hearings pressed him hard. Specter noted that his questioning of Hill was "legally correct" but "politically unwise," lamented the difficult job of "trying to find out who was telling the truth on an incident 10 years ago," and called on his own record of supporting liberalized abortion. He barely won, 51-49 percent.

Hatch's next election was in 1994, Simpson's in 1996.

Feminist anger at Hatch was not unusual but it was ironic. The record shows that Hatch did not ask Hill a single question, yet the impression that he tormented Hill was spread far and wide by feminists, allied liberal activists, and the media.

Hatch was, in reality, a leading sponsor of legislation to help women. In 1992 alone he sponsored a bill to protect women from ineffective or unscrupulous fertility procedures, cosponsored a bill requiring accurate mammography regulations and another to establish state cancer registries and require the National Cancer Institute to investigate factors contributing to breast cancer, and helped pass a bill providing apprenticeship programs for women in nontraditional occupations. All four bills became law with Bush's signature.

Perhaps most tellingly, Hatch bucked a trend on Capitol Hill by quietly setting an example of equality on his own staff. A Gannett News Service study of 11,500 congressional staffers found "a gender pay gap" between "highly paid men who hold most of the power, and lower-paid women whose careers can be stunted by an institutional glass ceiling."

The *Salt Lake Tribune* ran the article with a sidebar: "On Average, Hatch Pays Women More Than Men"—the only member of Utah's congressional delegation to do so. Hatch's staff consisted of twenty-six women paid an average of $30,300, and fourteen men, paid an average of $29,400.

While feminists and other liberal activists were angry at Hatch, average citizens—especially blacks, who comprised more than two-thirds of Washington's population—thanked him everywhere he went for helping Thomas. Some knowledgeable blacks had also come to appreciate that Hatch genuinely wanted to help them. He had long been a foe of racial-quota approaches to equality but was a forceful champion of job training programs and a youth-opportunity wage differential for first-time workers.

Hatch's friends in the black community included one of the city's little giants, Smallwood Williams, bishop of the Bible Way Church. Williams looked like a black Friar Tuck—short, stout, and bald. During the late 1980s, Hatch attended a service with a friend, Charles Coffer, a tall, handsome Capitol Hill policeman who belonged to Williams's church. Williams insisted that Hatch sit next to him in a high-backed chair facing the congregation and called on him for an impromptu address. Hatch returned occasionally and arranged for Williams to serve as Senate chaplain for a day.

Just days before Bush nominated Clarence Thomas to the Supreme Court, Bishop Williams died at age eighty-two. When his funeral was held, Hatch attended with Coffer.

Thirty-five hundred parishioners and VIP guests crammed the church and thousands of other mourners spilled into New Jersey Avenue and nearby streets.

Midway through the service, the conducting minister called for remarks from Eleanor Holmes Norton, the district's nonvoting member of Congress, then Jesse Jackson, who gave a fiery discourse with strong political overtones. Next the officiator, with no advance warning, announced that "one of the bishop's dear friends"—Hatch—would address them. Hatch eulogized Bishop Williams and gave a short sermon on the resurrection, quoting several scriptures from the Bible. As Hatch left the stand, Jesse Jackson, seated among perhaps two hundred other ministers, jumped up and grabbed his hand. "Senator," said Jackson, himself one of the country's premier orators, "you're a preacher!"

The support of average citizens, however, did not insulate Hatch from political vengeance. Liberals coupled his prominent role in the Hill-Thomas hearings with a speech of seemingly little importance in February 1990 about the Bank of Credit and Commerce International. His impeccable reputation for personal integrity was suddenly in free-fall.

Early in 1990, BCCI was known as a legitimate bank with offices in more than seventy countries. It was represented in Washington by superlawyer Clark Clifford—an advisor to every Democratic President since Franklin D. Roosevelt—and Robert Altman. Altman and Clifford were also top executives of First American Bankshares, Inc., which they did not know was secretly and illegally owned by BCCI. Only later would BCCI become a synonym for colossal financial fraud.

Hatch had become involved in December 1989 when several lawyers, including two former Justice Department officials and Altman, asked for his help. The Hatches had gotten to know Altman and his wife Lynda Carter ("Wonder Woman") socially, and that same December were among guests at a dinner party at the Altmans' $6 million Potomac estate.

Meeting in Hatch's office, the attorneys told him that BCCI was being prosecuted by the Justice Department in Tampa, Florida, for isolated incidents of money laundering by third-tier employees. The wrongdoing did not involve senior management, they assured Hatch, and the problems had been rectified. They said the bank was being singled out for harsh treatment because it was owned by Arabs. In January 1990, BCCI plea-bargained with the Justice Department, agreeing to pay a fifteen-million-dollar fine—three times higher than any previous penalty for money laundering. But several members of Congress, believing the punishment too mild, publicly attacked the Bush administration.

Altman and the other bank lawyers again met with Hatch, complaining that BCCI was being discriminated against. Hatch contacted top officials at the Justice Department, including the Attorney General's chief of staff, who assured him that the congressional criticism was unwarranted and encouraged Hatch's defense of the department's position.

Altman furnished Hatch a written explanation of the case, which became the basic draft for a Senate speech Hatch delivered on February 22, 1990, defending the Justice Department's settlement with BCCI. "The case arose from the conduct of a small number of BCCI's more than 14,000 employees," Hatch told his colleagues in a speech that covered more than a full page in the *Congressional Record*.

"Do not misunderstand me," said Hatch. "Money laundering is a serious crime and the BCCI case was an important prosecution," but "the senior management and board of directors of BCCI reacted responsibly and properly" when the situation became known.

Thus began the darkest chapter in Hatch's career. His political enemies quickly jumped on this opening. He had been badly misled and would rue the day he first heard of BCCI. Over the next year and a half, the BCCI case came into focus. Largely Arab-owned but headquartered in Luxembourg, it was alleged that the bank had systematically served terrorists and drug dealers along with corporate clients, made loans totaling in the billions to insiders, and bilked thousands of depositors overseas. Its operations, according to some banking experts, constituted the largest financial fraud in history.

In July 1991, regulators in seven countries shut down bank offices. The following December, BCCI pled guilty to fraud and racketeering charges in the United States and agreed to forfeit all U.S. holdings—$550 million—to the federal government. The forfeiture included First American Bankshares, Inc.

Altman and Clifford were now the targets of state and federal criminal investigations. Hatch's speech dragged him into the same spotlight, and the national media refused to accept Hatch's benign explanation that he was simply trying to help a friend and support the initial Justice Department settlement. His speech came long before he or most other citizens knew of the widespread BCCI corruption, and his support brought him no personal profit.

Two of Hatch's international connections lent impetus to the impression that he was not telling the full story: a relationship with a man named Mohammed Hammoud and another with a Mormon convert from Lebanon named Monzer Hourani.

Hammoud was a Shiite Moslem who claimed he could help win the release of American hostages in Lebanon. Between 1982 and 1989, Hatch met periodically and briefly with Hammoud to pursue that possibility—behavior consistent with both his penchant for going where angels feared to tread and his role in other covert U.S. activities abroad.

Michael Pillsbury had enlisted Hatch's help in restoring his security clearances, which finally occurred in 1992. He joined Hatch for a meeting with Hammoud in the senator's office in June 1989. Pillsbury had worked for Hatch and other GOP senators periodically and was still an occasional foreign policy consultant to Hatch, on a token retainer of $250 a month. Pillsbury was also writing a book for Hammoud. At the end of the June meeting, Hammoud mentioned that an Arab bank was being discriminated against in the United States. Hatch suggested Hammoud have the bank's lawyers get him more information. Hammoud did not name the bank, and Hatch does not recall speaking with him again.

The other events followed: Altman's appeal for help in December 1989, and Hatch's supportive speech in February 1990. The first time Hatch learned that Hammond had anything to do with BCCI was in May when he read an investigative article in *Regardie's,* a business magazine, identifying Hammoud as a resident of Lebanon with a 5-10 percent stake in First American and 3.56 percent share of BCCI. The article also listed other key figures owning parts of both BCCI and First American.

Hammoud was later accused by U.S. authorities of being a front man for BCCI, helping to hide the bank's involvement in sensitive transactions. Conveniently, Hammoud reportedly died under highly suspicious circumstances while undergoing an endoscopy by his doctor in Geneva in the same month the *Regardie's* article appeared. But life insurance companies refused to pay his family because the corpse was reportedly four inches shorter than the height recorded at Hammoud's last medical exam.

Monzer Hourani was an Arab American living in Houston. In 1985, a Mormon mission president in Houston had asked Hatch to befriend Hourani, one of the church's relatively few Arab converts, and this quasi-ecclesiastical responsibility had grown into a friendship. Hatch often telephoned Hourani, a large, friendly man in his forties, at his Houston home to remind him to attend church services. Hourani contributed to Hatch's reelection campaign in 1988 and the two corresponded, infrequently but with warmth. Hourani also attempted to help with the hostages.

In 1988, with Ethics Committee clearance, Hatch entered into a trust agreement whereby Hourani invested $10,000 for Hatch in a small, low-income condominium in Houston. As the extent of the BCCI scandal unfolded, a *Deseret News* reporter, unbeknownst to Hatch, had the property appraised in 1992 to see if its value had ballooned suspiciously, perhaps as a gift for Hatch's favors to BCCI. Instead, the condo's value had actually decreased to $8,000.

In early 1990, Hourani told Hatch that the savings and loan crisis in Texas was drying up financing for his construction projects. Hatch, without Hourani's knowledge, telephoned BCCI president Swaleh Naqvi in Europe on March 22.

Only four days earlier and a month after his speech defending BCCI, Hatch had become an original cosponsor of an anti-money laundering bill introduced by Democrat John Kerry of Massachusetts. BCCI, as it turned out, had its own compelling reasons for opposing the measure.

Hatch explained Hourani's plight to Naqvi and suggested Naqvi might wish to speak to Hourani about the potential benefits of doing business with a fellow Arab in the United States. At that point, Hatch had every reason to believe that the bank had corrected its problems and was suffering from discrimination.

The call was brief. Hatch did not detail Hourani's projects—he didn't even know what they were. Contrary to later press reports, he also did not ask for a loan or gift to Hourani. Naqvi was noncommittal, but Hatch told Hourani of the call, and Hourani mailed a proposal to the bank. Hatch never saw the proposal nor knew its specific purpose. Naqvi never answered Hourani.

The story might have ended there, except for another financial black hole: the savings and loan crisis, which cost U.S. taxpayers hundreds of billions as Washington took control of hundreds of failed institutions and paid off insured depositors.

During 1991, Senator Metzenbaum began a series of Judiciary Committee hearings on the S&Ls. Only institutions with strong Republican ties were investigated, however, leading to charges that Metzenbaum was trying to blame Republicans for the S&L debacle. Senate Republican leader Dole and others cried foul, and after weeks of debate, Metzenbaum agreed to consider a review of CenTrust Savings Bank of Miami, an institution with strong Democratic ties. Its failure was expected to cost taxpayers more than $2 billion. Metzenbaum suggested that Hatch do the initial inquiry, and Hatch's staff began the investigation.

In August 1991, Hatch released a fifty-seven-page report, with thirty-seven pages of appendices, calling for a more formal investigation of the outrageous spending of its chairman, David Paul, and why federal regulators had been unable to stop the mismanagement that led to the institution's failure.

The report highlighted two little-known facts: (1) BCCI had an ownership role in CenTrust and played a key role in covering up its financial problems, and (2) CenTrust's political action committee had contributed more than $328,000 to political candidates, mostly Democrats. Paul had served as honorary chairman of the Majority Trust, the former fund-raising arm of the Democratic Senatorial Campaign Committee. In 1987 and 1988 the committee was headed by Senator John Kerry.

Hatch's report was the first to establish BCCI's direct involvement in CenTrust's operations. It detailed a relationship between the bank and Saudi investor Ghaith Pharaon, who owned 28 percent of CenTrust and also owned substantial stock in BCCI. Hatch's report revealed that BCCI had illegally acquired ownership or control of at least 5 percent of CenTrust's voting shares.

David Paul's spending was a scandal in itself. From 1984 to 1989, Paul was paid $16 million in salary, bonuses, and dividends. The bank also lent him $6.1 million in mortgages to purchase and renovate a home on LaGorce Island near Miami—half of it extended from November 1988 to March 1989 while CenTrust was simultaneously losing $64 million. In January 1988, Paul purchased a Rubens painting for $13.2 million, buried the expense in a report for "furniture and fixtures," and hung the art in his personal residence in Miami Beach.

CenTrust, in fact, had spent $30 million on artwork by June 1989, along with $85,000 on Baccarat crystal for the bank's executive dining room, $35,000 on merchandise from Tiffany and Co., $22,000 on linens from Paris, and $232,000 on a forty-foot sailboat, the *Bodacious,* purchased by a 99 percent owned subsidiary.

A CenTrust corporate jet, kept at a Miami hangar for $301,000 *per month,* provided private transportation to a number of Democratic senators. Most of the trips were apparently related to fund-raising for the Democratic Senatorial Campaign Committee, which reimbursed the S&L for flight costs only at first-class airline rates.

On December 3, 1988, Hatch's report showed Paul threw a dinner party at his home on LaGorce Island that came to be known as the "French chefs' dinner." Initially charged to the bank, the dinner for fifty-six invited guests cost $122,726, including $36,600 in airfare and other fees to fly six chefs from Paris to Florida. The guest list included Ghaith Pharaon and two U.S. senators—John Kerry, ironically investigating BCCI at the time, and Wyche Fowler of Georgia.

Banking regulators tried to rein Paul in as CenTrust drowned in red ink. Instead of complying, he threatened them with political pressure, invoking the names of prominent Democrats, including U.S. senators. In addition to the jet, Paul let several Democratic senators make personal or fund-raising use of his ninety-foot yacht, the *Grand Cru.* Estimated operating costs on the $7 million yacht, technically owned by another Paul subsidiary, were between $3,000 and $6,000 for an eight-hour day, plus gas.

Hatch's report further documented that one of the senators hired a former CenTrust attorney, Steve Josias, for a temporary post in his office. The report said Josias used his position to force meetings with federal regulators about their CenTrust investigations, behavior that may have violated Senate ethics rules.

Because of the report's potentially embarrassing revelations, Hatch personally gave each senator it mentioned a prerelease copy of the portions in which they were named. Outrage exploded, and the press attacked Hatch's report as blatantly partisan. A *Wall Street Journal* headline, for example, said: "Hatch Adds Partisan Spice to BCCI Stew, Attempting to Link Democrats to Scandal."

No one, however, challenged the report's accuracy. The Senate Ethics Committee spent fourteen months probing ties between five senators and conservative Republican S&L owner Charles Keating. But neither the mainstream media nor Democrats, who controlled the Senate, showed any interest in following up in any way on the CenTrust report. There were no questions about the relationship between any member of Congress and CenTrust and no questions about why Congress had been unwilling to give CenTrust the same attention as it had given BCCI. In fact, Metzenbaum didn't even bother to answer Hatch's written request to the antitrust subcommittee to hold hearings on the report.

The media industry was struggling with tight budgets at the time of BCCI and CenTrust. Relatively few newspapers or TV stations were willing to devote the resources necessary to do investigative reporting on important subjects such as illegal toxic waste dumps, urban decay, or the S&L crisis. Such stories, at any rate, were less likely to offer the instant gratification of digging up dirt on public figures.

Orrin Hatch, perennially in disfavor with the liberal establishment, was an ideal target. He was powerful, conservative, and effective. His role in the Thomas-Hill hearings provided frequent fodder for pundits and talk-show hosts. Moreover, sources in Congress were beginning to leak false information about Hatch's relationship to BCCI to favored reporters. Each new revelation by a major newspaper or TV network, based on fact or not, was sent nationwide by the wire services and was followed by an obligatory round of stories in the Utah media, scarring Hatch's reputation.

In November and December 1991, major articles linking Hatch with the BCCI scandal appeared in the *Wall Street Journal,* the *New York Times,* and the *Los Angeles Times,* among others. On November 22, Tom Brokaw, anchoring NBC Nightly News, announced the lead story: "BCCI . . . is already the biggest banking scandal of the decade. . . . Tonight, a new name,

Senator Orrin Hatch, a Utah Republican, who played such a prominent role in the Clarence Thomas hearing. What is his connection?"

NBC failed to explain any connection between BCCI and the Thomas-Hill hearings, but the story ended with a bombshell: Law enforcement officials were investigating Hatch and "asking former bank insiders" about him.

Hatch, who saw the newscast, immediately called Attorney General William Barr to offer his cooperation if the story were true. A day later, the Justice Department notified Hatch he was not under investigation. But NBC refused to correct its false statement, which the rest of the media immediately picked up.

Stories about Hatch and BCCI became routine, even though few provided new information. False rumors recycled endlessly: Hatch had demanded a loan for Hourani; Hatch was BCCI's man in Washington; Hatch was Hammoud's close personal friend; Hatch had benefitted personally from the BCCI speech; Hatch had blocked, instead of cosponsored, Senator Kerry's money-laundering bill; and Hatch was under investigation by the Justice Department. All were untrue.

Hatch demonstrated an adage: the only way for a reporter to look on a politician is down. Perhaps understandably, he began to see a conspiracy to smear him.

In late November 1991, a reporter for a national weekly news magazine telephoned Hatch and began the conversation: "Senator, I am ashamed of my profession." The reporter then explained he had to follow up on the NBC report, even though he and other journalists knew it was not true.

"Do you know why you are under attack?" asked the reporter.

"I don't have the slightest idea," said Hatch.

"You're being paid back for Anita Hill and for your CenTrust report."

A Democratic senator told Hatch that a reporter for Roll Call, a biweekly tabloid that blanketed Capitol Hill, had boasted that he and his media friends were going to "get" Hatch. Apparently unaware of the two senators' friendship, the reporter said he would sit on his stories until Hatch's next reelection campaign in 1994. The reporter wrote numerous stories about Hatch and BCCI. When interviewed directly for this book, the reporter denied making such a threat. "I can only guess that Senator Hatch was referring to a discussion at a fund-raiser, which was about an issue unrelated to him," he said.

In the summer of 1992, the attacks stepped up. Senator Kerry, as chairman of the Senate Subcommittee on Terrorism, Narcotics, and International Operations, was nearing completion of his lengthy investigation of BCCI's U.S. activities and the government's handling of the case. Operating in Ted Kennedy's long shadow, the junior senator from Massachusetts was anxious to make a name for himself. His investigation, including repeated condemnation of the Bush administration, was bringing positive press coverage, earning him a reputation as one member of Congress willing to expose criminal activities of BCCI.

Ironically, Kerry had surfaced as a key player in Hatch's systematically ignored CenTrust report. Now, BCCI—for which there was an insatiable media appetite—apparently was the weapon of choice to get even with Hatch.

One Democrat unpersuaded by the BCCI allegations against Hatch was Kerry's fellow Bay State senator, Ted Kennedy. "It absolutely would be inconsistent with everything I know about his public and personal morality," said Kennedy.

"We're living in a world where, tragically, anything that's claimed is believed," he added. ". . . My father gave me very good advice: 'Teddy, don't bet on what a person says he's going to do or what he is about— bet on what you *believe* he is about. And you'll be more right than wrong.' I believe in Orrin."

Hatch also believed in Kennedy, and their friendship continued to grow, even during the tumultuous Clarence Thomas saga, when Hatch, as he often did, was accusing Kennedy of demagoguery. Hatch continued, gently but persistently, to press Kennedy to change his personal habits, and Kennedy privately assured Hatch his advice was not falling on deaf ears.

Then, in October 1991, just ten days after the Senate confirmed Thomas, Kennedy delivered a remarkable address at Harvard's Institute of Politics. It was the institute's twenty-fifth anniversary, and after extolling the institute's achievements and addressing current issues, Kennedy offered an emotional *mea culpa*.

> I am painfully aware that the criticism directed at me in recent months involves far more than honest disagreement with my positions. . . . It also involves the disappointment of friends and many others who rely on me to fight the good fight. To them I say: I recognize my shortcomings—the faults in the conduct of my private life. I realize that I alone am responsible for them, and I am the one who must confront them. Today, more than ever before, I believe that each of us as individuals must not only struggle to make a better world, but to make ourselves better too.

Kennedy said, "I have been given many gifts," including "extraordinary parents" and "extraordinary brothers and sisters—and their children and my own." Poignantly, he acknowledged, "Not least, unlike my brothers, I have been given length of years and time. And as I approach my 60th birthday, I am determined to give all that I have to advance the causes for which I have stood for almost a third of a century."

Kennedy's address came after polls showed him slipping in Massachusetts and six weeks before Willy Smith came to trial in Florida for rape. Some suggested that his speech was intended to inoculate him against the negative publicity likely to accompany the trial. But Kennedy's public declaration was in line with his personal assurances to Hatch. "Ted really seems intent on turning his life around," wrote Hatch privately. "I think he's going to prove the cynics wrong."

On December 6, Kennedy, having shed perhaps twenty pounds and appearing composed and confident, testified in the nationally televised trial in West Palm Beach. He expressed regret for waking up the two young men and taking them to Au Bar: "I wish I'd gone for a long walk on the beach instead."

There was no doubt Smith and Patricia Bowman had sex: a DNA match showed Smith's semen in her body and on her clothing. But had she consented? The jury felt the evidence raised a reasonable doubt and found Smith not guilty.

In February 1992, columnist Jack Anderson noted Kennedy had lost another thirty pounds—"always a precursor of a Kennedy comeback"—and was acting differently in other ways.

"Maybe it's because he has been caught rehearsing speeches in the Senate cloak room," wrote Anderson. "Maybe it's all those bills of his suddenly floating around the Capitol. Or maybe it's just the sight of him showing up on time for committee meetings. But all the signs are there that Capitol Hill is witnessing the resurrection of Ted Kennedy. He's back from the ashes."

Unlike many other comebacks, a Democratic leader said this one was "serious." Wrote Anderson: "Senators and White House advisors alike are asking: What the heck has happened to Ted?"

The answer came the following month. Hatch was speaking at a Republican fund-raiser in California in March when an aide sent word that Kennedy had "good news" and wanted him to call. Hatch phoned Kennedy's office and a secretary patched him through to Kennedy's home in McLean.

"Orrin," Kennedy explained, with a new lilt in his voice, "you're one of my best friends, so I wanted you to know that in a few hours we're going to announce that I'm going to get married again."

"Theodoe!" yelled Hatch. "That's wonderful! Who's the lucky lady?"

"Her name is Victoria Reggie. I've known her a long time and she is just wonderful. She has two beautiful children I also love very much."

Reggie was thirty-eight, a striking brunette; her two children were nine-year-old Curran and six-year-old Caroline. She and Kennedy had been dating since the previous June, though the two families had been friends for many years. Reggie was of Lebanese American ancestry, the daughter of a prominent politician and retired judge who had run the presidential campaigns of John, Robert, and Ted Kennedy in his home state of Louisiana. A high school valedictorian, Reggie had graduated summa cum laude from Tulane Law School and was a partner in a Washington law firm.

The following week, during a committee markup on a bill, Kennedy leaned over to Hatch.

"Orrin, you're making headway with me. I'm really trying to do the right things."

"I know you are, Ted, and I'm proud of you." Kennedy's physical appearance was much improved over previous months. He looked relaxed and, from all evidence, was no longer drinking to excess. "I must admit I am upset about one thing, though, Theodoe," added Hatch.

"What's that?"

"You didn't bring your fiancée in for my bishop's interview with her before popping the question."

Kennedy laughed.

"What does your family think of the marriage?" asked Hatch.

"My family is pleased, and my friends think I need a good lawyer. By marrying Victoria, I'll be satisfying both concerns!"

When Hatch met Victoria, his enthusiasm increased: "Ted seems to genuinely love her, and she certainly seems to love him. They are very good together."

They were married in Kennedy's home July 3 with only close relatives as guests. "I love Ted with all my heart, and I look forward to spending the rest of our lives together," said the bride in a statement released to the press.

Kennedy gave Victoria one of his paintings, a daffodil scene, as a gift. Guests received reproductions, inscribed with lines from Wordsworth:

> And then my heart with pleasure fills,
> And dances with the daffodils

The next June, Hatch would tell Vicki sincerely, "You have been so good for Ted. He's like a new man. I really love you for what you're doing for him."

Everyone noticed the changes. Kennedy seemed to mellow in the new marriage, the raw edge of recklessness gone. And Victoria good-naturedly supported his innocent indulgences, including Ted's annual

Christmas skit. In 1993, Kennedy pranced on stage dressed as Barney the purple dinosaur, with Victoria gamely at his side wearing a yellow braided wig over her dark hair.

The audience roared with laughter. "They don't call me tyrannosaurus sex for nothing," growled Kennedy in his best dinosaurese. Kennedy had changed. But not all *that* much.

Family milestones were also facing the Hatches. During the last week in May, Orrin and Elaine were in Utah for an annual seniors conference he had begun in 1987, to address issues facing older citizens. The next day, Orrin took his father fishing at Strawberry Reservoir. Almost immediately Jesse caught a two-pound cutthroat trout. Then Orrin landed a two-pound rainbow trout.

They were skunked the next several hours, however, and at about 1:30 P.M., Jesse, now eighty-seven, looked up at Orrin and said, "I'm tired. I want to go home."

"I never thought I'd see the day when Dad got tired of fishing," wrote Hatch. "It just about broke my heart."

In June, Hatch returned to Utah, concerned over Jesse's deteriorating health. "Dad had a very rough time getting out of his rocking chair," he wrote. Jesse had been falling a great deal; and as Orrin walked down the street with him, Jesse kept stumbling because "the upper trunk of his body kept falling forward."

Helen, eighty-six, was small and frail. Despite a mild stroke some years earlier, she had refused outside help. "I don't want independence taken from me," she told Hatch and his sisters. But when Jesse fell, she couldn't get him up by herself.

"I love them both so much and anguish over not being able to be there more often to help," wrote Hatch in a private memo. "I told Dad before I left 'I love you.' He said, 'I love you too.'"

Jesse had Pick's disease, a series of mini-strokes that attacked his brain. That summer he inexorably lost memory. Three of Hatch's sisters lived in Utah and intensified their care, and Hatch hired a neighbor to come in regularly.

Hatch paid tribute to Jesse in a Father's Day feature in the *Washington Times:* "My father was not a vocal man. His hard-working hands showed me more than words could ever do. He taught me a trade. We worked side by side. . . . His pride in his work rubbed off on me. He taught me the value of doing a good job. He never once complained about pain, sacrifice, or anything."

Jesse was dying of pneumonia when Hatch returned to Utah the first week in August. At his father's hospital bed, Hatch received an urgent call from his Washington office: Senator Kerry was trying to subpoena

Michael Pillsbury to discuss his knowledge of BCCI and Hatch's connection to it, and to get documents dating from Pillsbury's employment with Hatch.

The Ethics Committee, comprised equally of Democrats and Republicans and with clearly established procedures, was the Senate's established forum to investigate individual senators as the need arose. But in a virtually unprecedented move, Kerry was bypassing the Ethics Committee and using his own panel to go after Hatch, without even notifying the targeted senator.

Kerry made no effort to talk directly to Hatch, nor did Kerry's staff contact Hatch's staff. Instead, they immediately informed the press of Kerry's inquiry—producing yet another round of articles about Hatch and BCCI. But several senators from both parties insisted that Kerry turn over any information about Hatch's conduct to the Ethics Committee, forcing Kerry to back off.

The damage had already been done. The media bombarded Hatch with calls at his Utah condominium and even at the hospital. He recorded that some even accused him of hiding in the state and floating a false story about his father's illness.

Except for an occasional few hours of sleep, Hatch spent four days and nights with his father who was slipping in and out of consciousness. Helen sat at Jesse's side, holding his hand. Often he squeezed hers in return. They had been married sixty-nine years and had endured the Depression, the deaths of four children, and a life of hard work that had never been more than modestly comfortable. They counted their treasure in their five surviving children, thirty-four grandchildren, seventy-three great-grandchildren, and two great great-grandchildren.

At 3 A.M. on August 6, 1992, surrounded by Helen, his son, and his daughters, Jesse slipped peacefully away.

Many former Pittsburghers, along with servicemen and Mormon missionaries who had found a haven at the Hatches, attended Jesse's funeral two days later. Hatch gave the family tribute—"the most difficult assignment in my lifetime of difficult assignments"—and Vernon "Deacon" Law, the once-great Pittsburgh Pirates pitcher and Jesse's friend, also spoke. Jesse had just one flaw, Law quipped. He used to break the Sabbath by watching Law pitch on Sunday.

Helen was stoic through it all, telling Orrin, "I'll cry when I'm alone." Helen had perfect faith that their temple-sealed marriage would unite them for eternity, that it was only a matter of time before she would be with Jesse again.

Hatch's friends, especially Kennedy and retired senator Jake Garn, were supportive. Kennedy telephoned as soon as he learned that Jesse's death was imminent. Flowers came, and a warm note from Victoria:

"Teddy and I were talking last night and hurting for you during this time. Teddy was reminiscing about his own father, to whom he was so close, and was expressing to me how deeply he felt his loss and how much he understood what you are going through. . . . Please know that you are in our thoughts and prayers."

Among the letters of condolence that poured into Helen's house was one from the United Brotherhood of Carpenters and Joiners of America, Local No. 33L, in Pittsburgh. "[Jesse's] contributions to our organization as a member and as its president for many years have been and always will be greatly appreciated," it said. "Few men of his caliber come through and touch us in our lifetime."

And she cherished a letter from Peter Roff, a student who had come to Helen's door many years ago in Pittsburgh to answer an ad that offered a room for rent—the remodeled chicken coop after Orrin and Elaine moved out. Seeing a painting of Christ on a wall, he said, "One thing I should tell you, Mrs. Hatch, is that I'm a Jew."

"Heavens," answered Helen, "that makes no difference at all to us, just as long as you pay your rent and don't have young ladies in—which is what we'd expect of anyone else."

Roff had married as a student and the couple continued to rent from the Hatches. Now a letter came from his wife in Brooklyn:

> [Jesse's] passing was a deep sadness for us for which we still grieve. We often think that you and he were our second parents for us when we were starting out. Mr. Hatch was a wonderful role model for Peter, kind, patient, gentle, honest and religious. He always walked in God's way. Always a talent to work with his hands. He was a builder of houses and of people. Peter learned these fine qualities which . . . served him well as a rabbi, so you see Mr. Hatch's light was passed not only to his family . . . but also to all those many people his life touched.

Ted Kennedy came by Hatch's office to share memories of his own parents and how he had come to grips with mortality in his family. After Kennedy's visit, Hatch wrote,

> He is very kind this way and I really appreciated it. Politics aside, he has done this throughout his Senate career, and this is one reason why he is fairly well respected and liked.
>
> He knows I don't agree with him and I know he doesn't agree with me, but we have tried to develop a friendship that transcends politics and occasionally helps politics to transcend partisanship.

For Hatch, already burdened with sorrow, Capitol Hill offered mostly battering, not consolation. His integrity was under attack almost daily in the press. Death was part of God's plan, but the dismantling of his reputation was ordained by men and the media.

"Lawmaker's Defense of B.C.C.I. Went Beyond Speech in Senate," asserted the *New York Times* in a front-page story on August 26. An AP rewrite of the *Times* piece ran in the *Washington Post* under the headline: "Hatch Is Said To Play Wider Role on BCCI," with the tantalizing subhead, "Senator Reportedly Worked Behind Scenes."

Considering the situation out of control, Hatch, on August 12, took the unusual step of formally asking the Ethics Committee to investigate his office to see if he or any staff member had acted improperly.

"I am grieved that I have been smeared," wrote Hatch, expressing even more concern for Robert Altman and Clark Clifford, indicted in July for alleged criminality regarding BCCI. "I feel so sorry for both of them, because I believe they are both honest men. I really believe they were deceived about BCCI, as I was." Hatch could have lessened pressure on himself by pointing the finger at the two attorneys for having misled him, however unintentionally, but he refused to do so.

On September 30, Senator Kerry's subcommittee released an extensive report on BCCI and its activities in the United States, triggering another round of stories about Hatch. Amazingly, the document of nearly eight hundred pages contained only ten pages on BCCI's involvement with CenTrust. It ignored the members of Congress who had accepted CenTrust's favors, save for a single footnote which mentioned the irony of David Paul's inviting Kerry to the French chefs' dinner, also attended by BCCI-CenTrust middleman Ghaith Pharaon, at the very time Kerry was investigating BCCI.

After requesting the Ethics Committee's investigation, Hatch stopped talking to the media about BCCI until the inquiry was complete. His reluctance meant that the various allegations were rarely balanced with his side of the story.

In a private moment of despondency, he wrote, "It makes me wonder sometimes if I should continue in the Senate, but I really believe that I must, because many of the political approaches that would kill America would not be fought as effectively if I were gone. However, sometimes I yearn to be free of all this responsibility. It would be nice to once again have complete control of my life without the dirtiness of politics."

Encouragement from Kennedy and a few other close friends kept Hatch going. In August, Ted Kennedy phoned Hatch.

"Orrin, I've just been thinking about you," said Kennedy. "Don't get discouraged. Remember, that's just yesterday's story."

"Thanks, Ted," answered Hatch, "but unfortunately it's not that simple. This just seems to be a story that won't go away."

In September, Hatch wrote, "It is taking an inordinate amount of time to get the facts together on BCCI, but I'm making headway.... I have been told that some [people] hope I will get into a state of depression and quit the Senate. I have been somewhat depressed from time to time, but that is not going to happen. In fact, in the end, I intend to have even more strength to fight these opposition forces."

Friends established a defense fund, and contributions began to roll in to help Hatch pay for legal counsel. That, too, he believed, was "part of the game here": force him to raise and spend money on attorneys' fees that otherwise could go toward his 1994 campaign.

Glenn Simpson, a young reporter for *Roll Call,* the biweekly newspaper covering Capitol Hill, wrote more about Hatch and BCCI than any other journalist. His stories included various inaccuracies, errors that Hatch said Simpson refused to correct even after they were called to his attention.

Puzzled by Simpson's obsessive interest, Hatch believed he had found an explanation when a source told him Simpson was under contract with NBC News—another persistent Hatch critic—for stories on Hatch and BCCI. If this was the case, Hatch reasoned, then it was obviously to Simpson's financial benefit to keep the allegations of wrongdoing in the public eye.

Simpson, interviewed for this book, said no such contract existed. He acknowledged, however, that NBC paid him for assistance on another subject, raising at least the possibility that help on BCCI may have been thrown in unofficially as part of a quid pro quo.

A more likely explanation, though less satisfying for Hatch, was that his blood in the water had created a natural feeding frenzy among media sharks. No conspiracy was necessary to attract reporters to the Hatch/BCCI story. Most newsroom staffs saw themselves as models of political correctness and, in recent years, had included increasing numbers of pro-feminist reporters. Political correctness, almost by definition, meant that Hatch was to be regarded as sanctimonious, if not insufferable. Already seriously wounded politically by the Thomas-Hill hearings, Hatch was an irresistible target for the mainstream media.

Reporters pulled Hatch's records and scrutinized his annual public disclosure financial statements. Edward Pound of the *Wall Street Journal* spent four months investigating Hatch's entire tenure in Congress, interviewing dozens of former staff members, friends in Washington and Utah, former business associates and others. He interviewed Hatch several times and repeatedly badgered current and former staff members—cursing at least one when the sought-after dirt didn't materialize. When Pound's lengthy story was published in February 1993, his four months of drilling had produced only a dry hole.

The *Journal* headline read: "Lobbyist's Cozy Ties With Ex-Boss Sen.

Hatch Include Client Referrals, Political Fund-Raising." It was a yawner. Pound revealed that Hatch was still close to Tom Parry, a former chief of staff who had left Hatch's employ a decade earlier to set up a lobbying business. Hatch referred business to Parry, a major fund-raiser for Hatch, said the article, and Parry's clients believed they might get special consideration from the senator.

In the sixth paragraph, Pound acknowledged that Hatch's ties to Parry "don't appear to violate any laws or Senate rules," but he tried to flavor his story by tossing in some stale ingredients: BCCI, the travails of former aide Mac Haddow, and Hatch's "small financial stake" in a Utah corporation called Pharmics, Inc.

Others also asked about Pharmics. A year earlier, the *Los Angeles Times* ran a front-page story suggesting that Hatch's support for legislation protecting vitamins, minerals, and other dietary supplements from over-regulation by the Food and Drug Administration raised serious ethical concerns. The *Times* also implied strongly that Hatch's backing of the legislation was motivated by his personal financial interest in Pharmics.

What the *Times* and other newspapers routinely ignored, however, was that Hatch was merely a limited partner in a partnership that owned just over 2 percent of Pharmics stock. Further, Pharmics was primarily a real estate company, selling only two products that could possibly be affected by the legislation—an iron supplement and a vitamin C supplement. Neither product was a likely target of more FDA regulation and their sales would be affected little if any from the legislation.

In addition, according to Pharmics, the *gross* sales of those two vitamin and mineral products had never exceeded $42,000 annually. Consequently, their value to Hatch was negligible.

Given the facts, a fair-minded observer must conclude that Hatch had motives other than personal gain for opposing new FDA regulations. A more likely candidate was health-conscious Utah's interest in dietary supplements, a major industry with a value approaching $1 billion annually in the state. Hatch was lobbied hard by constituents to protect their rights to both produce and retain easy access to dietary supplements.

While barrels of ink were used trying to send Hatch down with BCCI's sinking ship, there were at least four reasons to doubt he had done anything worse than give a stupid speech:

- Deeply involved in other U.S. covert operations abroad, it was consistent for him to sound out Mohammed Hammoud on the possibilities of freeing American hostages in Lebanon. He did not know that Hammoud was a secret BCCI stockholder.

- In February 1990, the evidence was credible that BCCI was being picked on because of its Arab ownership. It was fully in character for Hatch to defend the Justice Department's initial settlement with the bank and help out his friend Robert Altman.

- Given Hatch's considerable missionary zeal, once he was contacted by a Mormon mission president regarding Monzer Hourani, he needed no other motive to keep tabs on Hourani than a desire to see him more fully involved in church activities.

- There simply was no evidence of Hatch ever using his Senate office knowingly for personal profit. The Hatch family, as senatorial families went, lived relatively simple, frugal lives. Whatever Hatch's faults, they did not include greed or dishonesty.

Caught in the maelstrom of BCCI and the trauma of his father's death, Hatch could not look back fondly on 1992. The year was so taxing that it was barely worth a smile when a tabloid headline screamed: "Five U.S. Senators Are Space Aliens!" Hatch was unmasked as one of the five, along with Sam Nunn, Alan Simpson, John Glenn, and Nancy Kassebaum.

Political cartoonist Pat Bagley did a takeoff on the spoof for the *Salt Lake Tribune*. A woman at a supermarket checkout, reading from the paper, says: "This tabloid has some weird story about Orrin Hatch being a space-alien!" The cashier's response: "Tell me when you get to the weird part."

Hatch continued to be a prodigious worker and effective legislator despite personal difficulties. The 102nd Congress passed eighteen Hatch bills, ranging from one making it more difficult for state lotteries to involve sports teams to another tightening protections against computer software piracy. Working with Jake Garn and other members of the Utah delegation, he also helped secure final authorization for the Central Utah Project. Bush signed the measure in October, authorizing $922 million more for the mammoth water reclamation system.

Even Democrats praised Hatch's work. David Lee, an attorney based in Washington for a Utah firm and one-time top aide to former Utah Democratic Congressman Gunn McKay, wrote Hatch's office in April. "Although I am a lifelong Utah Democrat," said Lee, "I have come to appreciate first-hand that there is no harder working or more capable Senator than Senator Hatch."

Veteran broadcaster Don Gale, president of the University of Utah's alumni association and editorialist on Utah's KSL radio and television stations, thanked Hatch for voting to override Bush's veto of a cable bill, then went well beyond that:

> It was not an easy thing for Senator Hatch to do. He is very loyal to the President. He often speaks out in support of the President when it might be easier to remain silent. . . . Whether or not you agree with the senator, he did what he thought was right. We recall other instances when Senator Hatch spoke out in favor of causes not popular with his political allies. He was a prime mover in getting a child care bill through Congress. . . . And Senator Hatch was a pillar of strength in the battle over funding for the arts. . . . We commend him for having the courage of his convictions in all aspects of his Senate service.

28

Tending the Home Fires

BILL CLINTON WANTED TO CAPTURE the presidency in 1992 more than George Bush wanted to keep it, or so it seemed. Bush ran a lackluster campaign, offered no compelling message of what he would do with a second term, and was handicapped by a shaky economy.

Hatch might have repeated his successful efforts for Reagan-Bush twelve years earlier, helping Bush-Quayle close the gap. But a bumbling campaign team used his talents sparingly and too late. Hoping against hope that Bush would pull out of his tailspin, Hatch sent letters and made phone calls of encouragement and advice. The President responded cheerfully:

"Your thoughtful letter means an awful lot to me," read a handwritten Bush note from Michigan in late September. "I am upbeat and determined. Damn the press, full speed ahead! But your great letter spurs me on."

A telephone call a week later reassured, "Don't worry, Orrin, I'm going to win." The President also sent Hatch a note on October 23: "I appreciate your suggestions and will keep them in mind. Less than two weeks left in this tough race and I am confident of a victory," and another dictated from Air Force One on November 1: "Your wonderful note of October 25 caught up with me in Wisconsin. . . . Like you, I'm convinced I'll make it."

Perhaps if Bush had written fewer notes and campaigned smarter, he would have won. As it was, Bush and Quayle got trounced November 3, winning just eighteen states and 168 electoral votes, to thirty-two states and 370 electoral votes for Clinton and his running mate, Tennessee Senator Albert Gore.

Independent Ross Perot made the strongest third-candidate showing since Teddy Roosevelt in 1912 but won no electoral votes and took second place only in Utah, the lone state where Clinton placed third.

Utah elected Republican Robert Bennett to the seat of retiring senator Jake Garn over Representative Wayne Owens. Democrat Owens, easily defeated by the son of former Utah Senator Wallace F. Bennett, had written the book on how to appear more conservative in Utah than in Washington. He had kept his constituents mollified by siding often with Republicans when his vote made no difference to the outcome of an issue. But when a vote was close and Democrats and unions needed him, Owens had usually been there. As a result he could point to a relatively high percentage of "conservative" votes, while keeping favor with Democrats and, especially, labor unions. But Owens had stumbled over an embarrassing flyer meant to raise funds only outside Utah that Republicans gleefully injected into the state contest.

The flyer's cover showed Hatch with Owens and a campaign quote from Hatch: "If you send Wayne Owens back there, every vote I cast is going to be canceled, virtually every vote."

Inside, the flyer agreed: "You can help cancel out every single one of Orrin Hatch's votes." It promised Owens would be "a real fighter for progressive causes in the Senate."

Among other things, the flyer boasted that Owens "voted to allow equal access to abortion for poor women," "opposed the 'gag rule' on reproductive counseling," and "co-sponsored the Federal Lesbian and Gay Civil Rights bill, the only member of the Utah delegation to do so."

Owens's "progressive" platform might have got him elected in Massachusetts, but it was anathema in Utah.

On election night, November 3, Orrin and Elaine joined Republicans at Salt Lake's Little America Hotel. "I was very dejected," he recalls. "I knew deep down that Clinton was going to win. But I kept hoping for a miracle."

Hatch characteristically went out of his way that night and the next day to extend condolences to Wayne Owens, who had been crushed by Bennett. Owens thanked Hatch, expressing gratitude that he had not attacked him during the campaign even though he knew Hatch was pulling for Bennett. They parted friends.

Near the end of the year, Hatch hosted a farewell dinner at a Washington hotel for his retiring colleague Jake Garn, now ending his Senate career of three terms. The two had become like brothers, and Hatch would genuinely miss Garn. His farewell gift was a binder containing good-bye letters from all their Senate colleagues, along with a landscape by Hatch's artist-cousin, Valoy Eaton.

Hatch was supposed to speak as well as host the evening. After others had offered tributes, however, Hatch said: "I'm not going to filibuster tonight. The totality of my speech is, I love you, Jake." The hundred and fifty guests applauded as the two men embraced in an emotional farewell.

They had been a powerful team for Utah, and now Hatch was the delegation's senior. Even before Garn's retirement, Hatch had created what *Utah Holiday* called the state's "most responsive congressional staff," making it easier to take up the slack while Bob Bennett got some seasoning.

Responsiveness to constituents was not just campaign rhetoric. For every Clarence Thomas or Oliver North Hatch had defended, he went to bat for a large number of average Utahns just as tenaciously. Hatch and his staff handled an estimated 13,000 to 16,000 individual cases annually, often involving citizens harried by federal bureaucrats. Hatch kept himself accessible, flying home to Utah nearly every other weekend, spending between 25 and 40 percent of his time in the state each year, and maintaining offices in Salt Lake, Ogden, Provo, and Cedar City.

Countless cases from his Salt Lake office lay to rest the tired claim that Hatch was interested only in national issues. He often went to extraordinary lengths to help individuals solve problems.

"Your name is magic!" wrote a Mr. Jensen, one of many who sought help with the Internal Revenue Service. "IRS told us that there was no appeal to their decision. When my wife said, 'I'm going to write Senator Hatch about this injustice,' there was a 180 degree turn around on IRS's part. . . . We appreciate your reputation and you!"

A newly divorced, unemployed woman, with Hatch's help, quickly got Social Security benefits for her Down's syndrome child—"a bright spot in my otherwise stressful situation."

Hatch arranged political asylum in the United States and found an anonymous donor to buy airline tickets to fly a Garcia family to safety from Marxist Nicaragua, where they were being severely persecuted and had even received death threats after joining the Mormon church. Many Latin American revolutionaries consider Mormons and Americans as virtually synonymous. A year later, the mother told Hatch's staff the family had two pictures on their living room wall: church founder Joseph Smith and Hatch.

When the Children's Dance Theater of Salt Lake was about to leave for a London tour, one dancer had no passport. Amy had given up hope of making the trip, but Hatch asked the federal passport office to cut its red tape, and the passport arrived in Utah by special delivery. Wrote program director Pia Byrd, "You've made one little girl very happy."

Then there was George Thomas Scott, who just wanted to be an American—and thanks in part to Hatch he was, for a single day, before he died. An emigrant from Scotland at age sixty-one, Scott married a Utah penpal, had ten years of idyllic marriage, and worked for an auto dealership. George and Jessie had their own home, a new car, and money to travel—dreams fulfilled in America that would have been impossible back in Scotland.

Becoming an American citizen was Scott's goal, but he was diagnosed with cancer and told he had four months to live. With the clock ticking, Hatch and his staff got immigration agents to expedite the paperwork. In November 1988, Scott, seventy-one years old and weighing eighty pounds, sat bright-eyed in his wheelchair in a judge's chambers, answering questions about his adoptive country and responsibilities of citizenship. He was too weak to raise his arm, but Jessie held it for him as George repeated the oath of allegiance.

"Congratulations," said the judge to Scott, who was grinning broadly, "you are now a U.S. citizen." Less than twenty-four hours later, Scott died in his wife's arms.

In 1993, for the first time since 1980, Democrats controlled both houses of Congress and the White House. And once more there was a rift between a Southern President and the special interests of the West. Bruce Babbitt, an elitist westerner who, as Arizona's former governor, had shown little empathy for those who rely on public lands to earn their living, was tapped by Clinton as Secretary of the Interior. Babbitt began where Jimmy Carter's team had ended, proposing a passel of land-use changes affecting timber, mining, wilderness, rural roads, water, and grazing.

"His land-management reforms would devastate our whole economy and ruin individual lives," charged Hatch. Rural families across the West worried that a way of life, already difficult for most, was about to be destroyed.

After Babbitt proposed to increase grazing fees on rangelands 130 percent across the board to sharply cut the subsidy for those using public lands, Hatch helped Senators Domenici, Wallop, Campbell, and others, to mount determined opposition, ending in a Senate filibuster. It prevented congressional endorsement of a modified plan which could have driven small ranchers off the range.

Hatch was a major supporter of the Utah Wilderness Act of 1984— designating nearly 800,000 acres of U.S. Forest Service land throughout the state as wilderness. It was the primary effort in Utah during the past decade to change the management of the state's public lands.

Most western senators, including Hatch, also echoed their region's peculiar worship of guns by opposing the Brady Bill, a measure providing a five-day waiting period for handgun purchases. Hatch believed the imposition of a waiting period would actually lead to more guns being sold—which initially appeared to be the case—including to citizens ill-equipped to use them safely. But massive public outrage over gun-related violence overcame Senate opposition and lobbying by the National Rifle Association, and Clinton signed the Brady Bill into law near the end of 1993.

Hatch continued to press for full implementation of a law passed in 1990, largely through his personal efforts, to compensate victims of nuclear fallout from weapons testing conducted in Nevada in the 1950s and 1960s. "Downwinders" in the region, including southern Utah, were betrayed by their country, Hatch believed, first by being bombarded with harmful or even fatal doses of nuclear radiation, then by a conspiracy of silence and denial in Washington.

Many downwinder families lost loved ones to cancer and other radiation-induced illnesses. After more than a decade of hearings, research, and sheer stubbornness by Hatch and others, a law was passed in 1990, including a formal government apology to victims and a trust fund to compensate those still alive. The first payments were made in 1992, varying from $50,000 to $100,000, and a majority of claimants approved for compensation had received payments by the end of 1993. When the Clinton administration tried to cut funding for the trust fund, Hatch won new assurances in 1993 that it would remain adequate.

Hatch also worked hard to attract new business to Utah and help existing businesses grow and deal with Washington. In 1993, Utah's economy was the envy of the nation. While most of the United States was in recession, Utah's labor force was in the sixth year of growth of 3 percent or higher—fastest in the nation. In August, Utah's unemployment was 3.4 percent, half the national average of 6.7 percent. While many states were in the red, the Utah legislature in 1993 had the enviable task of deciding what to do with a substantial surplus.

A key to Utah's success was its status as a "right-to-work" state, where workers could not be forced to join unions to keep jobs. Many firms had left unionized states in the Northeast and Midwest to relocate in Utah and other states protected by Section 14-b of the Taft-Hartley Act—a provision that Hatch had helped save during the 1977–78 fight against the Labor Law Reform Bill.

Democrats kept their edge in the Senate following the 1992 elections—fifty-seven seats to forty-three. However, twelve seats changed hands and the number of women jumped, fueled in part by anger over the Thomas-

Hill hearings. The House went from twenty-eight to forty-seven women, and the Senate from two to six—the most ever. Two new Democrats, Dianne Feinstein of California and Carol Moseley Braun of Illinois, the Senate's first black woman, were added to the Judiciary Committee. The *next* Anita Hill would not face an all-male panel.

Hatch faced a tough decision: Strom Thurmond, still going strong at age ninety, decided to leave his ranking position on the Judiciary Committee to take the same position on the Armed Services Committee. Hatch could continue as ranking Republican on Labor and Human Resources, where he and Chairman Kennedy had written so many laws, or take the spot Thurmond was vacating on Judiciary. It was an "extremely hard decision," reflected Hatch, but he chose Judiciary, foreseeing the "numerous judicial issues facing the nation in the next few years." Privately he wrote, "I will miss my friend Ted Kennedy as a daily partner."

Hatch landed a slot on the powerful tax-writing Finance Committee as his second panel and retained a lower-ranking slot on the Labor Committee as a third assignment. He also chaired the Senate Republican Conference Task Force on Hispanic Affairs.

Crime was an issue of uncommon importance before the Judiciary Committee. Hatch introduced the first crime-control bill in the 103rd Congress in January 1993 and was GOP floor manager of the $22 billion Biden-Hatch crime package approved by the Senate in November. It would put a hundred thousand more policemen on the beat, strengthen the federal death penalty—including for drug kingpins— toughen sentences for violent criminals, fund better state response to sexual assault and domestic violence, fight rural crime, provide funds to help curb gangs, and build more prisons.

Early in 1993 the American Civil Liberties Union sent a letter to all Senators on behalf of Hatch and Kennedy. Hatch and the ACLU rarely agreed on anything, but they agreed that religious freedom in America was at risk. In 1990 the Supreme Court (*Employment Division v. Smith*) had dismissed the protection of religious freedom as a "luxury" the nation could no longer afford. Since then a variety of unorthodox religious beliefs and practices had been restricted by local governments.

The court ruling stirred memories of the Holocaust among Jews, and alarmed leaders of the LDS church, whose members had suffered severe persecution during the nineteenth century—including an "extermination" order issued by Missouri's governor that resulted in Mormons being violently driven from that state in 1838. Hatch persuaded Kennedy to cosponsor the Religious Freedom Restoration Act.

"The Act does not affect any of the issues that fall under the rubric of separation of church and state," wrote the ACLU, "but simply restores the previously prevailing legal standard"—meaning that government had to show a "compelling" state interest that justified the restriction.

A companion bill was introduced in the House, and the two Senators, backed by the ACLU and many religious organizations, shepherded the legislation through Congress. Dallin H. Oaks, a member of the LDS church's Council of the Twelve, was among those testifying for passage, and another member of the Twelve, M. Russell Ballard, accompanied Hatch to the White House to watch President Clinton sign it into law in November.

Hatch's record of service to Utah apparently had put him in good political shape as he campaigned for reelection to a fourth term in 1994. He looked so strong early that year, in fact, that Democrats again were having considerable difficulty finding a credible candidate to run against him.

However, Utahns have a history of turning veterans out of office, and in the last half-century only one Utah senator—Wallace F. Bennett—had been elected to a fourth term. Democrats were counting heavily on sentiment generated by a move in Utah and elsewhere to limit service in Congress to about twelve years—two Senate terms.

"I'd be happy for Utah to pass a term-limitation proposal—just as soon as Massachusetts, New York, West Virginia, Maine, and others pass one," says Hatch. "But as long as Congress is run on a seniority system, I doubt that Utahns really want to disarm our state until other states whose interests are so opposed to ours also pass term limits."

Hatch's tenure was the subject of a point-counterpoint column in the *Salt Lake Tribune* in September 1993. Liberal Tom Barberi wrote that "Utah's Sen. Orrin Hatch is ranked 7th in the Senate for taking private industry [-paid] junkets," calling it "additional proof positive that we need term limitations for all elected positions."

Conservative Bud Scruggs—Hatch's 1988 campaign manager—defended the practice of private interests buying plane tickets so members can get out of Washington and "visit real Americans—tax payers rather than tax spenders." Scruggs added that "with the current left-wing consolidation of power in Washington, I'm not at all convinced it's time to pull the plug on Orrin Hatch."

Would Hatch consider throwing his hat into the presidential ring for 1996 should he win a fourth senate term? The prospect has been raised by others almost from the day Hatch arrived in Washington in 1977; but in an at-press-time interview for this book, Hatch still said his only ambition is to continue serving Utah in the Senate.

Orrin and Elaine flank Muhammad and Lonnie Ali on Temple Square in Salt Lake City, 1988. (Photo by Howard L. Bingham. Used by permission.)

Floating like a butterfly with pal Muhammad Ali.

Failed Supreme Court nominee Robert Bork and wife, Mary Ellen, at a fund-raiser for Hatch's 1988 campaign.

Taking Ali to his parents' Utah home for dinner.

Ali with Richie Hirschfield, Ali's one-time attorney and frequent companion. (Photo by Howard Bingham. Used by permission.)

The Senate's odd couple: Hatch and Massachusetts Democrat Edward M. Kennedy. "Orrin," wrote Kennedy next to one chummy photo, "If Ronald Reagan could see us now."

—Pointing out the error of his friend's ways.

—Borrring.

—Huddling in a committee hearing. (Photo by United Press International/ Bettmann Archive. Used by permission.)

—Actress Elizabeth Taylor lobbying for AIDS victims. When a similar photo ran in Kennedy's hometown *Boston Globe* in 1990, he sent a clip to Hatch, with a note: "I'm sure [Taylor] will be facing the other way on page one of the *Deseret News*!"

Convinced that "the future is in very small hands," Hatch, shown here at a northern Utah day-care center, played a pivotal role in crafting a national child-care law.

Supreme Court nominee—later Justice—Clarence Thomas and his tenacious defender embrace during Thomas's sensational confirmation hearings. At left is Thomas's wife, Virginia. Behind Hatch's left shoulder is Thomas's son, Jamal.

Disabled Americans and their allies applaud an emotional Hatch just after he helped pass landmark legislation in 1990 barring discrimination against them.

This *Washingtonian* magazine cartoonist, for one, wasn't impressed by Hatch's role in the 1991 Thomas-Hill hearings. (Cartoon by Richard Thompson. Used by permission.)

Turnabout is fair play: Hatch sent this photo to Candice Bergen (aka TV's Murphy Brown) after his name showed up on her sitcom dartboard. (Photo by United Press International/ Bettmann Archive. Used by permission.)

President Bush greets Orrin and Elaine Hatch and Jake and Kathleen Garn upon Bush's arrival in Utah in 1992.

Actor James Edward Olmos meets with Hatch, 1993 chair of the Senate Republican Conference Task Force on Hispanic Affairs.

Antonia C. Novello, the first woman and first Hispanic U.S. Surgeon General, flanked by Hatch and Senate GOP Leader Bob Dole of Kansas.

An emotional farewell to retiring Senator Jake Garn.

Elder M. Russell Ballard, a member of the LDS church's Council of the Twelve Apostles, with Hatch and President Clinton as Clinton signed into law Hatch's Religious Freedom Restoration Act.

Meeting on Capitol Hill with Ruth Bader Ginsburg, after Hatch played a key role in her elevation to the Supreme Court.

Orrin and Elaine at home in Vienna, Virginia, with their children and grandchildren. Other adults (*from left*:): Brent and Mia Hatch, Randy and Marcia Whetton, Alysa Hatch, Jess Hatch, Wendy and Scott Hatch, and Kimberly and John Catron.

29

A Season of Renewal

A t forty-six, Bill Clinton was the third youngest president in history and only the second Democrat in twenty-four years to capture the White House. When Clinton took office in January 1993, Orrin Hatch was fifty-eight but vividly recalled his own arrival in Washington as a callow senator sixteen years earlier. On a personal level he empathized with Clinton.

Many of the Clinton administration's key people would be coming before the Judiciary Committee, where Hatch had replaced Thurmond as ranking Republican. Conservatives urged Hatch to retaliate for injuries inflicted on Reagan and Bush's nominees over the last dozen years. But Hatch was determined to give Clinton a chance.

"I personally believe Clinton has intelligence enough not to be another Jimmy Carter," Hatch wrote privately soon after Clinton was elected. "Carter was a bright man but had an engineer mentality which required him to micromanage everything and therefore not do anything very well."

Zoe Baird, a Connecticut lawyer and the first woman ever nominated as attorney general, was first up. When Hatch met her early in January, he was "impressed," he wrote. "She is clearly intelligent and I think will make a good Attorney General. I also think we could not do any better. She at least has private sector experience and I hope that will guide her in her work there."

Baird, however, was destined to become a footnote. She and her husband had illegally hired two undocumented Peruvians. Although Clinton's transition team had brushed it off, public outcry was enormous. Others quickly backed off, but not Hatch. "I do not condone Zoe Baird's

399

hiring of unauthorized aliens to work in her household," he explained in a written statement. "But this admitted wrongdoing should be put in perspective. She has a fine overall record in the legal profession."

Critics suggested Hatch hoped to curry favor with Baird and other women by supporting her. But Hatch feared that a replacement for Baird would be less qualified. "Some of the outcry over hiring is, in fact, a smoke screen for differences in ideology," his statement continued. "Liberal special interest groups who are upset with her business background and her support for tort reform are now using the same tactics against her as they used against conservative Republicans."

But Hatch's defense was useless. Hours after her appearance before the Judiciary Committee, Baird became the first U.S. cabinet nominee in more than a century to withdraw her name. Other Clinton candidates likewise were tripped up when it was learned they too had hired undocumented workers.

Weeks later, Hatch was lunching at Maddox's in northern Utah when the White House tracked him down by telephone.

"Senator," said Clinton, "I just want you to know how much I appreciate the fair-minded way you have treated our nominees."

"Thank you, Mr. President," answered Hatch. "I'm going to help you all I can and hope you'll continue to choose people I can fully support. I sincerely want you to succeed."

"I really appreciate that," said Clinton. "By the way," he added with a laugh, "We've *got* to get rid of that baby-sitter statute"–against hiring undocumented workers for the home.

"Kennedy and I have been trying to do that for a long time," answered Hatch, "and if you'll join us, or let us join you, maybe we can change it."

Donna Shalala, a woman who had been chancellor of the University of Wisconsin's Madison campus, was nominated as Secretary of Health and Human Services. Shalala had a no-nonsense management style, had never married, and was considered the high priestess of political correctness, stating publicly that women in positions of authority should have feminist agendas. Despite their obvious differences, Hatch expressed a strong desire to work well together, and she did the same.

Clinton nominated Janet Reno, a Florida state official, who also had never married, as a replacement candidate for Baird. Reno, tall with a sunny disposition, had dedicated her life to the law.

Hatch liked her immediately, though they were poles apart politically. Reno had strongly supported the Equal Rights Amendment and many other liberal causes. But after studying her record carefully, Hatch concluded, "She appears to be a straight-shooter who has led a basically good life."

Reno's single status had sparked rumors that she was a lesbian. She disarmed the media when the subject came up, answering, "I'm just an old maid who happens to like men."

"That was a terrific response to the calumny," wrote Hatch, after wading through a three-volume FBI report on Reno.

Two or three people had made numerous allegations, none of which seemed to have any basis in fact. Hatch dismissed her detractors as "zealots who were maligning her without justification." He added that "It really unnerves me that we could have conservative people making these kinds of allegations without the necessary justification. I'm really burned about it."

Hatch drew the line at Lani Guinier, tapped by Clinton to head the Justice Department's Civil Rights Division. A radical black law professor, Guinier had attended Yale Law School with Bill and Hillary Clinton and remained good friends with them.

Guinier believed in a "concurrent majority," meaning that a minority with a "major interest" in an issue should have the right to veto the decisions of a numerical majority. This position flew in the face of Supreme Court one-person-one-vote rulings. She called for the election of "authentic blacks," who would not have to serve white constituencies against the interests of blacks in an area.

Guinier had criticized democracy as a form of government and said that health care, day care, job training, and housing were "basic entitlements." She also called repeatedly for racial quotas.

"Her ideas would polarize our country even more," said Hatch. "The more we get young blacks and other racial minorities thinking that they have to be insular polarities, the worse this country is going to become. . . . Ideally we should all be working together to help each other."

In his concern, Hatch organized meetings with Jewish and other special-interest groups, wrote articles, and spent hours talking to editorial writers across the country about Guinier. As a groundswell of criticism mounted, Clinton said he didn't realize how much he disagreed with Guinier and, despite political threats from black leaders, finally dumped her.

At almost the same time, Clinton nominated for assistant secretary in charge of fair housing at the Department of Housing and Urban Development someone even less acceptable to Hatch: Roberta Achtenberg. If confirmed, she would be the first avowed lesbian appointed to a high federal post.

However, it was not Achtenberg's sexual preferences that set Hatch against her but what he interpreted as her record of intolerance. As a member of the board of supervisors in San Francisco, Achtenberg had crusaded against the Boy Scouts of America because the organization was grounded in a belief in God and would not allow homosexuals to be Boy Scout leaders. "Do we want children learning the values of an organization that . . . provides character-building exclusively for straight, God-fearing male children?" asked Achtenberg.

Achtenberg reportedly got United Way to withhold funding, barred Scout troops from meeting in public facilities, and compelled San Francisco to withdraw millions of dollars from the Bank of America because the bank continued to support Scouting. The action against the bank, said Achtenberg, will "send a message to the youth of this city that this board will stand up for what is right."

To Hatch, this personal animus was evidence that Achtenberg lacked the tolerance required to ensure fair access to housing for all citizens. But in the floor fight, Jesse Helms called her "a damned lesbian" instead of confining himself to the relevant issues. His intemperance made it almost impossible to vote against her without appearing prejudiced, and she was confirmed 58-31.

In March, the only Democratic appointee left on the Supreme Court, Byron White, announced his retirement. A seventy-five-year-old moderate appointed by President Kennedy in 1962, he had served the nation well and had long been Hatch's friend.

Speculation over a replacement began immediately, and Hatch was besieged by the media for his opinion. He offered a number of names, saying it would be a great idea to put the first Hispanic on the court—something he had pushed for the last three vacancies. He suggested other candidates as well, including Ruth Bader Ginsburg of the D.C. appellate court where Bork and Thomas had recently served.

Ginsburg, sixty, a trailblazer in gender-discrimination law, had argued six women's rights cases before the Supreme Court in the 1970s, winning five of them. Despite a liberal reputation, she had been restrained and nonideological in her thirteen years as a judge, actually voting more often with Republican than Democratic appointees during the first eight years. She was married to a noted tax attorney and was the mother of two.

"I hope that President Clinton . . . will choose someone who appreciates, as Justice White does, that judges are not free to substitute their own policy preferences for the written law," said Hatch in a written statement. "In the confirmation process, whether a nominee is *politically* liberal or conservative is irrelevant. What matters is that we have judges who will neutrally and objectively interpret and apply the laws, not judges who will impose their own policy preferences."

Hatch had no litmus test for a justice but Clinton did: His nominee must not threaten the status quo on abortion. The President had struck out over Lani Guinier and over his promise to integrate gays into the military, but his Supreme Court choice, he promised, would be a "home run."

Then an eerie quiet settled over the White House for months as Hatch narrowed his own preferred list to two people: Ginsburg and Stephen Breyer, chief judge on the First Circuit Court of Appeals and former top aide to Kennedy. Reagan had placed Breyer on the federal bench after Hatch persuaded other Republican senators, who initially opposed Breyer because of his ties to Kennedy, to accept the appointment. Hatch lobbied other senators, as well as key advisors to Clinton, notably White House counsel Bernard Nussbaum, to encourage Clinton to select one of the two.

Meanwhile Nussbaum and key Senate liberals—Metzenbaum, Simon, and Leahy—settled on their own candidate: Interior Secretary Bruce Babbitt. Liberals wanted a political activist in the post, reasoning that Rehnquist would likely retire within a few years. If Clinton won a second term, he could appoint a new chief justice. Babbitt, they believed, would be a "smart" Earl Warren, a judicial activist who would help create policy preferences that liberals couldn't shove through Congress.

Although angry westerners probably would have given Babbitt anything—including the Supreme Court—to eject him from Interior, Hatch disagreed. He distrusted Babbitt's judicial philosophy and feared that his ardent environmentalism would hurt the West even more from the high court than from Interior. Hatch didn't worry long, for Breyer developed a "baby-sitter" problem—an undocumented woman had once worked for him. Even though he had honorably paid her Social Security, the White House was paranoid.

On Friday, June 4, Hatch telephoned Ginsburg, recounted his efforts to keep her on the White House short list, and told her she still had a chance. Ginsburg, who did not know she was still a candidate, was moved by Hatch's active support.

That weekend, the White House leaked word that Clinton was about to nominate Babbitt. On Monday morning, the *Wall Street Journal* headlined, "Babbitt is Now Top Contender For High Court," with this subhead: "Clinton Said to Be Ready To Name Interior Chief." But later that day, the White House called Hatch. He waited several minutes before Clinton, sounding extremely weary, said, "Hello." Clinton thanked Hatch for helping to confirm three new people for the Justice Department, then got down to business.

"Senator, I would like to run by you some of my feelings about the Supreme Court nominee, and get your reaction."

"By all means, Mr. President."

Clinton then asked what Hatch thought of Babbitt.

"Mr. President, if you want him, I will certainly help you. I think

Babbitt is basically a good man," responded Hatch. "But he's a politician, and there's a lot of concern that he might start legislating his own ideas instead of simply interpreting the law. Frankly, you'll probably have a harder time getting him confirmed than you would someone else." Hatch also noted that conservative publications had already started attacking Babbitt, and more of the same was inevitable.

That was not what Clinton wanted to hear. Upset, he pressed Hatch again. Hatch repeated his objections.

"What about Breyer?" asked the President.

"I think the Senate would confirm Steve Breyer one hundred to zero. That would be the home run you're looking for. He's really a fine man and is both well known and well liked on both sides of the aisle up here."

There was a pause on the other end, and Hatch ended it. "I hope you haven't discounted Ruth Ginsburg. She is also a very good person with a great intellect. She's viewed as pretty liberal, and that might be a possible political problem, but she really has a moderate record, and you could count on me to help lead interference for her in the Senate." Hatch also pointed out that Ginsburg and Breyer were both Jews. Some citizens believed the court should have a Jewish seat, and the last Jewish justice, Abe Fortas, had left the bench twenty-four years earlier.

Hatch offered a couple of other names: Jose Cabranes, a federal district judge in Connecticut, and Clinton's friend Richard Arnold, a member of the U.S. Eighth Judicial Circuit in Little Rock.

"Hispanic-Americans would go wild if you chose Cabranes," said Hatch. "It would really be a feather in your cap to put the first Hispanic on the Supreme Court. But Dick Arnold would also be excellent."

"I know of Judge Cabranes. You're right, he would be excellent," Clinton agreed. "And Dick Arnold is the best judge I know in the country."

"Then don't be afraid to pick him," said Hatch. "You ought to pick who you feel comfortable with and who you really feel will do a good job."

Clinton thanked Hatch for his candor, said his final list had three people on it, and promised to announce his decision within forty-eight hours. Hatch hung up, wondering who the third candidate might be.

Three days later, on June 10, as Hatch entered the Senate chamber, Paul Simon, glowering in annoyance, snapped, "Orrin, you've derailed Babbitt!"

Majority Leader Mitchell joined them: "Orrin, it is interesting to me how you have such great influence over this administration's picks for the Supreme Court."

"George," answered a bemused Hatch, "if I had any influence they would have picked *you*. . . . I really want to get rid of you up here because you're too effective."

Mitchell laughed.

Kennedy had repeatedly thanked Hatch for helping to keep his former staffer Breyer in the running. "You know, Ted," said Hatch, "probably Breyer's biggest disadvantage is that you, Dole, Thurmond, and I all like him."

Clinton caught considerable flak from Democrats and the media for allowing Hatch a voice in the selection. Reporters Carl Rowan and Jack Germond, on different TV talk shows, groused that the Utahn shouldn't be allowed to pick the Supreme Court nominee for a Democratic administration.

Midmorning on Sunday, June 13, the President called Hatch at home. "Senator," said Clinton, sounding both tired and resigned, I have decided to name Ruth Bader Ginsburg to the court."

"Mr. President," Hatch responded enthusiastically, "she is a wonderful choice. I know this has not been easy for you, but she will really serve our country well."

"I'm sure that's true," answered Clinton, voice lifting. "Could you be at the announcement ceremony tomorrow at two o'clock?"

Hatch said he would be there.

The public announcement on the White House south lawn the next afternoon became memorable for the press conference that did *not* follow it. Ginsburg, looking like an owlish schoolmarm in oversize glasses and dark brown hair pulled tightly into a bun, gave a stirring acceptance speech.

Clinton, moved by her eloquence and now confident he had his home run, invited questions from the crush of reporters. He was immediately brought back to earth by ABC's Brit Hume. Barely mentioning Ginsburg, Hume instead asked about Lani Guinier, Stephen Breyer, and "a certain zigzag quality in the decision-making process here."

The President's face reddened in anger. "I have long since given up the thought that I could disabuse some of you of turning any substantive decision into anything but a political process. How you could ask a question like that after the statement she just made is beyond me."

Democrats present applauded Clinton's sharp retort. Clinton simply added, "Good-bye. Thank you," and the press conference was over.

Clinton's relations with the media were bad already. He was inaccessible and had withdrawn some perks the White House press corps had come to expect. Reporters paid him back in spades. Recently Clinton had tried to improve relations by bringing back to the White House an old Republican media hand, David Gergen. Some speculated Gergen had programmed Clinton to shove it to the press in a bid for public support. While the public was divided on Clinton, it was united in its hostility toward the media.

The next day, Clinton again called Hatch, asking if he could expedite Ginsburg's Judiciary Committee hearings. Eighty-seven days had lapsed between Byron White's announcement and the naming of Ginsburg, and it was possible she wouldn't be seated for the court's opening session on the first Monday in October. Hatch promised to do what he could.

On Wednesday, Hatch attended a luncheon of the Senate Steering Committee, where conservative Republicans coordinated policy approaches. Some members suggested that, with a Democratic nominee now before the Senate, it was payback time.

"No," Hatch told his colleagues firmly, "that's the wrong way to look at it. We need to pick our fights, and this is not going to be one of them. We're going to show this nation that we're bigger than the Democrats. We are not going to play the same dirty rotten games they have played with our nominees."

Some of the Senate's strongest conservatives were there. No one openly objected.

Ginsburg, led by Hatch's unwavering support, sailed through the Judiciary Committee and was confirmed by the full Senate on August 3, 1993. She took her seat on the high court a week later.

The media was still pounding Hatch. On June 29 the *New York Times* reported that some Republican senators were unhappy with Hatch for being too easy on Clinton's nominees. Several—including Jesse Helms, who denied it to Hatch—speculated Hatch might be trying to curry favor with the Justice Department because of BCCI, said the *Times*.

In April the Senate Ethics Committee had finally announced it was opening a formal investigation of Hatch's ties to the corrupt bank, as he had requested the year before. The committee had an equal number of Democrats and Republicans—three each—and was chaired in 1993 by a tough former state attorney general from Nevada, Democrat Richard Bryan. Some suggested the Democrats had purposely delayed the investigation, hoping to embarrass Hatch during his reelection campaign.

No one doubted that, if they could knock off Hatch in 1994, Democrats would have a far easier time on Capitol Hill. Yet several Democratic colleagues personally offered encouragement the day the *Times* story appeared. Senator Carol Moseley Braun, a freshman Illinois Democrat, gave him a warm hug and said, "It's terrible what they're doing to you. If you need any help from me, just let me know."

Joe Biden ran into Hatch as both were hurrying to the floor for a vote. "Orrin," he said, "if there is anything I can do for you, I will. If I try too hard it will probably hurt you more than help, but I am willing to help in any way I can."

And that evening at 10:30, Kennedy phoned Hatch at home. "Vicki and I were just thinking about you," said Kennedy. "We are so sorry for what they're doing to you." Then Victoria got on the line and said, "We love you, Orrin."

Hatch was running up hundreds of thousands of dollars in attorney bills, covering every legal base and allegation that had been raised. He prayed supporters would keep donating to his legal defense fund. The stress, combined with his almost constant back pain, meant he slept badly most nights, tossing in anxiety.

"The game is to dishearten and discourage me so that I'll just give up and quit the Senate," wrote Hatch early in July. "But I'm going to disappoint them." Earlier he had written a candid appraisal of political life in a quick poem:

> This life of politics I find enervating—
> So many difficulties, so little time,
> With people claiming you as their own,
> Without regard to needs for family, friends and health . . .
> This way of life, this incapacitating strife
> Seems so debilitating, so depressing, yet—necessary . . .
>   The simple fact is, I'm here
>   And must give it everything,
>   So that my children, my wife, my friends,
> My state, my country, will continue
>   To preserve the liberties cherished by all.

On July 9, cares were cast aside in a day of celebration and refuge in the nearby Mormon temple as twenty-three-year-old Jess married Mary Alice Marriott, daughter of Richard and Nancy Marriott. The accompanying socials were so lavish that Hatch winced, but the bride's parents could afford it: They owned a sizable chunk of the Marriott Corporation, founded by Richard's parents, and were worth hundreds of millions.

Furthermore, in a gesture of solidarity in the newly extended family, four Marriotts, including Richard, Nancy, brother Bill, and mother Alice, donated $10,000 each—the legal maximum—to Hatch's legal defense fund.

Near the end of July a break came in the BCCI case. The Justice Department telephoned Hatch's attorney to say the department had found no wrongdoing on his part and had ended all consideration of his role with the bank. The department sent a follow-up letter, dated July 29, with the same message.

The exoneration lifted Hatch's heart. He could have won political points by releasing the news immediately. However, propriety constrained him until the Senate Ethics Committee concluded its investigation. He said nothing as the media continued to bash him.

But in the following weeks, he felt his old zest returning. He was increasingly confident that, in light of the Justice Department conclusion, the Ethics Committee would have to set politics aside and decide his case on the facts.

Some observers who had followed Hatch closely over the years called him "the Senate's last honest man." It was not a title Hatch claimed, but he knew he *was* honest.

As autumn leaves began to litter the Hatches' corner acre in Vienna, Hatch began to think less of BCCI and more of Senate fights still to be won and the 1994 reelection campaign to be waged out in Utah.

Elaine had held their family together valiantly during three Senate terms as Hatch conducted the people's business. She longed to hear him say, "Enough." But she stood faithfully beside him as preparations for the fourth campaign began. Elaine was proud of Orrin and knew he was affecting history in critical ways.

Evidences of Hatch's frequent absences had become something of a family joke. They had lived for seventeen years in their modest red-brick home in Vienna. Its shake roof was fading and splitting. Over the years, Elaine had done the most essential repairs and painting herself or hired help, but most rooms needed refurbishing. The kitchen still had its original dark cabinets and yellowish linoleum. Grandchildren played on the same faded brown carpet as their parents had.

In their backyard was a twenty-by-thirty-foot vegetable garden plot, dug years earlier with good intentions at Hatch's insistence. After a few seasons of carrots and cucumbers, it was quietly relinquished to the weeds. Hatch had not liked weeding the garden a half-century earlier in that patch of woods in Pittsburgh, and he liked it no better in Virginia. Time was too precious. There were family members to counsel, friends to call, and books to read.

If the house and yard had good reason to doubt his devotion, Elaine and the children—his real concern at home—did not. They had had to share him with the nation, and had borne the sacrifices—not always silently. But all six children had grown strong and secure, never doubting his affection. Helen and Jesse taught Hatch well: He never left home or parted from a family member without saying, "I love you."

A growing number of Hatches were now hearing that message: By the end of '93, Orrin and Elaine's five married children were returning for visits with fourteen grandchildren in tow.

Brent, thirty-five, had been a legal whiz kid in Washington and now was a partner in a Salt Lake firm, Johnson & Hatch. He had attended

BYU, served a Mormon mission in New York City, and returned to take a law degree at Columbia. Brent and his wife, Mia Ensslin Hatch, have three daughters and a son.

Marcia, thirty-three, also a BYU graduate, had taught elementary school for several years, like Elaine. Marcia and her husband, Randy Whetton, a chiropractor, have two daughters and two sons, and live in Yucca Valley, California.

Scott, thirty-one, had served a mission to Arcadia, California, graduated from BYU, and returned to the capital to work at a consulting and lobbying firm. Scott and his wife, Wendy Dalgleish Hatch, have one daughter and a son, both in danger of being spoiled by their nearby Hatch grandparents.

Kimberly, twenty-nine, had attended BYU, then married John Catron, an attorney. With their four daughters, they made their home in Los Angeles.

Alysa, twenty-four, served an LDS mission to Japan, then graduated from BYU early in 1993 in fashion merchandising. As the year closed, she was living at home in Vienna, fending off suitors, and helping to run a store selling time-management materials.

Jess, twenty-three, and Mary Alice were both undergraduates at BYU. He had served a mission to England and was a business major with an outside shot at getting a job with the Marriott Corporation.

Among treasured mementos from his children's lives, Hatch tucked away a recent note from Marcia, which offered a private view of how the children viewed their public father:

> I was sitting here thinking how much I love you. You are such a great dad. . . . You are always such a strength and support. You have often been an answer to prayer in my life. I know that you listen and follow the promptings of the spirit. . . . I can't imagine eternity without my whole family around me. . . . I wish I could see you and Mom more often . . . Dad, you make me very proud. I owe so much to you and I pray I will make you proud of me.

On November 19, 1993 a member of the Senate Ethics Committee called Hatch to say the panel had completed its investigation of his office and BCCI. Verdict: not guilty. The committee issued a formal statement the next day:

> On August 12, 1992, Senator Hatch requested that the Ethics Committee initiate an inquiry. . . . In addition, on October 1, 1992, Senators Kerry and Brown . . . provided the Ethics Committee with information obtained by [their] Subcommittee during the course of its

investigation of BCCI that was determined to be outside its jurisdiction.

In addition ... the Committee subpoenaed and reviewed documents of 8 individuals and entities and conducted 10 depositions, including the deposition of Senator Hatch. . . .

Finding

The Committee finds on the basis of available evidence that there is no credible evidence which provides reason to believe that Senator Hatch engaged in any conduct which would constitute a violation of any law of the United States or of any rule of the Senate, nor any reason to believe that the Senator engaged in any improper conduct.

That last paragraph had cost Hatch as much as a half-million dollars in legal fees, still being raised at the end of the year, along with untold stress and political capital.

"I want to thank those who stuck by me, especially my wife, Elaine," he told the press. "Without question, these have been the worst two years of our lives."

His friend Robert Altman, charged with receiving millions in bribes to help BCCI illegally and secretly take control of First American Bank, had been acquitted in August by a New York jury. Altman's aging partner, Clark Clifford, was considered too ill to stand trial, but there was no reason to believe he had been guilty either. Near the end of the year, Clifford telephoned Hatch, thanking him profusely for his "strength of character" in standing by them in their ordeal.

For Hatch, a painful chapter was ending. But legitimate questions went unanswered and would likely remain that way in a Democratic Congress unless the media determined otherwise.

Hatch had been subjected to a blatant double standard after having the effrontery to document the outrageous behavior of CenTrust and its plutocrat-president, David Paul. Unlike senators involved with Paul and CenTrust, Hatch had not accepted campaign contributions from anyone associated with BCCI or banks in which BCCI had an interest. He did not fly on corporate jets or play on corporate yachts provided by BCCI. He did not attempt to block hearings on the bank or smother reports which detailed BCCI activities in the United States. No senator involved with CenTrust asked the Ethics Committee to investigate his office. Hatch's key contact with BCCI—Robert Altman—was found not guilty on all counts by a jury of his peers.

David Paul, on the other hand, lavished on political friends hundreds of thousands of dollars of what ultimately became taxpayer money. He was closely involved with several senators, raised funds for Democrats, and was tight with the Democratic Senatorial Campaign

Committee. He lobbied members of Congress, sought legislative solutions to his problems, and used Congress to pressure bank regulators. Paul also went to trial. He was convicted on fifty-eight criminal counts of fraudulently misusing bank funds.

Yet senators close to him were never held accountable by Congress or the mainstream media. It was Hatch who was falsely accused, investigated, and all but convicted in the court of public opinion—while David Paul's Senate pals went about their business and the media slept.

Thanksgiving came just five days after the Ethics Committee officially cleared Hatch. Joining Orrin and Elaine around the dinner table were Alysa and a girlfriend, Scott, Wendy, and their two children, and two neighbor families. Elaine had prepared a traditional Thanksgiving feast: roast turkey, mashed potatoes and gravy, stuffing, corn and yam soufflés, salad, and pumpkin pie. Afterward, the men watched football in the family room, while the women did the dishes and visited. It could hardly have been more all-American. That evening, Hatch wrote his mother:

> I have much to be thankful for on this Thanksgiving. To have been blessed with wonderful parents, good brothers and sisters, a wonderful wife, six very fine children, and 14 grandchildren is almost beyond belief.
>
> To have been born in this wonderful nation, which has the greatest Constitution in the world, is a source of great blessing and comfort ... To be able to serve in the church ... To have obtained an education which has enabled me to become an attorney and use my legal skills in a variety of ways ... To have this opportunity to serve our country in the United States Senate ... It's wonderful to have a best friend wife, a best friend mother, now a spiritual best friend father who was certainly a best friend on earth. It has also been very comforting to have best friends at work, in the church, in the country, in fact in the world.

Friend. It was Hatch's most-used description for others. He had sought to forge friendships throughout his career, often across what others regarded as unbridgeable differences.

That, above all, was what made Hatch singularly effective in the Senate. As he said about Ted Kennedy: "We have tried to develop a friendship that transcends politics and occasionally helps politics to transcend partisanship."

Kennedy, for his part, after working with Hatch almost every weekday for nearly seventeen years, observed in an interview for this book, "It's been said that after reaching the Senate, some people blow and some people grow. Orrin has grown. He learned to fight for what he believed in and still maintain a sense of humor and decency. . . . He has been a very effective legislator."

Hatch viewed the Senate as he viewed life. It was not a zero-sum game in which one side had to win everything and the other side to lose everything. Except where a bedrock principle was involved, Hatch usually sought a way for *both* sides to win, believing that only then could the nation truly win.

When former First Lady Pat Nixon died in June, 1993, Orrin and Elaine flew to California for the funeral. After the services, VIP guests left in a long caravan, with Hatch in the second van. Just before pulling away, Hatch spotted former Senator George McGovern in the fourth van, and sent a legislative aide back to invite him to join them. One of the most liberal men ever to seek the presidency, McGovern had long since fallen from public view, but not from Hatch's view.

At midyear, Howard Metzenbaum announced he would not run for a fourth term in 1994. The Ohio liberal had been elected to the Senate the same year as Hatch, and for seventeen years had opposed almost every measure Hatch favored.

"I'll miss him," Hatch told an interviewer, who waited in vain for a punch line. "No, I'm serious. Howard represents the left end of the political spectrum, just as Jesse Helms represents the right end. Both views deserve to have their case made in the people's forum, which is Congress."

Hatch was basically an apolitical person in a highly politicized environment. He judged issues sharply, but he did not judge people. Helen taught him well. She had said, "Only God is in a position to look down on anyone."

Sana Shtasel was also right. Years earlier the ardently feminist Democratic staffer had sent Hatch a thank-you note for a poem he dedicated to her. "What I believe is ultimately important and enduring," she had written, "is caring for others regardless of any philosophical differences."

Orrin Hatch made many mistakes during his first three terms in the Senate. Most were a result of allowing his heart to overrule his head. He remained remarkably optimistic about others, sometimes in the face of strong evidence of bad faith. He arrived in Washington in 1977 as a guileless citizen-senator. Seventeen years of pitched Senate battles, in which he often led the charge, had failed to dampen his zest for the struggle or his conviction that others would come to view issues as he viewed them if only they had the full facts. And he had gone to extraordinary lengths to gather and present those facts to his fellow citizens.

In 1994 the challenges facing Hatch and the nation were more daunting than ever. While the economy looked strong and America was outwardly at peace, there were mountains of evidence that America was not at peace with itself. Since 1960, when Hatch was in law school, the nation's population had increased about 40 percent. But its rate of violent crime had gone up more than 500 percent, illegitimate births 400 percent, teenage suicide 200 percent. Divorce rates had quadrupled, the percentage of children living in single-parent families had tripled, and homelessness was a national disgrace. Wholesale abortion and AIDS were scourges.

Perhaps voters in Utah would give Orrin Hatch six more years to help America scale those mountains. Perhaps not. But as 1994 dawned, Hatch characteristically was not waiting for the November verdict. He was deeply engaged in the nation's business—cooperating with America's new young president and Senate colleagues when he could in good conscience, opposing them fervently when he could not.

Political victories were wonderful, of course. But the struggle itself was exhilarating and, for Hatch, even essential. He lived a creed expressed by Danish philosopher Søren Kierkegaard—a creed Hatch occasionally shared with others in their own times of challenge:

"To venture causes anxiety, but not to venture is to lose oneself."

Sources

T HIS BIOGRAPHY IS BASED MAINLY on primary sources, including personal interviews with Orrin Hatch and some ten thousand pages of private notes and correspondence written by him within days of most events recounted in the book.

Political opponents and other critics of Hatch, as well as family, friends and allies, have offered their own perspectives on him as a public figure and private individual, both in interviews and in print. While many sources are quoted by name, others have requested and been given anonymity. I conducted most interviews specifically for the book in 1993.

I also relied on extensive personal notes taken as a political journalist in Washington, D.C., for fifteen years. Much of the written documentation is currently located in the Library of Congress, the Marriott and law libraries at the University of Utah, and in family records kept by Orrin and Elaine Hatch and his mother, Helen K. Hatch.

The book refers often to Hatch's voluminous private writings. His missionary diary was the earliest of these writings. Next were personal memos begun when he was first elected to the Senate in 1976, then, ten years later, private letters to his college-age children, written confidentially at the time. I was given permission by Hatch to use all of these writings, virtually without restriction. Unless otherwise noted, quotations, narratives, and commentary by Hatch are from these sources, from a score of interviews I conducted with him in 1993, or from my personal observations.

Prologue
xii   *"an independent-minded and enigmatic politician";* Julie Kosterlitz, "Tough to Typecast" (profile of Orrin Hatch), *National Journal,* August 19, 1989, 2089.

Chapter 1   The Early Years
1   *. . . to include the notorious Harry Longabaugh, aka Butch Cassidy . . . ;* Charles Kelley, *Outlaw Trail* (Salt Lake City, Utah: Charles Kelly, 1938), 77.

   Jeremiah was widely known as a friend to the Indians, who . . . ; For the Hatch family's role in settling Ashley Valley, see the Hatch File, Historical Collection, Uintah County Library, Vernal, Utah.

2   *Jeremiah, whose own grandfather of the same name fought in . . . ;* (LDS) *Church News,* November 13, 1982.

3   *Joe also stayed in Vernal but his civic record was not so . . . ;* "Martha Luella Thomas and Josephus Hatch—Family History," July 1985, typescript, in Orrin Hatch family records and genealogy.

   Fifteen-year-old Jesse had his first full-time job . . . ; Information about Jesse's youth, his courtship with Helen Kamm, and their early family life, including memories of Orrin Hatch's childhood, comes from Helen Kamm Hatch, interviews, 1993; notes in my possession. Additional information on Hatch's youth came from 1993 interviews with sisters Nancy Hatch Scott and Frances Hatch Merrill.

11   *"She gave me a love for English literature which has been . . .";* Orrin Hatch, National Parent-Teacher Association, Questionnaire on "The Public School Teacher Who Most Influenced My Life," completed June 12, 1986.

   "In the first vote, [student] Senator Earl Lyons . . ."; The *Purbalite,* May 21, 1952; photocopy in my possession.

12   *"Basketball whiz . . . hardworking union man . . .";* The *Balthi,* 1952; photocopy in my possession.

Chapter 2   The Missionary
13   *Jerry Muir, the BYU boxing instructor, was all over the dazed . . . ;* "Jerry Muir" is a pseudonym. Hatch remained in the class for the rest of the year. They never liked each other or boxed again against each other, but Hatch respected Muir as a boxing instructor.

   When BYU's 6,325 students completed a survey during Hatch's . . . ; Ernest L. Wilkinson, ed., *Brigham Young University: The First One Hundred Years* (Provo, Utah: Brigham Young University Press, 1975), 613.

14   *He always ended by asking students for a standing vote . . . ;* Ernest L. Wilkinson and W. Cleon Skousen, *Brigham Young University: A School of Destiny* (Provo, Utah: Brigham Young University Press, 1976), 595.

   In a campus opinion poll a few weeks before the election, 41 percent; Ibid., 598.

16   *As a fourteen-year-old boy in upstate New York, Smith . . . ;* Joseph Smith—History 1:17-19. This account was canonized in 1880 as part of LDS scripture, *The Pearl of Great Price: A Selection from the Revelations, Translations, and Narrations of Joseph Smith . . .* (Salt Lake City, Utah: The Church of Jesus Christ of Latter-day Saints, 1981 edition).

17   *His mission president was a Utah dentist named Lorin L. Richards . . . ;* Florence Richards, interview, 1993; notes in my possession. She is also the source of other statements, either as attributed to her, or quoted from her late husband, in this chapter.

Chapter 3   From Henhouse to Courthouse
25   *Even among the weather-hardened farmers . . . ;* Elaine Hansen Hatch, interviews, 1993; notes in my possession. She also contributed information about her courtship with Orrin Hatch and details of the early years of their marriage in this chapter.

39 *Hatch tried a case before Willis Ritter, chief judge of the U.S. District Court . . .*; In addition to Hatch's memories of Ritter, Utah attorney Scott Savage told several Ritter stories and appraised Hatch's courtroom competence, as attributed, in this chapter.

41 *. . . to his neighbor and fellow church volunteer Frank Madsen . . .*; Frank Madsen, interview, 1993; notes in my possession. He also contributed additional information about Hatch's campaign and first election in Chapter 4.

42 *. . . but Nokes encouraged Hatch to do it . . .*; Jackie Nokes (widow of Grey Nokes), interview, 1993; notes in my possession.

Chapter 4   Orrin Who?

45 *Although Welch "has almost a Messianic complex . .";* Ernest L. Wilkinson, Diary, August 19–22, 1965, photocopy in Special Collections, Marriott Library, University of Utah, Salt Lake City.
    "The old-line party professionals tell me I have no chance . . ."; Salt Lake Tribune, May 11, 1976.
    Skousen wrote a campaign letter the next day . . .; Cleon L. Skousen, letter endorsing Hatch, May 12, 1976; photocopy in my possession.

47 *"Hatch hadn't formulated any issues, had laid none . . .";* Renee Pyott Carlson, The Best Man Doesn't Always Win (Privately printed, 1984; distributed by Signature Books, Midvale, Utah), 46.

48 *. . . "tall, physically attractive . . . and aware of this . . .";* Ibid., 85.

49 *. . . "a quick study" who had "assimilated in a few weeks . . .";* Ibid.

51 *One concerned Republican, in a letter to the editor . . .*; Lowell C. Brown, letter to the editor, Deseret News, July 15, 1976.

52 *Skousen wrote another letter on Hatch's behalf . . .*; Cleon Skousen, letter to Freemen Institute members, mailed ca. August 25, 1976; photocopy in my possession.

53 *"I feel so badly that I am the culprit . . .";* Helen K. Hatch, letter to the editor, Deseret News, September 10, 1976.
    On the same page appeared a witty letter that quoted Hatch's . . .; Henry Heath, ibid.
    "THE TIME HAS COME FOR ME TO DO EVERYTHING I CAN . . ."; Advertisement, Salt Lake Tribune, September 12, 1976.

55 *"Hatch was completely a blank page to me . . .";* Frank E. ("Ted") Moss, interview, 1993, notes in my possession.
    "I told him that Hatch might be more difficult than he figured . . ."; Dale Zabriskie, interviewed 1993; notes in my possession.

56 *"I have tried to get Orrin Hatch today to give him some advice . . .";* Wilkinson, diary, September 17, 1976.

57 *In a traditional luncheon debate before Utah clergy . . .*; Salt Lake Tribune, October 14, 1976.
    Moss asked Howe to meet with him and Gunn McKay . . .; Moss, interview, 1993.

58 *Moss's staff compiled an alphabetized briefing book on Hatch . . .*; This book and other relevant papers are in the Frank E. Moss Papers, Special Collections, Marriott Library, University of Utah, Salt Lake City.
    Pollster J. Roy Bardsley predicted that "an upset could be . . ."; Salt Lake Tribune, October 12, 1976.

59 *"We want to check government spending; they want to spend . . .";* Salt Lake Tribune, October 28, 1976.

60 *. . . including her father, Sidney Hansen of Newton . . .*; Deseret News, November 3, 1976.

Chapter 5   Settling In

62 *Oregon Republican Mark Hatfield took Hatch to the corner office . . .*; Hatch's personal writings, recording his reaction to the new environment, constitute the main source for this chapter with the exceptions noted below.

62   *While party balance was unchanged, noted the Congressional Quarterly . . .* ; "Largest Turnover in Senate since 1958," *1976 CQ Almanac*, 830.
66   *"It's one thing for an older fellow like myself . . ."*; Hubert Humphrey, undated memo to Orrin Hatch; photocopy in my possession.
69   *"I want to be known as a person who fights hard . . ."*; *National Journal*, March 17, 1979.
71   *"Mr. President, after a great deal of consideration . . ."*; *Congressional Record*, January 19, 1977.
73   *"We are different from previous generations . . ."*; *National Journal*, January 21, 1978.

Chapter 6   The Rookie
77   *"For five emotional minutes the chamber resounded with . . ."*; *Washington Post*, October 26, 1977.
78   *"[Humphrey] taught us all how to hope and how to love . . ."*; *Congressional Quarterly*, January 21, 1978, 114.
79   *Hatch quickly earned the reputation of being "bright, articulate, unafraid . ."*; Bruce H. Jensen, "Thunder on the Right," *Utah Holiday*, February 1978, 121.
     Redford said the "general view" of Utah's delegation . . . ; *Daily Universe* (BYU student newspaper), March 28, 1978.
     "My staff was going crazy when Orrin first arrived . . ."; Jake Garn, interview, 1993; notes in my possession.
80   *"Orrin had a save-the-world complex. He wasn't malicious . . ."*; Paul Laxalt, interview, 1993; notes in my possession.
81   *Moynihan, a New York Democrat, called a treaty amendment . . .* ; In addition to Hatch's private record, a photocopy of the transcript of Moynihan's original remarks is in my possession, and his revised remarks appear in the *Congressional Record*, March 20, 1978, S-4109; Hatch's rebuke appears on S-4111.
82   *"The Post called DeConcini "a 40-year-old freshman . . ."*; *Washington Post*, editorial, April 13, 1978; Hatch, letter to editor, April 13, 1978, typescript in Hatch correspondence.
83   *Meany publicly labeled Carter "indecisive" and graded . . .* ; *New York Times*, May 26, 1978.
84   *A U.S. News & World Report poll in 1978 named him . . .* ; *1979 Congressional Directory* (Washington, D.C.: U.S. Government Printing Office, 1979), 192.
86   *"Up until now the chief casualties in this congressional wrangling . ."*; "Why the Bitter Fight over a New Labor Law," *U.S. News & World Report*, April 10, 1978.

Chapter 7   The Labor Law Battle
89   *Rinfret's study warns that "the proposal would hit small business . . ."*; Richard Lugar, "That Labor Bill," *New York Times*, June 20, 1978.
96   *Lugar writes in the New York Times: "To say that there is no . . ."*; Ibid.
97   *This week's Kiplinger Washington Letter arrives in Hatch's office*; Kiplinger Washington Letter, June 16, 1978.

Chapter 8   Encounter with a Feminist
103 *"those who thought the question of [Kennedy's] philandering . . ."*; Suzannah Lessard, *Washington Monthly*, December 1979.
105 *"When it is not necessary to adopt a constitutional amendment . . ."*; Orrin Hatch, "An Intelligent Guide to the Equal Rights Amendment" (Washington, D.C.: Orrin Hatch, 1978).
106 *"We must place no time limit on the pursuit of equality . . ."*; Hearings on S. J. Res. 134, Joint Resolution Extending the Deadline for the Ratification of the Equal Rights Amendment, August 2-4, 1978, 2.
107 *Garn cited a survey by a California polling firm . . .* ; Ibid., 26. The polling firm was Decision Making Information, Los Angeles, the same firm used by Ronald Reagan.

"Based on experience since 1972," said Ginsburg . . . ; Ibid., 263.

Borrowing a phrase from Oliver Wendell Holmes, Ervin said . . . ; Ibid., 185.

108   *Early on the morning of August 4, 1978 . . .* ; The account of the hearings from Johnson's perspective, unless otherwise noted, is from her book, *From Housewife to Heretic* (1981; reprint ed., Albuquerque, N.M.: Wildfire Books, New Mexico, 1989), 130-38.

Then Johnson read a prepared statement, asking rhetorically . . . ; Quotations of testimony are from Hearings of the Subcommittee on the Constitution, photocopy of transcript, August 4, 1978, 307-58.

112   *"Utah Senator, Mormon Woman clash at Hearings on ERA"; Washington Star,* August 5, 1978.

"After watching you in the hearings, I have decided to nominate . . ."; Johnson, *From Housewife to Heretic,* 131.

114   *We are grateful for this great land and the freedoms . . .* ; *Congressional Record,* October 13, 1978, 36633.

The proposal, said the church, would strike at the family . . . ; LDS First Presidency statement, October 12, 1978, quoted in "The Church and the Proposed Equal Rights Amendment: A Moral Issue," copyrighted by *The Ensign,* the church's official monthly periodical for adults, February 1980. This twenty-three-page booklet outlines the Church's opposition to the ERA in question-answer form.

The church gave marching orders and supplied foot soldiers . . . ; For an analysis of the LDS church's fight against the ERA, see Linda Sillitoe and Paul Swenson, "A Moral Issue," *Utah Holiday,* January 1980, 18-34.

In answer to persistent questions, LDS leaders emphasized . . . ; "The Church and the Proposed Equal Rights Amendment," 17.

115   *"'If the missionaries ever come to my door, I wouldn't . . .'";* Transcript of news film clip of a Johnson speech in Kalispell, Montana, quoted in Sillitoe and Swenson, "A Moral Issue," 28.

"Her appearance before a congressional committee infuriated . . ."; *People,* December 3, 1979.

"I was pleased to see in your entertaining magazine . . ."; Ibid., December 24-31, 1979, 6.

116   *"He never did really get loud, but he got mean and personal.";* Cheryl Arvidson, interview, 1993; notes in my possession.

"We had some 'zinger' questions we wanted him to ask her . . ."; Randy Rader, interview, 1993; notes in my possession.

"They just didn't see it as the senator trying to engage . . ."; Steve Markman, interview, 1993; notes in my possession.

. . . the senator had "focused the media attention on her . . ."; Mary L. Bradford, "The Odyssey of Sonia Johnson," *Dialogue: A Journal of Mormon Thought* 14 (Winter 1981): 20.

"I think I'll always be a Mormon, no matter what."; In Sillitoe and Swenson, "A Moral Issue," 34.

117   *"Marriage also ceased to engage my attention. The idea . . .";* Preface to the 1989 edition of *From Housewife to Heretic.*

Chapter 9   Gentlemen of the Senate

119   *"Your endorsement was perfectly timed and politically potent.";* Brooke, letter to Hatch, September 29, 1978; photocopy in my possession.

120   *. . . $8,000–less than 2 percent–of the more than $500,000 . . .* ; Hatch's 1976 campaign spending report, filed with the Federal Election Commission; photocopy in my possession.

121   *"Crane wants exposure to establish his primacy . . .";* In *The American Political Report* (newsletter of the American Political Research Corporation), August 4, 1978, 3.

. . . polls "suggest that Carter is already unlikely to recover . . ."; Ibid., 1

122   Kaiser ended the piece by saying, "Hatch's rhetoric has earned . . ."; Washington Post, June 16, 1978.
123   . . . but Time magazine's cover used a sizeable photograph . . . ; Time, July 3, 1978.
       . . . "an issue of elementary human rights" and said . . . ; Washington Post, editorial, August 22, 1978.
125   Senator Birch Bayh, the bill's sponsor, wrote Hatch to thank him . . . ; Bayh, letter to Hatch, July 18, 1978; photocopy in my possession.
       . . . some called the final version the Humphrey-Hawkins-Hatch . . . ; Congressional Quarterly, October 21, 1978.
       Coretta Scott King called it "a major victory" . . . ; Ibid.
126   "Your presence was a turning point and did more good . . ."; Percy, letter to Hatch, December 1, 1978; photocopy in my possession.
       "I think our chances [of passing pro-union legislation] . . ."; U.S. News & World Report, November 20, 1978, 69.
127   An Arkansas newspaper dubbed him "a living monument . . ."; In ibid., p. 33.
       "If you look at the soft heads in Congress, most of them . . ."; Congressional Quarterly, August 5, 1978, 2027.
       The politics of Hatch and Heinz were also dissimilar . . . ; Alan Ehrenhalt, ed., Politics in America (Washington, D.C.: CQ Press, 1984), 1277, 1532.
128   Days later, influential columnists Jack Germond and Jules Witcover . . . ; Washington Star, November 26, 1978.
129   Conservative columnist Pat Buchanan contrasted Heinz's . . . ; photocopy of undated Buchanan column in my possession.
       "I know that you would do a good job," Lugar told Heinz . . . ; Lugar, letter to Heinz, December 29, 1978; photocopy in my possession.

Chapter 10   Bouncing Back

135   Early in 1979, National Journal chose Hatch as one of five . . . ; Richard E. Cohen, "Freshmen in the Senate Being Seen–and Heard," National Journal, March 17, 1979.
137   "The electoral college is a product of its time–America in 1787 . ."; Congressional Record, June 26, 1979, 16540.
       Journalist Edwin Yoder summarized the other side of the issue . . . ; Washington Star, February 22, 1979.
139   . . . system was "grossly unfair; it seems un-American to me . . ."; Congressional Record, March 15, 1979, 5196.
       . . . the vote later that day would be "perhaps the most . . ."; Ibid., July 10, 1979, 17702.
140   . . . Percy had taken the floor to thank Hatch for helping . . . ; Ibid., June 21, 1979, 15877.
       "I see no compelling reason for us to amend the Constitution . . ."; Ibid., July 10, 1979, 17757.
141   . . . both gave numerous two thousand dollar speeches . . . ; In 1979, Hatch earned $24,975 in honoraria, tenth among all senators and barely behind Garn who received $25,000, the maximum allowable under Senate rules.
142   "If he does, I'll whip his ass."; Washington Star, June 14, 1979.
       "What happened that night and the senator's attitude toward it . . ."; "The Kennedy Puzzle," Newsweek, September 24, 1979, 114.
143   "Thanks, but my father always said, 'If it's on the table . . .'"; Ibid.
       . . . had issued a withering attack on both Crane and his wife . . ."; Manchester Union Leader, March 8, 1979.

Chapter 11   Reagan and Other Rebels

147   "It's not the first attempted land grab," warned an editor . . . ; Ted Trueblood, "They're Fixing to Steal Your Land," Field & Stream, March 1980, 166.

"Back then, Orrin was a lot like Ronald Reagan," says Laxalt; Paul Laxalt, interview, 1993; notes in my possession.

148   *"Hatch writes well," Decker concluded. "He is clear and smooth."*; *Deseret News*, November 30, 1979.

154   *"If we had not let ourselves be bullied all over the Middle East . . ."*; *Utah Daily Chronicle* (University of Utah), January 14, 1980.

156   *"Help us to stamp out discrimination, but not by discriminating."*; My notes at the convention.

158   *"You can't have $140 billion in tax cuts, $100 billion . . ."*; *Salt Lake Tribune*, September 24, 1980.

       "Programs may sometimes become obsolete, but the idea of . . ."; *Salt Lake Tribune*, October 29, 1980.

Chapter 12   The Republicans Take Charge

162   *"If the Republicans take control of the Senate . . ."*; Jonathan Alter, "On the Hill: Borin' Orrin," *New Republic*, June 28, 1980, 9-12.

163   *"Despite a first-class intellect," wrote Al Hunt of the Wall Street Journal . . .* ; *Wall Street Journal*, February 24, 1981.

164   *"Hatch's assumption of control over labor legislation . . ."*; *Boston Globe*, November 8, 1980.

       "I believe in equality of opportunity, but not equality of condition . . ."; *Congressional Quarterly*, February 21, 1981, 350.

       . . . of a "last-gasp ultraliberal effort to impose the federal government . . ."; Ibid., October 10, 1981, 1953.

166   *"Asked about his priorities," wrote Hunt . . .* ; *Wall Street Journal*, February 24, 1981.

       "Sexual harassment in the workplace is not a figment . . ."; *Salt Lake Tribune*, April 22, 1981. This report also describes Schlafly's testimony.

167   *"The investigation showed that Hatch and Kennedy . . ."*; *Congressional Quarterly*, February 21, 1981.

168   *"It troubles me that we would require of a judge something . . ."*; *Congressional Quarterly*, July 11, 1981.

170   *"There are two things that are for sure," said Karen Mulhauser . . .* ; Ibid., September 12, 1981.

       "If this amendment becomes law, all abortions will be outlawed."; *Salt Lake Tribune*, November 5, 1981.

171   *but Reagan labeled Watt's detractors "environmental . . ."*; Ibid., December 27, 1980.

       "Please convey my best wishes to all my fellow 'Sagebrush Rebels.'"; *Salt Lake Tribune*, November 21, 1980.

172   *The Sagebrush Rebellion, he said, was in fact an attempted . . .* ; *Salt Lake Tribune*, March 13, 1981.

173   *Instead, Watt said meekly, the answer is "a good neighbor . . ."*; Ibid., December 24, 1980.

       "The President continues to be a Sagebrush Rebel and so does . . ."; Michael Reese, "Watt Defuses a Rebellion," *Newsweek*, September 21, 1981.

       "While we believe in the multiple use, the preservation and . . ."; *First Monday* (a newsletter published by the Republican National Committee), January-February 1982.

174   *"I say 'recognized,' not 'created,' because in my view that . . ."*; *Salt Lake Tribune*, December 13, 1981.

       "The only kind of gun control I believe in is a steady aim."; Undated Hatch speech on gun control.

175   *. . . First Presidency unexpectedly opposed MX deployment . . ."*; *Salt Lake Tribune*, May 6, 1981.

       The Mormon statement, said General Richard Ellis, head of . . . ; Ibid.

. . . editorial page carried a political cartoon depicting . . .; Ibid., May 13, 1981.

176   *"Mr. Hatch–an aggressive, ambitious man who, as much as . . ."*; Steven Roberts, "Point Man for the New Right," *New York Times*, November 22, 1981, Sec. 4, p. 5.

"The main ingredients of Hatch's senatorial style seem to be . . ."; Nadine Cohodas, "Orrin Hatch: The Mace and the Olive Branch," *Congressional Quarterly*, October 10, 1981, 1955.

The New Right's Paul Weyrich ruefully came to the same conclusion; Ibid., 1956.

Chapter 13   Winning a Second Term

177   *The Political Wit and Wisdom of Orrin G. Hatch and His . . .*; Copy in Special Collections, Marriott Library, University of Utah, Salt Lake City.

"As we review these critical issues, one overriding theme . . ."; photocopy of Wilson speech, Special Collections, Marriott Library.

180   *Early in 1982, forty-one-year-old Arthur Laffer, an economics . . .*; *U.S. News and World Report*, January 18, 1982.

183   *. . . "no one donates to him expecting favors because they . . ."*; *Salt Lake Tribune*, August 21, 1981.

Common Cause labeled the votes "expedient, self-interested . . ."; *Salt Lake Tribune*, September 27, 1981.

Hatch earned $46,330 in honoraria, keeping $29,700 . . .; Secretary of the Senate, Member Financial Records for 1981, notes in my possession.

"Economy," wrote the great fiscal conservative Edmund Burke, "is . . ."; Clews, letter to editors, January 26, 1982; photocopy in my possession.

184   *Wilson also believed Reagan and Congress should have cut the . . .*; *Salt Lake Tribune*, April 18, 1982.

Early in January, a poll commissioned by the Salt Lake Tribune . . ."; *Salt Lake Tribune*, January 17, 1982. The research firm of Bardsley and Haslacher conducted the poll.

185   *"I can't say I was stampeded by people . . . looking for . . ."*; Bill Keller, "Castoff Congressmen Find More Money and Less Misery Lobbying Former Colleagues," *Congressional Quarterly*, December 27, 1980, 3643–45.

"Along with his adherence to principle, he has the ability . . ."; *Salt Lake Tribune*, August 25, 1982.

. . . once saying the "Eastern elite" regarded the West as their . . .; Ibid., July 11, 1982.

"My Republican opponent," said Wilson, "has voted right down . . ."; Ibid., July 1, 1982.

Incumbents like Hatch who spent most of their money early, . . .; *Congressional Quarterly*, August 18, 1982.

"Let's assume that Ted goes back to Washington and he really. . . .; *Salt Lake Tribune*, July 2, 1982.

Hatch stressed that Utahns had a big investment in him . . .; Ibid., September 25, 1982. This source summarizes the Park City debate.

187   *On October 11 they squared off in Logan, just days after news . . .*; Ibid., October 12, 1982. Hatch's reaction to being booed is in his private notes.

188   *Defending Reaganomics, Hatch insisted the president was a . . .*; Ibid., 22 October 1982. This article includes Hansen's rebuke and Hatch's statement of response.

189   *"The biggest single factor was the economy," said one . . .*; Dan Jones, interview, 1993; notes in my possession.

. . . he later acknowledged to Hatch that funding had not been . . .; Wilson's comment is as reported by Hatch in an interview for this book after the campaign. Information on union assistance to Wilson is from Utah sources knowledgeable about that campaign.

. . . Newsweek dubbed him "Foreign Orrin."; *Newsweek*, October 11, 1982.

Chapter 14   Family Matters

192   *Fifteen-year-old Scott Hatch was in the kitchen with his mother . . .* ; Elaine H. Hatch, interviews, 1993; notes in my possession. Interviews with Elaine and Orrin provided most of the information in this chapter.

194   *One evening the family invited a reporter . . .* ; I was the reporter in question.

195   *One reporter astutely observed that guest-lists in "Embassy Row . . ."*; Al Hunt, *Wall Street Journal,* December 11, 1980.

197   *"I know I'm a member of the Capitol Hill family because my master . . ."*; Ralston Purina Company, St. Louis, Missouri, press release, August 12, 1986.

Chapter 15   Tackling Women's Issues

200   *But the coalition was weakening in 1982 and occasionally . . .* ; 1982 *Congressional Quarterly Almanac,* 40-C.

202   *. . . he argued that "the burden properly lies with proponents . . ."*; Orrin Hatch, *The Equal Rights Amendment: Myths and Realities* (N.p.: Savant Press, 1983), 85.
      . . . saying "there is something unseemly about the male members . . ."; Hearing on the Equal Rights Amendment before the Senate Subcommittee on the Constitution, May 26, 1983; photocopy of stenographer's draft in my possession. The quotations on pp. 202–4 are from this transcript.

205   *William F. Buckley called the Hatch-Tsongas exchange "marvelous" . . .* ; *Salt Lake Tribune,* June 21, 1983.
      George F. Will said Hatch "simply asked Tsongas what the amendment . . ."; *Washington Post,* June 2, 1983.
      "One can only reasonably conclude that . . ."; Hatch, *The Equal Rights Amendment,* 85.

206   *Thus, in the church's eyes, while abortion in most cases is . . .* ; "Church Issues Statement on Abortion," *Ensign* (official LDS monthly magazine), July 1976, 76. This statement allowed abortion to save the mother's life or in cases of conception by rape. By 1983, the official LDS *General Handbook of Instructions,* 77–78, added conception by incest as a defensible reason for abortion but broadened the list of those who may be liable to church disciplinary action to those who "encourage" abortion, as well as those who "perform, or submit to" abortions.
      As soon as the needle went in, she said, "I hated myself."; *Washington Times,* reprinted in hearings before the U.S. Senate, Subcommittee on the Constitution, Serial No. J-98-12, March 7, 1983, 257.

208   *In February, Hatch held two more days of hearings;* The following quotations from testimony are all from Hearings on the Equal Rights Amendment . . . , February 29 and March 7, 1983.

Chapter 16   Against the Tide

216   *He was a champion debater at Brigham Young University, for example . . .* ; Mark Hartshorn (Haddow debate opponent), interview, 1993; notes in my possession.

217   *There, on the bottom-left corner of the front page, was Haddow's . . .* ; *Washington Post,* June 18, 1986.

220   *"I've never known a person who's more misunderstood," said . . .* ; Steve Osborne, "Going to the Wall in Washington," *This People,* August 1983, 19–22, 52.
      "I don't know anyone easier to work for than Orrin Hatch . . ."; Ronald Madsen, interview, 1993; notes in my possession.

222   *"This is the most massive shift of power . . . [that] the U.S. Congress . . .* ; *Congressional Record,* September 29, 1984, S-12,418.
      "I feel deeply about civil rights," he said on the floor; Ibid., S-12,417. The quotations from Packwood and Kennedy (p. 223) are from the same page.

225   *"All of my children join with me in expressing to you . . ."*; Hak Ja Han Moon, letter to Hatch, August 24, 1984; photocopy in my possession.

Jeanette Williams, who had recently been in a serious car accident . . . ; Jeanette Williams, letter to Hatch, November 22, 1984; photocopy in my possession.

Chapter 17   Friends and Foes

229   *"There is a blind ideological aspect to some politicians . . .";* Edward M. Kennedy, interview, 1993; notes in my possession.
       "That took gall, guts, and an awful lot of sense," a labor lobbyist . . . ; Nadine Cohodas, *Congressional Quarterly,* October 10, 1981, 1953.
230   *"I enclose a piece of direct mail that is going out under your name . . .";* The letter, written on Dodd's personal stationery, was undated.
231   *"The Rise and Gall of Roger Stone" . . . ; Washington Post,* June 16, 1986.
232   *"I remember when legislation . . .";* Jan Bennett, interview, 1993; notes in my possession.
233   *That you would take the time to be so thoughtful speaks to . . .";* Shtasel, letter to Hatch, November 28, 1984.
       Her first speech after taking office in September 1985 was . . . ; Smeal's speech was reported in the *New York Times* and *Washington Post,* September 6, 1985. Hatch's press statement is in his files.
237   *"While a man can have no greater love than to be willing . . .";* Manuscript of speech, October 19, 1984.
238   *"They continue to write 'moving' editorials about me . . .";* Hatch recorded this joke in his personal notes.
242   *Rejoining the hearing, Hatch led Meese through a recitation . . . ;* Hatch recorded this line of questioning in his notes for the hearing.

Chapter 18   The Rehnquisition

245   *"Already we face a $170 billion bill each year just to pay . . .";* Congressional Record, March 25, 1986.
246   *"We fell one vote short. But without your leadership we would . . .";* Davidson, letter to Hatch, April 1, 1986; photocopy in my possession.
247   *Justice Rehnquist, with his wife, Natalie, and other family . . . ;* The summaries and quotations from testimony on pp. 247-51 are, except for the sources cited below, from Hearings before the Senate Judiciary Committee on the Nomination of Associate Justice William H. Rehnquist to be Chief Justice of the United States; photocopy of transcript in my possession.
248   *"Mainstream or too extreme–that is the question,"; Washington Post,* July 30, 1986.
       . . . the two Senators "are not exactly [the] Lewis and Clark . . ."; Ibid., August 3, 1986.
249   *Committee member Paul Simon, D-Illinois, however, says the public . . . ;* Judi Hasson, UPI story, wire version, as filed August 13, 1986.
       "Frankly, the only significant thing in the report is that . . ."; New York Times, August 13, 1986.
250   *The deed specifies that no part of the land "shall ever be used . . .";* Washington Post, August 3, 1986.
       He has "no knowledge of any covenant on the former home of . . ."; Ibid., August 4, 1986.
252   *Senator Laxalt said Rehnquist "had everything but the kitchen sink . . .";* 1986 CQ Almanac, 71.
       . . . called the negative votes a "moral defeat" for the . . . ; Richard Carelli, AP story, wire version, as filed September 17, 1986.
253   *Although Hatch was "only fourth in seniority among the Republicans . . .";* New York Times, August 2, 1986.
       "You have been a tower of strength on the Judiciary Committee . . ."; Rehnquist, letter to Hatch, August 1, 1986; photocopy in my possession.
       "Your comments during the committee hearings and your skilled . . ."; Reagan, letter to Hatch, August 15, 1986; photocopy in my possession.

"Washington is already fluttering with rumors about the court's . . ."; Newsweek,
September 22, 1986.
Lyle Denniston called Hatch "a tall, superbly dressed senator . . ."; Baltimore Sun,
September 22, 1986.
254 *"The 52-year-old Hatch . . . has been in the thick of . . .";* Legal Times, September 22,
1986.

Chapter 19   The Stingers
258 *"The CIA believed they had to handle this as if they were wearing . . .";* Washington
Post, July 20, 1992.
259 *"Your courage, honesty and frankness are highly appreciated . . .";* Salehi, letter to
Hatch, representing the Islamic Unity of Afghanistan Mujahideen (sic),
November 14, 1985.
260 *"I consider it very important for your [mission] to meet . . .";* Armacost, letter to Hatch,
January 2, 1986; photocopy in my possession.
. . . *calling it "one of the most significant experiences . . .";* Dee Benson, memo to
Hatch, ca. January 1986.
261 *"The decision, which has been closely held among the President's . . .";* Washington Post,
March 30, 1986.
Columnists Rowland Evans and Robert Novak reported that Reagan . . . ; Washington
Post, April 11, 1986.
"Tyler repeated in no uncertain terms that Pillsbury was not . . ."; Chris Williams,
memo to Hatch, May 15, 1986.
Time magazine later did a profile on him and another national . . . ; Time, May 23,
1988.
262 *"The State Department continues to divert attention from the problem . . .";* Hatch,
typescript of speech, August 13, 1986.
. . . *Hatch, "who helped persuade the Reagan administration to send . . .";* Washington
Post, September 9, 1986.
263 *"Savimbi captures two-thirds of his weapons from the MPLA . . .";* Orrin Hatch,
"Savimbi Deserves Support," typescript of speech, January 27, 1986.
264 . . . *as "a true revolutionary hero" and pledge "to do everything . . .";* Speech text
prepared for American Security Council dinner, Washington, D.C., February 4,
1986.
"Ever since Mengistu seized power in 1977 . . ."; Los Angeles Times, April 20, 1986.
265 *While the Sandinistas portray the contras as intransigent . . . ;* Washington Post, April 8,
1986.
"The fighting is going much better this year," one guerrilla . . . ; Washington Post,
October 14, 1987.
266 *An estimated million Afghans had been killed, and more than half . . . ;* The 1990 World
Book Year Book: A Review of the Events of 1989 (Chicago: World Book, Inc., 1989),
157.
Hatch's pivotal role in getting the Stinger into the hands of the . . . ; Washington Post,
July 20, 1992.

Chapter 20   Democrats Retake the Senate
270 *Hatch began with a question reportedly once asked of former . . . ;* Typescript of speech,
February 26, 1987.
271 *"Dr. Koop exhibits all the qualities that we want in our nation's . . .";* Typescript of
speech, May 20, 1987.
272 *Koop wrote warmly to Hatch, saying it was "so like" the Utahn . . . ;* Koop, letter to
Hatch, July 23, 1987; photocopy in my possession.
"Perhaps the most insulting slap in the face to his conservative . . ."; Family Protection
Report, July/August 1987; photocopy in my possession.

"If every member of the Senate were like Orrin Hatch, we'd . . ."; Reagan's original 5 x 7 speech cards, June 17, 1987; photocopy in my possession.

273 *"Our support of one another was not born out of political . . ."*; Deseret News, June 17, 1987.

"You may come to my office at S-243 at which location upon . . ."; Simpson, letter to Hatch, June 17, 1987.

A Washington correspondent for the Daily Herald in Provo, Utah . . . ; I was that journalist.

275 *"There's no question that Senator Hatch saved the deal by . . ."*; Joseph A. Cannon, interview, 1987; notes in my possession.

276 *In welcoming remarks, Hatch said as a "direct result" of what . . .* ; Typescript of Hatch's opening remarks, October 30, 1987.

"When I needed you, you were there," said Laxalt, "even though . . ."; Laxalt, letter to Hatch, September 1, 1987; photocopy in my possession.

Chapter 21   The Iran-contra Affair

278 *"These hearings will examine what happens when the trust which . . ."*; Opening statements and subsequent testimony cited in the chapter are from the Joint Senate-House Select committee Hearings into the Iran-Contra Affair, beginning May 5, 1987.

280 *That same week, a correspondent for the Wall Street Journal reported . . .* ; Wall Street Journal, May 18, 1987.

. . . who said Hatch "is not asking hard questions, but in fact . . ."; Ogden Standard Examiner, June 2, 1987.

A political cartoon by Herbert Block ("Herblock") in the Washington Post . . . ; Washington Post, July 14, 1993.

281 *McFarlane wrote to Hatch . . .* ; McFarlane, letter on personal stationery to Hatch, June 9, 1987; photocopy in my possession.

282 *"You are a man who has devoted your life in the most unselfish . . ."*; Reagan, letter to North, November 4, 1985, reprinted in North's autobiography, *Under Fire: An American Story* (New York: HarperCollins, 1991), 418-19.

284 *Forty-four percent of those responding to a Gallup Poll after . . . .* ; Poll, with a margin of error of plus or minus 5 percent, Newsweek, July 20, 1987.

285 *By early September, Hatch's office had received some eight thousand . . .* ; Suzanne Van Leishout (staff member), memo to Hatch, September 11, 1987.

Chapter 22   To Hang a Judge

286 *"Reagan and a few top aides immediately began discussing names,"*; George J. Church, "The Court's Pivot Man," Time, July 6, 1987, 10.

287 *. . . this headline appeared in full-page advertisements in . . .* ; Washington Post, September 15, 1987.

288 *"Robert Bork's America," said a demagogic Ted Kennedy . . .* ; U.S. News & World Report, September 14, 1987, 18. The NAACP statement is also quoted in this source.

Molly Yard, aging feminist and president-elect of NOW, called . . . ; Washington Post, July 20, 1987.

Bork, born sixty years earlier in Pittsburgh, had been an . . . ; Dave Beckwith, "A Long and Winding Odyssey," Time, September 21, 1987, 16. The biographical information on Bork in this section comes primarily from this source.

291 *Less than a year earlier, senators had voted unanimously to . . .* ; White House position paper on Bork nomination, issued in August 1987; Hatch made a memo to himself about the note on September 15, 1987.

Biden scrawled a misspelled note to Hatch, "Orin, are you . . ."; photocopy in my possession.

"My philosophy of judging is neither liberal nor conservative . . ."; All quotations from testimony in this chapter, unless otherwise noted, are from Confirmation Hearings on the Nomination of Judge Robert H. Bork to the Supreme Court, beginning September 15, 1987 (Serial No. J-100-64).

292   *Biden was pleased. "Every time I could get him to recant . . ."*; *Washington Post,* October 24, 1987.

    Veteran lobbyist and former Utahn Tom Korologos had been . . .; *Legal Times,* September 21, 1987.

    Korologos slipped Hatch a note before he delivered his . . .; photocopy in my possession.

    Hatch summarized his case for Bork this way: "By any standard . . ."; Typescript of speech, September 19, 1987; in Hatch's files.

293   *Biden, it seemed, had been liberally appropriating the words . . .*; Paul Taylor, "Biden: A 'Regular Guy' with Regular Guy Flaws," *Washington Post,* September 20, 1987.

    In fact, Biden had finished 506th out of 688 students . . .; Gloria Borger, "On Trial: Character," *U.S. News & World Report,* September 28, 1987.

294   *Hatch warned, "Political involvement in the selection of . . ."*; "Save the Court from What?" Review by Orrin Hatch, *Harvard Law Review* 99 (April 1986): 1347–61.

    Tribe: "I am concerned about a very simple 200-year-old . . ."; Hearings before the Senate Judiciary Committee, Serial No. J-100-64, 1306–7.

    "Senator, if Judge Bork is not in the mainstream, neither am . . ."; Ibid., 2104.

296   *"It is time to start the healing. I urge the President to . . ."*; *Washington Post,* October 24, 1987.

    Some members of the Judiciary committee "did not care if the . . ."; Ibid., December 5, 1987.

    . . . a hand-written note "to express both my gratitude and . . ."; Photocopy of letter, December 14, 1987, in my files.

297   *"At the first sign of trouble [White House officials] cut . . ."*; *Washington Post,* November 18, 1987.

    Irritated by the administration, he called the White House . . .; *Washington Post,* November 10, 1987.

Chapter 23   Float like a Butterfly

299   *"He impressed me as one of the sweetest-natured men I had . . ."*; Ruth Montoya, formerly Ruth Carroll, interview, 1993; notes in my possession.

301   *"There is a moral imperative to running against Hatch," said . . .*; *Washington Post,* June 3, 1987.

302   *"I think the difference between the incumbent and myself is hope . . ."*; *Salt Lake Tribune,* March 12, 1988.

303   *In a dramatic encounter during floor debate, as Helms . . .*; *Washington Post,* May 2, 1988.

    "An altar boy would probably fail a polygraph test," said . . . ; *1988 CQ Almanac,* 269.

304   *"Their differences were less philosophical than personal, . . ."*; Richard Fenno, Jr., *The Making of a Senator: Dan Quayle* (Washington, D.C.: CQ Press, 1988), 48, 75.

306   *Hatch "had been a resident of Utah less time than my six-year-old . . ."*; Lee Roderick, interview for Scripps League Newspapers, published under "Brian Moss Facing Long Odds Against Hatch," (Provo, Utah) *Herald,* July 26, 1988.

    "We're not going to blow it this time," Pennsylvania's . . . .; *Congressional Quarterly,* July 23, 1988.

307   *Insight noted that Ali had friends in both political parties . . .*; *Insight,* August 8, 1988, 48–49.

    As a child of eleven, he decided, "I'm gonna be a boxer and . . ."; Peter Tauber, "Ali: Still Magic," *New York Times Magazine,* July 17, 1988.

"I admire [the fact that Hatch] came up the hard way," said Ali; *Insight*, August 8, 1988, 49.

308   *"I want you to welcome a new friend . . . ; Salt Lake Tribune,* August 18, 1988. This story also quotes Ali's comments to the reporter and Hurtado.

309   *Hatch told an audience in St. George that Democrats, among . . . ; Salt Lake Tribune,* August 14, 1988.

311   *"The whole neighborhood came over to meet Ali and his darling . . .";* Helen K. Hatch, interview, 1993; notes in my possession.

312   *Early on, Moss said, "I believe the Moss name has a great deal . . ."; Salt Lake Tribune,* March 10, 1988.

   "the greatest thing about being [in Washington] and representing . . ."; Deseret News, October 30, 1988.

313   *"I knew you'd win,"* beamed Ali; *Salt Lake Tribune*, November 9, 1988.

   Days later, Wilson told Bill Loos, a fellow university staff . . . ; Bill Loos, interview, 1993; notes in my possession.

314   *"I have not asked for anything [for myself] over the . . .";* Letter to "Dear Nancy," January 13, 1989; photocopy of letter in my possession.

315   *. . . the probe probably cost in excess of $100 million. For . . . ; New York Times,* January 19, 1994.

Chapter 24   The Odd Couple

320   *"Orrin is well prepared and very persevering,"* said Kennedy; Edward M. Kennedy, interview, 1993; notes in my possession. Unless otherwise noted, additional quotations from Kennedy in this chapter are from this interview.

323   *"Tonight we celebrate your birthday, and it's my turn to toast . . .";* My notes from a framed copy of Patrick's toast on Kennedy's office wall.

   A study of Senate voting for 1989 showed that, among the . . . ; Undated one-page summary of Hatch's voting pattern compared with other senators for votes taken from January 3, 1989-November 21, 1989; in Hatch files.

   "I think my people are finally accepting it." . . . "My people . . ."; Deseret News, January 28, 1990.

324   *"I don't know why we so often let the labels of 'liberal' . . .";* Washington Times, January 21, 1986.

326   *"For persons who are members of minority groups with a history . . .";* Salt Lake Tribune, February 22, 1989.

327   *In an emotionally intense and moving final debate, Harkin . . . ; New York Times,* July 14, 1990.

   Hatch "came here as a very committed and brilliant conservative . . ."; National Journal, August 19, 1989.

328   *Hatch insisted: "When I believe something is right I will fight . . ."; Washington Times,* January 21, 1986.

   "This is not someone who has seen the liberal light," said . . . ; *National Journal,* August 19, 1989.

   . . . with Courtland Milloy of the Post saying Hatch "lied" about . . ."; Washington Post, October 10, 1989.

   . . . he said it was a "stupid letter" and that he had, in fact . . . ; Washington Post, October 17, 1989.

329   *. . . had been raised by Dave Kindred, a sports columnist for . . . ;* Kindred articles were syndicated in other newspapers, including the *Salt Lake Tribune,* December 11, 13, 14, 1988.

330   *. . . Hatch told reporters he was convinced he had "always been . . .";* Salt Lake Tribune, December 13, 1988.

"I've had hours and days of discussions with Ali and have no . . ."; Salt Lake Tribune, December 15, 1988.

"The United States is prepared to prove that Mr. Hirschfeld . . ."; Washington Post, April 17, 1991.

Chapter 25   Kinder and Gentler

332   "We are cannibalizing our children," said Dr. Edward Zigler . . . ; New York Times, June 19, 1989; reprinted in Congressional Record, June 22, 1989, S-7225.

333   "Some conservative [politicians] predict that Sen. Orrin . . ."; Suzanne Fields, "Hatch's Day Care Option," Washington Times, January 14, 1988.

"I believe it is far preferable for parents to care for their . . ."; Statement issued by Hatch's office, dated September 11, 1987.

"Since the 1950s, when the conservative movement coalesced out . . ."; George Will, "The 'Warm Fuzzies,'" Washington Post, January 10, 1988.

335   "Dear Orrin: To echo the famous cry of one who was betrayed . . ."; Phyllis Schlafly, letter to Hatch, January 30, 1989.

Dole compared Hatch to Donald Trump because "anything you . . ."; This exchange is quoted in an article by Julie Rovner, "Hatch: GOP's Child Care Maverick," Congressional Quarterly, June 24, 1989, 1544.

336   "[we] do not share a similar political philosophy in many areas . . ."; Congressional Record, June 23, 1989, S-7477.

Majority Leader Mitchell also praised Hatch for "the remarkable . . ."; Ibid., S-7487.

"The sleeper accomplishment of the 101st Congress–with all . . . ; Los Angeles Times, October 30, 1990.

. . . Judy Mann called child-care legislation "the big prize" . . . ; Washington Post, November 2, 1990.

337   "I was impressed with the employment provided–but more . . ."; Ensign, November 1989, 69.

338   . . . informed his members "with deep regret" that Hatch . . . ; Salt Lake Tribune, July 17, 1990. The article also quotes Hatch's statement.

339   "If President Kennedy is watching these proceedings today . . ."; This statement is Hatch's recollection of the exchange, verified in a subsequent interview with Clarence Thomas.

"Even after he knew me and liked me, he always asked tough . . ."; Clarence Thomas, interview, 1993; notes in my possession.

"The staff people get together and say, 'How do we do a number . . ."; Congressional Quarterly, January 27, 1990.

Finally, Biden conceded that the EEOC documents failed to . . . ; Senate Judiciary Committee, Hearing on the Nomination of Clarence Thomas to the U.S. Circuit Court of Appeals for the District of Columbia, February 6, 1990. This source also contains the statements by Thomas and Kennedy, p. 340.

"It's like a paralysis," said Sheldon Goldman, a political . . . ; 1989 Congressional Quarterly Almanac, 239. This source also includes Hatch's statement.

342   . . . John Sununu, after an April 1991 story in the . . . ; Washington Post, April 21, 1991.

343   "I'll tell Teddy Kennedy where George is. He's home sober . . ."; Washington Post, August 9, 1988.

344   "You know," Kennedy told Hatch somberly, "Eunice is . . ."; As per Hatch's recollection of the conversation.

345   "Teddy Sighted on Mars!" screamed one headline–not the . . . ; Washington Post, July 3, 1991.

As they left, Hatch put a hand on Kennedy's shoulder; As per Hatch's recollection of the conversation.

347   *On May 9, 1991, William Kennedy Smith was officially charged . . .* ; Washington Post,
      May 11, 1991.

Chapter 26   Clarence and Anita

350   *Thomas was a toddler in tiny Pin Point, Georgia, when his . . .* ; The biographical infor-
      mation on Clarence Thomas is drawn from Thomas's opening statement to the
      Senate Judiciary Committee hearings, beginning September 10, 1991, and Steven
      Roberts, "The Crowning Thomas Affair," *U.S. News & World Report*, September
      16, 1991.

351   *"Judge Thomas strikes me as a man who would get a note from . . ."*; USA Today, July 5,
      1991.
      "We're going to Bork him," said Patricia Ireland. . . ; Miami Herald, July 8, 1991.
      Another feminist leader, Flo Kennedy, agreed, "We have to Bork . . ."; Associated Press
      story, photocopy of wire version, July 5, 1991.
      "I don't recall seeing another young person as disciplined as . . ."; Washington Post,
      August 6, 1991.

352   *"I judge people by what they are now, not what they were . . ."*; As per Hatch's notes.

353   *Concern over Thomas's civil rights record at the EEOC was . . .* ; Formal statement by
      Hatch at the opening of Clarence Thomas hearings, September 10, 1991; photo-
      copy of typescript in my possession.
      Thomas declined to offer his views on abortion, saying it was . . . ; First set of Hear-
      ings before the Senate Judiciary Committee on the Nomination of Clarence
      Thomas to Associate Justice of the U.S. Supreme Court, September
      10-September 20, 1991.
      The voice was Ted Kennedy's. "We will have to respect . . ."; Washington Post,
      September 13, 1991.

354   *After Thomas's third day of testimony, a Washington Post . . .* ; Fred Barbash,
      "Nominee's Responses Presage Conventional, Unpredictable Justice," *Washington
      Post*, September 13, 1991.

355   *"No issue—none—has a greater impact on the lives and futures . . ."*; Michelman, testi-
      mony, September 19, 1991; in Hearings before the Senate Judiciary Committee.

356   *Kate Michelman reportedly told another pro-abortion woman in . . .* ; American
      Spectator, March 1992. Special issue on Anita Hill.

357   *Juan Williams, a reporter at the Washington Post who had known . . .* ; Washington
      Post, October 10, 1991.

358   *"The fact that I feel so very strongly about sex harassment . . ."*;   Second set of Judi-
      ciary Committee Hearings on the Nomination of Clarence Thomas to Associate
      Justice of the U.S. Supreme Court (focusing on allegations by Anita Hill),
      October 11, 12, and 13, 1991.

360   *. . . but she remained cool, conceded almost nothing, and calmly . . .* ; When I asked
      Hill for an interview to clarify her testimony, she declined. Hill, letter to
      Roderick, September 28, 1993.

361   *The two agents in Oklahoma, John B. Luton and Jolene Smith . . .* ; The affidavits are
      reprinted in the hearings, 116-17.

363   *Hatch said almost nothing to Hill during the hearing, except . .* ; Ibid., 111. These were
      Hatch's only comments to Hill.

365   *"Senator, you just saved his ass."*; As recorded in Hatch's notes; photocopy in my
      possession.

366   *"Black female brought suit against county and county officials . . ."*; 705 F. Supp. 1474,
      District Court, Kansas, 1988.

369   *"How important was Senator Hatch to my confirmation?"*; Clarence Thomas, inter-
      view, 1993; notes in my possession.
      Columnist George Will later noted that 'to believe that Hill . . ."; George F. Will, "Anita
      Hill's Tangled Web," *Newsweek*, April 19, 1993, 74.

... *the drumbeat of propaganda had paid off: A poll for* ... ; *U.S. News & World Report,* October 12, 1992; the Gallup and *Wall Street Journal* polls are cited in Ishmael Reed, "Feminists v. Thomas," *Washington Post,* October 18, 1992.

Thomas–determined to prove himself–hit the court running ... ; Paul M. Barrett, "Thomas Is Emerging As Strong Conservative Out to Prove Himself," *Wall Street Journal,* April 27, 1993.

370 *"A good, kind, gentle human being was destroyed, and that person* ..."; *U.S. News & World Report,* October 12, 1992.

Chapter 27   BCCI and Other Trials

372 *Polled a month after the hearings, 56 percent rated Hatch's role* ... ; *Deseret News,* November 10, 1991.

Simpson had gone too far during the hearings by referring to ... ; Second set of Judiciary Committee Hearings on the Nomination of Clarence Thomas to Associate Justice of the U.S. Supreme Court (focusing on allegations by Anita Hill), October 11, 12, and 13, 1991. 235.

Specter noted that his questioning of Hill was "legally correct" ... ; *USA Today,* April 23, 1992.

373 *A Gannett News Service study of 11,500 congressional staffers* ... ; *Salt Lake Tribune,* December 19, 1993.

375 *"The case arose from the conduct of a small number of* ..."; *Congressional Record,* February 22, 1990, S-1464.

376 ... *when he read an investigative article in Regardie's, a* ... ; Larry Gurwin, "Who Really Owns First American Bank," *Regardie's,* May 1990.

As the extent of the BCCI scandal unfolded, a Deseret News ... ; Lee Davidson, *Deseret News,* August 20-21, 1992.

379 *"Hatch Adds Partisan Spice to BCCI Stew, Attempting* ..."; *Wall Street Journal,* August 6, 1991.

380 *When interviewed directly for this book, the reporter denied* ... ; Name of reporter withheld, interview, 1993; notes in my possession.

381 *"It absolutely would be inconsistent with everything I know* ..."; Edward M. Kennedy, interview, 1993; notes in my possession.

"I am painfully aware that the criticism directed at me ..."; Typescript of speech delivered October 25, 1991; photocopy in my possession.

382 *He expressed regret for waking up the two young men and taking* ... ; *Washington Post,* December 7, 1991.

In February 1992, columnist Jack Anderson noted ... ; Ibid., February 23, 1992.

384 *"My father was not a vocal man. His hard-working hands showed* ..."; *Washington Times,* June 19, 1992.

386 *"Teddy and I were talking last night and hurting for you* ..."; Victoria Reggie Kennedy, letter to Hatch, undated; photocopy in my possession.

"[Jesse's] contributions to our organization as a member ..."; Robert Provolt, business representative, Lathers Local 33L, letter to Helen K. Hatch, September 23, 1992.

[Jesse's] passing was a deep sadness for us which we still ..."; Barbara and Peter Roff, letter to Helen K. Hatch, undated.

387 *"Lawmaker's Defense of B.C.C.I. Went Beyond Speech in Senate* ..."; *New York Times* and *Washington Post,* both August 26, 1992.

388 *Simpson, interviewed for this book, said no such contract* ... ; Glenn Simpson, interview, 1993; notes in my possession.

When Pound's lengthy story was published in February 1993 ... ; *Wall Street Journal,* February 18, 1993.

390 *"Five U.S. Senators Are Space Aliens!"; Weekly World News,* November 3, 1992.

Political cartoonist Pag Bagley did a takeoff on the spoof ... ; *Salt Lake Tribune,* October 22, 1992.

"Although I am a lifelong Utah Democrat," said Lee, "I have come . . ."; David Lee, letter to Hatch's administrative assistant, Wendy Higginbotham, on Jones, Waldo, Holbrook & McDonough letterhead, April 22, 1992; photocopy in my possession.

391 *"It was not an easy thing for Senator Hatch to do. He is very . . .";* Don Gale, transcript of KSL editorial, broadcast October 19, 1992.

Chapter 28   Tending the Home Fires

392 *"I am upbeat and determined. Damn the press . . .";* George Bush, letter to Hatch, September 2, 1992; photocopy in my possession.

"I appreciate your suggestions . . . Your wonderful note . . ."; George Bush, letters to Hatch, October 23 and November 1, 1992; photocopies in my possession.

394 *. . . had created what Utah Holiday called the state's "most . . .";* Utah Holiday, November 1985.

395 *Then there was George Thomas Scott, who just wanted to be . . . ;* JoAnn Jacobsen-Wells, "U.S. Citizenship Wish Filled—Briefly," *Deseret News,* July 4, 1990.

397 *"The Act does not affect any of the issues that fall under . . .";* Robert S. Peck, ACLU Legislative Counsel, letter to Senators, February 12, 1993.

398 *Liberal Tom Barberi wrote that "Utah's Sen. Orrin Hatch is . . .";* Barberi-Scruggs column, *Salt Lake Tribune,* September 19, 1993.

Chapter 29   A Season of Renewal

399 *"I do not condone Zoe Baird's hiring of unauthorized aliens . . .";* Statement by Hatch, January 20, 1993; photocopy of press release in my possession.

401 *Guinier had criticized democracy as a form of government and . . . ;* "Embattled Nominee Says She Wants Senate Hearing," *Deseret News,* June 3, 1993; Clarence Page, "Landmines Along Guinier's Trail," *Washington Post,* June 2, 1993.

402 *"Do we want children learning the values of an organization . . .";* San Francisco Chronicle, August 13, 1991.

Achtenberg reportedly got United Way to withhold . . . ; Ibid., December 22, 1992.

"I hope that President Clinton . . ."; Hatch statement, March 19, 1993.

408 *The department sent a follow-up letter, dated July 29, with . . . ;* G. Allen Carver, acting head of the fraud section, wrote to Hatch's attorney on July 29, 1993: "The Criminal Division's investigation . . . has been concluded insofar as he is concerned. We have determined that no further investigation is warranted."

409 *"I was sitting here thinking how much I love you. . ." ;* Marcia Hatch Whetton, letter to Orrin Hatch, November 8, 1992; photocopy in my possession.

410 *"On August 12, 1992, Senator Hatch requested that the Ethics . . .";* Hatch statement, November 20, 1993.

412 *"It's been said that after reaching the Senate, some people blow . . .";* Edward M. Kennedy, interview, 1993; notes in my possession.

"I'll miss him," Hatch told an interviewer, who waited in vain . . . ; I was this reporter.

413 *Since 1960, when Hatch was in law school, the nation's population . . . ;* William Bennett, "Index of Leading Cultural Indicators," study published jointly by Empower America, The Heritage Foundation, and The Free Congress Foundation, March 1993.

Index

433